Analyzing Congress

Second Edition

*The New Institutionalism in
American Politics Series*

Series Editor, Kenneth A. Shepsle

Analyzing Congress is part of *The New Institutionalism in American Politics*
series. The series applies analytical techniques to questions about political
processes, actors, and institutions. Each book provides students with the
tools for understanding the intricate relationships between political theory
and practice, and uses those tools to explore an abundance of real-world
examples.

Also available

Analyzing Politics by Kenneth A. Shepsle
Analyzing Elections by Rebecca B. Morton
Analyzing Interest Groups by Scott H. Ainsworth
Analyzing Policy by Michael C. Munger

Analyzing Congress

Second Edition

CHARLES STEWART III

MASSACHUSETTS INSTITUTE OF TECHNOLOGY

W·W·NORTON & COMPANY

New York   London

Copyright © 2012 by W. W. Norton & Company, Inc.

All rights reserved
Printed in the United States of America
Second Edition

The text of this book is composed in Galliard
with the display set in Modern 216 light
Composition by Westchester
Manufacturing by The Courier Companies, Inc.
Book design by Jacques Chazaud
Production Manager: Sean Mintus

Library of Congress Cataloging-in-Publication Data

Stewart, Charles Haines.
    Analyzing Congress / Charles Stewart III. — 2nd ed.
        p. cm. — (The new institutionalism in American politics series)
    Includes bibliographical references and index.
    ISBN 978-0-393-93506-6 (pbk.)
    1. United States. Congress.   I. Title.
    JK1021.S74 2011
    328.73—dc23
                                                        2011028353

ISBN 978-0-393-93506-6 (pbk.)

W. W. Norton & Company, Inc., 500 Fifth Avenue, New York, N.Y.
10110 www.wwnorton.com
W. W. Norton & Company Ltd., 10 Coptic Street, London WC1A
1PU

1 2 3 4 5 6 7 8 9 0

Contents

List of Figures

❦

List of Tables

Preface

When I began teaching congressional politics at MIT a quarter century ago, I asked the same question that generations of assistant professors have asked before me: How do I design my undergraduate courses to take maximum advantage of what I had read and thought about in graduate school? To help me answer this question, I investigated how others taught about Congress to undergraduates, including pulling out my own old undergraduate Congress syllabus. The conclusion I reached also was time worn: there was virtually no relationship between what I had done in graduate school, when I studied Congress, and what undergraduates were taught about Congress.

There were positive and negative sides to this revelation. The positive side is that I learned early on that undergraduate and graduate education *are* very different, and what one exposes graduate students to need not be taught to undergraduates. Undergraduate education is mostly about transmitting tried and true verities to students who will (with only minor exceptions) never take a course in the field again. For them, one wants to provide a firm foundation for a lifetime of citizenship. The danger with exposing undergraduates to the unformed ideas that permeate graduate education (and then later practicing research political science itself) is that they change very rapidly and so provide an unsure foundation on which to build a lasting base of knowledge.

The negative side is that congressional studies at the time was undergoing a sea change in theoretical orientation, followed rapidly by a change in empirical orientation, as well. While undergraduate education always plays catch-up with graduate education, in the mid-1980s the gulf between the two seemed especially great. David Mayhew's 1974 *Congress: The Electoral Connection* was no longer considered a dangerous economistic tract by graduate students. Newly minted Ph.D.s in the congressional field were becoming as familiar with game theory as previous generations had been in interviewing techniques. As the professional study of Congress pulled further and further away from the standard undergraduate curriculum in congressional politics, I worried that my undergraduates would realize that the older verities—with their accompanying behavioralist readings about Congress—were stale and irrelevant.

Out of that concern eventually grew this book. When I designed my first congressional politics subject[1] at MIT, I refused to use an established textbook—even though the established ones at the time (truth be told) were fine summaries of the best research of the day and had served me well in my undergraduate days, less than a decade earlier. Instead, I drew upon new monographs and journal articles. I paired articles from the older behavioral-ist approach with the new rational choice approach. I gave lectures on spatial voting theory. In short, I attempted to create an appropriate undergraduate version of a Congress course that was consistent and integrated with the new approach to legislative studies.

In particular, this book grew from my lecture notes, which originally were intended to provide students orally with the general material one typically gets from a textbook—a good mix of stylized facts, context, and analytical tools and insights. Because there always is more to convey in this regard than can be said out loud, I eventually started writing down my ideas, writing more than I could ever deliver orally in the course of a semester. Eventually, with the invitation of W. W. Norton to write a textbook on Congress, I went beyond simply fleshing out my lecture notes toward something more comprehensive.

The three major goals I set for teaching congressional politics at MIT in 1985 inform this book: (1) develop a broad perspective on congressional politics, (2) understand the professional development of the study of Congress, and (3) develop a working knowledge of how Congress operates.

The first major goal is to give students a broad perspective on congressional politics. I want students to be able to stand back from the chaotic swirl of legislative life and analyze it dispassionately. To do this, two subsidiary goals must be pursued. First, students need to understand that congressional politics is only a specialized case of the more general legislative politics. Congress is only one legislature among thousands that exist in the United States—and the United States is only one nation among dozens that have legislatures. Alas, the press of time (when I teach) and space (when I wrote this book) preclude exploring in any depth the comparative implications of studying Congress. At the very least, however, I want to pique the curiosity of students, who might be challenged to apply what they learn by studying Congress to the other legislatures they will encounter in life.

The second subsidiary goal in the pursuit of perspective is to introduce students to the theoretical and empirical tools necessary to analyze legisla-tive behavior scientifically. This is an important undertaking in all of politi-cal science; studying Congress can give students a window into how the scientific study of politics might be done. Indeed, the past quarter, century has seen an explosion in the development of systematic theoretical and empirical tools that have been applied in the legislative setting. These tools, in principle, are transportable to other legislative venues. I hope that, if undergraduates view analyzing Congress dispassionately, they will have few anxieties about approaching the analysis of other legislatures.

The second major goal of this book is to provide undergraduates and beginning graduate students an introduction to the *professional* study of Congress. This is likely to be a controversial goal, since most undergraduate study of Congress is imbedded within a traditional political science major, which in most places, still is regarded as one of the classic liberal arts disciplines. The goal of a liberal arts education is precisely *not* to develop a professional orientation, at least at the undergraduate level. Professional orientations are developed in graduate and professional schools. As convinced as I am of the power of traditional liberal arts curricula, I have learned at MIT the value of bringing undergraduates closer to the work of professionals in the field, which is a core idea in engineering education.

I teach at a place where it is expected that undergraduates will help you with your research, in league with graduate research assistants and colleagues. To make that succeed, I had to teach undergraduates about the major theoretical ideas and empirical techniques that are common currency among active legislative researchers. That necessity has guided the writing of much of this book. I am firmly convinced that if undergraduates can be brought closer to professional research, they will be excited by the palpable prospect that they, too, might join in the fun. The payoffs to that feeling are multifold. Not only might some of them go on to graduate school, having already experienced what typically is taught to beginning graduate students, but also the greater bulk of political scientists who go on to careers in law and business will have a better sense about how to meld theory and evidence and, in the end, might have a greater respect for the methods of the social sciences.

My final goal in writing this book is to help students build a firm working knowledge of the basic stylized facts of congressional politics. Although this book emphasizes theoretical and empirical abstractions more than other textbooks in congressional politics, political science at heart still is an empirical discipline, where mastering the particular facts about a particular case is valued. Therefore, while this book *emphasizes* abstraction and analysis, lots of facts remain to be learned, and the book is full of them.

To achieve these goals, I added a few special features to enhance the more typical material found in the chapters. First, the study of Congress is full of specialized terms—charitably we would call these *terms of art*, less charitably we would call them *jargon*. Throughout the book, whenever I first use a term that has a specialized meaning within the study of Congress (or a closely related subject, like elections or the Constitution), I highlight the word in **bold type**. I then collect all such words at the end of each chapter in a Summary of Key Concepts section.

Second, I include selected readings at the end of each chapter. I do so at my peril, because I know that some will read these selected readings lists with an Academy Awards mentality. Aware of this problem, I have approached the task with a few simple objective guidelines. First, I have sought to keep each list brief. Second, I emphasize books and articles that are frequently cited in articles that have appeared in the top political science journals. As an aid in making my judgments more systematic on this score, I actually engaged in a citation count exercise, to discover the most-cited works in congressional studies in the 1990s and 2000s. Almost all of the top fifty citation getters appear in the suggested reading sections. Those sections are rounded out, however, by a small number of readings that have not been widely cited (either because they are new or underappreciated) but nonetheless crystallize well an important theme of the chapter in question.

A third special feature of this book is a set of problems that appears at the end of many chapters. Political scientists who study Congress increasingly rely on spatial models to understand the dynamics of congressional politics, both inside the institution and in the electoral arena. Therefore, it is incumbent on all new students of congressional politics to be familiar with the basics of these models and master them. To master these models, it is insufficient simply to read about them; one needs to practice them systematically. Therefore, I include problems at the end of most chapters to allow the reader to practice or apply spatial models to the material just covered. Along the way, I also suggest some empirical exercises that will help students become familiar with common data sources and reference works that pertain to Congress.

The problems at the end of the first chapter are by far the most extensive, but they are also the most important. Chapter 1 introduces the spatial model, and all of the remaining chapters rely on some feature of the model for at least part of the discussion. That is why so many problems follow the first chapter. Other chapters contain a mix of problems that allow the reader to manipulate the spatial model in a relatively pure fashion, plus problems that challenge the reader to apply the model to a real-world setting. Doing the problems is an integral part of using this book, so I encourage all readers to try them.

For an instructor using this book in an introductory course on congressional politics, questions are likely to arise about how much to emphasize the spatial model and how early to push it. This book is written with the spatial model at the beginning because so much of the subsequent material relies on it. However, we all teach in the real world, and I understand that undergraduates in political science classes (even political science classes at MIT) generally do not expect large doses of formal theory at the beginning of what is advertised as a course about the U.S. Congress. Over the years I have experimented with the placement and emphasis of formal theory in my congressional classes, and here is the best advice I can give.

If your students are particularly averse to theory, then assign Chapter 1 in two pieces. Begin with the single-dimension spatial model, making sure that everyone understands the median voter theorem and all its ramifications. That is pretty much what is needed to handle the chapters on elections and voters. A small amount of the multidimensional spatial model creeps into the discussion of the constitutional origins of Congress in Chapter 2. That is where it would be useful to be familiar with the "chaos result" found in multidimensional models. However, the real-world chaos that faced the members of the Confederation Congress is intuitive enough to grasp that it is not critical to deeply understand multidimensional spatial models at this point. The real power of the multidimensional model comes later in the book, where I discuss the internal organization of Congress and the idea of "structure-induced equilibrium" looms large. Therefore, it is entirely reasonable to save the multi-dimensional material in Chapter 1 until you begin exploring congressional organization.

Finally, when I teach my Congress course, I emphasize the day-to-day politics of the institution. I encourage my students to watch C-SPAN regularly and to follow Congress religiously on the news. Compared to a quarter century ago, when *CQ Weekly Report* was always a week late in arriving by mail and few students had access to cable television, access to the new electronic media has produced an embarrassment of riches for following Congress in real time. To help focus attention to the news, I hold a weekly exercise I call the "Congressional Roundtable." Every student is required to find one interesting news item related to Congress, to post it on the class Web site, and to come prepared to discuss it during a twenty-minute period I set aside at the start of class once a week. Depending on the time of the year the class is taught, these weekly presentations help to drive home the fact that much of congressional politics is highly structured along the lines introduced in this book.

Needless to say, this book could not have been written without the help of the undergraduate and graduate students I have taught at MIT over the past three decades. It is thrilling to enter a classroom to know that you are nowhere close to being the smartest person in the room. Thrilling and challenging. In addition to challenging me intellectually, these students have challenged me to clarify my thinking and the communication of my ideas. A few of them— Dan Frisk, Mike George, Tony Hill, Russell Herndon, Doug Heimburger, William LeBlanc, Courtney Shiley, Erik Snowberg, Jonathan Woon, and Farhan Zaidi—read elements of the manuscript closer than average and pointed out errors and confusions. My friend Steve Ansolabehere read parts of the early chapters, also helping me to clarify my approach. And, Barry Weingast at Stanford gave me an office for a summer, where I was able to begin pounding out the chapters and talking about what I was writing. (Barry has been an inspiration over the years, as we've talked about the most effective ways to communicate basic findings of rational choice research to a broader audience.) A rump seminar of Stanford graduate students (which included my former colleague Brandice Canes-Wrone) also helped provide guidance at a critical stage. The unsung hero of that summer was my father-in-law, Carl Hess, who accompanied my wife and me to California to babysit our (then) thirty-month-old son during the day. Any parent reading this will know what special developmental activity parents and two-year-olds struggle through; the fact that Carl was doing adult duty during most of Cameron's waking hours at this stage was a godsend to the project. David Epstein kindly shared a set of exercises that has been incorporated here. Jeff Jenkins, Sean Theirault, Michael Press, David Canon, Scott Adler, and Keith Poole gave invaluable feedback about the first edition, which, I hope, made the second one better. Mea culpa for when I didn't heed their advice. Finally, T.J. Bright went beyond the call of duty in updating the tables and figures for the second edition.

Roby Harrington at Norton, who roped me into this project (with the assistance of Ken Shepsle, the series editor), and Steve Dunn, my editor at Norton, have been good-natured as this manuscript has taken a little longer to germinate than any of us had hoped. Ann Shin showed equal patience in facilitating the second edition. For their patience, I am immensely grateful. I promise the third edition won't take nearly so long!

In the end, of course, one eagerly takes the advice of friends and strangers, but they have to be held harmless against any misuse of that counsel. The same applies in this case.

NOTE

1. At MIT, classes (like Congressional Politics or Introduction to International Relations) are termed *subjects* and majors (like Political Science and Mechanical Engineering) are termed *courses*.

Analyzing Congress

Second Edition

～1～

An (Unusual) Introduction to the Study of Congress

Democrats lost a net of sixty-four seats in the U.S. House of Representatives in the 2010 congressional elections. The nation had not seen a defeat of this magnitude for the president's party in a midterm election since 1938, when Democrats lost seventy-two seats. Unlike 1938, when Democratic losses came at a time that the party held a historically large number of seats in the House already, 334, the 2010 losses shifted party control of the House to the Republican Party, giving the GOP more seats in that body than they had held since after the election of 1946. Senate elections went poorly for the Democrats, too, as they lost a net of six seats. However, because only one-third of the Senate is up for election every two years, Democrats continued to hold onto a slim majority.

As a result, momentum for policy change shifted sharply to the right. Republican leaders, bolstered by support from the Tea Party movement, promised to "Defund Obamacare," that is, to repeal the health care reform program that had passed the Democratically controlled 111st Congress, at the encouragement of President Obama, only months before the election. They also promised to roll back other major programs that President Obama and the Democratic Congress had championed, such as economic stimulus spending and more aggressive regulation of greenhouse gases.

How quickly electoral fortunes change! Just two years before, the terrible shape of the economy had made 2008 a good election year for Democrats. The size of the economic downturn was the second worst in American history, behind only the crash of 1929. In keeping with a pattern established in the 1880s, the party of the incumbent president—in this case, the Republicans—was punished at the polls, indicating the electorate's collective judgment that the party of George W. Bush was responsible for the economic mess and that the opposition Democrats were in a better position to pull the nation out of the economic tailspin.

The electoral gains of the Democrats were impressive in 2008. Their presidential nominee, Barack Obama, had garnered 4.6 percentage points more of the popular vote and 114 more electoral votes than the Democratic nominee four years before, Senator John Kerry (D-Mass.). Democrats in the House extended their margin over the Republicans by twenty-four seats, to take a 257–178 advantage; in the Senate, after a set of election challenges and vacancies were filled, Democrats held a "filibuster-proof" majority of 60–40. The Democrats' gains were even more impressive when we compare the results of the 2008 election with those of 2004. After the 2004 election, a conservative Republican was president, and Republicans held majorities of 232–202 in the House and 55–45 in the Senate. Thus, in addition to winning the presidency, between 2004 and 2008 the Democrats had managed to achieve a net swing of fifty-five seats in the House and sixteen seats in the Senate.[1]

It was not hard to draw parallels between the Democrats' position following the 2008 election and their position following the 1932 election—deep economic crisis, repudiated Republican incumbent, and Democratic gains in Congress following a switch in party control two years prior. In that earlier time, Democrats established themselves as the party of the "working man" that was willing to use the power and the money of the federal government to help the nation dig out of bad economic circumstances.

Financial crisis. Repudiated old Republican president. Charismatic new Democratic president. Large Democratic majorities in Congress. Promises for a more socially activist government. The field was clear for the Democrats to run up the score against the Republicans over the next two years as they did legislative battle.

Or was it?

Even with large majorities and a Democrat in the White House, passing legislation was anything but easy for congressional Democrats during the first two years of the Obama administration. The signature piece of the 111th Congress, health care reform, bogged down repeatedly, until the Patient Protection and Affordable Care Act narrowly passed, a full fifteen months (441 days) after Congress had first convened. Legislation to address the financial abuses that had led to the "Great Recession" also took months to pass and had to face criticisms that it was too favorable to the banking and finance industries. A popular bill to extend unemployment benefits also took months to pass. Other elements of the Democratic platform languished, including bills to address climate change, provide the District of Columbia with a vote in the House of Representatives, rein in warrantless wiretaps, and institute immigration reform.

How do we explain the vast gulf between promise and performance of the 111th Congress? How could a Congress with solid Democratic majorities working with a Democratic president have such a hard time passing Democratic legislation? Why did President Obama and Democratic leaders continue to seek bipartisan legislative solutions when they enjoyed comfortable majorities? Why did President Obama disappoint a core constituency of the Democratic Party, pro-choice activists, on the way to getting national health care legislation passed? Why did Democratic leaders not punish Senator Ben Nelson (D-Nebr.), who regularly opposed President Obama's proposals, or GOP leaders not punish the Republican senators from Maine, Olympia Snowe and Susan Collins, who occasionally gave the Democrats the needed votes to pass important legislation?

Did the electoral "shellacking" inflicted on the Democrats in the 2010 election come about because policies such as the health care reform went too far for most Americans, because they did not go far enough, or for reasons having no policy content at all? What role did campaign funds from corporations, unleashed by the *Citizens United* Supreme Court case, play in the historic gains made by Republican candidates? What role did the arch-conservative television network, Fox News, play in mobilizing pro-Republican voters? Did issues play any role at all in 2010, or were voters just angry that the economic recovery was not fast enough?

Questions such as these arise frequently in the analysis of the legislative process. How these questions are answered differs according to who responds. Activists, such as those attending the July 2010 Netroots Nation convention, might approach these questions quite differently from a journalist for the *Washington Post* or *slate.com*, and each would answer differently from the senators and representatives themselves.

How do *political scientists* answer these questions? Understanding how political scientists explain puzzling—and even not-so-puzzling—legislative outcomes is the purpose of this book.

The approach a political scientist takes to questions about how Congress behaves is typically quite different from how an activist, journalist, or politician approaches the same subject. Most people, when they try to explain why Congress does something, or fails to do something, rely on idiosyncratic explanations about the character of individuals. For instance, Markos Moulitsas, who founded the Netroots Nation convention as an extension of his liberal Daily Kos blog, seemed to lay the blame for the inability of Democrats to push through an even bolder legislative agenda during the 111th Congress on Democrats who were "inactive and incompetent." Against claims that Democrats were losing legislative battles on liberal items because they didn't have enough votes on their side, Ed Shultz, a liberal commentator, declared that all the Democratic leaders had to do to overcome a lack of votes was just go and get some more.[2] In other words, Democrats were losing because they were stupid and lazy.

Although the personal characteristics of politicians play an important role in determining the outcomes of legislative battles, political scientists tend not to start there. Rather, in most legislative battles of any consequence, political scientists tend to begin with more general, abstract factors that link a limited number of elements that are always at play, regardless of personal characteristics such as laziness and competence, with legislative outcomes.

What are the more abstract, general factors that political scientists would emphasize in explaining the Democrats' legislative difficulties after the 2008 election? One is institutional rules, a particularly salient one being the *filibuster* rule in the Senate, which requires sixty votes to stop debate and allow a vote on a bill being considered. This rule not only "raises the bar" needed to pass important legislation in the Senate from fifty[3] votes to sixty, but it also gives an inordinate amount of influence over the substance of legislation to the most conservative Democrats, or even to members of the minority Republican Party. The filibuster operates the same way, regardless of whether the majority party is Democratic or Republican, or whether the majority party is lazy or incompetent.

With the filibuster, in order to pass liberal legislation against an existing conservative status quo, the legislation has to appeal to the sixtieth-most-liberal senator in the 111th Congress, who, until the death of Edward M. Kennedy (D-Mass.), was Ben Nelson (D-Nebr.), who has been frequently courted by Republicans to switch parties, even though he has repeatedly said he is "more comfortable" with Democrats because of their stand on civil rights, social security, and Medicare. After Kennedy's death, the sixtieth-most-liberal senator became Olympia Snowe, one of the Republican senators from Maine. If the filibuster didn't exist, legislation passing the Senate would have to appeal to only the fiftieth-most-liberal senator—a senator such as Mary Landrieu (D-La.), who is still not the type of liberal activist who would appeal to attendees of the Netroots Nation convention, but would be much closer to the Democratic Party's mainstream.[4]

Understanding the constraints imposed by the filibuster—constraints that would stand regardless of the identities of the particular senators or president— it is easy to see how a political scientist would dismiss analysis implying that all Democrats had to do to win liberal legislative battles was "just get more votes." From where? From Republicans, who are even more conservative? More important, however, the political scientist would remark that the legislative histories of issues like national health care reform actually *were* governed by a desire on the part of Democratic leaders to "just get more votes." The problem is that to accommodate the filibuster, "getting more votes" meant making bills more conservative than liberals would have preferred, so that the "pivotal" votes of senators like Ben Nelson could be assured. Thus, the political scientist can show that the activist wants the impossible in a situation like this, which is "getting more votes" by making legislation more liberal.

The Democrats' travails in the 111th Congress and their fate in the 2010 midterm elections are nothing new, which you will see once you have become familiar with the basic analytical tools of political science, tempered by a bit of history to help see those tools in action. The analysis of Congress by a political scientist is similar to the analysis of the natural world by the natural scientist in one key respect: both the political scientist and the natural scientist begin by breaking reality into basic building blocks that later can be recombined to address particular real-world cases. The chemical engineer who wants to design a process to manufacture a new pharmaceutical must start, at least implicitly, with an understanding of chemistry at the atomic level. The biologist seeking a cure for cancer is likely to start with basic genetics. That the chemical engineer may have learned basic chemistry in high school or the biologist may have learned basic genetics as a freshman in college should not obscure the fact that their careers are possible only because they have mastered certain fundamental processes that they encounter in millions of particular examples every day.

Like the chemical engineer who starts with atoms and the biologist who starts with DNA, the political scientist wanting to understand how a legislature behaves begins with basic building blocks. Those building blocks are the motivations and aspirations of individuals. Individuals, called *legislators*, seek to achieve certain ends through their legislative activity. They rarely can achieve what they want by acting alone—it *is* a legislature, after all—but must act through the rules established by the legislature or imposed on the outside by a constitution. Other individuals, called *constituents* and *voters*, aim to achieve certain things through the efforts of their representatives. Representatives and constituents sometimes interact directly—as when a retiree tries to dislodge a check from the Social Security Administration. But mostly they interact in an institutional setting called *elections*. This interaction between individuals and institutions forms the core of the study of Congress.

The rest of this book is about the interplay between the individuals and the rules that together constitute the United States Congress and its electoral environment. To undertake this exploration most fruitfully, we must begin abstractly, laying out basic building blocks and then assembling them together systematically. The remainder of this chapter introduces the rudiments of rational choice theory as they have been applied to legislatures generally and Congress specifically. It is necessarily abstract, because we want to lay a firm foundation for later chapters in which we analyze more complicated features of Congress. This chapter is not *too* abstract, however, because we do not want to lose sight of the fact that ultimately we are interested in understanding a flesh-and-blood organization that dominates the news every day. If you want even *more* abstraction, a bibliography at the end of this chapter will help you explore in even more detail the topics introduced here. If you want *less* abstraction, just wait: subsequent chapters will return to the better-known world of history, elections, committees, and lawmaking.

The Politics of Lineland: Spatial Voting Theory in One Dimension

Goldylocks sat down at the bears' table and spied the bowls of porridge. The first one she tried was too hot. The second was too cold. The third bowl was just right, and she ate it right up.

What do the following stories have in common?

1. *The Supreme Court:* In 2010, a lawsuit was brought in the federal district court in San Francisco challenging California's Proposition 8, which made same-sex marriage illegal in that state. After the trial, Judge Vaughn R. Walker, who heard the case, issued a ruling that struck down Proposition 8 as inconsistent with the fourteenth Amendment to the U.S. Constitution. A number of commentators noted that Judge Walker's lengthy opinion seemed written particularly to appeal to Supreme Court Justice Anthony Kennedy. Here is how one Supreme Court watcher, Dahlia Lithwick, put it:

   Judge Vaughn R. Walker is not Anthony Kennedy. But when the chips are down, he certainly knows how to write like him. I count—in his opinion today—seven citations to Justice Kennedy's 1996 opinion in *Romer* v. *Evans* (striking down an anti-gay Colorado ballot initiative) and eight citations to his 2003 decision in *Lawrence* v. *Texas* (striking down Texas' gay-sodomy law). In a stunning decision this afternoon, finding California's Proposition 8 ballot initiative banning gay marriage unconstitutional, Walker trod heavily on the path Kennedy has blazed on gay rights: "[I]t would demean a married couple were it to be said marriage is simply about the right to have sexual intercourse," quotes Walker. " '[M]oral disapproval, without any other asserted state interest,' has never been a rational basis for legislation," cites Walker. "Animus towards gays and lesbians or simply a belief that a relationship between a man and a woman is inherently better than a relationship between two men or two women, this belief is not a proper basis on which to legislate," Walker notes, with a jerk of the thumb at Kennedy.

   Justice Kennedy? Hot sauce to go with those words?[5]

2. *Dick Morris and Robert Reich:* Following the 1994 election, which returned Republicans to control of the House of Representatives for the first time in half a century, President Clinton became very worried about his own reelection prospects in 1996. To help him position himself for the 1996 election, he brought in political consultant Richard Morris, who was known primarily for helping Republican candidates. One day, Morris visited Robert Reich, one of Clinton's oldest friends and the secretary of Labor. (As secretary of Labor, Reich was responsible for worrying about things such as job training and education, unemployment, and worker safety.) Here is how Reich recounted the dialogue between him and Morris during his visit:

   "You have a lot of good ideas," [Morris] says. "The President likes your ideas. I want them so I can test them." Morris speaks in a quick staccato that doesn't vary. Sentences are stripped of all extraneous words or sounds. The pitch is flat and nasal.

   "*Test* them?"

   "Put them into our opinion poll. I can know within a day or two whether they *work*. Anything under forty percent doesn't work. Fifty percent is a possibility. Sixty or seventy, and the President may well use it. I can get a *very* accurate read on the swing."

   "Swing?"

   Morris turns into a machine gun. "Clinton has a solid forty percent of the people who will go to the polls. Another forty percent will never vote for him. That leaves the swing. Half of the swing, ten percent, lean toward him. The other ten percent lean against him, toward Dole. We use Dole as a surrogate for the Republican candidate, whoever it may be. If your idea works with the swing, we'll use it." . . . "So, what are your ideas?" (Reich 1997, pp. 271–72)

3. *Fraternity brothers buy a car:* Three fraternity brothers—Bob, Carl, and Ted— agree to go in together to buy a car. None of them particularly cares about what kind of car it is or what amenities is has, just so long as it runs. After agreeing to buy the car, they realize they have not agreed on the only thing that is important to them: the price of the car. Since their fraternal bond will be irreparably broken if they back out of the deal to buy the car together, they agree to settle on a car price via a majority vote. Bob wants to spend $500 for the car, Carl wants to spend $1,000, and Ted wants to spend $2,000. Ted suggests they spend $2,000. Carl counters with $1,000, which Bob likes compared to the $2,000. Ted tries a compromise: How about $1,500? Both Bob and Carl say "too expensive." Bob tries another compromise: $750, Carl and Ted say "too cheap." One thousand dollars it is.

All of these examples (two real and one fanciful) have four things in common. First, each involves a choice to be made by a group of people through majority rule. Second, the available choices can be arrayed along a "more or less" or "greater or lesser" dimension: greater or lesser rights for gays and lesbians, more or less protection of laborers, and more or less spending on a car. Third, each example has someone directly in the middle of the dimension: Anthony Kennedy (who is typically on the winning side of 5–4 Supreme Court decisions), the 20 percent of swing voters (who might or might not support Bill Clinton in 1996), and Carl (who wants to spend $1,000 on a car). Fourth, in each example, the middle person (or persons) decides the outcome, or at least is *perceived* as deciding the outcome.

Two of these three examples involve an obvious political choice. It is common in politics to encounter political choices that easily can be arrayed along a single dimension, either a tangible dimension or an abstract one. Political discourse is littered with **unidimensional** descriptions of politics. When we talk about liberals and conservatives, we are engaging in a unidimensional political analysis. Liberals are on the left, conservatives on the right, and moderates in the middle. There are shades of ideological conviction—radical liberals, who are "far to the left," and reactionaries, who are "far to the right." A moderate might "lean to the left" or "lean to the right."

Single-dimensional analysis also undergirds statements such as "he's a friend of farmers" or "she's in the pocket of big business." Underlying these labels is the idea that we can rank people according to how willing they are to support the aspirations of farmers or business or any other group. "More or less," "friend or foe," and "left or right" are all statements that can be thought of in one-dimensional terms.

As we begin our introduction to the analytical study of legislative politics, I want us to start with this simple, single-dimensional way of thinking about politics. Two things will be gained by doing so. First, we can see how political scientists take a seemingly diverse set of political choices, boil them down to their unifying essence, then reach more general conclusions about practical politics. Second, we will begin to explore the most basic analytical tool currently used in the study of legislatures: **spatial voting theory.** We return to this tool time and again as we examine how the Constitution was constructed, how elections are waged, and how internal substructures like committees operate. It is a basic building block of the science of legislatures.

For the remainder of this section, I take the single-dimensional (or unidimensional) view of politics very seriously, exploring its basic elements and pointing out how it can be used to illuminate legislative dynamics. Having laid the groundwork in one dimension, in the next section, we take the spatial view to allow for politics in more than one dimension, when we move from the politics of Lineland to the politics of Flatland.

Before beginning an exploration of spatial voting theory, a word of advice: most works of history and political science can be read casually, with the reader making an occasional marginal comment or highlighting a particular phrase. The rest of this chapter is unlike most books in political science. It is more like a textbook in math or science. Like such textbooks, it builds from one idea to the next. Make sure that you have mastered one set of ideas before moving on. Also, read the following pages actively, with a pencil and pad of paper close by, so you can work out the ideas and examples that are explored. Unlike most topics covered in political science, there are right and wrong answers in the spatial theory of voting. You are more likely to understand why certain answers are right or wrong if you have worked through a number of examples. To help with this exploration, the end of the chapter includes a number of exercises.

The history of spatial voting theory

Spatial voting theory traces its roots back to the 1920s, to the work of Harold Hotelling, who examined (among other things) why merchants located their stores where they did. Why, Hotelling asked, did rival merchants tend to locate their stores close by each other? After all, if Mr. Sears and Mr. Penny located their stores across the street from each other, then a customer, looking for a bargain, easily could compare prices in the two stores and shop where the prices were lower. If the stores were located far apart, then it would be harder for customers to comparison shop, easier for stores to have captive customers, and therefore easier for stores to charge more for their goods.

In analyzing this "grocery store problem," Hotelling used the following reasoning. Assume that one main road runs into town, with the town's population located along the road at evenly spaced intervals. Two merchants with stores, Mr. Sears and Mr. Penny, sell identical goods at identical prices. It is costly for customers to travel to a store. (Travel costs are assumed to be directly proportional to the length of the road being traveled.) Because their goods and prices are the same, customers will patronize whichever store is closer. Where should Sears and Penny locate their stores?

They might choose locations similar to those in the top panel of Figure 1.1. Here, a point exactly halfway between Mr. Sears and Mr. Penny is indicated with a vertical line, Town residents who live to the left of the line will patronize Mr. Penny because his store is closer; residents who live to the right will patronize Mr. Sears. Note that, from the way the example is constructed, the halfway point between the two stores favors Mr. Sears, who will do a more active business than Mr. Penny.

FIGURE 1.1
Competition for Customers between Two Shop Owners

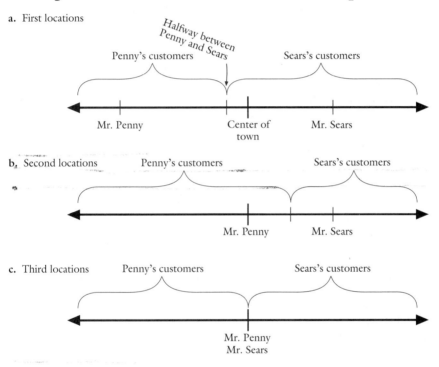

a. First locations

Halfway between Penny and Sears

Penny's customers

Sears's customers

Mr. Penny

Center of town

Mr. Sears

b. Second locations

Penny's customers

Sears's customers

Mr. Penny

Mr. Sears

c. Third locations

Penny's customers

Sears's customers

Mr. Penny
Mr. Sears

Had Mr. Penny chosen a better location, he could have lured more customers into his store. So, suppose Mr. Penny could costlessly move his store to the center of town, as in the middle panel of Figure 1.1. With Mr. Penny in the center of town and Mr. Sears still on the outskirts, Penny increases his business at the expense of Sears. Of course, Mr. Sears could recoup some of his losses to Mr. Penny, by moving right next door to him. With Penny and Sears located next to each other, in the center of town, they could split the town's business evenly. Note that neither merchant would have an incentive to move any farther, since doing so would only diminish that merchant's business. We would say that the location of the two stores is in equilibrium. In general, if stores sell identical goods at identical prices, and if customers do not like to travel, a rational process will lead competing stores to locate next to each other, in the center of town.

Hotelling noted the potential political application of this simple model of store locations. At the end of his essay about grocery stores, he wrote,

> So general is this tendency [of competitors to locate in close proximity] that it appears in the most diverse fields of competitive activity, even quite apart from what is called economic life. In politics it is strikingly exemplified. The competition for votes between the Republican and Democratic parties does not lead to a clear drawing of issues, an adoption of two strongly contrasted positions between which the voter may choose. Instead, each party strives to make its platforms as much like the other's as possible. Any radical departure would lose many votes, even though it might lead to stronger commendation of the party by some who would vote for it anyhow. (Hotelling 1929, pp. 54–55)

It took a quarter of a century before Hotelling's political musings were translated into explicit models of politics. But since the 1950s, Hotelling's insights have been fruitfully extended to two arenas of political decision making: mass elections and legislative decision making. Consider, first, the case of mass elections, first developed by Anthony Downs in 1957.

The question Downs sought to answer was this: If citizens cast their votes ideologically and if candidates can choose the types of appeals they make to voters to attract their votes, what types of platforms will candidates adopt? An answer to this question can be developed by relabeling Figure 1.1, so that the line no longer represents a road into town but the well-known liberal-conservative ideological continuum. Figure 1.2 accomplishes this relabeling. Instead of two merchants, Mr. Penny and Mr. Sears, we have two politicians, Ms. Penny and Ms. Sears.

In Figure 1.2a, Ms. Penny and Ms. Sears have located themselves a little way out toward the ideological extremes. Taking moderate-liberal and moderate-conservative positions, a point exactly halfway between Penny and Sears is indicated with a vertical line. Voters to the left of the line will vote for Ms. Penny because she is closer; likewise, voters to the right will vote for Ms. Sears. Note that, from the way the example is constructed, Sears wins the election.

Had Ms. Penny chosen a better ideological location, she could have received more votes. Consider if she had adopted a perfectly middle-of-the-road position, as in Figure 1.2b. Here, Ms. Penny could horn in on Ms. Sears's support, now winning a majority. Ms. Sears, not happy with the new state of affairs, could also moderate, taking a position nearly identical to Ms. Penny's, as in Figure 1.2c. With Penny and Sears located next to each other, they now split the votes evenly.

Penny and Sears have achieved a tie. This is the best that either one could do under the circumstances. If either Penny or Sears moves even a little and the other stays put, she will lose. Therefore, if voters base their voting decisions purely on ideological proximity and if candidates can adopt any ideological position they desire, there is a tendency in two-candidate races for both candidates to converge to the center and for elections to be tied.

FIGURE 1.2
Competition between Two Candidates for Votes

a. First locations

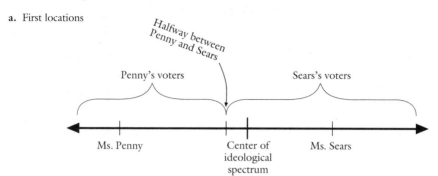

b. Second locations

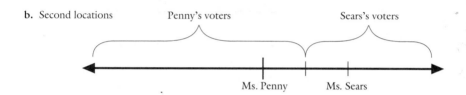

c. Third locations

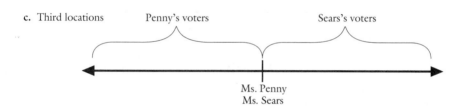

In 1958, Duncan Black performed a similar analysis, applying this single-dimensional voting model to committee deliberations. Now, the question was, If members of a committee have ideological preferences and are presented with two policy alternatives that can be described as lying along that ideological dimension, which alternative will be adopted by the committee? Similarly, if an agenda setter can decide which motions to propose to a committee, what should those motions be?

In applying the Hotelling-Downs logic to committees, one important difference must be taken into account at the beginning. Mass electorates and economic markets typically are so large that it makes sense to summarize preferences or geographic location with a line and assume that individuals are packed like sardines along it. Committees, by definition, are subsets of the electorate. Its members can be easily identified. Therefore, although we may construct a theoretically continuous dimension on which to situate committee members, we will (at least for the moment) specify the location of each member, as well as the location of the motions they vote on.

FIGURE 1.3
Voting in a Committee over Two Minimum Wage
Proposals, X and Y

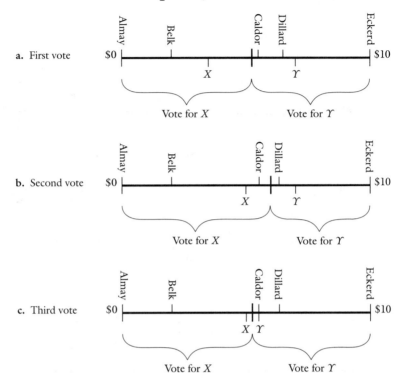

x must change its position to win

Figure 1.3 helps illustrate how the questions posed by Black might be answered in the context of a minimum wage debate. Suppose, now, we have a five-person committee whose members are arrayed as described in Figure 1.3a. The members are named Almay, Belk, Caldor, Dillard, and Eckerd. They are arrayed along a dimension that describes how high the minimum wage should be set. Almay believes the minimum wage should be abolished while Belk believes there should be a minimum wage but at a very low level. Dillard and Eckerd believe the minimum wage should be set very high, with Eckerd believing it should be $10/hr. Caldor is somewhere in the middle, preferring a minimum wage of $5.50 per hour.

Suppose this committee must choose how high the minimum wage is going to be, and the members are given a choice between alternatives labeled X ($3.50) and Y ($7.00) in Figure 1.3a. Which alternative will prevail?

Almay and Belk clearly prefer X over Y; Dillard and Eckerd clearly prefer Y over X. By a small margin, Caldor prefers the greater amount, Y, and so it prevails by a 3–2 vote.

Suppose it were possible to make amendments and that option X were changed to \$5/hr, leaving Y unchanged. What then? Figure 1.3b illustrates that this change would induce Caldor to switch her support, from Y to X, making X the winner.

Finally, allow one more amendment, this time moving alternative Y closer to the center of the *committee members' preferences*, equal precisely to Caldor's ideal minimum wage. This amendment is illustrated in Figure 1.3c. With Y now equal to Caldor's position, three members of the committee support Y, two support X, and Y wins. A little manipulation of the model reveals that no other amendment to X would allow it to unambiguously beat Y. The best supporters of X could hope to do would be to amend it so that it, too, perfectly corresponded to Caldor's position. Most people would regard such an amendment as trivial, since it would leave the committee with only one proposal, not two, located precisely at Caldor's ideal minimum wage.

It's no accident that the motions in this example tend to converge on Caldor's ideal minimum wage. Caldor is the *median* member of the committee. That is, as many members are to the left of her as to the right. In general, when a committee can be arrayed along a single dimension, anyone on the committee can make a motion, and voting can go on as long as the committee wishes; therefore, the position of the median committee member will prevail.

Each of these three simple examples—the location of a store, the ideological location of candidates, and the choice of a minimum wage—illustrates the power of the **median voter** in one-dimensional proximity models of economics and politics. The median voter result is so important in political science that if outcomes do not respect the median's preferences (assuming the issue can be fairly characterized as unidimensional), then there is a major puzzle to be explained. Even when results *do not* correspond perfectly with the median's preferences—and they rarely do—we can utilize the logic of the spatial voting setting to analyze what happened to cause policy to deviate from the median's preferences. Therefore, the median voter result is frequently the jumping-off point for many types of political and policy analysis.

In the preceding pages, we relied on some simple examples to illustrate spatial voting theory. Spatial voting theory relies on a more formal vocabulary, however; so we must proceed to state, a bit more precisely, what the theory is and how it works. Because the median voter result is so central to the political science of legislatures, it is in this context that we next delineate the special language one needs to understand and use the theory.

A more formal introduction to spatial voting theory

Three elements are necessary to undertake a spatial analysis of politics: (1) voter preferences, (2) issue alternatives, and (3) the rules by which the alternatives are voted on. The first two elements require some understanding of what the word *spatial* signifies in spatial voting theory.

We assume that **preferences** are *spatial* in the sense that they can be characterized in some *Euclidean space*. (Euclidean space is the intuitive, everyday coordinate system taught in high school geometry. For this reason, spatial voting theory is sometimes called *Euclidean voting*.) We also assume that all policy **alternatives** can be described spatially. If the space is one dimensional, then preferences can be arrayed along a line, as in the minimum wage example just explored. If the space is two-dimensional, then preferences can be described on an *x-y* plane.

When we think spatially, we need some idea of how many dimensions the space has. Often, it is enough to think unidimensionally, as when we say someone is a liberal or conservative or that a proposal is liberal or conservative. Most people are quite complicated, as are most policy proposals. So, in *reality*, we know that most people and proposals are not unidimensional. Yet, our willingness to summarize people and policy proposals with a single label speaks to the power of unidimensional spatial thinking in many circumstances. It often is a useful simplification.

In some cases, unidimensionality is not enough, even as a good summary. For decades the Democratic Party was composed of two regional factions, northern and southern. During that time, most Democrats favored some degree of government intervention in the economy and hence were varying degrees of "liberal." Yet, southerners and northerners differed in whether they believed the federal government should help blacks overcome the political barriers thrown up against them in the South. Very few southerners were antisegregation, but northerners varied greatly in how antisegregation they were. Any stylized story of Democratic Party politics during this time would miss a number of fundamentals if it didn't take into account both policy dimensions: race and the economy.

Similarly, a classic trade-off in politics is called *guns versus butter*, pointing to the often conflicting demands of domestic and military programs. Some believe in big government on both dimensions, such as the late senators Henry Jackson (D-Wash.) and Hubert Humphrey (D-Minn.); others believe in a large domestic presence and a more limited military, such as Senator Bernard Sanders (I-Vt.); still others believe in exactly the opposite, such as John McCain (R-Ariz.); finally, others believe in limited government activity in all realms, such as most libertarians such as Representative Ron Paul (R-Tex.). While it might be possible to summarize a person's feelings about military policy programs via one dimension (do they want more or fewer guns?) and all domestic programs along another dimension (do they want more or less butter?), it often does violence to the politics that emerge at the national level to further summarize feelings about domestic *and* military policy programs along a single dimension.

Important political insights can be gained by summarizing issues in a limited number of dimensions. Many important insights can be gleaned by just considering a single dimension; other important insights require a second. It turns out that few, if any, important *theoretical* insights emerge when we consider more than two dimensions. Therefore, in the pages that follow in this chapter, which explore theoretical topics, we confine ourselves to one-or two-dimensional examples. In the current case of exploring the median voter result, we will use just *one* dimension.

Preferences Two components of voter preferences need to be specified: the ideal point and the utility curve. The **ideal point** is simply the policy that the voter would most want enacted. An ideal point might be an actual number, such as when someone prefers a minimum wage of $5.50/hr or a $1,000 car, or may be a more abstract construct, such as a location on the liberal-conservative ideological scale. The **utility curve** describes how much pleasure the voter receives from policies, as a function of how far the policy is located from the voter's ideal point. Therefore, the utility curve is sometimes called the **utility function**. While the ideal point might or might not be a tangible location, the utility function describes a purely abstract concept of utility. By definition, the utility curve is at its maximum at the voter's ideal point.

Figure 1.4 illustrates a simple utility curve consistent with the committee voting example explored previously. To help motivate the example, assume that the policy being considered is the size of the minimum wage. Member *C* most prefers the minimum wage to be set at $5.50/hr, which is her ideal point.

The utility curve helps describe how *C* would evaluate various minimum wage proposals. Consider how *C* would evaluate minimum wages of $4, $6, and $7. Using the graph, we can characterize the utility that *C* receives from each alternative. The notation $U_c(\$4)$ indicates the utility member *C* receives from $4; $U_c(\$6)$ indicates the utility member *C* receives from $6; and so forth. Because $U_c(\$6) > U_c(\$4)$ (that is, the utility *C* receives from a $6 minimum

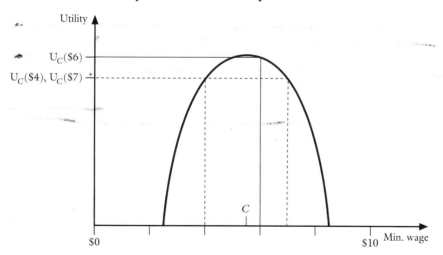

FIGURE 1.4
Symmetrical Utility Curve

wage is greater than the utility C receives from \$4), member C prefers \$6 over \$4. Because $U_c(\$4) = U_c(\$7)$, we say that C is indifferent between minimum wages of \$4 and \$7.

The utility curve in Figure 1.4 is symmetrical. That is, the amount of utility lost in moving to the right from C's ideal point is identical to the utility lost in moving the same distance to the left of C's ideal point. This is demonstrated easily when we analyze C's perspective on the proposals for \$4 and \$7, precisely \$1.50 less and more than her ideal point. Dashed lines rise vertically from \$4 to \$7 to intersect with the utility curve. They then proceed to the axis that measures utility, indicating that $U_c(\$4) = U_c(\$7)$ in both cases.

The utility curve in Figure 1.4 also is quadratic, meaning that utility declines in proportion to the *square* of the distance between C's ideal point and the alternative under consideration. For most applications, the precise functional form we use to describe a utility curve is not so important. However, the quadratic form has many nice mathematical properties that are useful when the spatial model is manipulated, and so we will rely on it in this book.[6]

If we want to describe the utility that member i receives from a proposal, x, and if member i's ideal point is written x_i, a quadratic utility function can be written as follows:

$$U_i = \alpha - \beta \, (x_i - x)^2$$

The letters α and β usually are arbitrary constants. For simplicity, therefore, α often is set to zero and β is set to 1, so that the quadratic utility function can be written more simply as

$$U_i = -(x_i - x)^2$$

When the utility function is symmetrical, voting reduces to a simple rule: vote for whichever proposal is closer to you. This rule does not hold if the utility function is asymmetrical. An example of an *asymmetrical* utility curve is drawn in Figure 1.5. It has a gradual slope to the left of the ideal point and then a steep drop-off to the right. This is the type of utility curve we might easily associate with the consumption of our favorite food. Consuming, say, a small amount of chocolate makes me happy—much happier than being entirely deprived of chocolate. Consuming a little more makes me happier still. As I eat more and more chocolate at a single sitting, I reach a point where I have eaten the perfect amount of chocolate. Let us say the optimal amount is a 6-ounce candy bar. Now, if I eat any more, I run the risk of getting a tummy ache. I find stomachaches to be so unpleasant that I would prefer to be relatively deprived at 5 ounces than to stuff myself with 7 ounces of chocolate. And, I would *certainly* prefer to forgo chocolate altogether rather than being force-fed 12 ounces.

FIGURE 1.5
Asymmetrical Utility Curve

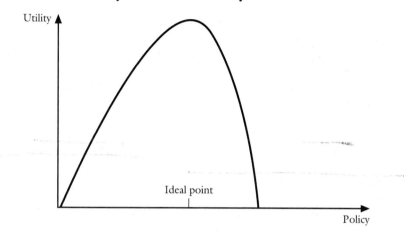

What is much more important to worry about than whether a utility curve is symmetric is whether the utility curve has **a single peak**. Figure 1.6 shows two utility functions that have more than one peak. One is ∪-shaped and, in a sense, describes someone with two ideal points. You can think about this person as someone who believes in an "all or nothing" way of doing business. The second utility function is bent a bit but still describes a person with a single ideal point. It would take us far afield to explore the problems that emerge when people have non-single-peaked utility curves or when they cannot be described as having a single ideal point. For this chapter, I will just note that non-single-peaked preferences are rare in the contexts of decisions

FIGURE 1.6
Two Non-Single-Peaked Utility Curves

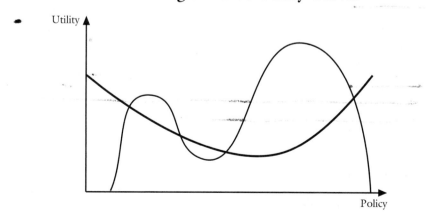

most members of Congress make; therefore, it is sufficient simply to acknowl-
edge the theoretical possibility of non-single-peaked preferences and move on.

Alternatives In spatial voting theory, alternatives can be expressed in the
same coordinate system as preferences. If committee members have preferences over the ideal minimum wage, then the alternatives will be different
levels of the minimum wage. If committee members have preferences over
the ideal degree of immigration restrictions, then the alternatives will be different levels of immigration restrictions.

In legislative decision making, one alternative in particular demands attention, the **status quo,** which is sometimes called the **reversion point.** The
status quo (or reversion point) is defined as the alternative that results if the
committee fails to agree to change policy. For example, if an appropriations bill
is not passed, then nothing can be spent on the items in that bill—the status
quo is $0. On the other hand, in most cases, when Congress considers a bill
to change income tax rates, if it fails to pass the new bill, then the tax rates
currently in effect remain—the status quo is whatever the rates are at the
time. In the example of the car purchase, if Bob, Carl, and Ted do not agree
on a car price, no car is bought. If a bill isn't passed to change the minimum
wage, it stays put.

The notion of the status quo is very important in spatial voting theory
because it helps to provide the frame of reference for the comparison among
alternatives. Members of Congress never vote for a policy alternative in a
vacuum. Rather, they are aware that something will happen if they fail to act
or if a motion is defeated. In some cases, the status quo is less obvious, such
as when the Senate votes on the confirmation of a Supreme Court nominee.
Whenever analyzing congressional voting, it is important to understand the
status quo to understand the ensuing behavior.

The Rules Two major features of the rules must be specified when using
spatial voting theory: (1) the majority requirement and (2) the agenda-
setting process. Most people are acquainted with *Robert's Rules of Order*,
which specifies how many votes are needed to pass certain motions. Most
regular motions and amendments require a simple majority to pass; a few special motions require more than a simple majority, such as two-thirds or three-
fourths of the votes. A requirement for greater than a simple majority is called
a **supermajority.**

Both houses of Congress have rules similar to those contained in *Robert's
Rules of Order*, although they are not identical. They certainly are more complex. As we will learn later in this book, the majority requirements for particular motions are very important in determining the policy that finally passes
in Congress. Not surprisingly, it is important to specify the majority requirements necessary in our theoretical treatments of voting, too.

The agenda-setting process also is important to characterize, both theoretically and practically. *Which* alternatives are allowed to be considered and
voted on can be the most important factors in understanding the laws that

Congress finally passes. Similarly, to take full advantage of spatial voting theory, we need to specify how motions are made; that is, who gets to make motions, under what circumstances, and when do motions stop.

In Chapter 9, we examine the voting rules of Congress and see that legislation is considered under many different rules. For now, we confine ourselves to the most basic of parliamentary rules: pure majority rule. Under **pure majority rule**, anyone can make a motion. (Alternately, everyone has an equal chance of being called on to make a motion at every stage of the legislative process.) After a motion is made, a vote is taken between the motion and the last motion that passed (i.e., the status quo). If the motion passes, it becomes the new status quo. Then, anyone can make a motion to change the status quo or to stop taking motions. Motions and voting continue until either a majority votes to stop or no motion can be found to beat the status quo.

Figure 1.7 reworks the single-dimension minimum wage example to show how pure majority rule might work. The committee is arrayed according to members' ideal points. In this example, the initial status quo, labeled with the letter φ, is at $3. Dillard is called on to make a motion and moves to change the status quo to $7. The $7 motion passes on a 3–2 vote. Caldor now is called

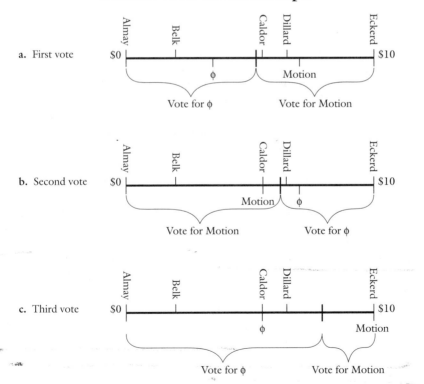

FIGURE 1.7
Median Voter Result Example

on to make a motion and moves to change policy to perfectly equal Caldor's ideal point, $5.50. This motion beats $7, 3–2. Eckerd then moves a minimum wage of $10, which loses 1–4. No other motion will beat $5.50, so voting ends.

Having now introduced some basic vocabulary, we are in a position to state more generally what was illustrated at the beginning of this section: if the number of voters is odd, if voters have single-peaked preferences in a one-dimensional space, and if they vote under pure majority rule, then the median voter's ideal point ultimately will prevail.

Figure 1.8 helps illustrate why the median voter result is true. Assume that we have lined up all the voters in the order of their ideal points and arrayed them evenly along the line in Figure 1.8. M marks the position of the median voter. If the total number of voters is N and N is odd, then the number of

FIGURE 1.8
Illustration of Median Voter Proof

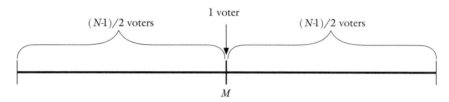

voters to the left and to the right of M is $(N-1)/2$. Recall that, for a motion to prevail, it must receive $(N-1)/2+1$ votes.

If the status quo is located to the left of M and M's ideal point is offered as a motion, we know that M will vote for it (because it is M's ideal point) and that everyone to M's right will vote for it (because M is located between them and the status quo). Therefore, the number of people voting for M's ideal point will be *at least* $(N-1)/2+1$. The same would be true if the status quo were located to the right of M and M's ideal point were offered as a motion. Similarly, if M's ideal point were the status quo and any motion to M's left were offered as an alternative, we know that M would vote to retain the status quo, as would everyone to the right of M. Again, M's ideal point always will receive at least $(N-1)/2+1$ votes against any alternative motion.

In the vocabulary of spatial voting theory, the median voter is the **Condorcet winner** of this voting exercise. The term *Condorcet winner* is named after the eighteenth-century French intellectual, the Marquis de Condorcet, who was very interested in understanding how voting systems operated. One of Condorcet's quests was to find voting systems that would automatically arrive at a result that could be beaten by no other motion, should such a result be possible to achieve at all. So, the median voter's ideal point is a Condorcet winner in the sense that, if it is moved, it always wins. Once achieved, it can never be upset via a majority vote.

A corrollary to the median voter theorem is nearly as important as the theorem itself: *under the same conditions that produce the median voter result, if the committee or electorate is given a choice between two alternatives and all actors have symmetric utility curves, the one closer to the median voter will prevail.* Hence, when we analyze voting in the unidimensional case, all we really need to know about an electorate or a committee is the location of the median. If the median prefers X over Y, then a majority of the electorate also will prefer X over Y.

This insight has both practical and theoretical implications. Practically, it means that we often can summarize the preferences of a group voting in one dimension by the location of one person, its median. The preferences of all the other members are irrelevant. Theoretically, the median voter result and its corrollary are important because they help to explain why group decision making may have so much stability, even with a lot of membership turnover. Under pure majority rule in a single dimension, outcomes will change only if the identity of the median changes, if either the median itself changes its mind or membership replacement shifts the ranking of the group such that the old median is not the new median.

I will stop here with the unidimensional case, picking it up again in later chapters. Let us now move to the multidimensional case, where just a little complexity will change the dynamics of the system considerably.

The Politics of Flatland: The Multidimensional Spatial Voting Model

Three friends, Abby, Bobby, and Carly, are movie buffs trying to decide on a movie to see. Three movies are playing in town: *Air Force II*, a violent thriller about an assassination plot against the vice president, with just one tasteful sex scene; *Rescue on Everest*, a high-altitude documentary featuring medium-paced outdoor footage and a small amount of violence but no sex; and *Porky's Vacation*, a low-energy flick featuring lots of bare skin and numerous sex scenes.

Abby usually prefers violent films but dislikes Hollywood's tendency to fill dull moments with sex and naked bodies. Bobby, too, likes violent films but also prefers films with naked, writhing bodies. Carly, a Media Studies major in college, is a devotee of erotic films, and even crass skin flicks, but is dismayed at the level of violence in society. Therefore, here is how they rank their preference for these three movies:

Abby	Bobby	Carly
Rescue on Everest	Air Force II	Porky's Vacation
Air Force II	Porky's Vacation	Rescue on Everest
Porky's Vacation	Rescue on Everest	Air Force II

Abby suggests they go to *Rescue on Everest*, to which Carly initially agrees. "Too chaste," says Bobby. "Let's go to *Air Force II*, instead."

"Too violent," says Carly, "but I would like to go to *Porky's Vacation*."

"That's better than *Everest*," says Bobby. "Sounds good to me. I guess *Porky's* it is."

"Not so fast," says Abby. "Too much sex, and boring to boot! If we're looking for a little sex, then I'd prefer *Air Force II*. What'dya say?"

Bobby replies, "*Air Force II* is clearly a better bet for me. Lots of carnage. Let's go."

Carly lets out a sigh. "I told you before that I don't like shoot-'em-up action films. If danger is what you want, let's go to *Everest*."

By now frustrated with the whole exercise, Abby grumbles, "I wanted to go to *Everest* in the first place, but you and Bobby wanted to go to *Porky's*. What gives? Maybe we should just play a computer game."

What gives, indeed? Abby and Carly agreed to see *Rescue on Everest*, but Bobby and Carly both agreed they'd rather see *Porky's Vacation*, followed by Abby and Bobby both agreeing they'd rather watch *Air Force II*, leading Abby and Carly to note their joint preference for *Rescue on Everest*. Back to the beginning. Why couldn't these three friends agree on an evening's entertainment?

The problem that Abby, Bobby, and Carly face is they are trying to decide a question that can be described along two dimensions, *violence* and *sex*. In the example, these two attributes are being traded off against each other on every move: having originally agreed with Abby to see *Rescue on Everest*, Carly discovered that she and Bobby would both prefer going to the movie with more sex (*Porky's Vacation*). The jilted Abby undid that coalition by offering Bobby a movie with more violence (*Air Force II*). Carly, who faced the prospect of now going to her least-favorite film (due primarily to its violence), got Abby to agree to go to a less-violent movie by suggesting one that also had less sex.

While this example is fanciful, it illustrates a generic problem that faces groups all the time. Whenever the rules of procedure are simple and the alternatives are complex, it often is possible to consider alternatives forever without settling on a single winner. When the procedures are complex, along with the alternatives, the decision-making process may eventually come to a stop, but the final result probably will have many detractors, perhaps even a majority of those who voted in favor of the final decision.

How do groups make decisions that can be described along more than one dimension? Such decisions face Congress all the time. The most interesting policy choices involve bundling together different features of a proposed action. A campaign finance reform bill might contain features to publicly finance elections *and* restrict the activities of political action committees. A welfare reform bill might address how much to spend on different public assistance programs, such as food stamps, housing vouchers, and medical assistance. A bill to regulate financial institutions might impose more or fewer restrictions on banks compared to insurance companies. A budget allocates spending into thousands of different types of accounts. While a single dimension is helpful in discussing certain types of policy making, staying with a single dimension will not be satisfactory for long.

In the preceding section we examined the unidimensional spatial model, reaching its most important finding, the median voter theorem. This theorem is reassuring, since it tells us that if a committee can vote long enough or candidates jostle for support long enough, majority rule eventually will reach a stable outcome, the Condorcet winner. The politics of Lineland has an **equilibrium of tastes**, with the normatively desirable property of being moderate.

In the example involving friends going to a movie, if the friends had made their decision along only *one* of the dimensions, ignoring the other, there would have been an equilibrium of tastes. For instance, assume that the friends had made their decision based *solely* on the amount of sex and that the amount of sex in each movie was ordered as follows: *Rescue on Everest* < *Air Force II* < *Porky's Vacation*. If *Porky's Vacation* has exactly the amount of sex that both Bobby and Carly like in a movie, they always will vote against Abby's efforts to see either of the other two. *Porky's Vacation* is the equilibrium of tastes. A similar example could be constructed if violence were the only dimension being considered.

Once we move away from the consideration of a single dimension, the assurance that we will encounter an equilibrium of tastes vanishes. In the movie example, *Porky's Vacation*, which was the equilibrium of tastes when sex was the only consideration, can be defeated in a majority vote when violence is added as a dimension. In the political world, with many dimensions on which to judge proposals, there also generally is no "natural" stable voting outcome and no "natural" process that will moderate outcomes. There is no equilibrium of tastes, no Condorcet winner.

To explore the multidimensional spatial voting model more closely and in a policy context, consider the situation where a legislature votes on how much to spend on two types of policy goods, national defense ("guns") and social welfare ("butter"). (You will be given the opportunity to explore the movie example in the problem set section.) As with the single-dimensional voting model, we assume all the legislators have an ideal point and a utility curve associated with deviations from that point. Because we now are in two dimensions, however, we need to describe the ideal point in terms of two goods, guns and butter, and we also need to draw a utility curve that describes how each legislator evaluates mixes of guns and butter that do not correspond with his or her ideal point.

Figure 1.9 illustrates one simple guns-butter example with three members of the legislature. Member *A* prefers little spending on defense and lots of spending on social welfare items. Member *C* prefers just the opposite, while member *B* likes a fair amount of spending on both guns and butter.

What does the utility curve look like? If we label Member *C*'s ideal national defense spending as Guns_c and *C*'s ideal social welfare spending as Butter_c, then Member *C*'s quadratic utility curve is defined as follows:

FIGURE 1.9
Ideal Points in Two Dimensions

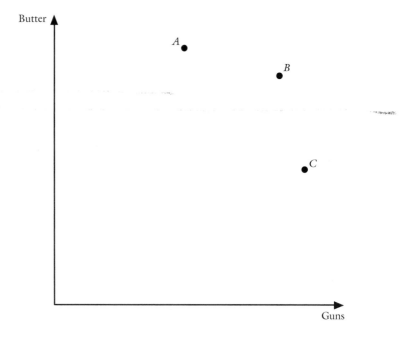

$$U_c(\text{Guns, Butter}) = \alpha - \beta \, (\text{Guns}_c - \text{Guns})^2 - \gamma(\text{Butter}_c - \text{Butter})^2$$

This is virtually identical to the one-dimensional utility curve we discussed earlier, with the addition of a term to account for the second dimension of the model. The letter γ (gamma) is a coefficient that measures how rapidly utility is lost as the amount of butter deviates from C's ideal amount of butter. Likewise, the letter β is a coefficient that measures how rapidly utility is lost as the amount of money spent on guns deviates from C's ideal amount of military spending. If β and γ are equal, then Member C is equally unhappy cutting military spending by \$1 as cutting social spending by \$1. If β is larger than γ, then Member C is made more unhappy by cutting military spending by \$1 than by cutting social spending by \$1. Finally, if γ is larger than β, Member C is more unhappy by cutting social welfare spending \$1 than by cutting military spending \$1. To aid in simplicity, let us assume for the moment that β and γ are equal. We can return later to explore what happens when they are not.

Figure 1.10 sketches out what Member C's utility curve looks like. The two policy dimensions, Guns and Butter, lie in the horizontal plane in the figure, while the axis measuring Utility is vertical. Note that the utility curve is actually three dimensional, so that it looks like half a football sticking up out of a table. We can slice horizontally into this football-shaped figure. Each of these slices produces a circle that represents all the combinations of guns and butter spending that give Member C an equal amount of utility.

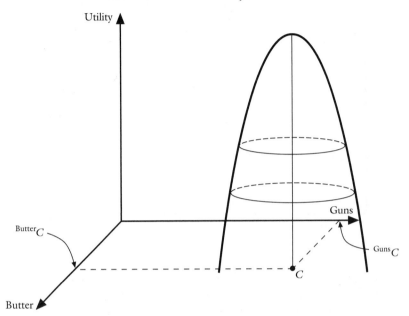

FIGURE 1.10
Member C's Utility Curve

It is more convenient to represent slicing into the "football" back onto the two-dimensional guns-butter coordinate system. I have done this in Figure 1.11. Here, I have drawn Member C's ideal point along with two circles that result when we horizontally slice into the utility curve in two places. The inner circle slices into the utility curve up high, and therefore it is relatively small. Every point along this circle represents a small *and identical* decrease in utility for Member C, compared to her ideal point. Point x_1 represents spending C's ideal amount on guns but a little too much on butter. Point x_2 also represents spending C's ideal amount on guns but now a little too little on butter. Note that x_1 and x_2 are on the same circle, and therefore Member C would derive the same amount of utility from either combination of guns and butter. Member C is *indifferent* between x_1 and x_2.

Point y_1 is even farther away from Member C's ideal point than either x_1 or x_2. Note that it lies on a circle that is larger than the inner circle. Therefore, any alternative that lies on this circle is valued less than any alternative that lies on the inner circle. Hence, while Member C is indifferent between x_1 and x_2 *and* indifferent between y_1 and y_2, we know that Member C would prefer *either* x_1 or x_2 over y_1 or y_2.

FIGURE 1.11
Examples of Indifference Curves

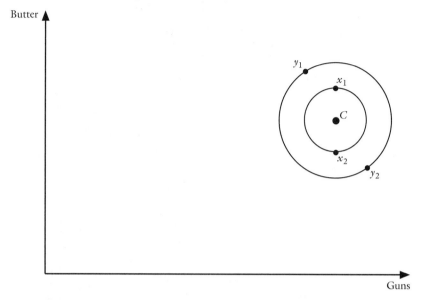

These circles have names. Because they represent alternatives toward which Member *C* is indifferent, they are called **indifference curves.** Because the indifference curves are circular, the voting rule is similar to the unidimensional case when we had symmetrical utility curves: vote for whichever alternative is closer.

Figure 1.12 restates Figure 1.9, this time adding an arbitrary status quo, ϕ, and then three indifference curves, one associated with each of the three members of the legislature. The indifference curve of Member *C* that the status quo lies on is labeled $I_c(\phi)$. Because every point inside this circle is preferred by Member *C* over any point on or outside the circle, we call the region inside the circle Member *C*'s **preferred-to set** against the status quo, labeling it $P_c(\phi)$.

Under majority rule, a motion needs a majority of votes in favor of it before it can defeat the status quo. Therefore, any motion that is going to defeat ϕ must lie in the intersection of at least two preferred-to sets. The three regions where the preferred-to sets overlap are shaded. The shaded region as a whole resembles a flower and is called the **win set** against the status quo, since this is where a motion could be offered against the status quo and win. (The notation for the win set is $W(\phi)$.) The small vertical petal is the intersection of Member *A* and Member *B*'s preferred-to sets, and thus represents the set of all points where, if a motion were made, Members *A* and *B* would vote in favor of the motion, but *C* would not. Each petal describes regions in which

FIGURE 1.12
Finding the Win Set

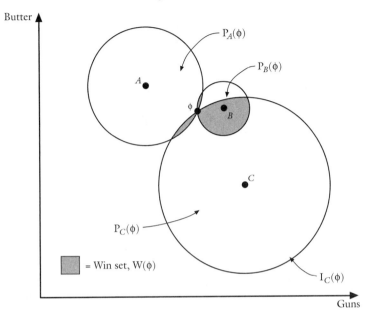

two-person coalitions would form to defeat the status quo. In this example, there is no region where all three members would vote together to overturn the status quo. So, every successful motion against the status quo will be resolved via a 2–1 vote.

If this hypothetical three-person legislature were to vote on the allocation of guns and butter, using pure majority rule, what decision would they reach? It is tempting to reason by analogy with the one-dimensional case and say, "The median eventually would prevail." If you examine Figure 1.12 closely, you see that Member B has median preferences on both the guns and butter dimensions. What if Member B is called on to make a motion and he moves that spending in both policy areas be equal to his ideal point? We know that the motion will prevail, because Member B's ideal point is in the win set of Figure 1.12. The most important question, though, is this: Once the legislature has agreed to set spending at B's ideal point, could yet another motion prevail to change spending further? In other words, is B's ideal point, which is the median on both the guns and butter dimensions, the Condorcet winner?

Figure 1.13 illustrates the answer to these questions: yes, there is a win set against Member B's ideal point; therefore B's ideal point is not the Condorcet winner. The win set against B's ideal point is a lens-shaped region to the "southwest" of B's ideal point in which Members A and C would vote

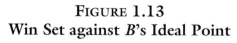

FIGURE 1.13
Win Set against *B*'s Ideal Point

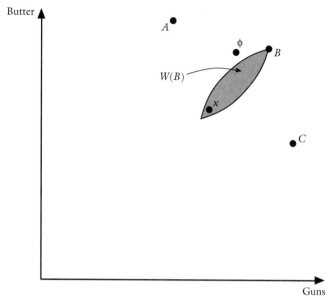

together to move policy away from *B*. (*B*, of course, will vote no because any deviation from his ideal point makes him worse off.)

Now, suppose a motion were made that was inside W(*B*). The policy location labeled *x* in Figure 1.13 is such a motion. Is there a win set against *x*? Figure 1.14 illustrates that the answer to this question also is yes. In this case, the win set is pretty large, occupying almost one quarter of the policy space.

Most interesting, however, is that the win set against *x* now contains the original status quo, ɸ. Think about this: we have seen that point B is preferred to ɸ by a majority vote and that *x* is preferred by a majority vote to B. By standard rules of logic, we tend to assume if someone prefers *Y* over *X* and prefers *Z* over *Y*, that person should also prefer *Z* over *X*. This is called the principle of **transitivity**.[7] Note that the example in Figures 1.13 to 1.15 violates this principle, since *B* is preferred to ɸ, *x* is preferred to B, but *x* is *not* preferred to ɸ.[8]

The violation of transitivity in this example is not a fluke or a contrivance. Rather, it is a fundamental characteristic of majority rule voting when the issues involved can be described along more than one dimension. Even if all the individuals have clearly defined, transitive preferences (as Members *A*, *B*, and *C* do in the example), there generally is *no* transitive preference ordering for the group. This, called the **chaos result** of public choice theory, is probably one of the most important insights of social science.

FIGURE 1.14
Win Set against *x*

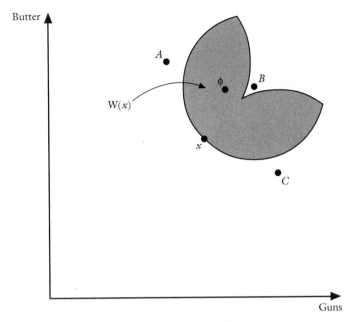

This insight is associated most clearly with the political scientist Richard McKelvey. Informally, the **McKelvey chaos theorem** may be stated as follows:

> If more than two decision makers are making decisions on a policy that can be characterized using more than one dimension, generally no motion can be made that cannot be beaten, via majority rule, by some other motion. In other words, there generally is no Condorcet winner in multidimensional voting setting. Furthermore, you can manipulate the agenda (i.e., the order of motions) in such settings such that *any* point in the policy space can be reached, at some point, through majority rule voting. (See McKelvey 1976)

The last sentence in the McKelvey chaos theorem sometimes is called the *anything can happen result*. To illustrate this point, consider Figure 1.15. Figure 1.15 takes the previous example, with the ideal points of Members *A, B,* and *C,* along with the status quo, ϕ, and labels a series of motions that move from ϕ to x_4.[9] So, we can start with a point that is "in the middle" of the preferences of the three legislators, lay out a voting agenda of proposals that win majority of support of the legislature, and very quickly move to an outcome that lies far away from anyone's ideal point. We could continue to propose motions that would prevail on a series of 2–1 votes that would establish a series

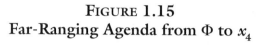

FIGURE 1.15
Far-Ranging Agenda from Φ to x_4

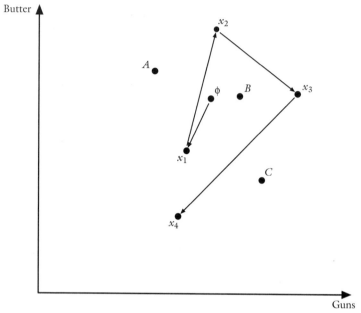

of new status quo points farther and farther from the region where the three decision makers are located, and where the original status quo was positioned.

To recap the multidimensional case, we have seen that the multidimensional case is quite different from the unidimensional one. There is no "equilibrium of tastes," as there is when there is one dimension of choice. Majority rule decisions are inherently unstable. Any result that eventually emerges through majority rule, in some sense, is arbitrary.

The McKelvey chaos theorem probably seems counterintuitive, since it does not describe most decision-making bodies we encounter in everyday life. Congress *does* pass legislation, school boards *do* pass budgets, and we are able to agree among our friends on where we will go to dinner and a movie on Friday night.

Therefore, the McKelvey chaos theorem is only the beginning of our analysis of legislative decision making. Political scientists and economists have killed a lot of trees trying to understand theoretically why real-life legislatures eventually come to closure in their decision making, even on complex items. In other words, they have spent a great deal of time dealing with the question of why so much stability is observed in legislatures when theory predicts massive instability (cf. Tullock 1981 and Shepsle and Weingast 1981).

Scholars first tried to answer this question by trying to see if some configurations of preferences might be naturally stable. There *are* such configurations of preferences, and a couple deserve comment. Figure 1.16a shows one such configuration. Here, the ideal points of the three legislators are situated perfectly along a single line. Using a compass and ruler, you can convince yourself that ideal point *y* is a Condorcet winner. If *y* is the status quo, any motion to move along the line in the direction of *z* will draw the disapproval of proponents for *x* and *y*; any motion to move along the line in the direction of *x* will draw the disapproval of proponents for *y* and *z*. Any motion off the line will likewise draw the disapproval of at least two members (*y* and one other) and might even draw unanimous disapproval.

FIGURE 1.16
Highly Symmetric Configurations of Ideal Points Create an Equilibrium of Tastes

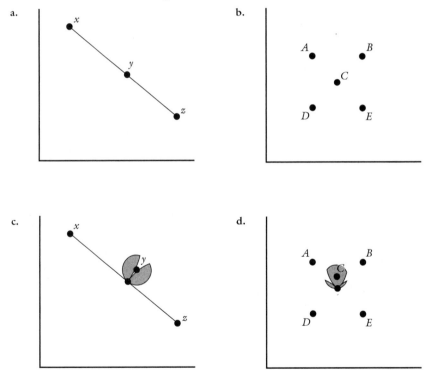

Geometrically, Figure 1.16a should be recognized as simply taking the unidimensional case and tilting it 45 degrees. If multidimensional politics collapses down to a single dimension, then there is a meaningful median, regardless of the angle at which the dimension is tilted.

Politically, this example can be thought of as a stylized version of political ideology. Political scientists classically have understood political ideology as the principle of attitude constraint (see Converse 1964). In Figure 1.16a, ideal points in the horizontal dimension are constrained by the linear relationship to lie in the particular place on the vertical dimension.

Figure 1.16b shows a more clearly two-dimensional example. Here, members *A*, *B*, *D*, and *E* reside at the corners of a box, with *C* being right in the middle of the box. Applying a similar type of analysis to Figure 1.16b as applied to Figure 1.16a would reveal that member *C*'s ideal point is a Condorcet winner, since any motion to move away from *C*'s ideal point will always elicit the opposition of at least three members (*C* and two others).

The primary reason that attempts to discover how an equilibrium of tastes might come about in multidimensional voting models have never gotten very far is illustrated in Figures 1.16c and 1.16d. In each of these panels, the ideal points identified as the Condorcet winners in Figures 1.16a and 1.16b move by only a tiny bit. After this move, a win set against the previous Condorcet winner can be drawn. Having drawn one win set, we reenter the land of chaos and "anything can happen" that we were trying to escape.

The general problem with trying to find useful equilibria of tastes in voting models is that they all have the quality of being *knife edged*. Just one person moves a microscopic amount and the equilibrium has vanished. Consequently, scholars have spent their time trying to find how decision-making equilibria might emerge independent of the preferences of the decision makers. Although we can contrive situations in which there *is* a natural equilibrium of tastes, the most useful place to look in explaining why congressional decisions are so stable is to look at institutions, such as committees and parties.

Politicians often take advantage of the fundamental chaos of politics to win political battles. A classic example of this phenomenon occurred in 1956, when Congress was considering whether to begin a program of federal assistance to local school districts. Several studies have addressed this episode (see Enelow 1981; Riker 1982, 1986; Poole and Rosenthal 1997, pp. 157–59). Here is the essence of the situation.

Before the 1950s, the federal government had never aided local school districts, except in a few limited cases. A majority of the Democratic Party wished to begin local school aid and had been working hard to achieve this result for many years. In 1956, the House Education and Labor Committee reported a bill to the House floor to achieve this goal. Figure 1.17a lays out the spatial logic of the situation. The status quo was far to the right of the issue space; the committee proposed a bill that was much closer to the median of the House than the status quo.

Because the committee bill was much closer to what a majority of the House wanted to achieve, we would expect federal aid to education to have passed the House in 1956. And yet, the House voted to reject aid to local school districts. What happened?

Adam Clayton Powell happened. Powell was the Democratic member of Congress representing Harlem in the House and, as a consequence, was probably the most prominent African American politician in the country in the 1950s. He was an ardent opponent of the system of segregation that existed in the South. His constituents expected him to fight hard to end segregation. So, when the aid-to-education bill was reported to the House floor, Powell proposed an amendment that would have barred money in the bill from going to school districts that ignored the recent Supreme Court rulings mandating the desegregation of public schools. In practical terms, this meant that virtually none of the money in the bill could have gone to southern school districts.

Powell's motion introduced a second dimension, racial desegregation, to the policy being considered. This changed the situation from being similar to Figure 1.17a and made it more like Figure 1.17b. Although Democrats from the northern and southern wings of the party almost all agreed that federal aid to education should be increased, they disagreed sharply on segregation. Southerners (S) represented a region of the country in which segregation was the core social institution; thus they all supported retaining the racial status quo. Northern Democrats (N) were a mixed lot, but they mostly favored ending segregation in the South (although some cynics would say they were less keen on ending segregation in the North). Republicans (R) also were a mixed lot on racial matters, but they mostly continued

FIGURE 1.17
The Powell Amendment in One and Two Dimensions

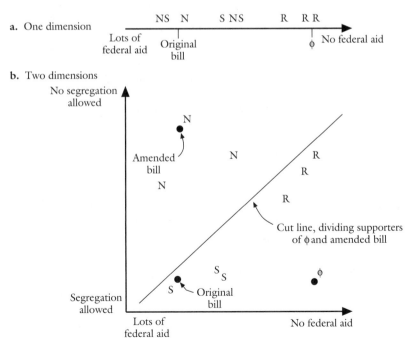

to adhere to their party's historical preference for racial equality, while taking conservative positions on matters of economics and welfare.

This is the world sketched in Figure 1.17b. Now in two dimensions, we see that the original bill simply moved policy directly to the left, leaving racial equality unchanged. The Powell amendment proposed leaving educational policy the same as the committee bill, only now moving racial policy in a strong desegregationist direction. Note what this amendment did. Without the amendment, the Democrats would have stayed together to support the committee bill. The amendment, though, asked them to make this comparison: educational aid with segregation or with desegregation. One bloc chose one way; the other bloc, the other.

With the bill amended, the comparison with the status quo had now changed, leaving only a minority of the House happy with changes on *both* policy dimensions. The amendment succeeded in peeling southern Democrats away from the pro-education aid coalition, leaving policy unchanged in the end.

The Powell amendment episode is a complicated one that we will revisit in later pages. What is important to know for the moment is that Republicans seized on the Powell amendment as an opportunity to kill federal aid to education. The Powell amendment was a **killer amendment**, because it took an otherwise acceptable bill and made it unacceptable to a majority. (The opposite of a killer amendment is a **saving amendment**, which takes a bill that is unacceptable to a majority and saves it by introducing a second dimension for consideration.) Because of the chaos theorem and "anything can happen result" discussed earlier, we know that killer amendments frequently are possible in any legislative setting. Whether they are offered and how they fare is a result of how a number of other factors come together, such as the rules under which the bill was considered and the overall distribution of preferences in the chamber at the time. But the *possibility* that a crafty opponent might successfully introduce an irrelevant policy dimension and derail a legislative vehicle is something that legislators always have to watch out for.

Two Unresolved Issues: Salience and Sophistication

In working through the material in the first part of this chapter, I have had to defer a couple of discussions for the sake of expositional clarity. Now, we return to them. In particular, I need to address two issues: (1) what happens in multidimensional voting models when one issue is "more important" than the other and (2) what happens when legislators try to misrepresent their true preferences and manipulate the voting situation.

Salience: The unequal importance of issues

Let us suppose that the government spends its money on just two goods: the administration of justice (courts, prosecutors, police officers, etc.) and national defense (ships, airplanes, soldiers, sailors, etc.). Let us further suppose that doing an optimal job of defending the nation's borders from attack is much more expensive than doing an optimal job of keeping the domestic court system going. Therefore, the ideal point for Legislator X for defense and justice spending is at $1 trillion for defense and $250 billion for justice. Suppose at Year 1 the government has fixed spending precisely at Legislator X's ideal point, so that the total budget is equal $1.25 trillion. The budget is balanced, meaning tax revenues are also $1.25 trillion. Finally, suppose that in Year 2 something dramatic happens to the ability to raise revenues, resulting in a drop in taxes to exactly $1 trillion dollars. The government has a balanced budget rule, so a total of $250 billion needs to be cut from either defense, justice, or both. Because total spending now may not exceed $1 trillion, what mix of spending on defense and justice would Legislator X most prefer?

When indifference curves are circular, as they were in the previous section, the answer to this question is straightforward. If Legislator X has a circular indifference curve around his ideal point, then he equally dislikes cutting $1 from either defense or justice. Therefore, if forced to cut total spending by $250 billion, Legislator X would choose to take half from defense and half from justice, resulting in an "induced" ideal point of $875 billion for defense and $125 billion for justice.[10]

Think about this: faced with a requirement to reduce total spending by 20 percent, Legislator X chooses to cut defense just a bit (12.5 percent) and to cut justice spending by a lot (50 percent). Does this seem realistic? Perhaps it does. But, perhaps it does not.

If it does not make sense, then that is likely because you suppose that $1 buys a certain amount of defense, in Legislator X's mind, and another amount of justice. It might be the case, for instance, that Legislator X believes that $1 buys as much justice as $5 buys of defense. In other words, he views the trade-off between defense and justice as weighing the purchase of goods that have different relative prices. Therefore, faced with the requirement of cutting overall spending by $250 billion dollars, he might choose some other allocation that takes into account the relative "unit price" of justice and defense. One such allocation may involve taking $200 billion from defense and $50 billion from justice, making the resulting budget consist of $800 billion for defense and $200 billion for justice.

If Legislator X makes the trade-off this way, we know that he values incremental changes in the defense and justice budgets differently, giving greater weight to a change in the justice budget than in the defense budget. This implies that the indifference curve around his ideal point is not circular, but elliptical, like that drawn in Figure 1.18. In that figure, two bundles of defense/justice spending are labeled b_1 and b_2. Point b_1 represents spending for justice at X's ideal level but with a cut of $100 billion in defense; point b_2 represents spending for defense at X's ideal level with a cut of $100 billion for justice. Notice how b_2 is on an indifference curve farther away from X's ideal point than b_1, even though each is equally far away from X's ideal point.

Recall from the previous section that X's utility function in this case can be written generally as

$$U_x(\text{Defense, Justice}) = \alpha - \beta(\text{Defense} - \text{Defense}_i)^2 - \gamma\,(\text{Justice} - \text{Justice}_i)^2$$

When $\beta = \gamma$, the indifference curves are circular. In this example, however, $\beta < \gamma$, accounting for the fact that a cut in justice is regarded more negatively than an equal cut in defense.

The term used to describe the state of affairs when $\beta \neq \gamma$ is **salience**. In this example, justice spending is more salient than defense spending because cuts in it are regarded more harshly than cuts in defense.

Elliptical indifference curves are a much more realistic way to describe how legislators evaluate the trade-offs between programs. There is no question, for instance, that a senator from Iowa regards a $10 billion cut in corn price supports to be more damaging than a $10 billion cut in urban mass transit subsidies. More commonly, we would say that price supports are more salient to farm-state senators than subsidies to subways.

FIGURE 1.18
Different Salience Weights along Two Spending Dimensions

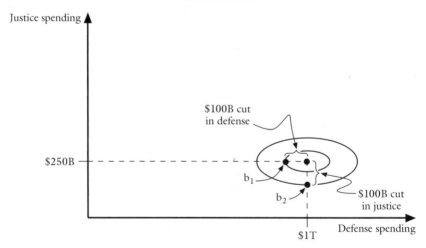

Salience comes into play even when we are not talking about money. For instance, for a generation now, Republicans have entered Congress with the support of the Right-to-Life movement, which is a strong opponent of abortion. For legislators who seek such support, abortion is more salient than other issues, such as the antitrust status of baseball. Likewise, a large number of new House members were elected in 1810 on a platform of making England pay for its supposed abuses of America's international shipping rights. (These were the "War Hawks" who supported the young Speaker of the House, Henry Clay.) To them, war with England was a more salient issue than other matters, like building roads in the western frontier.

In most cases, when a member of Congress has an intense interest in a particular project or program, that is because the member both wants the government to spend a lot of money on the program *and* the program is more salient to that member than other programs. Formally, these two characteristics imply that (1) the member has a higher ideal point on this dimension than other members of Congress (Iowa senators prefer a higher level of corn price supports than Rhode Island senators) and (2) the coefficient that measures the loss in utility due to deviations from the ideal point in that dimension is greater than the coefficent measuring utility loss in the other dimension.

The prevalence of elliptical indifference curves has an important, but subtle, effect on the nature of bargaining in Congress. At the core of legislative bargaining is coalition building. At the core of coalition building is groups of legislators agreeing to support each others' proposals when normally they would not. In bargaining, each group gives up something that is not of value to its members in order to get something that *is* valuable. If I am an Iowa senator, farm programs are valuable to me and urban mass transit subsidies are not. If you are a New York senator, the exact opposite is true. We can serve each other's political and policy goals by making a trade: I will support urban mass transit if you will support farm programs.

To understand the deal that we strike, it is important to know not only that we support high levels of spending for our pet programs but also what we will give up to get higher spending for our programs. If my indifference curve is circular, then I will be willing to accept spending $1 for your urban mass transit subsidies for each $1 of farm price supports you vote for. If you also have circular indifference curves, your calculations are the same, so that we reach a bargain that is some compromise in our two positions, with total spending equal to the average of our ideal points for our pet programs.

This is illustrated in Figure 1.19a, showing the ideal points for the Iowa and New York senators, along with a proposed compromise between the two. The indifference curves that go through that compromise indicate that the win set is empty. The bargain will stick between the two senators.

If the indifference curves are elliptical (or even if just one is), then the nature of the bargain will be quite different. If farm price supports are more salient to me than urban mass transit, then I am willing to accept more than $1 of extra spending for subways to purchase support for another $1 of extra spending for price supports. If you feel just the opposite, then we are both willing to accept even higher spending for the other's programs to win support for somewhat higher spending for our own program.

FIGURE 1.19
How Elliptical Indifference Curves Can Encourage
"Too Much" Spending

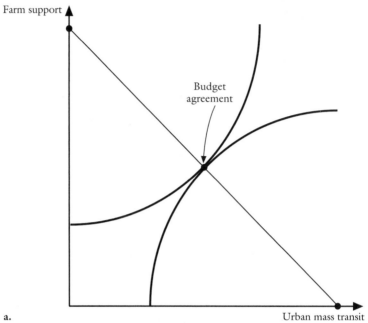

a.

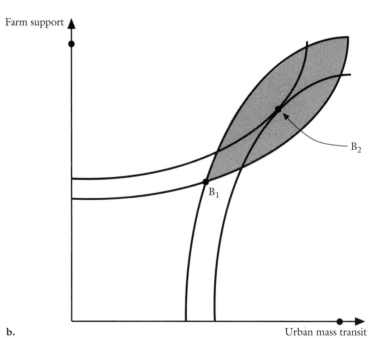

b.

Figure 1.19b illustrates this formally. The spending agreement from Figure 1.19a is labeled B_1. The elliptical indifference curves for the two senators go through B_1, and the shaded area is the resulting win set. Note that the win set is oriented to the "northeast" of B_1, indicating that any new agreement will require spending on both programs to go up. The new agreement that is reached will be something like the point labeled B_2. The new indifference curves that go through B_2 are drawn to show that this deal will stick and be in equilibrium between the two senators.

Political scientists and economists who study budgeting and public finance have used this type of analysis to help explain why it is so difficult to balance the federal budget (McCubbins 1991; Stewart 1991). A member of Congress who cares intensely about one program is willing to accept high spending on other programs, if as a result she can win the support of others to support her own programs. If this sort of behavior is common, and there is no credible mechanism to keep overall spending in check, then overall government spending will tend to balloon.

Sophisticated misrepresentation of preferences

Up to this point, I have been assuming that whenever legislators vote, they simply evaluate the utility they receive from the two proposals under consideration. Yet, we can think of cases where acting this way would strain credulity. Take the case of the Powell amendment again (refer back to Figure 1.17b).

One feature of this story I did not make clear earlier is that there are rules in the House specifying the order for voting on amendments; House members therefore knew that the Powell amendment would be dealt with in a certain order. They also knew that other votes would follow, depending on whether the Powell amendment passed or was defeated.

To simplify matters, House members knew that if the Powell amendment passed, then the next vote would be on whether to pass the aid-to-education bill, with the amendment integrated into the bill. If the amended bill passed, the aid-to-education bill that barred segregation would be the law of the land; if the amended bill failed, no federal aid to local schools would be provided and segregation would be allowed to continue (i.e., the status quo). On the other hand, if the *unamended* bill passed, the aid-to-education bill that allowed segregation would be the law of the land; if the unamended bill failed, no federal aid to local schools would be provided and segregation would be allowed to continue (i.e., the status quo).

This voting sequence is summarized in Figure 1.20 using a graphical representation called a *voting tree*. This voting tree is laid out from top to bottom, indicating at each level the choices facing the House. For example, the first level shows the first vote, the Powell amendment against the (implied) alternative of no Powell amendment.

A voting tree also has "branches" that help to summarize the sequence of votes, depending on which votes prevail at each step. Returning to Figure 1.20, at the bottom of each first-level branch, "No Powell amendment" and

FIGURE 1.20
Voting Tree for Powell Amendment

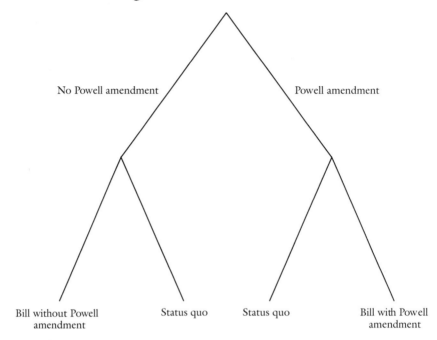

Rank-ordered preferences for three possible outcomes

Northern Democrats (N)	*Southern Democrats (S)*	*Republicans (R)*
Amended bill, with Powell amendment	Original bill, without Powell amendment	Status quo
Original bill, without Powell amendment	Status quo	Amended bill, with Powell amendment
Status quo	Amended bill, with Powell amendment	Original bill, without Powell amendment

"Powell amendment," there are two other branches that lead to the next votes, depending on which side wins the first vote. The left-hand branch, which is followed if the Powell amendment loses, shows that the second vote pits the unamended bill (aid-to-education, segregation allowed) against the status quo (no aid-to-education, segregation allowed). The right-hand branch, which is followed if the Powell amendment wins, shows that the second vote in this case pits the amended bill (aid-to-education, no segregation allowed) against the exact same status quo that is at the end of the left-hand branch (no aid-to-education, segregation allowed).

One of the things we notice when we construct a voting tree and study it carefully is that the most important decision that ultimately will be made pairs the status quo against a set of distinct alternatives in the last level of voting. In the case of the Powell Amendment illustrated in Figure 1.20, the status quo will *either* be paired against an aid-to-education bill that allows segregation (left-hand branch) *or* an aid-to-education bill that prohibits segregation (right-hand branch). Therefore, the most important question to ask of a voting tree is "what are the outcomes if *all* of the votes described on the last level are allowed to happen?" In Figure 1.20, this amounts to asking what happens if the unamended bill is voted on against the status quo (left-hand branch) and what happens if the amended bill is voted on against the status quo (right-hand branch).

As you can see by studying the figure, the answer to this question depends on knowing how House members rank-order three alternatives: the unamended bill, the amended bill, and the status quo. In this example, we can reduce this question further by asking how three blocs of House members—northern Democrats, southern Democrats, and Republicans—rank the three policy proposals that appear on the last level. We can use Figure 1.17 to calculate how each bloc ranked these proposals. For your convenience, I have recorded their rankings in the table at the bottom of Figure 1.20.

To make things simple, let us act as if there were an equal number of northern Democrats, southern Democrats, and Republicans. First, check out the final vote along the left-hand branch, which pairs the unamended bill against the status quo. The table in Figure 1.20 shows that if the unamended bill is paired against the status quo, the northern Democrats and southern Democrats favor the unamended bill, the Republicans favor the status quo, so the unamended bill passes 2–1. Now, check out the final vote along the right-hand branch. Here, the Republicans and southern Democrats prefer the status quo, while the northern Democrats favor the amended bill; therefore, the status quo passes 2–1.

Finally, return to the first stage of voting and ask, "What would a House member know about the vote on the Powell Amendment if he had the voting tree in his hand?" He would know that if the amendment loses, the House travels down the left-hand branch, in which the unamended bill is paired against the status quo, and that the unamended bill ultimately becomes law. He would also know that if the amendment passes, the House travels down the right-hand branch, in which the amended bill is ultimately paired against the status quo, and that the status quo prevails. Therefore, if (1) all House members are looking ahead (or "looking down the voting tree"), and (2) all House members are voting based on their policy preferences across the three alternatives, then the vote at the first level, which formally pairs the Powell amendment against the unamended bill, is *practically speaking* a vote that pairs the unamended bill against the status quo. Thus, he should not treat the first vote as simply a vote of the Powell amendment against no Powell amendment, but rather, as a vote about which branch of the voting tree to travel down.

Now, think about this: How should each of the blocs of House members vote at the first level, when presented with the alternative of Powell amendment against no Powell amendment? The answer depends critically on whether House members are looking down the voting tree. If they totally disregard the voting tree and vote based simply on how they feel about segregation, we know that northern Democrats and Republicans should vote for the Powell Amendment and southern Democrats should vote against it. However, by doing so, this forces the bill down the right-hand branch, dooming it to defeat. Thus, by ignoring the voting tree and supporting the Powell amendment, the northern Democrats *guarantee* that they will get their least-favorite outcome, the status quo.

If the House members pay attention to the voting tree, the northern Democrats recognize the trap at the first step, vote against the Powell amendment, force the bill down the left-hand branch, and at least salvage their second-preferred outcome: aid-to-education without the Powell amendment.

These two ways of considering the voting tree define two types of voting: **sincere voting** and **sophisticated voting.** Under sincere voting, all House members simply look at the two alternatives being paired, ask which they prefer more, and vote for that alternative, *regardless of which branch of the voting tree the bill is forced down.* Under sophisticated voting, House members start by asking, "What branch of the voting tree does this force the bill down, what is the outcome at the end of each branch, and which branch do I want the bill to travel along?" So, sophisticated voting involves taking into account the actions of others and all subsequent voting situations when voting on any particular measure.

Suppose someone wanted to vote in a sophisticated fashion. How easy is it to decide whether it is useful to do so? On the one hand, figuring out how to vote in a sophisticated fashion is difficult, because it helps to know, *with certainty*, not only the preferences of everyone else but also the willingness of everyone else to vote in a sophisticated fashion. If we assume that everyone is willing to vote in a sophisticated fashion, that everyone is a utility maximizer, that everyone knows everyone else's preferences, and that everyone knows the sequence of votes that will occur, it is not difficult to calculate the proper sophisticated strategy in any situation.

The method we use is called *backward induction*, which relies on this simple insight: on the last vote, everyone should vote sincerely, since there are no future votes to take into account. To see how it works, return to the Powell amendment voting tree in Figure 1.20.

Two final votes are possible: the status quo could be paired with either the unamended bill (the left comparison) or the amended bill (the right comparison). We know, from the rankings of the three blocs, that the status quo loses to the unamended bill but beats the amended bill. Now, go up a level, to the first vote. If the Powell amendment prevails, everyone knows that the status quo will be the ultimate outcome. If the Powell amendment loses, everyone knows that the unamended bill will be the ultimate outcome. Therefore, the vote on the amendment at the first stage *actually* is a vote between the status quo and the unamended bill.

We call a vote in favor of the Powell amendment at this first stage the *sophisticated equivalent* of the status quo, because voting for the Powell amendment has the same ultimate effect as voting for the status quo. Because the northern Democrats favor the unamended bill over the status quo, they oppose the Powell amendment, disregarding how they feel about it intrinsically. For both the southern Democrats and the Republicans, the sophisticated action is the same as the sincere action, hence they both have the luxury of appearing to vote sincerely at each stage of the process.

One of the things that makes the Powell amendment episode so interesting is that the question of whether northern Democrats should engage in sophisticated voting became a major issue. Many prominent liberal Democrats counseled against passing the Powell amendment, so that federal aid-to-education could at least achieve a toehold in national policy. The House Democratic leadership enlisted the aid of former president Harry Truman, whose credentials in opposition to southern segregation were secure, to appeal to northern Democrats to oppose the Powell amendment. In the end, some liberal northern Democrats *did* vote against the Powell amendment, in all likelihood because the appeals to sophisticated voting worked. (There also is evidence that some very conservative Republicans, who were in fact pro-segregation, voted *for* the Powell amendment, to kill the overall bill.) That more did not vote in a sophisticated manner represents practical problems with sophisticated voting. In particular, for a liberal northern Democrat, who had taken a strong stance against segregation, to oppose the Powell amendment would have required that northern Democrat to explain his actions to his constituents. Not all constituents understand the intricacies of legislative strategy, and so the willingness to engage in strategic voting varies among members of Congress, often based on how electorally secure they are (see Denzau, Riker, and Shepsle 1985).

The Powell amendment example is an easy way to show how backward induction works, since there are just two levels of voting. Yet, the default rules of the House allow for voting trees of five levels. Every bill that makes it to the floor may have an amendment and the amendment may have an amendment. In addition, you can move to substitute a whole new bill for the bill being considered, and the substitute can have an amendment. If this ever were to happen, voting would occur in this order:

1. The amendment to the amendment versus the unamended amendment.
2. The amendment to the substitute versus the unamended substitute.
3. The winner of step 2 against the winner of step 1.
4. The winner of step 3 against the unamended bill.
5. The winner of step 4 against the status quo.

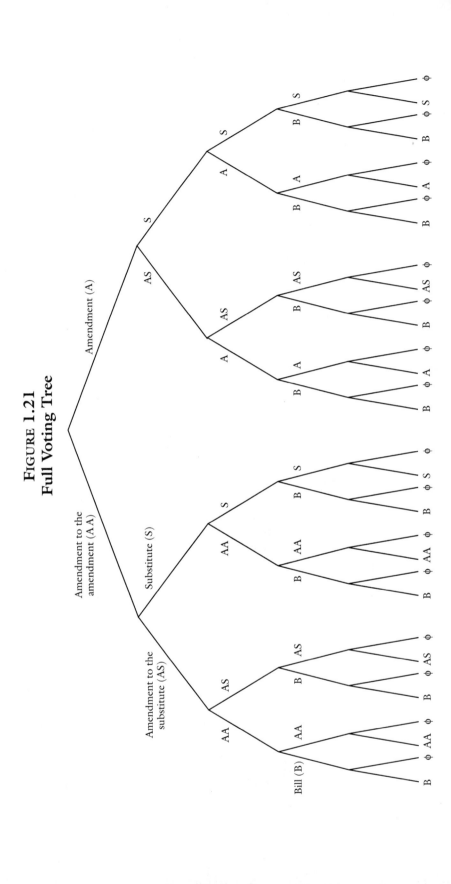

FIGURE 1.21
Full Voting Tree

This voting order gives rise to the voting tree in Figure 1.21. Despite the messiness of the voting tree, the logic of backward induction is easy (if tedious) to implement: figure out the winner at each of the end points of the voting tree, see how this affects the sophisticated equivalents of voting in the previous stage, and keep on doing this until you get to the top of the tree.

Spatial Voting Theory and the Study of Congress

The remainder of this book will be influenced heavily by the techniques and theoretical insights introduced in this chapter. Rational choice theory generally and spatial voting theory in particular provide an important set of building blocks for helping to better understand congressional behavior. The puzzles uncovered by spatial voting theory, particularly those concerning the inherent instability of democratic decision making, will be a constant topic of discussion as we try to understand how important institutional features of Congress operate, including the rules, the committee system, and the leadership system.

At this point, some may question how spatial voting theory is actually used to help explain the way real-world features of congressional politics work. Let me provide a brief road map to some of the following chapters and topics in the book. In Chapter 2, I will rely on the "chaos result" of instability in multidimensional voting settings to help explain why the Congress under the Articles of Confederation was so ineffective. I will also use the multidimensional model to explicate the basic issues facing the framers as they voted on important provisions of the Constitution, and show that the resulting document was a "centrist" compromise in a convention whose members had a diversity of views about the strength of the federal government and equality of representation in Congress. Finally, in Chapter 2, I use the multidimensional and unidimensional models to show precisely how bicameralism and the president's veto power influence the distribution of political power between Congress and the president, and between the two chambers of Congress.

Chapters 4, 5, and 6 explore a variety of topics pertaining to congressional voters, congressional candidates, and the competitive environment in which they interact. Running through each of these chapters is an assumption that voters are making decisions largely consistent with the spatial model—that is, they tend to favor candidates who are "close" to them, and that candidates are trying to position themselves in a way to take advantage of this prominent decision rule.

In Chapters 7 and 8, we turn our attention to two important institutional features *within* Congress: party leadership and committees. Members of political parties tend to hold ideal points similar to those of their co-partisans, but, as we have seen in this chapter, if issues are multidimensional, just having ideal points that are similar is not enough to ensure stable policy outcomes, or even outcomes that are "close" to the majority party. An important use of the unidimensional model in Chapter 7 will be to show how the agenda-setting power of the majority party in each chamber allows policies to migrate away from the chamber median and toward the median of the majority party. In Chapter 8, the multidimensional model will be used to show how sets of "interested" members of a chamber can also shade policy away from the chamber median and toward the median of the committee members who have jurisdiction over the issues overseen by different committees.

Finally, in Chapter 9, I use the spatial model, both the unidimensional and multidimensional versions, to show how certain chamber rules, like the filibuster, help to induce gridlock or move policy away from the preferences of medians.

The chapters that follow do not rely *entirely* on spatial voting theory. Indeed, the next two chapters will contain a lot of historical material that would appear in any textbook about Congress, regardless of its overall approach. However, because the spatial theory so elegantly captures the essence of what Congress does—makes choices across policy alternatives—the spatial theory is the infrastructure that guides all of the analysis that follows.

By and large, the inherent instability of democratic decision making is dampened in Congress because of how institutions operate. Many of the institutions and rules we will study in later chapters—particularly the committee system and rules of order—impose an artificial stability on decision making that would not exist without those rules and institutions. Because it emphasizes the essential role of institutions in inducing stability, public choice theory often is called the new institutionalism when it is applied to Congress and other governing institutions.

The term **new institutionalism** is more than just a relabeling of public choice theory. The term stands in contrast to behavioralism, which was the prevailing approach to Congress and most other American political institutions from the 1960s until the 1990s. Instead of focusing on how rules and institutions induce stability in democratic institutions, behavioralist research into congressional politics focused on the attitudes and beliefs of members of Congress to understand their behavior.

As I hope to make clear throughout this book, nothing is inherently wrong with understanding the values, attitudes, and beliefs of members of Congress if you want to understand their behavior. What the new institutionalism tells us, however, is that if you only understand what politicians believe and give no special attention to the arena in which they make their policy choices, you will wildly overestimate how easy it is for them to reach conclusions on issues and you will never understand why one policy alternative, rather than another, was chosen in the end.

The rest of this book adopts a new institutionalist approach to the study of Congress. We now know enough about the general approach and the specific vocabulary to get to work. As we proceed, we will build on the ideas first introduced in this chapter, in addition to the more traditional insights of political science history, to create a comprehensive view of how members of Congress make their policy choices.

Summary

This chapter provides a theoretical foundation for the study of Congress by introducing the basics of spatial voting theory. Spatial voting theory speaks generally about how members of a group make choices when they are rational and their choices can be described dimensionally.

Although the theory is abstract, it has many intuitive elements that make it easily applicable to the study of Congress. It is natural to think of decision makers as preferring alternatives that are "close" to them and opposing ones that are "far away." It also is natural to categorize politicians and voters as being "on the left," "on the right," or "in the middle"; and certainly, spending and taxing decisions are fought out along the lines of "more" or "less." Spatial analogies are natural in politics.

Spatial voting theory is more than an analogy, however. Taken seriously and analyzed precisely, nonobvious insights emerge when we construct simple models of legislative decision making and ask what happens when legislators are rational and vote according to spatial proximity. In this chapter, we first ask what happens when distance is considered along only one dimension, such as left/right. Here, the most important insight came from the median voter theorem. When voting is according to pure majority rule, the median voter eventually prevails. Even when voting is according to a procedure that is not *pure* majority rule, such as when a legislator who is not the median gets to decide which amendments are admissible, no policy change can gain majority acceptance unless the median voter agrees.

Even though the unidimensional spatial model is powerful, it fails to capture what happens when politicians consider complicated issues or try to navigate legislation that fuses seemingly unrelated issues, such as tax rates for married couples and subscription drug coverage for retired Medicare participants. These settings generally have no median. The lack of a median in multidimensional politics means that majority voting rarely will settle on stable policy solutions on its own accord. An equilibrium of tastes rarely is found in any complex democratic setting, whether it be a small committee, a large legislature, or even the whole citizenry. This lack of a median in multidimensional policy making and the "chaos result" that follows, in my opinion, is one of the deepest and most unsettling features of democratic politics.

Because Congress makes decisions in an extremely complex policy environment, multidimensional chaos always lies just below the surface. If Congress were a simple institution and operated according to pure majority rule, this chaos would be in our faces every day. Congress is not a simple institution, however. It has rules, committees, and party organizations (abetted by a shortness of time) that produce a structure-induced equilibrium, even when an equilibrium of tastes is elusive. In other words, policy change is rare in Congress, not because most members of Congress are content with the current state of affairs, but because the institutions that govern the legislative process allow so few alternatives that might win majority support to be considered in the first place.[11]

Further Reading

Black, Duncan. 1958. *The Theory of Committees and Elections*. New York: Cambridge University Press.

Downs, Anthony. 1957. *An Economic Theory of Democracy*. New York: Harper and Row.

Enelow, James M., and Melvin J. Hinich. 1984. *The Spatial Theory of Voting: An Introduction*. New York: Cambridge University Press.

Hotelling, Harold. 1929. "Stability in Competition." *Economic Journal* 39: 41–57.

Krehbiel, Keith. 1988. "Spatial Models of Legislative Choice." *Legislative Studies Quarterly* 13: 259–319.

———. 1998. *Pivotal Politics: A Theory of U.S. Lawmaking*. Chicago: University of Chicago Press.

McCubbins, Mathew D., and Thomas Schwartz. 1985. "The Politics of Flatland." *Public Choice* 46: 45–60.

Ordeshook, Peter C. 1986. *Game Theory and Political Theory*. New York: Cambridge University Press.

Poole, Keith T. 2005. *Spatial Models of Parliamentary Voting*. New York: Cambridge University Press.

Riker, William H. 1982. *Liberalism against Populism: A Confrontation between the Theory of Democracy and the Theory of Social Choice*. San Francisco: W. H. Freeman.

SUMMARY OF KEY CONCEPTS

1. A **unidimensional** spatial voting model is one that explores the dynamics of politics that have been simplified to unfold along one dimension, that is, a line.

2. **Spatial voting theory** is a means of analyzing how political actors make decisions, assuming that alternatives and the preferences of decision makers can be characterized in some issue space. Political actors prefer alternatives that are "close" to their ideal policies over those that are "far" from them.

3. The **median voter** is the decision maker situated so that as many individuals lie to his or her left as lie to his or her right. The median voter exists only in unidimensional voting.

4. A **preference** is a characterization of the desires of a decision maker, consisting of an ideal point and a utility function.

5. An **alternative** is a choice of outcomes available to voters. In a mass electorate, alternatives usually are candidates for office. In a committee, alternatives usually are policies.

6. An **ideal point** is a decision maker's most-preferred alternative in an issue space.

7. A **utility curve** (or **utility function**) measures how much the voter dislikes alternatives as they move away from his or her ideal point.

8. A **single-peaked utility curve** is shaped such that utility continually declines as alternatives move away from the ideal point.

9. The **status quo**, sometimes called the **reversion point**, is the policy that remains in effect if a motion fails to pass.

10. A **supermajority** is greater than 50 percent plus one and is usually specified. Prominent examples of supermajorities include the two-thirds requirement to override presidential vetoes and the 60 percent requirement to invoke cloture in the Senate.

11. **Pure majority rule** is a stylized mode of group decision making in which new motions to alter the status quo are allowed and majority votes are taken on those motions until the group decides, via majority vote, to stop taking motions.

12. The **Condorcet winner** is a policy alternative that always prevails in a majority rule vote against any other feasible policy alternative.

13. An **equilibrium of tastes** occurs whenever group preferences are arrayed in such a way that one or more alternatives is a Condorcet winner.

14. A decision maker's **indifference curve** is the set of all policy alternatives that she or he finds equally appealing, compared to a given alternative.

15. The **preferred-to set** is the set of all policy alternatives that a decision maker finds more appealing than a given alternative. The preferred-to set is the space interior to an indifference curve.

16. The **win set** is the set of all policy alternatives that could beat a given status quo in a majority rule contest.

17. **Transitivity** is a characteristic of preferences held by a decision maker considering multiple alternatives. Preferences among three alternatives are transitive if the following relationship holds: I prefer alternative A to B and alternative B to C, therefore I prefer alternative A to C. The preferences of individuals usually honor transitivity. The preferences of groups in multidimensional voting, revealed by majority voting, often violate transitivity.

18. The intransitivity of group preferences leads to a general **chaos result** in majority rule voting, in which any policy alternative can prevail at some point during a sequence of votes, using majority rule.

19. The **McKelvey chaos theorem** states that if more than two decision makers are making a decision about a multidimensional policy, generally at least one motion to change the status quo can defeat any status quo. Furthermore, the voting agenda can be manipulated such that any point in the policy space might be agreed on, at some point, through a series of majority votes.

20. A **killer amendment** is an amendment such that *without* the amendment, a given bill is expected to win, but *with* the amendment is expected to lose. The success of killer amendments as a legislative strategy often

depends on the willingness of bill supporters and opponents to engage in sophisticated voting.

21. A **saving amendment** is one that greatly increases the chance that a bill will pass; *without* the amendment, a given bill is expected to lose, but *with* the amendment it is expected to win. The success of using saving amendments as a legislative strategy often depends on the willingness of bill supporters and opponents to engage in sophisticated voting.

22. **Salience** is a feature of multidimensional decision making. Dimension *x* is more salient than dimension *y* to a decision maker who regards a movement away from his or her ideal point along the *x* dimension more negatively than an equal change along the *y* dimension.

23. **Sincere voting** is the practice of always voting in favor of the higher-ranked alternative in each round of voting, even if doing so guarantees that a lower-ranked alternative will ultimately prevail.

24. **Sophisticated voting** is the practice of voting in favor of a lower-ranked alternative in an early round of voting to prevent an even lower-ranked alternative from ultimately prevailing.

25. The **new institutionalism** is a general theoretical perspective on governmental decision making that emphasizes the essential role of institutions in inducing policy stability and shaping policy outcomes.

PROBLEMS

✔ **1.** Find the median voter on the following committees, with the ideal points as given:

     a. $A = 200$, $B = 100$, $C = 25$, $D = 16$, $E = 22$, $F = 63$, $G = 57$.
     b. $A = 200$, $B = 100$, $C = 25$, $D = 16$, $E = 22$, $F = 63$, $G = 75$.
     c. $A = 200$, $B = 100$, $C = 57$, $D = 16$, $E = 22$, $F = 63$, $G = 57$.

2. Suppose that each of the preceding committees voted on the following alternatives: $X = 60$, $Y = 65$. Assume that the utility curves are symmetrical and that voting proceeds under majority rule. Find the resulting policy outcome for each committee.

3. In the 2010 Cooperative Congressional Election Study, respondents were asked how they felt about certain controversial issues facing the country. The questions and the distribution of answers are given below. Based on this information, what is your best estimate about how the median American voter felt about these issues in 2010?

     a. *Abortion.* There has been some discussion about abortion during recent years. Which one of the opinions on this page best agrees with your view on this issue?

- By law, abortion should never be permitted (12.2%)
- The law should permit abortion only in case of rape, incest (28.6%)
- The law should permit abortion for reasons other than rape (15.5%)
- By law, a woman should always be able to obtain an abortion (43.8%)

b. *Jobs versus the environment.* Some people think it is important to protect the environment even if it costs some jobs or otherwise reduces our standard of living. Other people think that protecting the environment is not as important as maintaining jobs and our standard of living. Which is closer to the way you feel, or haven't you thought much about this?
- Much more important to protect environment even if lose jobs (14.5%)
- Environment somewhat more important (18.8%)
- About the same (28.4%)
- Economy somewhat more important (23.7%)
- Much more important to protect jobs, even if environment is worse (14.6%)

4. Consider committee members with ideal points arrayed as follows. What policy—either a single point or a range of points—constitutes a Condorcet winner?

a. $A = 200$, $B = 100$, $C = 25$, $D = 16$, $E = 22$.
b. $A = 200$, $B = 100$, $C = 25$, $D = 16$, $E = 22$, $F = 63$.
c. $A = 200$, $B = 100$, $C = 25$, $D = 16$, $E = 22$, $F = 63$, $G = 57$, $H = 22$

5. Figure P1.1 shows the ideal points of five committee members, $C_1, \ldots, C_5$, along with their utility curves, $U_1(X), \ldots, U_5(X)$. The letter ϕ indicates

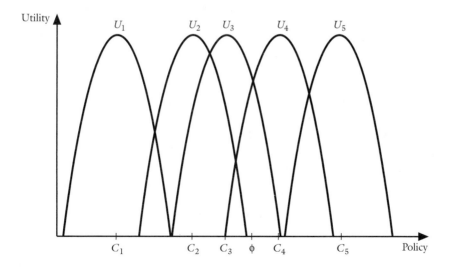

FIGURE P1.1

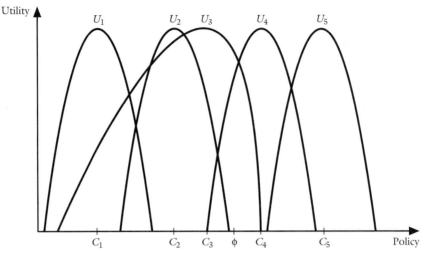

FIGURE P1.2

the *status quo* that obtains if the committee takes no positive action. Draw the win set against ϕ, $W(\phi)$.

6. Repeat Problem 5 with the set of utility curves depicted in Figure P1.2. How does the equilibrium outcome under pure majority rule differ between Problems 5 and 6?

Note: For the next three problems, use the setup provided in Figure P1.3. (You might want to make several copies of it.) In Figure P1.3, three ideal points are given for three legislators, C_1, C_2, and C_3. The points labeled ϕ_1, ϕ_2, and ϕ_3 will be used to indicate status quo points, where appropriate.

7. Using *circular* indifference curves, find the win set again for all three status quo points in Figure P1.3.

8. Construct a voting agenda such that the committee in Figure P1.3 can move from ϕ_1 to the point labeled Z using pure majority rule. (You will have to go "off the figure" to construct the agenda.)

9. Assuming *elliptical* indifference curves of the type described in the next sentence, draw the win sets for all three status quo points in Figure P1.3. The indifference curves are such that each committee member holds the *Y*-axis dimension more salient than the *X*-axis dimension, so the ellipses look like footballs laid on their sides.

10. Figure P1.4 shows the ideal points of seven committee members, $C_1, \ldots, C_7$, along with two status quo points, ϕ_1 and ϕ_2. Assume circular

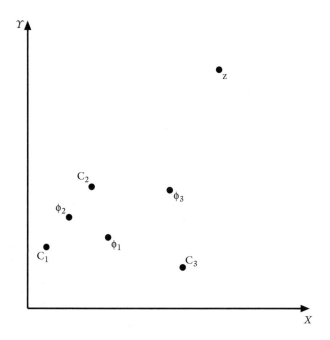

FIGURE P1.3

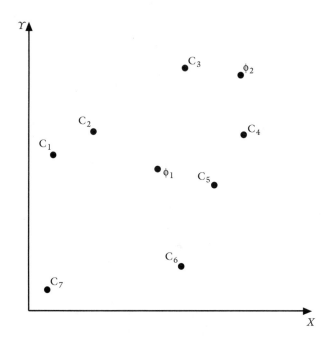

FIGURE P1.4

indifference curves. Show the regions that (1) a simple majority, (2) a two-thirds majority, (3) a three-quarters majority, and (4) a unanimous majority prefer compared to each status quo.

11. Assume there are three legislators who rank three alternatives, X, Y, and Z, as follows:

Legislator 1: X > Y > Z
Legislator 2: Y > Z > X
Legislator 3: Z > X > Y

Assume that the rules of the legislature specify that the first vote will be between X and Y, with the winning motion then put against Z. If the legislators vote sincerely, what is the outcome? What if they all vote strategically?

12. Redo Problem 11. This time, assume that the rules specify that the first vote will be between X and Z, with the winning motion put against Y. What are the sincere and strategic outcomes?

13. Consider the example that began the section on "The Politics of Flatland," in which three friends had to decide on a movie. Draw a multidimensional spatial representation of this example. That is, draw a figure that places the friends' ideal points in a two-dimensional space and then indicate where the three movies are located. (Hint: Begin by placing the friends' ideal points in the issue space and then locate the films. There is no one right way to draw this figure.)

14. The following exercise, which does not involve manipulating the spatial model, is intended to introduce you to the reference sources and datasets that describe basic features about congressional districts and members of Congress.

a. Who is the incumbent member of the House from your home district? (If you are a citizen of another country, choose any district you like.) What was his or her political background before being elected to the House? How electorally secure is the incumbent? If the incumbent were to be challenged for reelection, where might challengers from the opposite party come from? What issues does your House member focus on? What are the committee assignments or party leadership positions held by this member?

b. What is the political geography of your district? What are the major cities, if any? What are the major economic regions? Where is the greatest concentration of Republican and Democratic strength in the district? How does this district compare to the district drawn after the prior census?

c. Re-do your answers to 14a and 14b, as if you were taking the class in the fall of 1993.

NOTES

1. Accounting for the Democratic gains in the Senate following the 2008 election is complicated because one seat (Minnesota) wasn't determined until July 2009, owing to a disputed election, four Democratic senators resigned to take positions in the Obama administration (including Obama himself), and Arlen Specter (Penn.) changed party affiliations in April 2009. In addition, one Independent senator, Bernie Sanders (I-Vt.) is generally counted among the Democrats, as is Joseph Lieberman (Conn.), an "Independent Democrat." The net pickup reported here credits Specter's switch and treats the four resignations as if Democrats continued to hold those positions until replacements were chosen.

2. Philip Rucker, "Obama, Pelosi Urge Activists at Netroots Nation to Keep Fighting for Change," *Washington Post*, July 25, 2010.

3. Because Vice President Biden is a liberal Democrat, he can be counted on as a reliable vote to help out the Senate Democratic majority in the case of a tie. Therefore, the Democratic leadership would only need to get fifty senators on their side to pass liberal legislation.

4. Identifying who that fiftieth-most-liberal senator is at the time of writing is especially complicated, both because of the large number of vacancies that have occurred during the 111th Congress, and because there are four senators near the fiftieth position whose voting behavior is essentially identical—Tester (D-Mont.), Baucus (D-Mont.), Landrieu (D-La.), and Specter (D-Penn.).

5. Dahlia Lithwick, "A Brilliant Ruling: Judge Walker's Decision to Overturn Prop 8 is Factual, Well-Reasoned, and Powerful," slate.com, posted August 4, 2010.

6. One nice property, already mentioned, is that it is symmetrical. Another is that it is simple and seems to approximate the world reasonably well. It also has a first derivative, unlike the most simple of utility curves that rely on the *absolute value* of distance to gauge utility. This feature comes in handy in more advanced applications of the theory.

7. This is identical to the mathematical principal of transitivity, which can be written as follows: If $Y > X$ and $Z > Y$, then $Z > X$.

8. In keeping with the notation in the previous note, we have seen that $B > \phi$ and $x > B$ *does not imply* $x > \phi$ in a majority rule voting setting.

9. Using a compass and a ruler you can confirm that Members A and C prefer x_1 to ϕ, Members A and B prefer x_2 to x_1, Members B and C prefer x_3 to x_2, and Members A and C prefer x_4 to x_3.

10. This mix of spending for defense and justice is called an *induced* ideal point because it represents an ideal mix induced by an external constraint—the balanced budget constraint in this case.

11. Lest you consider this point a cynical indictment of representative politics in the United States, keep in mind that there are virtues in having a stable set of laws from year to year (not to mention day to day). It undoubtedly is good that the formal institutions of Congress limit the policy alternatives that might be considered at any given moment. What is open to debate is whether these formal institutions improve the *correct* limits on what will be considered.

∼ 2 ∼

The Constitutional Origins of Congress

The distinguishing institution of any democracy is its legislature. Legislatures, unlike executives, are by their nature *plural* institutions. Because legislatures have many members, they can mirror social divisions more completely and naturally than any executive, even an elected one. Consequently, citizens in a democracy usually first turn to the legislature to resolve conflicts. And because legislatures are the target of competing social demands, *how* they are designed to process those demands determines much of the character of nations' politics.

The constitution of a nation determines the most basic parameters of how a legislature operates. In some countries, such as Great Britain, the constitution is implicit. In most, such as the United States, the constitution is an actual written document that delineates the relative powers of the different parts of the government and specifies how people are chosen to occupy official positions. In theory, there is an infinite variety of ways to organize a democratic government and its legislature. In practice, democratic governments are organized in a number of different basic ways. Some have one legislative chamber, many have two, and a few even have three. Some constitutions make no distinction between the executive and the legislature while others (notably the United States) throw up formidable institutional barriers between the legislature and executive. Some constitutions specify fixed terms of office for their legislators; others allow the legislature to determine when elections will be held. Some countries elect their legislators from single-member districts, while others hold some sort of "at-large" election for their legislature.

The Constitution of the United States is the basic framework that organizes Congress, both internally and in terms of Congress's relationship with citizens. Because this book emphasizes institutional features of Congress in explaining its behavior, the natural starting point for an empirical investigation of congressional behavior is with the Constitution.

In this chapter, we examine the constitutional origins of Congress with two things in mind. The first is to understand why the national legislature that preceded the modern Congress—the institution that is known in the history books as the Continental Congress—failed. After all, if the Continental Congress had been successful in resolving the pressing conflicts that faced the new country, it is unlikely that the Constitutional Convention would have met at all. The second subject we will attend to is understanding why and how the Constitutional Convention agreed to change fundamentally the status of Congress, changing it from an assembly of ambassadors that could not act without the concurrence of the state legislatures, to an independent and sovereign legislature that no longer was tied strongly to the wishes of state officials. Such radical changes of governmental structure do not happen haphazardly. They happen only when political leaders deftly navigate the political constraints facing them. By understanding the political choices facing the framers, we will gain further insight into the compromises that established the framework of the modern Congress.

The Failure of the First Congress of the United States

The United States Congress is not like the mythical figure Athena, who sprang full-grown from the head of Zeus. The framers drew on a great deal of prior experience as they designed Congress. When the American Revolution began in 1775, the colonies already had 150 years of experience with local legislatures. Virginia, for instance, could claim a tradition of legislative self-governance through its House of Burgesses, which first met in 1619. In the Revolutionary period and beyond, the newly independent states developed these legislatures as the centers of political authority. The Revolutionary period also spawned a series of "national" congresses that met, first, to address the crown with a set of grievances, then to coordinate the fighting of the Revolutionary War, and finally to act as the first national legislature of the new nation.

As the Revolutionary War wound down, the thirteen former colonies joined together in a confederation. The document that delineated the first government of the United States was called the **Articles of Confederation.** The articles vested legislative authority in a Congress, which we will call the *Confederation Congress.*[1] The Confederation Congress was virtually the entire national government. The articles provided for no national courts; lacking a president, heads of executive departments were either members of Congress doing double duty or chosen by Congress.

Because Congress was the only formal institution of government under the articles, the dissatisfaction that led to the Constitutional Convention that met in Philadelphia in 1787 focused on the failings of the Congress to provide a national government that was credible to the outside world, could defend itself against internal insurrection, and could ensure smooth commercial relations among various parts of the country. In addition, the political leaders who instigated the convention were alarmed at what they regarded as the tendency of the state legislatures to ride roughshod over local minority and property rights.

In short, the political revolution that began at Lexington and Concord rested on a theory of government that exalted legislative institutions and distrusted single-headed executives. A decade of experience with such a government—in states and at the national legislature—acquainted political leaders with the dangers of entrusting governing purely to legislatures that, although they were supreme within the political system, nonetheless were prone to chaos.

The Constitutional Convention was called because of the perceived failures of existing legislatures. The solution to these failings constituted a new type of national legislature on the North American continent, one that was truly sovereign over citizens. At the same time, the compromises necessary to establish this new Congress embedded in the Constitution a set of complicated political relationships that balanced power at the national level and also established tensions between state and national political leaders.

The congress of the confederation[2]

The ending of the Revolutionary War removed from the colonies one looming problem, only to replace it with a collection of difficulties that, considered together, were at least as perilous. The severing of colonial ties with England, and the ensuing disruptions in export markets, created monumental economic difficulties for the new nation. The areas of the country that *did* develop new export markets found themselves at odds with each other and with regions that remained isolated from world trade. There was no permanent national capital. The Treaty of Paris, which ended the war between the colonies and England, specified a western frontier for the new nation that was permeable to foreign infiltration by the English, Spanish, and French to the north, west, and south. Native American tribes were willing surrogates for the European powers that wanted to challenge the hard-won independence on the frontiers. The English were recalcitrant in decamping from forts they held in upper New York state. The western territories (beyond the Appalachian Mountains) contained a hodgepodge of conflicting land claims that pitted states against each other. Towering debts had been built up fighting the war for independence, but no firm mechanism had been created for paying those debts. Beyond these massive problems of defending the borders and meeting a nation's obligations to the rest of the world, the new country was faced with more mundane tasks of delivering the mail, protecting mariners, and ensuring that a small, but far-flung, bureaucracy functioned effectively.

To address these problems, the Articles of Confederation were ratified in 1781, establishing the United States. The articles specified that delegates elected by each of the state legislatures would meet annually as "the United States in Congress assembled." According to the second section of the articles, each state retained "its sovereignty, freedom, and independence." Taken as a whole, the Confederation Congress was not designed to translate popular sentiments into bold action on a national stage. Rather, "the United States in Congress assembled" was a meeting place of coequal ambassadors from independent states whose primary responsibility was to protect the interests of state governments.

The articles did not rely on the general proclamation of sovereignty, freedom, and independence to its member states to keep its Congress in check. Instead, it further delineated a set of parameters for Congress's membership that kept its members closely tied to the state legislatures that elected them and cut off opportunities for congressional delegates to develop independent political followings back home. Congressional delegates were kept on a short leash. Each state could send up to seven (and no fewer than two) delegates to *Federalist 53* Congress each year. Terms were for one year; delegates were allowed to serve only three years out of any given six; state legislatures were allowed to recall their delegates in midterm for any reason; and each of the state legislatures was responsible for paying its delegates. Congress, at best, was bound to be *inexperienced* a way station for ambitious local politicians who wished to gain some experience with the wider world of North American politics. It was not designed to be the focal point of national power.

Historians have long attributed the demise of the Articles of Confederation to the weak links forged between the general government and citizens of the individual states. First, and most obviously, delegates to Congress were not popularly elected. Hence, there was no direct formal tie between delegates to Congress and residents of the various states. Second, laws passed by — *incorporation* Congress were not binding on the states. Congressionally passed laws were mostly exhortations to the states, which could choose to accept them or not. Most vexing for the new nation in this regard was the inability of Congress to get states to adopt the taxes necessary to pay off the debts incurred fighting the Revolutionary War and to meet obligations to other countries.

While the weak link between the Confederation Congress and the nation as a whole helped lead to its ultimate demise, Congress had a further problem: it had only a limited set of rules to guide its deliberations. The Confederation Congress never developed an effective committee system or effective rules of procedure. In later chapters, we will discover that the effective functioning of any legislature rests on rules of this sort. Therefore, although the Articles of Confederation cut off Congress from the well of popular support, Congress itself compounded its weakness by developing only the barest internal organizational structure.

Like virtually all large bodies, the Congress that existed under the Articles of Confederation found it useful to refer its business to a subset of its members, to committees. Unlike virtually all modern legislative bodies, however, the Confederation Congress granted virtually no independence to its committees. The foundation of the committee system, beginning even before the Articles of Confederation, during the War of Independence, was a series of ad hoc committees, usually consisting of three members, which were authorized to study matters that had come before Congress and report back their findings. Because they were ad hoc, these committees did not develop the level of expertise typically associated with functioning standing committee systems. Members appointed to consider a measure regulating the conduct of the army one week might not be appointed to the committee to consider a similar matter the next. Including the Revolutionary period, between 1774 and 1788, over 3,200 committees were thus appointed.

Over time, the business of Congress grew, so that members found themselves appointed to more and more committees. As certain matters began to recur, Congress experimented with a few standing committees, such as committees on naval affairs, military affairs, and foreign affairs. Yet, the work of these committees was closely scrutinized and second-guessed on the floor of Congress, leaving members of these committees to wonder whether their work on them was worth their effort. In addition, as the ineffectiveness of Congress grew more apparent to more people, absenteeism ran high, leaving even the "standing" committees short of members. Failing to develop a viable standing committee system, Congress then experimented with a series of executive boards and individual executives to run the government, but these executive devices spawned even more ad hoc committees to oversee (and second-guess) the work of the executives.

In short, working in an environment in which the floor was unwilling to grant its committees latitude to make deals and exercise independent judgment, committee members grew inattentive to their work. Faced with inattentive, ineffective committees, the floor had no reason to especially value the work of the committees it sanctioned, even though its members continued to express the desire to use the committee system to develop a system of expert policy advice within its halls. Organizationally, Congress was in an equilibrium in which virtually everyone agreed to the need to divide labor and allow committees to exercise independent judgment over policy, and yet no one was willing to relinquish his individual right to second-guess and hinder the work of committees.

Compounding the problems of having an ineffective committee structure were those that arose due to the lack of effective rules to control floor deliberations. During the Revolution, a simple set of rules was adopted by Congress that limited the number of times a member could speak on any question and specified that any motion made on the floor had to be dealt with immediately. Later rules, adopted as the war was winding down, fleshed out floor proceedings a little, but the principle of maximal flexibility remained. Thus, any item forwarded to Congress, whether by petition from state legislatures, citizens, or soldiers, could demand immediate consideration of the Congress. There was no way, for instance, to ensure that a bill to provide for the retirement of the war debt would be considered before a petition from a citizen group desiring to procure a captured cannon for the village green. Furthermore, the rules provided no way to limit debate or amendments, so that it was easy for opponents of measures to tie up the floor with a series of motions. Compounding this feature of the rules was the puzzling lack of any mention of a "reversion point" (see Chapter 1) to motions.

As we learned in Chapter 1, because legislative chambers generally have no "equilibrium of tastes," legislatures usually rely on institutions to provide stability to their proceedings. The signal characteristic of the Confederation Congress's rules is that they fostered instability, rather than reduced it.

One interesting example of how the Confederation Congress's rules undermined stability is how Congress reacted in the summer of 1783 to being attacked by mutinous troops from Philadelphia. Adjourning to the safety of Princeton, Congress eventually proceeded to consider where next to convene; that is, where to move the nation's capital. In the midst of great confusion about how to pick a permanent capital for the country, the decision was made to begin with New Hampshire and vote on locating the capital in every state down the seaboard. The last state to receive seven votes would get the capital.

In the ensuing voting down the coast, only New York and Maryland received as many as four votes. Lacking a location that could collect the support of even one-third of the delegations, a motion was made to narrow the choice to two possibilities: one on the Delaware River, near Trenton, and the other on the Potomac, near Georgetown. This motion led to an amendment, from a supporter of a site closer to Wilmington than to Trenton, to delete the language about Trenton or Georgetown, leaving instead general language about the rivers.

The rules specified that, in such cases, the motion would be on whether the *original* words (specifying Trenton or Georgetown) should stand, and it would take seven votes to keep the original wording. This motion to let the original proposal stand received five positive votes, with three states voting no and three being divided. Therefore, the original language was removed from the bill. But because no other sites were even remotely as favored as these two, the location of the new capital was left blank.

Later votes provided little relief to the problem. A motion to adjourn to Philadelphia and then to move to Trenton only elicited an amendment to strike Philadelphia from the motion. The motion to strike Philadelphia failed, but then the motion for Trenton-then-Philadelphia failed on a 5–4 vote. (Recall that it took seven votes for a proposition to prevail.) A motion to temporarily move to Annapolis lost 6–4. After letting the matter rest for a while, a compromise was reached to build two capitals, one near Trenton and the other near Georgetown, between which Congress would alternate. While awaiting the completion of these two capitals, Congress would alternate between Annapolis and Trenton. When the matter was called up for final passage, a delegate asserted his right to delay the vote for one day. In the end,

Congress began the alternation between Trenton and Annapolis, but returned to New York after this plan proved unsatisfactory.

This episode over the choice of a permanent capital highlights two serious failings of the Confederation Congress's floor proceedings. First, the original proposal on the floor had no privileged position. If any one questioned a particular provision on a bill, it would take a majority of all the state delegations to keep the bill's language intact, rather than a majority to strike the language.[3] Second, there was no provision for the "previous question." Any member of Congress could assert the right to delay a vote and, if so moved, make another motion that would have to be debated and voted on. Taken together, these failings made it easy for floor proceedings to devolve into chaos, with no clear reversionary point or policy anchor, and for individuals to delay action in the hope of gaining from the ensuing delay and confusion.

Congress's weak ties to popular politics and weak internal institutions produced endless rounds of gridlock on virtually all issues that confronted it. Not only did popular sentiment eventually turn against Congress, but delegates themselves became disenchanted with the body. Absenteeism became a serious problem. Most of the time, 10 to 20 percent of congressional delegates were absent, and absentee rates periodically climbed above 50 percent. Clustering of absences among particular state delegations sometimes meant that it was exceedingly difficult to gain the assent of seven states to pass minor legislation and all but impossible to gain the support of the nine states necessary to pass major legislation, such as tax bills.

In a related phenomenon, turnover was high, too. Although the three-year term limit would lead us to expect that at least one-third of Congress would leave each year, congressional turnover in the second half of the 1780s hovered in the 50–60 percent range from year to year.

Dissatisfaction with the national government and concern over the stability of state governments led to a movement, centered in individuals who had served in the Confederation Congress, to amend the Articles of Confederation. Their desire was to change the nature of the articles so that the national government would not be reliant on the state governments to give life to their statutes, political ties could be forged between national politicians and voters, and the national legislature would be given the framework necessary for it to develop differentiated governing institutions. Efforts to amend the articles first led to the Annapolis Convention, in 1786, called by political leaders in Virginia to examine deficiencies in the Articles of Confederation. The Annapolis Convention was met with disappointingly low attendance, but it led to a call for an amending convention in Philadelphia in 1787. This second convention turned into the Constitutional Convention of history and legend. It is to the politics of that convention and the resulting legislative institution that we next turn our attention.

What the Framers Wrought

The delegates who came to Philadelphia in 1787 were not the agitated revolutionaries who declared independence from England in 1776. For the most part they were seasoned veterans of state and national politics from the Revolutionary and post-Revolutionary era. Of the fifty-five delegates who attended, forty-six had served in a state legislature and forty-two had served in the Continental or Confederation Congress. By and large, they already were convinced of the need to change the Articles of Confederation so that the national government could be strengthened to provide more effective coordination of commerce among the states and secure the states against internal and external military threats. In addition, they were determined to reconfigure the national Congress so that it could develop stronger internal institutions than were possible in the incumbent national legislature.

While the delegates to the Constitutional Convention mostly agreed on broad general directions for the future of the Union, they disagreed on the specifics of how a new plan of government should be constructed. Such disagreement is prone to produce instability of the sort discussed theoretically in Chapter 1 and practically in the previous section. In addition to natural public choice instability, the Philadelphia delegates faced a looming external political problem—whatever they agreed to had to be ratified by a unanimous vote of the state legislatures. Because the logic of the Articles of Confederation was to make the national government an agent of the state legislatures, any plan to make it more independent of them was likely to be treated suspiciously.

The politics of the Constitutional Convention are well recorded in the annals of American history. Our interest here is more narrow than most historical accounts of the convention. This section addresses three topics especially important in the design of Congress: representation, the internal organization of Congress, and the power of Congress.

The first and the third of these topics—representation and the power of Congress—were controversies that occupied the attention of the delegates throughout the Constitutional Convention. Figure 2.1 sketches an overview of how these issues developed, using the spatial model introduced in the previous chapter. Voting in the Constitutional Convention was by state, so a spatial representation is provided of where state delegations tended to fall on two dimensions: the equality of representation and the strength of the national government. States are arrayed along the "equality of representation" dimension according to their state populations at the time; small-state delegations valued the equality of representation more than large-state delegations. States are arrayed along the "power" dimension according to their delegation's willingness to support measures that would further strengthen the power of the national government at the expense of the state governments.

The first major plan to be considered by the Constitutional Convention was the **Virginia Plan,** which originated from that state's delegation.[4] It

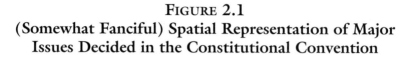

FIGURE 2.1
(Somewhat Fanciful) Spatial Representation of Major
Issues Decided in the Constitutional Convention

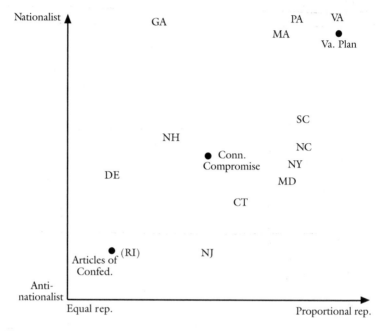

provided for a much stronger national government than had existed under the Articles of Confederation, including provisions such as a veto over state laws to be exercised by the national government. It also called for the representation of states in Congress in proportion to population. Although the Virginia Plan gained support from a majority of state delegations, it failed to receive universal support, signaling that such a radical departure from the Articles would not be ratified by the state legislatures. The convention proceeded to modify the Virginia Plan, mitigating its strongest nationalist tendencies through a series of amendments. Unhappy with their loss of relative power in the national government under the Virginia Plan, some small-state delegates proposed an alternative, the **New Jersey Plan**, which essentially restored the equal representation of states in Congress and granted the national government a few new powers, particularly the right to directly levy taxes.

Because this plan was barely different from the articles and because the Virginia Plan already had been modified to meet the objections of most delegates, the New Jersey Plan failed miserably. Yet the disenchantment of the smaller states with the direction of the convention presaged difficulties the Constitution would have in getting ratified. The Connecticut Compromise, therefore, provided for equal representation of the states in the Senate, thus pulling the final plan of the Constitution further back toward the representational plan favored by the small states, giving the Constitution a better chance of passing once it was sent to the states for ratification.

This summary only sketches out the gross politics of the Constitutional Convention using the standard spatial model. We now focus on the three sets of issues that were handled during the convention and affected the future of Congress: representation, national power, and internal organization.

Representation

Each state had one vote in the Confederation Congress. This equality of representation grew out of two factors, both practical. First, efforts to provide for weighted representation always washed up on the shoals of bad data. During and after the Revolution, there were no reliable censuses of the population or wealth of states that could be used to implement representation in Congress according to their "importance" to the Union. Second, the confederation of states that fought against England was built on a theory that treated each state as a sovereign entity whose members coordinated with other states only when it was in their own interest. Taking these two problems together, it is not surprising that whenever the topic of somehow weighting representation in the confederation congresses was broached, the issue always was deferred to the future.

Small states were the most insistent that power in the national government be shared equally. Yet most political leaders in these states realized that holding a hard line on this position would come at a cost. In particular, most of the large states, such as Virginia, Massachusetts, and Pennsylvania, contained important commercial centers through which international trade passed. Leaders of smaller states were willing to consider some form of weighted representation in the national government if the alternative was the larger states pulling out of the Union and boxing out their smaller neighbors economically.

The Virginia Plan was proposed by delegates from that state at the beginning of the Constitutional Convention to be a blueprint to guide the convention's deliberations. The plan was the brainchild of James Madison, who was among the most radical nationalists at the convention.

The Virginia Plan was strongly nationalist. It envisioned the national government as having the power, for instance, to veto the acts of state legislatures. It proposed replacing the single-chamber Congress of the confederation with a two-chamber (**bicameral**) Congress, a large lower house and a small upper house.

The nationalism of the Virginia Plan was manifested through the design of congressional representation in two ways. First, election to the large lower house would bypass the state legislatures; its members would be elected directly by the people. While state legislatures would nominate members of the small upper house, the lower house of the Congress actually would do the electing. The two chambers of Congress would then elect the president. Second, representation in both chambers would be weighted by population. In short, members of the new Congress would be encouraged to forge political ties directly to the voters rather than indirectly through the state legislatures, and regions of the country would be represented in proportion to what Madison considered to be each region's "importance" to the Union.

Convention delegates agreed to start their work by amending the Virginia Plan, which indicates the willingness of most delegates to move in the direction of weighted representation. As the work of the convention progressed, however, the dissatisfaction of small-state delegations persisted, climaxing with the New Jersey delegation offering an alternative: to keep the same representational structure of the Articles of Confederation and to make minor amendments within that structure concerning the power of the national government. The New Jersey Plan was defeated, but the political problem remained: how to convince the smaller states to accept a new constitution that reduced their voting power.

The compromise that ended the representational standoff is associated with the Connecticut delegation. The **Connecticut Compromise** provided for different methods of representation in the two chambers, by population in the lower house and equally in the upper house.

Two frequently overlooked points need to be made about the Connecticut Compromise. First, Connecticut's population was such that if Congress were apportioned according to population, it would have received roughly one-thirteenth of the members, the same proportion it would have received under equal representation. Connecticut's relative power under either system would have been roughly the same, and therefore it was a natural source of compromise. Second, as debate proceeded on the Virginia Plan, most delegates came to realize that so long as the "Senate" was much smaller than the "House of Representatives" and each state was guaranteed at least one representative in each chamber, representation in the Senate would have to be much more equal across the states than in the House.

For instance, under the apportionment of the House that eventually emerged, the largest state (Virginia) received ten seats and the smallest two states (Delaware and Rhode Island) received one each. The apportionment of a twenty-six-member senate would have given Virginia four seats, New Hampshire, Rhode Island, Delaware, and Georgia each one seat, and the rest of the states two or three seats (see Table 2.1). Therefore, the mathematics of the situation constrained the Senate to have a significantly more equal distribution of seats than the House. Consequently, Virginia did not lose much by agreeing to equalize representation in the smaller of the two legislative chambers.

TABLE 2.1

Constitutional Apportionment of the House Along with Hypothetical Apportionment of the Senate

State	House Members	Senators
New Hampshire	3	1
Massachusetts	8	3
Rhode Island	1	1
Connecticut	5	2
New York	6	2
New Jersey	4	2
Pennsylvania	8	3
Delaware	1	1
Maryland	6	2
Virginia	10	4
North Carolina	5	2
South Carolina	5	2
Georgia	3	1

The Power of the National Government

Another major issue that affected the flow of the Convention was the range of power given to the national government generally and to Congress particularly. Some, such as Madison, had become very suspicious of state governments, particularly state legislatures. Under the strains of the post-Revolutionary economic depression that gripped the country, many states adopted measures that strong nationalists considered grossly unsound, such as the nonpayment of debts and the establishment of paper money. As well, many state legislatures were unwilling to honor the international obligations that the Articles of Confederation or treaties had imposed on the states. For instance, states refused to honor their obligations under the Treaty of Paris to compensate English citizens for their economic losses during the Revolutionary War. In retaliation, England refused to vacate its military positions in upper New York state, imperiling the young nation's sovereignty.

Many of the delegates to the convention considered proposals such as Madison's to be power grabs by a political elite. They reacted strongly. The fact remained, however, that without the power to impose certain economic and foreign policies on the entire country, the Union was an empty shell. It was neither an effective free trade zone nor an alliance whose international obligations would be honored. Therefore, even the strongest opponents of Madison's grandest nationalist schemes were willing to accept some degree of enhanced power for the national government in commercial and foreign relations.

Most of the debate about the relative power of the national government concerned the organization of government as a whole and did not focus entirely on the organization of Congress. In the end, the national government was strengthened only slightly in comparison to the Articles of Confederation. Madison's plans to allow the federal government wholesale power to veto state laws were not supported. The new power given Congress was quite limited. States, which previously had been given the power to make treaties with foreign countries, were no longer allowed to do so; treaty making was reserved for the president and the Senate. States no longer could regulate the movement of goods across state borders; only Congress could do that. Beyond giving Congress sole authority over interstate commerce and shared authority (with the president) over treaty making, the shift in legislative authority granted Congress under the Constitution was a marginal change compared to the grant under the Articles of Confederation.

Internal Organization of Congress

One matter that entered the Constitution has rarely rated much comment in histories of the convention but should interest students of Congress greatly: the question of the internal organization of Congress. The Articles of Confederation were largely silent about the internal organization of the Confederation Congress, but the nature of the political union at that time made delegates to Congress reluctant to develop a strong set of internal rules. As discussed in the previous section, this situation made it difficult for Congress to develop an independent committee system or impose the will of the majority through rules of procedure. There were other difficulties, as well. For instance, as the problem of absenteeism became rampant, Congress began a series of debates about whether it could compel absent members to attend sessions. These debates were never conclusive, and the result was that Congress was helpless as it found itself regularly lacking the necessary quorum to do business.

That there was a consensus to strengthen Congress's internal organization is evident in how quickly the current provisions concerning its organization entered the Constitution. The proposal by the Committee on Detail that both chambers of Congress be allowed to make up its own rules, judge its elections, and arrest absent members and force them to attend sessions of Congress remained in the Constitution, virtually unchanged, throughout its months of deliberations.

By giving both chambers of Congress the unambiguous power to govern themselves without regard to the special rights of states or minorities within the legislature, the groundwork was laid for a much more independently powerful and coherent legislature in the future. Of course, nothing in the *granting* of such wide latitude in the Constitution required members of the new Congress to take full advantage of it. In future chapters, we will discover that members of the earliest Congresses under the Constitution, in fact, were quite solicitous of individual and states' rights when they first convened. But when

TABLE 2.2
Summary Comparison of the Confederation Congress with the Constitutional Congress

Item	Articles of Confederation	Constitution
General structure	Unicameral; each state gets one vote	Bicameral; each member gets one vote in the respective chamber
Apportionment	Each state allowed between two and seven members; each state casts only one vote	House apportioned with respect to population; Senate apportioned equally
Terms of office	One-year term; three-year term limit	House, two years; Senate, six years; no term limits
Mode of election	Elected, paid, and recallable by state legislatures	House, mass elections; Senate, state legislatures; members paid out of federal treasury; no recall; both chambers judge their own elections
Internal structure	No provisions	Both chambers given wide latitude to write rules and enforce them; both chambers may arrest members to compel attendance
Legislative powers	Provide approval to treaties and foreign agreements entered into by states and foreign countries; declare war; recommend tax levees to states to pay for military; adjudicate differences between states over land claims; regulate mail between states; regulate coinage, weights, and measures; raise and equip army and navy	Lay and collect taxes, not limited to military ends; ratify treaties; confirm executive nominees; regulate interstate and foreign commerce; declare war; provide post offices and post roads; regulate coinage, weights, and measures; raise and equip army and navy; provide for inferior federal courts; control federal district; "elastic clause"

new generations of congressional members entered, desiring to impose the will of the majority on the minority, there was no doubt that the *Constitution* would not stand in their way.

Summary

A summary comparison of the Congress of the Confederation with the Congress of the Constitution is given in Table 2.2. Note that in every particular, the plan for the new Congress implied a much more powerful and independent body than had existed under the articles.

The details of the constitutional provisions that emerged from the convention are well known to most Americans.[5] Congress consists of two chambers, a House whose membership is apportioned among the states proportional to population and a Senate whose members are drawn equally (two each) from each state. House members serve two-year terms; senators, six-year terms. One-third of the Senate is up for reelection every two years. (Unlike the Confederation Congress, no term limits are placed on members of the Constitutional Congress.) House members must be twenty-five years old and have been citizens of the United States for five years; senators must be thirty years old and citizens for seven years. Both members of the House and the Senate must be residents of the states they represent. (Although it is traditional—and politically expedient—there is no constitutional requirement that House members live in the *districts* they represent.) Originally, members of the House were elected directly by voters while senators were elected by state legislatures.

Article 1, Section 8, of the Constitution delineates Congress's legislative prerogatives. It first delineates a series of powers explicitly, such as the right to lay and collect taxes and to provide for post offices and post roads. These are often called Congress's **expressed powers**. Second, it contains two provisions that have been used over the years to expand the reach of Congress's legislative authority: the commerce clause and the elastic clause.

The **commerce clause** simply grants the power to "regulate commerce with foreign nations, and among the several states, and with the Indian tribes." Yet, as the United States grew as a commercial nation, very little that Americans did was not, at least loosely considered, part of commerce. Thus, for instance, the Civil Rights Act of 1965 prohibited discrimination in any setting where interstate commerce was conducted, even if the only interstate commerce being conducted in an establishment was someone using the phone to call someone else in another state.

Congress was also granted the power "to make all laws which shall be necessary and proper for carrying into execution the foregoing powers, and all other powers vested by this constitution in the Government of the United States, or in any department or office thereof." This **elastic clause**, or **necessary and proper clause,** also grants Congress great latitude to act. For instance, if Congress has the right to regulate the armed forces and make provisions for fighting wars, it is arguable that it has the right to build roads around the country on which armies might travel. That is, in effect, how the interstate highway system was built in the United States—it was built with reference to the need to move military equipment around the country in wartime, even though virtually all the traffic on the system was likely to be civilian.

The expansion of congressional authority under the commerce and elastic clauses has been controversial. Indeed, some of the most fundamental cleavages in American history have arisen over how broadly to read these constitutional provisions. In the early years of the Republic, for instance, there were great political divisions over whether Congress had the power to create and regulate banks. Banks are not explicitly mentioned in the Constitution (nor is Congress's right to grant charters of incorporation), but it was argued that the national regulation of banks was essential for Congress to regulate commerce and to have a safe place to keep tax collections. Others argued that the creation of banks was a state function and that the regulation of commerce or the collection of taxes did not require the creation of *national* banks. In more recent times, conservatives have tended to read the elastic and commerce clauses more narrowly than liberals. Indeed, this very debate could define what it means to be a liberal or conservative and, therefore, what it means to be a Democrat or Republican.

While both chambers may generally originate legislation, the Constitution lodges special legislative powers with both chambers. All revenue-raising bills must originate in the House.[6] The Senate is given special powers to act with the president in executive matters—to ratify treaties (two-thirds vote being required) and confirm executive appointments (where a majority vote is sufficient). All laws must pass both chambers in identical form before being sent to the president for his or her signature.

The requirement that the president sign legislation also makes the president a de facto third chamber of the legislature, though a chamber with no general agenda-setting power.[7] If the president refuses to sign a piece of legislation, two paths are possible. The first route is the **presidential veto**. Under the traditional veto, the president returns the bill to Congress, stating his or her objections to it. Both chambers of Congress must then give the bill a two-thirds vote of approval for it to become law. The second route is just to do nothing. If more than ten days are left in the congressional session, the bill becomes law without the president's signature after ten days. If Congress adjourns within ten days of passing a bill and the president does not sign it, the bill dies—this is called the **pocket veto**.

Constitutional amendments since 1787 have affected congressional prerogatives in matters great and small. At the grandest level, the Bill of Rights and certain other amendments most directly affect the types of laws Congress can pass. At a more minor level, only a few constitutional amendments have affected the organization of Congress. The most significant constitutional amendment affecting congressional organization was the Seventeeth Amendment, ratified in 1913, which provided for the popular election of senators. In a recent fluke of constitutional history, one provision of the Bill of Rights that had failed to be ratified in the 1790s was resurrected and ratified in 1992. This amendment, now the Twenty-seventh Amendment to the Constitution, prohibits members of Congress from voting themselves pay raises. Any increase in congressional pay that is voted in one Congress may not take effect until after the next congressional election.

In some ways, the Constitution represented a radical departure from the Articles of Confederation. In other ways, it was only an incremental change from the past. From the perspective of institutional political scientists trying to understand congressional behavior, two things stand out about the Congress of the Constitution compared to the Congress of the Confederation. First, the Congress of the Constitution was given more latitude to build internal systems to overcome problems of social choice instability than existed under the Articles of Confederation. Second, the Constitution created in Congress an institution that probably is the purest experiment with democracy we are ever likely to see, much more so than the Confederation Congress. This statement is not meant to be hyperbolic. Not only is the Constitutional Congress a representative institution, but more important to the theorist, members of Congress have absolute control over how they govern *themselves.* Fewer constraints are placed on the behavior of members of Congress than on any other collection of individuals in the country, making Congress a great laboratory for applying social choice analysis. This contrasts sharply with the Confederation Congress, whose members frequently were wracked with the question over whether they were allowed to govern themselves.

The Constitution of 1787 is a starting point for understanding all future congressional behavior. It is not the only starting point, since a wide variety of behaviors are consistent with the constitutional framework. And it is not a starting point always guaranteed to be honored by members of Congress. (For instance, almost every constitutional provision relating to Congress has been violated with impunity at some point in American history.) But, practically speaking, it is the starting point that helps to distinguish most quickly congressional behavior from the behavior of legislatures in other nations.

Spatial Analysis of Constitutional Features

The Constitution created an institutional setting for the national legislature that was quite different from the Congress of the Confederation. Two features are particularly important for legislating: bicameralism and the presidential veto. These two constitutional features are also good places to apply the ideas behind spatial voting theory that we encountered in Chapter 1.

Bicameralism

Bicameralism requires that before a bill can be sent to the president for his or her signature, identical versions of the bill must receive a majority vote in each chamber of Congress. To understand the essential institutional characteristics of bicameralism, we can ignore for the moment the effect of the president on legislation. In other words, in analyzing bicameralism formally, we assume that the president will sign anything both chambers of Congress pass.

The primary effect of bicameralism is to restrict the range of feasible policy change, compared to what either chamber would agree to do alone. This effect is easy to imagine intuitively when a different party controls each chamber of Congress and the policy issue in question is one that divides the two parties sharply, such as abortion. A majority in one chamber might want to make access to abortions easier while a majority in the other chamber might want to make access harder. Either chamber acting alone would change policy significantly, but because both chambers must agree on a policy change, there is stalemate.

Stated more precisely, *how* the range of policy change is restricted by bicameralism depends on the current policy and how majorities in the two chambers are arrayed around the status quo. Figure 2.2 helps illustrate this point in the unidimensional setting. Figure 2.2a shows a policy status quo (Q) and the location of the median member of the Senate (S) and House (H). (To emphasize the core qualities of bicameralism, we begin by assuming that both chambers vote using pure majority rule and that its members vote sincerely.) Immediately below the policy dimension is the length of the dimension included in the win set of the House, $W_H(Q)$, and the win set of the Senate,

FIGURE 2.2
Spatial Analysis of Bicameralism, a One-Dimensional Example

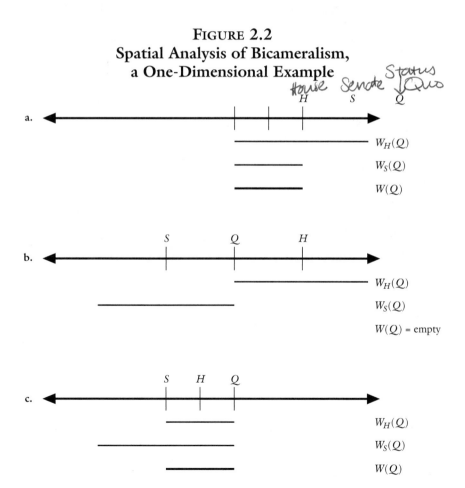

$W_S(Q)$.[8] To pass out of a bicameral Congress, legislation must be in the win set of *both* the House and the Senate. Therefore, the overall win set is the *intersection* of the two chambers' win sets: $W(Q) = W_S(Q) \cap W_H(Q)$.[9]

Unless we specify other details about how legislation is proposed, we do not know precisely *where* in $W(Q)$ the final bill will be located. However, we know that if the final bill is not *somewhere* in $W(Q)$, majorities of *both* chambers will not vote in favor of it. If the bill is to the left of Q, majorities of both chambers would prefer to leave the status quo unchanged, and so *neither* chamber would support a bill in that region. If a bill is located in the far right-hand part of the dimension, a majority of the House would vote to change the status quo, but a majority of the Senate would balk, due to the proposal's extremity. In this example, the overall win set $W(Q)$ is equal to the Senate's win set, since W_S is a subset of $W_H(Q)$.

The other two parts of Figure 2.2 demonstrate the effects of bicameralism when the other two configurations of preferences hold: (1) when the status quo is between the median senator and House member and (2) when the status quo is to the right of both the House and Senate medians. We can use the logic of the preceding paragraph to understand how policy movement is constrained in these two other scenarios. When the status quo lies between the median senator and the median House member, the intersection of the two chambers' win sets is empty. Although majorities in each chamber would vote to change policy, a concurrent majority cannot be found. In the case illustrated in Figure 2.2b, for instance, any policy shift that would please the median senator would displease the median House member and vice versa, so there is a policy stalemate. Finally, when the status quo is to the right of both the House and the Senate and the median House member is to the right of the median senator, it is the median House member who constrains the overall win set the most.

To summarize, when the medians of *both* chambers are on the same side of the status quo, the chamber whose median is closer to the status quo constrains where a bill changing the status quo is located. When the two chamber medians straddle the status quo, no bill can pass Congress.

Not surprisingly, when we consider how bicameralism operates when politics is described in more than one dimension, the results are a little less determinate. This is easily seen in the example illustrated in Figure 2.3, with a "Senate" and "House," each of which has a majority that generally disagrees with the majority of the other chamber. In Figure 2.3, solid circles represent the ideal points of three members of the "Senate," while open circles represent the ideal points of five members of the "House." Two of the three senators cluster in the southeast corner of the figure and three of the five House members cluster in the northwest. The status quo (Q) in the example is located between the two clusters, making it similar to Figure 2.2b, where the status quo was located between the medians of the two chambers. But because it is meaningless to speak of medians in a multiple dimension case, the conclusion we draw here is slightly different. The intersection of the two win sets now is not empty, but note nonetheless that the intersection is quite small compared to the separate House and Senate win sets. Therefore, in the multidimensional case, the imposition of bicameralism reduces the range of possible policy changes, but bicameralism itself does not cause absolute gridlock.

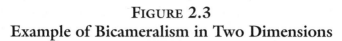

FIGURE 2.3
Example of Bicameralism in Two Dimensions

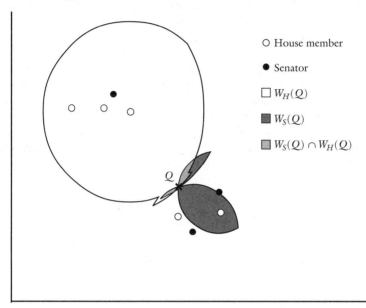

In general, the bicameralism of the Constitution reduces the maneuvering room that members of Congress have to change policy. When majorities of the House and Senate are similar but not identical, policy is anchored more by the chamber in which support for the status quo is the stronger, but the range of possible policy movement can be quite large. When House and Senate majorities support quite different policy alternatives, the resulting constraint on policy change can be quite severe.

The presidential veto

In addition to bicameralism, the other important legislative feature created by the Constitution was the presidential veto. It is easiest to intuit the effect of the presidential veto by considering the case when both chambers of Congress are controlled by a majority of one party, and the president is a member of the other party. For issues like abortion, if Congress under these circumstances wants to pass a bill the president strongly opposes, leaders in Congress need to round up more than the simple majority needed to get a law passed and signed by the president. Again, the range of policy maneuverability is restricted and stalemate is more likely.

As we did in the previous section, we can gain even greater insight into the veto using the spatial model. To do so we start simply, by imagining that the president's role is similar to that of a third body of the legislature. In other words, suppose Congress were *tricameral*, with one of its chambers consisting of only one member. Because majorities in the Senate and House must accommodate the president's preferences in order to pass legislation, the range of policy change that is possible at any given moment is further reduced.

In Figure 2.4, Figure 2.3 is augmented by adding a hypothetical "President." To add clarity to the figure, only the intersection of the House and Senate win sets is indicated to illustrate the policy regions where majorities of the two chambers could reach some agreement. The "President" is located in the southeast corner of the figure, near a majority of the Senate. The president's preferred-to set has been superimposed on the figure. Note that no region of overlap lies between the overall win set and the president's

Figure 2.4
Example of "Tricameralism," Treating the President as a Third Chamber of Congress

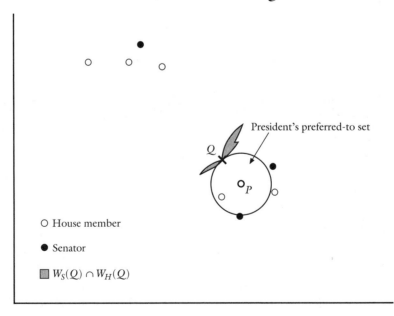

preferred-to set, other than a single point—the status quo. In this case, therefore, the addition of the president's preferences as a constraint has created policy equilibrium.

Yet we can say much more than simply that the veto allows the president to act like the third chamber of a tricameral legislature. First, the veto mechanism introduces an important *sequence* into the legislative process that can have significant policy consequences. With the exception of tax bills, the Constitution is mute about which chamber moves first in passing a bill, but it is clear about who moves last—the president. Along with this sequence, it gives complete latitude to Congress in deciding what the content of a bill will be while denying the president the opportunity to change the bill at all—he may not amend the bill, but may only sign it or return it to Congress with his objections.[10] This sequencing, in combination with the prohibition against the president's changing particular items in a bill, is referred to as the **presentation clause** of the Constitution, since it requires Congress to "present" all bills to the president.[11]

If the president vetoes the bill, then two-thirds of both Houses must vote to approve it for it to pass. The two-thirds veto override requirement further limits the possibility of major policy change in many settings, while also shifting some bargaining power back to the president under certain conditions.

These two important features of the veto—the presentation clause and the two-thirds veto override—have different effects on the operation of the veto power, so we consider them in turn.

In considering the effect of the presentation clause, I need to make explicit an important feature of the spatial models we have been considering. Notice that up to this point when I have talked about the theory of spatial voting, I have assumed that *all* decision makers know the preferences of all the other decision makers, *with certainty*. In the parlance of formal theory, this is the assumption of *complete information*. The assumption of complete information is a critical one when we analyze bargaining, since bargaining is easiest when "everyone understands everyone else." To understand the presentation clause, it is easiest, by far, to assume that everyone in Congress and the president have complete information about each others' preferences. This assumption is a bigger stretch in some situations than in others, which I discuss below. For the moment, we can still learn a lot by keeping it as simple as possible, by assuming complete information.

It is also significantly simpler to understand the presentation clause if we assume that Congress is unicameral. In understanding the core dynamics of the presentation clause, it is not important to specify the bargaining process between the House and Senate that produces a bill in the first place. Therefore, for the rest of this section, we will explore a simple, complete information veto model that helps to clarify the presentation clause, and then later, the two-thirds override.

We begin with the presentation clause. Leave aside the two-thirds override clause, to focus on the importance of allowing Congress to move first, presenting a bill to the president for his approval or disapproval. To see how this works, consider Figure 2.5, which shows a status quo, Q, the ideal point of the median member of Congress, C, and the ideal point of the president, P. As before, the win set of Congress, $W_C(Q)$, and the preferred-to set of the president, $P_P(Q)$, are indicated by the line segments below the ideal points. Any bill that finally passes must be in the intersection of these two sets. I have indicated this intersection, which is the overall win set, $W(Q)$, with a bold segment drawn directly on the line with the ideal points.

FIGURE 2.5
Effect of the Presentation Clause

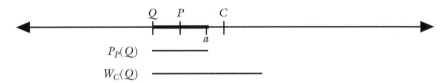

Notice that the overall win set includes the president's ideal point. That means that not only would the president sign a bill that placed policy at P (of course), but a majority of Congress would also vote for such a bill, if the alternative were Q. However, the median member of Congress gets to determine where the new policy is located, and she can do better than that. She cannot dictate that the new policy be located at her ideal point, C, because that is outside of $W(Q)$. However, the median can insist that the new policy be located at point a. This is the point, barely inside the win set, that both the president and a majority of Congress favor, compared to the status quo. Stated another way, this is the congressional median's best outcome, constrained by the need to improve the president's position, compared to the status quo.

Note what would happen if the presentation clause were reversed, with the president proposing a bill and Congress voting on whether to approve it but being given no power to amend it.[12] In that case, the president could present a bill to Congress that corresponded perfectly with his ideal point. Because that point clearly is better to a majority of Congress than the status quo, Congress would vote to accept it.

In this example, the policy difference represented by the physical distance between a and P represents the degree of agenda-setting power given to Congress through the presentation clause of the Constitution. If the Constitution had reversed the proposal power, policy outcomes would be different. In general, when a majority in Congress and the president both agree that policy should be changed "in the same direction," the bigger the gap between *C* and *P*, the greater the bargaining advantage to Congress.

So much for the presentation clause. What effect does the two-thirds rule have on the veto? As with previous analyses of constitutional features, it is useful to start with the unidimensional case. And because we know that bicameralism operates to constrict policy change compared to unicameralism, we can gain sufficient insight into this question by examining what happens when there is a unicameral legislature and then extrapolate to two legislative chambers.

The two-thirds rule requires us to shift our focus away from the chamber medians and toward the two members of the chamber who reside one-third of the way in from the two extremes of the issue dimension. Figure 2.6 shows a hypothetical legislature, this time indicating three members of the House: $\underline{H}$, who is the chamber median; H_*, who is located such that one-third of the House is to his left and two-thirds are to his right; and H^*, who is located such that one-third of the House is to her right and two-thirds are to her left.

$$H = median$$

FIGURE 2.6
Effect of Requiring a Two-Thirds Vote to Override a Presidential Veto

Note what would happen if the bill that passed the House corresponded with the House median's ideal point. Because the bill would move policy away from the president's ideal point, he would veto it. *H* and *H** would vote to "override" the veto, but H_* (and everyone to his left) would support the president, since H_* also is made worse off by the bill. The veto would be sustained and no policy change would emerge. A closer inspection of Figure 2.6 would reveal that *no* bill *H* would support would also be supported by H_*, and hence the status quo is in equilibrium.

Finally, Figure 2.7 illustrates a case where a successful override is possible but only if the House median is willing to be sophisticated. Suppose, for instance, the House passed a bill that corresponded with *H*'s ideal point. Again, the president would veto the bill, since it moves policy away from his or her ideal point. In the vote to override the veto, H_* would support the president, since he would regard the bill as changing policy too drastically.

FIGURE 2.7
Effect of the Two-Thirds Override Rule

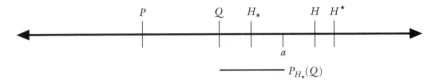

But suppose the House median were willing to support a bill located at point *a* in Figure 2.7. Again, the president would veto the bill. But because *a* is located within H_*'s preferred-to set, he would vote to override the veto.

In these two examples, the median member of Congress no longer is pivotal in determining whether legislation passes—the pivotal member has shifted to the extremes of the ideological distribution in Congress that is closer to the president's ideal point. We call this person, labeled H_* in Figure 2.7, the **veto pivot**.

This example illustrates a couple of real-life themes that continually emerge in the relations between the president and Congress because of the veto override provisions in the Constitution. The first point is obvious: the two-thirds rule means that the president's veto is not absolute, but in some cases, having the ability to override the president's veto is insufficient to overcome policy stalemate. The second point is more subtle: as illustrated in Figure 2.7, faced with a president likely to exercise veto power, whether legislation is successful depends on the willingness of members of Congress to be strategic and compromise.

Practically speaking, sometimes we see Congress and the president reach agreement on bills in the context of veto threats, and sometimes we do not. This suggests that important aspects of veto politics are not entirely accounted for by the complete information theoretical models we have been considering thus far—if they were, we would never see any vetoes. Contemporary scholarship has highlighted two additions to the complete information theory that help us understand what happens when lawmaking involving the possibility of a veto does not proceed smoothly. The first is called *sequential veto bargaining* (SVB), and the second is called *blame-game politics*.

Sequential veto bargaining refers to the dynamics that are often observed in real-world examples of veto politics, in which members of Congress and the president exchange words over what kind of bill the president is willing to accept. Not only do they exchange words, but also sometimes Congress passes a bill, the president vetoes it, the bill fails to be overridden, and thus the legislative process starts again. On the second (or third) try, Congress passes a bill the president signs.

One good example of this, explored in depth by Cameron (2000), was the set of interactions between leaders of the Republican-led 104th Congress and Democratic president Bill Clinton over welfare reform in 1995 and 1996.[13]

To summarize a protracted and very public tussle, Republicans acquired control of both the House and Senate following the 1994 election. For the first time since 1955, Republicans controlled both chambers of Congress. A confluence of factors emboldened the new Republican congressional majority to push through a significant contraction of the welfare state. From our perspective, the two most important ones were these. First, the Republican "Contract with America," on which Republican congressional candidates ran in 1994, promised a major retrenchment of welfare. Second, Clinton had run for president on a platform to "end welfare as we know it." Thus, Republican congressional leadership was convinced they could pass a welfare reform bill that Clinton would sign. Because of the overwhelming victory by Republicans in the 1994 midterm elections, Republican leaders also believed that Clinton was politically weak and therefore he was in no position to demand much moderation in the plans the Republican proposed.

The House, which has rules making it relatively easy for the majority party to dictate what's in a bill (we will review these rules later in the book), passed a welfare reform bill, H.R. 4, that almost all Democrats, including President Clinton, viewed as quite harsh. The vote on the bill was 234–199, far short of the 289 votes necessary to override a presidential veto. The Senate, whose filibuster rule (which we will also review later in the book) tends to give the minority party some leverage whenever legislation is considered in that chamber, passed a more moderate version of H.R. 4. The vote on the Senate bill was 87–12, well within the veto-proof range, indicating that many Democrats supported the more moderate Senate bill. A conference committee was appointed to hammer out a compromise between the two chambers. But because the differences between the House and Senate were so deep *among Republicans* about the bill's details, a stalemate resulted.

The stalemate prompted Republican leaders to try a different tack, which was to attach the salient features of H.R. 4 to a different bill, the huge Budget Reconciliation Act (H.R. 2491). Under the rules of both chambers, "reconciliation bills" such as H.R. 2491 are immune to most delaying tactics by the minority party. This cleared the way for the harsher features to pass both chambers—the reconciliation bill passed, by 52–47 in the Senate and 237–187 in the House. In each chamber, almost all Republicans favored the bill, while almost all Democrats opposed it. Clinton vetoed it. No attempt was made to override the veto, since it was clear from the original vote margins that Clinton would prevail.

Undeterred, congressional leaders took up H.R. 4 again, producing a compromise version in the conference committee that was quite similar to what was in H.R. 2491. The voting pattern on the conference report to H.R. 4 was virtually the same as on the Budget Reconciliation Act—the Senate favored it

52–47 while the House passed it 245–178, both on virtual party-line votes, neither margin veto-proof.

Clinton vetoed H.R. 4, too, and no override was attempted. But two weeks later, in his State of the Union Address, Clinton urged Congress to send him a bipartisan welfare bill, promising to sign it "immediately." This time, although Republican leaders continued to pursue significant welfare cuts, Democrats were brought into the conference committee negotiations in a serious effort to find a solution that would win broad support. This produced a final bill that significantly softened the most draconian features of the original House bill. Clinton announced that he would sign the bill, after which the House immediately passed it 328–101, followed by the Senate with a vote of 78–21. In each chamber, the Republicans again voted overwhelmingly for the welfare reform. What allowed these vote totals to change was that now Democrats were split 50/50 in each chamber.

In many ways, the situation here was quite similar to that sketched out in Figure 2.5. The status quo was far to the left, the median member of Congress was far to the right, and the president was between the two. Figure 2.5 could possibly be modified by relabeling C with H_*, that is, as the left-most veto pivot (see Figure 2.6). Either way, as the eventual outcome demonstrated, there was a point like a in Figure 2.5 that was a winnable compromise between Congress and the president. Why wasn't this agreement reached earlier, without all the dramatics?

Cameron emphasizes in the veto bargaining model that members of Congress are not always certain what the president's ideal point is. In this particular case, congressional Republicans figured that Clinton's ideal point was to the right of where it actually was, both because of his "end welfare as we know it" rhetoric and the stunning Democratic midterm losses in 1994. It is quite possible that Republican leaders *believed* that the two vetoed bills *did* represent an acceptable compromise to Clinton; his veto threats were simply "cheap talk." Clinton might talk tough, but he would capitulate once presented a bill to sign. What the twenty-month fight over welfare reform represented was Clinton establishing a reputation about where he actually stood on welfare reform. Vetoing two bills established that Clinton's ideal point on welfare reform was much closer to the status quo than his rhetoric (or Republican hopes) had previously suggested. Once that was established, an acceptable bill was produced and signed.

This case is extreme in its importance and protracted timeline but illustrates a dynamic that is surprisingly common when a Congress controlled by one party attempts to make a significant change to the law, and the president is from the other party. Indeed, Cameron (2000) estimates that in 20 percent of cases where major legislation is considered and there is divided-party government, something like the 104th Congress welfare reform case emerges. The fundamental reason is that when different parties control the Congress and the presidency, Congress often errs in estimating the president's ideal point and thus has to try again, if it wants to pass a bill.

During periods of divided government, Congress often passes important bills that the president later vetoes because congressional leaders simply misestimate the type of bill the president will sign. In most of these cases, congressional leaders and the rank and file are actually trying to pass some sort of bill; consequently, members of Congress update their estimate of what kind of bill the president will sign, make appropriate concessions to the president, and pass a new bill that the president signs. These are bills passed under veto bargaining, the welfare reform bill being an extreme example. Another important class of vetoed bills arises under divided government. These are bills that a majority of Congress has no intention of seeing the president sign. Such bills become instances of *blame-game politics.*

The theoretical underpinning of blame-game vetoes has been described by Timothy Groseclose and Nolan McCarty (2001). A real-life example arose in 1992 and 1993, involving campaign finance reform. The case started in 1992 (102nd Congress), a presidential election year. George H. W. Bush, a Republican, was president and running for reelection. Democrats controlled the House 267–167 and the Senate 56–44.[14] Campaign finance had long divided Democrats and Republicans. Democrats generally favored public funding of congressional elections, restrictions on spending by political action committees (PACs), and spending limits for congressional candidates. Republicans regarded these sorts of proposals as nothing more than "incumbency protection" devices or, in the case of public funding, an inappropriate raid on the treasury.

Campaign finance reform gained new momentum in the early 1990s in the wake of the "Keating Five" corruption scandal that was uncovered in 1989 and a scandal involving the House bank and post office in 1992, the so-called check-kiting scandal.

Congressional Democrats pushed an aggressive campaign finance bill through Congress in 1992. Even though Bush repeatedly stated that he would veto virtually any bill the Democrats would pass, Congress passed a bill in April 1992 that provided for a matching fund system for House candidates, a voucher system for Senate candidates to buy television ads, and a cap on what candidates to both the House and Senate could spend in their campaigns, among other things. Proceedings in both chambers were highly partisan, reflected in the votes on final passage of the conference report—259–165 in the House and 56–42 in the Senate, neither of which was even close to the two-thirds override threshold. President Bush vetoed the bill on May 9; the Senate vote to override was 57–42, nine votes short of the two-thirds requirement. Democrats made no follow-up attempt to pass a bill dealing with the president's objections. The two parties took the issue into the 1992 presidential election.

Democrat Bill Clinton won the 1992 election, running on a platform that included an attack on President Bush for his veto of the campaign finance bill earlier in the year. The partisan composition of the new 103rd Congress was virtually unchanged, with Democratic majorities of 258–176 in the House and 57–43 in the Senate. One could imagine that all Congress had to do was re-pass the previously vetoed bill and it would easily become law. Yet, even though the ideological environment seemed even more favorable for campaign reform, Congress was unable to pass a bill. The issue died in the 103rd Congress. What was going on?

Because this is a discussion of the veto, we focus on what happened in 1992. Events of the following Congress suggested that the bill Bush vetoed was actually more ideologically extreme than what a congressional majority favored; otherwise, a similar bill would have passed in 1993 when the veto threat was lifted. However, in the rhetoric that accompanied the bill, congressional Democrats emphasized neutral good-government goals of "cleaning up Washington" and "ending the influence of special interests." The substance of the bill was extreme, but the rhetoric was moderate. By taking this moderate rhetoric to the electorate, congressional Democrats sought to portray Bush as being more extreme than he actually was on campaign finance—if Bush vetoed such a reasonable bill, he *must* be in the pocket of special interests!

Thus, Democrats in 1992 had the best of all possible worlds—they could tar the president with charges that he was the enemy of good government while at the same time taking positions supporting provisions of a bill many Democrats had private doubts about. In this case, Democrats in the 102nd Congress were taking advantage of the incomplete information possessed by *the electorate* concerning campaign finance, attempting to make the president look extreme and Democrats moderate.

As Groseclose and McCarty note, an important feature of veto politics is that congressional majorities and the president are playing in front of a public audience, the electorate. The electorate is less informed about the policy positions held by the president than are members of Congress. When there is divided government, the majority party in Congress is tempted to take advantage of this informational asymmetry, using the shield of a threatened presidential veto to make the president of the opposite party look more extreme than he really is.

This has consequences for the types of bills Congress passes under divided government. For instance, it may drive presidents to sign legislation they oppose ideologically in order to take away from the opposite party an issue on which the president might be attacked, such as when presidents Reagan and Bush signed protectionist legislation, despite their well-known opposition to such policy. Alternatively, as with campaign finance reform, it may lead to the passage of ideologically extreme bills simply to create an issue on which Congress might campaign against the president in the future.

Groseclose and McGarty show that vetoes in presidential election years lead to a reduction in presidential popularity, so as a political strategy, blame-game veto politics seems to work. However, the research by Cameron that was cited shows that blame-game vetoes appear much less frequently than vetoes that are related to actual bargaining over the substance of legislation. Therefore, veto politics is usually not a cynical political game played between

Congress and the president, but it *is* a cynical game often enough that we should always be on the lookout for it, especially in presidential election years.

To summarize the discussion of the effects of the veto power in the Constitution, it is important to keep separate four effects that this power has on policy making in the national government:

1. In general, the insertion of the president into the legislative process further reduces how far policy can move, in addition to the restrictions imposed by the existence of bicameralism. The president has the effect of making Congress appear to be *tricameral.*
2. Within the constricted space of possible policy change, the presentation clause of the Constitution can give some advantage to legislative majorities in deciding how precisely policy will change.
3. The two-thirds rule mitigates the effects of "tricameralism" somewhat. It requires us to refocus attention away from the chamber medians and toward the ideological extremes on the "president's side" of the ideological spectrum.
4. The two-thirds veto override rule can be used by congressional majorities for political effect.

One final insight should be clear to anyone who has read thus far in this section: the precise impacts that bicameralism and the veto will have in any given situation are determined by the precise locations of preferences and alternatives. What I have done in this section is to demonstrate that spatial voting theory can be used to give greater specificity to our thinking about these constitutional features. Using these tools, we can make some general statements about constitutional features, but those statements rarely apply in all cases.

Policy observers frequently remark that the American political system tends toward "gridlock" and stalemate (see Sundquist 1992, 1993; Cutler 1980, 1988). These negative attributes of the political system sometimes are based on the ill will of political actors or even on the intransigence of the American people. Yet equally likely is that gridlock and stalemate were hardwired into the American political process by two of the most important features of American constitutional government, bicameralism and the presidential veto. As we have seen, stalemate is most likely whenever House and Senate majorities have quite different preferences. Because elections to the House, Senate, and the presidency by design are uncoordinated (due to their different constituencies and electoral calendars), therefore encouraging these institutions to embody different policy preferences, it is perhaps more surprising that we ever get policy innovation, rather than unremitting stalemate.

Summary

In the previous chapter, I provide one foundation for the study of Congress, by introducing spatial voting theory. In this chapter, I provide another foundation, by laying out the constitutional origins of the United States Congress.

The Congress that so dominates American politics in the current day had its origins not simply in the Constitution but also in a host of legislatures that preceded it. In a land filled with colonial legislatures, state legislatures, and town meetings, hardly an adult in the British part of the North American continent did not have an intimate working knowledge of how legislative bodies behaved. The legislative body that most vexed the drafters of the Constitution was the Congress provided for in the Articles of Confederation. The Confederation Congress was not just a weak institution, it was weak because its design encouraged the type of chaos that social choice theorists often treat as simply hypothetical.

The perspective on congressional politics I emphasize in these pages therefore provides added insight into the significance of the Constitution of 1787 for American political life. Not only did the Constitution delineate a host of political responsibilities for Congress and provide the possibility for many others about which it was not explicit, but the Constitution also established a Congress that was sovereign over the territory it governed and the legislators who served as its members. Probably the most important overlooked clause in the U.S. Constitution allows the two chambers to "determine the rules of its proceedings." This innocuous clause opened up far greater organizational possibilities than existed under the articles, since it was now clear that Congress could channel business in a way favored by majorities and harness the behavior of chamber minorities in new ways. In much of the history of Congress I explore in the following chapter, the rules of proceedings frequently form the focal point for many of the most contentious moments in that history.

Further Reading

Cameron, Charles M. 2000. *Veto Bargaining: Presidents and the Politics of Negative Power.* New York: Cambridge University Press.

Farrand, Max. 1986. *The Records of the Federal Convention of 1787,* rev. ed.; 4 vols. New Haven, Conn.: Yale University Press.

———. 1991. *The Framing of the Constitution of the United States.* New Haven, Conn.: Yale University Press.

Hammond, Thomas H., and Gary J. Miller. 1985. "The Core of the Constitution." *American Journal of Political Science* 81: 1155–75.

Jillson, Calvin. 1981. "Constitution Making: Alignment and Realignment in the Federal Convention of 1787." *American Political Science Review* 75: 598–612.

———— and Rick K. Wilson. 1994. *Congressional Dynamics: Structure, Coordination, and Choice in the First American Congress, 1774–1789.* Stanford, Calif.: Stanford University Press.

Krehbiel, Keith. 1998. *Pivotal Politics: A Theory of U.S. Lawmaking.* Chicago: University of Chicago Press.

Rakove, Jack N. 1996. *Original Meanings.* New York: Alfred A. Knopf.

Riker, William H. 1996. *The Strategy of Rhetoric: Campaigning for the American Constitution.* New Haven, Conn.: Yale University Press.

SUMMARY OF KEY CONCEPTS

1. The **Articles of Confederation** was the basic blueprint of the central government of the United States from 1781 to 1787. The design of Congress in the articles almost guaranteed that it would be weak and ineffectual.

2. The first plan considered by the Constitutional Convention in Philadelphia in 1787 was the **Virginia Plan,** which provided for a strong national government, with representation apportioned among the states in proportion to population. It initially was approved by the convention and formed the basis of the convention's early deliberation.

3. The **New Jersey Plan**, specifying a weaker central government and a Congress with representation apportioned equally among the states, was proposed in the Constitutional Convention by delegates from small states, to counter the Virginia Plan, and defeated.

4. The **Connecticut Compromise** was a plan proposed in the Constitutional Convention to meld elements of the Virginia and New Jersey plans, so that a constitutional proposal could emerge that stood a chance of being ratified by all the states. The Connecticut Compromise, which prevailed, specified a strong central government and a **bicameral** (i.e., two-chambered) Congress. Under this compromise, representation of the states in each chamber was specified differently—by population in the House and equally in the Senate.

5. The **expressed powers** granted Congress in the Constitution clearly delineate congressional powers, such as the right to declare war, raise revenues, and regulate the army.

6. The **commerce clause** is found in Article 1, Section 8, of the Constitution, allowing Congress to "regulate commerce with foreign nations, and among the several states, and with the Indian tribes." Creative interpretations of this clause have been used to justify much of the expansion of federal authority over the past century.

7. The **elastic clause**, or the **necessary and proper clause**, is found in Article 1, Section 8, of the Constitution, granting Congress the power "to make all laws which shall be necessary and proper for carrying into

execution the foregoing powers, and all other powers vested by this constitution in the Government of the United States, or in any department or office therefore." It has been the basis for much of the expansion of federal authority over the past two centuries.

8. The **presidential veto** allows the president to return to Congress a bill he does not approve of. The bill becomes law over the president's objections only if two-thirds of members of both chambers support the bill. The president has ten days (excepting Sundays), from the time he receives the bill from Congress, to exercise the veto. Otherwise, the bill becomes law.

9. A **pocket veto** occurs when the president kills a bill by holding onto it for ten days, during which time Congress adjourns.

10. The **presentation clause** of the Constitution requires all bills passed by Congress to be presented to the president for signature or veto.

11. The **legislative veto** is a device, declared unconstitutional, in which Congress reserves the right to veto actions of the executive branch without presenting that veto to the president for approval.

12. The **veto pivot** is the member of Congress who determines whether a veto can be overridden. In a unidimensional policy setting, if we array all legislators according to their preferences, the veto pivot is the member one-third of the way from the end of the dimension, on the same end of the dimension as the president.

PROBLEMS

1. Assume a nine-member House of Representatives considering a bill to change the minimum wage. Assume the current minimum wage is $8.00/hr. Members of the House are labeled $A, B, C, \ldots, I$. Their ideal minimum wages conform to the following pattern: $A = \$7.00/hr$, $B = \$7.50/hr$, $C = \$8.00/hr$, $\ldots I = \$11.00/hr$. Their utility curves are symmetrical.

a. What are the *highest* and *lowest* minimum wages that fall within the win set against the status quo minimum wage?

b. What is the minimum wage that passes if the House considers a bill under pure majority rule?

c. Assume a president who has veto power identical to that in the U.S. Constitution. What is the "best" minimum wage a majority in the House can achieve if the president's ideal points are located at the following points: (1) $7.00/hr, (2) $8.00/hr, (3) $8.75/hr, (4) $10.00/hr.

d. Add a second chamber to create a Senate that also has nine members who are labeled $R, S, T, \ldots, Z$. Assume no president. The ideal points in the Senate are located according to the following pattern: $R = \$6.50/hr$,

$S=\$7.00/hr$, $T=\$7.50/hr$, ..., $Z=\$10.50/hr$. If the Senate and the House must both agree to a change in the minimum wage through a majority vote (similar to the U.S. Constitution), what is the *highest* and *lowest* minimum wage that will pass in this bicameral legislature? (N.B.: Assume House ideal points given in 1.a above.)

e. Add back a president who has veto power identical to that in the U.S. Constitution for legislation that passes the bicameral legislature with ideal points specified above. What is the *highest* and *lowest* minimum wage Congress could achieve if the president's ideal points are located as follows: (1) $7.00/hr, (2) $8.00/hr, (3) $8.75/hr, (4) $10.00/hr.

2. In this question, use the spatial model to answer a set of questions that allow you to explore how real-world issues that come up in Congress are affected by the U.S. Constitution. This will require you to make estimates about the relevant locations of the ideal points of members of Congress and the president, plus the status quo/reversion point. Be prepared to justify those locations.

What is the equilibrium outcome of the following policies, given the current configuration of preferences in Congress and the presidency?

a. Tax cuts for single taxpayers making more than $500,000 per year.
b. Tax cuts for taxpayers making more than $75,000 per year.
c. Appropriations for a program that encourages African American and Latino citizens to vote.
d. Legislation restricting spending on abortions.
e. A constitutional amendment banning abortions.
f. Appropriations for the Department of Defense.

3. Imagine a country that consists of two states, Obamia and Bushington. This country has a bicameral legislature. The Senate consists of one senator from each state. The House is apportioned according to population, with Obamia having six representatives and Bushington having three. This Congress must allocate a total of $100 million in state highway assistance in a lump sum to the two states. All elected officials want as much money as possible appropriated to their own state. If Congress fails to pass an allocation, neither state gets any money. What range of allocations would be feasible under the following constitutional rules?

a. The allocation must be approved only by a majority of the House.
b. The allocation must be approved only by a majority of the Senate.
c. The allocation must be approved by majorities of both chambers.

4. Before the Civil War, Congress utilized the "balance rule" when it decided whether to admit new states to the Union. The balance rule stated that slave and nonslave states had to be brought into the union in pairs. The result was an equal number of slave and nonslave states in most Congresses, although nonslave states had a much larger aggregate population than slave states.

Figure P2.1 shows a hypothetical representation of the ideal points of members of Congress in the antebellum (pre–Civil War) Congress. (To keep this exercise manageable, only about half the states are shown.) The *y*-axis records preferences concerning slavery restrictions; the *x*-axis records preferences concerning government activism in the economy. For this exercise, assume that all senators and representatives from a state have identical ideal points. Next to the state symbols, a number represents the number of House members for the state in that Congress. The symbol ϕ records where the *status quo* policy is on these two dimensions.

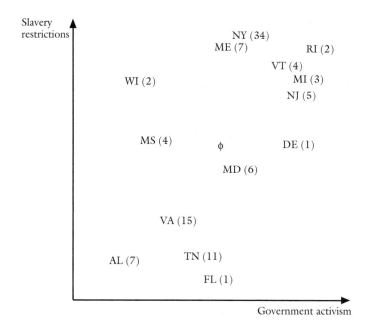

FIGURE P2.1

    a. What is the win set against the status quo in the House?
    b. What is the win set against the status quo in the Senate?
    c. What is the intersection of the House and Senate win sets?
    d. How is the win set in question c restricted if the president's ideal point coincides with the legislators from Virginia?
    e. How is the win set in question c restricted if the president's ideal point coincides with the legislators from New York?

NOTES

1. Historians and political scientists do not know quite what to call the Congress that served the United States between September 5, 1774, and the ratification of the Constitution in 1789. The Congress before the Articles of Confederation period usually is called the *Continental Congress*; after the adoption of the articles, Congress sometimes still is called the *Continental Congress*, while others call it the *Confederation Congress*. The reader should not be confused by this, either in the historical record or in this chapter, since even with several different names, Congress acted as a continuing, ongoing body from 1775 until 1789.

2. Much of this section is drawn from the analysis offered by Jillson and Wilson (1994).

3. Note, also, that it would take a majority of all state *delegations*, not just state delegations *present and voting*, to keep a provision in a bill. This feature of the rules greatly advantaged minority states whenever attendance was spotty. In theory, a state delegation that was alone in objecting to a provision in a bill could make an amendment to the bill's language. If the vote in favor of retaining the original language received the support of six states and the opposition of one state, the original language would still be stricken out. The next vote to include the provision favored by the minority-of-one state would then lose on a 1–6 vote, leaving the bill silent on the provision. It was quite easy, therefore, for minority states to hollow out the language of bills.

4. This spatial accounting of the politics of the convention is highly stylized and misses important details, some of which are examined further in this note. Students interested in how the convention unfolded are referred to Jillson (1981), Jillson and Eubanks (1984), and Rakove (1996).

   An important distinction to keep in mind is the difference between the preferences of the *convention delegates* and the potential *constitutional ratifiers* in each state. The delegates who were sent to Philadelphia by their respective states, on the whole, were much more nationalistic in sentiment than most Americans. They also were much better attuned to currents of national politics. Once the draft Constitution was released to the public, a national campaign occurred to convince state ratifying conventions whether to ratify it. In the course of these campaigns, pro- and anticonstitution forces were mobilized, and in some cases they managed to shift the terms of debate from what had been discussed in Philadelphia. My desire in this discussion is to focus on the politics of constitution writing as perceived by the members of the Federal Convention during summer 1787. An insightful study into how the campaign to ratify the constitution shifted the terms of debate was written by one of the fathers of rational choice theory (see Riker 1996).

5. The reader who wishes to reacquaint himself or herself with those provisions is invited to read the Constitution, which is reproduced in Appendix B.

6. Spending bills also originate in the House, but that is by tradition, not a constitutional requirement.

7. Note that, if we consider confirmation and treaty making legislative actions, then the president has tremendous formal agenda-setting powers in these realms.

8. Recall the corrollary of the median voter result from Chapter 1: for legislation to pass in a unidimensional world, the median voter must approve it. Therefore, the win set of a legislature in a unidimensional setting is the space that the median prefers compared to the status quo. The application of a ruler to Figure 2.2a will confirm that the win set of the House corresponds with the part of the policy dimension that is closer to the House median than the status quo.

9. Without further articulation of the rules that govern passing legislation, we cannot specify precisely where in W(Q) the final bill will be. We know only that,

for the bill to pass, it must lie within W(Q). In reality, all bicameral legislatures have rules that specify how different versions of the same bill are reconciled. In the U.S. Congress, the most important mechanism for reconciling differences between the two chambers is the *conference committee*. In Chapters 8 and 9, we examine the operations of conference committees in detail.

10. The president does have the option of not signing the bill, which can lead to two results. If the bill is held for ten days, it becomes law without a presidential signature unless Congress has adjourned in the meantime. If Congress adjourns before the ten-day period is up, the bill dies; this is referred to as a *pocket veto*. It is unusual enough for a president not to sign a bill that we ignore this constitutional wrinkle.

11. The presentation clause has been at issue in the use of the legislative veto. The **legislative veto** is a procedure that Congress frequently includes in laws that authorize executive branch agencies to issue regulations. The simplest way for a legislative veto provision to work would be for an agency to propose a regulation and then notify Congress. If one chamber passes a resolution opposing the regulation, it does not go into effect.

    In the 1983 court case *Chadha* v. *INS*, the Supreme Court ruled that virtually all variants of the legislative veto were unconstitutional because they violated the presentation clause. For a history of the legislative veto, see Fisher (1978).

12. While this hypothetical situation may seem farfetched, it is not too far removed from the politics of executive nominations, where the president proposes and the Senate votes up or down on the nominee.

13. Cameron (2000) contains an excellent summary of the quite complicated set of maneuvers about welfare reform in the 104th Congress, culminating in the passage of H.R. 3737, which provided for comprehensive welfare reform. Details may be found in the *CQ Almanacs* for 1995 and 1996. See "Welfare Bill Clears Under Veto Threat." CQ Press Electronic Library, CQ Almanac Online Edition, cqal95-1100649. Originally published in CQ Almanac 1995 (Washington: Congressional Quarterly, 1996). http://library.cqpress.com/cqalmanac/cqal95-1100649 (accessed August 20, 2010) and "After 60 Years, Most Control Sent to States." CQ Press Electronic Library, CQ Almanac Online Edition, cqal96-1092425. Originally published in CQ Almanac 1996 (Washington: Congressional Quarterly, 1997). http://library.cqpress.com/cqalmanac/cqal96-1092425 (accessed August 20, 2010).

14. Summaries of campaign finance reform attempts during the 102nd and 103rd Congresses can be found in the *Congressional Quarterly Almanac*, 1991–1994.

～ 3 ～

The History and Development of Congress

Congress was created to handle certain types of conflict that were bound to arise in the complex "extended Republic" the Constitution created. In Chapter 1, we discussed a generic danger inherent in any complicated society: Without well-constructed institutions, conflict can spiral out of control. Even among people of goodwill, a grand political bargain never can be struck that cannot be immediately undone. In Chapter 2, we saw that the "national" Congresses that existed before and during the Articles of Confederation were poorly constructed, further imperiling an independent United States.

With such introductory material behind us, we now can begin examining Congress systematically. In this chapter, I take as broad a view of Congress as I can, surveying over 200 years of congressional history, with the goal of understanding two general questions: First, within particular periods of congressional development, how have the basic institutional elements that define a legislature—rules of procedure, the committee system, and parties—been structured for Congress to do its work? Second, with these elements in place and fairly stable for long periods of time, what policy-making environment has characterized each of these periods?

In this chapter, the discussion is organized chronologically, as is traditionally done whenever a book or a book chapter has the word *history* in the title. History, after all, is about sequence. Still, to avoid telling a "one damned thing after another" series of stories about Congress, I impose a structure on the stories I tell. Congressional politics derives its energy from the electoral arena, so the best way to organize large swaths of congressional history is according to the ebb and flow of electoral dynamics. As it so happens, scholars of the electoral system have noted that American political history can be divided into eras in a surprisingly neat way. For long stretches at a time, the basic contours of nationwide partisan conflict remain fairly stable. The same (usually two) parties compete against each other, year in and year out, over the same issues. The same people—or demographic types—tend to support the same parties throughout. Shorter-term shocks to the political system, such as wars and recessions, may favor one party's fortunes over the other's, but a return to normalcy in the economy or society returns electoral competition to past patterns.

These relatively stable periods of party competition occasionally are broken, through calamitous political, social, or economic developments, such as the Great Depression or the Civil War. When the basic grounds on which the parties compete are shaken to the core, this opens up the possibility that *future* electoral competition will be quite different from the past; perhaps because new issues have entered politics, new groups have been mobilized into politics, or old groups have shifted partisan allegiances.

Scholars of the party and electoral systems call these long periods of stable partisan competition **party systems**. They call the calamitous periods in between **critical periods** and the elections that correspond to these periods **critical elections**. These same scholars largely agree that there have been five party systems, and some argue we are now in the sixth. Those systems are the following:[1]

1. **Experimental system,** 1789–1820, characterized by elite politics and contested by the Federalists (more elite) and Republicans[2] (less elite).
2. **Democratizing system,** 1828–1854 or 1860, emerging from a multifactional politics in the 1810s and 1820s and an expansion of the electorate, contested by Whigs (pro-commercial) and Democrats (pro-agrarian).
3. **Civil War system,** 1860–1893, formed around the Civil War and resulting in a largely regional politics contested by Democrats (southern) and Republicans (northern).
4. **Industrial system,** 1894–1932, organized mostly according to those advantaged by the rise of industry (Republicans) and those disadvantaged by it (Democrats), with the same regionalism remaining from the previous party system.
5. **New Deal system,** 1932–1972 energized by new voters who were mobilized in 1930 and 1932, pushing the Democrats to the "left" and the Republicans to the "right," with regional vestiges of the two previous systems still in place.
6. **Candidate-centered system,** 1972–?, prompted by political upheaval of the 1960s, which eliminated the regional vestiges of the previous two-party systems, in favor of a more ideologically aligned set of parties. Party allegiances of individual voters are much weaker than they used to

be. Organized parties have become stronger, but they are more often in the service of individual candidates.[3]

This periodization is a useful starting point for organizing a discussion of over two hundred years of congressional history, for two reasons. First, a periodization like this is helpful because congressional politics derives its energy from elections. If electoral competition is stable, then politics should be stable—and the institution of Congress likewise will be stable.[4] When elections are in a state of flux, this also presents opportunities to members of Congress (MCs) who wish to use the institution of Congress to further the agendas of emerging political blocs to advance those agendas.

Second, and speaking more practically, it is striking how relatively stable Congress has been during the partisan systems identified by electoral scholars and how fluid Congress has been surrounding the critical periods of change and realignment. While any periodizing scheme comes with the danger that it will overly simplify the dynamics of politics, one can go a long way by noting that the evolution of congressional politics closely parallels the evolution of party politics.

I take only one major deviation from the mainstream of party scholarship in the pages that follow. The "New Deal realignment" stood prior electoral politics on its head, replacing one long-standing majority party (the Republicans) with another (the Democrats). Yet this electoral realignment changed only congressional personnel. The institution itself was not changed very much in any fundamental sense. Hence, my own periodization of *congressional* politics merges together the industrial and New Deal systems into what Shepsle (1989) called the *textbook* system of congressional politics.

Figure 3.1 sketches out the five major periods of congressional history— what I call **congressional systems**, in deference to the term *party systems* used in the study of political parties. Each congressional system is characterized by a combination of an electoral equilibrium that supports an organizational equilibrium.

Figure 3.1
Congressional Historical Eras and Electoral Discontinuities

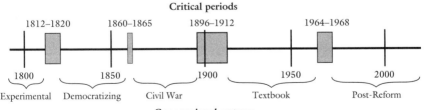

Table 3.1

Summary Characteristics of Organizational and Electoral Features during Congressional Systems and Electoral Features during Critical Periods

Dates	Electoral Dynamics		Organizational Dynamics		
	During Critical Period	During Congressional System	Rules	Committees	Party Leadership
1789–1812 (Experimental system)		Elite electorate; Federalists support commercial development, Republicans support agrarian development	Floor supreme; "previous question" developed in the House	Ad hoc select committees dominate	Formal organization inchoate; House speaker turnover common; weak Senate leadership
1812–1820	Electorate expands; Federalists discredited; slavery introduced as issue; Napoleonic Wars end				
1820–1860 (Antebellum system)		Mass electorate; Whigs support commercial development; Democrats support agrarian interests	Committees take agenda control in both chambers	Standing committees dominate selects; committee chairmen sometimes compete with House speakers for power	Regional divisions complicate selection of House speaker; Senate leadership remains weak
1860–1865	South excluded from national elections; party support highly regionalized				

1865–1896 (Civil War system)	Democratic strength in the South; Republican strength in the North; Republicans support commercial development; Democrats tilt toward the agrarian; knife-edge partisan margins	"Reed Rules" in the House	Parties take control of committee rosters; appropriations devolution	Party polarization; party leaders dominate in both chambers
1896–1912	Economic dislocations create Progressive and Populist movements, where Republicans are strong			
1912–1968 (Textbook system)	Same regional orientation as before; Democratic party picks up significant progressive and urban wings	Battles over filibuster prominent in the Senate	Committees dominate decision making; congressional careers are committee centered; committee consolidation in 1946	Party cohesion diminished; party leaders brokers

(Continued)

TABLE 3.1
Summary Characteristics of Organizational and Electoral Features during Congressional Systems and Electoral Features during Critical Periods (*continued*)

Dates	Electoral Dynamics		Organizational Dynamics		
	During Critical Period	*During Congressional System*	*Rules*	*Committees*	*Party Leadership*
1968–1974	Antiwar sentiment divorces supporters of strong defense from the Democrats; civil rights movement divorces southern whites from Democrats but reinforces black affiliation with Democrats				
1974–now (Candidate-Centered system)		Republicans conservative; Democrats liberal; regionalism per se deemphasized	Floor proceedings opened up	Committees continue to dominate, but leadership responsive to parties	Resurgent; partisan voting blocs more cohesive; leaders more assertive

Table 3.1 summarizes the basic contours of these equilibria. I have also characterized the basic elements of the critical election periods that set off each separate congressional system.

The remainder of this chapter is divided according to the congressional systems just identified. Each section discusses the electoral "crisis" that demarcated the new congressional system from the old. The major institutional features that grew up during these congressional systems and were supported by the electoral system as it emerged then are discussed.

The Experimental Era, 1789–1812

I term the first congressional system *experimental* because that is precisely what the earliest members of Congress did—they experimented. As mentioned in the previous chapter, the Congress under the Articles of Confederation tried many different divisions of labor. The states, too, had many different ways of organizing their legislatures (Harlow 1917; Jameson 1894). The Constitution gave each chamber of Congress the right to make its own rules and organize its own internal affairs. Neither chamber immediately hit on a grand organizing principle that was left unchanged for very long.

In the background of congressional organization was the electoral environment. Well before the advent of the mass media, or even universal suffrage, politics was an elite business in the late 1700s. Most states had property restrictions governing who could vote, and therefore electorates were fairly small. Table 3.2 shows the size of voter turnout in the earliest elections for which we have data. Identifiable party factions did not form immediately, but by the elections of 1794 and 1795, the party labels *Republican* and *Federalist* were used nationwide to identify the partisan affiliations of congressional candidates. Federalists formed around a core of supporters of Alexander Hamilton, the first secretary of the Treasury, who favored strong national programs to provide for the commercial development of the United States and stronger ties to Great Britain. Republicans formed around a core of supporters of Thomas Jefferson, the first secretary of State, who put greater faith in state and local governments than Hamilton and opposed Hamiltonian plans for commercial development. Finally, the Republicans tended to side with France in the European conflicts of the day.

The legislative theory that governed the basic flow of legislation in the earliest years of Congress has been termed *Jeffersonian*, after followers of Jefferson who believed that the whole Congress, and not subsets like committees, should hold a tight rein over legislation (Cooper 1970). For most of this period, legislation proceeded as follows. A subject would be introduced on the floor of one of the chambers, say, the House, and a general debate would ensue. As the debate wound down, someone would make a motion that the matter be referred to a committee to consider the matter in light of the debate and report back to the chamber. In the earliest years, this ad hoc (or **select**) **committee** then would report back to the chamber with a more refined set of ideas, leading to further debate. Then, another committee would be appointed to draft a bill for final passage. The bill would be reported back to the House for final debate, possible amendment, and final passage.

TABLE 3.2

Turnout as a Percentage of the Adult Population in the Elections of 1790 and 1791 (2nd Congress) and 1800–1801 (7th Congress), for States with Complete Electoral Returns

	1791–1793	*1801–1803*
Connecticut	6.5	9.2
Delaware	—	33.4
Maryland	30	21.6
Massachusetts	15	20.1
New Hampshire	12.3	11.8
New York	12.7	26
Rhode Island	—	12.9
Virginia	5	—
Georgia	5	31
New Jersey	18	34.6
Vermont	—	22.5
Kentucky	—	24.6
Tennessee	—	40.2

Source: Dubin (1998).

As time progressed, the two ad hoc committees involved in turning an inchoate proposal into legislation would be reduced to one, with the initial committee being authorized to report back immediately with a bill. Even with this minor streamlining, the logic underlying the flow of legislation remained unchanged: from the floor, where basic principles were established, to committee, where details were specified, and then back to the floor, where the law finally was approved.

As typical of most legislatures with a lower and upper chamber, the lower chamber of the U.S. Congress (the House) was much more active in origi-nating legislation than the Senate. In those few cases where the Senate ini-tiated legislation, the flow of business paralleled the House: Senate floor debate ⇒ ad hoc committee ⇒ Senate floor debate and passage. In most cases, however, the Senate simply received the House bill, referring it imme-diately to an ad hoc Senate committee, which was directed to consider the bill and report back to the Senate with a recommendation about what action to take. The Senate, which met in secret until 1795, often had little to do while waiting for the House to send it legislation. Therefore, it frequently adjourned early so that senators could attend to business or listen in to the public House sessions.

The second major institutional feature of Congress of interest is its leadership structure, and here both chambers exhibited a simple set of practices early on. The House speaker possessed some authority to help guide legislation, through the power of recognition and right to appoint committees.[5] Yet it is commonly agreed that only one speaker before 1812—Theodore Sedgwick (Fed. Mass.; 6th Congress, 1799–1801)—used his parliamentary assets in a brazenly partisan fashion. The vice president, as the constitutionally designated presiding officer of the Senate, was never given parliamentary rights even closely resembling the House speaker's, nor was the president pro tempore. The failure to trust the vice president with strong parliamentary authority is easily understandable. Vice presidents, then and now, do not face the same electoral imperatives as senators, nor is there a guarantee that the vice president will share the same political goals as a majority of the Senate. The failure to grant considerable authority to the president pro tempore is more of a puzzle, since such a leader could be chosen by a majority of the Senate for overtly political reasons and share the electoral environment of the full chamber.

The strongest legislative leaders identified during this period were not members of Congress at all. The first, Alexander Hamilton, derived his leadership authority from his position as the first secretary of the Treasury and the source of the most credible recommendations for getting the young nation's financial house in order. Yet political divisions quickly emerged precisely over Hamilton's active role in guiding legislation; by the 3rd Congress (1793–1795) the House had created a permanent, **standing committee** on Ways and Means to provide financial advice to the House, skirting Hamilton's influence. Thomas Jefferson also provided legislative leadership to the House following his election as president in 1800, which corresponded with the Jeffersonians taking control of both the House and Senate. Like Washington before him, Jefferson relied on his secretary of the Treasury (Albert Gallatin) to provide strategic leadership to his partisans in Congress. Furthermore, Jefferson was willing to intervene in the choice of House leaders, arranging for the appointment of his floor leader as chairman of the Ways and Means Committee.

The Democratizing System, 1820–1860

The electoral developments that helped end the Experimental system were associated with the War of 1812 and its aftermath. The period preceding the war itself witnessed the ascent of one of the most innovative House leaders in its history, Henry Clay, who led off a decade of institutional flux when he seized the speakership on the first day he was a member of the House (1811) and then actively orchestrated the declaration of war against England in 1812. On ascending to speaker, Clay promoted a change in the House rules that gave the speaker greater latitude in controlling debate on the floor and particularly limiting the tactics that opponents of legislation might use to obstruct business (Binder 1996, 1998). Combining a firm control over floor debate with deft attention to the composition of committees, Clay and his followers held the legislative upper hand to an unusual degree in American history.

From the perspective of the development of Congress, the most important direct effect of the War of 1812 was to fundamentally upset the incumbent structure of national partisan politics in three ways. First, the Republicans by and large supported going to war against England while the Federalists did not. The patriotic fervor whipped up during the war had the effect of undercutting popular support for the Federalists. Even worse for the Federalists, however, was the Hartford Convention called by a host of New England Federalist politicians in 1814 to discuss their grievances with the national government, which arose through the conduct of the war. Secession was discussed, although rejected. Even though the Hartford Convention was a failure, it made the Federalists seem not only antiwar, but anti-American. Popular support for the Federalists vanished, leaving the Congress a virtual one-party legislature by 1815.

The War of 1812 destroyed what was left of the two-party system organized along the Federalist-Republican axis, replacing it with a structure of politics that was factional, not partisan. Foreign policy receded into the distance as the major organizing issue of partisan conflict. The slavery issue came rapidly into view and quickly dominated national politics. The debate over the first Missouri Compromise, which began in 1819, caused regional animosities to erupt and linger for the first time in American history. Those animosities were an active feature of congressional voting patterns and electoral competition until the 19th Congress (1825–1827). National leaders, men such as Henry Clay and Martin Van Buren, worked hard to forge new partisan organizations that spanned the two regions and, in the end, created parties in which regional issues such as slavery and the tariff were submerged. Nonetheless, the transregional coalitions that the two political parties (Democrats and Whigs) developed into were fragile. Regional issues were just below the surface, providing the possibility that a regionally based factionalism could split either party (or both) at any given moment.

The breakdown of the old partisan system in the 1810s sowed the seeds for new legislative behavior. Going forward, fear that the submerged regional animosities suddenly might surface greatly influenced legislative behavior until the Civil War.

The most important formal institutional development in Congress during the second congressional system was the establishment of standing committee systems in both chambers. Gradually throughout the early nineteenth century, the House had been abandoning its reliance on ad hoc select committees for separate bills and petitions, adding instead a host of standing committees. During the 1810s and 1820s, momentum in favor of the standing committees gathered quickly so that by 1830, all senators and House members were members of standing committees. By then, select committees in both chambers were the exception rather than the rule.

Why did both chambers move so swiftly to install standing committees as the normal route for the consideration of legislation? Although this organizational change arguably is the most consequential in the history of Congress, virtually no contemporary members of Congress commented on the changes, either in the press accounts of the day or in the journals and letters they wrote. Therefore, scholarship into the development of the committee system during this period has been partially speculative. Yet, piecing together fragments of direct evidence, along with puzzling through this period aided by theory, political scientists have developed four general explanations about why the congressional committee system became entrenched, and why this entrenchment occurred in the 1810s and 1820s, rather than before or after.

1. *The role of Henry Clay.* Henry Clay and his War Hawk allies took Congress by storm upon entering the House in 1811. Determined to go to war against England and united as a bloc, the Clay-led House majority easily controlled the House politically in the early 1810s. However, as the war started going poorly, support for Clay waned. Later, once the war was over, it became impossible to hold together this political coalition by relying on a shared antagonism toward England. As a vehicle to bind together his political coalition, Clay doled out valued committee assignments to potential allies. In other words, strengthening the House committee system was a major vehicle by which Clay bolstered his political strength. Once strengthened, it was difficult to pull back this power from the committees (Gamm and Shepsle 1989; cf. Jenkins and Stewart 1997).

2. *Workload demands.* Much of the growth of the committee system in the 1810s and 1820s came through the creation of committees that pored over requests from constituents for special consideration from the federal government. Some of these requests concerned the distribution of public land in the newly acquired territories west of the Mississippi River; others concerned the payments of pensions to survivors of veterans of the Revolutionary War and the War of 1812; and still others simply handled claims against the federal government to redress economic harms caused by actions of the federal government. All these matters eventually were referred to new claims, lands, and pension standing committees in the two chambers.

3. *Oversight of the executive branch.* The War of 1812 led to the growth in size and complexity of the national government. The greatest growth in the size of the House committee system came through the creation

of six committees in 1816 that were charged with the task of auditing the various departments of the national government.

4. *Institutional competition.* During the 1810s, a host of factors prompted senators to become more active in initiating legislation and aiding constituents. This activism, in turn, prompted Senate leaders to propose a streamlining of Senate legislative procedure. At the start of the 16th Congress, the Senate took a major detour in its institutional development, replacing its scores of select committees with a much smaller number (twelve) of standing committees (Swift 1997). Nearly overnight, the Senate thus acquired a set of committees in which policy expertise could be developed independent of the House and the executive branch. The House, in turn, responded by finishing its conversion to standing committees, due to its members worried about losing the upper hand in policy disagreements with the Senate.

Each of these explanations can be grounded in the rational calculations of individual members of Congress. The explanation that emphasizes the role of Henry Clay highlights the strategic calculations an individual leader might make to advance his own political ambitions. The explanations that emphasize growing workloads address a problem common to all organizations—how to parcel out the work while retaining control over the decisions finally made. The institutional solution sought by both chambers of Congress in managing its workload—referring its work to committees composed of members rather than delegating to the executive branch—illustrates how Congress usually trusts advice from political peers (who share the same electoral imperatives) over advice from political outsiders (whose goals often differ significantly from those of legislators).

In overseeing the executive branch, Congress faced the problem of how to exert policy control over an entity that had grown unwieldy as a consequence of the war effort. Thus, in its earliest days, Congress was faced with what economists call a ***principal-agent problem.***[6] And finally, as the two chambers engaged in a type of institutional arms race, expanding each standing committee system apace, we witness members of both chambers trying to keep control over policy making to themselves, lest they lose initiative and influence to their rivals.

Each of these explanations for the expansion of the committee system resonates with research into the more modern Congress—as well it should. The legislators who endowed Congress with a strong, well-articulated committee system in the 1810s and 1820s were practical politicians trying to achieve a mix of electoral and policy goals. It is not surprising that the mix of motivations identified by historians of Congress to explain this committee system development mirror the motivations of modern legislators who have tried to reform the committee system more to their liking.

At the same time the standing committee system was developing into a complex and defining feature of the American Congress, the party leadership system was developing in fits and starts. The House and Senate each had different manifestations of this phenomenon, but the result was the same: once the era we are examining came to a close in 1860, neither chamber had developed a party structure or leadership apparatus that rivaled the committee system.

In both chambers, the looming reality that hung over party leadership from 1820 to 1860 was the regional divide opened by the Missouri Compromise and the issue of slavery. Although the Whig and Democratic parties, which grew up during this period, were national parties, each had northern and southern wings, leading to the possibility that the parties themselves could fly apart, with the regional wings defecting, joining the corresponding regional wing of the opposite party. Additionally, the national party system was fertile ground for the development of third parties, such as the American ("Know-Nothing") and Free Soil parties.

Party chaos in the electorate often translated to party chaos in Congress. One important manifestation of this chaos occurred in antebellum elections of the House speaker. Under the rules of the House, speakers must be elected by a majority of the chamber present and voting. Whenever one party is clearly in the majority and members of that party are loyal to it, electing the House speaker is trivial: the majority party nominates its leader, then votes as a unified front for his election. The majority is guaranteed. But if there is no majority, or if the majority has warring factions, then electing the House speaker is anything but trivial. In these circumstances, we may observe multiple candidates for speaker from a single party and multiple ballots to resolve the contest.

This is what we observe in the antebellum period. From 1820 to 1860, the House elected a speaker twenty-two times. Nine times it took more than one ballot to make a selection. The average number of ballots needed to finally select a Speaker in these nine elections was thirty-three. The most protracted and bitter contests occurred in the 26th Congress (1839), when it took fourteen days and 11 ballots to elect a speaker; the 31st Congress (1849, eighteen days, 63 ballots); the 34th Congress (1855, two months, 133 ballots); and the 36th Congress (1859, two months, 44 ballots).

A good example of how regionalism could intrude into the established party system was the balloting for speaker in the 34th Congress. The 34th Congress was elected in 1854 and 1855,[7] on the heels of the passage of the Kansas-Nebraska Act.[8] Much like the reaction to the Missouri Compromise in 1819, the Kansas-Nebraska Act brought underlying regional animosities to the fore. Complicating divisions over slavery, however, was an anti-immigrant political movement whose followers often are called the *Know-Nothings*, but whose politicians marched under the banner of the American Party. Americans came mostly from the North, but they had southern adherents, too.

In reaction to the Kansas-Nebraska Act, a hodgepodge of northern representatives—former Whigs and Democrats—came together under a loose alliance that identified itself simply in opposition to the Kansas-Nebraska

Act. While this group would form the core of the Republican Party, at this time they were simply labeled the *Opposition*. While the Democrats were the largest party in the 34th House, they were not a majority. Without a majority party to organize the House, the only thing obvious at the beginning of the 34th Congress was that the balloting for speaker would be protracted.

The Democratic Party, which had been reduced to a southern core with a few middle-Atlantic and Midwestern sympathizers, was cohesive and nominated a single candidate, William Richardson, from Illinois. The anti-Nebraska forces were split along two dimensions: between North and South *and* between American and Opposition blocs. Consequently, four major opponents emerged to battle the Democratic speaker candidate on the first ballot: Nathaniel Banks (American-Mass.), Humphrey Marshall (American-Ky.), Lewis Campbell (Opposition-Ohio), and Henry Fuller (Opposition-Pa.).[9] On the first ballot, Richardson received seventy-two votes; Campbell, fifty-two; Marshall, thirty; Banks, twenty; Fuller, seventeen; and sixteen other candidates split the vote of the thirty other House members.

The top part of Figure 3.2 uses a one-dimensional spatial model to show how the voting emerged on this first ballot. The upper panel shows the estimated ideal points along a left-right dimension of all the House members who supported each of the five major candidates for speaker on the first ballot.[10] Triangles show the left-right ideal points of the candidates. While the left-right spatial location of the candidates for speaker helps to explain who voted for whom on the first ballot,[11] regional and nativist (anti-immigrant) factors, which are accounted for by other dimensions in the policy space, intervened as well. So, for instance, southern Americans (who were mostly on the left of the dimension) supported Marshall, while northern Americans supported Banks. The non-American, Opposition vote likewise was split between the westerner Campbell and the easterner Fuller.

Over the next two months, leaders of the various factions tried out new speaker candidates, attempting to find the right combination of ideological correctness and regional appeal that would attract a majority of the chamber. Eventually, the Democrats settled on William Aiken of South Carolina and an Opposition-American alliance emerged that supported Banks. Still, enough slavery extremists on both sides of the issue refused to accede to these compromise candidates (particularly Banks), so that neither could quite get a majority. The contest was resolved only after the House finally agreed to settle the matter via a plurality vote (i.e., victory to the highest vote getter, regardless of whether the vote was a majority).[12]

The lower part of Figure 3.2 shows the left-right location of Aiken and Banks, along with the ideal point locations of their supporters. The final vote is described almost perfectly by the one-dimensional spatial model. However, it took over a hundred ballots before bargaining among factional leaders could achieve a reduction of the choice to just two major candidates. Banks, in turn, rewarded his supporters by favoring anti-Nebraska men in the appointment

FIGURE 3.2
Spatial Summary of the Vote for House Speaker in the 34th Congress

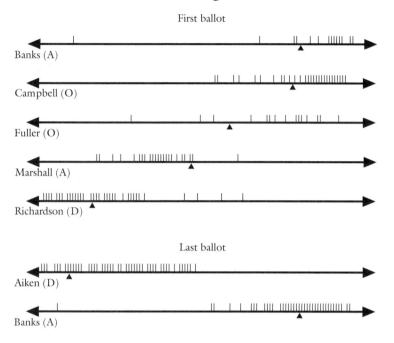

of committees, even though he sought to placate the South by appointing one of their own, John A. Quitman (D-Miss.) to chair the Military Affairs Committee.

Lacking a speaker, the Senate did not have quite the pyrotechnical displays in choosing its party leaders. Still, the underlying regional tensions manifested themselves within the Senate by the choice of the vice president. The choice of vice president was critical for the maintenance of the balance rule that emerged following the Missouri Compromise of 1820 (Weingast 1998). The **balance rule** operated by admitting Missouri and Maine together as slave and free states and then setting in motion a pattern of always balancing the admission of slave and free states. Thus, even though the House would grow to possess a large antislavery, northern majority due to population growth in the North, the Senate maintained an even balance between the two regions. Helping reinforce this balance rule was a practice developed by the two parties of balancing their presidential-vice presidential tickets between North and South, too.

Table 3.3 shows the balancing of tickets of the Whig-Republicans and Democrats from 1836 to 1860.[13] Except for the regionally structured campaign of 1840, almost always, whenever a party chose a northerner for

TABLE 3.3
Regional Balance in Party Tickets, 1836–1860

	Democratic Party		Whig-Republican Parties	
Year	President	Vice President	President	Vice President
1836	Van Buren (N.Y.)	Johnson (Ky.)	Webster (N.H.)	Granger (N.Y.)
			Harrison (Ohio)	Granger (N.Y.)
			White (Tenn.)	Tyler (Va.)
1840	Van Buren (N.Y.)	None*	Harrison (Ohio)	Tyler (Va.)
1844	Polk (Tenn.)	Dallas (Pa.)	Clay (Ky.)	Frelinghuysen (N.J.)
1848	Cass (Mich.)	Butler (Ky.)	Taylor (Va.)	Fillmore (N.Y.)
1852	Pierce (N.Y.)	King (Ala.)	Scott (Va.)	Graham (N.C.)
			Whig-American	
1856	Buchanan (Pa.)	Breckinridge (Ky.)	Fillmore (N.Y.)	Donelson (Tenn.)
			Republican	
			Fremont (Calif.)	Dayton (N.J.)
1860	Douglas (Ill.)	Fitzpatrick (Ala.)	Lincoln (Ill.)	Hamlin (Maine)

*State parties chose their own vice-presidential nominees.
Source: Aldrich (1995, Table 5.1).

president, it chose a southerner for vice president and vice versa. The most egregious violation of this pattern occurred at the end of the time period, when the Republicans ran two sets of northern candidates in the 1860 presidential election. So, what mortified southerners about the election of Abraham Lincoln was not only his moderation on the issue of slavery expansion but that his party had disavowed the balance rule, eliminating the pro-southern veto that had been institutionalized at the national level for almost half a century.

That the vice president was chosen to help the parties deal with their electoral needs, rather than to help lead the Senate from within, is one reason the vice president, although the constitutional head of the Senate, never developed as the actual leader of the Senate. The experience of John C. Calhoun (vice president in the 19th, 20th, and 21st Congresses) helps demonstrate the strategic disadvantage facing vice presidents who wished to take the legislative lead. At the start of the 19th Congress, the Senate rules specified that the "presiding officer" would appoint Senate committees. Heretofore, the vice president had rarely functioned as the Senate's presiding officer, leaving the matter to the president pro tempore or some other senator who happened to be holding the chair. Calhoun, however, upset this practice by insisting on appointing the Senate committees himself. His committee assignments reflected strongly his policy views, which, by and large, were radically different from those of the mainstream of the chamber.[14] Consequently, the Senate took the right of making committee assignments away from the vice president, vesting it first in the president pro tempore, and then in a ballot of the whole Senate.

At the dawn of the Civil War, the organizational character of both chambers was similar in many respects, even as they differed in obvious ways (like by size and regional composition). A large committee system had developed in both chambers and much of the original legislative work was lodged there. Committee membership was fluid, reflecting partially the high turnover of members, but also reflecting the fact that slightly different factions controlled each chamber from one Congress to the next, requiring the reshuffling of the power system, much like cabinet portfolios are shifted every time a government in a parliamentary system faces an election. Party leaders tried valiantly to overcome deep regional animosities, but the need to manage regional cleavages undermined leadership positions as foci of real power. Leaders were chosen, on an ad hoc. Congress-by-Congress basis, to help manage the regional crisis of the moment.

The Civil War System, 1865–1896

The obvious political break point in the middle of the nineteenth century was the Civil War, fought from 1861 to 1865. Although the political consequences of the war for the nation as a whole were immense, the changes that were wrought in Congress have been underappreciated by historians and political scientists. As far as Congress is concerned, the most important electoral discontinuity brought by the Civil War was the exclusion of the South from the national electorate, depriving the Democratic Party of its long-running majority on the national scene, allowing the Republican Party to rule in a virtual one-party state for a decade.

The war helped make partisan affiliations within the electorate even more regionally structured than they had been in the past, producing a "solid South," loyal to the Democratic Party for the next century; a (less) solid North, tending toward the Republican Party; and a highly competitive Ohio River Valley, which could go either way. Additionally, while the Republican Party held sway over Congress and the presidency in the 1860s, it worked to undo the effects of the "balance rule" that had operated before the Civil War. In particular, through a series of highly partisan maneuvers, the Republican Congress admitted to the Union a host of low-population western states that had strong Republican tendencies (like Nevada), keeping from statehood some higher-population states with Democratic tendencies (like Utah). The strongly Republican Dakota territory was split in two, creating two new low-population Republican states where there had been a single medium-population Republican territory.

The most important consequence of this strategy of "stacking the Senate" (Stewart and Weingast 1992) was that once the southern states were readmitted to the Union under Reconstruction, Republican and Democratic strength in Congress was matched perfectly, even though the Democrats returned to majority party status in the mass electorate. This creation of a Democratic-dominated House and Republican-dominated Senate produced what was then the longest period of chronically divided control of the federal government in the nation's history, a period unmatched until recently. Republicans and Democrats found themselves locked in intense partisan combat at the polls and on the floor of Congress. This combat not only affected which policies were passed (or failed to pass due to deadlock) but significantly affected the internal organization of Congress.

In both chambers the committee systems had been fully fleshed out during the antebellum period. The post–Civil War period brought greater structuring of the committees along partisan lines. This is illustrated in Figure 3.3, which shows the percentage of committee chairmen in both chambers who belonged to the majority party. Before 1860, that figure only occasionally approached 100 percent. After a period of transition in the 1860s, that figure generally hovered around 100 percent. Before 1860, the party composition of the committees changed yearly, usually driven by the necessity to knit together intraparty coalitions to help organize both the House and Senate. From roughly 1870 until the present, the majority party almost always has held more than half the seats on all the committees and almost all the committee chairmanships. The only systematic deviation from this pattern occurred in the Senate, which had so many committees after the 1880s that it sometimes had more committees than members of the majority party, prompting the appointment of minority party committee chairmen simply to fill out the committee rosters.

Corresponding to a stronger partisan structuring of the committees in both chambers was the generally stronger and more central role played by party leaders. On the House side, the job of the party leader was simplified as a consequence of the stronger regional alignment of the parties. Democrats mostly represented the South and farmers; Republicans mostly represented the North and urban dwellers. There were enough exceptions to make the parties less than perfectly homogeneous, but now the homogeneity was sufficient to keep intraparty struggles from breaking out on the floor. Contrasting with the antebellum period, only once since 1859 has a contest for the speaker of the House been fought out on the floor.[15]

Because the Senate lacks a focal organizing vote like the House's speakership balloting, the stronger tug of partisanship in the Senate after the Civil War had fewer obvious organizational manifestations. It was easier to organize the Senate in most Congresses, too, only this did not show up in balloting for speaker. The one exception came in the 47th Congress, when the number of Republican and Democratic senators was evenly matched and the Senate deadlocked briefly over which party would get to control majorities on the committees.

FIGURE 3.3
Percentage of Standing Committee Chairs Held by Members of the Majority Party, 1st to 49th Congresses (1789–1887)

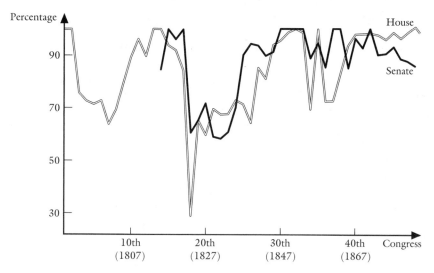

During the post–Civil War period, the Senate emerged as one of the centers of partisan power in the United States. Reformers derided the Senate as a "Millionaires Club," since so many of its members had become rich, particularly through financing and building the railroads. What this slogan misses is a more subtle characteristic of the Senate after the Civil War: the millionaires who populated it were also many of the most important party officials of their eras. They gained election by consolidating political power in their states. By controlling state politics first, they dominated elections to state legislatures. In a very real sense, therefore, the constitutional theory that senators would be responsive to states primarily through their legislatures was turned on its head—the state legislature in many cases was responsive to the senator (Riker 1955).

The greater cohesion of the two parties' individual constituency bases, coupled with the close partisan margins produced by the elections, opened the way for party leaders to acquire greater power to lead their parties. The classic example of this came in the passage of the **Reed Rules** during the 51st Congress (1889–1891).

The elections of 1888 had returned a bare majority for the Republicans. The partisan margin stood at 173 seats for the Republicans and 156 for the Democrats, with one vacancy. Following that election, fifteen Republicans who had been declared losers by state election officials appealed those decisions to the House where, according to the Constitution, the House could determine who rightfully held the seat. During this era, contested elections more often than not were decided in favor of the party holding a majority in the House, presumably even in cases where the minority party candidate was the rightful winner (Polsby 1968). Understanding the partisan nature of contested elections cases, it is not surprising that Republicans who lost by narrow margins would appeal to a Republican-controlled House. And given the close partisan margin already in the House, it is not surprising that Democrats would skeptically regard any proposal to resolve a contested election case in favor of a Republican.

One of the Republicans who appealed his electoral defeat to the whole House was Charles B. Smith, who had lost his election to James M. Jackson in the 4th District of West Virginia by only three votes—19,834 to 19,837. After considering his contest, the House Elections Committee recommended that Smith be seated. On calling up the resolution to seat Smith instead of Jackson, the Democrats objected that the election challenge was being unjustly decided. Speaker Reed, who was presiding at the time, ignored the protests of the Democrats and led a roll call to seat the Republican Smith. At the end of the roll call, the votes were in: 161 voted to seat Smith, 2 voted against seating Smith, and 165 members of the House failed to respond to their name when it was called. Among all Republicans who were members of the House at that time, they voted 161–0 to seat Smith, with 5 absent; 1 Democrat voted in opposition to seating Smith, and 160 were absent.

Because 163 members had voted and 165 were silent, a quorum (i.e., half the members of the House) was absent. Under the Constitution, half the elected members of the House must be voting for the House to transact any business. According to the Constitution, the only thing Speaker Reed could do in the absence of a quorum was adjourn the House, try to get a quorum, and try the vote to seat Smith another day.

Reed chose a different tactic, though. Although 165 House members had failed to vote, that did not mean that 165 House members were absent. Indeed, most of the 165 nonvoters were in the House chamber at the time the roll call was taken. These Democrats had participated in a so-called **disappearing quorum**, whereby members refrained from voting, hoping the lack of a quorum would kill the measure. Here is an excerpt from the *Congressional Record* that describes what Reed did next:

THE SPEAKER. On the question the yeas are 161, the nays 2.

MR. CRISP. No quorum.

THE SPEAKER. The Chair directs the Clerk to record the following names of members present and refusing to vote: [Applause on the Republican side.]

MR. CRISP. I appeal—[applause on the Democratic side]—I appeal from the decision of the Chair.

THE SPEAKER. Mr. Blanchard, Mr. Bland, Mr. Blount, Mr. Breckinridge of Arkansas, Mr. Breckenridge of Kentucky.

MR. BRECKINRIDGE, of Kentucky. I deny the power of the Speaker and denounce it as revolutionary. [Applause on the Democratic side of the House, which was renewed several times.]

MR. BLAND. Mr. Speaker, I am responsible to my constituents for the way in which I vote, and not to the Speaker of this House. [Applause on the Democratic side.]

THE SPEAKER. Mr. Brookshire, Mr. Bullock, Mr. Bynum, Mr. Carlisle, Mr. Chipman, Mr. Clements, Mr. Clunie, Mr. Compton.

MR. COMPTON. I protest against the conduct of the Chair in calling my name.

THE SPEAKER (proceeding). Mr. Covert, Mr. Crisp, Mr. Culberson of Texas [hisses on the Democratic side], Mr. Cummings, Mr. Edmunds, Mr. Enloe, Mr. Fithian, Mr. Goodnight, Mr. Hare, Mr. Hatch, Mr. Hayes.

MR. HAYES. I appeal from any decision so far as I am concerned.

THE SPEAKER (proceeding). Mr. Holman, Mr. Lawles, Mr. Lee, Mr. McAdoo, Mr. McCreary.

MR. MCCREARY. I deny your right, Mr. Speaker, to count me as present, and I desire to read from the parliamentary law on that subject.

THE SPEAKER. The Chair is making a statement of the fact that the gentleman from Kentucky is present. Does he deny it? [Laughter and applause on the Republican side.]

A few days after Reed had established the precedent of breaking the disappearing quorum, the rules were changed to strengthen the hand of the speaker and the majority party against attempts by the minority to delay legislative action. Two changes were made. First, the rules were changed to prohibit members from making dilatory motions. A **dilatory motion** is made purely for the purpose of delaying action, such as endlessly moving to adjourn or making a host of trivial amendments to a bill. With this rule change, a speaker could swiftly move to take a vote on a measure and avoid motions from the minority.

Second, the quorum in the Committee of the Whole was reduced from a quorum of the whole House (165 at that time) to a plain 100. In Chapter 7, we examine in some detail how the Committee of the Whole operates. For now it is sufficient to know that **Committee of the Whole** is the legal fiction that the House uses to expedite the consideration of legislation and the debate of amendments. As the name implies, the Committee of the Whole consists of all members of the House. The rules generally are more relaxed in the Committee of the Whole, but the rules also allow for less debate for each motion that's made. The speaker also does not preside when the House is meeting in Committee of the Whole, allowing this person to take care of his or her own and party's political business while the House works on legislation. Because the Committee of the Whole is not, technically, the House, any amendments it approves must again be approved by a formal session of the

House. However, amendments that are defeated in the Committee of the Whole may not again be considered by the House. Thus, the Committee of the Whole is a powerful legal fiction. By reducing the quorum in the Committee of the Whole to one hundred, it was made much more difficult for the minority party to grind business to a halt by being absent from the chamber.

Reed also developed the Rules Committee as a strategic partisan weapon (Bach and Smith 1988). Before Reed's speakership, the Rules Committee had little work. Its primary task was the consideration of any rule changes proposed. Because most of these changes occurred at the start of a session, the Rules Committee usually worked hard in the opening weeks of a Congress to modify the rules and then went into legislative hibernation.

The problem Reed solved with the deft use of the Rules Committee was that of scheduling. Under the rules of the House, all bills that are reported out of committee go onto a long list, called the **House Calendar**.[16] Under the rules, the House was supposed to consider legislation in the order in which it appears on the calendar, meaning the first matter reported from committee is supposed to be considered first by the House. Naturally, with such an ordering device, it is possible for important legislation to become bogged down behind trivial matters. By the 1880s, the House had tried to deal with this problem by allowing certain committees—notably Ways and Means and Appropriations—to report their bills to the House floor at any time. Thus, at least money matters could get considered whenever they were ready, jumping over other, nonfinancial legislation. However, even this device was unsatisfactory, since it gave significant agenda-setting power to the chairs of the Ways and Means and Appropriations Committees. Aware of the power they wielded, they often roamed the House floor with a few bills stuffed in their pockets. If it looked like something was going to come to the floor that he objected to, the chairman of the Ways and Means Committee could gain recognition, bring up a tax bill, and block the consideration of the other business.

Reed's solution to the agenda-setting problem was to endow the Rules Committee with another role: that of reporting out resolutions setting the time for the consideration of legislation. These resolutions were called **special orders**, but now are popularly known as **rules**. As the chair of the Rules Committee, then, Speaker Reed took back from his committee chairmen some of the authority to direct the legislative agenda.

Thus, through a combination of factors—electoral and institutional—the parties following the Civil War were distinct and cohesive. A common statistic used to illustrate this fact measures the incidence of party unity voting. In **party unity voting** at least half the members of one party take a position on a roll call vote that is in disagreement with at least half of the members of the other party. The incidence of party unity voting in the House graphed in Figure 3.4 is simply the fraction of all votes taken during a particular Congress in which a majority of the Democrats opposed a majority of the Republicans. During the Civil War congressional system, partisan unity was high by historical standards and grew throughout.

FIGURE **3.4**

Prevalence of Party Unity Votes in the House of Representatives, 35th–110th Congresses (1857–2008)

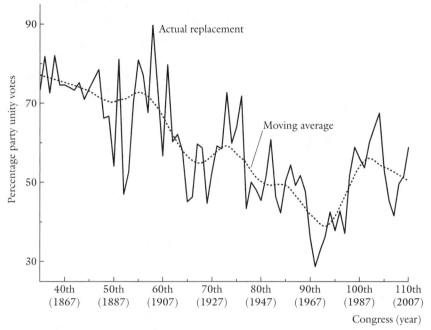

Source: http://pooleandrosenthal.com/party_unity.htm. Moving average calculated using loess smoothing.

The Textbook Era, 1912–1968

Two related electoral developments in the 1890s provided the basis for undermining the Civil War system and ushering in the Textbook system. Those two developments were the elections of 1894 and 1896 and the rise of the Progressive fissure within the Republican Party. Political scientists have identified the elections of 1894 and 1896 as providing the clearest example of a set of critical realigning elections. Both followed the Panic of 1893, a severe economic downturn that was so bad it was known as the Great Depression, until an even worse depression came along in 1929. The Panic of 1893 occurred under the presidency of a Democrat, Grover Cleveland. Consequently, the Democrats were hammered in the midterm election of 1894, falling from a 220–126 membership edge in the House in the 53rd Congress (1893–1895) to a 104–246 deficit in the 54th (1895–1897).[17]

The social upheaval spawned by the Panic of 1893 carried over into the presidential election of 1896. In that election, the two parties took strong and distinct stances on two important issues of the day: the protective tariff and the gold standard. Based on the positions historically held by the two parties, but thrown in sharper relief by the effects of the Panic, the Republicans nominated William McKinley on a platform that promised to raise tariffs to protect American industries against import competition; the Democrats nominated William Jennings Bryan on a platform promising a further easing of tariffs. Bryan's candidacy is better known, however, for his zealous stance against the gold standard, exemplified by his fiery "Cross of Gold Speech" made at the Democratic convention. In short, the Republicans held to a doctrine of "hard money" (i.e., a gold standard), while the Democrats favored the striking of silver coins and the deflation of the currency.

The stances taken by the two parties' presidential candidates in 1896 had the effect of shifting partisan support in the country in subtle ways. The regional voting realignment is summarized in Table 3.4, which reports the average vote received by Democratic, Republican, and other party candidates in different regions between 1886 and 1900. The election of 1896 did nothing to change the stranglehold that the Republican Party held over New England or the Democrats over the South. The industrial and more prosperous agricultural regions—the Northeast, and East North Central states—moved from being competitive to being strongly Republican. Voters in the least prosperous agrarian regions—the West North Central and the far West—shifted some of their support away from the two major parties in favor of more populist parties that responded directly to the economic dissatisfaction in these regions: the Progressive, Populist, and Silver parties.

By the net nationwide movement of about 7 percent of the vote in favor of the Republicans, the elections of 1894 and 1896 transformed Congress from an institution characterized by close partisan margins to one in which the Republican Party was clearly dominant nationally. In most regions of the country, the Republicans also were the dominant party, but not in all. Democrats still held tight to the Deep South, and they continued to hold a slight edge in the Border states. Overall, most congressional districts became safely aligned with one of the parties, depending on the region (Price 1975a, 1975b, 1977).

An important change in election laws nationwide had a further effect on electoral dynamics in Congress. During the 1880s and 1890s, almost every state adopted ballot reforms to clean up voting fraud and regulate party competition (Katz and Sala 1996). While the laws differed in their particulars from state to state, most adopted two ballot reforms that changed the electoral landscape of Congress for good. First, all states adopted the **Australian ballot**, which was the innovation of having the state (rather than the parties) print up ballots which were then cast in secret. Second, nearly all states required political parties to hold primaries to choose party nominees for Congress. The first reform helped loosen the tie between voters and parties by making it

TABLE 3.4
Mean Party Vote in House Elections by Region, 1886–1900

	New England	Northeast	E. North Central	W. North Central	South	Border	West
Republicans							
Avg. 1886–1892	51.8	47.5	48.1	46.5	20.0	40.8	49.9
Avg. 1894–1900	61.0	55.8	53.2	40.0	19.2	45.2	48.5
Diff.	9.2	8.4	5.1	−6.5	−0.8	4.5	−1.4
Democrats							
Avg. 1886–1892	44.9	48.6	47.3	44.0	71.7	55.9	46.0
Avg. 1894–1900	35.7	40.1	43.8	41.1	69.0	50.4	36.8
Diff.	−9.2	−8.5	−3.5	−2.9	−2.7	−5.5	−9.3
Other parties							
Avg. 1886–1892	3.3	4.0	4.7	9.6	8.4	3.4	4.1
Avg. 1894–1900	3.4	4.1	3.0	19.0	11.8	4.4	14.8
Diff.	0.0	0.1	−1.7	9.4	3.4	1.1	10.6

Note: The regions are coded as follows. *New England*: Conn., Maine, Mass;, N.H., R.I., Vt.; *Northeast*: Del., N.J., N.Y., Pa.; *East North Central*: Ill., Ind., Mich., Ohio, Wisc.; *West North Central*: Iowa, Kans., Minn., Mo., Nebr., N.D., S.D.; *South*: Ala., Ark., Fla., Ga., La., Miss., N.C., S.C., Tenn., Tex., Va.; *Border*: Ky., Md., W.Va.; *West*: Calif., Colo, Mont., Nev., N.M., Ore., Utah, Wash., Wyo.

Differences are affected by rounding.
Source: Brady (1988, Table 3.2).

easier for voters to pick and choose among candidates for various offices. The second reform helped loosen the tie between politicians and parties by making it easier for renegade party members to contest the party's nomination for Congress.

The combination of ballot reforms and partisan realignment in the 1890s ended up giving members of Congress greater latitude in plotting their own electoral careers. With open primaries the norm, party organizations no longer could automatically cut short the congressional career of an incumbent who had served in the House "long enough," in favor of someone else in the party who had patiently waited his turn. And with safer electoral margins, House incumbents could be assured that they would be around for a long time, making a career in the House possible for more people. Consequently, turnover in House membership dropped significantly at the onset of the twentieth century (see Figure 3.5).

Before exploring the effects of lower turnover rates on congressional politics, we return briefly to a development alluded to earlier: the ideological fissures created in the Republican Party (particularly) as a consequence of the election of 1896. The Panic of 1893 had its greatest long-term negative economic consequences on the upper Great Plains states and the far West. These regions had provided strong support for the Republican Party, stretching back to the admission of these states before and after the Civil War (Stewart and Weingast 1992). The conservatism of Republican Party leaders in the face of the economic distress of this region undercut support for the GOP in the Great Plains. Even though Great Plains voters were disenchanted with the Republican Party, they were unlikely converts to the Democratic Party, which still bore the stain of the Civil War and slavery in the minds of many western voters. Instead, this region became ripe territory for parties espousing a populist message, distinct from Democratic candidates who might run on similar platforms. Rather than draw from a previously Democratic base, the populist parties appealed mostly to disaffected Republicans. In some cases, the parties' candidates were successful—most of the "third party" House members from the 1890s and 1900s came from the Great Plains and the mountain West.

Trying to outflank the more populist parties, Republican candidates in western states also tried to appeal to the antiestablishment vote. Therefore, even among many western Republican members of Congress, party loyalty was not all it had been only a decade before. Therefore, although the Democrats and Republicans, on the whole, were cohesive, congressional Republicans harbored a small wing of approximately twenty members dissatisfied with the conservative tendencies of the party mainstream, a wing that would destabilize the party in significant ways (Holt 1967; Hechler 1940).

Cracks in the Republican facade appeared in the election of 1894 and 1896, although more than a decade would transpire before those cracks showed up on the floor of Congress. The populist-conservative Republican divide came to a head under the speakership of Joseph "Uncle Joe" Cannon (R-Ill.). Cannon was a conservative House speaker (58th-61st Congresses, 1903–1911)

FIGURE 3.5
Membership Turnover in the House of Representatives, 2nd–110th Congresses (Elections of 1790–2008)

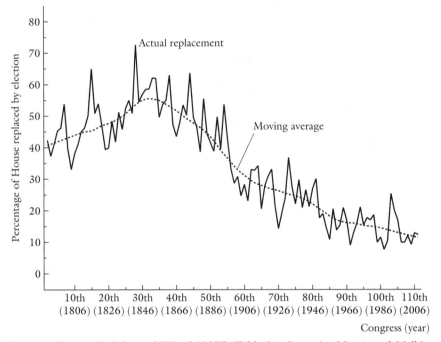

Sources: Fiorina, Rohde, and Wissel (1975, Table 1); Ornstein, Mann, and Malbin (2008, Table 2–7). Moving average calculated using loess smoothing.

who had little patience for the form of progressive Republicanism exemplified in the person of President Theodore Roosevelt. Cannon adhered to a classical doctrine of **party responsibility**: parties, in Cannon's view, should clearly distinguish themselves from each other. Having staked out a position, each party should work to achieve that position. Should a policy course prove unworkable or unpopular, the right thing for a party to do would be to tough it out in the electorate. His beef with progressives within his own party was twofold. First, he simply disagreed with much of what they stood for, such as greater regulation of business and reform of the political system. Second, he objected to progressives' muddying the Republican message. If Progressive Republicans had a problem with the mainstream of the party, they should leave. Cannon had been willing to implement his views on party responsibility through his actions as speaker, blocking legislation of which he disapproved and punishing renegade Republicans through his committee assignments.

Dissatisfaction with Cannon among the insurgents grew throughout the first decade of the twentieth century. One complaint that the insurgents lodged against Cannon was that he presided over the Rules Committee with an iron fist, using it to keep off the floor any legislation of which he personally disapproved. Dissatisfaction over Cannon's tight control over the agenda resonated beyond the small group of insurgents who were most at odds with Cannon, since virtually all committees had seen legislation favored by a majority get bottled up by the Rules Committee. The insurgents' idea was to remove the speaker from the Rules Committee, making it less of a leadership tool. Cannon was easily able to rebuff this proposal, but he was unable to keep total control over the agenda.

At the end of the 60th Congress (1909), Cannon agreed to the creation of a parliamentary device, Calendar Wednesday, that gave a small degree of agenda control back to the various legislative committees. **Calendar Wednesday** operated like this: at a set time each Wednesday (hence, the name), each committee of the House would be called on, alphabetically. When a committee was called, the chairman of the committee could bring up a bill that had been approved by his committee. The House then would get two hours to consider the bill. After a committee's bill had been considered, it would have to wait its turn until it came up on the alphabetical list again.

The Calendar Wednesday provision proved so cumbersome in getting alternative legislation to the House floor that the insurgents quickly abandoned it and returned to their designs on the speaker's powers more broadly. The elections of 1908 helped the insurgent cause significantly. Following the election, there were 219 Republicans and 172 Democrats. If thirty insurgent Republicans could be convinced to side with the Democrats in changing the House rules, the anti-Cannon forces would have a 202–189 margin. While the insurgent Republicans were not in the parliamentary driver's seat, their chances against Cannon were the best they had ever been.

At the opening of the 61st House (1909–1911), the insurgent Republicans were loyal to their speaker, voting unanimously for Cannon against the Democratic speaker nominee Champ Clark, of Missouri. Right after Cannon's election as speaker, he entertained a motion that the House adopt the rules of the 60th Congress as the rules of the 61st. This always had been considered a pro forma motion, allowing the House to proceed immediately with the business of organizing committees without having to reconsider its rules from scratch. This time things were different: the insurgents joined with the Democrats to oppose this motion, leaving the House without formal rules. Champ Clark then moved that all the past House's rules be adopted, with three changes: first, the speaker no longer would be allowed to appoint committees; second, the speaker would be removed from the Rules Committee; and third, the Rules Committee would be enlarged from five to ten members.

Clark's motion also was narrowly defeated, 180–203, this time because Cannon had convinced a small group of conservative Democrats to support him rather than Clark. Representative John Fitzgerald (D-N.Y.) authored a compromise that allowed the House to proceed with its business. Under the compromise a consent calendar was created, allowing minor, uncontroversial legislation to come to the floor more easily.

Agitation among insurgent Republicans and Democrats for further reform continued apace. Finally, St. Patrick's Day 1910, Representative George Norris (R-Nebr.) tried again, offering a resolution to reform the House rules similar to the one Clark had offered on opening day. Cannon ruled Norris's motion out of order. Norris appealed Cannon's ruling, arguing that a motion to amend the rules always was in order, being privileged by the Constitution. A majority of the House supported Norris's appeal, 182–160. It then proceeded to debate Clark's motion, spending twenty-nine hours in continuous session. At the end of that time, the House voted 191–156 to strip the speaker of his committee-appointing power and his membership on the Rules Committee. Rebuffed, Cannon immediately offered to entertain a motion declaring that the speakership was now vacant. Representative Albert S. Burleson (D-Tex.) obliged the speaker, but the insurgent Republicans returned to the fold to table this motion. In the end, much of Cannon's formal power had been stripped from him, but he was still Speaker.

Speaker Cannon was swept out of the House in the 1910 election, along with enough of his Republican colleagues that the Democrats won control of the House for the first time in two decades. It was up to the Democrats to figure out how to bypass the speaker in nominating committees and controlling the House agenda. In theory, the full House now made committee appointments. In practice, the Democrats decided to establish the Democratic members of the Ways and Means Committee as its **Committee on Committees**. The Republicans decided to use a separate Committee on Committees.

For controlling the House agenda, the Democrats decided to use the Democratic caucus. The House Democratic **caucus** is simply the organization of all House Democrats. The caucus passed a rule requiring all Democrats to vote for any measure supported by two-thirds of the caucus—to oppose the caucus would result in being "read out of" the party. Historians have credited the caucus's activity with the passage of the Underwood tariff, the Federal Reserve Act of 1913, and antitrust legislation in 1914 (Sundquist 1981, pp. 165–76).

The 62nd and 63rd Congresses were heady ones for the Democrats. Yet, as the decade of the 1910s proceeded, the unity of the party waned. The Republicans, temporarily in the minority, attacked the Democrats' use of the caucus to control the agenda and promised to abandon "King Caucus" once they returned to power. The Republicans returned to control the House in 1918, and they made good on their promise not to control the House floor via the caucus mechanism.[18]

As 1920 drew near, the House had reestablished a new institutional equilibrium to replace the one in place before the revolt against Cannon. The party mechanisms that had coordinated the policy-making process, periodically using coercion against reluctant rank-and-file members, no longer existed.

Leadership in the House was dispersed, shared between formal party leaders and the chairmen of the committees.

Lacking a strong mechanism to exchange party loyalty for plum committee assignments and punish disloyalty by yanking those assignments, the two parties adopted a strong form of the seniority system which remained entrenched until very recently. The **seniority system**, as it developed in the 1910s, had two components. The first was a property rights system in committee assignments: although a member could not just choose which committees to serve on, once on a committee, he or she could not be taken off involuntarily. The second was a rigid mechanism to pick committee chairs: the member with the longest continuous service on a committee got to chair it whenever the chairmanship came open. From 1912 to the 1970s, these two prongs of the House seniority system were almost never violated. Combining the longer House careers that became more common after the election of 1896 with the seniority norm that emerged after 1912, we see the core elements of the "textbook Congress" that ruled American policy making for much of the twentieth century.

In the Senate, the electoral changes begun in the 1890s also had an influence on politics in the chamber, although the contours of those changes are less well known among students of Congress. The election of 1896 also made the Senate even more safely Republican than it had previously been. At the same time, the insurgent movements that arose from the Panic of 1893 eventually had the effect of changing the electoral environment of the Senate profoundly. The most obvious formal transformation of the Senate came in the passage of the Seventeenth Amendment to the Constitution in 1913.

Proposals to institute the popular election of senators had been floated since at least the 1860s, but the western reform movements of the 1890s increased agitation for this change. Not surprisingly, the House was much more eager to pass the popular election of senators than the Senate. As early as 1893 the House passed a resolution proposing an amendment to the states, but it died in Senate committee. By 1910, twenty-eight of the forty-six states had laws providing for the nomination of Senate candidates in party primaries. The legislatures were not bound by the primaries, however; in some cases, senators were elected who had not even appeared on the ballot. Agitation for reform continued, leading to the submission of a resolution to the states in 1912 that became the Seventeenth Amendment to the Constitution when it was ratified in 1913 (Riker 1986).

The effects of the Seventeenth Amendment were not dramatic, but they were substantial nonetheless. Scholars have identified three long-term effects of the amendment. First, the amendment mitigated against the older trend of senators being selected from political dynasties. After the Seventeenth Amendment passed, more ordinary folks were elected. Second, the Seventeenth Amendment facilitated the incorporation of the Senate into the standard political career ladder. Before the popular election of senators, it was common for new senators to enter the Senate directly from the private sector. Afterward, entry from the realm of politics became much more common. Third, the Seventeenth Amendment forged a stronger link between shifting partisan fortunes in the states and the partisanship of the senators elected from the states (Cook and Hibbing 1997).

Within the Senate, the most important formal change came on the floor rather than in committee. As the twentieth century came into view, the committee environment of the Senate was quite different from that in the House: the Senate had more standing committees than the House and nearly as many seats on committees to fill. Consequently, senators hardly could be considered to be "specializing" by doing committee work—in 1910 the average senator served on 7.3 committees, compared to 2.0 for the average House member.

The real innovation in Senate rules during this period was curbs put on the filibuster in 1917. **Filibuster** refers to the Senate practice of using that chamber's lax rules of debate for parliamentary advantage. In particular, before 1917 the Senate had no procedure in its rules to cut off debate nor did it have a very strong **germaneness rule** (Binder and Smith 1997).

The use of the filibuster became an issue in 1917, in a famous case involving the Neutrality Bill of 1917. The bloc holding up the Neutrality Bill was limited to eleven, but by coordinating their speaking and holding the floor at the end of the 64th Congress, they were able to keep the bill from coming up for a vote, thus killing it. President Woodrow Wilson made the opposition of this band of "eleven willful men" a national issue. Feeling electoral pressure and called into special session by Wilson, the Senate hurriedly passed Rule XXII of the Senate.

Rule XXII provided a way to limit debate on a bill, called **cloture**. The cloture requirement has changed several times since then, but the idea was simple: debate could be cut off in the Senate only after sixteen senators had signed a petition asking that debate be cut off *and* two-thirds of the Senate actually voted to stop debate.

The Candidate-Centered Congress

Each of the electoral watersheds discussed thus far, which ended up altering congressional politics in important ways, developed over a fairly well-defined period of time. The most recent electoral watershed has been less well bounded chronologically, and some scholars even deny its existence. Keeping this in mind, if we were to examine the electoral bases of the two political parties in 1960 and 2000, we would discover that support for the two parties' congressional candidates changed in important ways. Most obviously, the regional organization of the two parties' core support eroded. No longer did a "solid South" stand behind a bloc of Democratic officeholders. More subtly, but equally significant, nonsouthern farming areas and suburbs no longer were uniformly Republican. To a first approximation, the transformation that occurred can be summarized as follows: the old party division, organized along a combination of economic and regional lines, was replaced with a new division, organized ideologically. This new organization of the party system in turn has produced a new ordering of congressional politics. Some of that internal reshuffling is still occurring in the twenty-first century.

The purpose of this section is to delineate how a realignment of partisan sentiments in the congressional electorate developed into a realignment of congressional politics from the 1960s to the present. Much of the material in the chapters that follow examines the congressional politics of this era. Therefore, I do not dwell on the details of contemporary congressional politics. Rather, I focus on the transition to the current era and point out the major trends that provide the context for later discussion.

The Civil War established a basic regional structure to the American party system that persisted for over a century. A salient substantive feature of that regional structure was to endow the Republican Party with a history of support for civil rights measures and endow the Democratic Party with a history of opposition to these measures. As politics moved forward from 1865, however, other issues, independent of race, muscled their way onto the national agenda and into the platforms of the parties. The most important set of these issues pertained to the degree of federal involvement in economic development and, more generally, the strength of the federal government in addressing national social concerns. As the twentieth century unfolded, the Democratic Party became more associated with federal government activism, with the Republican Party associated with a less active federal government.

By the middle part of the twentieth century, tensions within both parties, but especially among Democrats, began to build over how to reconcile their historic stances on race with their more modern stances on social policy. The Democratic base contained two blocs of voters who were at odds: liberal (mostly northern) voters who favored an activist federal government and civil rights for blacks, and conservative (mostly southern) voters who favored a less-activist federal government and opposed extending civil rights protections to blacks. The Republicans were less conflicted, but they, too, contained a combination of "liberal" and "moderate" voters on questions of social activism who mostly favored civil rights for blacks. Figure 3.6 illustrates these divisions schematically in terms of the spatial model.

During the 1930s and 1940s the various administrations led by Franklin Roosevelt succeeded in expanding significantly the role of the federal government in everyday national life. Consequently, Congress found itself frequently considering some policy change along the "social program" dimension illustrated in Figure 3.6. As drawn, the median voter along the left-right dimension may be either a southern Democrat or an eastern Republican. While not nearly as frequent an occurrence, civil rights questions often were

FIGURE 3.6
Schematic View of the Spatial Location of Members of Congress in 1960

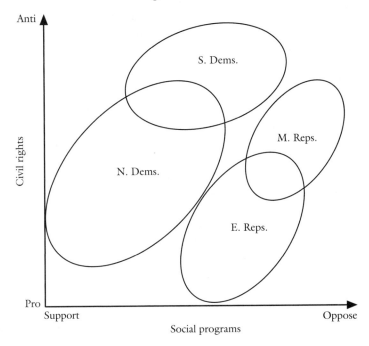

on the agenda, too. As Figure 3.6 is drawn, we would expect the pivotal voter on a civil rights issue to be either a northern Democrat or a midwestern Republican. Therefore, Figure 3.6 illustrates in a simple form the basic coalitional problem that both parties often faced: to pass legislation, it was necessary to build coalitions across parties. Conversely, whenever a coalition was built around a piece of legislation, members of each party were likely to find themselves on both sides of the issue; hence, deep partisan divisions.

Such divisions were in evidence earlier (see Figure 3.4, which shows the prevalence of party unity votes in the House). After rebounding somewhat during the early New Deal years, levels of party unity voting continued to drop throughout most of the middle twentieth century, which is consistent with the notion that most coalitions were being built with members from both parties on each side.

Another indicator of the lack of party cohesion measures support for something called the *Conservative Coalition*. *Conservative Coalition* is a phrase developed to describe the most common form of cross-party coalition formation in the mid-twentieth century: one bringing together southern Democrats with Republicans (of all stripes). A *Conservative Coalition vote* is defined as any roll call vote in which a majority of northern Democrats votes against a majority of southern Democrats *and* Republicans.[19] Figure 3.7 reports the percentage of all roll call votes in any particular year in which the Conservative Coalition appeared. This cross-party voting pattern rarely appeared before the mid-1940s, but from then until the early 1980s, roughly one-fifth of all roll calls witnessed the coalition's appearance.

Although the regular appearance of the Conservative Coalition continued into the 1980, the seeds of its destruction were sown in the 1960s. The most dramatic factor undermining the regionally based party system no doubt rests in the consequences of the passage of the Voting Rights Act of 1965 and the resulting shift in voting patterns in the South (Carmines and Stimson 1989). The Voting Rights Act had one major direct effect and one major indirect effect.

The major direct effect of the Voting Rights Act was the enfranchisement of southern African Americans, who had grown to support the Democrats gradually beginning with the presidency of FDR. Eventually southern blacks flocked to the polls to vote in Democratic primaries. Savvy Democratic politicians, even those who in the past had opposed civil rights legislation, had to become responsive to the desires of this expanded Democratic electorate.

Figure 3.7
Appearance of the Conservative Coalition, 1929–2008

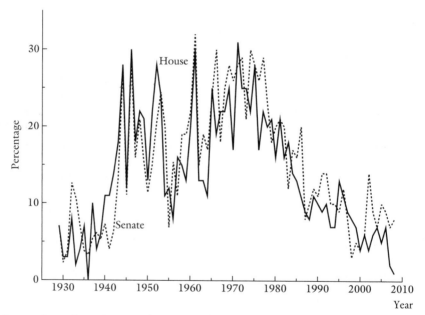

Source: http://voteview.com/partycount.htm.

Thus, the major direct effect of the Voting Rights Act was to make southern Democratic voters (and hence, politicians) more pro–civil rights and more pro-activist federal government.

The major secondary effect of the Voting Rights Act came on the heels of making the southern Democratic Party more like its northern wing. Die-hard southern conservatives, abandoned by their party, were ripe for the picking by the Republican Party. The result of all this shifting around was that by 2000, the parties were aligned as sketched in Figure 3.8: Democrats were liberal on *both* civil rights *and* social welfare issues, and Republicans were conservative. Although there still was some regional differentiation, the differences were not so great as they had been twenty years before. Rather than being regionally structured, the parties had become ideologically structured.

In the transition from regionally to ideologically structured parties, the internal organization of Congress came under strain as well. Most of these strains came about because the operation of the seniority system tended to favor members of Congress who came from one-party regions of the country; for the Democrats, this meant conservative southerners. For much of the 1950s

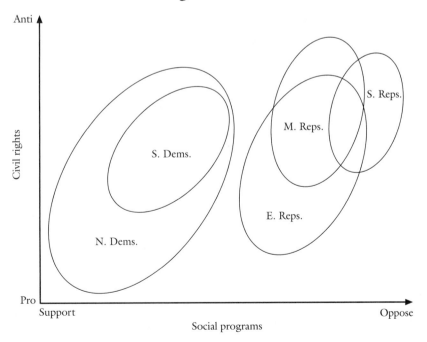

FIGURE 3.8
Schematic View of the Spatial Location of Members of Congress in 2000

and 1960s, this resulted in southern Democrats chairing more than their share of committees and thus taking more of a lead in legislating than the average Democrat was comfortable with.

On the leadership side, both parties adopted strategies to share leadership across their major regional divides. Among Democrats, this led to the creation of the "Boston-Austin connection," so-named because of the pattern of naming the top two Democratic leaders, one from New England and the other from the middle South. Among Republicans, this led to a pattern of balancing leadership tickets between representatives from the Northeast and the Midwest, creating a "Wall Street-Main Street" axis.

Because the Democratic Party controlled Congress for virtually all the post–World War II period (until 1995), the electoral strains eventually were resolved as the Democrats changed how they organized the House for business. The early 1970s saw a flurry of activity aimed at "reforming" the institutions of Congress, increasing the capacity of Congress to act in the policy realm, and increasing the power of the Democratic caucus over its committees. Two of these reforms in the House were the most important. First, the right to make committee assignments was taken away from the Democratic members of the Ways and Means Committee and given to a party committee dominated by the speaker and other Democratic Party leaders. Second, the seniority system was altered to provide for an automatic ballot each Congress to ratify nominees for committee chairs. In the first year the mechanism was used, three House committee chairs were deposed and replaced by other Democrats.

Few formal changes were made in the leadership structure of either chamber, but the informal leadership practices changed. In particular, both parties became increasingly willing to give their leaders latitude to enforce party discipline and set the legislative agenda more aggressively, so that more legislation would bear an obvious partisan cast.

The current period of the Candidate-Centered Congress, therefore, is quite different from the previous period of the Textbook Congress. Candidates of the two parties are much more ideologically cohesive than they were in past generations. When they enter Congress, they are more likely to view their own party as a team whose job it is to defeat the other team, electorally and in policy terms. Committees are structured with a greater eye toward advancing the majority party's agenda. Seniority is no longer the ironclad mechanism that awards committee leadership positions. Now, it is more likely for committee chairs to ascend the hierarchy because they have proven to be effective deal makers, articulate partisan advocates, and generous funders of the campaigns of co-partisans. Congressional leadership is also much more likely to bypass committees altogether, often negotiating the details of important legislation in a process directed by party leaders or their surrogates.

The greater coherence of the parties and the prominence of party leaders in the legislative process do not mean that co-partisans march in lockstep, like parliamentarians in much of the rest of the world, or that party leaders have suddenly been empowered to coerce the rank and file to take actions against their will, simply at the whim of the leaders. Because the current electoral environment is very candidate centered, party leaders are likely to see their authority challenged internally when their actions put the electoral prospects of their members at risk. Members of Congress still have significant latitude to stake out positions at odds with the national party when local electoral realities intervene.

This greater partisan coherence is the making of the members of Congress themselves, which means the current institutional equilibrium could change when the electoral equilibrium next becomes upset. Still, the organizational environment that members of the contemporary Congress have chosen for themselves is now quite distinct from the Congress of the mid-twentieth century. It is this new, more partisan institution that the rest of the book will focus on understanding.

Conclusion

The purpose of this chapter has been to lay out, in bare details, the historical background of congressional political development. In reading such a history, it is easy for the trees to obscure the forest. The most important historical themes to take away from this discussion are these: first, a logical linkage lies between changes in the electorate and changes in internal congressional politics. The two do not change in lockstep, but the two sides of the congressional equation never stay out of balance for long. Second, at any given moment in congressional history, the institution has developed according to a logic that is broadly consonant with the outlines of Chapter 1. At every time and in every place, members of Congress have seen the institution as a vehicle for achieving their larger political goals. As the American political universe has evolved, those goals have changed and so too has Congress. Nonetheless, it is important to understand that at any given moment—and not just in the present—the institution of Congress has evolved based on choices, and those choices are grounded in the politically sophisticated calculations of expert politicians. The following chapters take us closer to the present (with a few backward glances) to understand more completely contemporary congressional politics.

Further Reading

Aldrich, John H. 1995. *Why Parties?* Chicago: University of Chicago Press.
———. 1999. "Political Parties in a Critical Era." *American Politics Quarterly* 27: 9–32.

Binder, Sarah A. 1997. *Minority Rights, Majority Rule: Partisanship and the Development of Congress.* New York: Cambridge University Press.

Burnham, Walter Dean. 1970. *Critical Elections and the Mainsprings of American Politics.* New York: Oxford University Press.

Chambers, William Nisbet, and Walter Dean Burnham. 1967. *The American Party Systems.* New York: Oxford University Press.

Cooper, Joseph. 1971. *The Origin of the Standing Committees and the Development of the Modern House.* Houston: Rice University.

Gamm, Gerald, and Kenneth Shepsle. 1989. "Emergence of Legislative Institutions: Standing Committees in the House and Senate, 1810–1825." *Legislative Studies Quarterly* 14: 39–66.

Harlow, Ralph V. 1910. *The History of Legislative Methods in the Period before 1825.* New Haven, Conn.: Yale University Press.

Polsby, Nelson W. 1968. "The Institutionalization of the U.S. House of Representatives." *American Political Science Review* 63: 144–68.

Price, H. Douglas. 1977. "Careers and Committees in the American Congress: The Problem of Structural Change." In *The History of Parliamentary Behavior,* edited by William O. Aydelotte. Princeton, N.J.: Princeton University Press.

Riker, William H. 1955. "The Senate and American Federalism." *American Political Science Review* 49: 452–69.

Schickler, Eric. 2001. *Disjointed Pluralism: Institutional Innovation and the Development of the U.S. Congress.* Princeton, N.J.: Princeton University Press.

Stewart, Charles III and Barry R. Weingast. 1992. "Stacking the Senate, Changing the Nation: Republican Rotten Boroughs, Statehood Politics, and American Political Development." *Studies in American Political Development* 6: 223–71.

Sundquist, James L. 1981. *Decline and Resurgence of Congress.* Washington, D.C.: Brookings Institution Press.

Swift, Elaine E. 1997. *The Making of an American Senate.* Ann Arbor: University of Michigan Press.

SUMMARY OF KEY CONCEPTS

1. A **party system** is a long period of time characterized by a stable set of political parties that contend against each other along a well-established set of issues; groups in society also tend to maintain stable affinities with one of the parties.
2. A **critical period** is a brief period of time when the stable set of relationships defining a party system is unsettled, because of economic or other social crises.

3. **Critical elections** are elections when a critical period's instability is manifested through a significant shifting of underlying allegiances among parties or a significant change in a party's electoral fortunes.

4. The **experimental party system** (1789–1820) was characterized by elite politics and contested by the Federalists (more elite) and Republicans (less elite).

5. The **democratizing party system** (1828–1854 or 1860) emerged from a multifactional politics in the 1810s and 1820s and an expansion in the electorate, contested by Whigs (pro-commercial) and Democrats (pro-agrarian).

6. The **Civil War party system** (1860–1893) was formed around the Civil War, resulting in a largely regional politics contested by Democrats (southern) and Republicans (northern).

7. The **industrial party system** (1894–1932) was organized mostly according to those advantaged by the rise of industry (Republicans) and those disadvantaged by it (Democrats), with the same regionalism remaining from the previous party system.

8. The **New Deal party system** (1932–1972) was energized by new voters who were mobilized in 1930 and 1932, pushing the Democrats to the "left" and the Republicans to the "right," with regional vestiges of the two previous systems still in place.

9. The **candidate-centered system** (1972–?) emerged during the political upheaval of the 1960s. Eventually, the regional vestiges of the party system were replaced by a more ideological organization of the parties. Party organizations have become stronger but are often put in service of the political aims of individual members.

10. **Congressional systems** are long periods of time when an electoral equilibrium, which corresponds closely with the current party system, supports an organizational equilibrium.

11. A **select committee** is a committee appointed on an ad hoc basis to consider a particular issue or bill. Until the 1810s and 1820s, almost all business in Congress was handled through select committees.

12. A **standing committee** is a committee with a stable jurisdiction and permanent status, by virtue of being written into the chamber's rules.

13. The **principal-agent problem** has been identified in economics as arising when an individual (principal) hires another (agent) to act on the principal's behalf. Principal-agent problems arise when there is imperfect information, allowing the agent to shirk. In the study of Congress, the principal-agent problems emerge principally in the control of a chamber over its committees and the control of voters over their representatives.

14. The **balance rule** was a practice adopted in the pre–Civil War Congress, admitting free states and slave states in pairs, to keep the balance of such states even in the Senate.

15. The **Reed Rules** were a set of practices and formal rule changes associated with Thomas B. Reed's speakership in the 51st Congress

(1889–1891), intended to strengthen the hand of the majority party in the House.

16. The **disappearing quorum** was the practice of minority party members in the House refusing to answer their names during a roll call vote, so that it would appear that a quorum was not present to conduct House business. This practice was abolished by the Reed Rules.

17. A **dilatory motion** is a motion made purely for the purpose of delay, such as a series of amendments that change a bill only slightly or repeated motions to adjourn.

18. The **Committee of the Whole** is a convenient parliamentary fiction, in which the whole House constitutes itself as a committee, allowing it to debate measures less formally and with a smaller quorum.

19. The **House Calendar** is the list of all bills reported from committee and eligible for floor action, except bills pertaining to taxing and spending.

20. The **Union Calendar** is the list of all bills pertaining to taxing and spending reported from committee and eligible for floor action.

21. A **special order** (or a **rule**) is a resolution passed by the House that determines the details of how a bill will be debated and considered for amendment.

22. A **party unity vote** is a roll call vote in which a majority of the members of one party vote against a majority of the other party. (Sometimes, the threshold is higher, such as 90 percent.) The fraction of times party unity votes appear in a Congress is a measure of overall partisan polarization. The fraction of times an individual legislator sides with his or her party on party unity votes is a measure of the party loyalty of that member.

23. The **Australian ballot** is produced by the government and cast privately.

24. **Party responsibility** is a doctrine holding that parties should take clear issue positions, its members should act consistently with those positions in the legislature, and party members should accept electoral reward or punishment, depending on whether their preferred policies succeed or fail.

25. **Calendar Wednesday** is a parliamentary device created in the House in 1909 to facilitate committees bringing legislation to the floor. Each Wednesday, the clerk calls the roll of the committees alphabetically, at which time committees can bring up bills. This procedure usually is dispensed with through unanimous consent.

26. Each party in each chamber of Congress has a **Committee on Committees**, which is responsible for assigning its party's members to legislative committees.

27. A **caucus** is a meeting of all of the members of a particular party in one of the chambers of Congress. Caucus meetings discuss legislative strategy and make nominations for leadership positions. Sometimes, a party will designate its all-encompassing gathering a **conference**.

28. The **seniority system** is a practice in both chambers of Congress that allocates valuable committee positions, such as chairs, to members according to the member's length of service on a particular committee.

29. The **filibuster** is the practice of prolonged debate solely to delay action.
30. A **germaneness rule** limits debate and amendments to the subject at hand.
31. **Cloture** is the procedure to limit a filibuster and bring a matter to a vote.

NOTES

1. Classic treatment of critical realignment theory includes Burnham (1970), Chambers and Burnham (1967), Key (1955), and Sundquist (1973). The most significant application of this theory to congressional development is Brady (1988).
2. Do not confuse the supporters of Jefferson, who were called *Republicans*, with the modern political party that goes by the same name. Because of the possible confusion across historical eras, some scholars refer to the earliest Republicans as either *Jeffersonians* or *Democrat-Republicans*.
3. Since the publication of the first edition of this book, the evidence that we now live in a sixth party system is even stronger; whether we now are entering a seventh party system seems an appropriate question. On evidence of the emergence of a clearly distinct sixth party system in 1972, see Aldrich and Niemi (1996) and Aldrich (1999). The strongest argument against this view comes in a masterful critique of the entire critical elections synthesis of American political history by David Mayhew (2002).
4. By *stable*, I do not wish to imply that congressional politics is quiet or conflict free during these periods. A better adjective may be *predictable*.
5. The first rules adopted by the House of Representatives called for committees to be chosen by a ballot of the whole House. However, this provision quickly proved unworkable—the House was spending almost all of its time electing committees and doing little actual work—and was changed to provide for the Speaker to appoint the committees unless the House directed otherwise.
6. The classic and simplest example of a principal-agent relationship exists between an employer and an employee. The employer wants a certain amount of work done as well as possible while the employee presumably wants to do only well enough to please the boss. The boss cannot always observe directly what the employee is doing and so the employee has an incentive to *shirk*. In wisely designing the principal-agent relationship, the boss attempts to align the incentives of the employee more directly with the desires of the boss. So, for instance, the boss might pay the employee as a function of the profits of the firm to encourage him or her to work hard and keep costs down.

    A similar relationship exists between chamber majorities and anyone to whom it delegates legislative decision making. Committee members and members of the executive branch do not automatically share the policy goals of the chamber majority. Comparing committees with executive branch officials, committees have the advantage in that they are more easily monitored by the whole chamber, and committee members more readily share the electoral goals of other chamber members. Executive branch officials often possess greater expertise, so the trade-off generally is between greater expertise from people the chamber cannot trust and less expertise from people the chamber can trust more. The classic way of solving this dilemma, which is evident in the earliest days of congressional development, is to delegate the ultimate authority over giving the chamber advice to a committee composed of peers and then authorizing the committee to consult with executive branch officials and anyone else it chooses.

7. Until the late nineteenth century, several states held elections in odd numbered years.

8. The Kansas-Nebraska Act repealed the Missouri Compromise, organized two new western territories, and allowed residents of the territories to decide for themselves whether to allow slavery.

9. In addition to these five candidates, each of whom received at least seventeen votes, sixteen other House members received at least one vote on the first ballot.

10. Throughout this book, I rely on the research of Keith Poole and Howard Rosenthal, who developed a statistical technique to estimate the ideal points of members of Congress based on their observed roll call votes. I discuss this technique in Chapter 9. For this discussion, all you need to know is that Poole and Rosenthal's technique uncovers the ideal points of members of Congress, assuming they are voting according to the logic of the spatial model discussed in Chapter 1. While their technique uncovers ideal points in a multidimensional space, the first dimension by far has the greatest power in explaining how people vote on particular roll calls. In the modern era, members who are on one end of the space tend to be known as extreme liberals while those at the other end of the space tend to be known as extreme conservatives. Therefore, it is convenient to think of the first dimension as simply the well-known left-right, or liberal-conservative, continuum.

11. In other words, the further left (right) the speaker candidate is, the further left (right) are that candidate's supporters.

12. See Leintz (1978) for the most comprehensive review of speakership battles during this period. Also see Jenkins and Nokken (2000).

13. This discussion of the president-vice president balance rule is taken from John Aldrich (1995, pp. 129–31).

14. Calhoun by this time had emerged as the strongest exponent of a strong view of states' rights and a limited federal government. The Senate, of course, was tightly balanced between states' rights and national rights points of view, and so Calhoun's unabashed stacking of the Senate committees strongly angered northern senators and even discomforted moderates in the chamber.

15. That one exception was in 1923 (68th Congress) when Progressive Republicans nominated their own candidate for Speaker and threw the House into a nine-ballot, two-day struggle over organizing.

16. There actually are two main House calendars: the House Calendar, for all regular legislation, and the **Union Calendar**, for financial matters. Other calendars also are maintained to order the consideration of minor or odd legislative matters, like the District of Columbia or matters considered under suspension of the rules.

17. Other parties held ten seats in the 53rd Congress and seven in the 54th.

18. Vestiges of this promise remain today in the names of the party organizations in the House. The Democrats still call themselves the Democratic *caucus*, while the Republicans call themselves the Republican **conference**, under the theory that *conference* implies simple consultation among coequal members, while *caucus* implies the use of nefarious coercive means to extract compliance out of party members.

19. An example of a Conservative Coalition vote was the roll call taken on House passage of the Elementary and Secondary Education Act in 1965. On that vote, northern Democrats voted 187–3 in favor, southern Democrats voted 41–54 against, and Republicans voted 35–96 against.

Be warned that the label *Conservative Coalition* is controversial, since it implies that the voting pattern of northern Democrats opposing Republicans and southern Democrats comes about through conscious coalition-building behavior. During the height of the coalition's life, leading conservatives vehemently denied that this pattern was anything other than like-minded members of Congress just voting together (see Manley 1977).

— 4 —

The Choices Candidates Make: Running for Congress

he most fundamental way democracies translate popular sentiments into public action is through elections. In a well-functioning democracy, elections will appear to come off like clockwork: they come along at the prescribed time, multiple candidates compete for the right to hold office, and voters go to the polls on election day to record their choice. Elections work because everyone knows and follows the rules of the game automatically. End of story.

The perspective on elections I want to emphasize in the next three chapters is slightly different from the common textbook or civics view of how elections work. The common view implicitly supposes that all the principal actors in congressional elections—voters and candidates—act out of a sense of civic duty or deeply held convictions about the public good. It is enough that an individual "wants to make a difference" to explain why someone runs for Congress. And, it is enough that a voter wants to "make a statement" or "be a good citizen" to explain why someone votes on election day.[1] Elections look automatic because, in one way or another, everyone wants "to do the right thing" with respect to the electoral system.

I would like to avoid focusing on the glib claims of politicians and voters about their acting in the public interest. Rather, I suggest in this chapter that the most fruitful focus in studying congressional elections is on what political actors themselves—elites and mass alike—are trying to get out of the electoral system. I certainly will not deny that candidates and voters, at least in part, are public spirited. Nonetheless, the primary momentum behind the system of congressional elections in the United States derives from self-seeking behavior on the part of candidates and voters. If we do not at least start with the ambitions of candidates and voters, we will be lost.

Candidates and voters are different types of political animals. Most candidates for political office, particularly federal office, are professional politicians. While they all have some other "real-world" job, they differ from most people in that they derive special satisfaction from acting in the political realm. Politics is different from most settings in the business world or among family and friends. Politicians survive in the political world by learning to read the political portents around them. They learn to anticipate the actions of others, whether a mass of voters or a small number of individual rivals for office, and make decisions based on the anticipated actions of others. In other words, they are *strategic*.

Voters are not strategic. By and large, they respond to the choices presented them. Voters are neither stupid nor uninformed. Rather, the roles laid out for voters and candidates are quite different, as are the settings in which they act. To get on the ballot to run for office, an individual must make a choice. Unless that individual has a martyr complex or a special desire to shake hands, an individual will not choose to go on the ballot unless it seems like running for office will pay off somehow. Even a highly ambitious local politician may choose to wait it out, hoping to avoid a certain defeat in the present or find a more fertile political field to plow in the future. At the same time, the number of likely candidates for the House or Senate from any district or state is likely to be relatively small in any given election year. All the serious candidates at least know of each other, often can make good estimates of the future behavior of the others, and know that the course of action they themselves choose will have a material effect on the actions of the other potential candidates (and vice versa). Potential candidates for Congress are strategic because it is worth their while to be strategic.

Contrast this with voters. The costs of voting are very low but so are the direct benefits that accrue to any single voter by voting. Assuming that a citizen turns out to vote in an election pitting a Democrat against a Republican, there is only one course of action that makes sense for the voter—vote for the one he or she likes best.[2] There are so many other voters in the district or state that if an individual voter chooses an outrageous course of action, such as writing in Donald Duck, that action will have no effect on the eventual outcome of the election. Indeed, there are so many other voters in any district or state that one might wonder why one should vote at all. I will leave this important point to ponder for the next chapter. For the moment I will simply remark that all a voter needs to do is wait for the candidates to present themselves, make a choice based on whatever criteria he or she chooses, and vote for the one he or she likes best. This may be a well-considered, informed choice, but it is not strategic.

Because candidates and voters are so fundamentally different, we must discuss them differently. At the same time, we always need to be aware that we can not entirely discuss candidates without understanding what voters are like and vice versa. That is, the strategic interactions among potential candidates for office take place in the context of trying to anticipate who the voters will prefer in November. Voters make their decisions after watching the preelection, primary, and general election processes and (at least in part) judge the field on how they made decisions about how to enter the race and run their campaigns.

In these three chapters, we explore the dynamics of congressional elections by focusing sequentially on three major topics of congressional elections. The first broad topic is the strategic decisions made by the most critical actors in elections—the candidates. After exploring in Chapter 4 who runs for Congress and why, we turn our attention in Chapter 5 to the other side of the electoral coin—the choice made by voters. Finally, the electoral arena in which voters and candidates act is heavily regulated. Therefore, in Chapter 6, we examine the regulation of congressional elections, through mechanisms such as campaign finance and redistricting laws, to understand how these regulations influence electoral outcomes.

Strategic Choice and Political Careers

Candidates for Congress do not automatically appear on the ballot. To appear on a ballot, a candidate must make a series of strategic choices that are conditioned on (1) what she or he expects other potential candidates might do and (2) the benefits and costs that will be encountered in the process of running and then either winning or losing. The choices candidates make are heavily conditioned by outside factors. This is illustrated by two examples, one historical (Abraham Lincoln) and the other contemporary (the 1994 House election).

Abraham Lincoln is revered in American history for his presidential service during the Civil War. He steadfastly defended the principle of an inviolate American Union against secessionists, who wished to leave the Union, and radical northerners, who wished to treat the states of the Confederacy as a vanquished foreign land as the North rolled to victory. Lincoln's presidential service is well chronicled. Less well known is his first service in the national government, as a member of the House from 1847 to 1849. Given Lincoln's later tireless defense of the principle of an inviolate Union, why did he leave the House after only one term, just as the political struggle to keep the Union together was getting interesting?

In 2010, public opinion polls indicated that voters held members of Congress in particularly low esteem. In a Gallup/USA Today poll that year, 22 percent of adults said they approved of the job that Congress was doing, 31 percent believed that "most members of Congress" should be reelected, and 50 percent stated that their own member of the House deserved reelection.[3] Yet, in that year's congressional election, 85 percent of House members and 84 percent of senators running for reelection won. Given the public's low regard for incumbent members of Congress and less-than-enthusiastic support for individual incumbents, why did virtually everyone running for reelection win?

Abraham Lincoln's short congressional career is a testimony to how service in Congress can be influenced by the electoral environment in which candidates run.[4] Lincoln was a Whig; Whigs generally supported the principle of **rotation in office**.[5] In the part of Illinois that Lincoln represented, the Whigs practiced a particularly strong version of rotation. Lincoln's two immediate Whig predecessors from the 7th district of Illinois had pledged to serve only a single term, and Lincoln was obliged to do the same. Even though there is evidence in Lincoln's own hand that he would have preferred to stay in Washington for another term, when he returned home he discovered local Whigs engaged in a mad scramble for the nomination, under the assumption that Lincoln would keep his word. Thus the activity of local party elites kept Lincoln from being given the chance to succeed himself in the House.[6]

Given his great political ambitions, Lincoln was left with the option of seeking other offices, which he did. He unsuccessfully sought the position of commissioner of the General Land Office, in 1849, and turned down an offer to become the governor of the Oregon territory, in 1849.[7] Twice in the 1850s he sought to become senator from Illinois but failed each time. It was as a private citizen, then, that Lincoln was nominated and elected president in 1860.

The paradox of the 2010 election—that everyone hated Congress but incumbent members of Congress were overwhelmingly reelected—illustrates a number of things about contemporary congressional elections. In this context, however, one important thing it illustrates is the way unpopular incumbents may avoid electoral defeat by preempting the electoral process altogether. Thus, even though 84 percent of the House was reelected in 2010, thirty-six House members (8 percent of the House) chose not to seek reelection in the first place. Overall, 28 percent of the House did not return after the 2010 election, with retirement, not electoral defeat, being a major instrument of turnover. Therefore, the unpopular House of Representatives in 2010 was met with unusually high membership turnover, but this turnover was instigated as much by the choices of incumbents about running for reelection as by the choices of voters to oust unpopular incumbents.

To understand how elections help channel popular sentiment into Congress, it is necessary to break up into its basic components the larger question of why people run for Congress. Just as we discovered in Chapter 1 that legislative decision making may be fruitfully understood by breaking any issue into its components, by understanding the emergence of congressional candidates' demands we identify the most basic considerations weighing on candidates (both potential and actual) and build from there.

At the root of candidate decision making is a cost-benefit calculation. The calculation is so basic and generic, that it can be written simply.[8]

$$E(a_i) = P_i U_i - C_i \tag{4.1}$$

$$E(a_i) = P_i U_i - C_i$$

[handwritten: must be > 0]

where

E(a_i) = The expected utility of choosing to run for office i;
  P$_i$ = The probability of winning in the race for office i;
  U$_i$ = The utility associated with serving in office i;
  C$_i$ = The cost of running for office i.

In words, anyone who contemplates running for office must weigh the likelihood of winning, the value of the office, and the cost of achieving the office. It is obvious that the right-hand side of equation (4.1) must evaluate to a sum greater than zero in order for someone to run for office i: the value of office (discounted by the probability of winning) must exceed the cost of running for office. What is less obvious is what constitutes the costs of running and the benefits of office, and what affects the probability of winning. A discussion later in the chapter fleshes out these categories so that we might understand the candidate calculus more precisely.

An important factor that affects both the costs of running and the probability of winning is whether an incumbent currently holds the office. That is, if the person using equation (4.1) is a private citizen, we can be pretty sure that he or she will have a more difficult time running for Congress if facing an incumbent running for reelection than if the incumbent has retired and the seat is open. The same is true if the person holds a lower political office, such as a city council or state legislative seat, or is a member of the House who is contemplating a run for the Senate.

Furthermore, if we think carefully about equation (4.1), we begin to realize that the costs involved in running for office come from a number of different sources. There are the obvious costs of running for office—those associated with fund-raising and a wrecked family life. A nonobvious cost of running for office is important in considering the dynamics of congressional politics—the **opportunity costs** that arise when someone gives up one political office to run for another. In an environment in which incumbent politicians tend to get reelected regularly, giving up a seat to run for another represents a real cost to that politician in terms of whatever utility he or she would have received by staying put, rather than seeking higher office.

The comments in the previous two paragraphs suggest that different types of candidates approach equation (4.1) differently. We can divide congressional candidates into three types: incumbents, challengers, and candidates for open seats. The last section of this chapter examines factors particular to each of these types of candidates.

But before plowing into a full-blown analysis of the implications of equation (4.1), we must attend to one important structural feature of running for office in the United States. Officeholding in the United States has a fairly clear hierarchy. Among elected offices in the federal government, the pyramid is absolutely clear: at the top is the presidency, followed by the Senate, then the House. Within states, a similar hierarchy holds, with governors on top, state legislators next, and various local offices down below. The ambiguity arises not within the hierarchies but in understanding how the hierarchies mesh: the governorship of any state is more sought after than membership in the state House of Representatives, but which is better, to be a senator from New York or the governor? These ambiguities aside, the hierarchy of elected office derives from structural features in the American political system, producing a regularized system of **progressive ambition** within the United States. So, before settling down to examine the implications of equation (4.1) for the study of congressional elections, we first turn our attention to examining how this system of progressive ambition works.

Progressive Ambition in the United States

State politicians begin shuffle step to move up the line

By declaring her candidacy for governor, U.S. Rep. Barbara B. Kennelly, D-1st District, started a chain reaction Monday that could touch politicians with aspirations ranging from Congress to the common council in Middletown.

Four Democrats immediately confirmed they are candidates to succeed Kennelly in Congress, where she has represented the Hartford region since January 1982. At least six others said they might also enter the race.

Democrats predict the most wide-open contest in the 1st District, one of the nation's safest Democratic seats, since 1970, when another Hartford congressman, Emilio Q. Daddario, ran for governor.

Because half the potential candidates already hold office, the stampede for the congressional race will open up other opportunities further down the political food chain.

"There's a domino effect all the way down to the city council in Middletown, West Hartford and several other communities," said Roy Occhiogrosso, an aide to state Senate Democrats. The candidates who said they are committed to seeking Kennelly's seat are Secretary of the State Miles S. Rapoport, 47, of West Hartford; former Senate President Pro Tem John B. Larson, 49, of East Hartford; state Rep. James McCavanagh, 57, of Manchester; and Daniel I. Papermaster, 33, of West Hartford. Papermaster is a lawyer who oversaw Hartford's successful bid for the 1996 presidential debate.

On the list of those considering a run are Senate President Pro Tem Kevin B. Sullivan, 48, of West Hartford; state Sen. Eric Coleman, 46, of Bloomfield; state Rep. Richard D. Tulisano, 57, of Rocky Hill; and former state Treasurer Joseph M. Suggs Jr., 57, of Bloomfield. . . .

Rapoport said this week belongs to Kennelly, but he planned to officially announce his candidacy next week. McCavanagh has similar plans. Larson said he may wait until after the municipal elections.

"Did he say what day?" state Rep. Susan Bysiewicz, D-Middletown, asked about Rapoport's plans.

Hers is not an idle interest.

Bysiewicz is ready to announce for Rapoport's job, as soon as Rapoport announces for Kennelly's job. Occhiogrosso said he suspects that somewhere in Middletown, probably on the common council, someone is thinking about Bysiewicz's seat in the General Assembly.

Rep. Ellen Scalettar, D-Woodbridge, is another would-be secretary of the state awaiting Rapoport's official announcement. Others are likely to emerge.

And so it goes.

Jonathan Pelto, a political consultant, said he already has heard from potential clients three levels down the food chain. All their plans, he said, were predicated on Kennelly's seeking higher office. Sullivan's plans are being closely watched in West Hartford—and not only by the other three residents of that town who are potential competitors for Congress.

Names also are starting to surface as potential successors to Sullivan if he runs for Congress, instead of re-election to the state Senate. The chain reaction makes for good political gossip.

"It's a long chain," said one West Hartford Democratic activist, who was amused by the ripple effect. "At the end of the chain, I think the guy that cuts my lawn changes, too." (Mark Pazniokas, "State Politicians Begin Shuffle Step to Move up the Line," *Hartford Courant*, September 23, 1997)

The career ambition of politicians is the engine of electoral dynamics. The United States has an overabundance of people who want to serve in politics and are exceptionally skilled at seeking office. They seek political power but not blindly. Seeking power is costly. There is a word for people who pursue goals without regard for the cost—*bankrupt*. (Another word might be *masochist*.) Potential aspirants for office, therefore, are most likely to act on their goals if the costs are relatively low or the chances of success are relatively high.

The sheer number of elected positions in the United States, coupled with the system of federalism that overlays the political landscape, provides a natural way for politically ambitious people to seek political career advancement at a relatively low incremental cost. In particular, it is common to witness rookie House and Senate members who started their political careers in a local elected office, moved on to a state office, and then used the state office as the springboard to Washington. At each step along the way, the latitude afforded the office sought gradually increased; each step along the way constituted moving on to "higher office." Equally important, however, is that, at each step along the way, the constituency of the old elected position was a subset of the constituency of the new position. A career in elected office, therefore, often is a matter of winning a majority in a small constituency, shoring up that constituency through diligent service, and then using the smaller constituency as a base in trying to win in a larger constituency. Joseph Schlesinger, in his 1966 study of political ambition in the United States, coined the phrase *progressive ambition* to describe the aspirations of politicians who desire to use service in a lower office as a stepping stone to higher office.[9]

One simple example of how progressive ambition often works is the electoral career of Senator Scott P. Brown (R-Mass.), who received national attention in early 2010 when he was elected to fill the vacancy caused by the death of Senator Edward M. Kennedy (D-Mass.). As a young boy, Brown held campaign signs for his father, who was a long-time city councilor in Newburyport, Massachusetts. Yet the younger Brown did not "catch the bug" for politics until he was a young man living in Wrentham, Massachusetts, where he was elected in 1992 as a property tax assessor.[10] Three years later, he was elected a town selectman.

In 1998, at the end of his selectman term, Brown ran for a seat in the Massachusetts House of Representatives. Brown's hometown of Wrentham was one of the four small towns that composed the district. He won a bare majority in a three-way race against a Democrat who came from a smaller town, Norfolk, and an independent from the district's largest town, Walpole. Brown's firm electoral base in his hometown is illustrated by his receiving 20 percentage points more votes in Wrentham than party registration in the town would have predicted.[11] Brown's electoral success grew in his two reelection campaigns, in which he garnered 66 percent of votes cast in 2000 and 76 percent in 2002.

In late 2003, the state senator from Brown's district resigned.[12] Brown's House district was almost entirely within the Senate district, comprising almost a quarter of the Senate district's voters. Brown easily won the Republican primary against a perennial candidate with no prior electoral experience. He then faced Democrat Angus McQuilken in the general election. McQuilken, likewise, had no prior electoral experience, serving instead as the chief of staff of the state senator who had just resigned the post. Brown won the special election by 349 votes, out of over 37,000 cast. Pivotal to Brown's victory was the support he received from the towns in his existing House district, collecting 17 percentage points more of the vote than we would predict, given the partisanship of those towns. Brown went on to defeat McQuilken more handily (by over 2,600 votes) in the November 2004 general election, to win opposed in 2006, and then to win against a different opponent by over 14,000 votes in 2008.

Thus, when Brown faced off against the Democratic nominee for U.S. Senate, Martha Coakley, in the special election in January 2010, he already had an eighteen-year career within the classic model of successful progressively ambitious candidates. His constituencies fit within each other like nesting dolls, and he used the goodwill he had generated at each step along the way to gain a critical increment of votes as he sought to move to higher office. Brown's opponent for the U.S. Senate fit within the progressive ambition model, too, having served as the (elected) district attorney of Middlesex County (1999–2007), the largest county in the state with a quarter of its population, before being elected state attorney general in 2006.

Usually, when two candidates who are currently serving in elective office face off against each other in the search for a higher office, the one who comes from the larger constituency is advantaged. Because Coakley's political base was in an area, Middlesex County, that was ten times more populous than Brown's state Senate district, one would not be faulted for predicting that Coakley should have beaten Brown in the special election to succeed Senator Kennedy. Indeed, Brown's victory surprised many professional observers, causing him to become a national phenomenon and harbinger of better electoral fortunes for Republicans in the November 2010 general election. Other factors intervene in determining the outcome of elections, including

TABLE 4.1
Prior Careers of the Massachusetts Delegation to Congress, 111th Congress (2009–2011)

District	Name	Year First Elected to Congress	Prior Elective Experience	Occupation Immediately Prior to First Congressional Election
1	John Olver	1959	State House, 1969–1972 State Senate, 1973–1991	State Senate
2	Richard E. Neal	1989	Springfield City Council, 1978–1984	Springfield Mayor
3	James McGovern	1997	None	Staff member for Rep. Joseph Moakley
4	Barney Frank	1981	State House, 1973–1980	State House
5	Niki Tsongas	2007	None	College dean
6	John Tierney	1997	None	Lawyer
7	Ed Markey	1976	State House, 1973–1976	State House
8	Michael E. Capuano	1999	Alderman, Somerville, 1977–1979, 1985–1989 Mayor, Somerville, 1990–1998	Mayor
9	Stephen F. Lynch	2001	State House, 1995–1996 State Senate, 1997–2001	State Senate
10	William Delahunt	1997	State House, 1973–1975 Norfolk County Dist. Atty., 1975–1996	District Attorney
Senate	Edward M. Kennedy*	1962	None	Asst. District Attorney
Senate	Scott P. Brown*	2010	Wrentham Selectman, 1995–1998 State House, 1999–2004 State Senate, 2004–2010	State Senate
Senate	John F. Kerry	1985	Lt. governor, 1982–1984	Lt. governor

*Kennedy died August 25, 2009. Governor Deval Patrick appointed Paul G. Kirk, Jr., to fill the vacancy on September 24, 2009, pending a special election to fill the seat permanently. Brown was elected to fill the vacancy on January 19, 2010.

Source: *Biographical Directory of the United States Congress, 1774–present,* http://bioguide.congress.gov/biosearch/biosearch.asp.

national partisan tides, which were overwhelmingly in the Republicans' favor in early 2010. The point is to note that although much of the public considered Brown to have come out of nowhere to succeed Ted Kennedy in liberal Massachusetts, and to characterize him as a an everyman nonpolitician, his success derived in part from his opportunity to hone his political skills through seeking election in a series of interlocking and ever-larger constituencies.

The circumstances of a politician's rise up the ranks are dependent enough on local conditions that not everyone follows a paradigmatic career path to Congress, as Brown did. Yet, a quick look reveals patterns similar to that of Scott Brown. For instance, Table 4.1 summarizes the electoral careers of Brown's Massachusetts colleagues in 2010. Seven of Brown's ten colleagues in the Massachusetts House delegation first entered Congress directly from lower elective office. John Kerry, Brown's Senate colleague, entered the Senate directly from being the lieutenant governor of the state.

Senator Kennedy, whom Brown replaced, seems an exception to the pattern followed by most members of Congress, since he entered the Senate directly from the lowly position of (appointed) assistant district attorney in the county that encompasses Boston. Of course, with the name of Kennedy, he had other political advantages that helped him move into the Senate seat that his brother, John, vacated when he was elected president in 1960. Still, knowing that he wanted to enter politics, Edward Kennedy had taken a job, assistant district attorney, that is a frequent entry-level position for young lawyers interested in a political career—a job that provides an easy introduction to the legal community and an opportunity to score points with voters by putting miscreants behind bars. Certainly, Kennedy had no interest in spending his career chasing petty criminals through the Boston courthouses. His first job was a political steppingstone to bigger things.

Massachusetts is known as an unusually political state, so to illustrate the enduring hierarchical nature of political ambition in the United States, we finally turn our attention to the House freshman class of 2011 (elected in 2010). This is an appropriate class to illustrate the endurance of the structure of progressive ambition in American politics, since incumbents were widely discredited in 2010 and many successful House candidates ran on "outsider" and "antipolitician" themes. If any modern group of House members should have broken the political careerist mold, it should have been these.

The 112th Congress had ninety-four new House members. Of these, fifty-nine were either serving in some elective office at the time of their election to the House or had served sometime in the past. Finally, four had served either in some appointed political position (like police chief or U.S. attorney) or on the staff of a political official (such as governor or U.S. senator). Thus about two-thirds of the House freshman class in 2011 were on a political upward track, which is a stunning fraction in a year when politicians were said to be discredited as a class.

Very little research has been done about progressive ambition in the United States before the twentieth century. What limited information we have suggests that some of the patterns we observe in modern times had antecedents. Certainly the origins of members of Congress have always been in local politics. For instance, of the eighty-eight rookie members of the House elected in 1880 to the 47th Congress, seventy-one had served in politics prior to being elected to the House.[13] Among rookie senators in the 47th Congress, fourteen of the sixteen new senators came from a political background. Moving further back in time, among the sixty-five members of the First

Congress under the Constitution, sixty-two had a background either in state government or the government under the Articles of Confederation.

Although Congress has always drawn the bulk of its members from lower political offices, one important thing that has changed with the times is the degree to which Congress is a place where politicians want to settle down. For the first half of American history, Congress, both the House and Senate, served as a stepping-stone to further political office for professional office seekers, either back in the states from which they came or in an appointive position in the federal bureaucracy or judiciary.

For example, virtually all the members of the first Congress (1789–1791) had a background in state government or in the old government of the Confederation. Most of those, when they eventually left Congress, would hold yet another political office, most likely back home. To be precise, thirty-five of the first sixty-five House members and sixteen of the first twenty-six senators left Congress to pursue another political career. By the end of the nineteenth century, things had begun to change a bit, with the Senate becoming the ultimate political destination for many of its members, but the House was still a way station. Of the eighty-eight rookie members of the 47th House mentioned earlier, thirty-nine would move on to another political office after leaving the House. Yet only four of the sixteen U.S. senators who were first elected to the Senate in the 47th Congress would go on to another position in politics.[14]

The most comprehensive analysis of political ambition in Congress during the nineteenth century was conducted by Samuel Kernell (1977). Kernell's goal was to explain why the average level of turnover in the House dropped steadily from 57 percent each election in the 1850s to 27 percent in the first decade of the 1900s. Most of the drop in turnover during this period can be attributed to changes in the ambition structure of American politics, with a substantial portion attributable to a drop in partisan competition in congressional districts and a small residual due to the decline of the norm of rotation.[15]

Thus, while romantics may believe otherwise, the United States always has had a political class, even though its size and composition have changed with the times. In modern times, this phenomenon has led to the creation of a label—*career politicians*—to describe people so interested in public office and good at achieving it that they spend their adult lives in elective office. Americans have not always had career politicians in this sense. The notion of a "career" as we understand it is mostly a twentieth-century phenomenon and the compensation of public officials used to be so little that politicians always had to keep a hand in their "real" jobs. Still, it is important to recognize that members of Congress have always viewed this service in the context of a political career.

The career of Abraham Lincoln is one example of how political ambition can operate in the face of severe external constraints, such as the practice of rotation in office. First, Lincoln's political life was spent continually expanding his constituency base: before he even tried for elective office, he traveled around southern Illinois, practicing law in local towns, following itinerant judges. As Lincoln traveled, he made political contacts and gradually developed a personal following. Lincoln's first political step was running for the state legislature. This state legislative district provided the political base on which Lincoln built his later run for the U.S. Congress. But this is where the nineteenth-century path diverges from the twentieth century. Barred by his local party (which controlled renomination) from running for Congress again, Lincoln sought to stay in politics by seeking *appointed* office, within the system of spoils that operated at the time. Finding nothing to his liking, Lincoln continued to build his popular base in ways that are well recorded in the history books.

The Costs and Benefits of Running for Office

Equation (4.1) lays out the basic calculation for a politician in deciding whether to run for office and which office to run for. Within the system of progressive ambition just discussed, the calculation usually performed looks something like this:

$$E(a_L) = P_L U_L - C_L \qquad L = \text{lower office}$$
$$E(a_H) = P_H U_H - C_H \qquad H = \text{Higher office} \qquad (4.2)$$

where the L subscript refers to the lower office and H refers to the higher office. To be even more specific, when thinking about (potential) candidates for the House, the higher office is the House while the lower office typically is some state or local position. When thinking about the Senate, the lower office includes not only state and local positions but the House as well.

In examining equation (4.2), it is easy to see why even ambitious politicians will seek higher office after only careful consideration, because it is so risky. It is obvious that the costs for running for higher office are higher than running for lower office, if for no other reason than a congressional district is bound to be several times larger than even the largest district of a lower office.[16] Likewise, before even taking into account what happens during a campaign and leaving aside the cost of running for office, we know that the probability of winning is going to be much lower for the higher office than the lower one. Without getting too much ahead of the discussion, consider two factors that will affect the probability of winning: (1) the number of potentially viable opponents and (2) the heterogeneity of political interests in the district.[17] *(L being diverse)*

An incumbent politician in a lower elected office is "king of the hill" with respect to politics at that level in that location. But if the "king" wants to branch out, he has to contend with dozens of similarly successful and qualified opponents. A state senator from Wyoming, for instance, has to worry about the other twenty-nine state senators who also might run for the U.S.

House. Likewise, as we burrow down further in the hierarchy of elective office, we encounter constituencies that are more and more heterogeneous.[18] A politician who has succeeded at that level may, or may not, be successful in broadening his or her political base. By running for higher office, the politician is taking the risk of being unsuccessful in convincing different types of voters to vote for him or her—he or she cannot know the result without trying. Therefore, to the degree that any politician who has a firm political base contemplates running for office in a larger constituency that is likely to have different political interests, the a priori probability of winning in the new constituency, on average, must be lower than the probability of winning in the old one.

Running for higher office is daunting, but many people do it. Therefore, we should not dwell too long on the fact that, for most politicians most of the time, $E(a_L) > E(a_H)$. Instead, we should understand the different components that make up the cost, benefit, and winning probability calculations. Table 4.2 makes an initial attempt at disaggregating the different components of equation (4.2).

TABLE 4.2
Factors That Affect the Calculus of Progressive Ambition

B_L vs. B_H	P_L vs. P_H	C_L vs. C_H
Scope of legislative authority	Party identification in the districts	Opportunities forgone
Political and policy resources within the institution	Partisan tides	Number and quality of challengers
Pay and perquisites	District changes	Fund-raising efficiency
Value in achieving even higher office	Scandals	Efficiency of translating money and volunteer time into votes

In examining Table 4.2, keep in mind that each of the factors listed comes into play cross-sectionally and across time. Consider the first entry in the table. It is obvious that different political offices come attached with different degrees of political power. The differences that occur in relative power among different political offices (e.g., U.S. House, U.S. Senate, state house, state senate, mayor, city council) at any given point in time are the *cross-sectional* differences in power. Therefore, if we were to look at the array of public offices contained within a House district, the largest gap in office-specific benefits probably would be between service in a position such as a school board member and service in the House. Therefore, if the decision to run for higher office were based *solely* on relative benefit, we would expect to see lots of school board members running for Congress, fewer mayors, and still fewer state senators.[19]

If we step away from any individual congressional district and cast our gaze across all congressional districts, we see how another set of cross-sectional differences in the relative benefits derived from various political offices come into play. In some regions of the country, mayors are enormously powerful (think of Chicago). In other regions, mayors are mostly ceremonial (think of most of New England). Even within states, some cities have strong mayors (like Boston) while others have extremely weak ones (like Cambridge, Massachusetts). Consequently, to the degree that the decision by a mayor about whether to run for Congress is made based on the value of the mayorality compared to Congress, weak mayors should be more likely to run than strong mayors, small-city mayors should run more frequently than large-city mayors, and so forth.

Finally, the value of a congressional seat relative to that of other political offices has changed *across time*. As the value changed, it opened up a different set of lower offices as stepping-stones to Congress.

Therefore, we can think of each of the factors listed in Table 4.2 as varying cross-sectionally and across time. Let us examine each of them in turn.

The relative benefits derived from office

Scope of legislative authority The authority of Congress certainly has changed over the past two centuries and, as it has, so too has the value of serving in Congress. In the early days of the Republic, the federal government was relatively weak, with little reach into citizens' lives. One consequence was that members of Congress cycled quickly through the institution, looking for better opportunities elsewhere. For instance, during the 1810s, 18 percent of all House members who were eligible for reelection voluntarily left the House. In his study of the House of Representatives early in the nineteenth century (1801–1828), James Sterling Young (1966) concluded that House members served short tours of duty in Washington precisely because real political power resided elsewhere—back home in state governments—and therefore ambitious politicians returned home as soon as possible.

In the last two-thirds of the twentieth century the federal government's reach grew significantly, and along with it grew the legislative responsibilities of Congress. One consequence of this is surely that retirement rates have been much lower in recent decades than in the earliest years of the Republic. For instance, in the 1980s only 6 percent of all House members eligible for reelection retired. Political scientists such as Morris Fiorina (1977) have attributed low congressional turnover in recent years directly to the expansion of the federal government's power and hence Congress's.

Political and policy resources within the institution Congress employs resources—money and personnel—to effect the political and policy goals of its members. So too do other legislatures. The scope of congressional resources devoted to policy and politics is staggering. In fiscal year 2010, the Legislative Branch Appropriations Bill amounted to over $3.6 billion. The legislative branch employed over 25,000 people. The average senator employed over forty people in his or her personal office, the average House member, seventeen.

These statistics dwarf all state legislatures, but they dwarf some more than others. Eight states, for instance, have full-time, year-round staff for all the members of the state legislature. At the other end of the spectrum, two states (Wyoming and South Dakota) have no personal staff for their legislators. Therefore, an ambitious politician in the Wyoming state senate will be relatively more covetous of the institutional resources of an MC than a state senator in a state like California, New York, or Massachusetts.

Pay and perquisites Related to resources that can be marshaled in policy making are the private resources—pay and perquisites—that can be gained by serving in Congress compared to other offices. All members of Congress receive generous compensation. The salary alone for members of Congress in 2010 was $174,000.

As with institutional policy-making resources, local offices vary tremendously in what they pay their legislators and other political officials. The only state officials whose pay even approaches MCs are the governors of some large industrial states, whose pay is well over $100,000 per year. (In 2010 the highest-paid governor was California's Arnold Schwarzenegger at approximately $174,000.) State legislators are paid nothing close to MCs. California's legislators, who are the nation's best paid, still make only about two-thirds the salary of MCs (over $116,000).

While many MCs will protest that they are not in politics for the money, the most comprehensive study of pay-induced career decisions about members of Congress bears out the conjecture that congressional pay is related to the choice of whether to run. Examining the number of retirements in the House from 1900 to 1980, John Hibbing (1991) discovered that in election years following a congressional pay increase, the number of retirements decreased significantly; when the congressional pension plan was significantly improved, the next election tended to exhibit more retirements.

The value in achieving even higher office Precisely because of the system of nested constituencies, offices are seen as springboards for other offices. If we suppose that ambitious politicians have long-range career plans, like other professionals, then certain offices will be valuable because of what they lead to, not because of what they are intrinsically. As I mentioned previously in noting the career path of Senator Edward Kennedy, the office of assistant district attorney is a common stepping-stone to one's first elected office, so common that the heir to the country's most valuable political name was willing to take the position even though it was beneath him socially.

The value of congressional seats as grooming stations certainly has changed over the years. In the 1810s, Henry Clay coveted his House seat—and particularly his role as House Speaker—because it allowed him to take an active role in directing American foreign policy during the war against England. Because, at the time, the position of secretary of State was seen as the stepping-stone to the presidency, Clay's presidential ambitions helped determine the value of his House seat—the House seat was seen as a stepping-stone to being secretary of State, which was a stepping-stone to the presidency. Once it was clear that he would never be elected president, Clay was elected to the Senate, where he could take an even more central position in the regional politics of the day, but now out of the presidential spotlight. In the mid-twentieth century, as three out of four presidents (Truman, Kennedy, and Johnson) arose from the Senate, presidentially ambitious politicians momentarily reaimed their fire at the Senate, away from state government, in their hunt for the great White House.

The probability of victory

The factors that go under the heading of the probability of victory are those structural situations that constrain how well a candidate could do in a district even if he or she were to run the "best" race possible. Such factors, outside the control of the (potential) candidates in the short term, include partisan, geographic, and personal considerations.

Party identification Although allegiance to political parties has waned over the past half century, partisanship still is the strongest cue to which voters respond. Consequently, an ambitious politician needs to weigh the benefits likely to derive from a successful contest for a House and Senate seat by the likelihood that someone from that party could win in that particular district.

The strength of party affects both the willingness of lower-level politicians to try for Congress and the level at which they try. A Republican state legislator in the inner suburbs around Boston, for instance, would have virtually no chance winning a U.S. House seat, given the strength of the Democratic party in and around Boston. Winning the Senate would be difficult for the same Republican state legislator, but if running for Senate, at least he or she could find a base of strength in the more Republican areas of the state. Consequently, we should not be surprised when incumbents in lower offices "leapfrog" intermediate elections, if the more proximate constituencies contain hostile partisan terrain.

Although partisanship is fairly stable in most regions in the short term, population characteristics evolve in most locales, and often this evolution can shift the partisan base from under an incumbent. This evolution has been most evident in recent years in the gradual growth of the Republican Party in the traditionally Democratic South. As Republican Party identification in the South has grown since the early 1960s, so too have incumbent Democrats found it not worth their while to seek reelection while Republicans have begun to build progressive political careers in the South. The result has been a slow but profound shift in the partisanship of representation from the South over the past generation.

Partisan tides Not only do districts differ with respect to their receptiveness to candidates of the two parties, but partisan fortunes also fluctuate

TABLE 4.3
Midterm Loss of Seats by the President's Party

President	Party	Elected	Next Midterm Election	Percentage of Vote Received by House Candidates of President's Party			House Seats Lost by President's Party (no.)	Senate Seats Lost by President's Party (no.)
				Presidential year	Midterm year	Difference		
Truman	Dem.	1948	1950	51.6	48.9	-2.7	29	6
Eisenhower	Rep.	1952	1954	49.3	47.0	-2.3	18	1
Eisenhower	Rep.	1956	1958	48.7	43.6	-5.1	48	13
Kennedy	Dem.	1960	1962	54.4	52.1	-2.3	4	-3
Johnson	Dem.	1964	1966	56.9	50.5	-6.4	47	4
Nixon	Rep.	1968	1970	48.2	44.5	-3.7	12	-2
Nixon	Rep.	1972	1974	46.4	40.5	-5.9	48	5
Carter	Dem.	1976	1978	56.2	53.4	-2.8	15	3
Reagan	Rep.	1980	1982	48.0	38.2	-9.8	26	-1
Reagan	Rep.	1984	1986	47.0	40.7	-6.3	5	8
Bush	Rep.	1988	1990	45.5	38.4	-7.1	8	1
Clinton	Dem.	1992	1994	50.8	46.9	-3.9	52	8
Clinton	Dem.	1996	1998	48.5	47.8	-0.7	-4	0
Bush	Rep.	2000	2002	47.3	49.6	+2.3	-8	-1
Bush	Rep.	2004	2006	49.2	45.6	-3.6	30	6
Obama	Dem.	2008	2010	57.5	48.0	-9.5	63	6
Average				50.3	46.8	-4.4	24.6	3.4

Source: Orstein, Mann, and Malbin (2000); *Statistical Abstract of the United States.*

at the national level from year to year. The most regular fluctuation in party fortunes comes in **midterm elections** (i.e., elections held between two presidential elections). Table 4.3 illustrates how partisan tides have disadvantaged the president's party in the second half of the twentieth century, showing a pattern that stretches back to at least the Civil War. In more recent years, the president's party has lost an average of twenty-six House seats in midterm elections and almost four Senate seats. Some years are worse than others—note the devastating years of 1958, 1966, 1974, and 1994 and compare them to the milder rejections of 1962, 1986, and 1990. The most dramatic exceptions to this pattern were in 1998 and 2002, when the party of the president actually gained seats in the midterm election.

The implications of the midterm loss pattern are twofold. First, in general, politicians of the president's party always are cautious at midterm—incumbents retire at a slightly higher rate and challengers appear at a lower rate. Second, some years are known ahead of time to be worse than others, which redoubles the midterm effects. The best example of this was 1974, an election held in the midst of the Watergate scandal. With the popular press predicting the demise of the Republican Party due to the scandals emanating from the Republican White House, Republican politicians at all levels ran for the hills (see Jacobson and Kernell 1981).

Districting changes The Constitution provides for a decennial census for the purpose of redistributing House seats among the states in proportion to population. (See Chapter 6 for a discussion of districting issues.) Even when states experience no greater-than-average population changes over the course of a decade, the population typically redistributes itself enough within all states to make some redrawing of districts necessary, to meet the Supreme Court's requirement that districts be equal in population.

 Redrawn districts rarely are politically neutral. As a different set of congressional districts is overlaid on existing local political boundaries, political options are opened and foreclosed for different groups of aspiring politicians.

A good illustration of this effect is the redistricting of northern Virginia over the last four decades of the twentieth century, following the rapid growth of the Washington, D.C., suburbs with respect to the rest of the state, and the rapid growth of the outer ring of Washington suburbs compared to the older suburbs of Arlington and Alexandria. Figure 4.1 shows the evolution of northern Virginia's districts from the 1970s to the 1990s. The solid lines show the congressional districts. The counties are shaded according to Republican strength in the 1996 presidential election—the darkest counties are strongly Republican, the white counties are strongly Democratic, and the lighter-shaded counties are moderately Republican.

The two districts from northern Virginia were the 10th and 8th congressional districts.[20] Both districts had been relatively unchanged from the 1950s through the 1980s. Each had a Democratic urban area bordering the District of Columbia connected to a mostly Republican suburban area. In

FIGURE 4.1
Northern Virginia's Congressional Districts, 1970s, 1980s, and 1990s

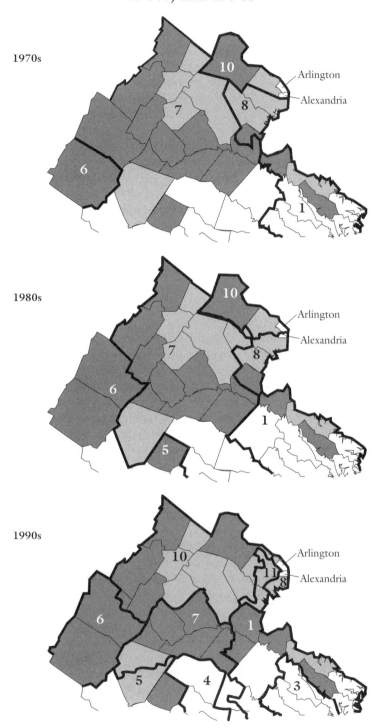

the 10th district, the urban area was Arlington County,[21] the 8th district's urban core was Alexandria. The 8th district's suburban area was the southern half of Fairfax County (an enormous bedroom community of Washington), Mount Vernon, and a collection of other "colonial" suburbs. The 10th district's suburbs were the northern half of Fairfax County and the smaller (in population) rural area of Loudin County.

When districts were redrawn after the 1980 census, the Virginia legislature chose to keep them almost unchanged, which kept the political fortunes of the two incumbent House members virtually unchanged. Both Frank Wolf (10th district) and Stan Parris (8th) were long-term incumbent Republican House members. But because the two districts included substantial cores of Democratic strength, neither had ever been able to win election easily and both had faced a long line of well-financed Democratic challengers.

The population continued to surge in northern Virginia during the 1980s. Unlike most population shifts around the country, which tended to favor the Republican outer suburbs and disfavor inner-city areas, the population surge in northern Virginia was more politically balanced. So, as Wolf and Parris were gaining more Republican-minded constituents in the outer reaches of their districts, they also were gaining Democrats in the inner reaches around Arlington and Alexandria. The precariousness of the two men's political standing was driven home in 1990, when Parris lost the general election to a Democrat, Jim Moran.

After the 1990 census results were announced, the previous strategies of redrawing districts in northern Virginia were no longer possible. Population grew *so much* that another district had to be added. How was this growth accommodated? In two ways. First, the 8th and 10th districts were redrawn to accommodate the political needs of the incumbents. Democratic Arlington was shifted to the 8th district, which also had most of its Republican areas excised. Consequently, the 8th district became highly urban. The 10th district, free of Arlington, was catapulted far to the west to pick up counties even more Republican than Fairfax County. Second, a new district, the 11th, was created in the region immediately to the west of Arlington and Alexandria. In politically contestable territory, this new district inherited the political dynamics of the two older 8th and 10th districts.

Following the 2000 census, these three districts were virtually unchanged, only reinforcing the patterns introduced by the post-1990 districts.

What effects did the redistricting after the 1990 census have on candidate strategies in these two districts? There are at least two answers. First, by recombining the northern Virginia populations to transform two competitive districts into one safe Republican district and one safe Democratic district, it made the political careers of the two incumbents, Wolf and Moran, virtually bulletproof. Wolf's average reelection margins in the old, competitive 10th district had been 60 percent until the 1990 election, growing to 71 percent afterward. Moran, who was elected in a district that had given Democrats 44 percent of the vote on average in the previous decade, and who had himself beat Parris with only 52 percent of the vote, found himself in a new district in which his average vote share was 64 percent.

In the notation of equation (4.2), $P_{\text{continued reelection to the House}}$ went up for both incumbents. Consequently, both probably became less likely to voluntarily relinquish their office, either to retire or seek higher office. Likewise, $P_{\text{knocking off the incumbent}}$ dropped for anyone considering a run against the two, leading to a considerable drop in the quality of the challengers they faced.

Second, the creation of a new congressional district in an area that had been represented by a series of long-serving incumbents opened up political opportunities in the 11th district. The district, as drawn, was expected to lean Republican. As a consequence, five prominent Republicans contested the 1992 primary to be the first representative from the district. Unfortunately for the Republicans, a Democrat, Leslie Byrne, won the seat in 1992, riding the coattails of President Clinton. This result brought another strong, locally prominent Republican, Tom Davis, to the fore to oppose Byrne in 1994. The Republican won in 1994 and continued to do so until he retired in 2008. Following Davis's retirement, a Democrat, Gerry Connolly, took the seat in a close-fought election.

During the time when Parris and Wolf were heavily entrenched incumbents, their invincibility suppressed higher political ambitions among northern Virginia's Republicans. In other words, the probability that an ambitious young Republican could knock off either Parris or Wolf in a party convention[22] was virtually nil. Therefore, almost no one tried; politically ambitious Republicans from northern Virginia either cast their eyes away from Washington or left politics after hitting a glass ceiling. By moving the two local congressional incumbents out of the way, the 1990s redistricting created a short-term turbulence in the probability of winning higher office among Republicans in central Fairfax County. This, in turn, led to the ready appearance of attractive local Republican candidates who fought to rise through the ranks to claim a higher political reward.

Scandals Aside from the normal controversy that attends anyone in political life, periodically members of Congress are faced with problems that make them stand out. A political scandal, such as charges of bribery and sexual impropriety, that calls into question the ability of an incumbent MC to perform her or his official duties can change the political landscape quickly and significantly. In the most comprehensive study of the effects of political scandals on House elections, Peters and Welch (1980) discovered that being caught up in a scandal costs incumbents between 6 and 11 percentage points in the polls the next time they run for reelection. Abramowitz (1988) found similar results for the Senate.

The Peters and Welch estimate of a 6–11 point vote loss due to political scandal undoubtedly underestimates the electoral seriousness of scandals. That is because we observe this vote loss only among incumbents who choose to run for reelection even though their names have been tarnished.

A potential challenger, observing a scandal, is likely to revise the estimate of how successful one would be, should one run. Hence, scandals are likely to bring out a better crop of challengers. Fearing a grueling reelection battle, and knowing that the probability of reelection has dropped, an incumbent is more likely to retire from Congress than risk reelection.

The costs of running for office

Rounding out the calculus of election are the costs associated with running for office. The most obvious costs in running for Congress are the money, time, and personnel needed to mount a credible campaign. Less obvious, but perhaps more important, is the cost of opportunities forgone by deciding to run—or not run—for office. We begin with these opportunities forgone.

Opportunity costs One cost of running for reelection usually overlooked is what economists call *opportunity costs.* The opportunity cost of doing X instead of Y is the additional benefit that would have been gained if Y had been done. Put concretely in terms of congressional careers, a member of Congress who decides to run for reelection forgoes other opportunities, at least in the short run, such as races for higher office, jobs in the private sector, and spending more time with his or her family. Congressional Representative A, in deciding to run for the Senate, forgoes the benefits that would have come from staying in the House. Because the reelection rate is so high, choosing not to run for reelection constitutes a real risk for most elected politicians trying to move up the electoral ladder. Giving up a lower office is a cost in and of itself.

Opportunity cost calculations affect not only decisions about whether to run for some other office but also decisions about whether to leave politics for the private sector. Many members of Congress in their mid-forties and fifties would be extremely valuable additions to law firms and lobbying operations, and these firms would be happy to pay enormous salaries to lure these incumbents to their firms.[23] In general, then, the decision to run for reelection instead of seeking some other opportunity—electoral or otherwise—is made in the context of the value to the member of Congress of doing something else.

Number and quality of other candidates It goes without saying that it costs money to run an election campaign. What may be less obvious is that how much it costs will depend on whom one is running against. For a holder of a lower office, running in a general election against an incumbent is likely to be much more expensive than running in a general election against the nonincumbent candidate of the opposite party when the incumbent retires.[24] Incumbents, likewise, face a costlier reelection battle when they are running against challengers who have lots of political experience—and so know how to raise money—than when they face neophytes.

Fund-raising efficiency Fund-raising is a necessary evil in American politics. Although all successful high-level politicians are better than average at doing it, not everyone is equally good, and not everyone enjoys it equally as much. Some revel at the opportunity of jawboning prominent individuals and interest groups for campaign funds; others hate it. The ones who enjoy fund-raising and are good at it are more likely to run over a long course of elections, while the ones who are particularly bad at it eventually decline to run.

Spending efficiency The other side of the campaign finance coin is the efficiency with which campaign contributions can be turned into political support. Districts vary in how they are configured: geographically, demographically, and with respect to the media. In some states, for instance, television markets coincide closely with congressional districts, and so television advertising (a very efficient method of reaching voters) easily can be relied on. Other states, however, are less well served by existing television markets, either because many districts are crowded into single media markets (e.g., in New York City) or because so many large-city markets serve highly rural states (e.g., Wyoming). Where "wholesale" campaign techniques are easily implemented, the fund-raising advantages of incumbents can be amplified to lower the cost of running for reelection and thus increase the incidence of incumbent longevity (Campbell, Alford, and Henry 1984; Stewart and Reynolds 1990; Ansolabehere, Gerber, and Snyder 1999).

One factor that influences the efficiency of translating resources into votes is the size of the constituency that an incumbent must reach. Most obviously, senators generally represent much larger constituencies than House members, must exert more effort in fund-raising to gain reelection, and thus feel the costs of running for office more acutely than House members. Less obviously, even House districts experience vast variations in how many voters turn out to vote. For most of the twentieth century, the South was uniformly Democratic and therefore general elections were often uncontested. (Even primaries were rarely contested.) Not surprisingly, southern members of Congress tended to retire at low rates, in part because the number of mobilized voters needed for reelection was minuscule.

The "calculus of election" discussed in this section is generic to all ambitious political candidates and so has a place in the decisions that all candidates for Congress—or potential candidates—undertake. Moving beyond the generic calculus, however, different types of candidates weigh the different factors differently. The most basic differentiation of candidates' calculi comes about because some are incumbents and others are not. Among the nonincumbents, some are considering (or actually) running against an incumbent, while others are running for an open seat, with no incumbent present. Therefore, we turn our attention to the particularities of these different candidates' considerations.

Incumbents, Challengers, and Open Seat Candidates

Incumbents

The power of incumbency has been the subject of much discussion since the success rates of **incumbents** running for reelection began rising so rapidly in the mid-1980s. While the **reelection rate** (the rate at which incumbents running for reelection win back their seat) in the House averaged 91 percent from 1946 until 1980, it began creeping steadily upward in the 1980s, until it reached 98 percent in 1988.[25] Since 1990, the average reelection rate has been 95 percent. Even before the House reelection rate flirted with the 100 percent mark, scholars began to notice that a measurable and significant **incumbency advantage** had emerged around the mid-1960s. The incumbency advantage is defined as the increment of the vote that an incumbent running for reelection receives by virtue of being the incumbent, rather than the incumbent's party's nominee in an open seat race. From the mid-1960s to the end of the 1980s, as estimated by Andrew Gelman and Gary King (1990) the incumbency advantage in House elections was about 8 percent; which boosted most incumbents from being electorally marginal to being electorally safe. More recent research confirmed a similarly sized incumbency advantage through the first decade of the twenty-first century.

Although the incumbency success rate certainly increased in the 1980s and a large incumbency advantage began appearing in the mid-1960s, one should be cautious in inferring that the result was a reduction in turnover in the House and Senate. Indeed, the **turnover rate** (the percentage of the chamber that leaves at the end of each election) remained virtually unchanged during this period. At least two factors help explain this paradoxical phenomenon. First, although incumbents started winning by larger electoral margins, large electoral margins in one election became less of a guarantee of a large electoral margin (or even victory) the *next* election (Mann 1978; Jacobson 1987). Second, retirement from the chamber began to take up the slack from electoral defeat in accounting for turnover in the chambers. In the 1950s and 1960s, the House averaged twenty-eight retirements and thirty-four electoral defeats each election, resulting in an average turnover level of sixty-two seats. In the 1980s and 1990s, the House averaged thirty-seven retirements and twenty-four defeats, resulting in virtually the same net turnover level—sixty-one seats. Turnover stayed the same, but its composition changed. In the first decade of the 2000s, the average number of retirements (27) and defeats (14) fell significantly, leading to an average overall turnover level of only forty-one seats per election.

Even though incumbents periodically *do* lose reelection, and even more retire before being tossed out, the most important question facing incumbent members of Congress each two or six years is whether to retire from the chamber, either to retire outright or to seek higher office in the Senate or presidency. Because reelection rates are so high, it is not surprising that so many incumbent MCs choose to run for reelection. But, the probability of reelection is not absolute, so *some* factors must be especially compelling in getting MCs to retire.

Much research has gone into explaining why some incumbents retire and others seek reelection. Among the factors shown to affect the retirement are the following:

- *Congruence between party and ideology.* In recent years, as part of an "ideological rationalization" of party membership, electorally vulnerable Democrats representing conservative districts and Republicans representing liberal districts have retired at a higher rate than incumbents whose partisanship is congruent with the district's ideology.
- *National partisan tides.* All things being equal, members of the president's party retire at a higher rate than members of the opposition party during the midterm election season.
- *Opportunities for higher office.* MCs—particularly senators—have left Congress at higher rates when the governorship of their state opened up. The most frequent leavers are those whose governors are prevented by term limits from running again and whose governors belong to the opposite party.
- *Scandals.* Incumbents embroiled in ethical scandals leave at higher rates. The most dramatic illustration of this was the aftermath of the 1992 "House Bank Scandal." Only 9 percent of House members with no bank overdrafts retired from politics in 1992, while 26 percent of those with over a hundred overdrafts did (Stewart 1994).

Challengers

Much of what was said about the decisions of incumbents about retiring also applies to challengers and candidates for open seats. In many cases, potential challengers and open seat candidates also are politicians incumbent in some other office, and so the decision calculus is fundamentally identical. Therefore, I leave as an exercise to the reader the task of detailing how to apply the previous section's discussion to candidates who might challenge an incumbent or run for an open seat following a retirement. I will confine my remarks here to the special issues attending challengers and then to open seat candidates.

Challengers come in all shapes and sizes. The most important feature of challengers, from the perspective of the quality of representative democracy, is whether they have a chance to defeat the incumbent.[26] As I suggested earlier, challengers who already hold some elective office tend to fare much better than those who do not. This pattern holds even in years such as 2010, when the electorate supposedly holds grudges against "professional politicians." Table 4.4 reports the percentage of challengers of both parties who were successful in 2010, breaking out the percentages according to whether the challenger previously had held elective office. Two patterns stand out. First,

2010 was a very good year for Republicans, so that the percentage of Republicans winning in each category of challenger was higher than for Democrats. For instance, no Democratic challengers without previous electoral experience won, compared to 12 percent of Republican challengers with no prior experience. Second, within each party's challengers, those with experience did much better than those without. This is especially striking among Republicans, in which over half the challengers with prior electoral experience (56%) won, compared to only 12 percent of Republican challengers with no prior experience.

TABLE 4.4
Success of High- and Low-Quality Challengers in 2010

	Democratic Challengers against Republican Incumbents		Republican Challengers against Democratic Incumbents	
	No Prior Office	Held Prior Office	No Prior Office	Held Prior Office
Challenger won	0%	13%	12%	56%
Total challengers	111	23	179	52

The seminal study of the effects of "challenger quality" on congressional elections is Gary Jacobson and Samuel Kernell's *Strategy and Choice in Congressional Elections* (1981). Jacobson and Kernell were inspired to conduct their investigation into the effects of challenger quality on congressional elections in the wake of inconsistencies between aggregate-level election outcomes and evidence about congressional elections adduced from public opinion polls. The disjuncture between findings at these two levels were especially stark in the 1974 election.

The 1974 election represented the low-water mark for the Republican party in the twentieth century, up and down the ballot. The aggregate congressional vote for Republicans, 41 percent, was the lowest received by either of the two major parties in the twentieth century. As a result, Republicans won only one-third (144) of the seats in the House. Political commentators attributed the Republican drubbing in 1974 to the massive unpopularity of the incumbent Republican president (Nixon) and the related implication of the Republican Party in the Watergate scandal. Yet, at the same time, public opinion analysts discovered, at best, a weak relationship between how voters felt about President Nixon and how they voted in the congressional race. Nixon haters were not especially anti-Republican in how they voted for Congress; Nixon lovers were not especially pro-Republican. Given the enormity of the Watergate scandal, it seems intuitive that the Republican Party should have suffered at the polls in 1974 because of it. Individual voters did not appear to tie together their hatred of the incumbent Republican president with a hatred of Republican congressional candidates, yet Republican candidates did poorly. What gives?

Jacobson and Kernell argue that the answer to this question lies in the strategic calculations of Republican and Democratic elites early in 1974. By the time the 1974 general election had rolled around, the strategic calculations of incumbents and challengers had made the final outcome a virtual certainty. Early in 1974, Republicans who might seek election in November checked the political winds, found them threatening, and decided to lay low for a year or two. At the same time, ambitious Democrats who already held some lower elective office recognized the opportunity and started running early for higher office. Therefore, the worst that could have been said about many Republicans who ended up on the ballot in 1974 is that they were untried, naive, and inexperienced. They may have been relatively untainted by scandal, in fact, since they did not come from political backgrounds. They were innocents, but they also were inept. Republican congressional candidates were slaughtered by the Democrats, who had experience, rather than purity, on their side.

What difference does prior electoral experience make among challengers? Much of the answer to this question has already been given earlier in this chapter. Because the American political opportunity structure is pyramidal, these "high-quality challengers" are already proven vote getters in their communities. Other political elites are more willing to swing support their way. Sophisticated contributors are more likely to contribute "seed money" to their campaigns. And finally, because most quality challengers must give up a relatively safe electoral career in a lower office to run for Congress, the very fact that such a challenger appears in a congressional race virtually guarantees that the office is ripe for the picking.

Some students of American politics tend to regard the strategic role challengers play in the outcome of congressional elections as undermining democracy. Should not voters have the best alternatives presented to them every year, regardless of national tides or the electoral advantage built up by the incumbent over time? This is a serious question, for which there is no easy answer. A glib answer is to say that if incumbents always knew that they would face well-financed and experienced challengers, they would be more responsive to their constituents. Thus, even if a steady succession of quality challengers never defeated a particular incumbent, at least the constant competition would keep him or her honest.

Yet the glib answer overlooks important features of democratic politics. One important feature keeps high-quality challengers from facing off against incumbents in every election and likely would continue to keep them away from elections even if their participation were heavily subsidized: no one can force anyone to run for office. Any desire to ensure that high-quality challengers always face off against incumbents is probably chimeral. Second, incumbents who knew they would have to face a steady stream of high-quality challengers into the infinite future would tend to retire earlier, cutting short most congressional careers. While many people consider shorter congressional careers to be an intrinsically good thing, others do not. And in any event, this second consideration points out that nothing would ever prohibit incumbents from choosing to retire rather than face a well-regarded challenger. Open seat elections provide voters with even greater opportunities to change the political course. Yet when retirements increase, the number of incumbents held accountable by the voters decreases. It is not obvious that encouraging more retirements would improve the representative character of Congress. Furthermore, incumbents running for reelection are more ideologically congruent, on average, with their districts than candidates for open seats or challengers (Ansolabehere, Snyder, and Stewart 2000b).

Because the American structure of political opportunity is hierarchical, it is possible for changes in the parameters of state and local elections to affect whether high-quality challengers appear in congressional elections. The movement among the states to limit the terms of their *state* legislatures, which grew in popularity in the early 1990s, may have a second-order effect on congressional elections by dumping into the pool of potential congressional challengers a number of former state legislators who *must* run for higher office if they are to stay in politics. Recent research by Birkhead, Uriarte, and Bianco (2010) suggests an interesting pattern. These authors find that for the 1996–2006 period, term limits induced more state legislators to run for Congress. However, these term-limited candidates mainly forced aside other potential high-quality challengers, who were now *deterred* from running against the incumbent. Therefore, the net effect of term limits has not been to increase the supply of high-quality challengers running against incumbents; it has only made it more likely that the high-quality challenger facing an incumbent House member will be a state legislator.

Open seat candidates

Every two years on average, six senators and thirty House members retire from Congress, leaving their seats open. While small in number, these open seat races in recent years have provided about half the new members of Congress. Because open seat races, by definition, involve no incumbent, their dynamics are fundamentally different from those involving a challenger and an incumbent.

Beginning in the mid-1960s, the degree of competition within most congressional districts began declining, as measures of the incumbency advantage grew. A major contributor to the decline in this competition was the decreasing number of high-quality challengers who opposed incumbents. Still, overall congressional turnover did not decline as precipitously as the decline in high-quality challengers. As a consequence, from the 1960s into the early 1990s, competition that once was dispersed among all congressional elections was redistributed and concentrated more and more on open seats. In other words, congressional races involving an incumbent became less and less competitive, while races without an incumbent became more competitive.

Campaign money has flowed to **open seat candidates** in a manner consistent with the trends in competitiveness (see Figure 4.2). Ever since the federal government started keeping records, spending by incumbents has risen steadily while spending by challengers has stagnated, producing a dramatic disparity between incumbents and challengers. At the same time, spending in open seat elections has kept pace with incumbent spending. Even though spending in open seat races tends to favor the candidate of the party that previously held that seat, the advantage is not nearly as great as that held by incumbents over challengers.

FIGURE 4.2
Campaign Spending in House Races, 1976–2008, in 2008 Dollars

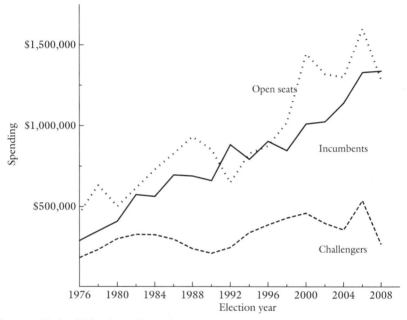

Source: Federal Elections Commission data.

An open seat provides the best opportunity for the party that previously had not held a congressional seat to take it over. How successful have out parties been in this regard? The answer is not very, despite a trend in the 1970s and 1980s for out parties to do slightly better across time. Still, the out party tends to be unsuccessful in taking over seats when they become open for one important reason: the out party typically is the minority party in the district already.

One factor that separates open seat elections from those involving an incumbent running for reelection is the primary. When the incumbent retires, the primaries become more important, because they are more likely to be contested. Still, because most districts tend to lean perceptibly toward one of the two parties, it is unusual to have two strongly contested primaries whenever a congressional seat comes open. What is more common is for the district's majority party to hold a highly contested primary, with the minority party nominee winning an uncontested or poorly contested primary (Schantz 1980).

Because open seat congressional elections tend to be more competitive than elections with an incumbent running, many people have supported **term limits** as a mechanism to increase the retirement rate and, thus, to increase the number of open seat elections. Having worked through the decision calculus of various types of congressional candidates, you now should appreciate how term limits might, or might not, increase the competitiveness of congressional elections. A naive prediction about term limits is to suppose that competition for congressional seats *must* increase if the number of open seats is increased by term limits. After all, competition currently is greater for open seats than for incumbent-contested seats. Why would creating more open seats not just increase the level of competition even more?

The reason that simply creating more open seats through term limits will not *guarantee* more competition for House seats is that term limits would *regularize* the appearance of open seats. Right now, local political elites might try to *estimate* when the local member of Congress will retire, but they rarely know definitely that he or she will retire by a certain election.[27] Hence, potential candidates for Congress at least must test the waters periodically, on the off chance that the incumbent will retire *this* time around. Uncertain about when the incumbent will retire, more anxious challengers might take on the incumbent, to test his or her vulnerability. If everyone *knows* the incumbent must retire after six terms, this would focus attention on what happens after the sixth term and might discourage challengers from testing the waters against the incumbent after the first through fifth terms—why not wait until the seat becomes open?

At the same time, term limits might actually increase competition in the elections *before* the incumbent must retire. Consider the situation from the perspective of an ambitious potential candidate. You could wait to run against all the other ambitious politicians in your area when the incumbent retires, madly scrambling for the nomination, or you could run against the incumbent in the election before he or she must retire and have a shot with fewer other opponents to distract you. Which would you choose? Furthermore, knowing that you are likely to challenge the incumbent in the election before retirement is mandatory, some other slightly more ambitious local politician might jump in the race *two* elections before the incumbent must retire. Before you know it, you could have competition against the incumbent all the time, with ambitious challengers running against the incumbent in the hope of avoiding the chaos of an open seat race that everyone has been anticipating for many years.[28]

Therefore, whether term limits would increase or decrease electoral competition for Congress is an empirical question that depends on things such as the number of potential candidates for Congress and their feelings about taking risks.

Conclusion: The Engine of Ambition in Congressional Elections

"Ambition lies at the heart of politics" (J. Schlesinger 1966, p. 1). This chapter has been about how the individual ambitions of politicians provide the energy to propel the congressional election system. The universe of congressional elections revolves around incumbents, who make up the bulk of congressional candidates and whose skills and command of resources make them the obvious first movers in congressional elections.

While a focus on the strategic interactions of candidates and potential candidates may make it seem that the engine of congressional elections is isolated from the world of the voters, nothing could be further from the truth. All the actions and reactions of candidates for office are predicated on the desire (eventually) to please the most voters and win election. Having focused on the strategic interactions in a rarefied stratum of American politics, it is time to turn our attention to the voters and understand how they react to the machinations of local political elites.

Further Reading

Ansolabehere, Stephen, James M. Snyder, Jr., and Charles Stewart III. 2000. "Old Voters, New Voters, and the Personal Vote: Using Redistricting to Measure the Incumbency Advantage." *American Journal of Political Science* 44: 17–34.

Banks, Jeffrey S., and D. Roderick Kiewiet. 1989. "Explaining Patterns of Candidate Competition in Congressional Elections." *American Journal of Political Science* 33: 997–1015.

Black, Gordon S. 1972. "A Theory of Political Ambition: Career Choices and the Role of Structural Incentives." *American Political Science Review* 66: 144–59.

Bond, Jon R., Cary Covington, and Richard Fleisher. 1985. "Explaining Challenger Quality in Congressional Elections." *Journal of Politics* 47: 510–29.

Canon, David T. 1990. *Actors, Athletes, and Astronauts: Political Amateurs in the United States Congress.* Chicago: University of Chicago Press.

Ferejohn, John A. 1977. "On the Decline of Competition in Congressional Elections." *American Political Science Review* 71: 166–76.

Gelman, Andrew, and Gary King. 1990. "Estimating Incumbency Advantage without Bias." *American Journal of Political Science* 34: 1142–64.

Jacobson, Gary. 1987. "The Marginals Never Vanished: Incumbency and Competition in Elections to the U.S. House of Representatives, 1952–82." *American Journal of Political Science* 31: 126–41.

———. 1989. "Strategic Politicians and the Dynamics of U.S. House Elections, 1946–86." *American Political Science Review* 83: 773–93.

Jacobson, Gary, and Samuel Kernell. 1981. *Strategy and Choice in Congressional Elections.* New Haven, Conn.: Yale University Press.

Johannes, John R., and John C. McAdams. 1981. "The Congressional Incumbency Effect: Is It Casework, Policy Compatability, or Something Else? An Examination of the 1978 Election." *American Journal of Political Science* 25: 512–42.

Mann, Thomas E., and Raymond E. Wolfinger. 1980. "Candidates and Parties in Congressional Elections." *American Political Science Review* 74: 617–40.

Mayhew, David R. 1974. "Congressional Elections: The Case of the Vanishing Marginals." *Polity* 6: 295–317.

Riker, William H., and Peter C. Ordeshook. 1968. "A Theory of the Calculus of Voting." *American Political Science Review* 62: 25–42.

Rohde, David W. 1979. "Risk-Bearing and Progressive Ambition: The Case of Members of the United States House of Representatives." *American Journal of Political Science* 23: 1–26.

Schlesinger, Joseph. 1966. *Ambition and Politics: Political Careers in the United States.* Chicago: Rand-McNally.

SUMMARY OF KEY CONCEPTS

1. **Rotation in office** is the practice of limiting the number of terms a legislator may serve in office by the party that nominates him or her, to share the benefits of office among a number of party members.

2. An **opportunity cost** is the benefit forgone from one alternative when it is passed up in favor of another.

3. **Progressive ambition** describes the career goal of politicians who view service in a lower office as a stepping-stone to higher office.

4. A **midterm election** is a congressional election held in a nonpresidential election year, such as 2002 or 2006.

5. An **incumbent** is the individual who currently holds an elected position.

6. The **reelection rate** is calculated by dividing the number of representatives in a chamber who are reelected in a particular year by the number of representatives who sought reelection.

7. The **incumbency advantage** is the extra increment of electoral support an incumbent receives purely by virtue of being an incumbent.

8. The **turnover rate** is calculated by dividing the number of representatives in a chamber who do not return to Congress following an election (for any reason including defeat and retirement) by the number of representatives in the chamber.

9. A **challenger** is a candidate who runs against an incumbent for election to Congress.

10. An **open seat candidate** runs in a congressional race in which the incumbent is not running for reelection.

11. A **term limit** is a constraint on the number of times an incumbent may run for office and serve. States may not constitutionally impose term limits on members of Congress, although they may impose term limits on their own state legislators.

PROBLEMS

The following set of questions is intended to help you explore the calculus of running for Congress. To explore these questions, pick a member of the House or the Senate. This could be your own representative, or someone in whom you are interested. Pick the representative wisely, because you will be prompted to explore more about this person in problems associated with later chapters.

Using online news sources, such as Lexis-Nexis, Google News, congress-specific online sites such as CQ or Roll Call, or printed volumes such as the *Almanac of American Politics,* answer the following questions:

1. For the most recent election, when did the incumbent member of the House or Senate announce that he or she was running for reelection or retiring? What were the issues or other factors that the member mentioned as entering into this decision? What other factors did the press mention as entering into the decision?

2. For the most recent election, who were mentioned as possible challengers to the incumbent? What were their backgrounds? Did these people end up running? If so, when did they announce, and what issues or other factors did they emphasize in their campaigns? If they did not run, what factors entered into that decision?

3. For the House district or state you have chosen, who would be the most viable candidates to contend for the seat in the next election, should the challenger run for reelection, or should the seat come open? What makes them viable candidates?

NOTES

1. The traditional civics view of congressional elections has a difficult time dealing with the motivations of one important type of political actor—the political contributor. Do contributors give money to candidates because they are public spirited (giving to candidates they agree with) or because they want to buy influence and access to politicians (giving to candidates with the best chance of winning)?
2. Political scientists and economists have spilled a lot of ink contemplating the meaning of this sentence. I will defer to the next chapter a full exposition of the calculus of turning out and voting.

3. These numbers were taken from the Gallup/*USAToday* poll and constitute the average response to these three questions during all 2010. An archive of Gallup/ *USAToday* poll results can be found on the Gallup Poll Web page, http://www .gallup.com.

4. Few of Lincoln's biographers deal fully with his congressional service. For some who did, see Riddle (1979), Finley (1979), and Beveridge (1928). See also Silbey (1986), Howe (1979), and Donald (1995).

5. The principle of rotation in office constrains incumbents to hold a particular elected office for a limited number of terms. When rotation in office was common in the United States, the most frequent limitations were either two or three terms. Rotation in office is enforced by the party simply refusing to renominate an incumbent after she or he has served the maximum number of terms. Therefore a system of rotation relies on party leaders being able to keep people off the ballot, which is impossible in the modern system of primary elections where any party member may get on the nomination ballot regardless of the desires of party leaders. On the rise and fall of rotation in office, see Kernell (1977).

6. In the end, it was probably just as well that Lincoln was not given a second chance at running for Congress. The year 1848 was not especially good for Whigs, and the Whig nominee to take Lincoln's place lost to the Democratic nominee, Thomas Harris. Harris, not laboring under a one-term limitation, ran for reelection in 1850 but lost to the Whig, Richard Yates.

7. It is supposed that Lincoln turned down the opportunity for political leadership in Oregon because that territory was Democratic in sentiments. Once admitted to the Union, it was unlikely to elect a Whig to any prominent positions, and hence the job would have been a dead end for someone as politically ambitious as Lincoln.

8. This formulation of the expected value calculation that candidates use to evaluate whether to run for office is common in the literature. Two examples of how this formulation has been used to good effect in the analysis of candidate decisions are found in G. Black (1972) and Rohde (1979).

9. Schlesinger actually delineated three types of political ambition. *Discrete ambition* describes a politician who seeks office for a single term and then retires. *Static ambition* pertains to a politician who seeks an office as the ultimate end, with no desire to move on. *Progressive ambition* describes cases where a politician holds an office and then tries to move on, using that office as a springboard.

   Most members of Congress never try for higher office. It would be a mistake to regard most MCs as lacking progressive ambition, however. Ask yourself the following question: If most members of the House were offered a seat in the Senate, *without cost or risk to themselves*, would they take the seat? It is clear that the answer is yes. The reason we do not see House members running for the Senate in droves is because of the risks and costs involved in running. Therefore even without rampant, cutthroat competition for Senate seats by House members, Congress as a whole clearly operates in an environment of progressive ambition.

10. http://www.masslive.com/news/index.ssf/2009/11/republican_scott_brown_ seeking.html, last accessed September 6, 2010.

11. This last claim is based on a simple regression analysis that uses Brown's percentage of the votes cast in each of the district's precincts as the dependent variable and the following variables as independent variables: percentage of voters who are Republicans and dummy variables for the towns of Norfolk, Walpole, and Wrentham.

12. This senate district was the Norfolk, Bristol, and Middlesex District. His previous state house district was the Norfolk County 9th.

13. Information about political careers of members of Congress was taken from the *Biographical Directory of the United States Congress* and Inter-University Consortium for Political and Social Research and Carroll McKibbin, *Roster of United States Congressional Office Holders and Biographical Characteristics of Members of the United States Congress, 1789–1991: Merged Data*, Computer File, 8th ICPSR ed. (Ann Arbor, Mich., ICPSR, 1991).

14. It is impossible to give a similar accounting of the eventual political careers of contemporary members of Congress because most have not finished their political careers. Still, the eventual political careers of MCs first elected in 1952 give us an idea about how things had changed since the 1880s. Of the eighty-two rookie House members in 1953 which included future-speaker Thomas P. (Tip) O'Neill, fifty-nine went no higher than the House of Representatives; twenty-three of the twenty-nine first-term senators found the Senate to be their last political office. (One of the six rookie senators who went on to higher office was John F. Kennedy, who was elected president in 1960.)

15. In other words, part of the reason more House members were reelected as the nineteenth century progressed was that congressional districts as a whole came to be dominated by one of the two political parties. Therefore, fewer incumbents were defeated for reelection by a candidate of the opposite party. Rotation in office, on the other hand, was the practice of requiring incumbents to step down after serving a small number of terms, so that someone else of the same party would have a chance. (Recall that this is why Abraham Lincoln served only one term in the House.) With the rise of primary elections in the late 1800s to determine the party nominees, party organizations lost the ability to enforce the practice of rotation and so it died out.

16. The one major exception to this sentence is in California, where there currently are fewer state senators (forty) than members of the U.S. House (fifty-three).

17. See G. Black (1972) for a discussion of how the size of a political unit and degree of political competition affect the riskiness of political ambition.

18. This point was a central feature of James Madison's argument in favor of the Constitution found in *The Federalist* #10:

> The smaller the society, the fewer probably will be the distinct parties and interests composing it; the fewer the distinct parties and interests, the more frequently will a majority be found of the same party; and the smaller the number of individuals composing a majority, and the smaller the compass within which they are placed, the more easily will they concert and execute their plans of oppression. Extend the sphere and you take in a greater variety of parties and interests; you make it less probable that a majority of the whole will have a common motive to invade the rights of other citizens; or if such a common motive exists, it will be more difficult for all who feel it to discover their own strength and to act in unison with each other.

Viewed from the perspective of a politician trying to succeed within the Madisonian world, life in a larger collection of citizens is more politically perilous than life in a smaller society.

19. Of course, the point of this chapter is that the decision to run for higher office is not based *solely* on the relative benefit of serving in different offices. Another reason we see no constant onslaught of school board members running for Congress is that most school board members probably are not progressively ambitious.

20. The same logic that makes San Francisco the hub of *northern* California, rather than of *middle* California makes the Washington suburbs of Virginia *northern* Virginia, not *northeast* Virginia. Although the 7th congressional district (in the 1970s and 1980s) included the northern-most portion of the state, it was not considered to be part of northern Virginia politically, and hence I ignore it for the remainder of this discussion.

21. Do not be deceived by Arlington's small size on the map and its designation as a county. Arlington was—and is—a city in how it behaves, looks, and feels politically. It is densely populated, like a city, and home to an ever changing ethnic mix of residents.

22. Until recently, Virginia was one of the few states still to have party nominating conventions, rather than primaries. Virginia law has changed, resulting in a growth in the number of primaries there, but conventions still are common, too.

23. The number of House and Senate members leaving Congress to pursue a lobbying career fluctuates from year to year. The *Washington Post* (December 29, 1996, p. A04) reported that only three of the fifteen retiring senators in 1996 (20 percent) remained in Washington after leaving the Senate. This is compared to seventeen of the twenty-three senators (52 percent) who remained inside the Beltway after retiring or being defeated in 1992 and 1994.

24. You may want to think about this problem, however: If you were an incumbent in a lower office of a congressional district held by a politically safe member of the opposition party, would it cost you less to run against the incumbent or to wait until the incumbent retired? If we consider only the general election, the answer is obvious. Unseating an incumbent costs more than winning against the nominee of the incumbent's party once the seat comes open. However, when the seat comes open, a scramble is likely for the nomination of *both parties*. Therefore, if you choose to run now—and oppose the incumbent in the general election—you probably can get the nomination at a low cost. If you wait—and choose to oppose the nominee of the incumbent's party in the general election after the incumbent's retirement—you may have to fight a highly contested primary to get the nomination. Therefore, it is not obvious whether taking on incumbents or waiting for them to retire is always the lower-cost strategy. Unfortunately, not enough empirical research has been done to answer this question, so the answer remains a matter of speculation.

25. The reelection rate in the Senate likewise crept up, averaging 75 percent from 1946 to 1988, but reaching 97 percent in 1990. From 1992 to 2008 the average was 86 percent.

26. The discussion here focuses on challengers of the opposite party from the incumbent. Incumbents rarely are seriously challenged in primaries, but when they are, the same logic also applies.

27. A good example of how political careers are never certain is the machinations of Representative Joseph Kennedy of Massachusetts. In summer 1997, amid much speculation that he would run for Massachusetts governor in 1998, he announced that he would stay out of the governor's race, pleading that negative press about his family would make such an endeavor foolish. In the same press conference, Kennedy announced he instead would run for reelection to the House in 1998. Massachusetts political commentators took Kennedy at his word and immediately declared him invincible for reelection to his House seat. Yet, within two months of his notice to run for reelection, volatile turnover among Kennedy's congressional staff had caught the eye of Boston political reporters, who began speculating about Kennedy's eminent retirement from the House. In the end, Kennedy *did* retire in 1998, leading to a ten-person scramble for his seat in the Democratic primary, in a highly Democratic district. He was replaced by Mike Capuano, the mayor of Somerville.

28. Banks and Kiewiet (1989) make a similar argument in their analysis of why incumbents almost always are challenged for reelection and why weak challengers frequently do the challenging. Weak challengers try to avoid open seat elections, when they know that a number of high-quality candidates are likely to enter the primaries. Even though opposing an incumbent is a long shot for a low-quality

challenger, it may be a better shot than taking on a whole host of high-quality candidates when the seat comes open. This phenomenon helps explain why the typical losing incumbent is a first-term member: periodically, low-quality challengers get lucky and win. Such a winner is likely to be a more vulnerable incumbent in the next election, particularly against a high-quality challenger. Hence, in the *next* election the formerly low-quality challenger (now the incumbent), faces a high-quality challenger, ofttimes losing.

~5~

The Choices Voters Make

I n the previous chapter, we began a discussion of the dynamics of congressional elections by focusing on the choices made by candidates and potential candidates for Congress. In this chapter, we examine the choices made by voters (and potential voters) in response to the choices made by actual candidates.

Voters and candidates play quite different roles in congressional elections, as befits what each has to gain by participating in elections. For a candidate—or potential candidate—a political career is at stake, and therefore candidates tend to devote considerable resources and time to understanding what other candidates are up to and what the electorate prefers. Candidates are positive actors in the system. For a typical voter, relatively little is at stake in a congressional election, particularly compared to other choices voters make about their lives. Therefore, voters tend to devote few resources and little time to understanding the alternatives presented them on election day. Consequently, voters tend to be relatively passive actors. In the language of previous chapters, candidates are strategic while voters are not.

Even though voters tend to be passive compared to candidates, they are not entirely passive—they do make choices after all. For whatever reason, many people *are* interested in politics generally, and congressional elections particularly, and they adopt low-cost strategies to inform themselves about the alternatives facing them. The purpose of this chapter is to explore what these strategies are.

A natural progression of topics helps us focus on the choices that voters make in congressional elections. First is the choice about whether to vote at all: with a minority of the eligible electorate turning out to vote in most congressional elections, it is important first to understand the fluctuations in turnout. Second is the choice of which candidate to support. Finally is the special problem of voters evaluating candidates in two different types of electoral arenas, the general election and primary elections.

The Decision to Vote

A common conversational topic among professional and sidewalk political commentators is the low level of voter turnout in the United States. There is no denying that voting participation levels in the United States pale in comparison to these levels in almost every other democracy in the world. The typical comparison that is made between the United States and other countries is between turnout in American *presidential* elections and turnout in other countries' parliamentary elections. Things are even worse when we do the right comparison: between participation in *congressional* elections and other countries' parliamentary elections.

Turnout in American presidential elections has averaged 58 percent since the end of World War II. Turnout in congressional elections held concurrently with presidential elections (**on-year elections**) has averaged 53 percent in the same period. Turnout in intervening years (**off-year elections**) has been even worse, 42 percent since 1946. As Figure 5.1 illustrates, turnout in all American national elections drifted downward after 1960. Since the mid-1990s, turnout has drifted back upward in on-year elections, but not on off years.[1]

Turnout in congressional elections has been low and getting lower, but not uniformly so. Even in off-year congressional elections, turnout in some congressional districts can be high; in others, low. Figure 5.2 describes turnout across all House districts in 2006 and 2008 as a percentage of the voting age population in each district. Just as the number of people who vote in congressional elections varies from year to year, as much variation occurs from district to district in any election year. To understand voting turnout, we need to understand what gives rise to both the temporal and spatial variations.

Regardless of how we cut it, turnout is low in congressional elections. Yet even though popular pundits regard voter turnout as a glass half empty, social scientists tend to view the glass as not only half full but miraculously so. This is because if we view citizens as rational egoists, then the glass should be totally empty. That is, no one should vote. That anyone votes at all—indeed that millions of people vote every two years—is the puzzle to be explained. Therefore, in examining turnout we begin with this puzzle, argue why citizens should tend to stay home on election day, and then discuss possible explanations for why theory does not seem to square with the evidence. After examining the puzzle of turnout, we look at the practical

FIGURE 5.1
Turnout in Congressional Elections, 1930–2008

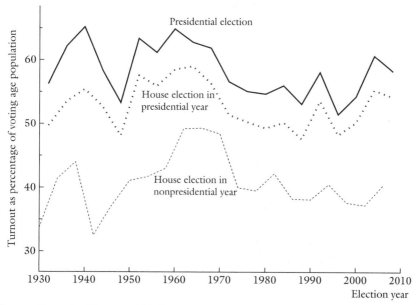

Source: Ornstein, Mann, and Malbin (2008, Table 2-1); *Congressional Directory*, 111th Congress; *Dave Leip's Atlas of U.S. Presidential Elections*, www.uselectionatlas.org.

political question that makes the question of turnout so important: What difference does it make that some people vote and others do not in congressional races?

The calculus of nonvoting

The puzzle of voting, or the calculus of nonvoting, is a topic whose emergence coincided with the appearance of rational choice theory in political science in the 1960s. Before then, virtually everyone took for granted that good citizens generally wanted to vote and would vote if given the opportunity. The failure of many people to vote in national elections was attributed to poor information or a lack of citizen duty among nonvoters. (Of course, everyone recognized that the failure of African Americans to vote in the South was due to the fiercely enforced laws effectively barring their participation.) When economists began to take on the topic of voting, which previously had been in the sole domain of political scientists, they pointed out that most people, political scientists included, had thought about the problem all wrong. Rather than just taking for granted the proposition that all citizens naturally wanted to vote in congressional elections, these scholars reframed the question to ask, under what conditions will a rational egoist vote?

└ maximize
self-interest

FIGURE 5.2
Variation in Turnout among House Districts, 2006 and 2008

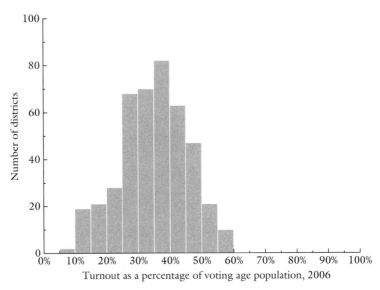

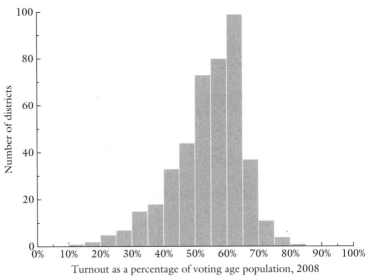

Source: *Congressional Directory,* 111th Congress.

The answer that this question elicited, "virtually never," has been provocative enough to animate many voting studies ever since. The goal in this section is to explore why this outrageous answer should be taken seriously and suggest ways in which the fact that many people *do* vote can be squared with the axiom that individuals are rational egoists.

The rational choice analysis of voter turnout can be divided into two general approaches, which I will term the *investment* and *consumption* approaches. The investment approach supposes that voters invest their time in voting to receive a future payback. This payback can be either directly tangible, such as getting a street paved or a local industry supported, or intangible, such as getting Congress to pass a law that embraces some general principle. The consumption approach supposes that voters view participating in the electoral process as intrinsically rewarding, in much the same way that residents of a community enjoy rooting for the home team or an individual likes to drink Coca Cola.

The investment approach to the calculus of nonvoting, the more pessimistic of the two, can be expressed as follows.[2] Consider the cost-benefit analysis that a representative citizen, Citizen, might conduct in deciding whether to vote in a two-candidate race. That cost-benefit analysis can be summarized as follows:

The expected net benefit of voting = The benefit the individual receives as a consequence of the election outcome − The cost of voting

Citizen will vote if and only if the expected net benefit of voting is greater than 0. When will this be true? When will Citizen vote?

To answer this question formally, we need to peer further inside the benefits Citizen would receive as the consequence of an election. Here, we make a couple of simple assumptions, which leads to some simple notation. Assume, first, that we are talking about an election that pits two candidates, D and R, against each other. Second, assume that if D is elected, Citizen will receive a stream of benefits for the term of office that D serves, $B^D_{Citizen}$. The benefits that Citizen will receive if R is elected will be similarly written as $B^R_{Citizen}$. Finally, assume that Citizen would prefer for D to beat R because $B^D_{Citizen} > B^R_{Citizen}$. If we abbreviate the cost of voting as c, we are set in terms of notation.

If Citizen abstains from voting, then $c=0$. The benefits Citizen will receive will depend solely on who wins, D or R. If D and R tie, the benefit is ambiguous, but by convention, say the tie is resolved with a coin toss. Then, half the time Citizen will receive $B^D_{Citizen}$ and half the time, $B^R_{Citizen}$; thus, on average, $(B^D_{Citizen} + B^R_{Citizen})/2$. These *net* benefits if Citizen abstains from voting are summarized in the first column of Table 5.1.

Now, keeping the world exactly the same as it was before, if Citizen votes, two things change about the outcome. First and most obvious, Citizen must pay the cost of voting, c, whatever it may be. Second and less obvious, Citizen has an opportunity to change the outcome of the election and thus the benefit associated with the election. However, this opportunity is confined to two situations: (1) if the election were to be tied so that Citizen's vote would tip

TABLE 5.1
Benefit to Citizen from Abstaining or Voting in an Election

State of the World without Citizen's Vote	Net Benefit if Citizen Abstains	Net Benefit if Citizen Votes	Condition under Which Citizen Should Vote
D wins by more than 1 vote	$B^D_{Citizen}$	$B^D_{Citizen} - c$	Never
D wins by exactly 1 vote	$B^D_{Citizen}$	$B^D_{Citizen} - c$	Never
D and R tie	$(B^D_{Citizen} + B^R_{Citizen})/2$	$B^D_{Citizen} - c$	$(B^D_{Citizen} - B^R_{Citizen})/2 > c$
R wins by exactly 1 vote	$B^R_{Citizen}$	$(B^D_{Citizen} + B^R_{Citizen})/2 - c$	$(B^D_{Citizen} - B^R_{Citizen})/2 > c$
R wins by more than 1 vote	$B^R_{Citizen}$	$B^R_{Citizen} - c$	Never

the scales in D's direction and increase Citizen's benefit, since by definition $B^D_{Citizen} > (B^D_{Citizen} + B^R_{Citizen})/2$; (2) if, without that vote, candidate R would win by precisely one vote, then Citizen's vote for D would produce a tie, a tie would produce a coin toss, and on average Citizen would receive $(B^D_{Citizen} + B^R_{Citizen})/2$, which is greater than $B^R_{Citizen}$. The second column of Table 5.1 summarizes Citizen's net benefits from voting, taking into account the cost of voting in each situation and the possibility of changing the outcome in two cases.

It is clear from Table 5.1 that if *forced* to vote, Citizen would never be worse off by voting for D and, in two cases, definitely better off by voting for D. That is, if forced to vote, Citizen would pay the cost of voting regardless of the outcome; therefore, the cost of voting is irrelevant in figuring out how to cast one's ballot. In no case does voting for D make it more likely that R will win, and in two cases D is more likely to prevail.

Even here, we can glimpse the turnout problem: only if the outcome were to be tied without that vote or if R were to win by one vote would Citizen regard the vote as making a material difference. If a majority of any size already are voting for D, then one more vote for D makes the outcome no more likely nor does it grant any greater benefits to Citizen. Likewise, if a majority greater than one already is voting for R, then one more vote for D makes no difference, either.

How often will Citizen's vote be so privileged that it will make a difference in this way? How often will Citizen be pivotal? In a House district or state, the probability of a tie or a one-vote victory for the other side is virtually nil. Therefore, if we forced Citizen to vote, to a first approximation that vote would never make a difference and we would have forced the voter to bear a cost for no personal benefit.

Of course, in this thought experiment, we *are not* forcing Citizen to vote, we are asking *whether* Citizen will vote. But the logic and mode of analysis in figuring out whether someone will vote are virtually the same as the consequences of forcing Citizen to vote. If, in Table 5.1, we compare the net benefits that arise when Citizen does and does not vote, we discover a few things. First, if majorities for D or R are "sufficiently large" (meaning any majority for D or a two-vote or larger majority for R), then Citizen is made to pay a cost, c, but receives no added benefit. Second, if D and R otherwise would tie without that vote, then Citizen is better off by voting if and only if $(B^D_{Citizen} - B^R_{Citizen})/2 > c$. Intuitively, this means that Citizen is better off voting to break a tie if D and R are sufficiently different from each other to overcome the cost of voting. Third, if R would win by one vote if Citizen abstained, then Citizen also is better off voting if and only if $(B^D_{Citizen} - B^R_{Citizen})/2 > c$, with the same intuition attached.

For Citizen to vote in this world, two things must coincide: the outcome must be known to be a (virtual) tie *and* D and R must be "sufficiently" different. Even if the two candidates offer quite different visions of the future from Citizen's perspective, the chance of a tie is all but nil, hence the chance of Citizen voting is all but nil.

You may think, "That depends on Citizen's *knowing* whether the election will be a tie without that one vote. You never know the outcome of an election until all the votes are cast." True enough. It is possible to take this objection into account by specifying the subjective probability in Citizen's mind that the outcome will be a tie without that one vote. But the strength of the analysis remains unchanged: the possibility that a single vote will make a material difference in an election is limited, and hence the pull for any individual to abstain is strong.[3]

"my vote doesn't matter" ✗

This version of the investment calculus of nonvoting is distasteful to many people for many reasons. Scientifically, the theory is unsatisfying because the prediction that no one should vote flies in the face of the observation that many people do vote. Thus, the pure investment theory needs to be modified to account for the fact that many people vote. The most commonly followed path of modifying this logic was formally suggested first by Riker and Ordeshook in 1968. The Riker-Ordeshook approach relies on positing that voting itself brings satisfactions to many people. These satisfactions include

- Compliance with the ethic of voting and duties of citizenship.
- Affirmation of allegiance to the political system.
- Affirmation of a partisan preference.
- Engaging in research, deliberation, discussion, and the like.
- Affirming one's efficacy within the political system. (Riker and Ordeshook, 1968, p. 28)

Therefore, we could modify the earlier equation to read as follows:

The expected net benefit of voting = The benefit the individual receives as a consequence of the election outcome − The cost of voting + The immediate satisfaction of voting

Because the pure net benefit of voting is likely to be about 0, the expected net benefit of voting is determined primarily by the immediate satisfaction that people derive from voting.[4]

This appeal to "citizen duty" to explain voting frequently has been attacked as being ad hoc, that is, taken out of thin air to salvage a theoretical path clearly off base. Nevertheless, this reformulation can help us organize our thinking about the turnout puzzle while retaining the lens of methodological individualism. If the material benefit from voting, compared to abstaining, is likely to be negligible, then the question of turnout becomes whether the immediate satisfaction from voting exceeds the immediate cost of voting. And if the immediate satisfaction exceeds the immediate cost, then the decision to vote is more of a decision about consumption than about investment.

The study of consumer behavior is full of examples where individuals make decisions that look irrational if they are taken as long-term investment strategies but look understandable if the benefit being derived is immediate.

If cigarette-induced lung cancer is a leading cause of death in the United States, why do so many people smoke? If sugar is so bad for the teeth, why do so many people drink Coke? If football is such a mindlessly violent game, why do so many people watch it?

There is no accounting for taste. Although, at a deep philosophical level, we find it hard to explain why individuals like cigarettes or particular brands of soda pop or television shows, we know it is possible to understand *which* cigarettes, colas, and shows they will consume or *how much* they will consume, assuming people *want* to consume these things. Economists have gained ground by putting bounds around the deeper questions of consumer choice so that they can ask much simpler (yet important) questions about that choice. For instance, we may not be able to explain *why* people watch football, but we do know that more people will watch it on free, broadcast television than if they must watch it through pay-for-view cable. Price influences the quantity consumed.

In the same way we can make significant progress in predicting *who* will watch football (e.g., more seventeen-year-olds than eighty-five-year-olds, more men than women) and how many will stop watching when the cable company charges more to watch it, we also can predict who is likely to vote and how many will stop voting when the costs are raised.

Empirical research into voter turnout confirms that sometimes it appears to be an investment decision and other times it is like a consumption decision. Consider, first, evidence about investment behavior. The investment theory of turnout pins the probability of voting on the relative difference in the outcomes and the cost of voting. Evidence gleaned from public opinion surveys and other studies suggest that influences similar to these do have an impact on whether people vote.

Consider the difference between the candidates. Public opinion researchers rely on an ingenious measure, the **feeling thermometer,** to elicit a summary positive-negative evaluation about congressional candidates. The measure is called a *feeling thermometer* because the respondent is asked to rate, on a 0–100 scale (0 being "cold," 100 being "warm"), how she or he feels toward a candidate. When this is asked about the two congressional candidates in a respondent's district, the difference in the two rankings gives us a useful measure of how differently the two candidates are evaluated in the citizen's mind. Table 5.2 reports the likelihood of voting in all congressional elections from 1978 to 2004 as a function of how differently the respondent evaluated the two parties' House candidates in that district. Just over half the respondents who saw virtually no difference between the two candidates reported having voted, whereas four-fifths of those noting big differences between the two candidates voted.[5]

The most comprehensive study of voter turnout, Raymond Wolfinger and Steven Rosenstone's *Who Votes?* (1980), confirms that turnout is tied to the perceived tangible benefits one receives from the political system. The evidence they offered was not related to perceived candidate policy differences, however, but rather evidence about the relationship between the self-interest of voters and their tendency to participate in electoral politics. In particular, government employees vote at much higher rates than employees in the private economy. While government employees may have a stronger sense of civic duty than other people, what is most likely to be going on is that government employees have a greater immediate stake in the outcome of elections and hence are more willing to bear the costs of voting than voters in the private economy. Certain segments of government employees—particularly the largest segment, teachers—are well organized and therefore have effective mechanisms to encourage higher turnout. Wolfinger and Rosenstone did not separately analyze the turnout patterns of retirees, yet it is entirely plausible that the extraordinarily high turnout levels among recent retirees is due to their reliance on two mammoth government benefit programs—Social Security and Medicare—that increasingly are under scrutiny from budget cutters (Campbell 2003).

A great deal of scholarship has measured the costs of voting and their effects on voter turnout. The United States stands almost alone among democratic nations in erecting a large number of barriers between its citizens and the voting booth. Those barriers start with the overall philosophy about *who* is responsible for taking the initiative to register people to vote, citizens or the government, and end with particular laws that positively interfere with the ability of citizens to vote. In most states, citizens must take the initiative to re-register to vote when they move, however, in most other democracies, it is the responsibility of local governments to register people. Registration requirements and procedures vary from state to state and sometimes from county to county. In a highly mobile society, therefore, citizens must bear real costs, no matter how small, to find out how to register and then to do it.

TABLE 5.2
Probability of Voting as a Function of House Candidate Evaluations, 1978–2004

Difference in Feeling Thermometer Ratings	Probability of Voting for a House Candidate	Number of Observations
Small (0–10 points)	57%	3,490
Medium (11–35 points)	75%	3,094
Large (36–100 points)	80%	1,835

Note: Voting is measured by the respondent's self-report of whether she or he voted for one of the House candidates running for election in that district. The underlying "feeling thermometer" ratings ask the respondent to rate, on a 0–100 scale, how she or he "feels" toward both the Democratic and Republican candidates in the district. The difference is the absolute value of the difference in the two evaluations. Note the extreme overreport of turnout, which is typical of such survey results.

Source: Cumulative American National Election Study 1948–2004 (Version of 10/2005).

Having registered, voters have to make sure they are not removed from the voter rolls if they fail to vote in a series or elections.

In the political jurisdictions where the barriers to voting are highest, turnout tends to be lowest. Earlier research by Rosenstone and Wolfinger (1978) showed a statistical relationship between lower voter turnout in the 1972 election and the condition of voter registration laws in the states. States that kept their registration books open until election day was imminent, mandated that election offices be open forty hours per week, required that election offices be open evenings and weekends, and allowed absentee registration had higher turnout than states that did the opposite. From their statistical estimates Rosenstone and Wolfinger predicted that voter registration laws alone reduced turnout in the 1972 election by over 9 percentage points.

In 1993, Congress passed the National Voter Registration Act (NVRA), popularly referred to as the "motor voter" law because it mandated states to institute systems of mail-in registration and make registration forms available in a wide range of government offices, including driver's license offices. An insufficient number of national elections (i.e., two) has occurred since the passage of the motor voter law to draw any firm conclusions about the long-term effect of making voter registration more accessible to citizens. Knack's (1995) study of the effects of state-level "motor voter" laws discovered that it took about five years for the full effect of the laws to be felt and that, in steady state, the laws increased registration levels by about 10 percentage points overall (cf. Highton and Wolfinger 1998). Subsequent research has concluded that the NVRA definitely increased *registration* but did not increase turnout (Brown and Wedeking 2006).

If turnout is like an investment decision, then anything that raises the electoral benefit or lowers the voting cost should increase voter turnout. One reason political reformers supported passage of the motor voter law was that they wanted to lower the cost of voting and thus boost turnout. Congressional candidates, on the other hand, have mixed incentives as far as stimulating overall turnout is concerned—they want to maximize turnout among supporters while minimizing it among opponents. Candidates seem to respond to the net cost of the voting equation by trying to lower the cost of voting to their supporters rather than trying to raise it for their opponents. Efforts to bring supporters to the polls, called *get-out-the-vote* (GOTV) drives, range from simply calling supporters on election day and reminding them to vote to rounding up supporters and delivering them physically to the polls. (Gerber and Green 2000, 2005). In some cases, it may be possible to demobilize voters by attacking one's opponents, in a strategy termed *going negative* (Ansolabehere and Iyengar 1995).

When elections are predicted to be close, candidates invest more time and effort into GOTV activities, since the added effort is more likely to be pivotal. The payoff to GOTV activities in close races is illustrated in Figure 5.3, which graphs turnout in House elections in 2006 and 2008 against the resulting percentage of the vote received by the winner in each race. Note that even in 2008, when a surge of turnout was generated by the presidential

FIGURE 5.3
Turnout and Winning Percentage of the Vote, House Elections, 2006 and 2008

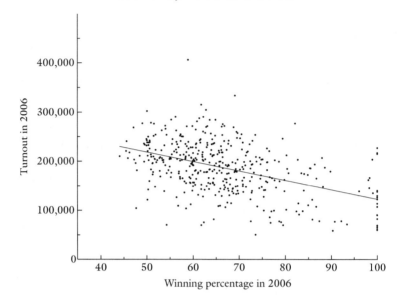

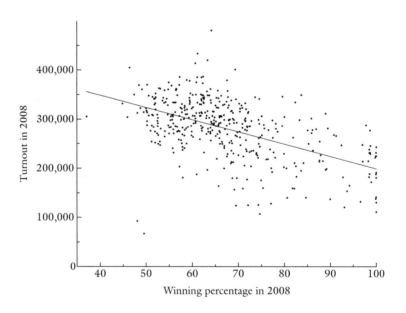

election, there still was a negative correlation between turnout and the winning percentage. Of course, these two graphs also demonstrate a great deal of variability in turnout across House districts, and therefore closeness is not the only influence on turnout levels. Still, closeness counts for something in turnout, as it does with hand grenades (Cox and Munger 1989).[6]

In examining barriers to voting imposed by voter registration laws and attempts to overcome those barriers undertaken by candidates, we treat the costs of voting as a concern largely beyond the control of the voter. Certainly all voters are not alike. Some can more easily overcome these costs; for others, the costs identified are not as great.

For instance, better-educated, higher-income citizens are more likely to vote than poorly educated, lower-income ones. In their exhaustive study of voting in the 1972 election, Wolfinger and Rosenstone (1980) reported that 53 percent of respondents to a Census Bureau survey who had not graduated from high school reported voting, 69 percent of high school graduates voted, and 83 percent of those who at least had some college turned out. Likewise, voter participation ranged from 46 percent in their lowest-income category to 86 percent in the highest-income category.

Well-educated, high-income individuals have advantages over others that aid them in overcoming the costs of voting. Most important, they *know* how to participate in democratic politics. At the same time, people with higher education and income levels have more flexibility with their lives, and thus participation in politics exacts lower opportunity costs.

One puzzle about the relationship between education and voter turnout emerges within the rational choice framework, however. Wolfinger and Rosenstone also report that highly educated citizens express greater affinity to democratic symbols and more of a sense that their participation makes a difference in the political system. Silver, Anderson, and Abramson (1986) also found that survey respondents who report that they voted when they in fact did not tended to be better educated. What is puzzling is that education *should* demystify the political system, so that well-educated citizens should be aware of the implications of the Riker-Ordeshook logic of nonvoting. That the world seems to operate in the opposite direction is probably testimony to the strong socializing (and conservative) goals of civics education in the United States.

An important, and nonobvious, contributor to nonvoting that Wolfinger and Rosenstone reported was the high levels of mobility among Americans. When people move, they are required to bear the cost of registering and figuring out local election laws and politics yet again. Long-time residents of a community already have paid many of the costs of participating politically.

The idea of a consumption side of the turnout equation requires us to consider the link between a person's interest in politics, however it comes about, and the tendency to vote. At the most cursory level, there clearly is a link between an interest in politics and voting. For instance, in 2006, 91 percent of respondents to the Cooperative Congressional Election Study who reported they were "very much" interested in politics and current affairs voted in the congressional election; only 45 percent of respondents who were "not much" interested voted.

The Riker-Ordeshook argument requires us to examine a particular link between an interest in politics and voting—the link that runs from a sense of civic duty to the act of voting. Do some citizens reap a psychic reward for voting that transcends the long-term material benefit they derive? The psychic reward phenomenon is a little more difficult to demonstrate directly, since no national polls regularly ask people whether voting itself makes them "feel good." However, if such a thing as psychic reward is associated with voting, that reward also probably is associated with things such as a person's feelings about patriotism, national symbols, and the government. People who are more patriotic than others, value national symbols such as the flag more than others, and trust the government to do the right thing more than others are likely to derive greater pleasure from voting than are others, as well.

Table 5.3 shows how voting in the 2002 congressional election correlated with answers to questions intended to capture feelings of these sorts. In general, people who believed government was not too complicated, reported a strong love of country, and experienced an extremely good feeling when they saw the American flag, voted at higher rates than people who expressed opposite feelings.

The effects of nonvoting

Does it matter that some vote and not others? Like many questions in the social sciences, this question has an easy answer that dissolves under close scrutiny. The easy answer is that it must matter that some people vote and others do not, since voters and nonvoters are dissimilar. If people with more education, higher income, and greater social stability are more likely to vote, should that not bias elections in a conservative direction?

While it is certainly true that the electorate (i.e., those who turn out to vote) is slightly more conservative than the general adult population, research aimed at gauging the effects of this bias largely has come up empty. Wolfinger and Rosenstone's (1980) analysis of voting in the 1972 election estimated that, on net, turnout patterns gave the Republican party a boost of a couple of percentage points nationwide. Voters and nonvoters are different, but not *that* different, from one another.

Research by James DeNardo (1980) suggests another reason that differential rates of turnout in congressional elections may not bias outcomes in a conservative direction. As already suggested, turnout rates vary in two ways: reasons particular to individuals (through education, income, interest in politics, etc.) and reasons particular to specific election campaigns (how close they are, how active the candidates are, etc.). For nearly half a century, the Democratic Party was the majority party as far as composition of Congress was concerned. This means that naturally there were more Democratic districts in which incumbents were relatively safe (i.e., won by large margins) than Repub-

TABLE 5.3
Relationship between Attitudes toward the United States and Voting Turnout in the 2002 Congressional Election

Question: How do you feel . . . when you see the American flag flying?

	Percent Voting
Extremely good	65
Very good	61
Somewhat good	59
Not very good	54

Question: How strong is your love of country?

	Percent Voting
Extremely strong	67
Very strong	61
Somewhat strong	46
Not very strong	43

Source: 2002 American National Election Study.

lican districts. This balance of power produced relatively more districts in which Republicans ran poor candidates, drawing fewer Republican voters to the polls. Thus, although demographic characteristics tended to advantage conservative Republican voters in terms of turnout, the nature of electoral competition in congressional districts tended to advantage Democrats.

Of course, with the success of Republicans in House elections over the past two decades, this countervailing Democratic advantage in turnout may have ended. The general point remains, however: demographics are not the only factor causing variations in turnout rates. The candidates themselves contribute significantly to these variations, and ofttimes they contribute in ways that counteract "natural" demographic factors.

Another way to focus the question about the effects of voter turnout in congressional elections is to ask about the different electorates in on- and off-year elections. In the 1950s and 1960s, scholars coined a phrase to describe the difference in presidential- and nonpresidential-year elections: **surge and decline** (Campbell 1966). The idea behind identifying the surge-and-decline phenomenon was to point out that the electorate in presidential years included many people who usually were not very interested in politics, who surged into the electorate in response to the unusually high level of political information surrounding the presidential election but were absent two years hence in the off-year congressional election. Because the hard core of voters, who participated in both off- and on-year elections, appeared to be stable in its political attitudes, it was concluded that volatility in congressional elections from election to election was due to the fickleness of citizens who voted only in presidential years.

More recent scholarship has demonstrated that the earlier conjecture was largely incorrect. While the added increment to the electorate in presidential years is composed of voters who are different from the hard-core base, again the differences are not so great as to account for the great swings that occur from election to election. Therefore, the regular midterm loss of seats to the president's party is not due directly to the ebb and flow of turnout.

Saying that fluctuating turnout at the national level from election to election has little effect on aggregate election outcomes is not the same as saying that fluctuating turnout in individual districts has no effect on outcomes. Indeed, it does. Safe incumbents tend to win in low-turnout elections, which leaves a pool of unmobilized voters in most districts who are ripe for the picking by the "right" challenger. Closely contested races tend to be high-turnout affairs. Yet when we survey all 435 House elections and the 33 or 34 Senate elections, we see that sometimes the turnout surge induced by a hot challenger helps the Republican candidate, other times the Democrat; sometimes a liberal and sometimes a conservative. Therefore, the surge-and-decline effect that we should be more aware of when we examine individual congressional districts is one that is independent of the ebb and flow of presidential politics per se.

Deciding Whom to Support

Among those who vote in congressional elections, how do they choose among the alternatives? The theory of public choice provides two general answers to this question, for which there is ample supporting evidence. The first answer is that voters should support candidates ideologically similar to them and oppose candidates ideologically dissimilar. This is no more than a restatement and application of the Downsian spatial model. The second answer is that regardless of the criteria voters use to make up their minds, those criteria should be easy to use, since a hard-to-use criterion would simply discourage citizens from voting altogether. Both answers point toward two significant explanations for voting behavior in congressional elections: ideology and party identification.

Ideology

Ever since the French Revolution, much of Western politics has been summarized along a left-right continuum. In the United States, this divide is often relabeled *liberal and conservative*. Whatever we call it, allusion to politics occurring along a dimension should alert us to a spatial explanation for voting in congressional elections. If the spatial model is at all relevant in explaining voting in congressional elections, liberal citizens should support liberal candidates, conservative citizens should support conservative candidates.

Evidence taken from the 2006 congressional election is typical of all public opinion research on the subject of **ideology**: When voters can identify themselves and the House candidates with an ideological label, they in fact vote for the candidate whose ideology more closely aligns with their own. In the case of the 2006 election, respondents were asked to place themselves on a 101-point scale, with 100 indicating they were very conservative and 0 indicating they were very liberal. Respondents were also asked to rate the Democratic and Republican House candidates on this same scale. Of those who rated the Republican as being ideologically closer, 84 percent voted for the Republican candidate; 86 percent of those who rated the Democratic as being ideologically closer voted for the Democrat. (Virtually no voters rated themselves equally close to both candidates.)

One implication of the Downsian spatial model of candidate competition examined in Chapter 1 was that candidates should converge toward each other and toward the median of the electorate. If there is evidence that voters support ideologically compatible candidates, is there also evidence that candidates converge to the center? Here, data limitations hinder our ability to draw strong conclusions. Public opinion researchers have rarely administered the same survey instruments to samples of voters and candidates, and therefore we have little direct evidence about whether both candidates in congressional races converge to each other and to the median voter. In the 1990s a citizens group began to query all congressional candidates—incumbents and challengers, winners and losers—about their issue stances. This group, Project VoteSmart, has made the results of these surveys available to average citizens, but researchers have used responses to these surveys to study candidate convergence (see Erikson and Wright 1997; Ansolabehere et al. 2000b).[7] We have always known that liberal constituencies tend to elect liberal members of Congress and vice versa. Now, however, we also know that the correlation of the ideology of the *losing* candidate with the district she or he runs in is very low and that candidate convergence is rare. Convergence happens in those relatively unusual situations where district partisanship already is closely split.[8]

Party identification

There is some evidence that the Downsian ideological proximity model works in explaining the decisions of congressional voters. Yet there is at least one problem with the evidence: the model works among voters who know the ideology of the candidates and can place themselves ideologically. However, many people refuse to describe themselves in ideological terms and even more are unable to describe the ideological disposition of congressional candidates. Still, many of these people vote. On what basis do they make up their minds?

The party membership of the candidates is a highly reliable voting cue for voters who eschew an overtly ideological evaluation of the candidates. It is a cue entirely consistent with the Downsian spatial voting model, since Democrats tend to be liberal and Republicans tend to be conservative.[9] It is highly reliable in at least three senses: (1) all congressional candidates are identified by their party membership on the ballot, (2) most voters align themselves with one of the two major parties, and (3) party labels, of voters and candidates, tend to be stable over time. Therefore, a busy electorate may be able to proxy its ideological leanings by relying on party as a voting cue.

In 2006, 90 percent of self-described Democrats and 87 percent of Republicans voted for congressional candidates of their own parties. This degree of party loyalty has not always attended congressional elections. Figure 5.4 shows the percentage of voters in House and Senate elections whose votes were consistent with their **party identification**. The degree of party loyalty among congressional voters declined during the 1960s and 1970s, leveling off in the 1980s. However, since the early 1990s, the degree of party loyalty in congressional (and presidential) elections has grown to a level unprecedented in the history of public opinion polling on the question. (Also see Bartels 2000.)

Even so, a factor that continues to limit the importance of party in congressional elections has been the decline in the percentage of voters identifying with one of the two political parties (see Figure 5.5). In the 1960s and

FIGURE 5.4
Party Line Voters among All Voters, 1952–2008

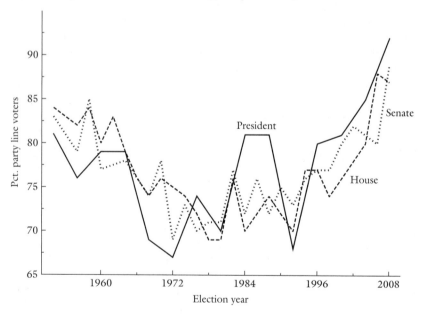

Source: Ornstein, Mann, and Malbin (2008, Table 2-19); American National Election Study (1952 and 2008 data); Cooperative Congressional Election Study (2006 data).

FIGURE 5.5
Percentage of Survey Respondents Declining a Party Label, 1952–2008

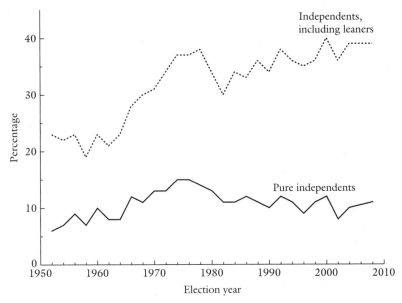

Source: Stanley and Niemi (2010).

1970s particularly, the percentage of voters who called themselves *independents* grew substantially. In the 1980s, the decline of partisan identification reversed course, so that now the documentation of the continued growth of independents depends on how one chooses to measure them. If you take people at their word and classify people who initially call themselves *independent* as independents, then the number of independents has started creeping up again. (This is the dotted line in Figure 5.5.) If you give people who call themselves independents a chance to say which party they usually support and take the residual of "pure" independents as your measure of independence, then the number of independents has been flat since the 1980s.[10] In any case, to the extent voters eschew party labels, they will have fewer obvious and commonly shared cues on which to base their voting decisions. Since party identification in recent years is at a lower level than it was immediately after World War II, this suggests that voters may not be able to exercise informed judgments about congressional candidates like they once could.

Because partisanship and ideology are so closely linked, it is natural to ask whether the effects of partisanship remain after controlling for ideology and vice versa. The answer to this question is yes, the effects of ideological proximity remain after controlling for partisanship and vice versa. Representative

TABLE 5.4
Party and Ideological Distance as Explanatory Factors in 2010 House Elections

| | Ideologically Closer To | | | |
Party Identification	Democrat	Don't Know	Neither	Republican
Democrat	97%	94%	87%	65%
	(4,994)	(7,484)	(787)	(513)
Independent	89%	45%	50%	5%
	(1,710)	(5,011)	(566)	(3,310)
Republican	43%	6%	21%	2%
	(252)	(5,926)	(453)	(6,087)

Note: Entries in cells are the percentage of respondents reporting they voted for the Democratic candidate for the House. Numbers in parentheses are the number of observations on which the percentages are based. Independents leaning toward one of the parties are grouped with that party. "Don't Know" respondents on the ideological dimension are respondents who could not place both candidates and themselves on the ideological scale.

Source: Cooperative Congressional Election Study, 2010.

results are reported in Table 5.4, showing the percentage of respondents to the 2010 Cooperative Congressional Election Study who voted for the Democratic House candidate as a function of their ideological proximity to the candidates and their party identification. Looking across all the rows, we see that, within partisan categories, voters were more likely to stay loyal to their party's candidate when that candidate agreed with the voter ideologically. For instance, Democratic identifiers who were ideologically closer to the Democratic candidate supported the Democrat 97 percent of the time, whereas they supported the Democrat only 65 percent of the time if they were ideologically closer to the Republican candidate. Looking down each column, we see that within ideological proximity categories, Democratic self-identifiers were more likely to vote for Democrats than were Republican identifiers. For instance, among those for whom the Republican was ideologically closer than the Democrat, 98 percent of the Republican identifiers supported the Republican candidate, whereas only 35 percent of the Democrats supported the Republican candidate, despite the Republican being ideologically closer.

Therefore, most of the time ideological proximity and partisan self-identification work together in the minds of voters. When ideology and partisanship work at cross-purposes, some voters opt for the partisan options, while others opt for ideological congruence. Either way, by relying on partisanship and ideology, voters can choose candidates who agree with them without investing too much effort in knowing the details of how candidates stand on particular issues.

The Problem of Multiple Constituencies:
Primaries *versus* the General Election

The focus of this chapter has been on the general election. This is appropriate, since the greatest competition for congressional seats typically is in
the general election, in which the Democratic nominee faces off against the
Republican nominee, plus a loose collection of "third party" nominees. An
incumbent running for reelection rarely faces serious opposition for renomination. Primary contests for the opposition party rarely are hotly contested,
either.

In the roughly 10 percent of cases where the congressional seat has become
open, more candidates are likely to file in an attempt to obtain their party's
nomination. In those cases, at least one, and possibly two, hot congressional
nomination battles are likely to occur in the district.

Unfortunately, neither the theoretical nor empirical literature about congressional elections help us very much in understanding primary elections.
One of the two most important voting cues in the general election—party
identification—is obviously missing in a nomination primary. Furthermore,
the ideological space is truncated within the two parties, making it difficult
both for candidates to distinguish themselves ideologically and for voters to
base their choices on ideology.

Therefore, while nomination battles generate much heat, little light is shed
on the candidates by which the average adherent of a party might make an
informed choice. Not surprisingly, then, primaries typically are low-turnout
affairs. Just how low is difficult to say, due to less centralized reporting of
election results for primaries than for general elections. Data reported by the
Center for the Study of the American Electorate (CSAE) illustrates how low
turnout is likely to be in primaries, compared to the general election. In 2010,
for instance, 29 million voters are estimated to have participated in statewide
party primaries that would have chosen nominees for House races. Keep in
mind that many of the voters participating in these primaries would not have
had a meaningful vote to cast for the congressional nominees because party
nominations when a incumbent is running for reelection are rarely contested.
Therefore, this 29 million figure is a generous estimate of turnout in congressional primaries. Contrast that with the estimate that 91 million people voted
in the general election, a number more than three times the primary turnout.
While this 91 million figure is also a bit of an overestimate, because of the
frequent lack of challengers when incumbents are running for reelection, it is
much less of an overestimate than the primary number. Therefore, the primary
electorate in 2010 was *at most* only one-third that of the general electorate,
a typical pattern for recent years.[11]

These prefatory comments about primaries suggests some generalizations
that we can make about the contrast between the primary and the general
electorates. The first is about turnout. Just as turnout in general elections

fluctuates as a function of the closeness of the race, so does turnout in primaries. Another factor influences turnout in primaries: when the nomination
"means something," turnout is likely to be up, too. Nominations are likely
to be "meaningful" when there is a chance that the nominee might win the
general election, either by defeating the incumbent from the other party or
winning an open seat election. As with general elections, the higher turnout
in meaningful primaries is partly due to voters believing their votes will
count more, but it is mostly a result of candidates and their backers putting
extra effort into turning out their supporters.

The second important point about primaries concerns the composition of
the respective electorates. It is trivial to point out that the primary electorates
are smaller than the general electorates, since primary electorates are by definition subsets of general electorates. But dividing the electorate into partisan
subsets does more than simply cut the general electorate in two. First, a certain fraction of the electorate does not identify with one of the political parties, so depending on the particular laws in each state and the willingness of
people to register for a party of which they are not particularly fond, roughly
one-third of the citizenry (i.e., the Independents) are excluded from the primary process by its very nature.[12]

By this fact alone the primary electorate is more ideologically polarized than
the general electorate.

Adding to the mechanical polarization of the electorate that primaries
produce, voters in primaries tend to be ideologically extreme, both from the
perspective of the entire electorate *and* from the perspective of co-partisans.
That is, voters in Democratic primaries tend to be more liberal than Democrats generally; Republicans who vote in primaries tend to be more conservative than Republicans generally.

This pattern is easily interpreted within the cost-benefit analysis of voting
that we examined early in this chapter. Primaries generally are low-information
affairs for the general population, in which the easiest voting cues are unavail-
able. Therefore, it may make no sense for an individual only casually interested in politics to vote. People with ideologically extreme views tend to
intrinsically enjoy politics more than moderates and be disposed already
to gather the information necessary to participate in primaries.

A glimpse of this pattern is presented in Table 5.5, which summarizes the
ideological disposition of citizens in 2010, broken down according to their
interest in news and public affairs. Among those who expressed interest in
public affairs "most of the time," 43 percent placed themselves in one of the
two extreme ideological categories, compared to 16% who expressed interest
"hardly at all." Probably most telling of all, among those who expressed the
most interest in public affairs, only about one in twenty could not place
themselves on the seven-point ideological scale, compared to over one-fifth
of those who expressed the least interest in politics.

The research done on the characteristics of primary electorates compared to general electorates principally focuses on *presidential* elections. Yet

TABLE 5.5
Ideological Extremity of Citizens in 2010,
by Interest in Public Affairs

Interest in Public Affairs	Very Liberal or Very Conservative	Somewhat Liberal or Somewhat Conservative	Moderate	No Answer to Ideology Self-Placement
Most of the time	43%	33%	22%	2%
Some of the time	19%	37%	38%	6%
Only now and then	16%	28%	44%	12%
Hardly at all	16%	23%	38%	23%

Note: Percentages should be read across the rows. For instance, 19 percent of those who were very interested in politics and public affairs in 2006 were either very liberal or very conservative, 42 percent were somewhat liberal or conservative, 37 percent were moderate, and 2 percent did not answer the ideological self-placement question. Percentages do not add to 100 percent because of rounding.

Source: 2010 Cooperative Congressional Election Study.

because presidential primaries often are held concurrently with congressional primaries and in any case appeal to the same people, it is likely that we make few mistakes in generalizing from presidential elections to congressional elections on this topic.

If primary electorates are more ideologically extreme than the general population, it is natural to ask whether this has an effect on the types of candidates nominated for Congress. A simple application of the Downsian model might suggest that candidates vying for a party's nomination in a primary would aim their ideological appeals to the median of the candidates' *party*. If the parties are divided on the left and the right, then the resulting nominees from each party will tend to be ideologically divergent. This is a direct contradiction of the plain vanilla Downsian model, which predicts that candidates who face off in a general election will converge ideologically. At the same time, primary voters tend to be fairly politically sophisticated and often recognize the value of picking a moderate nominee to better compete in the general election. No direct empirical research focuses on this point in congressional primaries, but research about the behavior of partisan elites in the presidential nomination process suggests that voters in presidential primaries are willing to trade off the ideological purity of the candidates they support for their electability in the general election.

By ending this chapter with a discussion of primary electorates, we emphasize one frequently overlooked feature of congressional elections: members of Congress must respond to different constituencies, just as different constituencies may respond differently to them.

In *Home Style*, Richard Fenno (1978) examined the interaction between incumbent members of the House and their constituencies and discovered that

<h3 style="text-align:center">Figure 5.6
Nested Constituencies as Seen by the Incumbent</h3>

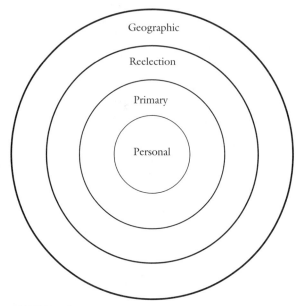

Source: Fenno (1978).

MCs tended to think of four nested constituencies when they considered their districts (see Figure 5.6). The **geographic constituency** is the legally defined constituency within the bounds of the district. The member is supposed to represent this population, but it is so heterogeneous that to think of it as an undifferentiated mass is rarely useful. Nested inside the geographic constituency is the **reelection constituency**. This is the group of voters that the incumbent relies on in the general election. The group often is a heterogeneous collection of voters, some of whom may be from the other party, that over the years the incumbent has cultivated and expanded.

Burrowing down another level is the **primary constituency,** the core of voters the incumbent relies on year in and year out. It may be the constituency that actually turns out in the party primary to (re)nominate the candidate, but its most important characteristic is its core nature. This is the constituency that defines who the candidate is and is unlikely to change much from election to election. Finally, there is the group of family, friends, and close associates who constitute the **personal constituency.** The incumbent can rely on them to give sage political advice and keep the candidate in tune with important developments in the district.

As we burrow down into this nested set of constituencies, we come upon collections of potential voters who evaluate congressional candidates differently. The personal and primary constituencies have the most information about the candidate and are likely to provide the most loyal support. The reelection constituency is more likely to be fickle, being composed of many people who need to be reacquainted with the candidate each two or six years. Because much of the reelection constituency is politically inattentive most of the time, the candidate works hardest to maintain and expand this group. The danger, of course, comes in trying to expand into new constituencies while maintaining the support of the primary supporters. As mentioned before, primary constituents tend to be more politically sophisticated than most voters and therefore appreciate the need for candidates to reach to the district mainstream to shore up political support. Still, the need to keep the primary constituents onboard always provides a constraint on the political flexibility of incumbents.

Summary

In this chapter, we examined the world of congressional elections, mostly through the eyes of voters. The most puzzling aspect of voting in congressional elections is the decision to vote at all. Voting is irrational, if we consider it to be a narrowly self-interested act of material investment. It is clear, however, that many citizens derive pleasure, for whatever reason, from the simple act of voting. This pleasure undoubtedly is the fundamental reason millions of Americans go to the polls every other year to choose Congress. Even though the great mass of congressional voters views politics as a type of consumption behavior, examining the self-interested calculations of voters is helpful in understanding why turnout fluctuates, across districts and from year to year. Turnout in a district is likely to fluctuate, for instance, as the two candidates are more or less ideologically distinct or the contest itself is more or less competitive.

Having decided whether to vote rather than abstain, American voters use two powerful and stable decision rules to help them decide whom to support. The first is ideology, or the practice of simplifying political life into liberal-conservative, left-right terms. The second is party identification, which is a standing decision to support a political party's candidates based on a variety of past factors, including early life socialization and the later life assessment of the parties' competence. Ideology and party identification easily are incorporated into the theory of spatial voting, and utility maximizing more generally.

In this and the previous chapter, we emphasized electoral factors associated with the individual participants in the voting arena: the candidates and the voters. In the next chapter, we step away from the personalities involved, exploring how the regulation of the electoral playing field affects contests for Congress.

Further Reading

Ansolabehere, Stephen, and Shanto Iyengar. 1995. *Going Negative*. New York: Macmillan.

Campbell, Angus. 1966. "Surge and Decline: A Study of Electoral Change." In *Elections and the Political Order*, edited by Angus Campbell, Phillip E. Converse, Warren E. Miller, and Donald E. Stokes. New York: Wiley.

Downs, Anthony. 1957. *An Economic Theory of Democracy*. New York: Harper and Row.

Erikson, Robert S., and Gerald C. Wright, Jr. 1997. "Voters, Candidates, and Issues in Congressional Elections." In *Congress Reconsidered*, 6th ed., edited by Lawrence C. Dodd and Bruce I. Oppenheimer. Washington, D.C.: Congressional Quarterly Press.

Feddersen, Timothy J. 2004. "Rational Choice Theory and the Paradox of Not Voting." *Journal of Economic Perspectives* 18: 99–112.

Ferejohn, John A., and Morris P. Fiorina. 1974. "The Paradox of Not Voting: A Decision Theoretic Analysis." *American Political Science Review* 68: 525–36.

Green, Donald P., and Alan S. Gerber. 2008. *Get Out the Vote: How to Increase Voter Turnout*, 2nd ed. Washington, D.C.: Brookings Institution Press.

———. 2009. *Politics of Congressional Elections*, 7th ed. New York: Pearson.

Miller, Warren E., and Donald E. Stokes. 1963. "Constituency Influence in Congress." *American Political Science Review* 57: 45–56.

Riker, William H. and Peter Ordeshook. 1968. "A Theory of the Calculus of Voting." *American Political Science Review* 62: 25–42.

Rosenstone, Steven, and John Mark Hansen. 1993. *Mobilization, Participation, and Democracy in America*. New York: Macmillan.

Wolfinger, Raymond, and Steven Rosenstone. 1980. *Who Votes?* New Haven, Conn.: Yale University Press.

SUMMARY OF KEY CONCEPTS

1. An **on-year election** is a congressional election held the same year as a presidential election.
2. An **off-year** or **midterm election** is a congressional election held in the even numbered year between presidential elections.
3. The **voting age population** (VAP) is the number of residents in a given geographic jurisdiction who are eligible to vote by virtue of age, approximately equal to the number of citizens eighteen years of age and older.

4. A **feeling thermometer** is a device used in survey research to gauge how positively respondents regard political notables and groups. It is calibrated so that the "coolest" feelings are recorded as 0 and the "hottest" feelings are recorded as 100; respondents are allowed to give any response in that range.

5. **Surge and decline** describes a regularity in voter turnout, in which the electorate is large ("surges") in on-year elections and smaller ("declines") in midterm elections.

6. **Ideology** is the integrated assertions, theories, and concepts that constitute one's political beliefs. Political actors use this to simplify complicated political positions and ideas. In the United States, it is seen in the application of labels such as *liberal* and *conservative* to individuals who hold particular views about the economy and social policy.

7. **Party identification** refers to the tendency of citizens to express a political allegiance to a political party. A voter's party identification is the strongest predictor of whom he or she will support in an election.

8. An **open primary** is a nominating election in which members of either political party, or independents, may participate.

9. A **closed primary** is a nominating election in which only party members may participate.

10. A representative's **geographic constituency** is defined by law, consisting of all residents of a district.

11. The **reelection constituency** are the voters a representative relies on for support in the general election.

12. The **primary constituency** are the voters a representative considers his or her core supporters among the mass public, usually the voters he or she relies on to retain the party nomination.

13. The **personal constituency** are a representative's close associates in a district who provide his or her most candid political advice and enduring political support.

PROBLEMS

The following questions are intended to help you explore patterns of electoral support for members of Congress—in this case, senators. They ask you to perform some very basic statistical analysis. They can be approached using a spreadsheet program, such as Microsoft Excel, although you can also use a statistical package (SPSS, Stata, SAS, etc.) if you are comfortable using one.

Download the dataset containing Senate election data by visiting the following URL: http://www.mit.edu/~17.251/acdata.html. Keep the data that pertain to one state, presumably your home state. Graph the relationship between the percentage vote share received by the Democratic candidate in the most recent Senate election in your state against each demographic variable in the dataset. (In Excel, this involves inserting a series of scatter charts into the spreadsheet.) If you would like, insert a linear trend line into each chart. Write a short analysis (2–3 pages) of the patterns you observe in these graphs, attempting to address the following questions:

1. Which groups supported the Democrat, and which did not? (In other words, do the votes for the Democrat rise or fall as the demographic variable rises?)

2. Focusing on the relationship between the Senate vote share and the variable that measures average support for Democratic presidential candidates, did the Democratic candidate for Senate tend to over- or underperform Democratic candidates for president? Are there any counties that appear to be outliers?

3. Redo the previous set of charts, this time examining the vote share for the Democratic candidate who ran before the most recent election. (For instance, if the most recent Senate election in your state was in 2010, then the election referred to here was either in 2008 or 2006, depending on which seat class the state belongs to.) Are the overall patterns of support for the two Democratic candidates the same?

Note: You may also do this analysis from the perspective of Republican candidates. If you do, make sure you approach all three questions from the perspective of the same political party.

NOTES

1. The reader is cautioned about the slipperiness of turnout statistics. The measure of voter turnout that most academic researchers and the Census Bureau use takes as the denominator the number of individuals who are *eligible* to vote, whether they have registered or not. The population of eligible voters is called the **voting age population** (VAP). Some researchers have begun adjusting VAP by removing estimates of the ineligible population—felons, aliens—to create an estimate of the voting *eligible* population (VEP). All turnout rates discussed in this chapter are in terms of VAP. Local officials and secretaries of state, always eager to demonstrate the democratic fervor of their state and local populations, tend to report a less-revealing statistic: turnout as a percentage of *registered voters*. Of course, turnout as a percentage of registered voters always will be higher than turnout as a percentage of the voting age population. Because voter registration (until recently) was a high hurdle in many states, someone who registered at all demonstrated a commitment to vote. Therefore, the difference between the two turnout statistics was sometimes quite high. For instance, turnout in the 2008 presidential election in Massachusetts was 60 percent of its VAP. Turnout as a percentage of registered voters was a whopping 72 percent.
2. The intellectual history of the calculus of nonvoting is long and rich. The pages that follow are a composite of arguments that appear across three decades of

scholarship. For the reader interested in exploring this topic in detail, the best place to start is with Downs (1957). Riker and Ordeshook (1968) extended the Downsian argument, paying attention to the role that "citizen duty" pays in encouraging citizens to vote. Rosenstone and Hansen (1993) is the best empirical analysis of voter turnout to date.

3. At the risk of piling on, we add the following feature onto congressional elections to make a prediction of abstention virtually guaranteed: keep in mind that congressional elections involve electing hundreds of legislators to go to the capital and act in concert to produce policy. A congressional voter gets to vote in only one of hundreds of legislative elections. Even if a citizen in a congressional district could vote to break a tie in that district, it is unlikely that the legislator so elected would turn around and vote to break a tie in the legislature. Therefore, not only is a single voter virtually never pivotal in a district but that vote is even less often pivotal in determining the overall complexion of the legislature.

4. Ferejohn and Fiorina (1974) provide an alternative way to think about why rational people would vote, by applying the "minimax regret" criterion to the decision to vote.

5. The most striking thing about Table 5.2 may be the massive overreporting of voting implied in the tables. Turnout rates derived from surveys always overestimate actual turnout, as many nonvoters do not wish to appear to be bad citizens.

6. The lines drawn in each of the two graphs in Figure 5.3 represent the results of a linear regression in which the dependent variable was turnout and the independent variable was the winning percentage. Here are the full results of those regressions (standard errors in parentheses):

	2006	*2008*
Intercept	314,616	448,351
	(12,240)	(13,358)
Winning percent	−1,919	−2,494
	(181)	(195)
r^2	.21	.28

Hence, each 1 percent increase in winning percentage was associated with an average turnout drop of 1,919 in 2006 and 2,494 in 2008, compared to average turnouts in these two years of 186,991 and 280,348.

7. Project VoteSmart's Web site is www.votesmart.org.

8. The classic study of the relationship between the policy preferences of constituents, compared to congressional candidates is by Miller and Stokes (1963). Achen (1978) provides a major critique of this study.

9. This consistency has grown over time, as the conservative southern Democratic wing of that party has disappeared and the remaining southern Democrats have become more like northern Democrats. Yet even in the era when there was a large conservative wing in the Democratic Party, the party label was consistent in this sense: southern Democrats tended to be more liberal (or at least less conservative) than southern Republicans. So long as voters confine their choices to the candidates before them, we can be less concerned about the heterogeneity of the parties at the national level.

10. One may ask why we would want to push survey respondents who initially call themselves *independents* into one of the partisan categories, then treat these "leaning independents" as partisans. The most common justification for treating leaning independents as partisans is that they tend to behave like partisans.

It is likely that many people who are identified as "Independent Republicans" and "Independent Democrats" are averse to identifying with one of the parties because of a personal aversion to political parties and not to an aversion to the ideas that the parties espouse.

11. The URL for the CSAE Web site is http://www1.american.edu/ia/cdem/csae/. The turnout figure for the 2010 general election was taken from the United States Election Project, http://elections.gmu.edu/Turnout_2010G.html.

12. Some states allow anyone to vote in a party's primary—these are so-called **open primary** states, such as Wisconsin. A **closed primary** is one in which participation is restricted to voters who are registered as members of that party. Research has found very little cross-party voting in open primary states, as there is very little voting among pure independents.

6

Regulating Elections

I n the spring of 1993, President Clinton backed down from one of the most divisive issues of his young presidency, the nomination of Lani Guinier to head the civil rights division of the Justice Department. Even though the job of the civil rights division is to step into the middle of racially based controversies, the nominee to head this division has rarely rated attention on the front page of the newspapers. What, then, made Guinier objectionable to enough senators that Clinton was forced to abandon his friend's nomination?

Guinier's nomination inspired a firestorm of protest because of her legal writings about how legislatures are elected and organized in the United States (Guinier 1989, 1991a, 1991b, 1995). In the matter of elections, she argued that the American tradition of electing members of legislatures through single-member districts severely disadvanged racial minority candidates. As a remedy for this bias, she advocated a variant of **proportional representation**, called **cumulative voting.**[1]

The senatorial attack on Lani Guinier highlighted, at least for a moment, the regulation of congressional elections. Regardless of how one evaluates the particulars of Guinier's arguments, in one important respect she was right and her senatorial adversaries were wrong. She was right in noting that no way of electing a legislature (or even organizing one) is neutral. Choices must be made about how to structure electoral competition, including how to group candidates into districts, if districts are used at all. While it is difficult to structure electoral competition for Congress to resist popular tidal waves, the details of the electoral system certainly influence the details of representation, including precisely how large the majority will be, how vigorously elections will be contested, and what will be the precise racial, sexual, or ideological composition of Congress.

Ironically, at the same time many senators were attacking Lani Guinier for her supposed support of manipulating the electoral system in favor of racial minorities, the Senate was considering campaign finance reform legislation that would (arguably) manipulate the electoral system in favor of incumbent senators. In 1993, the Senate passed a campaign finance reform provision that would have capped the amount of money congressional candidates could spend in running for office. It further would have taxed the campaign receipts of any candidate unwilling to abide by these limits. Because research has long shown that challengers usually must outspend incumbents to have any chance of winning, this provision was seen by Republicans (who were the minority party in Congress at the time) as a mechanism for locking in the incumbency advantage, and thus Democratic control of Congress.

Both the Guinier and the campaign finance episodes bring us into the realm of regulating congressional elections. In some respects, regulating congressional elections is just like regulating anything else: rules are promulgated to induce a certain type of behavior, agencies are established to police the rules, and political pressures are brought to bear in writing the rules and enforcing them. But in one important respect, regulating congressional elections is fundamentally different, since the regulators are also the regulated. Also, because the regulation of congressional elections can have such important consequences and because it encourages self-seeking behavior, this subject elicits more popular attention than most formal, structural matters affecting the federal government.

The rest of this chapter is about how congressional elections are regulated. The first section lays out some basics that precede even campaign finance laws or drawing election districts. The second section explores issues affecting congressional districts, including a discussion of how proportional representation might work if applied to Congress. The third section turns its attention to election financing, both behavior under the current system and prospects for reform.

In this chapter, it is important to keep in mind the grand theme of this book: congressional behavior primarily is the result of political actors striving for political advantage. Since the electoral system determines who wields the most authoritative power in the American system, here is where the scramble for political advantage often is most acute.

Running for Congress: The Basics

The Constitution is the starting point for understanding the regulation of congressional elections. Members of the House must be twenty-five years old and citizens of the United States for seven years. Senators must be thirty years old and U.S. citizens for nine years. Both House members and senators must reside in the states they represent. The practice of representatives residing in the *districts* they represent is a custom but not constitutionally mandated. Given the highly particularlistic view of representation in the United States, it is not surprising that this custom has emerged and that an incumbent MC feels compelled to move when a district's lines are changed to exclude his or her residence.

The Constitution gives both houses of Congress the right to judge outcomes of elections to their respective chambers. Consequently, courts infrequently have commented on electoral matters, even though they began doing so more often in the last half of the twentieth century.[2] Therefore, while Supreme Court pronouncements on electoral matters since the 1960s have shaped the electoral landscape in two areas discussed here—congressional districting and campaign finance—it was virtually mute before then. Consequently, the Court still has never ruled on some areas of electoral regulation.

After the Constitution, the next important basic building block in regulating elections is federalism. Although Congress is a national institution, many important regulations are imposed on congressional candidates by the states. These regulations include "resign-to-run" laws, restrictions on access to the ballot, the method of nomination for office, and the timing of primaries and the general election. Other regulations primarily are national in origin, most notably campaign finance regulations. The regulations that got Guinier noticed—the drawing of legislative districts—actually is shared between the states and the federal government, since Congress has mandated single-member districts in various laws since 1842 and has prohibited the dilution of minority votes since the Voting Rights Act of 1965 but still left it to the states to draw the districts.

In Article 1, Section 4, the Constitution gives the states the right to regulate the "times, places, and manner" of holding congressional elections but reserves for Congress the right to overturn any of these state-passed regulations.[3] Congressional intervention into election laws has been minimal, confined to the following provisions in recent years (see 2 U.S.C. 1–9):

- Members of the House must be elected from single-member districts.
- If a state loses representatives after a census but is unable to redistrict in time for the next election, all that state's representatives shall be elected at-large in the state; if the state gains seats in the House but cannot redistrict in time, the additional member(s) shall be elected at-large.
- Candidates for at-large House seats shall be nominated in the same manner as candidates for governor in the state.
- Congressional elections shall occur on the Tuesday after the first Monday in November of even-numbered years.
- Voting for representatives must be by written, printed, or machine ballot.

With Congress mute on so much of election law, states have dominated, producing wide variation in the details of how members of Congress are elected. Among the most significant of these laws are filing fee and petition requirements for getting on the ballot. They range from Indiana, which requires a candidate simply to pledge loyalty to his or her party, to Florida, which requires candidates to post a filing fee of over $10,000. Another important law passed by states is the filing date to run for Congress. In 2010, for instance, someone running for Congress from Illinois had to file to run for office no later than November 2, 2009. That same person could have waited until July 30, 2010, if he or she were a resident of Delaware.[4] Finally nine states, all but one being in the South, maintain runoff primaries. Under a **runoff primary** system, to be nominated, a candidate must receive a majority of votes in a primary. If no one receives a majority, then a runoff is held a few weeks later between the top two candidates, with the winner of that election becoming the party nominee. Most states, however, maintain a **plurality primary** system, in which the person with the most votes is nominated, even if he or she does not receive a majority.[5]

All of the rules just discussed have identifiable effects on the outcomes of congressional elections. For instance, filing fees serve as a fixed cost in running for election, much the way that fixed costs serve as a barrier to entry for companies trying to get into a new market. As these barriers rise in congressional elections, two things happen. First, challengers are discouraged from running against incumbents, and so incumbents face fewer high-quality candidates. Second, because incumbents are reelected more easily, fewer of them retire instead of facing an overly costly reelection battle. In a study of the electoral effects of ballot access rules in the 1980s, Ansolabehere and Gerber (1996) discovered that states with the highest barriers had triple the number of uncontested races compared to states with the lowest barriers and that retirement rates for members of Congress from states with low ballot access barriers were about three times higher than for members who represented high-barrier states.

The timing of filing deadlines has a different effect on the quality of electoral competition. As discussed in Chapter 4, much of the fate of incumbents running for reelection is in the hands of challengers, with high-quality challengers posing a greater threat than low-quality challengers. In states with late filing deadlines, potential high-quality challengers have more time to see whether a challenge to the incumbent is likely to pay off. Likewise, in states with late filing deadlines, incumbents have a greater opportunity to retire from office rather than run again if the political signs turn negative in the election year.

This is a pattern that Gary Jacobson and Michael Dimock (1994) found when they researched the electoral effects of the 1992 "House Bank Scandal." Very briefly, the House Bank Scandal involved a number of House members writing bad checks on their bank accounts then not being held accountable for their overdrafts. From our perspective, what is important is that the names of everyone who had written bad checks and the number of checks they had written was published in April 1992, right in the middle of the filing season for Congress. Among the incumbents who wrote more than 100 bad checks but who were from states with filing deadlines *before* April 15, 21 percent faced a high-quality challenger in the party primary. Among incumbents who wrote more than 100 bad checks but were from states with filing deadlines *after* April 15, 57 percent had primary battles against high-quality challengers.

Finally, the effects of a runoff primary are easily illustrated through the single-dimensional spatial model in Figure 6.1. Three candidates are in this example: A, B, and C. Voters are located uniformly along the dimension as shown. They all vote and they all vote sincerely. In Round 1, no candidate receives a majority. While each candidate receives a similar number of votes, A receives the most. Therefore, if this were a plurality election, A would be the nominee. However, this is a runoff example, so C, who receives the fewest votes, is knocked out. In Round 2, the competition is between A and B. Because B is closer to the median voter, B is the nominee.

FIGURE 6.1
One-Dimensional Example of a Primary Runoff

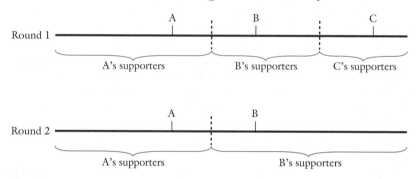

Runoff systems always end up pitting two candidates against each other if no one receives a majority in the first round. The result is that the most extreme candidate in Round 1 cannot receive the nomination in either round. This does *not* mean that the candidate closest to the median always gets the nomination, as the example in Figure 6.2 shows. Here, the median candidate is "squeezed" on both sides by more extreme candidates. In the second round, candidate C (the slightly less extreme of the two extremists) gets the nod.

Figure 6.2
A Runoff Primary That Knocks Out the Median Voter as a Candidate

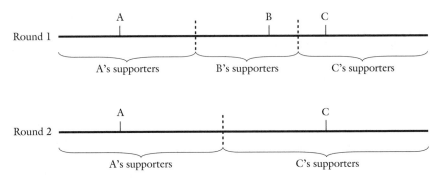

Congressional Districting

Because new congressional districts must be redrawn after each decennial census, redistricting is the most prominent state-controlled process that governs congressional elections. The drawing of strangely misshapen districts—**gerrymandering**—is the electoral manipulation about which voters are likely to know the most. In the late twentieth century, the Supreme Court and the Congress entered into the redistricting game—the Court, by mandating certain equal-population criteria, and the Congress, by the passage of the 1965 Voting Rights Acts and subsequent reauthorizations of the act.

Nothing in either democratic theory or practice *mandates* that members of a legislature be elected from districts. However, the practice is so firmly rooted in American political history that when someone such as Lani Guinier suggests otherwise, she is ripe for attack from political enemies. Guinier's writings were stimulated by the difficulties in finding ways of drawing legislative districts in the United States to bring ethnic minorities into legislatures in numbers closely proportional to their numbers in the population *without* violating other representational principles that Americans also hold dear. Because non-district-based representation systems continue to be proposed as remedies for specific shortcomings in how Americans elect legislatures, we conclude this section with a discussion of Guinier's favorite system, the method of cumulative voting.

Districting: some general principles

We begin by introducing five principles of districting that either govern current court rulings and legislation or are mentioned frequently as desirable features of districting schemes. These principles are compactness and contiguity, equal population, the preservation of existing political communities, partisan fairness, and racial fairness. After discussing each, we turn our attention to conflicts among the principles and the decision rules that usually resolve these conflicts (see Butler and Cain 1992).

The principles of compactness and contiguity are geometric. In a *contiguous* district all the pieces are connected to each other. A system with contiguous districts usually is synonymous with geographically based districting, since such districts aggregate voters according to similar geography rather than similar political characteristics.

Natural geography, of course, often conspires against contiguity. For instance, Staten Island, a part of New York City with a population of 469,000, is too small to have a House member all its own. Therefore, it must be joined with another part of New York state to make a district. The problem, of course, is that there is no land connection between Staten Island and the rest of New York state. That Staten Island is part of a noncontiguous congressional district is a concession to geographic reality.

Yet it is also possible to manipulate such "natural" geographic discontinuities. How, for instance, *should* Staten Island be joined to the rest of New York? In 2001, it was joined with the precincts in Brooklyn connected to Staten Island over the Verrazano-Narrows Bridge, in a second-best concession to the principle of contiguity. But in the 1970s, Staten Island was included in a district with the lower tip of Manhattan. In this case, the only connection between the two parts of the district was a ferry ride across the harbor.

Compact is defined in *Webster's Tenth Collegiate Dictionary* as "occupying a small volume by reason of efficient use of space." Compact districts are valued because they benefit both sides of the representation equation, the representative and the represented. When a district is compact and not strung out over a great distance, contact between representatives and voters is facilitated. Great distances need not be traversed for a representative to visit constituents, for instance. In addition, when a district is compact, it is easier for constituents to know who their representative is—they are less likely to be confused by assuming that a representative who attends to a problem in a neighboring community will also attend to problems in one's own.

A major problem with compactness, theoretically, is recognizing when it exists. To illustrate this problem, Figure 6.3 shows six stylized congressional districts, each of which is roughly the same area. Intuition tells us that certain of the districts, such as the circle and triangle, are less "straggling and rambling" than some of the others, such as the puzzle piece and the serpent. Yet beyond intuition, political scientists, mathematicians, geographers, and lawyers have been stymied in developing a rigorous definition of compactness. Each district pictured in Figure 6.3 would be considered "compact" by some formal definition that has been proposed and used to judge districts.[6] For figures of equal area, a circle always will be the most compact district. The conflict comes over judging districts that are not circles, that is, all real-life districts.

The greatest practical obstacle to compactness is the actual distribution of population. As we discuss later, modern congressional districts are meant to encompass people not geography. If states' populations were distributed equally

FIGURE 6.3
Stylized Legislative Districts

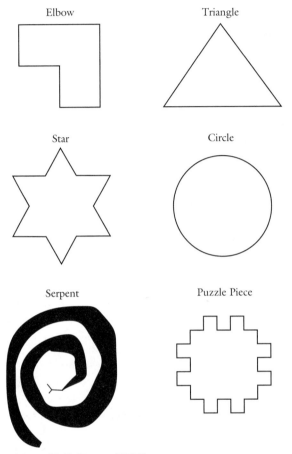

Source: Adapted from H. P. Young (1988).

across the landscape and state boundaries corresponded to neat geometric shapes, then the only problems in judging whether districts are compact would be theoretical.

The meaning of *equal population* is self-evident. With districts of equal population, the opinion of a voter in one district is often said to be "worth" the same amount as that of a single voter in another district.

A number of difficulties emerge with this simple view of population equality. First, as a historical matter, what the Constitution tries to equalize is not the voting power of individual voters but the voting power of states. Districts are nowhere mentioned in the Constitution, and not until 1842 did Congress pass a law requiring the use of single-member districts for House elections. Until that time, it was common for House members from some states to be elected either **at-large**, with several members elected from a single district that encompassed an entire state, or in **multimember districts**, with more than one member being elected from one of several districts in a state.

Although Congress regularly passed laws requiring nearly equal populations among congressional districts, from the 1840s to the 1910s, the House never barred membership to anyone because he was elected from an unequally populated district. For years, the Supreme Court acquiesced to malapportionment as well. For instance, as late as 1946, the Court ruled in *Colgrave* v. *Green* (328 U.S. 549) that if Congress failed to pass a law mandating equally populated districts and if this failure violated basic tenets of democracy, then such violation should be dealt with by the people voting Congress out of office.[7] The emergence of a legally mandated and enforceable rule about equal population did not occur until the case *Baker* v. *Carr* (369 U.S. 186) in 1962, which we discuss later.

The requirement that each state be allowed at least one member of the House is an important constraint that produces a serious malapportionment of members among the smallest states. In 2010, Montana had 994,000 residents while Wyoming had 568,000; both had a single House member.

Before the equal population revolution of the 1960s, the biggest obstacle to equally populated congressional districts was the state legislatures that drew them. The range of populations among some congressional districts was massive, including Illinois's range of 112,000 to 914,000 in the 1940s and Georgia's range of 272,154 to 823,860 in the 1960s. The population imbalance among congressional districts in the twentieth century always benefited rural districts. That is, rural districts tended to be smaller than urban districts. Because the relative power of a voter in an electoral system is inversely related to the number of voters in a system, rural voters tended to win out against urban voters.

The Supreme Court began considering legislative districting cases in the 1960s, gradually altering the political question doctrine that had kept it from deciding cases such as *Colgrave* in earlier years. That is, the court eventually decided to make a distinction between protecting political rights and wading into politically divided policy questions. Because voting is a political right, the Supreme Court became more willing to take action when presented with what it considered a discriminatory set of legislative districts.

The first districting cases accepted by the Supreme Court concerned state elections. In **Baker** v. **Carr,** 369 U.S. 186 (1962), the Supreme Court took on the Tennessee legislature, whose largest House district was twenty-three times larger than its smallest and whose largest Senate district was six times larger. In *Gray* v. *Sanders,* 372 U.S. 308 (1963), the Supreme Court struck down Georgia's county-unit system for electing governors, articulating the **one person-one vote** doctrine that has governed apportionment cases ever since. Finally, in *Wesberry* v. *Sanders,* 376 U.S. 1 (1964), the Supreme Court entered the issue of congressional districts, ruling that Georgia's districts did not pass constitutional muster.

Having articulated a one person-one vote doctrine, the next question was, How much variance is allowed in the population of congressional districts? Do states need to draw districts that are precisely equal in population, even splitting up precincts to achieve such equality, or is some variance allowed? Although no court has ever ruled that perfect equality is required, line drawers have an incentive to approach equality, since federal courts seem to favor population equality when they are forced to decide among competing plans contested in court.

The principle of *preserving existing political communities* means that existing political boundaries—such as cities, counties, or precincts within a city—will be respected when districts are drawn. Sometimes, it also means that identifiable demographic communities (racial communities, religious communities, and the like) will be kept together, even when they extend beyond a single political boundary. Iowa's 1990 districts are an example of districts drawn to respect existing political boundaries. In this case, Iowa has a law that requires congressional districts to respect county boundaries.

In some ways it is difficult to square this principle with the tenets of liberal democracy, which are those most associated with the rational choice theory that motivates this book. That is, the principle of preserving existing political communities elevates collectives of individuals over the individuals themselves. Still, if one wanted to enhance the representation of individuals *as individuals*, some strong arguments can be made for keeping intact existing communities. For instance, existing political subdivisions, such as counties, already have political groups organized to influence politics within those subdivisions. Political parties often have precinct, ward, and town committees. Citizen groups usually center their activities around the communities where their members live. Because political participation is costly and individuals rarely have the resources to organize effective mass political activity alone, making legislative districts coincide with existing political communities may facilitate contact between voters and their representatives, since voters can rely on organizations that already exist to make their desires known.

Although the previous three principles describe the *forms* of electoral systems, the next two are about the *outcomes* of elections. The first of these is partisan fairness. *Partisan fairness* can be divided into two related ideas: symmetry and proportionality. Symmetry demands that if the Republicans receive X percent of the vote and consequently receive Y percent of the seats in Congress, then the same relationship should pertain to the Democrats. In theory, if both parties receive the same number of votes in the election, then the legislature should be split 50–50. On the other hand, proportionality requires a one-to-one correspondence between the percentage of votes received for a party's congressional candidates and the percentage of seats the party receives in Congress.

Of these two components of partisan fairness, symmetry is easier to achieve than proportionality. To see the difficulty of maintaining strict proportionality with a system of single-member districts, consider the following extreme example. Imagine that the Democrats were to win every district in one election with exactly 51 percent of the vote. The party would have a bare majority of votes but all the seats. Now, suppose that in the next congressional election, 2 percent of the vote shifted in favor of the Republicans, allowing that party to win with 51 percent of the vote in each district. The Republicans would have garnered all the seats and a bare majority of the vote. This system is symmetrical—51 percent of the vote yields all the seats for the majority party—but not even close to proportional.

The previous paragraph proposes an extreme case for the purpose of illustration. What is the actual case in the United States? Figure 6.4 illustrates the proportionality of the system by showing a scatter plot based on House elections from 1946 to 2010, with the percentage of seats won by the Democrats on the *y*-axis and the percentage of votes received by Democratic candidates on the *x*-axis. The dotted line is at a 45° angle, which is where the scatter would lie if the American system were proportional. The solid line fit through the scatter is the least-squares best fit to the data. The slope of this line is approximately 1.7, meaning that each 1 percent increase in the Democrats'

Figure **6.4**
Votes and Seats in House Elections, 1946–2010

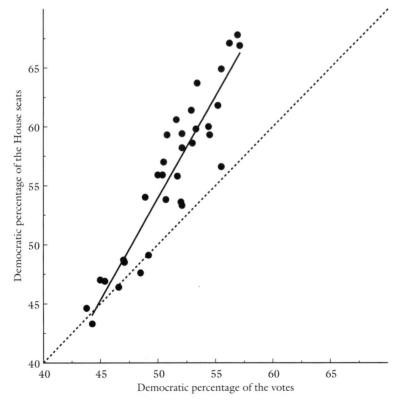

votes has yielded, on average, 1.7 percent increase in the number of Democratic seats in the House. (This 1.7:1 ratio is one measure of the **swing ratio**.)

It is tempting to use Figure 6.4 to estimate whether the House electoral system also passes the symmetry test. To do this, one would check to see whether the regression line runs through the 50–50 point. Simple inspection reveals this is not the case—at 50 percent of the vote, the least squares line predicts Democrats will receive about 54 percent of the seats. However, because so few elections have taken place since 1946 when Democrats have received half the vote or less, a rigorous statistical test of this regression would conclude that House districts, on the whole, have treated Democrats and Republicans symmetrically. Because of the paucity of House elections fought in the 50 percent range, more sophisticated statistical techniques are needed to uncover whether there has been symmetry in House districts for the past half-century. The most sophisticated studies have indicated that House districts mostly have treated the two parties symmetrically, with perhaps a small bias in favor of Republicans early in the century and a small bias favoring Democrats in more recent years.

Perhaps the most controversial districting principle in recent years has been that of *racial fairness*. As a general principle, it has garnered widespread support across the country only in the past three or four decades. Even then, dissension continues over how, in practice, to implement this principle, as was evidenced in the nomination controversy surrounding Lani Guinier.

Laws governing the implementation of the principle of racial fairness center on the Voting Rights Act (VRA) of 1965 and its various reauthorizations. The 1965 act outlawed legislative districts that diluted minority voting power. Before the 1965 VRA, southern states employed a host of mechanisms to mute the ability of black voters to influence local politics, including poll taxes, literacy tests, and outright physical intimidation. Racially biased districts also helped to keep down minority participation. A good example of this type of districting was Mississippi's congressional districts drawn following the 1960 census, shown in Figure 6.5. The map in Figure 6.5 shades Mississippi's counties according to the proportion of their population who were African American. Note that blacks lived in higher proportions in western Mississippi, close to the Mississippi River. Note, too, that districts tended to be oriented east to west. By dispersing the predominantly black western counties into four congressional districts, the Mississippi legislature created a series of districts of which only one had a majority black population: the 1st, with 51 percent. This districting ignores the reality that 42 percent of Mississippi's population was African American in 1960 and two majority-black districts could have been drawn by respecting county boundaries and containing more equal populations than the actual plan. Figure 6.6 shows this hypothetical districting of Mississippi with two majority-black congressional districts—the 1st (62 percent black) and the 2nd (52 percent black).

Controversy over the VRA arose after the most egregious cases of racial vote dilution were addressed and more difficult issues emerged. One precipitating event in the further controversy over implementing the principle of

FIGURE 6.5
Mississippi's Congressional Districts in the 1960s

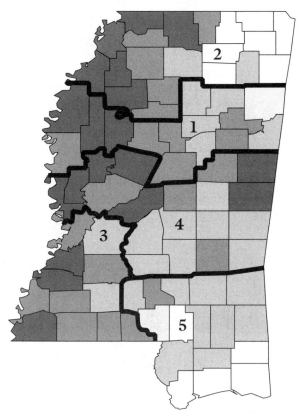

racial fairness came in 1980, when the Supreme Court ruled, in *Mobile* v. *Bolden*, that to successfully challenge a districting plan, minority voters had to show that the plan *intentionally* diluted minority votes. When Congress extended the Voting Rights Act in 1982, it altered the burden of proof in redistricting cases so that minority voters had to show only that districting plans had the *effect* of diluting minority votes, regardless of intent. Coupled with a change in how the Justice Department implemented another section of the Voting Rights Act, states in the post-1990 redistricting round were induced to craft plans that maximized the number of districts in which racial minorities were a majority. These were called **majority-minority districts.**

Many redistricting plans that emerged following the 1990 census were challenged by white voters, who claimed that districts maximizing the chance of electing African Americans to the House violated *their* civil rights. The most important Supreme Court case was **Shaw v. Reno,** in which a 5–4 majority ruled that if a district was drawn *primarily* with race in mind, it was constitutionally suspect. This case threw open to review a series of districting plans in Florida, Illinois, Louisiana, Texas, and North Carolina.

FIGURE 6.6
An Alternative Districting of Mississippi in the 1960s

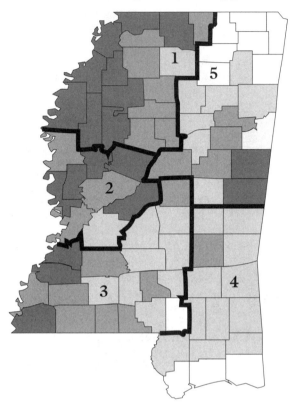

The decade of the 2000s brought the issue of partisan gerrymandering to the fore, owing both to the politics surrounding the redistricting that immediately followed the 2000 census and to attempts to redistrict mid-decade.

The 2000 census continued the pattern of Democratic-leaning states losing population while Republican-leaning states gained. This meant that the fastest growing parts of the county—the parts where the population mobility virtually requires that new congressional districts be drawn from scratch—had districting processes that were dominated by Republican state legislatures and governors. The net result was that a handful of seats shifted toward the Republican Party because of redistricting between 2000 and 2002. Districting schemes intended to disadvantage Democrats were particularly evident in Michigan, Ohio, and Pennsylvania, states that lost seats after the 2000 census (Jacobson 2009, pp. 9–10).

The Pennsylvania plan was challenged by Democrats in the Supreme Court in *Vieth* v. *Jubelirer*. Plaintiffs were relying on the decisions in a 1986 case, *Davis* v. *Bandemer*, which ruled that a partisan gerrymander would be unconstitutional *if* it were egregious. However, the *Davis* ruling did not establish the standard by which a redistricting plan would be judged egregiously partisan, and the 5–4 majority in the *Vieth* case failed to find a way to call the Pennsylvania plan an unconstitutional partisan gerrymander. Indeed, given the vehemence by which four of the five-member majority attacked the *possibility* that standards to assess partisan gerrymanders might be established, it seems unlikely that partisan gerrymander cases will be successful any time soon.

Perhaps more consequential were three efforts to redraw district lines a second time, after the initial post-census redistricting. In Colorado, the Republican-dominated state legislature redrew districts following the 2002 election, attempting to reinforce the state's 5–2 Republican advantage in the House delegation. The Colorado state Supreme Court, however, ruled that under the Colorado constitution, districts could only be drawn once, immediately following the census. So the Colorado effort was overturned.[8]

Not so in Texas, where a new Republican majority in the state legislature that was elected in 2002 undid the congressional districts that had been drawn in 2001 by a Democratic-controlled legislature. Democratic state legislators resisted these efforts in dramatic style, first keeping the legislature from achieving a quorum when many of them fled to Oklahoma, and then preventing a quorum in a special session called specifically to redistrict, by fleeing to New Mexico. Eventually, however, these parliamentary tactics were overcome, and the new districts took effect for the 2004 election. Republicans achieved a 21–11 margin in the House delegation following the 2004 election, undoing a Democratic margin of 17–15 in 2002. Of course, Democratic sympathizers attributed this shift of six seats to a partisan gerrymander. Yet it is at least as likely that this shift was caused because the 2003 plan undid a partisan gerrymander that was passed to favor Democrats in 2001.

The Texas districts drawn in 2003 were challenged as an unconstitutional partisan gerrymander and, again, the Supreme Court rejected this complaint in *League of United Latin American Citizens* v. *Perry*, this time on a wider 7–2 margin. However, the court also ruled that one of the districts diluted the voting power of Hispanics, thus violating the Voting Rights Act. This district, the 23rd, was redrawn as a result.

One set of unintended consequences of the 2003 Texas redistricting fell on the head of Tom DeLay, the Texas Republican who was also U.S. House majority leader and the mastermind of the redistricting process of his home state. First, in order to accomplish the gerrymander, DeLay agreed to reduce the percentage of Republican voters in his own district, so that other Republican voters in the Houston area could be more efficiently distributed to other districts. This had the effect of making DeLay more vulnerable if the election tide turned against Republicans, which it did in 2006, resulting in DeLay's defeat by a Democrat, Nick Lampson. Second, DeLay's fund-raising efforts on behalf of redistricting were eventually judged to be contrary to federal law. DeLay was eventually indicted and convicted of felony campaign finance violations, as a consequence.

A set of factors similar to the post-2000 redistricting may have influenced redistricting in the wake of the 2010 census, although it is too early to issue a final judgment. As in 2000, the 2010 census revealed a net population shift from Democratic-leaning states to Republican-leaning states. The Republican landslide of 2010 affected state legislatures, too, meaning that a significant number of states saw Republican majorities in control of redrawing districts.

However, a number of factors complicated redistricting following the 2010 census. The first was the dramatic increase in the size of the Hispanic population nationwide. Hispanic voters became increasingly Democratic in the 2000s, so that an increase in Hispanic population would seem to bode well for Democrats in states where this growth was the fastest. The fact that Hispanic populations grew the fastest in some Republican-leaning states, such as Florida, Georgia, and Texas, complicated the work of Republican legislators who were trying to disadvantage Democrats. With a Democratic U.S. Justice Department in charge of enforcing the Voting Rights Act in southern states and ensuring that minority voting strength is not "diluted," it would be difficult for Republican legislators in many of these states to ignore the growing political clout of Hispanic voters.

The second complicating factor was the number of states that had divided party control of redistricting—twenty of the fifty states—with Republicans controlling the process in another twenty states and Democrats controlling in ten. Therefore, while the parties entered the post-2010 redistricting season intent on improving the prospects of their candidates, there may be limits to how far partisan gerrymandering can go in this decade.

Districting: the conflict of principles

When each principle is considered separately and abstractly, there is little controversy about the principles of compactness, contiguity, equal population, the preservation of existing political communities, partisan fairness, and racial fairness. They become controversial on implementation, however, since each tends to conflict with another. Table 6.1 gives some (limited) examples of this conflict.

The principle most difficult to maintain in practice is compactness and contiguity, particularly compactness. This is a special problem in the United States, since the most intuitive standard that most Americans use to judge legislative districts is compactness: districts that are gangly or have ragged edges are immediately suspected of being manipulative.

Compactness has been a central issue in voting rights cases ever since the *Shaw* v. *Reno* case, when a Supreme Court majority expressed dismay over the "bizarrely shaped" districts that were being drawn to enhance the number of majority-minority districts. Figure 6.7 shows the districts from two states, Florida and North Carolina that gained notoriety for their creative district drawing in 2001. (Note particularly the 12th district of North Carolina and the 3rd district of Florida.)

TABLE 6.1
Conflicts among Districting Principles

	Compactness and contiguity	Equal population	Respect existing political communities	Partisan fairness
Geographic considerations	State boundaries and population distribution may be uneven			
Equal population	Equality may produce unwieldy districts; compactness may undercut equality			
Respect existing political communities	Existing political divisions may be unwieldy	Strict equality usually requires dividing up existing communities		
Partisan fairness	No necessary conflict	No necessary conflict	No necessary conflict	
Racial fairness	Dispersed minority populations may encourage rambling districts	No necessary conflict	Community boundaries may have been drawn for racial reasons	Racial and party fairness may conflict

Source: Adapted from Butler and Cain (1992, p. 83).

FIGURE 6.7
House Districts in Florida and North Carolina

A. North Carolina

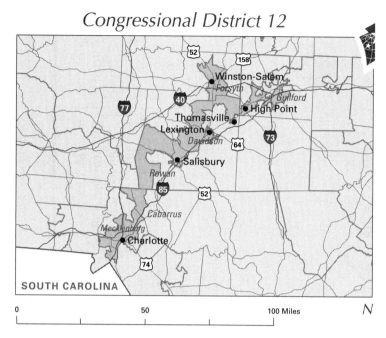

Congressional District 12

B. Florida

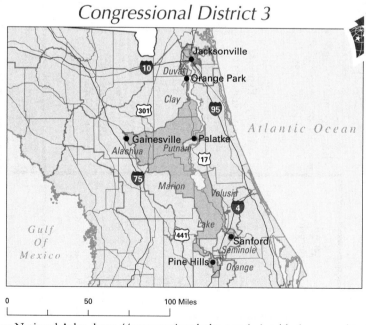

Congressional District 3

Source: National Atlas, http://www.nationalatlas.gov/printable/congress.html

FIGURE 6.8
The Original Gerrymander

The American political vocabulary has a name for districts that are especially misshapen, the *gerrymander*, named after Elbridge Gerry. Gerry, the governor of Massachusetts, drew a state senate district in 1811 that joined together two far-flung Federalist enclaves to carve out a Jeffersonian district between them. Figure 6.8 shows that district. The irony, of course, is that, compared to the districts in Figure 6.7, the original gerrymander was pretty tame.

Gerrymanders originally were drawn to favor one party over another, by creating a few districts in which the disfavored party's supporters were concentrated, allowing the favored party to win a few more districts. Through a combination of court cases and effective use of technology by legislatures, gerrymanders have emerged to protect more than just parties, including incumbents and members of racial groups.

Alternatives to districting

The United States inherited from England a tradition of district-based representation. Yet when we survey Western-style democracies, we discover that this form of representation, while widespread, is not the only way to choose members of the national legislature. Japan, for instance, elects members to the lower house of its parliament (the *Diet*) through a series of multimember districts. Israel operates with a **party list system**, under which the country's many political parties each offer up a list of candidates, ranked 1 to *n*, where *n* is the number of people in the parliament (the *Knesset*). Voters do not vote for candidates directly but vote instead for one of the parties. The more votes a party gets, the more candidates it can send to parliament, with the allocation of seats to parties following closely the proportion of the vote. This is the simplest form of proportional representation.

Reformers in the United States have long advocated various forms of proportional representation, whereby voters express support for parties rather than individual candidates, and seats are divided among parties in proportion to their support in the electorate. Others have advocated variants of multimember district elections. Proportional representation often is favored by people, such as Lani Guinier, who want to assure greater proportionality between population characteristics, such as race, and membership in Congress without drawing bizarrely shaped districts.

A prominent variant of multimember district elections that functions much like proportional representation—the type favored by Guinier—is cumulative voting. The idea behind *cumulative voting* is that it gives voters the opportunity to register not only their preferences among candidates but also the intensity of those preferences.

Under cumulative voting, legislators run in multimember districts. Voters choose individual candidates, with a twist: unlike most multimember district elections, where one can vote only once for a candidate, voters under cumulative voting may either spread out their votes among a series of candidates, or bunch (i.e., *cumulate*) their votes on one candidate. For instance, in a district with three representatives, a voter would be allowed to cast three votes however he or she wished, including casting all three votes for a single candidate.

Here is an example of how cumulative voting might work. Suppose a racially polarized electorate of one hundred people, seventy whites and thirty blacks, could elect ten representatives to a legislature. Under cumulative voting, each voter would get ten votes to cast across all candidates in the race. Assume that ten black and ten white candidates ran for office. The easiest strategy for voters to pursue would be for each voter to allocate one vote to each candidate of his or her own race. This would result in each of the white candidates receiving seventy votes (one from each white voter) and the black candidates each receiving thirty votes (one from each black voter; see Table 6.2). Thus, the entire legislative delegation would be white, since all ten of the white candidates would receive more votes than any of the black candidates.

Black voters would do better, however, if they could coordinate their strategies. For instance, if the black voters all agreed to spread their votes evenly among the first four black candidates—candidates A, B, C, and D—then each of these four candidates would receive seventy-five votes, with the white candidates each receiving seventy votes.[9] The first four black candi-

dates would be elected, with six of the ten white candidates also being chosen, presumably by lot. Faced with such a strategy, white voters also could
organize, for instance, adopting a strategy of spreading their votes as evenly
as possible among nine of the ten white candidates. As Round 3 in Table 6.2
indicates, such a strategy would end up with each of the white candidates
receiving seventy-seven or seventy-eight votes, each black candidate still
receiving seventy-five votes, and the legislature now consisting of nine whites
and one black. (Again, we leave unstated the strategy that voters use to coordinate their voting strategies and how the tie is broken among the four black
candidates with seventy-five votes.)

Table 6.2
Cumulative Voting Example

	Votes Received in Each Round			
	1	*2*	*3*	*4*
Black candidates				
A	30	75	75	100
B	30	75	75	100
C	30	75	75	100
D	30	75	75	0
E	30	0	0	0
F	30	0	0	0
G	30	0	0	0
H	30	0	0	0
I	30	0	0	0
J	30	0	0	0
White candidates				
K	70	70	78	100
L	70	70	78	100
M	70	70	78	100
N	70	70	78	100
O	70	70	78	100
P	70	70	78	100
Q	70	70	78	100
R	70	70	77	0
S	70	70	77	0
T	70	70	0	0

One can imagine a number of strategies emerging within each racial
community as it tried to improve its chances against the other community.
Eventually, however, voters would be driven to try the strategy summarized by Round 4: the black voters would evenly spread their votes among

three candidates and the white voters would evenly spread their votes among seven candidates. Each candidate would receive one hundred votes; the legislature would consist of seven whites and three blacks—a mirror of the entire society.

Note a couple of things about the cumulative voting system. First, the composition of the legislature tends to reflect the sharp cleavages in society. In this example, we chose that cleavage to be race, but in principle it could be anything—social class, religion, economic interest, or the like. Second, cumulative voting allows the composition of the legislature to mirror society without drawing bizarrely shaped districts. Finally, the cleavages reflected in the legislature are those that voters care to organize around, not the ones the legislature chooses to privilege. For instance, in the preceeding example, should society no longer be racially polarized but polarized around religion, then the legislature would tend to reflect religious divisions, with racial composition being determined almost randomly.

The purpose of this section has not been to argue for the clear superiority of cumulative voting (or any proportional system) over the Anglo-American system of **first past the post**. Even if it was such an argument, the Anglo-American system is so ingrained in most Americans that it is difficult to imagine a state legislature doing something else. Rather, the purpose has been to illustrate another method of electing legislators that may respect certain widely shared districting principles better than the status quo. There may be other systems, too. As American society becomes more complex and the representative system is subjected to more constraints, certain forms of proportional representation may provide a creative solution to increasingly intractable problems.

Campaign Finance

The second major way congressional elections are regulated is in the area of campaign finance. In Chapter 4, we discussed the effects of campaign spending on election outcomes. In this section, we discuss how campaign finances are regulated, reforms of campaign finance that have been proposed, and the likely effects that such reforms would have on electoral competition.

How campaigns are financed has elicited perennial controversy in American politics. Campaign finance was linked to the issue of civil service reform following the Civil War, since so much campaign money was funneled through political appointees—one estimate reported that 75 percent of contributions to Republican candidates for Congress in 1868 came through assessments to officeholders who owed their positions to patronage. Once such contributions were made illegal, the parties shifted their focus in fund-raising to corporations and wealthy individuals. Increasing popular alarm over reliance on such a small donor base eventually led to two laws, the Corrupt Practices Acts of 1911 and 1925, which regulated contributions to and expenditures of congressional candidates.

The Corrupt Practices Acts were paper tigers, in large part because the limits to spending were set ridiculously low, which led candidates and their supporters to search actively for ways around them. (For instance, the 1925 law limited the spending of Senate candidates to $25,000, with $5,000 for House candidates.) It became common for candidates to report that they had no contributions or expenditures in their election efforts, arguing that their campaign committees had operated without their "knowledge or consent."

The next period of great concern over campaign finance began in the 1960s, culminating with the passage of the Federal Election Campaign Act (FECA) in 1971; the FECA was significantly amended in 1974, in the wake of the Watergate scandal. The 1974 amendments were so thorough that we can treat this as the beginning of the modern era of federal campaign finance regulation. The FECA contained a number of provisions that pertained generally to all candidates for federal office—the House, Senate, and the presidency—and a number that pertained only to Congress or to presidential campaigns.

The FECA established spending limits, expenditure restrictions, contribution limits, and reporting requirements for congressional candidates. It also established a system of public financing for presidential campaigns. Provisions of the FECA are summarized in Table 6.3. The act provided that candidates for the House could spend no more than $70,000 in the general election; Senate candidates were subject to a variable limit that increased as a function of state population. The FECA limited *how* candidates could spend their funds as well. For instance, House candidates were limited to $52,150 in media expenses, $31,290 of which could go for radio and television. All expenditures had to be reported to the Federal Elections Commission (FEC) and made public at regular intervals during the campaign season. Finally, the FECA outlawed direct contributions to candidates by corporations or labor unions but did allow these bodies to sponsor **political action committees** (PACs) to raise money and disburse it among candidates for electoral purposes.

TABLE 6.3
Provisions of the 1971 Federal Election Campaign Act and the 1974 Amendments

Original Provisions	*Effect of* Buckley *v.* Valeo
Expenditure limits	
Overall spending limit (Congress, president)	Struck down, except as condition to receive public funding
Limits on candidates' own resources	Struck down entirely
Limit on media expenditures	Struck down entirely
Independent expenditure limits	Struck down entirely

(Continued)

TABLE 6.3
Provisions of the 1971 Federal Election Campaign Act and the 1974 Amendments (*Continued*)

Original Provisions	Effect of Buckley v. Valeo
Contribution limits/Individual limits: $1K/candidate/election	Affirmed
PAC limits: $5K/candidate/election	Affirmed
Party committee limits: $5K/candidate/election	Affirmed
Cap on total contributions individuals could make to all candidates: $25K	Struck down
Cap on spending "on behalf of candidates" by parties	Affirmed
Federal Election Commission	
Receive reports; implement FECA	Upheld
Appointed by Congress	Violates separation of powers
Public funding (presidential elections)	
Check-off provision to fund system	Upheld
Partial funding during primaries; total funding during general election	Upheld
Spending limits as price of participating	Upheld
Disclosure	
All expenditures	Upheld
Contributions over $200	Upheld

The FECA was almost immediately challenged in federal court, reaching the Supreme Court in 1976 through a case called **Buckley v. Valeo** (424 U.S. 144–235). James Buckley, a Conservative Party senator from New York, challenged the FECA on constitutional and administrative grounds. Buckley argued that the disclosure provisions overreached Congress's authority to regulate its elections. Perhaps most significant, however, Buckley argued that the spending and contribution limits conflicted with First Amendment guarantees of free speech.

In the *Buckley* decision, the Supreme Court upheld the contribution and spending reporting requirements, in general. It also upheld the limit on the size of campaign contributions, arguing that the limits did not unduly restrict the overall political expression of contributors. It struck down restrictions on expenditures by candidates *and* restrictions on expenditures by independent political groups, however. The Court wrote that

> a restriction on the amount of money a person or group can spend on political communication during a campaign necessarily reduces the quantity of expression by

restricting the number of issues discussed, the depth of their exploration, and the size of the audience reached.

Finally, although the Court agreed that it was permissible to restrict the size of contributions to campaigns, it was unconstitutional to restrict the size of contribution a candidate could give to his or her own campaign.

The *Buckley* decision also addressed the issue of public financing of campaigns.[10] The Court denied the constitutionality of campaign spending limits in general, but it did allow them under one special condition: it was permissible to restrict how much a candidate spent in a campaign if such a restriction was a precondition for the receipt of public campaign funds. In particular, the spending limits imposed on presidential campaigns were ruled permissible because they applied only to candidates who applied for and received federal funds. A presidential candidate is allowed to break the limits, the Court ruled, if he or she is willing to forgo public funds. (Cases where presidential candidates for nomination refused federal campaign funds included John Connolly, 1976; Ross Perot, 1992; Steve Forbes, 1996 and 2000; and George W. Bush, 2000. Barack Obama refused federal funds for both the nomination process and the general election in 2008.)

This part of the *Buckley* decision is important because it establishes a precondition for the restriction of how candidates spend their campaign funds in congressional elections. Congress could limit how much a congressional candidate spent in a campaign *only* if it offered federal campaign funds *and* the candidate accepted the funds. The same would apply, for instance, if Congress wanted to restrict how much candidates could spend on radio and television advertising.

Bipartisan coalitions of representatives and senators advocated the further expansion of campaign finance regulation during the 1990s, culminating in the passage of the Bipartisan Campaign Reform Act (BCRA) in 2002, popularly known as the McCain-Feingold election reform law. (McCain's legislative partner was Russell Feingold [D-Wisc.].) BCRA was quite long and complicated, but it had four sets of provisions that changed the campaign finance landscape extensively. These changes are summarized in Table 6.4. First, it raised various contribution limits and indexed them to inflation. For instance, unlike the fixed limit of $1,000 per individual/candidate/election, in 2010 the limit was raised to $2,400. Second, it prohibited national party committees from raising funds outside the fund-raising and reporting regulations of the FECA, known as "soft money." The implications of this change are discussed below. Third, it instituted a set of regulations on issue ads and electioneering communications, such as requiring entities that paid for ads to identify themselves, and for candidates to explicitly endorse the content of the ads. Fourth, it instituted a "millionaires' amendment," which raised the limits on contributions to House and Senate candidates who faced wealthy, self-financed opponents.

McCain-Feingold faced a vigorous challenge in court, spearheaded by Senator Mitch McConnell (R-Ky.), who was a long-time opponent of campaign

TABLE 6.4
Major Provisions of the 2002 Bipartisan Campaign Reform Act (BCRA) (McCain-Feingold)

Provision	Prior Law	BCRA
Contribution limits		
Individual contributions to candidates	$1,000/candidate/election; not indexed for inflation	$2,000/candidate/election; indexed
Individual contributions to state party committee	$5,000/yr to federal account; not indexed	$10,000/yr to federal account; not indexed
Individual contribution limits to national party committee	$20,000/yr to federal account; not indexed	$25,000/candidate/election; indexed
Individual aggregate contribution limit	$25,000/yr to PACs, parties, and candidates, not indexed	$95,000/two-year cycle, with sublimits to candidates and PACs
Soft money		
National party committees	May raise soft money so long as funds are deposited in non-federal accounts	Prohibits solicitation of soft money
State and local party committees	May spend soft money on the state portion of mixed state/federal activities	Generally bans soft money spending on federal activities
Role of federal candidates/officeholders	May participate in fund-raisers without restrictions	Generally bans federal candidates or officeholders from raising soft money
Advertising		
Candidate appearance in ads	No requirements	To receive lowest unit rate for broadcast ads, candidate image and statement of approval must appear
Sponsor identification	Express advocacy ads must clearly state who paid for them	Enhances identification requirements
Wealthy candidates		
	Buckley v. *Valeo* prohibited limits on use of personal funds to run for office	Raises contribution limits for candidates who are facing opponents who are spending their own funds, above certain thresholds

finance reform and who also led a diverse coalition of interests against the bill—a coalition as diverse as the National Rifle Association and the American Civil Liberties Union. Although some minor provisions of the law were struck down, on the whole, in 2003 it was upheld by a 5–4 ruling by the Supreme Court, in the case of *McConnell* v. *Federal Election Commission.*

(Unintended) consequences of the FECA

It usually is difficult, if not impossible, to state clearly the "intent" of a piece of legislation. This certainly is true of the FECA. Some, particularly reformers, argue that the FECA was enacted to "clean up" the campaign finance system, to force candidates to broaden their bases of support in seeking campaign contributions, to diminish the role of money in elections, to diminish the role of "special interests" in elections, and to elevate the will of "the people" over that of "the bosses." More skeptical observers argue that the FECA was intended to limit electoral competition by reducing the amount of money available to campaigns and by increasing the administrative burden on small parties and underdog candidates. Whatever the "true intent" of the FECA, provisions of the act, aided by the *Buckley* decision, have changed the way that campaigns are run in the United States.

In understanding how the FECA has changed the electoral landscape, it is important to recall that the FECA is applied to the most ambitious politicians in the United States and their supporters. These politicians are intent on winning elections and have an incentive to discover and exploit loopholes and strategic opportunities that the campaign finance laws provide. Likewise, individuals and groups who try to influence government decisions also have an incentive to exploit the campaign finance system to their advantage.

Four developments bear special attention in discussing the consequences of modern campaign finance regulation: the rise of political action committees, "millionaire candidates," soft money, and independent expenditures in congressional elections. The first development is the growth of an old organizational form that was given new life under the FECA. The last three developments grew out of the *Buckley* decision and its protection of the political expression rights of individuals.

Political action committees Political action committees got their start in the 1940s when Congress denied labor unions the right to use their own resources for direct political activity. This restriction led the Congress of Industrial Organizations (CIO) to create an organization called the *Political Action Committee* (PAC), in 1943. When the CIO merged with the American Federation of Labor in 1955, to form the AFL-CIO, they established its successor, the Committee on Political Education (COPE). Both PAC and COPE raised money from union members and distributed it among sympathetic candidates.

Eventually business groups and other private associations also got into the political action committee business, but not until after the FECA did PACs reach full flower. The 1971 FECA encouraged labor unions and corporations to create separate entities, with funds segregated from the parent organization, that could raise money for political candidates. While unions and corporations are not allowed to contribute their own funds directly to candidates, they are allowed to use their funds to establish and administer PACs.

Tables 6.5 and 6.6 document the growth in political action committees. The FEC categories used in Tables 6.5 and 6.6 are mostly self-evident. Because the trade/membership/health category consists mostly of private professionals (such as doctors, dentists, or lawyers) and the cooperative category consists mostly of agricultural producers, they often are grouped together with corporate PACs when researchers wish to describe the extent of business-related money in politics. Nonconnected PACs often are the most politically controversial, since this category contains most of the well-known, highly ideological PACs.

The number of PACs reached a plateau of about 4,500 in 1984, which held for the next two decades, but it began to grow in 2004, following the passage of BCRA. Similarly, the growth of PAC spending hit a plateau in the 1990s,

TABLE 6.5
The Growth of Political Action Committees, 1974–2008

			PAC Type				
Year	Corporate	Labor	Trade/Membership/ Health*	Nonconnected	Cooperative	Corporation without stock	Total
1974	89	201	318				608
1980	1,206	297	576	374	42	56	2,551
1990	1,972	372	801	1,321	60	151	4,677
1992	1,930	372	835	1,376	61	153	4,727
1994	1,875	371	852	1,318	56	149	4,621
1996	1,836	358	896	1,259	45	134	4,528
1998	1,821	353	921	1,326	45	134	4,528
2000	1,725	350	900	1,362	41	121	4,499
2002	1,741	337	956	1,401	41	118	4,594
2004	1,756	328	986	1,650	38	109	4,867
2006	1,808	312	1,019	1,797	40	115	5,091
2008	1,779	296	1,063	1,919	42	111	5,210

*Until 1978, this category contained all other PACs.

Source: FEC, "Growth in PAC Financial Activity Slows," news release, April 24, 2009. http://www.fec.gov/press/press2009/20090415PAC/20090424PAC.shtml. Last accessed May 18, 2010. Figures for 1974 and 1980 taken from Federal Election Commission, "FEC Releases Semi-Annual Federal PAC Count," press release, January 19, 2000. The 1974 and 1980 figures were calculated using a different method than for 1990–2008, but are roughly comparable.

TABLE 6.6
Contribution of PACs to Candidates,
1980–2008 (millions of dollars)

	PAC Type						Total Spending	
Year	Corporate	Labor	Trade/ Membership/ Health	Nonconnected	Cooperative	Corporation without stock	Nominal dollars	2008 dollars
1980	21.6	14.2	17.0	5.2	1.5	0.7	60.2	146.2
1990	58.1	35.7	44.8	15.1	3.0	3.4	159.1	246.1
1992	68.4	41.3	53.7	18.1	3.0	4.0	188.7	270.3
1994	64.4	40.7	50.3	17.5	2.9	3.8	179.6	245.3
1996	69.6	46.3	56.0	22.0	2.8	4.0	200.7	262.2
1998	71.1	43.2	59.0	27.1	2.2	4.0	206.6	262.4
2000	84.0	50.0	68.1	35.6	2.2	4.8	244.8	299.2
2002	91.6	51.8	71.5	44.6	2.5	4.0	266.0	312.8
2004	104.3	50.3	78.1	49.8	2.7	3.8	288.9	324.3
2006	122.0	53.9	95.1	66.7	3.2	4.4	345.2	363.2
2008	145.0	60.9	107.8	62.6	6.7	4.9	387.9	387.9

Source: FEC, "Growth in PAC Financial Activity Slows," news release, April 24, 2009. http://www .fec.gov/press/press2009/20090415PAC/20090424PAC.shtml. Last accessed May 20, 2010.

when measured in constant dollars, but then grew rapidly in the first decade of the twenty-first century.

PACs elicit much concern among the public and journalists, although the source of that concern often is poorly focused and vague. Some object simply to the amount of money PACs raise and disburse, which seems to be the least of the problems that PACs generate. While sums approaching $388 million—the amount contributed to all political candidates by PACs in 2008—are substantial, the amount of money given by PACs to candidates still is only a couple of dollars per voter. Also, PAC dollars still are dominated by individual contributions. In the 2008 congressional election, for instance, PACs contributed a total of 380 million to House and Senate candidates, compared to individual contributions of $800 million.

PACs behave differently from individuals, however, and this different behavior provides some insight into how relatively well-off organizations consider politics compared to the relatively well-off individuals who contribute to campaigns. But to understand this behavior, we need to consider *why* someone—a group or an individual—might contribute to a political candidate in the first place.

It is helpful to divide the motivation for making political contributions into two types. On the one hand, some contribute to political candidates because of an agreement on political issues; a contribution may be a show of solidarity with a cause, a policy, a party, or the like. While winning is nice, this is not the primary point of such contributions. We call these *consumption-oriented contributions.*

On the other hand, some contribute to political candidates not because of an intrinsic agreement on issues but rather from the desire to achieve something else out of politics, such as access to decision makers. It may make sense to contribute to a political candidate you normally disagree with if this contribution would give you access to the candidate once in office. This is especially true if the candidate is assured of reelection, such as an electorally safe incumbent. In such a case, if you contribute to the candidate's opponent, you do not increase the chance that someone who agrees with you will win office, but you surely decrease the chance of the winner giving you an audience should you seek something out of government. We call these *investment contributions.*

PACs tend to be investment contributors; individuals tend to be consumption contributors. The dominance of investment behavior among PACs is evidenced in their preference for incumbents over challengers. For instance, in the 2008 congressional election, PACs favored incumbents over challengers by a ratio of over 9:1; individuals favored incumbents by a ratio of only 2:1. The investment mentality also is illustrated by the tendency of PACs to favor contributions to candidates in close elections—that is, where small contributions have a greater chance of swaying outcomes—compared to individuals.

Therefore, if there is normative concern about the relative influence of PACs compared to individuals in congressional elections, the concern is best directed at the strategic advantages that PACs hold over individuals in the electoral arena. Individuals clearly are not powerless in the political contribution game—they dominate in sheer numbers and money, after all. Individual contributions are not focused as well as PAC contributions to influence outcomes, however, nor is the average individual as well situated to follow up a contribution with a visit to a congressional office as a PAC.

Even if reformers sometimes overstate the evil consequences that PACs bring to congressional politics, the growth of PACs since the early 1970s is further evidence that people who try to influence politics will find new ways to do so when old doors are barred. In particular, the growth of PACs in congressional elections is the direct result of two other restrictions placed on campaign finance: (1) the limitation of $1,000 that an individual can give a candidate (individuals may give unlimited amounts to PACs) and (2) the public financing of presidential elections, which prohibits politically interested groups from contributing to the presidential candidates of their choice, after the conventions are over.

Millionaire candidates The 1971 FECA sought to limit the sway that personal fortunes could have over elections by restricting what candidates could contribute to their own campaigns. In the *Buckley* decision, the Supreme Court identified this as a direct assault on the First Amendment and ruled it unconstitutional. A direct consequence of this decision has been to disadvantage millionaire *friends* of candidates, in favor of millionaires who want to be candidates.

The reliance on the personal fortunes of candidates in congressional elections is illustrated in Table 6.7, which reports sources of campaign receipts for the 2008 congressional election. In 2008, as in most years, the candidates themselves were a significant source of campaign money among challengers and open seat contestants. Indeed, among Senate challengers, candidate contributions to their own campaigns almost equaled contributions from all other individuals combined.

The data in Table 6.7 suggest one reason that candidates may rely on their own personal fortunes to run for office: incumbents dominate the PAC contribution market. Therefore, challengers and open seat candidates, particularly those without widespread name recognition to begin with, must rely on their own resources to jump-start their campaigns.

The virtual monopoly that incumbents hold over PAC contributions gives wealthy individuals an advantage in running for federal office a fact that reformers often use to argue for the elimination of PACs. This monopoly, combined with the restriction on contributions from other people, gives wealthy people an advantage, particularly in running for open seats or to challenge incumbents. This advantage is particularly ironic, however, since the $1,000 contribution limit in part was justified on the basis of requiring candidates to build widespread supporter-contributor bases when they ran

TABLE 6.7
Sources of Campaign Receipts for Congressional Races, 2008

	Incumbents		Challengers		Open Seats	
	$ millions	%	$ millions	%	$ millions	%
House						
Individuals	290.4	53.0	147.5	65.8	90.9	55.3
PACS	251.8	45.9	24.2	10.8	24.7	15.0
Candidate	4.9	0.9	51.8	23.1	48.9	29.7
Other loans	1.4	0.2	0.6	0.3	0.0	0.0
Senate						
Individuals	134.8	66.2	88.7	70.1	46.6	77.2
PACs	60.0	29.5	8.5	6.8	10.7	17.8
Candidate	8.8	4.3	20.4	16.1	3.0	4.9
Other loans	0.0	0.0	8.8	7.0	0.1	0.1

Note: Candidate sources include candidate contributions and candidate loans.

Source: Federal Election Commission, "Congressional Candidates Raised $1.42 Billion in 2007–2008," press release, December 29, 2009. http://www.fec.gov/press/press2009/2009Dec29Cong/2009Dec29Cong.shtml. Last accessed May 21, 2010.

for office. What could be a narrower contributor base than the candidate alone?

The rise of self-financed "millionaire candidates" following the passage of the FECA was one of the motivators behind the "millionaires' amendment" attached to the 2002 BCRA. McCain-Feingold raised the individual contribution limits that applied to candidates *if* they faced a candidate who contributed more than a threshold amount of his or her own personal funds to the campaign. However, in 2008 the Supreme Court ruled 5–4 in *Davis* v. *FEC* that the millionaires' amendment was a violation of the First Amendment, thus unconstitutional, forcing the FEC to cease enforcing it.

Independent expenditures Although the Supreme Court has allowed some regulation of how federal candidates finance their campaigns, the *Buckley* decision makes it clear that the Court would have little tolerance for heavy regulation of individuals and groups who want to influence congressional elections independent of the campaigns themselves. Concern over these **independent expenditures** has waxed and waned as amounts fluctuated over time. Some of the concern arose because much independent spending has been ideologically driven and some commentators simply disagree with the groups doing the spending. This was the case, for instance, when the National Conservative Political Action Committee (NCPAC, pronounced "nickpack") poured so much money into the 1980 congressional and presidential elections.

In addition to this sort of ideological concern, independent expenditures raise two other interesting issues. First are the matters of accountability and negative campaigning. While in certain situations benefits may accrue to waging a negative campaign (see Chapter 4), candidates often worry that the strategy of going negative could backfire. Some candidates worry about being tarred with the negative image of a mudslinger. Independent groups can remove this burden from a candidate. They can make outrageous charges against an opponent. The benefited candidate then can distance himself or herself from the mudslinging. Voters who may want to punish mudslinging are limited in their response—they can vote against the candidate who is supposed to benefit from the mudslinging, but they cannot vote against the group actually doing the mudslinging.

Second is the matter of evading the intent of campaign finance laws. Here, we return to a theme of this section: because campaign professionals view their jobs as winning elections, they have incentives to probe the bounds of campaign finance law for weaknesses and loopholes that make doing their job easier. As greater scrutiny is given to what the candidates themselves do, campaign professionals have incentives to encourage independent expenditures. Of course, because independent expenditures, by definition, cannot be closely coordinated with the strategies of individual campaigns, they probably are less effective in benefiting individual candidates. But if fewer restrictions are placed on how groups raise and spend money "independent" of individual campaigns, then eventually independent spending on behalf of candidates could come to dominate direct spending by candidates.

Soft money Related to the issue of independent expenditures is **soft money**. The FECA allowed political parties to raise unlimited amounts of money from groups and individuals for **party building activities,** such as voter registration drives and advertising generally on behalf of a party's platform.

The amount of soft money raised by the parties rose significantly between the passage of the FECA and 2000, and outpaced growth in funds they raised that were regulated by federal law ("hard money"). For instance, between 1992 and 2002, hard money raised by the two major parties went from $434 million to $658 million, a growth of nearly 50 percent in a decade. In comparison, over the same period, soft money raised by the parties grew from $86 million to $496 million, a growth of nearly 500 percent over the same period.

Soft money was a major theme of Senator John McCain's (Ariz.) run for the Republican presidential nomination in that year. Although he failed to gain the nomination, his leadership in the issue helped achieve passage of the Bipartisan Campaign Reform Act (BCRA) in 2002, discussed above.

Among other things, McCain-Feingold prohibited state and local parties from raising soft money and using it in federal elections. After the passage of McCain-Feingold, growth in federally regulated fund-raising by the parties continued at roughly the same pace as before, rising to a total of $1.6 billion in 2008.

Soft money always aroused suspicions among those who believe that unregulated, unlimited campaign contributions fostered the corruption of the political process. In addition, the skyrocketing growth in soft money before the passage of BCRA shifted the balance of power between individual candidates and the national parties. Candidates labored under fund-raising restrictions that did not apply to the parties. Thus, while the soft money prohibition can be considered a "good government" measure, we should not overlook the fact that eliminating soft money tilted the fund-raising playing field slightly back in the favor of individual candidates, at the expense of the parties.

Campaign finance reform Campaign finance reform is a perennial favorite of voters and politicians. Polls regularly report that voters are disgusted with the current state of campaign finance; almost every year, some campaign finance reform is considered in Congress, to no avail. In this section, we review some of the more popular proposed reforms and discuss who likely would benefit from their enactment. In beginning this discussion, bear in mind the history of campaign finance reform thus far and the difficulty in predicting with certainty the effects of such reform.

Although reformers are a creative bunch and have proposed a wide series of campaign finance reforms in recent years, we focus on three hardy perennials: limits on expenditures, limits on political action committees, and public financing of elections.

Expenditure limitations Many citizens believe that too much money is spent on elections and, therefore, would like to limit it somehow. One way of addressing this point is to question its premise, that "too much money" is spent on elections. How would one judge what is too much money in elections? Compared to what is spent on public relations in the private sector, for instance, campaign spending is a drop in the ocean. For instance, in 2008, total campaign spending for Congress, in all elections, amounted to $1.4 billion. In contrast, spending on all commercial advertising and marketing in the United States, amounted to $412 billion, with $249 billion of that attributed to advertising.[11] The largest advertiser, Procter & Gamble, alone spent $4.8 billion.

The *Buckley* decision placed heavy limits on the ability of Congress to control how much candidates spend on their congressional campaigns. Indeed, the Court ruled that Congress may limit campaign spending only if public funding is offered to candidates first. Therefore, in discussing spending limits we must assume that a system of public finance has been instituted, too. We defer a discussion of public financing of elections per se until later.

How would limiting campaign expenditures change congressional elections? Reformers would have us focus on the reduction of "corruption" among political interests and candidates as the proper way to assess the effects of limiting expenditures. With less spending would come less pressure on candidates to raise money in the first place. (How much less would depend on the details of the public finance provisions.) Since the drive to raise increasingly large amounts of money is said to produce all sorts of evil under the current system,[12] anything to diminish this drive should be regarded as good.

Assessing claims about reduced corruption is difficult. Limiting spending on legislative campaigns has never been *seriously* tried, and so there is no experience to go on.[13] Among scholars who studied the subject is also skepticism that levels of outright corruption would be high in any case (Thompson 1994). Therefore, judgment and predictions about the effects of limiting expenditures on political corruption are mostly a matter of personal tastes and prejudices.

Reducing campaign corruption surely would not be the only effect of limiting campaign spending. Scholars and (especially) politicians have worried that spending limits would affect who won and lost in elections. At first blush, it seems obvious how these effects would work. On further consideration, however, such effects are not so cut and dried.

Incumbents running for reelection regularly spend more money than their opponents. This spending gap frequently is cited as a major source of the "incumbency advantage" in congressional races. Therefore, if spending limits were set low enough that they actually constituted a real constraint on spending, then the limits would have the greatest effect on incumbents, narrowing the spending gap between incumbents and challengers.

Figure 6.9 illustrates how this analysis typically works. The graph summarizes the relationship between campaign spending in House races and election outcomes. In particular, the *x*-axis indicates the ratio between incumbent and challenger spending in the 1996 House race; the *y*-axis indicates the percentage of the vote received by the incumbent. The solid line graphs the average relationship between the two variables, calculated using simple linear regression.

Figure 6.9 indicates what the average ratio of incumbent-to-challenger spending was in 2008, roughly 5.0:1. This translates into an average vote share for the incumbent of just over 60 percent. Because the incumbent's vote share rises (on average) as this spending ratio rises, if we close the spending gap between incumbents and challengers, we also close the vote share gap. Therefore, if spending were limited in such a way that the average incumbent would

FIGURE 6.9
Campaign Spending and the Vote in House Races in 2008

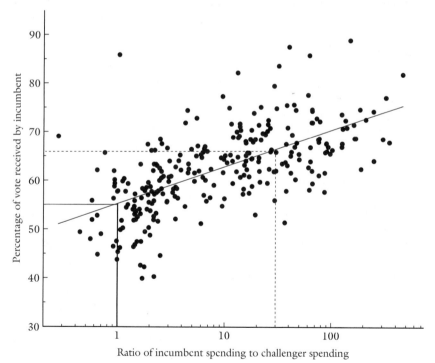

Ratio of incumbent spending to challenger spending

Source: Federal Election Commission, "Congressional Candidates Raised $1.42 Billion in 2007–2008," news release, December 29, 2009. Last accessed January 12, 2011.

now spend only twice what the average challenger spent, then the average incumbent would receive only 56 percent of the vote. Likewise, if challenger and incumbent spending were set to be equal, then incumbents would receive, on average, a 54 percent vote share. So, equalizing spending would not equalize votes, *on average*, but would push more incumbents into the vulnerable range and presumably push more below the 50 percent threshold.

So, Figure 6.9 formally illustrates what incumbents worry about informally, that by limiting spending, incumbents would lose much of their electoral advantage. Hence, incumbents tend to oppose spending limits. Not all incumbents oppose them, however. In particular, before they gained control of the House in the 1994 election, Republicans (incumbents and challengers alike) tended to favor spending controls more than Democrats, since Republicans tended to be challengers and Democrats tended to be incumbents. Of course, the 1994 election changed this situation.

The analysis illustrated in Figure 6.9 is the starting point for understanding how election outcomes might be changed if spending were limited, but it is only a starting point. That is because this analysis does not take into account the strategic behavior of congressional candidates faced with spending limits. Remember, the goal of candidates is to win elections, within the constraints of the law. With spending limits, candidates would be encouraged to seek other ways of winning votes that did not cost money or that were more efficient uses of money. Two obvious methods of substitution present themselves. The first is volunteer labor. Before the rise of mass media, the most successful politicians were those who could marshal volunteers to distribute literature, hold signs, and get people to the polls on election day. Spending limits once again would put a premium on having connections with pools of potential volunteers, such as labor unions, churches, and retirement centers. The second obvious way to change behavior would be to shift into more efficient uses of campaign money. Studies of candidate spending habits have suggested that incumbents, especially, use significant portions of their campaign coffers for noncampaign activities: they have nicer campaign offices, give more elaborate parties, and own more cars than they need to get reelected. Thus, spending limits, to a degree, would simply make campaigns leaner operations.

On the whole, both substitutions—to volunteer labor and to more efficient uses of money—on net, would benefit incumbents. Incumbents, by definition, already have ties with the community, developed through years of electioneering. And they have already won election in the district, so they presumably already know what would be the most effective uses of their campaign dollars; most challengers still need to learn that. Therefore, while spending limits might still diminish the incumbency advantage somewhat, the most important effects of limits would be to change behavior altogether; and in such a changed environment, incumbents would still be advantaged.

Because of the *Buckley* decision, it is impossible for Congress simply to impose spending limits on national elections. Therefore, limits always are bundled with possible inducements to candidates to accept those limits. These inducements typically involve some sort of campaign subsidies, whether they be outright public funding of campaigns (see the discussion that follows) or subsidies of particular campaign costs. (A popular cost subsidy is reduced postage or television advertising rates for candidates who agree to limit their expenditures.)

Political action committees In the eyes of reformers and most of the public, money contributed to congressional candidates by political action committees is suspect. It is often referred to as *special interest money.* Political scientists who study campaign finance tend not to be so alarmed by the activity of PACs, for two reasons. First, individual contributions dominate PAC contributions, even among incumbents. Second, studies repeatedly have failed to find PAC contributions systematically changing the voting habits of MCs. Research has shown, rather, that PAC contributions are primarily effective through two avenues. First, contributions grant PAC representatives access to legislators during the bill-drafting stage. Second, because PACs are more strategic in their contributions than individuals, their contributions to candidates can have a greater effect, on the margin, in affecting electoral outcomes. Through this second avenue PACs are influential, not because they buy the votes of legislators, but because their contributions might help to elect more candidates who already support their side of the issues.

Reform groups such as Common Cause support the greater regulation of PACs—or their elimination altogether—because of their supposed corrupting influences on elections. Members of Congress who have become interested in this issue have responded out of different motivations, however. Because PACs tend to contribute more readily to incumbents than to challengers (see Table 6.7), the party out of power tends to favor hobbling PACs more than the party in power.

527 organizations Nonprofit political organizations that are organized for the purpose of influencing nominations or elections of candidates are often organized under a provision of the U.S. tax code called Section 527. The activities of Section 527 groups have been controversial for years and became the subject of attempted legislation in the early 2000s, after the passage of McCain-Finegold. Unlike PACs, Section 527 groups are able to accept unlimited contributions from individuals, labor unions, and corporations. They are allowed to spend the proceeds to influence elections, so long as they do not coordinate their activities with the candidates themselves. McCain and Feingold, along with House members Chris Shays (R-Conn.) and Martin Meehan (D-Mass.), introduced legislation several times after 2002 to regulate Section 527 groups, to essentially treat them as PACs. As such, they would have been subject to contribution disclosure laws and contribution limits. Despite the fact that legislation to regulate Section 527 groups has enjoyed some degree of bipartisan support, it has always met insurmountable parliamentary hurdles.

The largest Section 527 groups are quite large, visible, and support both parties. In 2008, the largest liberal Section 527 group was America Votes, which raised $17.6 million; the largest conservative group was GOPAC, at $9.3 million. Independent groups can be a powerful force in elections, precisely because they can take more aggressive positions that candidates themselves might avoid, out of fear of offending centrist voters. At the same time, Section 527 groups, and independent groups of all sorts, can be a threat to individual candidates, even ones they are ideologically sympathetic to, because of this independence. If a message backfires, it can be the candidate who is blamed, instead of the group, which the candidate may sincerely wish to avoid associating himself with. As a consequence, it is not surprising that members of Congress periodically take aim at the activities of these groups. Thus far, however, they have failed to seriously damage them.

Public financing Proposals to finance campaigns publicly range from total subsidies for major party nominees to matching fund schemes. Reform organizations favor public financing both intrinsically and because of the secondary benefits it would provide. For those who believe the search for campaign money corrupts politics, public financing is an obvious solution. For those who believe that too much money is spent on campaigns or is spent on the wrong things, public financing becomes the vehicle through which other types of policy changes are allowed.

Support and opposition within Congress for public financing of campaigns derives from two sources: from lofty political principles and from narrow self- (or party) interest. Many supporters simply agree with reform organizations about the corrupting influence of money on politics. At the same time, support also is concentrated among Democrats, who tend to support domestic government spending programs more generally and often believe that Republicans share a long-term fund-raising advantage over Democrats. Opposition to public financing is centered not only among those who oppose government spending generally but also among those who worry about the intrusion of the state in political competition. The presidential system of financing elections already advantages the major parties, and it is likely that a congressional system would advantage them, too. But Republicans have tended to oppose public financing because generally Democrats have crafted the plans, and they are distrustful that Democratic proposals would treat them neutrally.

As with spending limits, it is possible to analyze the probable effects of public financing both strategically and nonstrategically. Suppose, for instance, a public finance plan included one-for-one matching of individual contributions, up to a certain limit. The matching feature might encourage candidates to cut back on their fund-raising efforts, since they could raise as much as in the past with less effort. Yet, because each unit of effort in individual fund-raising now would be twice as effective as before, candidates might put *more* effort into individual fund-raising, resulting in more money poured into campaigns, not less. Depending on the marginal returns to a unit of effort put into PAC fund-raising, a matching feature might encourage less PAC fund-raising and more individual fund-raising.

The legal future of campaign finance Ever since the current regulatory regime covering campaign finance began in 1972, it has been attacked on First Amendment grounds. Although traditionally liberal groups such as the American Civil Liberties Union have sometimes joined in the opposition, in general, attacks on the overall regulation of campaign finance have been led by conservative groups, who have found First Amendment objections to be the most powerful in court cases.

Ever since the *Buckley* decision in 1976, Supreme Court minorities have expressed their discomfort with campaign finance regulation quite strongly. As the conservative bloc on the court has solidified, the anti–campaign finance regulation minority has, in some instances, become a majority. This has led many court observers and campaign finance experts to predict that the limits and disclosure regulations embodied in laws like the FECA and BCRA will eventually be overturned.

Some people believe that the first step in the eventual dismantling of the campaign finance regulatory system in the United States occurred in early 2010, when the Supreme Court decided the case ***Citizens United*** v. ***FEC*** on a 5–4 vote.

Before *Citizens United*, FEC regulations generally prohibited corporations and labor unions from using their own money for **express advocacy**, that is, for explicit calls for the election or defeat of named candidates. If a corporation or labor union wanted to do this, it had to establish a separate organization, a PAC, and solicit funds from individuals. This segregated money could be used directly to influence voters in campaigns. In addition, before *Citizens United*, the FEC barred corporations and labor unions from running "electioneering communications" that mention candidates (but do not advocate their election or defeat) within sixty days of a federal election or thirty days of a primary.

The Supreme Court ruled in *Citizens United* that such restrictions were unconstitutional abridgements of the First Amendment right to free speech. The decision evoked a strong backlash from supporters of stringent campaign finance laws, especially Democrats. The intensity of the dispute was illustrated when President Obama attacked the decision in the 2010 State of the Union Address, which prompted Justice Samuel Alito, who was in the audience for the speech, to mouth the words "not true" when Obama described the decision.

The eagerness of the Supreme Court majority to strike down a long-established practice within campaign finance regulation—one that preceded the FECA itself by approximately half a century—was a sign to most observers on both sides of the issue that the same majority was just as eager to strike down less hoary practices, such as the 1972 FECA and its 1974 amendments. Just how far the Court is willing to go—whether, for instance, the justices would allow disclosure requirements to remain while striking down contribution limits, "stand by your ad" regulations, and so on—is now open to question.

Although large majorities of Americans appear to support amending the Constitution to overturn the *Citizens United* decision, the hostility toward campaign finance regulation among Republican congressional leaders, especially those in the Senate, seems to suggest that the *Citizens United* decision will stand, and its progeny will loosen campaign finance regulations further.

It is too early to assess the full impact of *Citizens United*. Opponents of the decision tend to overstate its importance, since they tend not to make a distinction between the activity that would have occurred anyway under pre–*Citizens United* regulations and the *marginal* effect of the ruling itself. The decision reflects a clear willingness of the current Supreme Court to extend the rights of electioneering citizenship to corporations. Whether corporations, who must market their wares to both Democrats and Republicans will jump into the electoral arenas in a highly partisan fashion awaits experience with campaigning in a post–*Citizens United* world.

Conclusion

Elections do not just happen in the United States—they are planned, structured, and regulated. It would be too extreme to argue that the outcomes of congressional elections are *determined* by these plans, structures, and regulations. It is not too extreme to suggest that elections are materially influenced by how the states and the federal government organize electoral competition. For example, that House elections are run in single-member districts is an important contributor to the resilience of the two-party system; a proportional system would allow more opportunity for minor parties to win seats in Congress and thus establish themselves permanently. The reliance on single-member districts has virtually determined the strategies that states have adopted to respond to the Voting Rights Act. Reliance on private financing of elections provides an opportunity for incumbents to reinforce whatever natural advantages they already may have in their districts.

Because the details of how electoral competition is organized has such a strong influence on congressional politics, it is no surprise that popular reforms often meet stiff opposition in Congress. And because competition for national office is so intense, it is no surprise that candidates always will try to gain advantage under any new, reformed system. Therefore, the history of electoral reform is bound to be one of unforeseen consequences.

Further Reading

Ansolabehere, Stephen, John de Figueiredo, and James M. Snyder, Jr. 2003. "Why Is There So Little Money in U.S. Politics?" *Journal of Economic Perspectives* 17:105–30.

Ansolabehere, Stephen, and James M. Snyder, Jr. 2008. *The End of Equality: One Person, One Vote and the Transformation of American Politics.* New York: Norton.

Butler, David, and Bruce Cain. 1992. *Congressional Redistricting: Comparative and Theoretical Perspectives.* New York: Macmillan.

Guinier, Lani. 1995. *The Tyranny of the Majority: Fundamental Fairness in Representative Democracy.* New York: Free Press.

Jacobson, Gary C. 1980. *Money in Congressional Elections.* New Haven, Conn.: Yale University Press.

———. 1990. "The Effects of Campaign Spending on House Elections: New Evidence for Old Arguments." *American Journal of Political Science* 34: 334–62.

Lowenstein, Daniel Hays, Richard L. Hasen, and Daniel P. Tokaji. 2008. *Election Law: Cases and Materials,* 4th ed. Durham, N.C.: Carolina Academic Press.

Snyder, James M., Jr. 1990. "Campaign Contributions as Investments: The United States House of Representatives, 1980–1986." *Journal of Political Economy* 98: 1195–227.

Thompson, Dennis. 1994. *Ethics in Congress.* Washington, D.C.: Brookings Institution Press.

SUMMARY OF KEY CONCEPTS

1. **Proportional representation** is a class of electoral systems that assigns seats in a legislature to parties or individuals in proportion to the number of votes they receive.

2. **Cumulative voting** is one method of proportional representation, in which voters are allowed to allocate a number of votes (usually equal to the number of seats open for election in a district) among a number of different candidates, including casting more than one vote for a single candidate. This is the method of proportional representation favored by Lani Guinier.

3. A **runoff primary** system requires a candidate to receive a majority of votes cast to receive the party's nomination. If a primary does not produce a majority winner, then a runoff primary is held between the two

top vote getters, with the majority winner in that contest receiving the nomination. This system commonly is used in southern states.

4. In a **plurality primary** system, a party nominee is chosen as the candidate with the greatest number of votes, even if that number is less than a majority cast. This is the most common primary system in the United States.

5. A **gerrymander** is a legislative district drawn to maximize the number of winning candidates who come from a particular group, usually a political party. Gerrymanders often are identifiable through their bizarre shapes.

6. An **at-large district** places all House members from a state in a single, statewide district. At-large districts were commonly used prior to 1850 but have become rare. House members who represent states with only one representative are often said to be elected at-large.

7. A **multimember district** is represented by more than one representative. States generally are prohibited from drawing multimember districts for members of the U.S. House, but many state legislatures have members elected from multimember districts.

8. *Baker v. Carr* is a Supreme Court case decided in 1962 that ruled that the population imbalance of Tennessee's state legislative districts was so great that the districts were unconstitutional. The decision was the first of a series of cases that established the general principle of population equality in drawing legislative districts.

9. The doctrine of **one person-one vote** holds that legislative districts should be drawn to produce districts that are (nearly) equal in population.

10. The **swing ratio** is the predicted change in the percentage of legislative seats held by a political party when that party receives 1 percentage point more of the popular vote.

11. In a **majority-minority district**, minority (e.g., black, Hispanic) voters constitute a majority of the district's population. State legislators were encouraged to draw majority-minority districts following the passage of the Voting Rights Act.

12. *Shaw v. Reno* was a case decided by the Supreme Court in 1993, ruling that districts drawn primarily with race in mind were constitutionally suspect.

13. A **party list system** is an electoral system in which voters cast their ballots in favor of a particular party. A party sends members to the legislature based on the number of votes it receives. The identity of a party's elected legislators is determined by their rank on a *party list*, which records the candidates who are eligible for election.

14. A **first past the post** electoral system elects legislators in single-member districts, the winner being the candidate who receives a plurality of the votes.

15. A **political action committee** (PAC) is an organization set up to raise and dispense money to candidates, to aid their election. The growth of PACs in federal elections was encouraged by the passage of the Federal Election Campaign Act.

16. ***Buckley*** v. ***Valeo*** is a Supreme Court ruling, handed down in 1976, that constrains the types of limits that Congress can put on campaign finance. It approved reporting requirements and contribution limits in the Federal Election Campaign Act but prohibited spending limits except in cases where candidates accepted public financing in return for abiding by those limits.

17. An **independent expenditure** is the use of money, usually by a PAC or other political organization, to aid a candidate for office. Under federal law, such monies must be disbursed without the knowledge of the candidate who benefits and without coordinating the expenditure with the candidate's own campaign organization.

18. **Soft money** refers to political contributions that political parties can seek, from groups or individuals, in unlimited amounts to fund "party building activities." Contribution restrictions on soft money are much less than those on funds given directly to candidates.

19. **Party building activities** are actions taken by political parties to aid the electoral fortunes of their candidates generally without targeting the campaigns of specific candidates, such as voter registration drives and mobilization efforts. Fund-raising for these activities is less closely regulated than fund-raising to benefit specific candidates.

20. ***Citizens United*** v. ***FEC*** is a Supreme Court ruling issued in 2010 that held that restricting corporations and labor unions from using their own funds to engage in express advocacy is an unconstitutional infringement of the First Amendment's right to free speech.

21. **Express advocacy** is a form of political advertising that explicitly argues for the election or defeat of a candidate. Whether an ad engages in express advocacy often comes down to whether it uses one of a set of "magic words," such as "elect," "defeat," or "vote for."

PROBLEMS

Note: The following problems ask you to evaluate outcomes in legislative elections using different voting rules. Refer to Figure P6.1, which shows the ideological location of five candidates (A, B, . . . , E) in an electorate that consists of 1,125 voters. Directly below the indicated location of each candidate is the relative position of the candidate. For instance, Candidate A's ideological position corresponds with the position of the 220th voter, counting from the left; Candidate B's ideological position corresponds with the position of the 445th voter, counting from the left; and so forth.

1. Which one candidate wins the legislative election, under the following rules?

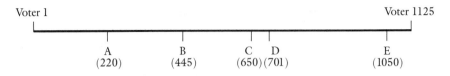

FIGURE P6.1

a. The candidate with a plurality of the votes wins.

b. If no candidate receives a majority in the first round, the two top vote getters compete in a runoff. The runoff winner is elected.

c. If no candidate receives a majority in the first round, the lowest vote getter is eliminated; those who voted for the lowest vote getter then have their votes redistributed to the candidate most ideologically compatible. If no one receives a majority in this round, the lowest voter getter is eliminated; and so on. The first candidate to reach a majority of the votes, through successive iterations of this process, is declared the winner.

Note: The following problems break the ideological spectrum in the middle, separating the electorate into two parties, the L Party and the R Party (refer to Figure P6.2). L Party and R Party voters may vote only for candidates of their own party in the nomination phase but in the general election phase may cross over and vote for the nominee of the other party.

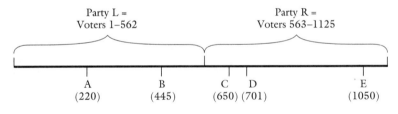

FIGURE P6.2

2. Which candidates are nominated and then prevail in the general election, under the following election rules? Does it matter whether you assume voters are sophisticated or sincere?

a. Nomination is by plurality rule.

b. Nomination is by runoff, with the two top vote getters meeting in a runoff election if no one receives a majority in the first phase.

3. Refer back to the electoral system described in Figure P6.1. If this district elected the top *three* vote getters to the legislature, who would be elected?

Note: The following problems refer to Figure P6.3 which shows the distribution of voters in three legislative districts. The bar graphs illustrate how many voters reside in each of five ideological regions in each district. (For the sake of simplicity, assume that the voters within these ideological regions are evenly

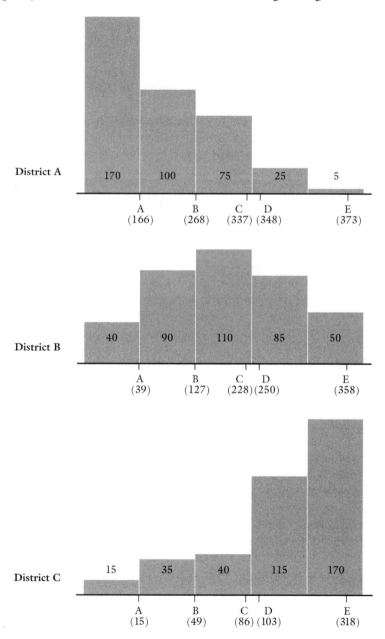

FIGURE P6.3

spaced within the region.) For instance, in District A, 170 voters are on the far left and 5 voters are on the far right; in District B, 40 voters are on the far left and 50 are on the far right; and so on. Note that if you were to combine the ideological distributions of these three districts, you would have a uniform distribution of ideological locations in the combined district. Finally, note that, as with Figure P6.1, the location of five candidates is indicated in each district.

4. Who is the winning candidate in each district, given the following electoral rules?

a. The candidate with a plurality of the votes wins.

b. If no candidate receives a majority in the first round, the two top vote getters compete in a runoff. The runoff winner is elected.

5. Suppose a perfectly square state was composed of one hundred perfectly square precincts, all of whose voters were perfectly loyal to a single party. Three such stylized districts are drawn in Figure P6.4. A precinct with a *D* inside indicates that the ten voters who live in the precinct are all perfectly loyal Democrats; a precinct with an *R* inside indicates that the ten voters who live in the precinct are all perfectly loyal Republicans.

a. Draw five contiguous districts in each state that you would defend as being compact. Calculate the winning party in each district and the overall partisan mix in the resulting legislature.

b. Draw five contiguous districts in each state to maximize the number of seats won by one of the two parties.

6. From www.opensecrets.org, find campaign contribution data for the member of Congress from your home district. (If you are a citizen of another country, choose any district you like.) Write a short paper (2–3 pages) in which you address the following questions:

a. How well does the contribution pattern from PACs match the economic, demographic, and political characteristics of the member's district? (Refer back to Question 14 from the problems at the end of Chapter 1, if you did that question.) How does it match the profile of the member's committee assignments?

b. How does this pattern compare to the earliest election on file for this member at www.opensecrets.org? (If yours is a first-term member, do the comparison using the previous incumbent to hold the seat.)

c. What is the mix in fund-raising between PACs and individual contributions, comparing the most recent election with the earliest election on file? (Again, if yours is a first-term member, do the comparison using the previous incumbent to hold the seat.)

State 1

D	R	D	R	D	R	D	R	D	R
R	D	R	D	R	D	R	D	R	D
D	R	D	R	D	R	D	R	D	R
R	D	R	D	R	D	R	D	R	D
D	R	D	R	D	R	D	R	D	R
R	D	R	D	R	D	R	D	R	D
D	R	D	R	D	R	D	R	D	R
R	D	R	D	R	D	R	D	R	D
D	R	D	R	D	R	D	R	D	R
R	D	R	D	R	D	R	D	R	D

State 2

D	D	D	D	D	D	D	D	D	D
R	R	R	R	R	R	R	R	R	R
D	D	D	D	D	D	D	D	D	D
R	R	R	R	R	R	R	R	R	R
D	D	D	D	D	D	D	D	D	D
R	R	R	R	R	R	R	R	R	R
D	D	D	D	D	D	D	D	D	D
R	R	R	R	R	R	R	R	R	R
D	D	D	D	D	D	D	D	D	D
R	R	R	R	R	R	R	R	R	R

State 3

R	R	R	R	R	R	R	R	R	R
R	R	R	R	R	R	R	R	R	R
R	D	D	D	D	D	D	D	D	R
R	R	D	D	D	D	D	D	R	R
D	D	D	D	D	D	D	D	D	D
R	R	D	D	D	D	D	D	R	R
D	D	D	D	D	D	D	D	D	D
R	R	R	R	R	R	R	R	R	R
D	D	D	D	D	D	D	D	D	D
R	R	R	R	R	R	R	R	R	R

FIGURE P6.4

d. Produce a plot of this member's receipts, expenditures, and cash on hand for each of the past five election cycles, or as far back as the incumbent's career in the House goes. How has this pattern changed over time, and how has it related to the incumbent's electoral vulnerability?

NOTES

1. In the matter of how legislatures are organized, Guinier argued that the standard majority requirements further diminished the influence of racial minorities, even beyond that proportional to their strength in the legislature. So she also advocated mechanisms that would encourage majority-race legislators to include minority-race legislators in ruling coalitions. Such proposals are beyond the subject matter of this chapter, and so I do not pursue them here.

2. Neither chamber of Congress has been eager to enforce the Constitution's electoral rules, even when violations have been clear. The most frequently cited example of this was Henry Clay's election to the Senate in 1806, at the age of twenty-nine.

3. Before the popular election of senators, accomplished in the Seventeenth Amendment, Article 1, Section 4, prohibited Congress from regulating where senators were elected, which effectively prohibited Congress from determining where state capitals were located.

4. Federal Election Commission, "2010 Congressional Primary Dates and Candidate Filing Deadlines for Ballot Access," http://www.fec.gov/pubrec/fe2010/2010pdates.pdf. Last accessed January 14, 2011.

5. Louisiana is known for having its own unique system. In that state, all candidates for Congress, regardless of party, are put on a single "primary" ballot. If one candidate receives a majority in the primary, he or she is elected to Congress. If not, the top two candidates are required to compete in the general election. A useful biennial reference book for state-by-state ballot access requirements is the *Book of the States*, published by the Council of State Governments.

6. See H. P. Young (1988) for a review of mathematical measures of compactness.

7. The case of *Colgrave* v. *Green* involved Illinois, where district populations varied from 112,000 (the 5th District) to 914,000 (the 7th District).

8. Georgia also redistricted in 2005, following a Republican takeover of the state legislature in the 2004 election. This episode has received considerably less attention than the one in Colorado, and certainly in Texas, perhaps because the Georgia redistricting was implemented less dramatically and really affected only two districts. See Hood and McKee (2009).

9. I leave unspecified how the black voters would evenly distribute their votes among these four candidates. For instance, the first fifteen black voters could each give three votes apiece to candidates A and B and two votes apiece to candidates C and D; the next fifteen voters could then give two votes apiece to candidates A and B and three votes apiece to C and D. Other strategies are possible too. *Which* strategy is adopted is not so important as *some* strategy being adopted.

10. Even though only presidential campaigns are eligible for public funding under the FECA, the prevalence of public financing of elections among subsequent congressional reform proposals makes this part of the decision also relevant for congressional elections.

11. "Third Annual Outsell, Inc. Study Forecasts $412.4 Billion in 2008 Advertising and Marketing Spending," July 14, 2008, http://www.outsellinc.com/press/press_releases/ad_study_2008. Last accessed January 21, 2011.

12. The forms of evil range from simple corruption, such as promising political favors in exchange for a contribution, to the diversion of a candidate's time away from the substance of politics and governing.

13. One could argue that the modern presidential campaign finance system would be a good model to use to judge the anticorruption claim. Certainly, Watergate has not repeated itself. However, the number of presidential candidates who have fallen under that system is so small, compared to the number of congressional candidates in any given year, that experience with the presidential system is of only limited utility in judging whether this is a good way to control corruption more generally.

— 7 —

Parties and Leaders in Congress

Political parties are one of the two major structural features of Congress— indeed, of virtually any legislature. Their centrality is symbolized by the first official act of the House of Representatives on its convening every two years. In a ritual bordering on the religious, the chairs of the two parties' caucuses rise and give rousing speeches, each extolling the virtues of that caucus's nominee for speaker of the House. Then, in great solemnity, each House member's name is called by the House clerk, and each shouts out his or her choice for speaker. When the roll is called, all the Democrats vote for the Democratic nominee, all the Republicans for the Republican nominee, and the majority party will have elected one of its own as speaker. Once the new speaker is sworn in, a subsequent series of perfectly partisan roll calls enshrines the majority party's choices into the top administrative offices of the House (like House clerk and sergeant at arms) and determines the rules that the chamber will follow for the next two years. Committees then are appointed, all with majorities and chairs coming from the majority party.

A student of politics who had only a cursory knowledge of the United States would witness this pomp and circumstance and conclude that the American Congress was much like the other parliaments of the world, wherein the majority party controls the organization of the chamber and, consequently, legislative outcomes. But looks can be deceiving. Even in the most strongly partisan eras in American history, national political parties have been weak by international standards. Party leaders in Congress have never been able to assume they could corral all their members to walk in lockstep on important policy questions. Consequently, the weakness of political parties has always been a puzzle to be addressed by scholars, just as it has been a hurdle to be overcome by party leaders.

In this chapter, we examine the puzzle of political parties and party leadership in Congress. In the first two sections, I review the lay of the land with respect to the political parties, describing the evolution of congressional parties and the basics of congressional political party organization. In the third section, I address an important question that recently has been the subject of intense debate among scholars—whether parties are independently powerful and, if so, under what conditions parties might exert that power. In the fourth and final section, I address the issue of *why* political parties might be given the power to influence the legislative process in the ways examined previously.

The History of Political Parties in Congress

Partisan warfare in the United States is currently dominated by Democrats and Republicans, with a principal battlefield being the halls of Congress. By its very nature, Congress always has been the home of contending opinions, but Congress has not always been the home of two political parties. Parties emerged within a decade of the Constitution's ratification, but they were not there at the beginning. Partisan strife has tended to be organized in a bipolar fashion but not always. A few times in the past, the two-party system in Congress collapsed—sometimes because one party completely dominated national politics, other times because the party system became so fractured that the parties themselves could be said to have disappeared.

Party fortunes have fluctuated in complicated and interesting ways throughout American history. Here I examine the number of parties and what each stood for throughout American history. Mostly I examine the major parties, but a detailed understanding of partisan battle throughout congressional history requires us to understand something of the minor parties, too.

In Figure 7.1 presents one measure of the fluctuating fortunes of the two-party system in Congress by graphing a summary measure of the "effective" number of political parties in each Congress for the past two centuries.[1] The solid line shows the House while the dotted line shows the Senate. Presently I discuss the evolution of the political parties and, in the process, details of the figure. For the moment, simply note that the relative balance of the two parties varied significantly in the eighteenth and nineteenth centuries, becoming notably stable in the twentieth century, especially following the onset of World War II. For much of the pre–Civil War period, we had either a one-and-a-half party system (a system dominated by one majority party and exceedingly weak opposition) or a two-and-a-half party system (dominated by two major parties and vexed by one or more minor parties).

As discussed in Chapter 3, congressional behavior derives its momentum from the electoral arena, and from time to time that arena gets fundamentally changed. An important way in which change has occurred has been

FIGURE 7.1
Effective Number of Political Parties in Congress, 1789–2010

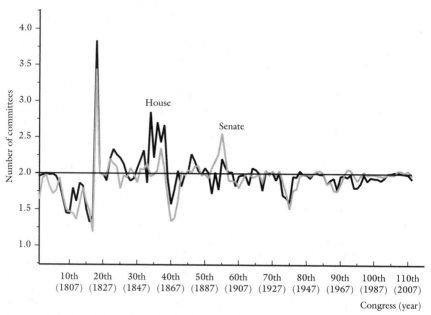

Source: Calculated from data obtained at voteview.com.

through the appearance and disappearance of major political parties. Table 7.1 lists the major parties and the periods of their dominance (see Martis 1989; A. M. Schlesinger 1971). When congressional candidates began regularly taking on party labels in 1794, the labels that were first applied were *Republican* and *Federalist*. Not to be confused with the modern Republican party, the earliest Republicans were followers of Thomas Jefferson. (To help avoid this confusion, sometimes the earliest Republicans are referred to as *Jeffersonians* or *Democrat-Republicans*.) Its political strength resided mainly in agricultural areas, and its supporters tended to oppose an activist national government. Federalists took their political cues from Alexander Hamilton, were more commercial and urban in orientation, and were more comfortable with the national government taking the lead in supporting commercial development. Federalists and Republicans contested fairly evenly until 1800, when Federalist fortunes began a steady decline (refer to Figure 7.1).

The War of 1812 killed off the Federalists, but nothing immediately took its place as an opposition party. For about a decade virtually all members of the House and Senate were nominal Republicans. However, the Republicans themselves were heterogeneous to an extreme, so it is probably more accurate to describe the period around the 1820s as one of *factional* rather than

TABLE 7.1
Major Political Parties in Congress, 1789–Present

Period	Party of the "Right"	Party of the "Left"
1789–1823 (1st–17th Congresses)	Federalists*	Republicans*
1823–1837 (18th–24th Congresses)	Multifactionalism based on old party labels and new individual alliances	
1837–1857 (25th–34th Congresses)	Whigs	Democrats
1857–present (35th Congress–present)	Republicans	Democrats

*During the first two Congresses, Martis (1989) identifies only pro- and anti-administration factions in both chambers. The pro-administration faction evolved into the Federalists and the anti-administration faction evolved into the Republicans.

partisan battle. The extremity of factionalism is illustrated in Figure 7.1 by the spike around 1820, which represents the 18th Congress (1823–1825) when the old Republican Party was split along cleavages that emerged in antici-pation of the presidential election of 1824. Although the vast majority of members of Congress in the 18th Congress nominally were Republican, the Republican members were split among supporters of John Quincy Adams, William Crawford, and Andrew Jackson (Martis 1989, p. 29).

Politicians such as Andrew Jackson and Martin Van Buren reestablished the Republicans, now named the *Democrats*, as a party somewhat in the Jef-fersonian mold while others, notably Henry Clay and Daniel Webster, estab-lished an opposition, called the *Whigs*. The Whigs, too, had many principles in common with earlier partisan forebears, in this case the Hamiltonians and the Federalists. One principal difference between the newer Whigs and the older Federalists was that the Whigs had a strong antipolitician streak, and its followers frequently favored rotation in office. (Recall the history of Abraham Lincoln's House career, reviewed in Chapter 4, which featured Lincoln rotat-ing in and out of the House due to local Whig nominating practices.)

One key feature of Whig-Democrat partisan conflict was that both parties were transregional, meaning each had strong northern and southern wings. This nationalism of both parties came under increasing strains in the first half of the nineteenth century, as tensions over slavery and different paths of economic development tore at national politics. Some of this tension was evident through the emergence of minor parties, such as the Anti-Masons and the American (Know-Nothing) Party. Because of the common appearance of smaller parties in the two decades before the Civil War, Figure 7.1 reveals that Congress really was a "two-and-a-half party" system during this time. (I return later to a more

detailed discussion of what these third parties stood for and how—or whether—
they operated as an independent political force in Congress.)

A distinctly regional and antislavery party, the Republicans, emerged in
the early 1850s. Within just a couple of elections the Republicans had supplanted the Whigs as the principal opposition party to the Democrats. The
Republicans inherited much of the political legacy of the Whigs, particularly
a belief that the federal government deserved a strong role in the nation's
commercial development. However, the antislavery stance of the most radical Republicans garnered the most attention, particularly in the months
leading up to the Civil War.

From 1856 to the present the primary axis of partisan conflict in Congress
and in the nation has pitted Republicans against Democrats. Since then the
relative fortunes of the two parties have waxed and waned. More interesting,
the core policy stances of the two parties have shifted, too. For instance, at
its founding, the Republican Party was known for its greater support of civil
rights for blacks, while the Democratic Party often was violently anti–civil
rights. Today the tables have been turned, with Democrats more often associated with advocating the political interests of African Americans. Similarly,
the Democrats and Republicans have swapped positions on the question of
how active the federal government should be in promoting commercial and
economic development, with the Democrats favoring more activism and
Republicans taking a more laissez-faire attitude.

In addition to the two major parties, Congress has also had minor, **third
party** members. Such members have been relatively uncommon although
not quite rare. Between the 1st and 111th Congresses, 36,555 people occupied House seats.[2] (Of course, this number involves a significant amount of
double counting.) Of these, only about 1,000 members have come from
minor parties. Likewise, of the 8,821 Senate seats occupied since the 1st Congress, only about 300 have been held by minor party senators.

Even though their numbers have been small, in a few Congresses these
minor parties were important because either they held the balance of power
between the two major parties or the issues they espoused gained national
attention. Table 7.2 lists the third parties that have sent more than ten members to Congress over the years and summarizes what they stood for. Most
minor parties have had narrow regional followings. They tended to stake
out positions best characterized by describing what they were against: the
anti-Masons were against elite political groups, Unionists were against secession, the Americans were against immigration, and so forth. In the twentieth
century, the minor parties tended to take positions against more generalized
sets of evils, like political corruption and big business.

The two major parties have tended to stake out positions at the extremes
of whatever passes for ideological debate in any era. In the current era, for
instance, Republicans are to the "right" and Democrats are to the "left."
Where have the minor parties been? All over the ideological map. Some, such
as the Nullifiers in the 1830s, staked out an extreme position on an important

TABLE 7.2
Principal Minor Parties with Members in Congress, 1789–2011

Party	Years of Greatest Strength	Regional Strength	Issue Positions
Anti-Masonic	1829–1841	Western N.Y., Penn.	Anti-elitist
Nullifier	1831–1839	S.C.	States' rights
Unionist	1861–1865	South	Antisecession
American (Know-Nothing)	1845–1861	National	Anti-immigrant
National (Greenback)	1879–1889	South, Midwest	Currency reform
People's (Populist)	1891–1903	Prairie	Agrarian reform
Progressive	1913–1919	Midwest, West	Political reform
Farmer-Labor	1923–1945	Minnesota	Economic reform

Source: Martis (1989).

FIGURE 7.2
Spatial Location, Relative to the Major Parties, of Minor Parties in the 23rd and 65th Congresses (House of Representatives; NOMINATE scores)

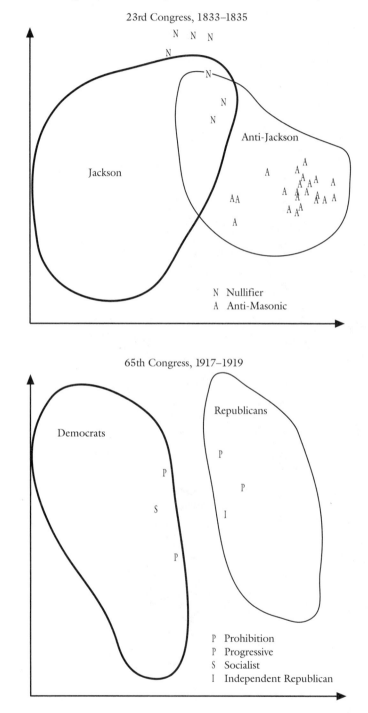

23rd Congress, 1833–1835

Jackson

Anti-Jackson

N Nullifier
A Anti-Masonic

65th Congress, 1917–1919

Democrats

Republicans

P Prohibition
P Progressive
S Socialist
I Independent Republican

issue of the day—the issue of states' rights, particularly the right of state legislatures to declare federal laws inoperative within their state's boundaries. Others, such as the Progressives at the turn of the twentieth century, introduced new issues into national discourse and managed to play off the two major parties against each other.

Figure 7.2 sketches out the spatial locations of the minor parties in the House relative to the major parties in two Congresses, the 23rd (1833–1835) and 65th (1917–1919).[3] The spatial locations are taken from a statistical technique developed by Keith Poole and Howard Rosenthal (1997) we will explore in more detail in Chapter 9 called NOMINATE scores. NOMINATE scores estimate the ideal points of members of Congress based on the roll call votes they cast. In both parts of this figure, the general spatial locations of the two major parties are indicated with irregular figures while the locations of individual members of minor parties are indicated with letters.

In the 23rd Congress, Poole and Rosenthal tell us that the primary (x-axis) dimension of contention split supporters and opponents of Andrew Jackson, while the second (y-axis) dimension divided representatives over regional issues, especially slavery. Note that the Nullifiers, as previously mentioned, staked out the most extreme set of positions in the 23rd Congress over regional issues. This is illustrated by their placement toward the top of the first panel in Figure 7.2. They were so extreme, in fact, that they were never pivotal on regional votes. However, they were centrist with respect to the major issues of factional cleavage so, ironically enough, they may have played a larger role in determining policy outcomes in issues about which its members gained little electoral support. Conversely, the Anti-Masons were ideologically indistinguishable from the extreme of the anti-Jacksonians, who eventually formed the core of the Whig Party. Ironically, the Anti-Masons were more likely to be pivotal on regional issues, which was not the set of issues that got them elected to Congress.

Thus, the 23rd Congress (1833–1835) is a good example of the difficult position that ideologically extreme or narrowly focused minor parties can find themselves in. Neither the Nullifiers nor the Anti-Masons were ever so large or strategically placed as to significantly affect the policy areas they most cared about. It therefore is not surprising that elements of both movements were rapidly absorbed by the major parties in the localities where they arose.

The fate of the Progressives and other minor party House members in the 65th Congress (1917–1919) illustrates how small numbers of minor party members can be influential in Congress out of proportion to their numbers. The House in the 65th Congress was nearly evenly split between Democrats (215) and Republicans (214), with a scattering of Prohibitionists, Progressives, Socialists, and Independent Republicans. Note that in the 65th Congress, these minor party members resided in the middle of the primary ideological axis over which the two major parties contended. Unlike the 23rd Congress, minor parties in the 65th Congress were pivotal.

The Democrats ended up organizing the House in the 65th Congress with eleven votes to spare, due largely to capturing the votes of nearly all the minor party House members in the vote for speaker. No doubt this helped move ahead the agenda of the Progressives during the 65th Congress in areas like women's suffrage and prohibition, issues the minor parties cared about tremendously but that the Democrats probably cared about less than they cared about organizing Congress for their own policy reasons.

Historians and political scientists long have been interested in the politics of minor parties in the United States. For some, this interest represents a break from the tedium of analyzing the same two major parties, year in and year out. For others, it represents a glimpse at what might have been, had political circumstances been slightly different at various times in history. Very little effort has gone into analyzing the strategic role of minor parties of the sort just suggested for the 23rd and 65th Congresses. Yet spatial voting theory suggests that even the most interesting and flamboyant minor party will be only a side show unless it can either (1) prove pivotal in the partisan battles waged by the two major parties or (2) be able to trade off support for its own narrow interests in return for taking positions friendly to one of the two parties (ideally, the majority party).

Party competition in the United States has been waged almost exclusively between two parties—with notable exceptions as described—but nonetheless leavened by minor ("third") parties. Because other Western nations with which we compare ourselves sometimes have more than two parties, it is natural to ask why we tend to have just two and why others, like France, Germany, and Israel, have more.

The most common explanation for two-partyism in the United States is provided by **Duverger's law**, which can be expressed as follows (see Duverger 1954; Rae 1967; Riker 1982): electoral systems with **plurality elections**[4] in single-member districts will tend to produce two-party competition.

The operation of Duverger's law depends on the rational behavior of party elites intent upon winning the election. Its dynamic can be illustrated with a simple example. Suppose, contrary to the expectations of Duverger's law, three parties are in a district: a leftist party supported by 25 percent of the electorate, a centrist party supported by 35 percent, and a rightist party supported by 40 percent. If all the parties' supporters remain loyal, then the rightist party's candidate would win the election with 40 percent of the vote—not a majority but a plurality. If we assume that the leftist party supporters would rather see a centrist represent the district than a rightist, then in the next election it would not surprise us to see the left and center parties combining forces to defeat the rightists, 60–40. If the left-center coalition endures, it may even become a party of its own.

If a dynamic such as this prevails in all districts, each district will have a two-party system. Yet nothing in this dynamic *requires* the two parties to be the same everywhere. Suppose, for instance, that we had another district where the mix of supporters for the left, center, and right parties was divided 40–25–35, with the left party starting out with the plurality. A right-center coalition might emerge in this district the next time around.

Nations sometimes develop such locally idiosyncratic two-party systems. Canada, for instance, for many years tended to experience two-party competition in national parliamentary races and two-party competition for provincial parliamentary races, but the two national parties were not always the same as the two parties that fought it out in provincial elections.

The United States has the further feature of the electoral college, which has tended to operate much like a plurality legislative system, because most states allocate all their electoral votes to the presidential candidate who receives the most votes. This has seriously undermined the long-term strength of minor parties in presidential elections. Therefore, the most likely explanation for why most congressional elections involve two parties is a straightforward application of Duverger's law district by district. That is insufficient for understanding why the *same* two parties compete virtually everywhere. The same two parties compete everywhere likely because of the *presidential* election system.

Parties as Organizations

Following the discussion of the electoral bases and policy stances of the major congressional parties throughout history, the most obvious mark that the parties make on Congress comes through the electoral process: almost all winners of congressional elections have a party label. The more members who share a single party label in Congress, the better are the chances that the party's favored policies will fare well.

An interesting and equally consequential mark of parties on Congress is organizational. Today in both chambers, the majority party controls all the positions of power such as Speaker of the House, and all the important ceremonial posts, such as president pro tempore of the Senate. This control can have two important consequences, which we explore later in this chapter. First, positions of power represent goodies that can be distributed among political supporters, like any other type of spoils. A party that controls a chamber of Congress can allocate opportunities to its members to appoint friends and supporters to jobs in Congress. In modern times, the allocation of such rewards has been muted and quasi-professionalized; the spoils system of the past largely is in the past. In earlier years, however, when a party controlled the organization of a chamber, that control included the ability to sweep out incumbents who printed congressional documents, transcribed congressional debates, folded documents, and worked as committee clerks, replacing them with supporters of the new majority party.

Second, and more important, the majority party can use the positions it controls to set the legislative agenda to coincide with its own partisan agenda. Even though the majority party does not dictate the outcome of roll call votes, it has a greater chance to influence what gets voted on than the minority. Indeed, it can be argued that the greatest benefit to being in the majority is precisely this, determining the legislative agenda.

Two ways in which the organization of the majority party functions to advantage the majority are in scheduling legislation and in distributing positions of policy leadership within the chamber.

Scheduling business

The amount of business facing both chambers is vastly greater than the amount of time available to consider it. And everyone recognizes that some pieces of legislation are more important than others. Despite the numerous ways to regulate the scheduling of legislative business, the primary vehicles in both chambers revolve around the parties.

In the modern Congress, each chamber schedules its business differently. (See Chapter 9 for a more detailed discussion of legislative scheduling.) The House regulates access to the floor for the most important legislation via its Rules Committee. The majority party's numerical advantage on the Rules Committee historically has been greater than the majority party's advantage in the whole chamber. Furthermore, for the past quarter century, membership on the committee has been restricted to loyal partisans of both sides. Less important legislation comes up through two special expedited processes, unanimous consent and suspension of the rules, both of which are guarded by the **speaker of the House**. On the whole, therefore, access to the House floor for all legislation *and* the rules under which important bills are considered are dominated by the majority party. Needless to say, this advantages the majority party in its efforts to push forward its agenda and to resist legislative embarrassment by the minority party.

In the Senate, the flow of legislation is less stacked in favor of the majority than in the House. Party leaders still dominate the scheduling of Senate legislation. Important Senate legislation is considered under complex deals that are formalized as unanimous consent agreements. (Unanimous consent agreements will be discussed in further detail in Chapter 9.) The party leaders typically serve as the focal points in crafting these agreements. As legislation proceeds and adjustments need to be made on the fly to the floor schedule, the majority and minority leaders are responsible for moving the action along. Indeed, by tradition, the Senate majority leader has the **right of first recognition** by the Senate presiding officer: if no one else holds the floor, whoever is presiding over the Senate will recognize the majority leader if he or she requests it. Once recognized, the leader can make a motion (usually for **unanimous consent**) that will guide how the Senate will proceed with its business.

Business has not always been dominated by the party leaders. Before roughly 1880, business got through the floor via a variety of paths, some controlled by party leaders, others by committee leaders. The Rules Committee in the House began its domination of legislative scheduling in the 1890s. Senate leaders were later in grabbing control of the Senate's agenda, but by the 1930s, Senate party leaders were the most active in leading the Senate in its allocation of time.

Distributing leadership among and within the committees

The hallmark of the congressional legislative process is its committee system (see Chapter 8). While membership on the committees formally is established by the majority votes of each chamber, in practice, committee positions are determined by party committees and party caucuses in each chamber. Most important, committee and subcommittee chairs are drawn exclusively from among the majority party. Finally, in setting subcommittee jurisdictions and memberships, the dominant factors are the majority party members of each committee.

[handwritten margin note: all an exercise of power]

Not only does the majority party control all the committee leadership posts but it long has allocated to itself proportionately more seats on committees than their membership in the chambers, particularly in the House. This is illustrated in Table 7.3, which reports the party ratios on each committee in the 112th Congress (2011–12). In the House, the Republicans held a 242–193 edge over the Democrats, so the ratio in the chamber of Republicans to Democrats was 1.25:1. Except for the Committee on Ethics, Republicans held majorities greater than this floor ratio. The Rules Committee, with jurisdiction over the flow of important legislative business onto the House floor, and House Administration, with jurisdiction over House business operations, had over twice as many Republicans as Democrats.

In the Senate the overrepresentation of Democrats was less extreme in the 112th Congress. Indeed, the Democratic edge on five committees—Agriculture, Budget, Commerce, Foreign Relations, and Small Business—was less than the party ratio advantage they held in the chamber. This makes sense from the perspective of the different agenda-setting mechanisms in the two chambers. In the House, where committees effectively are gatekeepers over the entire legislative process, party ratios on committees help the majority party use committee gatekeeping to partisan advantage. In the Senate, where it is easy to bypass committees to get items considered by the whole body, trying to exert partisan agenda control at the committee level hardly seems worth the effort.

[handwritten margin note: committees more impt @ the House—why have committees in a Senate simulation]

The effects of majority party overrepresentation can be shown using the spatial model. Suppose that all of one party's members are on the ideological right and all the other party's members are on the ideological left, as in Figure 7.3. For convenience, the seven members of the legislature from the leftist party are designated *D* and the eight members from the rightist party, *R*. If we were to give the R Party a bare majority on a five-member committee, to match the bare majority it holds in the chamber, and if we choose every third member of the legislature to serve on the committee, we would have Committee I in the figure. Note that this committee's median is very close to the chamber median. Now, suppose we decide that the majority party should have a larger majority on this committee than the majority it holds in the chamber. Further suppose we replace one of the Democrats (it does not matter which) with an R Party member drawn from the middle of that party.

TABLE 7.3

Party Ratios on Congressional Standing Committees in the 112th Congress (2011–2012)

House
(242 R, 193 D; Ratio: 1.25:1)

Committee	Rep.	Dem.	Ratio:1
Agriculture	26	20	1.30
Appropriations	29	21	1.38
Armed Services	35	27	1.30
Budget	22	16	1.38
Education and the Workforce	23	17	1.35
Energy and Commerce	31	23	1.35
Ethics	5	5	1.00
Financial Services	34	27	1.26
Foreign Affairs	26	20	1.30
Homeland Security	19	14	1.36
House Administration	6	3	2.00
Judiciary	23	16	1.44
Natural Resources	27	21	1.29
Oversight and Government Reform	23	17	1.35
Rules	9	4	2.25
Science, Space, and Technology	23	17	1.35
Small Business	15	11	1.36
Transportation and Infrastructure	33	26	1.27
Veterans' Affairs	15	11	1.36
Ways and Means	22	15	1.47

Senate
(53 D, 47 R; Ratio: 1.13:1)

Committee	Dem.	Rep.	Ratio:1
Agriculture, Nutrition, and Forestry	11	10	1.10
Appropriations	16	14	1.14
Armed Services	14	12	1.17
Banking, Housing, and Urban Affairs	12	10	1.20
Budget	12	11	1.09
Commerce, Science, and Transportation	13	12	1.08
Energy and Natural Resources	10	8	1.25
Environment and Public Works	10	8	1.25
Finance	13	11	1.18
Foreign Relations	10	9	1.11
Health, Education, Labor, and Pensions	12	10	1.20
Homeland Security and Governmental Affairs	9	8	1.13
Indian Affairs	8	6	1.33
Judiciary	10	8	1.25
Rules and Administration	10	8	1.25
Small Business and Entrepreneurship	10	9	1.11
Veterans' Affairs	8	7	1.14

FIGURE 7.3
Effect of Majority Party Overrepresentation on Committees in the Agenda-Setting Process

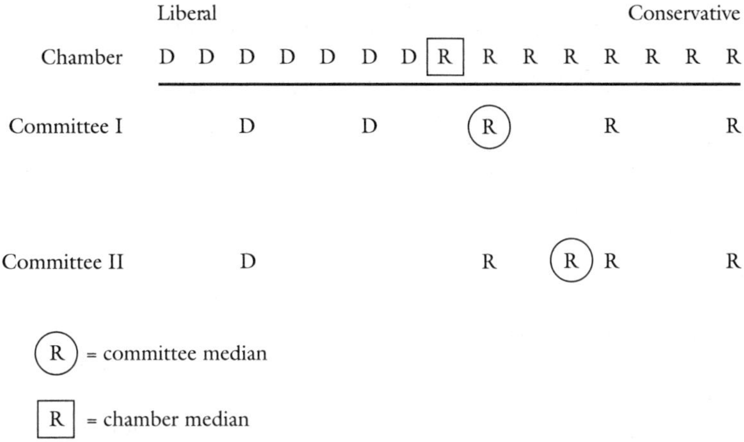

	Liberal													Conservative
Chamber	D	D	D	D	D	D	D	☐R	R	R	R	R	R	R
Committee I			D		D		(R)		R		R		
Committee II		D					R	(R) R			R		

(R) = committee median

☐R = chamber median

This would yield a committee such as Committee II in the figure. Note that Committee II's median is well to the right of Committee I's, by virtue of the extra member from the majority party.

In addition to the organizational advantages seized by the majority party in setting the legislative agenda, the party structures are important organizing principles for the conduct of business in Congress. Even when they do not necessarily convey a partisan advantage to the majority party, two important legislative activities have been centralized within partisan congressional organizations: promoting attendance and facilitating bargaining.

Promoting attendance and spreading information

The job of a member of Congress involves juggling many competing demands, some of them within Congress itself, others outside Congress. Party organizations are responsible not only for communicating with its members which issues are particularly important for the future health of the party but also for making sure that its members are physically present in the chamber when important votes are taken.

Facilitating inter- and intraparty bargaining

Leaders of the congressional parties serve as representatives of the party. They tend to hold preferences typical for the party, which puts them in the perfect position both to be the focal point for negotiations among members of the two parties in Congress *and* to help facilitate bargaining among different factions and interests within a party. Furthermore, negotiations between Congress and the president tend to be spearheaded by party officials.

The party organization of the contemporary Congress

The functions served and services rendered by party organizations are handled within a structure that gradually has grown in scope, complexity, and sophistication over the past two centuries. Table 7.4 delineates the current set of party leadership offices and organizations and identifies the incumbents as of the 112th Congress (2011–2012). This table organizes party positions hierarchically, starting with constitutional positions and proceeding down through the ranks.

Although the Constitution does not specify that the constitutional officers will be party positions, they have been so for most of American history, so I place the constitutional head of each chamber at the top of the table. The House has only one constitutional head, the Speaker, who has been from the majority party, except in those rare instances when no single party held a majority of the seats. The relationship between party and constitutional leadership is a bit more complicated in the Senate, where the Constitution specifies, in effect, two leaders—the vice president, who also serves as the **president of the Senate**, and the **president pro tempore**, who formally serves in his absence. Because the vice president is elected independent of the senators, there is no guarantee that the president of the Senate will be from the majority party. Of fifty Senates in the twentieth century, fifteen were formally led by a vice president of the minority party. *Biden, 114th congress*

The speaker not only holds constitutional leadership of the House but he or she also has been given substantial authority in the House rules over the years to convert that formal leadership into effective leadership. As discovered in Chapter 3, however, that power has waxed and waned. For instance, until 1911, speakers appointed all committees, which gave them great influence over the general flow of legislation and, as important, great influence over how rank-and-file members actually spent their time on Capitol Hill. From 1858 to 1911, Speakers also chaired the Rules Committee, which gave them enormous influence over the flow of bills onto the House floor. The revolt against Speaker Cannon in 1911 took from the speaker these powers, and from then until the early 1970s, the influence of speakers over the details of legislation and the flow of business was diminished. The Democratic Party in the early 1970s restored to the speaker some (although not all) previous authority in these areas. When the Republicans took control of the House in 1995, they continued along the same lines. Now, committee assignments for the majority party are made in a committee in which the Republican speaker has the most influence; majority party Rules Committee members now are appointed by the speaker. (The minority party leader has analogous power within that party.)

TABLE 7.4
Congressional Leadership Organization at the
Start of the 112th Congress (2011–2012)

| | House | | Senate | |
	Democrats	Republicans	Democrats	Republicans
Constitutional head	—	*Speaker* John Boehner (OH)	*President* Joseph R. Biden, Jr. (DE) *President pro tempore* Daniel Inouye (HI)	—
Floor Leader	*Minority leader* Nancy Pelosi (CA) *Assistant leader* James E. Clyburn (SC)	*Majority leader* Eric Cantor (VA)	*Majority leader* Harry Reid (NV)	*Minority leader* Mitch McConnell (KY)
Whip	*Minority whip* Steny Hoyer (MD)	*Majority whip* Kevin McCarthy (CA)	*Assistant majority leader* Richard Durbin (IL) *Chief deputy whip* Barbara Boxer (CA)	*Minority whip* John Kyl (AZ) *Chief deputy whip* Richard Burr (NC)

(Continued)

TABLE 7.4
**Congressional Leadership Organization at the
Start of the 112th Congress (2011–2012) (*Continued*)**

	House		Senate	
	Democrats	*Republicans*	*Democrats*	*Republicans*
Caucus	*Caucus* Chair: John Larson (CT) Vice chair: Xavier Becerra (CA)	*Conference* Chair: Jeb Hensarling (TX) Vice chair: Cathy McMorris Rodgers (WA) Secretary: John Carter (TX)	*Conference* Chair: Majority leader Vice chair: Charles E. Schumer (NY) Secretary: Patty Murray (WA)	*Conference* Chair: Lamar Alexander (TN) Vice chair: John Barrasso (WY)
Policy Committee	*Steering and policy committee* Chair: Speaker Co-chairs: Rosa Delauro (CT), George Miller (CA)	*Policy committee* Chairman: Tom Price (GA)	*Policy committee* Chair: Charles E. Schumer (NY)	*Policy committee* Chair: John Thune (SD)
Committee on Committees	*Steering and Policy Committee*	*Steering Committee* (28 members) Chair: Speaker		
Campaign Committee	*Democratic Congressional Campaign Committee* Chair: Steve Israel (NY)	*National Republican Congressional Committee* Chair: Pete Sessions (TX)	*Democratic Senatorial Campaign Committee* Chair: vacant	*National Republican Senatorial Committee* Chair: John Cornyn (TX)

Looking to the Senate, however, the Speaker's power at its nadir always exceeded the power of the Senate leaders at its zenith. Of the president of the Senate, Woodrow Wilson said, "The chief embarrassment in discussing [the vice presidency] is, that in explaining how little there is to be said about it one has evidently said all there is to say" (Wilson 1963 [1885], p. 162). The same could be said (or not said) of the president pro tempore, as well.

Prior to the Civil War, from time to time, the Senate gave to the "presiding officer" the right to make committee assignments. However, that grant of power quickly ran afoul the basic political problem with the vice president having real influence in the chamber: this person need not agree with the majority of senators on policy, since the vice president is party to an external political alliance with the *president.* In modern times, Lyndon Johnson hoped to strengthen the vice presidency within the Senate when he was elected in 1961 as John F. Kennedy's running mate. Johnson's hopes were not far-fetched, since he previously had served as the chamber's majority leader and, being a Democrat, was a member of the Senate's majority party. Johnson nonetheless was rebuffed, as the Senate Democrats elected Mike Mansfield (Mont.) their leader, relegating Johnson to ceremonial irrelevance. [VP isn't impt. in Senate (or in general?)]

The real power in the Senate, therefore, resides at the second rung down in Table 7.4, among the **floor leaders**. Formally, each party in each chamber elects a floor leader. By tradition, the leader of the majority party in each chamber is called the **majority leader**, while the leader of the minority party is called the **minority leader**. (During their decades-long status as the minority party, the House Republicans became tired of the term *minority.* Hence, they adopted the term *Republican leader* as the minority leader title. The Democrats took up a similar practice following the 1994 election, when they returned to the minority in each chamber.) [floor leader maj./min. leader]

As the term implies, the floor leaders take particular responsibility for the legislative product of their parties. While other partisan officers below them are responsible for most of the legislative heavy lifting, the floor leaders serve as point people in the legislative process. Some of the influence is formal. For instance, all floor leaders also are members of party councils that decide legislative strategy and distribute committee assignments. Perhaps the most important role all the floor leaders serve is a public relations function, communicating the interests of their party members to others in Washington and throughout the country. [Collective representative, by necessity (at least Speaker!)]

On the Senate side, the party leaders play an added legislative role distinct from that played by House party leaders. Senate leaders are responsible for helping negotiate **unanimous consent agreements**, which are the vehicles that provide for the consideration of most of the important legislation on the Senate floor. In the Senate, where the rules give small, intense minorities many opportunities to obstruct the legislative process, having the responsibility to clear the consideration of legislation is an important task, Underlining this responsibility is a tradition in the Senate, whereby the majority leader is given the right of first recognition by the presiding officer. While the same courtesy does not extend to the minority leader, practically speaking, very little proposed by the majority leader has not been cleared by the minority leader. (The deference given to the party leaders by the presiding officer is symbolized by the seating pattern in the Senate chamber. In the front row of the chamber, on the center aisle, the Democratic leader sits to the right of the presiding officer, while the Republican leader sits on the left.)

Each of the parties has a **whip** organization, which are the eyes, ears, and arms of the parties. The term *whip* is taken from English fox hunting. Apparently, none of the animal participants in a fox hunt wants to be there: the foxes, obviously, do not look forward to being mauled by the hounds, and the dogs would rather be doing doglike things in the woods, ignoring the scrawny foxes they are supposed to chase. Fox hunts can deteriorate into chaos, and so people on horses must keep all the dogs and the fox moving together, roughly in the same place. The individuals are called *whippers-in*.

Just like the potential chaos of a fox hunt, passing legislation can devolve into chaos. Although members of the parties mostly agree among themselves on grand principles of policy, they often disagree on details. The whip operations allow for the parties to gather information about how their members stand on particular measures, informing both party and committee leaders about the courses of action most likely to elicit support from the party rank and file. Once legislation is considered, events can move too quickly for everyone to follow. Therefore, the whip operations also communicate with the party's members, notifying the rank and file of the evolution of legislation and the party's stance on legislation (including amendments). Finally, the complex lives of members of Congress often mean that legislators can be far from Capitol Hill at critical legislative moments, particularly at roll calls. The whip operations also serve the prosaic function of promoting roll call attendance among party members.

At the top of the whip operations stand individuals in each chamber's party designated the party whips. Below the whip is a complex and fluid whip organization. Indeed, the whip organizations have been the most fluid of all major organizational elements in Congress for the past quarter century. In addition to the whip (and chief deputy whip, which most of the parties now have) are deputy whips, regional whips, and class whips. The whip operations as a consequence, can get quite large. For instance, in the 106th Congress, the House Republicans identified forty-one representatives as holding some formal position in the whip organization, while Senate Republicans had a total of ten senators in their whip operation.

Below the positions of constitutional head, floor leader, and whip, the party apparatus becomes more collective. For instance, the membership of the two parties in each chamber constitutes each party's **caucus**. (Note that only the House Democrats actually refer to themselves formally as a *caucus*. The House Republicans and both parties in the Senate refer to the collection of partisans as their **conference**.) Each party has a caucus chair separate from any of the leaders mentioned previously. The formal role of the **caucus chair** is to preside over meetings of the caucus and speak when a party position has been announced. Usually, the chairs of the House caucuses make the nominating speeches for Speaker candidates at the start of each Congress. Most important, the chairs (and particularly the secretaries and vice chairs) of the caucuses have been grooming grounds for up-and-coming party leaders. They also have provided the parties opportunities to elevate to national prominence party members with particular demographic characteristics. For instance, as the Democrats sought to appeal to professional women politically, it seemed natural to symbolize this appeal through naming women to caucus offices.[5] Not to be outdone, Republicans have followed suit. For instance, Republicans in 1999, hoping to blunt an image of hostility toward African Americans, elevated the lone African American House Republican, J. C. Watts (Okla.), to chair their caucus.[6]

Below the caucus, the parties have experimented with mixes of "policy" committees, "steering" committees, and committees on committees. **Policy committees** give party activists and strategists opportunities to explore substantive issues that might benefit the party. On the other hand, **steering committees** generally function as a sounding board for the senior party leadership.

One set of party committees deserves mention: each party in each chamber sponsors a **campaign committee**, whose function is to recruit candidates and raise funds for congressional races. Aside from the caucuses, these committees are the oldest institutional manifestations of the parties, tracing their lineage back to the mid-1800s. In recent years, these committees have taken on greater prominence in the biennial congressional elections, for both their recruitment and fund-raising functions. In 2010, for instance, the disbursements of these committees amounted to about one third of the campaign spending in congressional races. The House Republicans especially were noted for raising the activity and sophistication of their campaign committee to new heights in the early 1980s. Indeed, the recruitment and support of candidates is widely viewed as an important foundation on which Newt Gingrich built political support within the Republican Party for his eventual rise to speaker. Republicans in the Senate and Democrats in both chambers caught on, so that the chairs of these four committees now are very prominent in the halls of Congress.

The gratitude of members of Congress for the funds raised has been shown by the elevation of campaign committee chairmen to higher party office. Tony Coehlo of California, for instance, in 1986 went from chair of the **Democratic Congressional Campaign Committee** (DCCC) to become the House majority whip. Senator Charles Schumer's (D-N.Y.) tenure as chair of the **Democratic Senatorial Campaign Committee** (DSCC) from 2005 to 2009 was so successful that he was elevated to chair the Democratic Steering Committee in the 112th Congress (2011–2012).

But whoever lives by the sword can die by the sword. In the aftermath of the 1998 congressional election debacle for the Republican Party, the chairs of their two party campaign committees met vigorous challenges for reelection. John Linder of Georgia was defeated for reelection as chair of the Republican Congressional Campaign Committee (now the **National Republican Congressional Committee**), being replaced by Tom Davis of Virginia. Mitch McConnell of Kentucky, chair of the Republican Senatorial Campaign Committee (now the **National Republican Senatorial Campaign Committee**), survived a challenge from Chuck Hagel of Nebraska. Conversely, Martin Frost, Democrat from Texas, felt the gratitude of his colleagues in 1999 when he was elevated from chair of the DCCC to chair of the Democratic caucus.

The party apparatus just described helps deliver a set of private and public goods to members of the respective parties. The party structures, in turn, have important effects on the politics of the chambers in unexpected ways. Two of these are discussed here: how the party structures help embody factional divisions in the parties and how the structures help define one of the two major career paths in each chamber.

Overcoming factional divisions

The first nonobvious effect of party organization is that the "team" put in place when party leaders are elected represents a power-sharing arrangement among party factions. Who is included on the team provides a clue about which interests are "up" and which are "down." The most famous example of such a power-sharing arrangement was the "Boston-Austin connection" that grew up within the leadership of the Democratic Party from the New Deal until the 1980s. As the name implies, the Boston-Austin connection described the tendency of the Democrats to cement their northern and southern wings through the election of a northerner and a southerner to the two most prominent party leadership positions in both chambers.

The operation of the Boston-Austin connection is seen most easily in the pairing of the top two Democratic positions in the House from the 1940s until the late 1990s. The genesis of the connection came in 1940, when Sam Rayburn of Texas was elected speaker of the House and John McCormack of Massachusetts replaced Rayburn as majority leader.[7] When Rayburn died in 1961, McCormack was elevated to speaker and Carl Albert of Oklahoma was elected majority leader. (While Albert did not represent Austin, or even Texas, his district was adjacent to Rayburn's.) When McCormack retired at the end of the 91st Congress, Albert was elevated to speaker. But the first violation of the Boston-Austin pattern in over thirty years occurred with the election of Hale Boggs of Louisiana to the position of majority leader in 1971. However, following Boggs's death in 1972, Thomas P. ("Tip") O'Neill, from Cambridge, Massachusetts, was elected majority leader, reestablishing the Boston-Austin link. The connection continued once O'Neill ascended to speaker in 1977 and Jim Wright, from near Fort Worth, was elected majority leader.

The Boston-Austin connection was severed completely in 1987, when Wright became speaker, but a westerner, Tom Foley, of Washington, was elected to the number 2 spot. When Wright stepped down as speaker in 1988, under pressure in the midst of a scandal, Foley replaced him as speaker, but Foley's replacement as majority leader was Richard Gephardt, from Missouri. When the Democrats went into minority status in 1995, Foley also was defeated for reelection. This defeat allowed Gephardt to ascend to the top Democratic post; the Democratic second in command became David Bonior, of Michigan.

For the half century the Boston-Austin connection was in operation, it helped to cement an understanding within the party that its leadership would keep the House from wandering off to the two extremes, either to the far left favored by northern Democrats or the far right favored by southerners. Particularly before the passage of the 1964 Civil Rights Act, the pairing of leaders from a racially conservative northern city and a racially moderate southern state helped to defuse race as an issue within the Democratic Party. As the parties began to realign in the mid-1960s, the logic behind the Boston-Austin connection unraveled. Ideological, not regional, balance became the operative principle. Hence, current Democratic leadership teams are not geographically based but based on a pairing of liberals and moderates.

Republicans have had policy divisions within their ranks, but they have not been so serious as those of the Democrats. Therefore, they lack the equivalent of a Boston-Austin connection. The closest thing is a weak variant of the "Main Street-Wall Street" division, which sometimes has split the party. That is, the Republican Party often has been characterized as embodying the sometimes-conflicting interests of finance and large-scale capital (Wall Street) versus the farm and small business (Main Street). Some hint of a pairing reflects the Main Street-Wall Street division in the Republican Party's history. For instance, from 1943 to 1975, one top Senate leader tended to be from the Midwest (Main Street) and another from either California or the East (Wall Street). A similar pattern in the House, if it ever existed at all, died when the Joseph Martin (Mass.)–Leslie Arends (Ill.) leadership pairing ended in 1959.

Leadership ladders

A second indirect effect of the way the party organizations have developed is that leadership ladders emerged in each of the parties. This career ladder has been in existence the longest among the House Democrats. Since 1933, every House Democratic majority leader has stepped into the speaker's chair once the upper position became open. Since 1962, most Democratic Party leaders gained their position by being first elected party whip. The Republican leadership path has been more varied, Robert Michel of Illinois was elevated from whip to minority leader in 1981, on the retirement of John Rhodes of Arizona. When Michel retired in 1995, his whip, Newt Gingrich of Georgia, moved up to replace him. However, when Gingrich left the House in 1999, the Republican Party leader, Dick Armey (Texas) was passed over in favor of J. Dennis Hastert (Illinois), who had been the chief deputy whip for the Republicans. John Boehner was elected to head the House Republicans following the 2006 election on an upset victory over then-minority whip Roy Blunt (R-Mo). When the Republicans regained the majority following the 2010 election, he was elevated to speaker without challenge.

Not surprisingly, the leadership career ladder in the Senate emerged more gradually than in the House and shows signs of deemerging in recent years. Three Senate Democratic leaders in a row (Johnson, Mansfield, and Byrd) ascended to that position from the number 2 slot. Their two successors, George Mitchell (Maine) and Tom Daschle (So. Dak.) vaulted into the top position from outside the ranks of party leadership altogether. Likewise, of the eight most recent top Republican leaders, four (Dirksen, Scott, Lott, and McConnell) have risen from the second-ranked position, while three others (Knowland, Baker, Dole, and Frist) have not. However, Harry Reid (Nev.) rose to the position of Democratic leader having been Democratic whip, so this line of succession is not completely dead.

Perhaps because the job of party leader is less routine than the job of committee member (or committee chair), the career path on the leadership side is less direct and secure than a career path a member can follow within the committee system. Yet, to the degree that lower-level party leaders know they automatically will be favored to move up in the hierarchy should they function to the mutual benefit of all the party rank and file, party leadership emerges as an incentive system that functions to tie the particular success of party leaders to the general success of the whole party.

On the Strength of Parties

To even the casual observer of congressional politics, the important place of parties in the legislative firmament is obvious. Therefore, it probably comes as a shock that the question of whether parties really are important in legislating frequently has arisen in the study of Congress. No one denies the obvious: the parties, as organizations, are the primary vehicles for the organization and smooth functioning of both chambers. What *is* in question is whether the activity of the parties makes any substantive difference in the long run. This section first explores reasons that doubt has been expressed about the efficacy of parties, then examines important responses to these doubts.

Point: Parties are weak

Doubt about whether parties really matter legislatively rests on a collection of empirical and theoretical arguments advanced by scholars over the years. The empirical arguments are the oldest and the most intuitive.

Consider **party unity**, the tendency of members of one party to vote cohe-
sively within its ranks against the cohesive ranks of the opposition. Aside
from the vote for speaker and other occasional procedural matters, almost no
roll calls end up pitting all the Democrats against all the Republicans. In the
111th Congress (2009–2010), for instance, only 36 percent of all roll call
votes in the House saw at least 90 percent of the Democrats voting one way
and at least 90 percent of the Republicans voting the other. By a weaker
threshold of party cohesiveness—at least half of a party voting against at
least half the opposition—evidence of party unity has not been all that stunning. About 75 percent of the House roll calls were party unity votes, by this
criterion, in the 111th Congress.

This seemingly low level of party unity voting still is high by the standards
of the mid-twentieth century. Figure 7.4 plots the historical evidence: party
unity voting rates in Congress since 1887. High levels of party unity were
commonplace in the nineteenth century but declined over time in the twentieth, enjoying an up-tick as the century closed.

So we frequently observe a lack of cohesion among members of both political
parties in both chambers. Despite the frequent lack of cohesiveness among the
congressional parties, one could retort that the parties vote in a quasi-cohesive

FIGURE 7.4

**Party Unity Voting in the House and Senate, Using
the 50 Percent Criterion, 50th–111th Congresses**

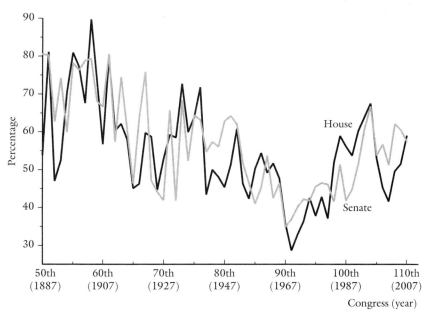

Source: voteview.com.

fashion at least *most of the time*. That must account for something. Here, we turn to theory to cast doubt on the pull of political parties in Congress.

To frame the theoretical question, it may be useful to consider this counterfactual example: suppose we regularly observed large majorities of Democrats voting together against large majorities of Republicans. Could we *then* infer that the political parties were strong in Congress? The spatial theory of voting suggests not.[8] Suppose ideal points were arrayed as illustrated in Figure 7.5. In this example, the Democrats are on the left and the Republicans are on the right. (The two triangles describe the distribution of ideal points among the Ds and Rs.) There is a small amount of overlap between the two parties but not much. Also included is a hypothetical status quo and motion. The dashed line indicates the "cut point" between the motion and the status quo; that is, the point at which everyone on the left favors the motion and everyone on the right favors the status quo. If this vote were taken in the House, for instance, and everyone voted sincerely, then the final outcome would pit almost all the Ds against almost all the Rs. Yet this cohesiveness would not be the result of the party doing anything *as a party*. Rather, this cohesiveness would be entirely because the two parties' members already had sorted themselves along the left-to-right continuum. Ideologically presorted parties plus motions with cut lines in the middle of the ideological space produce observed cohesion. Unless party leaders work to achieve a level of cohesion that exceeds what would occur if preferences were simply left to run their course, it is hard to argue that this is a case of party *strength*.

To judge that the parties are independently powerful, we need to do more than show party solidarity. We need to show that party members, at least some

FIGURE 7.5
Conditions Necessary for "Strong" Parties

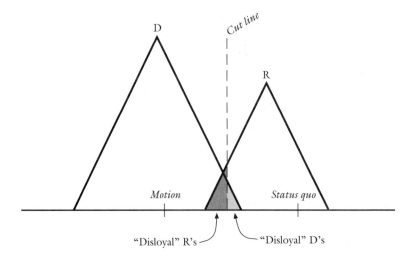

of the time, vote contrary to their preferences, in ways desired by the parties. In terms of the example in Figure 7.5, this would require the potentially disloyal Republicans (i.e., Republicans located in the shaded area of the figure) to support the party; likewise for disloyal Democrats. Whether and how often this happens in practice is an important question to which we will return.

Counterpoint: Parties are powerful

> When 435 Members pack into the House chamber this week to decide whether to impeach President Clinton, all eyes will be fixed on the shrinking number of undecided moderate Republicans and Democrats. . . . While roughly 400 Members have already declared their positions on the articles of impeachment reported out by the House Judiciary Committee, more than two dozen Republicans and a handful of Democrats are still in play. . . . Majority Whip Tom DeLay (R-Texas), the powerful vote counter who desperately wants Clinton impeached, has denied threatening any Members. But the message is being sent through conservative activists that any moderate defector can expect the flowing stream of campaign contributions to dry up and a primary challenge to emerge if they defect. "The only unanswered question," as one GOP leadership aide said, "is 'Will the pressure work?'" ("A Score of Moderates to Watch: Twenty Members Key to Clinton's Fate," *Roll Call*, December 14, 1998)

Members of Congress receive all sorts of pressure to vote particular ways—from constituents, interest groups, contributors, their staff, and party leaders. As this quote suggests, the pressure extends even to (or especially to) momentous constitutional decisions like impeachment. The quote also provides an interesting lens into partisan "pressure" as it is said to exist. The majority whip, Tom DeLay, who was presumably in a position to exert "pressure" on reluctant Republicans, found it necessary to disclaim any direct partisan activity in the late-1998 impeachment votes. At the same time, one of his (unnamed) aides also felt it necessary to note that the word had been channeled through Republican interest groups and campaign contributors that a pro-impeachment vote was expected out of moderate Republicans. In the end, moderate Republicans overwhelmingly supported impeaching President Clinton, suggesting that party pressure, at least in this instance, worked.

If party pressure exists in a systematic fashion, the quote also suggests that it may come from a variety of directions. Even when party pressure has been successfully exerted, members of the party leadership honestly may be able to say that *they* had not twisted arms.

As often happens in the social sciences, it is exceedingly difficult to study whether party pressure actually is effective in any particular instance (not to mention across several instances) because party pressure may come in so many forms and its effects may be so diffuse. If we are to search for evidence of party pressure in congressional decision making, the best research strategy probably is *not* to ask members of the House whether party pressure was exerted on any particular vote or if party loyalty was demanded in exchange for a good committee assignment, for example. Instead, we should look for the *effects* of party pressure, should they exist.

The most obvious place to look for evidence of party pressure is in the roll call record. Stories abound of party leaders "twisting arms" in important legislative battles. A classic example of such a story was contained in the vote to pass President Clinton's budget plan in 1993:

> When the clock ran out, all eyes in the House were on the scoreboard. Democrats still needed two votes to pass President Clinton's economic plan. Democratic leaders hovered around freshman Rep. Marjorie Margolies-Mezvinsky of Pennsylvania, who had deserted Clinton the first time his economic package came before the House. Finally, after the automatic voting system had been shut down, she walked to the rostrum along with Pat Williams, the Democrat who represents the entire state of Montana. They signed their names on the back of green voting cards. Green for yes. "They sort of jumped together," said a House staff member who was counting votes. "Butch Cassidy and the Sundance Kid." ("A Day of Tension, Cajoling—and Relief," *Washington Post*, August 6, 1993, p. A1)

Marjorie Margolies-Mezvinsky previously had won election to the House in 1992 in a very narrow race, having promised to vote against tax increases. Unable to win passage of their president's economic package, House Democratic leaders finally appealed to Margolies-Mezvinsky to switch sides, causing her to renege on a promise to her constituents. As she walked down the aisle to change her vote, a House Republican taunted her with "Good-bye, Marjorie." Indeed, she was unable to overcome her pressured loyalty to leadership and was defeated for reelection in 1994.

Stories like this fill the newspapers whenever a major policy change is enacted by Congress, particularly changes that are highly partisan. Still, an old saying goes "dog bites man isn't news; man bites dog *is* news." An episode like Margolies-Mezvinsky's party-induced change of heart may be noteworthy because of its rarity, not because it reflects how business regularly is done in Congress. Consequently, congressional scholars look for broader measures of legislative behavior in order to judge whether and when parties successfully exert pressure on their members or materially influence the legislative agenda.

We can study the average behavior of all members of Congress across all the roll call votes taken to gain a broader perspective on whether a party exerts an independent pull on the behavior of its members. Here we have to be careful, though, lest a naive reading of the roll call record make us overly eager to embrace evidence of effective party pressure. We do know, for instance, that the average Democrat tends to vote frequently with other Democrats against the way that most Republicans are voting. But we also know that most Democrats are from Democratic districts and that most Republicans are from Republican districts. So when we observe members of the two parties frequently voting against each other, this hardly is evidence of party pressure or power—it may be evidence of constituency "pressure" or even simply evidence that districts tend to elect like-minded representatives to Congress.[9]

Political scientists James Snyder and Timothy Groseclose (2000) suggest a more sophisticated way of using the roll call record to uncover evidence of party voting. Suppose political parties from time to time *do* induce some of their members to vote the party line, contrary to their own personal preferences. When would they do so? Because any rewards or punishments party leaders could use to pressure their members are scarce, party leaders cannot exert pressure on every roll call vote. Parties are likely to exert pressure to win roll call votes. Therefore, party leaders who already know that their position is going to win or lose on the floor are unlikely to work very hard to change the behavior of "disloyal" members. Similarly, if the vote is "too close to call" at the beginning of the legislative battle, we would be more likely to expect the party leaders to roll out the big guns, twist some arms, and try and wring a little loyalty out of at least some of their members.

This observation prompts Snyder and Groseclose to explore the roll call voting behavior of Republicans and Democrats when roll calls are close and when they are lopsided. Looking at all roll call votes from 1871 to 1996, they found that over half of all close roll call votes exhibited statistically significant signs of party influence, independent of the preferences of the party members. Breaking down the study into smaller time periods, they found evidence of party pressure in 73 percent of roll call votes at the beginning of the twentieth century, but only 35 percent in the 1970s and 1980s. In the 1990s, the incidence of party pressure rose to the 60 percent range.

Another place to look for evidence of the independent power of parties is through the agenda process. Political parties in Congress often are said to be *procedural coalitions*, which means that party leaders may excuse some disloyalty on substantive votes, particularly for electoral reasons, but they expect great loyalty on procedural issues, such as passing resolutions to consider legislation, passing the rules of the chamber, and the like. Given all the previous discussion, you might suspect that expecting loyalty on procedural matters is not neutral from the perspective of public policy, and you would be right.

Consider the following example of how the exercise of procedural power by a political party might work to the advantage of that party, even if its members are allowed to "vote their conscience" when roll calls are held on the floor. The majority parties in both chambers of Congress, in fact, hold procedural advantages in deciding what will get to the floor of that chamber for a final vote—particularly in the House. For instance, the House Rules Committee, which effectively controls the House agenda, had a larger number of Republicans on it in the 106th Congress (1999–2000) than it would have been entitled to if seats had been distributed on the committee in the same ratio as Republicans in the House. Presumably, this allowed the Republican Party to control the House floor agenda.

FIGURE 7.6
How Agenda Control Might Enhance the Success of the Majority Party in Policy Making

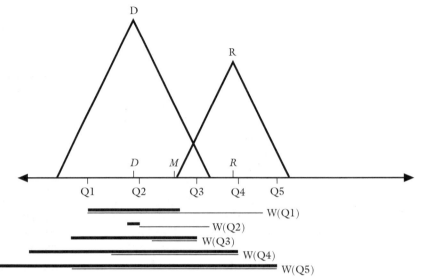

Note: Thin lines indicate the relevant win sets against the status quo; heavy lines indicate the relevant preferred-to set of the Democratic median.

Here is an example that illustrates a simple version of how such agenda control might work. Suppose that preferences are arrayed as illustrated in Figure 7.6. Democrats are the majority and to the left; Republicans are the minority and to the right. (This is the same distribution of ideal points you saw in Figure 7.5.) The location of the Democratic and Republican medians, along with the overall median for the chamber (designated M), are indicated. The figure indicates five different status quo points, $Q1, Q2, \ldots,$ $Q5$. For each status quo a thin line indicates the win set that beats it. Thick lines indicate the preferred-to set of the Democratic median against each status quo.

In each case, if the voting rule is pure majority rule, the median gets his or her ideal point passed into law. But suppose that instead of pure majority rule, the rules governing motion making are highly partisan, as follows: the median of the majority party gets to make a motion on how to change policy from the status quo; the motion then is voted on in a take-it-or-leave-it fashion. If the majority party median does not want to propose a motion, he or she does not have to. For the status quo to change, both the floor median *and* the majority party median must prefer the proposal to the status quo.

Inspection of this figure shows that except when the status quo is at Q2, the intersection of the win set and the Democratic median's preferred-to set is not empty; thus in most cases a motion will be made. The Democratic median can't always get his ideal point, however. Notice that when the status quo is at Q3, $W(Q3)$ does not include $P_D(Q3)$. Even here the Democratic median can offer the left-most point of $W(Q3)$ as a motion and it will pass.

From the perspective of party power and cohesiveness note the following features of Figure 7.6. First, whenever policy is changed, at least a majority of Democrats support the change. Sometimes a majority of Republicans also support the change (as when the status quo is at Q1), but typically a majority of Republicans are in opposition. Second, whenever policy is to the right of the Democratic median, the agenda mechanism always either preserves the status quo or allows policy to move to the left. *Policy never moves to the right, even when a chamber majority might support a rightward move.* Third, whenever policy is to the left of the Democratic median, policy will move to the right but never further right than the Democratic median, even when a chamber majority would support a movement even further to the right.

The preceding describes the operation of **negative agenda control**. If the majority party can do no more than keep off the floor any policy proposal that most of the majority party opposes, then policy gradually will gravitate toward the mainstream of the majority party. Along the way, you will never observe the majority party losing a vote.

Using reasoning like this, political scientists Gary Cox and Mathew McCubbins (1999) have argued that a simple test of whether majority parties in Congress actually exercise influence over the substance of legislation is whether the majority party wins more roll call votes than the minority. They argue that we should examine roll calls and see whether the final outcome of each vote goes contrary to the desires of most of the majority party. (If most of the majority party *does* lose a roll call vote, this is called *rolling* the majority party.) If something akin to pure majority rule or random floor access dominates procedural matters, then the majority party frequently will be rolled. If something akin to the example in Figure 7.6 operates, then the majority party rarely will be rolled.

How often is the majority rolled and how does this compare to the frequency of the minority being rolled? One answer is provided in Figure 7.7, which reports the "roll rates" of the majority and minority parties in the House and Senate from the 1860s to the 2010s. With only three exceptions in the House and four in the Senate since the Civil War, the minority has always been rolled more often than the majority on roll call votes. Close comparison of the House and Senate graphs in Figure 7.7 reveals that the majority party is rolled a little more and the minority party a little less in the Senate, which is consistent with the notion that agenda control mechanisms are more robust in the lower chamber. The important point is that even in periods when the parties were less unified than they are today, and even in the chamber that is more prone to anti-majority-party revolts on the floor, the majority party in both chambers is consistently able to steer the agenda away from votes that divide them.

FIGURE 7.7

Roll Rates of the Majority and Minority Parties in Congress, 37th–111th Congresses, 1861–2010

A. House

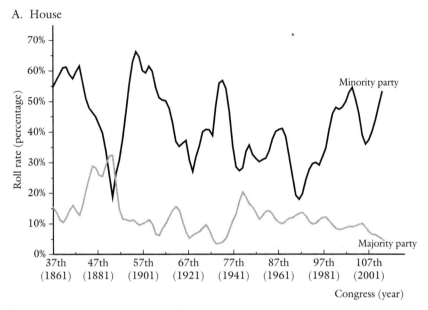

B. Senate

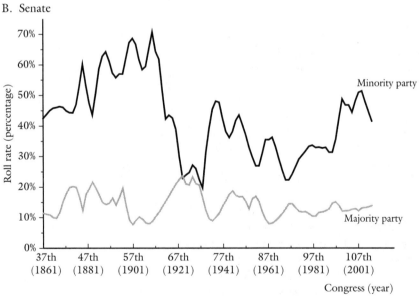

Source: Calculated by the author from data provided at voteview.com.

Perhaps the best example of the power of agenda control in recent years came in the 112th Senate (2001–2002), which started off split fifty-fifty, with Vice President Albert Gore (Dem.) breaking ties in organizational votes in favor of the Democrats, so for a brief moment Democrats controlled the Senate. When Dick Cheney (Rep.) assumed the vice presidency on January 20, 2001, he was able to side with the Republicans, so control shifted to the GOP. Then, on May 24, 2001, Senator James Jeffords of Vermont quit the Republican Party and became a Democrat, giving the Democrats a clear 51–49 majority in the Senate, allowing them again to control Senate organization and giving the Democratic leader, Tom Daschle (S.D.) first-mover advantage in setting the Senate agenda. For the period between January 20 and May 23, when Republicans controlled the Senate, a Democratic majority was on the winning side of roll call votes 53 percent of the time; after May 24, under Democratic control, they were on the winning side 84 percent of the time.

Thus two strands of research provide evidence that the majority party has powerful means to influence the policy process directly. This research cautions us, however, against assuming that the evidence of party pressure will be uniform—sometimes the evidence will be on the floor, other times before the bill even gets to the floor.

The Benefits of Strong Parties in Congress

In concluding this chapter, it would serve us well to consider *why* political parties might exert influence on legislative outcomes. Even if the research just reported stands the test of time, party "pressure" and party-based gatekeeping are costly to members of the majority party, particularly majority party "moderates,"[10] in terms of policy. On a vote-by-vote basis, why do members appear to "knuckle under" to the party? On a more long-term basis, why do the party rank and file support the creation of a party organization that will coerce them some of the time?

In recent years, political scientists have wrestled with this question, providing a number of explanations that share one common feature: they suggest that legislative political parties provide collective goods that individual legislators could not provide on their own. These explanations differ, however, in *which* collective good they emphasize.

For instance, Mathew McCubbins emphasized the *electoral* goods that the legislative party organizations provide (Kiewiet and McCubbins 1991; Cox and McCubbins 1993). What McCubbins and his collaborators have in mind is not the obvious electoral benefit that the party organizations provide, campaign contributions, but something more subtle. McCubbins notes that for all the talk about the decline of political parties in the United States, voters still rely heavily on political party as a voting cue (recall the discussion in Chapter 5). Furthermore, year-to-year fluctuations in electoral outcomes definitely have a partisan cast, with each candidate of a particular party gaining, or losing, due to national partisan tides.

To the degree these partisan tides are due to voters making judgments about the collective performance of Congress and to the degree that voters know who controls Congress, the party rank and file may want to endow its leaders with special authority to make the legislative trains "run on time." Viewed this way, the various powers given party organizations, like committee appointments and scheduling, make sense as mechanisms for creating a relatively coherent legislative program that bears the stamp of the majority party and then gets it enacted on the floor.

The role of the parties in this view is much like that of a national office of a hamburger franchise. The McDonald's corporation has made a fortune by franchising thousands of stores that offer a uniformly high-quality product anywhere in the United States. Achieving this uniform high quality is no easy task. Each store owner, at least in theory, has an incentive to free ride on the McDonald's reputation: cutting corners, lowering costs, luring in unsuspecting customers, and making even more money. The contract between McDonald's and its franchisees not only prohibits such free riding but contains mechanisms to enforce the contract (like inspectors and auditors) and punish noncompliance.

While the analogy between legislative parties and hamburger franchises is not perfect, it helps to think about the relationship between the rank and file and party leaders in this way. The rank and file gives over to its leaders certain authority to try to create a relatively uniform, positive image of the party that is of benefit to all party members. It cedes to those leaders the right to punish (at least mildly) recalcitrants, just as franchise contracts contain performance penalties for slackers. Because of this analogy, the McCubbins argument sometimes is termed the *brand name* explanation.[11]

It is not hard to be skeptical about this argument, for at least two reasons. First, considerable research ties congressional electoral partisan tides to the *president's* performance, but little finds a correlation between *congressional* performance and partisan tides in congressional elections. Second, very few voters actually know which party controls Congress. If they lack this important fact at their fingertips, how can the supposed rewards of a good brand name be distributed?

Even so, recent history is full of a sufficient number of political stories consistent with the brand name explanation that this argument cannot be dismissed out of hand. For instance, in 1980 and 1982, the Republican Party ran a series of television ads featuring an actor who resembled W. C. Fields, intending to evoke an image of the Democratic Party as bloated and out of control, playing on the physical resemblance between Fields and Democratic Speaker "Tip" O'Neill (Mass.). Likewise, Speaker Newt Gingrich (Ga.) became the symbol of a Clinton-obsessed Republican Party that was more interested in Clinton's sex life than in legislating in the 1998 congressional election. More recently, the unifying theme in the 2010 midterm election among Republican candidates was animosity toward Democratic speaker Nancy Pelosi (Calif.), who was identified as the legislative brains behind President Obama's legislative victories. Campaign strategists certainly believe that if the public develops a negative perception of the other party's congressional leaders, especially one based on their legislative activities, all the better for their party's candidates.

While it is possible to examine the common electoral goods that party leaders can bring their followers, it is also possible to point out the *policy* goods that the party apparatus can provide. One of the most important public goods that party leaders can provide their followers is the service of *coordination*. Legislative coordination is particularly important whenever a policy issue before Congress is complex. In such cases, we know (from the theory presented in Chapter 1) that even if a majority agrees that *something* should be done to change policy, there is no guarantee that a majority will settle on anything in particular.

In discussing the coordination problem, political scientists often resort to a game in Game Theory called the **battle of the sexes**. Here, briefly stated, is how that game works.

Imagine a couple, Agnes and Bob. Agnes likes professional wrestling more than anything else in the world except, of course, hanging out with Bob. Bob, on the other hand, adores going to the ballet more than anything else in the world, except spending the evening with Agnes. To complete the setup, Agnes really hates ballet and Bob hates wrestling. However, Bob likes Agnes more than he hates wrestling, so he would rather endure a night at a wrestling match than a night sitting at home alone. Likewise for Agnes: she would rather go to the ballet with Bob than sit at home alone for the evening.

Because Agnes and Bob are so absorbed in their special pastimes, after-hours life for them consists of only four possibilities: (1) Agnes and Bob can go to the ballet together, (2) Agnes and Bob can go to the wrestling match together, (3) Bob goes to the wrestling match while Agnes goes to the ballet, or (4) Agnes goes to the wrestling match while Bob goes to the ballet. Here is the summary of how they each rank these four possible ways of spending an evening:

Rank	*Agnes*	*Bob*
1	Go to the wrestling match with Bob	Go to the ballet with Agnes
2	Go to the ballet with Bob	Go to the wrestling match with Agnes
3	Go to the wrestling match alone	Go to the ballet alone
4	Go to the ballet alone	Go to the wrestling match alone

Agnes and Bob meet at the local diner for breakfast. After eating, they part ways, calling after each other, "see you tonight!" Only after they leave each other do they realize that they did not settle on what they would do after work. Assuming that they cannot phone each other during the day, what should Bob and Agnes do after work?

Both Agnes and Bob would be pretty miserable going to his or her favorite activity alone: for both, this is her or his third choice. If both decide to be nice and show up at the favored venue of the *other* person, they are even worse off, since the risk is that Agnes would show up at the ballet alone and Bob at wrestling. If only they could figure out how to coordinate during the day. Only then could they guarantee achieving one of their two top outcomes. Without coordination, they are virtually doomed to endure their two least favorite nights out.[12]

This sort of coordination dilemma faces the parties as they decide how to construct complex legislative packages. The story of the "Powell amendment" in Chapter 2, in part, was one of coordination. Democrats, as a whole, had the votes necessary to pass a federal aid-to-education bill. The tricky question was knowing *which* bill would pass: a bill without a prohibition against school segregation or one with the prohibition. The leadership of both parties swung into place, as activists on both sides of the issue tried to get their members to coordinate their behavior in the face of potential strategic voting. In this case, the Powell amendment story is of *failed* coordination, since the Democratic leadership could not convince a large enough bloc of Democrats to oppose the renegade Powell. Nonetheless, had the Democratic leadership *not* played a role in this case, including efforts by President Truman and former first lady Eleanor Roosevelt, federal aid to education would have had absolutely no chance of passage.

One final argument recently has been put forward in the discussion of the independent efficacy of political parties in Congress, the **conditional party government** argument by David Rohde (1991). Rohde argues that, at least as far as legislative coordination is concerned, the political parties vary across time in the degree to which they can serve the coordinating and sanctioning roles we associate with strong parties. One important *condition* must be met before the rank and file will give over to its leaders the tools necessary to exercise strong leadership: the party must be cohesive. Without widespread cohesion within a party about legislative goals, giving party leaders a large arsenal of carrots and sticks would be counterproductive. The rank and file either would rebel or (assuming that the lack of cohesiveness was electorally based) meet widespread electoral defeat.

Looking across history, we see general support for Rohde's argument. The times in American history, such as the 1880s and 1890s, when the parties were the strongest in Congress are also the times when the two parties' constituency bases were the most internally consistent. In recent years, the electoral context of the two parties has rationalized, making the electoral environments of Democrats and Republicans more internally homogeneous than they have been for nearly a century. This no doubt has paid off in terms of greater cohesiveness among Democrats and Republicans in Congress in recent years, which, in turn, has provided the founda-

13. A party's **whip** is the official responsible for communicating the desires of party leaders to the rank and file, polling party members on important matters, and communicating with the party leaders about the desires of the rank and file.

14. A **caucus** is a meeting of all of the members of a particular party in one of the chambers of Congress. Caucus meetings discuss legislative strategy and make nominations for leadership positions. Sometimes a party will designate its all-encompassing gathering a **conference.**

15. The **caucus chair** presides over party caucus (or conference) meetings and serves on the party's leadership team. The caucus chair often is a stepping-stone to even higher party office or serves to highlight a party's concern with the issues associated with particular demographic groups.

16. The **policy committee** is a party organ in a chamber consisting of top leaders who examine policy on behalf of a party, occasionally suggesting or endorsing new initiatives.

17. The **steering committee** is a party organization consisting of the top leaders responsible for managing the party's internal affairs. For the Democrats in the House and Senate, the steering committees recently have served as the Committee on Committees, a function the Republicans usually reserve for a separate, dedicated committee.

18. A **campaign committee** consists of members of a party in one of the chambers of Congress responsible for helping to recruit party candidates and raise funds for them. These committees are the **Democratic Congressional Campaign Committee** (DCCC), the **Democratic Senatorial Campaign Committee** (DSCC), the **National Republican Congressional Committee** (NRCC), and the **National Republican Senatorial Committee** (NRSC).

19. A **party unity** vote is a roll call vote in which a majority of the members of one party vote against a majority of the other party. (Sometimes, the threshold is higher, such as 90 percent.) The fraction of times party unity votes appear in a Congress is a measure of overall partisan polarization. The fraction of times an individual legislator sides with his or her party on party unity votes is a measure of the party loyalty of that member.

20. **Negative agenda control** is activity by the majority party to keep off the floor bills that could pass, even though most of the majority party opposes the bill.

21. The **battle of the sexes game** is a non-zero-sum, two-person strategic game used to illustrate the losses individuals endure when they wish to coordinate their behavior around a single choice but cannot do so with certainty, owing to the inability to bind one or both actors to a strategy beforehand.

22. **Conditional party government** is the tendency of the political parties in Congress to be responsible (i.e., work in favor of a single coherent policy) only when the preferences of party members are relatively homogeneous.

NOTES

1. This measure of the "effective" number of parties is constructed as follows. Call f_i the fraction of the seats held in a legislature by party i and indicate the number of parties in the legislature with n. Then, the effective number of parties is defined as

$$\left(\sum_{i=1}^{n} f_i^2 \right)$$

For instance, if there are three parties of equal size, then $n = 3$ and $f_1 = f_2 = f_3 = 1/3$; thus, the effective number of parties is $1/(1/9 + 1/9 + 1/9) = 3$. If party 1 holds 50 percent of the seats, party 2 holds 30 percent, and party 3 holds 20 percent, then the effective number of parties is $1/(0.5^2 + 0.3^2 + 0.2^2) = 2.63$. A similar measure of the market concentration of firms is called the *Herfendahl index*. See Rae (1967, Chap. 3) for a discussion of various ways to measure the number of parties in a political system.
2. This number is the sum of the number of people elected to the House in its history. Therefore, it is greater than the number of *individuals* elected to the House.
3. Estimates of spatial positions are taken from Poole and Rosenthal's NOMINATE scores (see Poole and Rosenthal, 1997, and www.voteview.com).
4. *Plurality election* means that the candidate who receives more votes than anyone else wins an election.
5. One embarassment in doing this is that, by tradition, the number 2 position in the caucus is titled *secretary*. Democrats, hoping to be seen as champions of women in nontraditional roles, quickly saw the problem with this title and switched it to *vice chair*.
6. The House Democrats had to manage a sticky situation on the symbolic politics front when they were relegated to minority status following the 2010 election. Traditionally, when the majority party had been overturned, in the upcoming Congress, all the party leaders would retain their rank, just move down a rung in term of job titles. For instance, the former speaker would become the new minority leader, the former majority leader would become the new minority whip, and the old majority whip would be out of a job. However, if the Democrats had followed this tradition, they would have had to remove from leadership the highest-ranking African American in the government, James Clyburn (D-S.C.), who had previously served as the Democratic Party's majority whip, so that Steny Hoyer (D-Md.) could move from being majority leader to minority whip. Rather than risk an embarrassing fight between Hoyer and Clyburn, Nancy Pelosi (D-Calif.), who was stepping down as speaker to become minority leader, created a new position, "assistant Democratic leader," to rank immediately behind the minority whip, but at least initially without any known job description.
7. Although McCormack in fact was from Boston, Rayburn was from Bonham, Texas, several hundreds of miles from Austin, which is quite outside Rayburn's district. The term *Boston-Austin connection* represents a bit of poetic license.
8. The argument that follows is made most forcefully and persuasively by Krehbiel (1998).
9. In his book on the passage of the 1946 Employment Act, Stephen Kemp Bailey characterized how internal pressure might work when he discussed the relationship between Senator C. Douglas Buck (R-Del.) and the DuPont corporation, the largest employer in his state:
To suggest that Buck as a Senator was a "tool" of the Du Ponts is to misinterpret the nature of what Lynd has called the "business-class control system." It was

not the pressure of Du Pont *on* Buck, but the pressure of Du Pont *in* Buck which was at work. (Bailey 1950, p. 192)

10. By *moderates*, I mean members of the party in the middle of the overall ideological continuum. When Democrats are the majority party, these are "conservative" Democrats; when Republicans are the majority, these are "liberal" Republicans.

11. As with all analogies, it is dangerous to push this one too far. In particular, it is difficult for an individual franchisee to change the contract, as it would be impossible for a majority of franchisees to revolt against national headquarters and demand new management if sales were to slump in a particular year.

12. Of course, if Agnes and Bob make a habit of forgetting to settle on their night's activities before parting for the day, they might adopt strategies to do better than they might do in this one-shot example. For instance, if Agnes and Bob both flip coins, then half the time they end up together at one of the two locations, half the time they are alone. A better strategy probably would be to call each other during the day.

— 8 —

Committees in Congress

RQ:
Hyp:

> In form, the Committees only digest the various matter introduced by individual members, and prepare it, with care, and after thorough investigation, for the final consideration and action of the House; but, in reality, they dictate the course to be taken, prescribing the decisions of the House not only, but measuring out, according to their own wills, its opportunities for debate and deliberation as well. The House sits, not for serious discussion, but to sanction the conclusions of its Committees as rapidly as possible. It legislates in its committee-rooms; not by the determinations of majorities, but by the resolutions of specially-commissioned minorities; so that it is not far from the truth to say that Congress in session is Congress on public exhibition, whilst Congress in its committee-rooms is Congress at work. (Wilson 1963 [1885], p. 69)

With the words "Congress in session is Congress on public exhibition, whilst Congress in its committee-rooms is Congress at work," American political science was born. While this assertion is a bit hyperbolic, it holds a grain of truth. Political science as a discipline arose only toward the end of the nineteenth century, on the heels of a transformation of American higher education and the professions. That transformation involved, in part, the creation of research universities in the model of those found in Germany. Among the first to adopt this model was Johns Hopkins University, and among its first Ph.D.s in political science was a young southerner named Woodrow Wilson.

Wilson's dissertation, later published as *Congressional Government*, would have been memorable even if he had not gone on to be the president of the United States. Wilson's analysis represented a bold move in the intellectual analysis of American political institutions. He brushed aside the hagiography that had attended most learned discourse on the institutions handed down in the Constitution. (Notice that Wilson was writing on the eve of the centennial of the U.S. Constitution, and so Constitution worship was in the air.) In *Congressional Government*, he held up Congress to judgment against what Wilson regarded as the highest good that a national legislature could stand for. Because the Constitution had placed Congress at the heart of the national governing system, he imagined that the keystone of all national institutions should have certain characteristics: it should be deliberate, draw the attentive citizenry into its deliberations, respect the political equality of its members, and allow voters to judge directly whether policy had been beneficial to the nation, so that voters could reward or punish those who were responsible.

As the epigraph to this chapter suggests, Wilson found Congress lacking. Rather than being dominated by the deliberations on the floors of the two chambers, congressional business was dominated by the secret, idiosyncratic machinations of its committees. Rather than integrating national power, Congress dispersed and *dis*integrated national power. By relying on committees and stealth, Congress was irresponsible, not responsible.

In the century since Wilson wrote, political scientists have written volumes about the behavior of congressional committees. Even though Wilson's words were controversial at the time and his analysis has come under tough scrutiny, his identification of congressional committees as the working centers of Congress was absolutely correct. Corresponding with their critical positions in the legislative process, congressional committees are the most-studied part of Congress.

The purpose of this chapter is to introduce congressional committees, both the contours of committee behavior and the theoretical perspectives of their study. You may think: "Woodrow Wilson first identified congressional committees as the keystone of congressional activity. I understand why I need to know something about what congressional committees do and how they do it. But why do I need to know something about the *theoretical perspectives* surrounding the study of committee behavior?"

By examining theoretical perspectives on committee behavior, we gain a better understanding of *why* congressional committees behave as they do and can judge whether committees contribute to or detract from the democratic-representative character of Congress. Although scholars of Congress all agree with Wilson about the importance of committees, many regard his normative views about congressional committees as theoretically confused.[1] It can be argued that Wilson underappreciated how a division-of-labor system (which is what congressional committees are formally) actually operates in a complex organization. All complex organizations operate through delegation, so the right question in judging the quality of committee deliberations is not whether their legislative products were rubberstamped on the floor but whether the resulting legislative product was "better" than what would have emerged without the use of committees. It is impossible to judge the contribution of congressional committees to legislating without specifying theoretically what we could expect committees to accomplish in a relatively pure, theoretical environment.

The plan of this chapter is as follows: the first section explores the most important empirical features of the committee system, reviewing its basic shape, its historical development, and important patterns associated with committee membership and leadership. The second section focuses briefly on the differences between the House and Senate committee systems, highlighting along the way committees in both chambers that deserve particular attention. The final section steps back from the empirical aspects of committees to explore the important ways in which theorists of legislative behavior have approached the committee system over the past century.

The Committee System

Congress relies on many different types of committees, so I will start empirically, by discussing what the different types of congressional committees do. We then turn to the historical development of the committee system. Following that is an examination of the important topics of committee membership, including committee appointments, the selection of committee chairs, and the transfer of members between committees. This section concludes by examining two important features of the committee system: subcommittees and committee staff.

Committee basics

Committees in the United States Congress are organized according to some basic features, which are summarized in Table 8.1. Most committees are organized within a single chamber, although the membership of some—joint committees and conference committees—spans the two chambers. Committees also vary according to their persistence. Some, most notably the standing committees, can be considered permanent. The House Ways and Means Committee, for instance, has been in continual existence since the 1790s. Others are short term, created to study a particular issue (like most **select** and **special committees**) or finalize a particular piece of legislation (**conference committees**). Finally, while most congressional committees are created primarily to consider legislation, a few are not legislative, being either investigatory or administrative.

Standing committees are the best known of the congressional committees, being responsible for almost all legislation. They are written into the rules of both chambers and thus have a sense of permanence about them.[2] Not only do the identity and jurisdictions of standing committees typically remain unchanged from Congress to Congress but most members also continue from one Congress to the next, as do the staff.

TABLE 8.1
A Morphology of Congressional Committees

Type of Committee	One Chamber or Two	Permanent or Ad Hoc	Legislative or Not
Committee of the whole	One	Ad hoc	Legislative
Standing	One	Permanent	Legislative
Select and special	One (usually)	Both	Usually not legislative
Joint	Two	Permanent	Usually not legislative
Conference	Two	Ad hoc	Legislative

Until 1946, neither chamber was very precise in specifying the jurisdictions of its committees. Instead, both relied on decades of informal practice to guide the reference of bills to committees. That changed with the Legislative Reorganization Act of 1946, which rationalized the committee system considerably. The rules of both chambers now delineate in fine detail which matters belong to which committees. Table 8.2 shows the jurisdictions of the two "taxation" committees in the House (Ways and Means) and Senate (Finance), as defined in the rules of the 112th Congress. Note that even these committees, which have relatively simple jurisdictions, can lay claim to matters far removed from their obvious jurisdiction (which in this case is taxing and finance), such as Social Security. Even though the jurisdictions are clearly defined in the House and Senate rules, vigorous "turf wars" are fought among the committees for the right to consider legislation, in cases where jurisdiction is unclear or overlapping (King 1994, 1997).

Select and special committees[3] have many of the features of standing committees but lack their formal permanence and usually the ability to report legislation. From the mid-1800s to the present, both chambers have tended to rely on select committees to investigate matters that emerge unexpectedly on the political agenda and are expected to recede from the agenda shortly.

Some of the most notable committees in various historical eras have been select committees. For instance, in the early 1970s, elements of the Watergate scandal were exposed through the Senate Select Committee on Presidential Campaign Activities, chaired by Senator Sam Ervin (D-N.C.). More recently, in the 106th Congress (1999–2000), the Senate appointed the Special Committee on the Year 2000 Technology Problem to investigate and report back on the nation's readiness to deal with the so-called Y2K bug.

Select committees provide members with political advantages that standing committees lack. Because they focus on a single issue, it is easier for the

TABLE 8.2
Jurisdictions of the House Ways and Means and Senate Finance Committees, 112th Congress (2011–2012)

House Ways and Means Committee (Rule 10.1 (t))	Senate Finance Committee (Rule 25(i))
Customs, collection districts, and ports of entry and delivery	Bonded debt of the United States
Reciprocal trade agreements	Customs, collection districts, and ports of entry and delivery
Revenue measures generally	Deposit of public moneys
Revenue measures relating to insular possessions	General revenue sharing
Bonded debt of the United States	Health programs under the Social Security Act and health programs financed by a specific tax or trust fund
Deposit of public monies	National social security
Transportation of dutiable goods	Reciprocal trade agreements
Tax-exempt foundations and charitable trusts	Revenue measures generally
National social security	Revenue measures relating to the insular possessions
	Tariffs and import quotas and matters related thereto
	Transportation of dutiable goods

Source: House Rules; *Senate Manual.*

press to cover the proceedings of select committees and communicate them to the general public. Therefore, membership on select committees can be highly sought after among members who desire a public platform. The publicity select committees generate often redounds to the benefit of committee members, especially the chairs. The Senate Watergate committee was popularly known as the *Ervin Committee*. The Senate special committee that investigated organized crime in the 1950s was popularly known as the *Kefauver Committee* after its chairman, Estes Kefauver (D-Tenn.).

Select committees are popular among members of Congress because they allow them to pursue politically interesting issues without having to forgo membership on other committees. The rules and party practices of both chambers restrict the number of standing committees on which members can serve. So a representative who wants to switch over into another area of specialty typically has to quit one committee to acquire membership on another. Members of select committees escape these rules, so that a senator who wants to spend time on an issue away from his or her standing committee assignments can do so without jeopardizing longer-term legislative interests. For this reason, the party leaders in both chambers are under great pressure to expand the number of select committees and even, at times, designate certain committees that should be standing as select. One example of this latter phenomenon is the designation of the Senate Indian Affairs committee as a select committee in 1977, and then its designation as a "permanent select committee" in 1985.[4]

Table. 8.3 lists the standing and select committees that existed in the House in the 112th Congress (2011–2012). Table 8.4 lists the Senate committees. The remainder of this and the next section reviews important features of these committees. For the moment, simply note the following. First, the committees in both chambers vary considerably in size, jurisdiction, staff and financial resources, subcommittee complexity, and degree to which the majority party dominates the membership. Second, in both chambers, the majority party (the Democrats in the 112th Congress) hold a majority of seats on almost all committees[5] and a member of the majority chairs all committees.

In addition to the well-known standing and (lesser-known) special committees, both chambers of Congress use other committees to transact specialized business. The joint rules of the two chambers, for instance, currently make provision for three **joint committees**: the Joint Economic Committee, the Joint Committee on Taxation, and the Joint Committee on the Library of Congress. Joint committees are composed of members from both chambers, with the chair (typically) rotating between the two. Only one joint committee has ever been given jurisdiction over legislation, the Joint Committee on Atomic Energy, which existed from 1947 until 1979.

Over the past century, the number of joint committees has been reduced and their jurisdictions farmed out to the separate standing committees of the two chambers. A small skirmish broke out in the 104th Congress over this trend, when the House leaders wanted to eliminate the Joint Committee on Printing (which oversees the Government Printing Office) and the Senate leaders wanted to keep it. The skirmish was part of a larger effort, supported by a vocal group within the Republican caucus, to streamline the operations of the House and eliminate vestiges of what they considered to be past Democratic wastefulness.

While joint committees such as Printing and Library generally labor under obscurity, two joint committees, on Taxation and Economics, do their work closer to the limelight. The Joint Economic Committee (JEC), which was created by the 1946 Employment Act, was intended to be the depository of macroeconomic expertise on Capitol Hill. For many years, the JEC's hearings

TABLE 8.3
Committees in the 112th House (2011–2012)

Name	Chair	Reps.	Dems.	Party Ratio*	Staff	Sub-committees	Budget ($m)
Agriculture	Frank D. Lucas, Okla.	26	20	1.3:1	53	6	12.2
Appropriations	Harold Rogers, Ky.	29	21	1.4:1	142	12	28.5
Armed Services	Howard P. "Buck" McKeon, Calif.	35	27	1.3:1	59	7	15.1
Budget	Paul Ryan, Wisc.	22	16	1.4:1	75	0	12.1
Education and the Workforce	John Kline, Minn.	23	17	1.4:1	76	4	16.7
Energy and Commerce	Fred Upton, Mich.	31	23	1.4:1	111	6	22.4
Ethics	Jo Bonner, Ala.	5	5	1.0:1	22	0	5.9
Financial Services	Spencer Bachus, Ala.	34	27	1.3:1	68	6	17.4
Foreign Affairs	Ileana Ros-Lehtinen, Fla.	26	20	1.3:1	88	7	17.9
Homeland Security	Peter T. King, N.Y.	19	14	1.4:1	62	6	16.9
House Administration	Daniel E. Lungren, Calif.	6	3	2.0:1	44	2	10.5
Judiciary	Lamar Smith, Tex.	23	16	1.4:1	82	5	16.8
Natural Resources	Doc Hastings, Wash.	27	21	1.3:1	62	5	15.7
Oversight and Government Reform	Darrell E. Issa, Calif.	23	17	1.4:1	99	7	21.2
Rules	David Dreier, Calif.	9	4	2.3:1	37	2	6.8
Science, Space, and Technology	Ralph M. Hall, Tex.	23	17	1.4:1	52	5	13.3

Small Business	Sam Graves, Mo.	15	11	1.4:1	30	5	6.9
Transportation and Infrastructure	John L. Mica, Fla.	33	26	1.3:1	84	6	19.8
Veterans' Affairs	Jeff Miller, Fla.	15	11	1.4:1	38	4	7.3
Ways and Means	Dave Camp, Mich.	22	15	1.5:1	96	6	19.6
Permanent Select Committee on Intelligence	Mike Rogers, Mich.	12	8	1.5:1	32	3	10.3

*The party ratio (Republicans: Democrats) in the chamber was 1.3:1.

Sources: Clerk of the House, *List of Standing Committees and Select Committee of the House of Representatives*, March 18, 2011, http://clerk.house.gov/committee_info/scsoal.pdf; H. Res. 147 (112th Cong., 1st sess.), for committee budgets, except Appropriations; H.Res. 22 (112th Cong., 1st sess.), for Appropriations; *Congressional Staff Directory: 2010/summer.* (2010). Washington, DC: Congressional Quarterly Press.

TABLE 8.4
Committees in the 112th Senate (2011–2012)

Name	Chair	Dems.	Reps.	Party Ratio*	Staff	Sub-committees	Budget ($m)
Agriculture, Nutrition, and Forestry	Debbie Stabenow, Mich.	11	10	1.1	48	5	9.6
Appropriations	Daniel K. Inouye, Hawaii	16	14	1.1	74	12	15.2
Armed Services	Carl Levin, Mich.	14	12	1.2	51	6	16.3
Banking, Housing, and Urban Affairs	Tim Johnson, S.D.	12	10	1.2	61	5	14.8
Budget	Kent Conrad, N.D.	12	11	1.1	53	0	15.4
Commerce, Science, and Transportation	John D. Rockefeller IV, W.Va.	13	12	1.1	69	7	15.9
Energy and Natural Resources	Jeff Bingham, N.M.	10	8	1.3	52	4	13.5
Environment and Public Works	Barbara Boxer, Calif.	10	8	1.3	43	7	12.4
Finance	Max Baucus, Mont.	13	11	1.2	77	5	18.3
Foreign Relations	John F. Kerry, Mass.	10	9	1.1	64	7	15.1
Health, Education, Labor, and Pensions	Tom Harkin, Iowa	12	10	1.2	87	3	21.0
Homeland Security and Governmental Affairs	Joseph I. Lieberman, Conn.	9	8	1.1	121	6	23.7
Indian Affairs	Daniel K. Akaka, Hawaii	8	6	1.3	20	0	5.1
Judiciary	Patrick J. Leahy, Vt.	10	8	1.3	122	7	22.9

Rules and Administration	Charles E. Schumer, N.Y.	10	8	1.3	24	0	6.3
Small Business and Entrepreneurship	Mary L. Landrieu, La.	10	9	1.1	31	0	5.9
Veterans' Affairs	Daniel K. Akaka, Hawaii	8	7	1.1	27	0	5.5
Select Committee on Ethics	Barbara Boxer, Calif.	3	3	1.0	15.0	0	—
Select Committee on Intelligence	Diane Feinstein, Calif.	10	9	1.1	41.0	0	14.6
Select Committee on Aging	Herb Kohl, Wisc.	11	10	1.1	20.0	0	6.6

*The party ratio (Democrats: Republicans) in the chamber is 1.1:1, a figure that includes Senators Sanders and Lieberman as members of the Democratic Party.

Sources: Senate Web site; S.Res. 81 (112th Cong., 1st sess.) for committee budgets; H.R. 1105, 111th Cong., 1st sess. (for Appropriations budget); *Congressional Staff Directory: 2010/summer.* (2010). Washington, DC: Congressional Quarterly Press.

have been the location of the best continuing macroeconomic seminar in Washington. Many closely followed economic indicators are released to coincide with JEC hearings on how the economy is evolving. In recent years, the chairman of the Federal Reserve Board has used his regular appearance before the committee to issue statements about how the Fed perceives the direction of the economy, information investors always are eager to hear.

The Joint Committee on Taxation (JCT) gets less press attention than the Joint Economic Committee but much more attention from lobbyists and others concerned about the details of the tax code. The Joint Tax Committee, which for years was known as the Joint Committee on Internal Revenue Taxation, is composed of the senior members from the House Ways and Means and Senate Finance Committees. While both chambers' taxation committees have guarded their legislative prerogatives fiercely over the years, the staff of the JCT has served both committees by providing expert tax advice to the writers of revenue legislation. It, in effect, is Congress's own Treasury Department, one of the reasons that members of Congress have held their own against successive administrations when tax bills have been written.

Conference committees also are composed of members from both chambers, but that is where the similarity with joint committees ends. A conference committee is an ad hoc committee, appointed by the presiding officer of each chamber, that reconciles differences between the House and Senate versions of the same legislation. For that reason, we can consider them committees that legislate. Unlike true legislative committees, conference committees have no staff or permanent membership. The membership of conference committees typically is dominated by members of the standing committees in the two chambers that originally considered the legislation in the House and Senate and most often by members of the *subcommittees* that originally considered the bill.

In the case of simple legislation, this means that the number of conferees is relatively small. More complex legislation might have larger conference committees. Examining the 94th (1975–1976), 96th (1979–1980), and 97th (1981–1982) Congresses, Longley and Oleszek (1989) found that the *total* size of conference committees ranged from thirteen, in the case of transportation and environmental conferences in the 97th Congress, to twenty-four, in the case of agriculture issues in that Congress. House delegations in that period ranged from a low of seven to a high of twenty-four; Senate delegations ranged from five to sixteen. House delegations typically exceeded Senate delegations in size, with the typical number of House members ranging between nine and fifteen and the number of senators ranging between six and thirteen.[6]

Occasionally, a bill will involve a number of issues and committees, resulting in a mammoth conference committee appointed among members of many standing committees and viewpoints. A good example of this was the conference committee appointed in 1981 to finalize budget cuts under the Reconciliation Act. This conference involved more than two hundred fifty members of Congress, divided further into fifty-eight separate conference subgroups.

The number of House and Senate members on conference committees need not to be the same. Equality in numbers between the two chambers is not critical, since a majority of *each* chamber's delegation must approve the conference committee's report before the bill can go back to the two chambers. Therefore, most important in the composition of conference committees is the degree to which each chamber's conference committee delegation represents that *chamber*.

Conference delegations typically represent the winning coalition in the chamber on that bill. However, the presiding officer's prerogatives to appoint conferences can be used for personal (or party) advantage. An example of this was the House conference delegation appointed by Speaker Hastert on the 1999 bill establishing a "patients' bill of rights" for participants in health maintenance organizations (HMOs). Hastert, an opponent of many provisions in the House-passed bill, appointed a conference delegation composed of members who had *opposed* the House bill. While this move generated an angry response from the original House bill sponsors, who were Republicans, they could do little about it.

Reliance on conference committees declined precipitously during the first decade of the twenty-first century, leading some to claim that the conference was becoming outdated (Oleszek 2010). Like so much of contemporary congressional politics, blame has been laid at the feet of partisan polarization, plus the willingness of senators to use the filibuster to prohibit conference committees from being appointed. In the absence of conference committees, ironing out legislative differences between the chambers gets pushed to informal negotiation, which is more likely to be led by party leaders than by committees.

Finally, the House frequently uses a fictional committee to transact most of its business. Usually, when the House is considering legislation, it operates as a Committee of the Whole. As the name implies, a Committee of the Whole consists of all members of the House, However, because the committee, formally, is not the House itself, the Committee of the Whole device allows the House to proceed with routine legislative business without having to compel all of its members to be present for all the debate and parliamentary fisticuffs. Because it is a committee, the rules of procedure are less formal than if the House were meeting in formal session, and it is easier for floor majorities to work their will without getting tied into parliamentary knots.

As mentioned in Chapter 3, the Reed Rules of 1888 changed the quorum of the House Committee of the Whole to 100, rather than a constitutional majority, which is now 218.[7] Furthermore, expedited amendment and debating procedures in Committee of the Whole allow the House to get a lot of business done very quickly.

Because the Committee of the Whole is not the House per se, everything the committee does must be ratified by the House in formal session. Most important, all amendments passed in the Committee of the Whole face a second vote in the formal House session. Amendments that lose in the Committee of the Whole are not voted on again by the House. Since most amendments to bills attack the legislative product of a standing committee, this voting procedure gives the legislative committees a second chance to beat back challenges to their work, should they lose the first time.

Historical development of the committee system

When Congress convened in April 1789, it had inherited from the Confederation Congress the practice of referring different bills to ad hoc select committees (see the discussion in Chapter 2). Both chambers of the new Congress continued the practice into the new regime. Eventually both chambers migrated into a new practice, in which select committees were supplanted by permanent standing committees.

Figure 8.1 graphs the number of select and standing committees in both chambers of Congress from 1789 to the present. At first blush, the gross development of the two chambers' committee system is similar: early on, both relied heavily on select committees, but as time passed, reliance on select committees waxed and the prominence of standing committees waned. Examined in more detail, the paths from reliance on select to standing committees took different directions in the two chambers, reflecting the different styles of legislating that developed in the two bodies.

The House adopted its initial parliamentary practices primarily from the Confederation Congress. It would *begin* the deliberation of legislation in Committee of the Whole. Once a majority view had emerged on a particular topic, a committee would be appointed to consider the matter further, in greater detail. However, the committee could write a bill only if it had been given explicit authority to do so. More often, the committee would report back to the House with its recommendations, after which further debate might develop on the floor. *Then* another select committee—perhaps with the same membership as the original one, but not necessarily—would be appointed to draft a bill and report it back to the House. Committee bills were considered on the House floor with no special parliamentary protections, and they frequently were amended.

The select committees appointed in the House in its earliest years were on a very short leash. The early legislative process in the House under the Constitution was not much different from the process under the Articles of Confederation, subjecting the House to the same problems that had emerged in the extinct Confederation Congress. One important difference, however, is that the earliest House was willing to act as if Alexander Hamilton, George Washington's Treasury secretary, was the prime minister for the first two Congresses. Hamilton was the key player in drafting the details of the young nation's financial plans and shepherding them through passage in Congress. He even was given access to the House floor to lobby representatives in favor of the administration's plans.

So long as a majority of the House was politically sympathetic to the president and his Treasury secretary, this arrangement was better than a committee system for the development of complex legislation. It left House members free to focus on what they specialized in, the political consequences of government action, while allowing Treasury officials to focus on what they specialized in, public finance.

FIGURE **8.1**

The Number of Committees in the House and Senate, 1789–2010

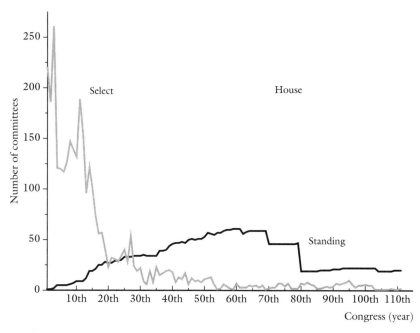

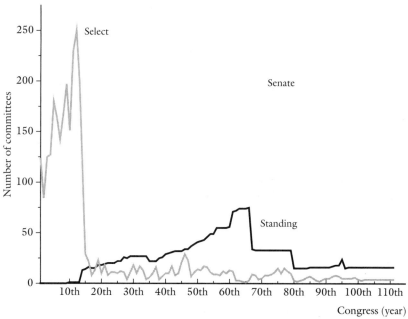

Sources: Canon, Nelson, and Stewart (2002); Nelson and Stewart (2010).

Relations between the administration and the House began to deteriorate as the political majority in the House shifted away from the party of Hamilton (eventually called the *Federalists*) and toward the party of Jefferson (eventually called the *Republicans*). This led, in the 4th Congress (1795), to the establishment of the first legislative standing committee, on Ways and Means, which was responsible for reviewing all financial legislation that came before the House: taxing, spending, and banking.[8] Even with the establishment of the Ways and Means Committee, the House proved hesitant to devolve front-line responsibility for legislation to other standing committees. Nonetheless, over the next thirty years, it regularly was faced with crises in which the reliance on closely watched ad hoc select committees was roundly criticized. The 1810s were particularly challenging to the House, on both policy and political grounds. Hence, by 1820 almost all original oversight over legislation in the House had been given to standing committees, with select committees reserved for special investigations or hot political topics, such as the issue of slavery in Missouri.

In the Senate, committees of all kinds were slower to develop. In fact, examining Figure 8.1 closely, you will see that in the earliest years, while the number of select committees was declining in the House (reflecting a gradual shift of work from select to standing committees), it was growing in the Senate. This also reflects a shift in the general legislative style of the Senate, which developed somewhat independent of the House. In its earliest years, the Senate was content to leave to the House the job of taking a first crack at legislation. Therefore, in its earliest years, the Senate was much less busy than the House.[9] Political realities slowly shifted around senators, as they began to feel many of the same political pressures from back home as House members. This, in turn, led to a gradual shift in attention to the origination of legislation and an increase in the number of select committees appointed in the Senate.

The onset of standing committees was more sudden in the Senate than in the House, so much so that the source of this shift remains a bit of a mystery. In 1816, the Senate changed its rules so that it went, overnight, from having no standing committees to having twelve. From that time forward, the evolution of the committee system in the Senate paralleled that of the House.

Figure 8.1 also reveals that the committee systems in both chambers have been pruned back occasionally, especially in the 1920s and 1940s, with smaller cutbacks in other years. Each of these retrenchments, large and small, is the obverse of the dynamic that leads to the gradual expansion of the standing committee system in normal times.

The existence of a standing committee dedicated to a specific topic, in turn, leads to the specialized organization of politics around that topic. For instance, when the House created a committee on Revolutionary Pensions in 1831 (half a century after the end of the Revolutionary War), it created expectations among a certain class of citizens that their requests for pensions for military service in the Revolutionary War would be considered sympathetically. It also created expectations among a small set of House members that they could reap political benefits by responding to these requests through serving on the committee. And it created expectations among lawyers working on behalf of claimants that they could rely on a one-stop forum for their clients. Even as the number of Revolutionary War veterans (and their dependents) dwindled, the committee stayed in business. It was finally abolished in 1881, a century after the Battle of Yorktown.

The most significant reorganization of the congressional committee system occurred in 1946, taking effect with the 80th Congress in 1947. The Legislative Reorganization Act of 1946 mandated the reduction in the number of committees in both chambers, from thirty-three to fifteen in the Senate and forty-eight to nineteen in the Houses; codified committee jurisdictions; and expanded the congressional support staff system, including that in the committees. Most of the abolished committees found their jurisdictions transferred wholesale to a new standing committee, where the former committee reemerged as a new subcommittee. Thus, a second-order consequence of the Legislative Reorganization Act of 1946 was the heightened importance of subcommittees within the overall committee system.

Since 1946, both chambers periodically have changed the committee system on the margin. The Legislative Reorganization Act of 1970 made some formal changes to the overall committee system, including requiring House committees to have formal rules and opening up committee proceedings to the public. The subcommittee bill of rights, discussed later, expanded even further the importance of subcommittees in the House in the early 1970s. The takeover of the House by the Republican Party in the election of 1994, for the first time in almost half a century, led to the abolition of three standing committees, a reduction in committee membership and staff, a change in committee procedures, and tactical warfare with the Senate over the continued existence of joint committees.

Committee reforms in the 104th Congress

The committee system in Congress tends to be fairly stable for long periods of time, for a variety of reasons. Among these are that the political goals of the great bulk of members do not change all that rapidly, the committee system is adaptable enough for members to satisfy most of those goals without altering the system, and the system itself creates political resources that members are willing to defend.

This last factor most often is overlooked by observers of Congress. Serving on committees is valuable to all members of Congress, for both policy and political reasons. The policy advantages are obvious. Committee service focuses the attention of members of Congress on a narrow range of topics, not only allowing them to acquire expertise but also identifying a few domains in which each member can exert effort and plausibly claim to have made a difference in policy making. Less obvious are the political benefits, but they are substantial, too. Two types of political benefits draw our attention, external and internal. Committee service opens up avenues for soliciting campaign assistance from donors, particularly political action committees. In total, some committees are just better positions from which to raise funds (like Commerce) than others (like District of Columbia). Still, even serving on a low-ranking committee helps align committee members with political action committees associated with issues in the committee's domain. For example, serving on the House Science Committee facilitates contribution links with telecommunications firms and companies with large research and development components. And service on the Agriculture Committee facilitates contacts with farm organizations and agribusiness concerns.

Internally, the simple process of continued service on a committee allows committee members to accrue political benefits over time. The longer a member serves on a committee, the more favors he or she has been able to do for colleagues who do not serve on the committee but care about its output nonetheless. Favors are an important currency in any legislature, and they can be swapped across time. Continued service on a single committee makes it easier for rank-and-file committee members to acquire a valuable legislative resource. Most important, perhaps, is that with a functioning seniority system, the longest-serving members of committees also ascend into positions of leadership, and from these positions of leadership, they are able to acquire even greater policy influence and more political resources.

Hence, even though committee reform is a topic always on the lips of *someone*, it is rarely on the top of the agenda of a lot of members. A few times in congressional history—in the 1880s, the 1920s, the 1940s, and the 1970s—political events have conspired to overcome institutional inertia and prompt major reforms of the committee system. The months following the 1994 congressional election was another such period.

The Democratic Party had controlled the House of Representatives, nonstop, from 1955 to 1995. In 1994, Republican candidates for the House (incumbents and challengers) ran on a platform called the *Contract with America*. Most of the planks in the contract pertained to policy differences between Democrats and Republicans, such as crime, welfare, and "personal responsibility." But some of the planks also addressed the organization of the House itself. The contract promised that the Republicans would pass the following congressional reforms on the first day of Congress:

- Require all laws that apply to the rest of the country apply equally to the Congress.
- Select a major, independent auditing firm to conduct a comprehensive audit of Congress for waste, fraud, or abuse.
- Cut the number of House committees and committee staff by one-third.
- Limit the terms of all committee chairs.
- Ban the casting of proxy votes in committee.

- Require committee meetings to be open to the public.
- Require a three-fifths majority vote to pass a tax increase.
- Guarantee an honest accounting of our Federal Budget by implementing zero base-line budgeting.

Note that many of these items targeted committees directly—their number, the size of staff and budgets, practices such as proxy voting and closed meetings, and the terms of committee chairs.[10] The reforms actually passed by the Republicans when they took control of the House corresponded very closely to the promises made in the contract. Those reforms are summarized in Table 8.5.

TABLE 8.5
Changes to the House Committee System in the 104th Congress (1995)

Committees eliminated
    District of Columbia (jurisdiction transferred to Government Reform and Oversight)
    Merchant Marine and Fisheries (jurisdiction transferred to several committees)
    Post Office and Civil Service (jurisdiction transferred to Government Reform and Oversight)
    Several committees renamed

Staff cut by one-third

Subcommittee limits
    Committees generally restricted to five subcommittees
    Exceptions are Appropriations (13), Government Reform and Oversight (7), Transportation and Infrastructure (6)

Subcommittee staff now controlled by committee chair (not subcommittee chair)

Assignment limits: members may serve on no more than two standing committees and four subcommittees

Proxy voting banned

Committees must publish roll call votes on all bills and amendments

Rolling quorums banned

Meetings may be closed to the public in only very limited cases

Committees must allow broadcast coverage and still photography in all open sessions

Multiple referrals eliminated; speaker still may serially refer bills and parts of bills to different committees

Three of these changes were particularly important: the reduction in the number of staff members, the reduction in the number of committees, and the imposition of term limits for chairs. The reduction in the size of staff and the number of committees was justified as a way to reduce a bloated congressional bureaucracy and end pandering to special interests. All the committees eliminated—District of Columbia, Merchant Marine and Fisheries, and Post Office and Civil Service—had strong supporters among the Democrats. Imposing term limits on committee chairs was justified in two ways. First, it was consistent with the more general Republican promise to return Congress to control by "citizen legislators," not "career politicians." Second, it was consistent with a desire among the most dedicated conservatives to rein in the independence of the committees so that they might do the bidding of the Republican caucus more expeditiously.

One consequence of these committee changes was to shift power from the committees to the Republican leadership. The reduction in staff and the number of committees allowed the leadership to redistribute resources (committee assignments and staff resources) in ways consistent with the party's legislative agenda. The imposition of term limits for committee chairs also helped centralize power in the parties. Most obvious, the term limits reduced the flexibility of the chairs and gave the party leadership new opportunities to change committee leaders if it so desired. Less obvious, this provided an avenue for party leaders to impose new political burdens on rank-and-file committee members who aspired to be future chairs. The effect has shown up in elections, when Republican Party leaders began demanding that all committee chairs and candidates for chair come up with campaign funds to assist party candidates, especially vulnerable Republicans running for Congress.

One interesting example of this came at the start of the 107th Congress (2001–2002), when thirteen Republican House Committee chairs reached the three-term limit imposed by the party when they took control of the chamber at the start of the 104th Congress. This was the first chance to observe what criteria the Republican Party leadership would use to select committee chairs—seniority or something else? In a study of the process leading to the selection of the thirteen new committee chairs, Brewer and Deering (2005) discovered that the criteria shifted from seniority alone (with a few notable exceptions) to seniority *plus* fund-raising acumen. In particular, of the thirteen new committee chairs selected that Congress, barely half— seven—were the most senior member of the committee. Of the remaining six, five had been the candidate who had contributed the most money, out of their own fund-raising efforts, to other Republicans running for the House. Prior to the 107th Congress, fund-raising on behalf of Republican House candidates had never been a factor in choosing who would chair House committees (also see Heberling and Larson, 2007).

Democrats also have continued to deepen the ties between the core of the Democratic caucus and the behavior (and identity) of committee chairs. This was seen clearly following the 2006 election, when Democrats regained control of the House, in the 110th Congress. In addition to retaining practices begun by the Democratic caucus before 1994, to keep committee chairs loyal to the principles of the caucus, new speaker Nancy Pelosi announced (apparently without informing senior Democrats ahead of time) that she would retain the six-year term limit on committee chairs that the Republicans had adopted following the 1994 election. Hence, the Democrats have set up the same dynamic a few years down the road, of inducing a new herd of candidates for senior committee posts to ingratiate themselves to their party, through their campaign fund-raising prowess.

As a general matter, bringing leadership of the committees under tighter reins from the parties has created greater fluidity at the tops of the committees, and greater uncertainty about who will be the next chair (or ranking minority member) of the committee. One illustration that seniority is now just one of a handful of criteria for the selection of committee leaders is how often seniority has been violated in the selection of chairs and ranking minority members. From the 104th Congress (1995–1996) to the 112th (2011–2012), Republicans changed standing committee leadership fifty-nine times; in thirty-one of these cases (53%), the most senior Republican was not chosen to lead the Republican contingent of the committee. The Democrats, in comparison, changed leaders forty-eight times (thus, less turnout overall), violating the seniority norm only nine times (19%). In contrast, over the eight preceding Congresses (96th—103rd, or 1979–1980 to 1993–1994), with three fewer committees, the Republicans changed committee leadership only forty-four times, two times (5%) violating seniority; Democrats changed leaders forty times, violating seniority six times (15%).

What is still unclear is how these changes have affected the quality of legislation, and the relative influence of the House over the details of legislation, compared to the Senate. The Senate has endured many fewer changes to its committee structure, although Republicans adopted the same six-year term limits for Senate chairs as the House. One could certainly argue that partisanship is running rampant in many parts of the Senate committee system, but the shift in the House away from encouraging long careers and hard detailed policy work toward party orthodoxy and the "big picture" has perhaps made the House more like the Senate.

Membership

Membership on committees is formally at the discretion of the chambers that establish and maintain the committees. In practice, the actual locus of power in determining who will serve on what committees has shifted about in both chambers over time.

Originally, both the House and Senate appointed their committees by ballot. Constantly balloting for committees proved such a burden that the House changed its rules in the 1st Congress, allowing the speaker to make committee appointments. This rule stayed in effect until 1910, when, as a part of the revolt against Speaker Cannon, the House formally took back authority to make committee assignments. In practice, this means that the two House parties took it on themselves to appoint their share of committee seats. Both parties established committees on committees that were responsible for making party committee assignments. The Republican Party established a separate committee within its House organization to make its assignments. Originally, power in this committee was distributed so that states with a large number of Republicans were allocated the best assignments. Over the past two decades, the Republican Party has dropped this practice, opting for a more egalitarian committee on committees, that nonetheless now gives added weight to the speaker's preference. The Democrats, on the other hand, originally gave the authority to make committee assignments to the Democratic members of the Ways and Means Committee. (Democratic members of Ways and Means, in turn, were appointed via a ballot of the Democratic caucus.) Liberal reformers in the 1950s and 1960s charged that the Ways and Means Committee was too conservative in making Democratic assignments. Therefore, in the 1970s the Democrats, too, adopted a separate committee on committees that was more representative of its party rank and file.

The Senate continued to appoint its committees by ballot into the 1840s. In December 1845, the party caucuses developed committee lists and the Senate adopted those lists, prearranged by party. Thus began the dominance of party organizations in the making of Senate committee assignments—a dominance that continues to this day.

Stating that party organizations are *practically* responsible for making committee assignments implicitly raises a question that precedes the making of assignments: Who determines how many members of each party will serve on each committee? As parties have developed to take on greater responsibility for organizing Congress, the majority parties, at a minimum, could allocate a majority of committee assignments to their members. Ever since the Legislative Reorganization Act of 1946, the parties have been able to go one better, by allocating a disproportionate share of seats on the most powerful committees, such as Ways and Means and Finance.

This is illustrated in Figure 8.2 which shows the percentage of seats held by the majority party since the beginning of the twentieth century on the two tax-writing committees, House Ways and Means and Senate Finance. From the 80th Congress to the present, the majority party almost always has held considerably more seats on the House Ways and Means Committee than in the full House. This disproportionality grew particularly large in the past two decades. In the Senate, this disproportionality has not been so great and actually disappeared in recent years.

Ultimately, setting the party ratios on committees is a job for the majority party since, by definition, it has the votes to impose its will. The minority is left with only two lines of recourse, public complaint and delay. In the House, the minority party periodically engaged in delaying tactics to protest its treatment by the majority in the distribution of committee assignments. Because the avenues for delay are even greater in the Senate than in the House, the majority party has tended to treat the minority more equitably, even when it allocated for itself a disproportionate share of the good committee assignments.

Chapter 7 discussed the effects of this partisan committee stacking in terms of the spatial model. In those committees responsible for issues that most clearly divide the parties, partisan committee stacking deflects the location of the committees' median members away from the chamber median toward that of the majority party median.

The appointment of members and chairs Although majorities of the two chambers formally control who serves on the committees, in practice, committee membership is controlled by the parties and leadership committees within each that actually make the assignments. Chapter 7 noted the identity of each party's committee on committees (see Table 7.4).

While the committees on committees have significant latitude in moving members among committees, a few practices, both formal and informal, constrain how this is done. First, with only a few exceptions, once a member is on a committee, he or she can veto efforts to be removed from the committee. Thus, transfers between committees among veteran members of Congress usually are worked out between the rank and file and the leadership. The vesting of a property right in committee assignments arose in the early twentieth century, due to the demand among rank-and-file members for a more predictable career path within Congress. Keep in mind that this was a time when legislative careers were lengthening rapidly, leading rank-and-file members of Congress to use their congressional service to further political goals.

Violations of committee assignment property rights are rare enough that they usually elicit considerable note in the press when they do occur. The best-known case of a member being removed from a committee involuntarily occurred at the beginning of 1983, when Phil Gramm (Tex.) was removed as a Democratic member of the House Budget Committee, due to his collaboration with Republicans in 1981 and 1982 to promote President Ronald Reagan's economic plans. Even though Gramm's actions were particularly egregious—he served as a spy for the Reagan administration during budget negotiations in 1981—it still took the Democratic caucus over a year of discussion and debate before it decided to remove Gramm from the committee. In response to being deposed from the Budget Committee Gramm resigned from the House, changed parties, ran as a Republican to fill his own vacancy in the House, won, and then returned to the House to take his seat again on the Budget Committee, this time as a member of the GOP.

The property rights system in committee assignments is an informal practice that restricts how party committees can make committee assignments.

FIGURE 8.2

Percentage of Seats Held by the Majority Party on House and Senate Taxing Committees

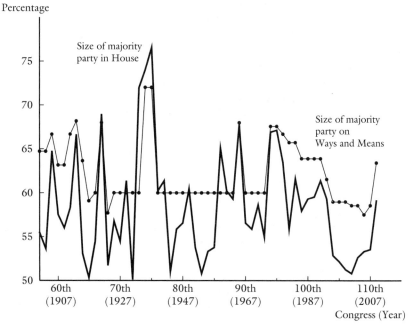

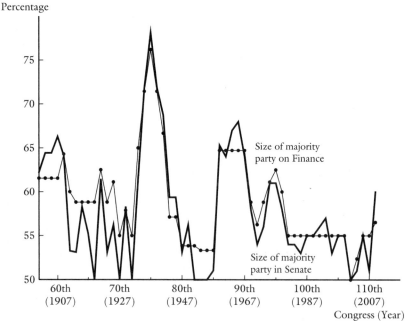

Sources: Ornstein, Mann, and Malbin (2008, Table 1-19); Canon, Nelson, and Stewart (2002); Nelson and Stewart (2010); House Clerk and Secretary of the Senate, 112th Congress.

The formal rules of the chambers and parties also limit how assignments are made. On the House side, both parties have divided the committees into categories—exclusive versus nonexclusive or major versus minor—and require members to spread their memberships around these committees. **Exclusive committees** have tended to be Appropriations, Rules, Ways and Means, and Energy and Commerce (and Financial Services for Democrats). Membership on any exclusive committee generally precludes membership on any others. Those not blessed with a membership on an exclusive committee generally are limited to service on two committees, with the parties sometimes differing with respect to what combinations of committee assignments are allowed. These rules generally allow members to serve on one attractive **nonexclusive committee** and then require them to serve on an unattractive nonexclusive committee.

On the Senate side, restrictions on committee membership are found primarily in the *Senate Manual* (rules). Senators generally are limited to membership on two major committees and one minor committee, but the rules are crammed full of exceptions. Augmenting these formal restrictions, both parties have honored the *Johnson rule* since at least the early 1950s in the assignment of senators to committees. The **Johnson rule**, named after Lyndon Johnson, who was Senate majority leader when the rule was last instituted, restricts a senator from serving on a second "good" committee (like Appropriations) until all senators from his or her party have at least one good committee assignment. This rule was instituted primarily to keep veteran senators from hogging all the good committee assignments, and it allows the freshmen to participate more fully in the legislative process.

Choice of chairs Just as committee assignments are formally under the control of chamber majorities, the chairs of the committees are formally appointed by majority vote in each chamber. But, as with committee assignments more generally, the actual designation of committee chairs is determined outside the rules.

Historically, the most important statement about committee chairs was that the chair (and, by extension, the ranking minority member) was allocated through the operation of the seniority rule. Broadly stated, the **seniority rule** grants the chair of a committee to the member of the *majority party* who has served on the committee the longest. The seniority rule came into full flower in the 1910s, as authority over committee appointments slipped out of the hands of party leaders, especially in the House. From then until 1995, violations of the seniority rule were rare.[11] Since then, violations have become more common, to the point that one could argue it is dead within the House Republican Party, and on life support among House Democrats. It continues to be robust in the Senate.

The demise of the seniority rule was a slow-moving development. It first came under fire in the 1950s, when Democratic liberals complained that the operation of the rule tended to favor southern Democrats, who on average were more conservative than the mainstream of the Democratic Party. After battling the seniority rule for two decades, reformers managed in 1974 to change House Democratic caucus rules to allow the Democratic caucus to confirm committee chairs via secret ballot.[12]

The Republican Party ended up going the Democrats one better in its assault on the seniority system. In the 1970s, while Democrats were changing how committee chairs were selected, the House Republicans adopted a rule that allowed for the caucus ratification of ranking minority members or chairs. In the election of 1994, the Contract with America promised that the Republicans would institute term limits on committee chairs, should they gain control of the House. They kept their promise to change the House rules by setting six-year term limits for committee and subcommittee chairs.

Not only did the new Republican majority enact a new rule in the 104th Congress limiting the service of committee chairs but party leaders also insisted that committee chairs had to act as agents of the party caucus by violating the seniority principle in filling a number of new chairs (Aldrich and Rohde 1997, 2009). The Republican leadership appointed chairs of three important committees—Appropriations, Energy and Commerce, and Judiciary—by jumping over the next in line, choosing instead long-serving committee members who were more in sync with the urgency felt by the party to enact the Contract with America. Additionally, Republican leaders required the chairs of the Appropriations subcommittees to sign a "letter of fidelity," promising to enact budget cuts demanded by leadership. Finally, although the committee chairs were given the authority to appoint the chairs to subcommittees, the choices had to be cleared with Speaker Gingrich, who was reported to have insisted that seniority be bypassed in making some of these appointments.

Because the clock for term limits on committee chairs started with the 104th Congress, the term limit rule became the "ticking time bomb" (Rae and Campbell 1999, p. 16) within the caucus that finally went off when the 107th Congress convened. Would the party follow through? In a word, "yes," though the rule ended up being interpreted in a way that allowed chairs who were forced to step down to assume the leadership of another committee. Still, as mentioned above, when the 107th Congress rolled around, the Republican Party was faced with replacing thirteen committee chairs, mostly because of term limits—the biggest committee leadership turnover unrelated to a turnover in majority status since 1941. Candidates to fill the vacated chairs were required to apply for the positions, interview with the committee on committees, and await their fates. Six of the thirteen committee chairs chosen at the start of the 107th Congress were not the most senior members of the committee; at the start of the 108th Congress (2003–2004), two of the four new committee chairs chosen were also not the most senior member. In general, since the 1994 Republican revolution, only half the Republican committee leaders—either chairs or ranking minority members—have been the most senior member.

The lack of a firm-and-fast seniority rule on the Republican side has shifted the choice to other criteria, including ideology, fund-raising acumen, and the indefinable quality of being a "team player."

What about the Democrats? In a sense, the Democrats continued their practice of honoring seniority, except in exceptional circumstances—in this case, ranking minority members. Democrats did not adopt term limits for ranking members. While in the minority, only three of the twenty-nine vacancies that occurred in ranking minority member positions were not filled by the second-ranked Democrat.

When Democrats assumed control of the House after the 2006 election, in the 110th Congress, there were some signs that the Democrats might borrow more heavily from the Republican playbook. First, Speaker Nancy Pelosi announced, without consulting with other Democrats, that she would retain term limits for committee chairs—a decision she backed down on at the start of the 111th Congress. Also at the start of the 111th Congress, Henry Waxman (D-Calif.), the second-ranking Democrat on the Energy and Commerce Committee, challenged the longest-serving member of that committee, John Dingell (D-Mich.), for the chair, and won. The fight was close, being decided on a 137–122 vote, and revealed that some elements of the Democratic caucus, particularly African American members, continued to value the seniority system per se.

Senators have put less effort into regulating the election of committee chairs, in part because almost half the majority party senators get to chair a committee. Indeed, committee chairs are acquired so easily in the Senate that it is common for a freshman to chair a Senate committee whose House counterpart had to wait decades before ascending to the top. Perhaps more important in the Senate is the operation of the rule that restricts senators to chairing only one committee at a time and the further practice within both parties that allows senators not only to claim the chair of a committee by virtue of seniority but also to depose a sitting chair based on claims of seniority.

The case of what happened when Robert Byrd (D-W.Va.) stepped down as chair of the Senate Appropriations Committee at the start of the 111th Congress (2009–2010) illustrates this point. Byrd was the longest-serving senator in American history. First elected in 1958, he had been a member of the Appropriations Committee, either as chair or ranking member, since 1987. Ninety-one years old at the time, he had long been in declining health, and his Senate colleagues were increasingly concerned that he was incapable of handling the rigors of the position. Soon after the 2008 election, Byrd announced he was stepping down as chair,[13] setting off a scramble not only for that position but for three additional committee leadership positions.

The second-ranking Democrat on the Appropriations Committee was Daniel Inouye (D-Hawaii), who is also the second-longest serving senator in American history, after Byrd. Inouye chaired the Commerce Committee, which he was quick to relinquish, in favor of chairing Appropriations. Jay Rockefeller (D-W.Va.), who was second-ranking on Commerce, was chairing the Select Intelligence Committee, which he gave up to chair Commerce. Next on the Intelligence list was Diane Feinstein (D-Calif.), who was then chairing the Rules and Administration Committee. She, too, gave up her leadership position in favor of chairing Intelligence. Looking over to Rules and Administration, the three top Democrats were otherwise occupied. The longest-serving member on the committee was Byrd, who was incapacitated. Second-ranked was Inouye. Christopher Dodd (D-Conn.) was ranked third and could have claimed the chair of Rules and Administration, but he was already chairing the Banking Committee—a more powerful committee even in normal times, but especially powerful in light of the 2008 financial meltdown. Charles Schumer, who was chairing the Joint Economic Committee, gave up that position to claim the chair of Rules and Administration, leapfrogging over three other more senior members who already had better leadership positions.

Hence, the decision by one senator to step down from chairing a committee can lead to a cascade effect on other committees. This particular case was extreme because the Senate Appropriations Committee is so powerful, but variants of this form of musical chairs almost always occur whenever the leadership of one committee changes, due to the death, resignation, or defeat of a senator.

Jockeying for committee chairs in the Senate usually is not as complicated as this, but the example illustrates how the small size of the chamber interacts with the seniority system to produce a moderately complicated senatorial dance whenever committee leadership positions are shuffled. For the student looking at this as an indicator of how power is distributed in the Senate and how policy making proceeds, the lesson should be obvious: on the whole, committee power in the Senate is distributed according to longevity of service and only indirectly according to the policy preferences or political abilities of majority party senators.

Moving to and fro—evidence of committee value

The committee system is more than a mechanism for helping MCs deal with the crush of legislative business. Committee service also focuses their legislative attention. In some cases, this focus corresponds with the *policy interests* of legislators. At other times, it serves primarily their *electoral interests*. For whatever reason, MCs care deeply about the committee assignments they receive and jockey mightily for better ones.

Members of Congress long have cared about how committee assignments are made. Nowadays, in both parties and both chambers, committee assignments are made by party committees. These assignments are made for a variety of reasons, but two factors stand out. First, the party committees weigh the electoral vulnerability of their members in making assignments. This has two major implications. First, the most electorally marginal members of the two chambers are unlikely to be assigned to committees that handle matters central to the parties or in which they are expected to resist lobbying pressures. In this way, the parties protect their most vulnerable members from political embarrassment. Second, the party committees also try to match their members to the interest of their constituents in making committee assignments. A member whose district includes a large army base, for instance, will have a better chance of getting on the Armed Services Committee than a member without a large military presence.

The second major factor in making committee assignments is party regularity. At the most extreme, the parties can threaten their most heterodox members with the loss of committee assignments if they do not shape up. We already have seen an example of this, concerning Phil Gramm in the early 1980s. Rewarding party regularity and punishing irregularity rarely is as dramatic as this, but it still plays an important role in determining who gets on the most important and powerful committees, such as Appropriations, Ways and Means, and Rules.

An MC who serves on a committee can focus attention on a fairly narrow set of legislative matters and, as a consequence, become a legislative expert on those matters. Additionally, the MC becomes skilled in navigating that policy domain to the benefit of his or her constituents. For that reason, MCs jealously guard their committee assignments—the assignments themselves are valuable and they grow in value over time. Thus, over the past century, a type of property right in committee assignments has emerged in both chambers—members are allowed to hold onto their committee seats from one Congress to the next and may not be removed *unless* the party ratios change so dramatically between Congresses that junior members of the minority party find their seats abolished altogether.

At the same time, someone who has learned the ropes on Committee A still may believe that service on Committee B is more valuable. For instance, all but the most senior members of the House Interior Committee would fall over themselves at the prospect of becoming the most junior member of the House Ways and Means Committee.

That MCs usually find value in the committees they serve on, that they often (but not always) would like to serve on even more powerful or valuable committees, and that they can veto transfers between committees has an interesting empirical implication for studying Congress. If these conditions hold, then the net traffic of MCs through the committee system tells us something about the relative value of the different committees in Congress. A number of scholars developed techniques to use patterns of transfer between committees to ascertain the relative attractiveness of committees at any point in time. These techniques range from simple ratio measures to more complex econometric methods.[14] The results from a more sophisticated econometric method are reported in Table 8.6.

Note a few things about these rankings. First, even though members of the Senate and House are drawn from different electoral environments, the rankings of the two sets of the committees are largely consistent. The committees that handle the purse strings are the most attractive in both chambers. The Rules Committee fills a special role in the House, which explains its third ranking there, but even without a special institutional position in the Senate, the Committee on Rules and Administration also is especially attractive.[15] Ranked at the bottom of both lists are mostly constituency-oriented committees, like Agriculture, Veterans Affairs, and Post Office and Civil Service.

There is one very interesting anomaly in Table 8.6, compared to how this ranking looked when Stewart and Groseclose (1999) first applied their ranking technique to congressional committees from the 81st to 102nd Congresses (1947–1992). The value rankings of the Senate Foreign Relations and Judiciary Committees have dropped like a rock. This indicates that senators are leaving these two committees at higher rates than before, in return for new assignments on other committees. One would expect Foreign Relations and Judiciary to be especially attractive in the Senate because of the upper chamber's constitutional role in helping to guide foreign policy and confirming judges. On the other hand, battles over judicial nominations have risen in frequency and intensity over the past two decades, as has partisan conflict over foreign policy. Therefore, service on these two committees is now regarded as a burden to many senators, who now seek to spend their committee efforts in more fruitful pursuits.

In general, both senators and representatives have similar career patterns through the two respective committee systems. They start out with committees suited to their particular policy, constituency, and electoral interests. Over time these interests tend to broaden, leading to a migration up the committee system to places where broader interests can be accommodated.

Subcommittees

Up to this point, focus has centered on the committee system at its most basic unit of analysis—the committee itself. Committees, however, evolved a further division of labor that has become politically significant in recent years: subcommittees. It is tempting to consider subcommittees as a type of fractal expression of the committee system. That is, subcommittees, in a sense, are just a replication of the committee system, one level lower. They grew up within the committees and out of the same impulse that gave rise to the committees themselves—a desire to take advantage of the division of labor.

No comprehensive history or accounting has been done of the rise of subcommittees in either chamber of Congress; so, any general statement about their early history is largely speculative. Within the original records of the committees themselves are occasional references to permanent subcommittees as far back as the 1870s. Even before then, the committees that considered a large number of constituent claims—such as the House Committee on Claims or the Committee on Invalid Pensions—essentially did their work via one-man subcommittees, who were assigned the task of investigating claims

TABLE 8.6
Relative Attractiveness Ranking of House and Senate Committees, 104th–111th Congresses

Rank	*House Committee*	*Senate Committee*
1	Ways and Means	Finance
2	Energy and Commerce	Appropriations
3	Rules	Armed Services
4	Appropriations	Rules and Administration
5	Foreign Affairs	Commerce, Science, and Transportation
6	Financial Services	Health, Education, Labor, and Pensions
7	Judiciary	Energy and Natural Resources
8	Standards of Official Conduct	Banking, Housing, and Urban Affairs
9	House Administration	Homeland Security and Governmental Affairs
10	Budget	Budget
11	Armed Services	Foreign Relations
12	Natural Resources	Judiciary
13	Transportation and Infrastructure	Agriculture, Nutrition, and Forestry
14	Oversight and Government Reform	Veterans Affairs
15	Science and Technology	Small Business and Entrepreneurship
16	Veterans Affairs	Environment and Public Works
17	Education and Labor	
18	Small Business	
19	Agriculture	

Note: Committee on Homeland Security is omitted because it is a new committee, established in the 109th Congress.

Source: Data gathered by the author. Ranking method described in Groseclose and Stewart (1998) and Stewart and Groseclose (1999).

and shepherding the bill that disposed of the matter through the committee and the full chamber.

Subcommittees first became major features of the House committee system in the mid-1880s, when the major committees (i.e., Agriculture, Military Affairs, Naval Affairs, Foreign Affairs, Indian Affairs, and Commerce) acquired the right to report appropriations bills within their jurisdictions, thus upstaging the House Appropriations Committee. These committees each established subcommittees (usually chaired by the parent committee's chair) that considered the appropriations bill and acted, for all intents and purposes, like a mini-appropriations committee. (The Senate followed suit in the 1890s, with the same effects on subcommittees.) When the two chambers reestablished their Appropriations Committees in 1919, both coincidentally expanded their Appropriations Committees and began the practice of granting great autonomy to the Appropriation subcommittees.

Subcommittees became a practical reality throughout the entire congressional committee system following the Legislative Reorganization Act of 1946, which consolidated the standing committee system. In many cases, when one committee was combined with another, a subcommittee arose in the new committee with the same jurisdiction as the old committee.

Throughout this early development of subcommittees in Congress, one basic rule governed their development: the subcommittees were creatures of the committees, just as the committees were the creatures of the parent chambers. Therefore, the rules of the two chambers did not even mention subcommittees, and the practical use of subcommittees varied committee by committee. Most subcommittees were created and operated at the sufferance of the committee chair, who determined the jurisdiction, composition, and workload of all the subcommittees. Some committees had subcommittees with set jurisdictions; others had subcommittees that were assigned numbers, but no jurisdictions.

The consolidation of the committee system in 1946, combined with the expansion of the role of the federal government at that time, led to a more expanded role for subcommittees within the legislative life of Congress, especially the House. This led to increasing tensions between House leaders and the rank and file in the 1950s and 1960s. Part of the tension was ideological: Congress in these years was controlled by the Democratic Party and the Democratic Party, in turn, was wracked by divisions between its southern and northern wings. Southerners disproportionately chaired committees and northerners disproportionately filled out the Democratic backbenches. In a few notable cases, conservative southern committee chairs used the subcommittee system to their political advantage, mostly hampering the legislative agenda on civil rights and social welfare.

But the tension was not entirely ideological. As power flowed from the committees to the subcommittees, all members of Congress wanted a hand in the exercise of power, for both policy and electoral reasons. That the organization and operation of the subcommittees was beyond the short-term control of the rank and file was inconsistent with the majoritarian impulses of the institution.

Therefore, in the 1970s, both chambers of Congress adopted reforms that spread control over the subcommittees more evenly among the rank and file. The House Democrats adopted a series of reforms in the early 1970s that, taken together, have been referred to as the **subcommittee bill of rights**. Some of these reforms included restricting the number of subcommittees a Democrat could chair, guaranteeing subcommittees control of their own staffs; allowing the Democratic caucus of each committee to select subcommittee chairs; requiring bills to be referred to subcommittees based on set, written rules; and requiring almost all committees to *have* subcommittees.

The subcommittee bill of rights ushered in an era that congressional observers termed a period of **subcommittee government**. This term is applied more accurately to House politics from the mid-1970s to the mid-1990s than to the Senate. During the period of subcommittee government, formal and informal power was pushed to the subcommittee level. Because subcommittee jurisdictions are drawn very narrowly, it is easy for interest groups and government agencies to develop cozy relationships with subcommittees. (See Table 8.7 for a list of subcommittees in the 112th Congress.) The charge was eventually made that subcommittee government facilitated special interest legislation and made it more difficult for rank-and-file members of Congress to influence the details of legislation. Republicans went one step further, claiming that this cozy relationship between interest groups and subcommittees encouraged government bloat. Finally, the proliferation of subcommittees led to the proliferation of subcommittee *meetings*, which further created a sense that legislative life was out of control.

In the mid-1990s, with the ascendance of the Republican Party in the House, this era of subcommittee government ended—or at least changed significantly. On taking control the House following the 1994 elections, the House Republicans undertook a number of changes to undercut what they regarded as abuse of the subcommittee system. The number of House subcommittees was reduced, from a total of 115 to 84. The names and jurisdictions of many subcommittees were altered, expressly to undercut the power of subgovernments that the subcommittees may have given rise to. For instance, the subcommittees of the House Agriculture Committee traditionally had been organized along agricultural commodity lines. In the 100th Congress (1987–1989), the House Agriculture Committee had the following subcommittees:

- Conservation, Credit, and Rural Development
- Cotton, Rice, and Sugar
- Department Operations
- Domestic Marketing, Consumer Relations, and Nutrition
- Forests, Family Farms, and Energy
- Livestock, Dairy, and Poultry
- Tobacco and Peanuts
- Wheat, Soybeans, and Feed Grains

In the 106th Congress (1999–2001), the subcommittees had been changed to the following:

- Department Operations, Oversight, Nutrition, and Forestry
- General Farm Commodities, Resource Conservation, and Credit
- Livestock and Horticulture
- Risk Management, Research, and Specialty Crops

TABLE 8.7
Subcommittees of Standing Committees in the 112th Congress (2011–2012)

House	Senate
Agriculture	**Agriculture**
• Department Operations, Oversight, and Credit	• Commodities, Markets, Trade and Risk Management
• Conservation, Energy, and Forestry	• Conservation, Forestry and Natural Resources
• General Farm Commodities and Risk Management	• Jobs, Rural Economic Growth and Energy Innovation
• Nutrition and Horticulture	• Livestock, Dairy, Poultry, Marketing and Agriculture Security
• Livestock, Dairy, and Poultry	• Nutrition, Specialty Crops, Food and Agricultural Research
• Rural Development, Research, Biotechnology, and Foreign Agriculture	
Appropriations	**Appropriations**
• Agriculture, Rural Development, Food and Drug Administration, and Related Agencies	• Agriculture, Rural Development, Food and Drug Administration, and Related Agencies
• Commerce, Justice, Science, and Related Agencies	• Commerce, Justice, Science, and Related Agencies
• Defense	• Department of Defense
• Energy and Water Development, and Related Agencies	• Department of Homeland Security
• Financial Services and General Government	• Department of the Interior, Environment, and Related Agencies
• Homeland Security	• Departments of Labor, Health and Human Services, Education, and Related Agencies
• Interior, Environment, and Related Agencies	• Energy and Water Development
• Labor, Health and Human Services, Education, and Related Agencies	• Financial Services and General Government
• Legislative Branch	• Legislative Branch
• Military Construction, Veterans Affairs, and Related Agencies	• Military Construction, Veterans Affairs, and Related Agencies
• State, Foreign Operations, and Related Programs	• State, Foreign Operations, and Related Programs
• Transportation, and House and Urban Development, and Related Agencies	• Transportation, and House and Urban Development, and Related Agencies

Armed Services
- Emerging Threats and Capabilities
- Military Personnel
- Oversight and Investigations
- Readiness
- Seapower and Projection Forces
- Strategic Forces
- Tactical Air and Land Forces

Budget [No subcommittees]

Education and the Workforce
- Early Childhood, Elementary, and Secondary Education
- Workforce Protections
- Higher Education and Workforce Training
- Health, Employment, Labor, and Pensions

Energy and Commerce
- Commerce, Manufacturing, and Trade
- Communications and Technology
- Energy and Power
- Environment and the Economy
- Health
- Oversight and Investigations

Ethics [No subcommittees]

Armed Services. Airland; Emerging Threats and Capabilities; Personnel; Readiness and Management Support; Seapower; Strategic Forces

Banking, Housing, and Urban Affairs. Economic Policy; Housing, Transportation, and Community Development; Financial Institutions and Consumer Protection; Security and International Trade and Finance; Securities, Insurance, and Investment

Budget. No subcommittees

Commerce, Science, and Transportation. Aviation Operations, Safety, and Security; Communications, Technology, and the Internet; Consumer Protection, Product Safety, and Insurance; Competitiveness, Innovation, and Export Promotion; Oceans, Atmosphere, Fisheries, and Coast Guard; Science and Space; Surface Transportation and Merchant Marine Infrastructure, Safety, and Security

(Continued)

TABLE 8.7

Subcommittees of Standing Committees in the 112th Congress (2011–2012) *(Continued)*

House	Senate
Financial Services • Capital Markets and Government Sponsored Enterprises • Domestic Monetary Policy and Technology • Financial Institutions and Consumer Credit • Insurance, Housing and Community Opportunity • International Monetary Policy and Trade • Oversight and Investigations	*Energy and Natural Resources.* Energy; National Parks; Public Lands and Forests; Water and Power
Foreign Affairs • Africa, Global Health, and Human Rights • Asia and the Pacific • Europe and Eurasia • The Middle East and South Asia • Oversight and Investigations • Terrorism, Nonproliferation, and Trade • The Western Hemisphere	*Environment and Public Works.* Children's Health and Environmental Responsibility; Clean Air and Nuclear Safety; Green Jobs and the New Economy; Oversight; Superfund, Toxics and Environmental Health; Transportation and Infrastructure; Water and Wildlife
Homeland Security • Cybersecurity, Infrastructure Protection, and Security Technologies • Transportation Security • Oversight, Investigations, and Management • Emergency Preparedness, Response and Communications • Border and Maritime Security • Counterterrorism and Intelligence	*Finance.* Health Care; Taxation and IRS Oversight; Fiscal Responsibility and Economic Growth; Energy, Natural Resources, and Infrastructure; Social Security, Pensions, and Family Policy; International Trade, Customs, and Global Competitiveness

House Administration
- Elections
- Oversight

Judiciary
- The Constitution
- Courts, Commercial and Administrative Law
- Crime, Terrorism, and Homeland Security
- Immigration Policy and Enforcement
- Intellectual Property, Competition, and the Internet

Natural Resources
- Energy and Mineral Resources
- Fisheries, Wildlife, Oceans and Insular Affairs
- Indian and Alaska Native Affairs
- National Parks, Forests and Public Lands
- Water and Power

Foreign Relations. Western Hemisphere, Peace Corps, and Global Narcotics Affairs; African Affairs; International Operations and Organizations, Human Rights, Democracy, and Global Women's Issues; International Development and Foreign Assistance, Economic Affairs, and International Environmental Protection; Near Eastern and South and Central Asian Affairs; East Asian and Pacific Affairs; European Affairs

Health, Education, Labor, and Pensions. Children and Families; Employment and Workplace Safety; Primary Health and Aging

Homeland Security and Governmental Affairs
- Ad Hoc Subcommittee on Contracting Oversight
- Ad Hoc Subcommittee on Disaster Recovery and Intergovernmental Affairs
- Investigations
- Federal Financial Management, Government Information, Federal Services, and International Security

(Continued)

TABLE 8.7
Subcommittees of Standing Committees in the 112th Congress (2011–2012) (*Continued*)

House	Senate
Oversight and Government Reform • Federal Workforce, U.S. Postal Service and Labor Policy • Government Organization, Efficiency and Financial Management • Health Care, District of Columbia, Census and the National Archives • National Security, Homeland Defense and Foreign Operations • Regulatory Affairs, Stimulus Oversight and Government Spending • TARP, Financial Services and Bailouts of Public and Private Programs • Technology, Information Policy, Intergovernmental Relations and Procurement Reform	*Judiciary.* Administrative Oversight and the Courts; Antitrust, Competition Policy and Consumer Rights; Crime and Terrorism; Immigration, Refugees and Border Security; Privacy, Technology and the Law; The Constitution, Civil Rights and Human Rights
Rules • Legislative and Budget Process • Rules and Organization of the House	*Rules and Administration.* No subcommittees
Science, Space, and Technology • Energy and Environment • Investigations and Oversight • Research and Science Education • Space and Aeronautics • Technology and Innovation	*Small Business and Entrepreneurship.* No subcommittees

Small Business

- Agriculture, Energy and Trade
- Contracting and Workforce
- Economic Growth, Tax and Capital Access
- Healthcare and Technology
- Investigations, Oversight and Regulations

Transportation and Infrastructure

- Aviation
- Coast Guard and Maritime Transportation
- Economic Development, Public Buildings, and Emergency Management
- Highways and Transit
- Railroads, Pipelines, and Hazardous Materials
- Water Resources and Environment

Veterans' Affairs

- Disability Assistance and Memorial Affairs
- Economic Opportunity
- Health
- Oversight and Investigations

Ways and Means

- Health
- Human Resources
- Oversight
- Select Revenue Measures
- Social Security
- Trade

Veterans' Affairs. No subcommittees

Staff and resources

Given the time demands on members of Congress, it should not come as a surprise that they delegate most committee work to others. Each committee has a staff and a budget for its operations. Even the smallest committee, the House Committee on Standards of Official Conduct (Ethics), had a budget of $5.6 million in the 111th Congress and a staff of twenty-three. At the other extreme, the House Appropriations Committee's budget was $31.3 million, supporting a staff of 142.

Tables 8.3 and 8.4 list the budgets and staff sizes of the House and Senate committees. Careful study of these tables reveals an important change in the relative capabilities of the committees in the two chambers over the past couple of decades. Whereas in years past, every House committee had a larger staff and budget than its Senate counterpart, this is no longer the case. Where this pattern remains as true now as in the past is with Appropriations—both the staff and budget of the House committee are roughly twice the staff and budget of the Senate committee. The House also still has a staff advantage on the other financial committees, Ways and Means (compared to Senate Finance) and Budget. But beyond these, House committees no longer enjoy an across-the-board resource advantage compared to committees in the Senate.

What do the committee staffs do? Always wary that they not overstep the bounds that separate them from their bosses, committee staffs are responsible for actually carrying out the three major tasks of each committee—organizing hearings, drafting legislation, and keeping in touch with the myriad collection of outsiders (lobbyists, constituents, and executive agencies) who want to influence committee behavior. Some have viewed the central role of committee staffs as usurping congressional power (see Malbin 1980). However, the professional success of committee staff members depends on the continuing political success of their bosses. Therefore, it is more accurate to say that committee staff members operate as agents of their political bosses, rather than loose cannons who "usurp" legislative power.

However, having asserted that committee staff are keenly attuned to the desires of the committee members, I have only pushed the question back one step: What do staffs do and for whom do they work? Even if committee staff members are faithful servants of their bosses, staff resources are not distributed evenly, with predictable consequences for the distribution of power within and between committees.

Control over committee staff has been a contentious issue throughout congressional history. Until the beginning of the twentieth century, individual members had no personal staffs. The only hope for clerical (and political) assistance at taxpayers' expense came by virtue of chairing a committee—committee chairs (usually) were entitled one clerk. When Congress changed the law and allowed individual members to have staff support, the dynamics concerning committee staff changed somewhat. Committee staff no longer are solely the political henchmen of the committee chairs. Still, tensions continue to emerge in fights over who controls committee staff (Fox and Hammond 1977).

These fights generally break over three lines of cleavage: (1) between the chair and the rest of the committee, (2) between majority and minority party members, and (3) between the full committee and individual subcommittees. Ever since the 1960s, each cleavage has erupted behind the scenes of Congress. Originally, all the committee staffs of both chambers were controlled by the chairs. Now, rules in both chambers allow sharing staff between the chair of the full committee and the chairs of the subcommittees and between majority and minority party members. The sharing rules are so fluid that there is no need to talk about the details of them here. Just note that the allocation of committee staff is another thing that has no equilibrium of tastes and therefore members of Congress fight about it—and change it—all the time.

House-Senate Comparisons

As the previous discussion indicates, the committee systems in the two chambers have evolved separately, as befits the slightly different tasks delegated the two chambers by the Constitution and the slightly different sets of political imperatives members of the two chambers face. On the whole, the House is more reliant on its committees than the Senate. House members devote relatively more time to committee business than senators, and the House as a whole devotes more of its resources to committees than the Senate. (Conversely, senators are more likely to rely on their personal staffs, making the Senate as a whole oriented more around the personal offices of its members.)

Constitutional differences between the chambers also affect the relative importance of different committees in the two chambers. For instance, the constitutional provision requiring all revenue bills to originate in the House has given the House's revenue committee, Ways and Means, considerable clout within the chamber. What is more, the preeminence of Ways and Means extends to relations with the comparable committee in the Senate, Finance, such that the Ways and Means Committee is considered the more expert and politically powerful committee of the two.

The converse of the revenue situation is executive business, which has been given to the Senate by the Constitution. Most obvious, the job of ratifying treaties has led the Senate to a preeminent position in foreign policy. However, as we have seen, this role has not led the Senate Committee to be especially sought after. Less obvious, the appointment power that the Senate shares with the president has given Senate committees considerable clout in making policy and Senate committee members important positions in distributing patronage. For instance, before civil service protections were extended to the Post Office, the Senate Committee on the Post Office and Post Roads had an important role in determining who would be the local postmaster in virtually every community in America. Their role was so significant that senators were the real appointees of most postmasters—the presidential nomination was a mere formality. In the twentieth century, with the explosion of the federal court system, the Senate Judiciary Committee has come to play an important role in appointing, or blocking the appointment of, federal judges.

House committees of note

Within each chamber, some committees are more important than others, as is evident both from their jurisdictions and the transfer patterns summarized in Table 8.6. The discussion of House-Senate committee differences concludes by highlighting some committees of note in both chambers, either because they find themselves frequently in the news or because they have special influence on the legislative process behind the scenes. Most of these committees deal with the nation's finances, but a couple deal with the business of the chambers. We begin with the House committees.

Rules Committee The House Rules Committee was established as a standing committee in 1880, even though it had existed as a select committee in most Congresses until that time. Before 1880, however, the select Rules Committee established at the beginning of most Congresses was charged with reviewing the rules of the House and recommending any changes that might be considered wise. Beginning in the early 1880s, though, the Rules Committee began taking on a different role in the House. At that time, it became the originator of resolutions, technically called *special orders* but now referred to as *rules*. In this context, a rule is a resolution that sets the parameters under which a bill is considered on the House floor. Although the full House gets to vote on these rules, the Rules Committee's role in bringing these resolutions to the floor makes it especially powerful. First, if a rule is *not* brought to the floor, it is very unlikely that a bill will even be considered. Second, on important legislation, the rule often will contain language that restricts how amendments may be considered—if they may be considered at all. While, in principle, the House can overturn a rule recommended by the Rules Committee, the complexity of the rule's language and the importance of the Rules Committee's power to the majority party make it unlikely that the Rules Committee's recommendation will be overturned.

The Rules Committee has not always been a tool of leadership. In the 1950s and 1960s, it was a famous conservative bottleneck, as the liberal Democratic majority tried to move social legislation out of committee onto the House floor. Beginning in the early 1960s, the party caucuses started to control the membership of the Rules Committee more directly. Now, its members are appointed by the top leaders of both parties. Because the majority party members of the committee are appointed by the speaker, it has become a de facto arm of the majority party leadership, quite a different role for the committee from its function in the mid-twentieth century.

Appropriations Committee The House Appropriations Committee was created in 1865 to consider all the annual appropriations bills. Prior to then, the appropriations bills were considered by the Ways and Means Committee, but the fiscal strains of the Civil War were too much for one committee to have jurisdiction over taxes, spending, and banking; and so Ways and Means found its jurisdiction spread among three committees.

The power of the House Appropriations Committee is immense, as a consequence of its jurisdiction. Not only does the jurisdiction of House Appropriations give it significant clout in Congress, but the practice of allowing the House to consider appropriations bills before the Senate also gives this committee a "first mover" advantage enjoyed by no other congressional committee.[16] This committee gives the annual bills the closest scrutiny of any congressional entity, a power that strikes fear in the hearts of agency bureaucrats who must justify their appropriations requests before it each year. The House Appropriations Committee also tends to cut the president's budget requests for most items, which, practically speaking, sets a floor under the amount of money that eventually will be appropriated for federal agencies.

The House Appropriations Committee, along with the Ways and Means and Rules Committees, has long been considered one of the "exclusive" committees of the House, meaning that members of these committees may serve on one and only one committee. Table 8.6 shows it to be the fourth most-attractive committee in the House. The power of the committee extends to its subcommittees, which are organized to correspond with the annual appropriations bills. The chairs of those subcommittees are so powerful that they are often referred to as the *College of Cardinals*. Recognizing their power, the two parties treat the chairs of Appropriations subcommittees just like the chairs of a full committee, in that the chairs of Appropriations subcommittees also must be formally ratified by the majority party caucus.

As powerful as the Appropriations Committee is, its influence in the House has waxed and waned over the years. Twenty years after it was created, the committee was stripped of its jurisdiction over most appropriations bills, with the bills being given to the legislating committees. (For instance, the Army appropriations bill was taken from Appropriations and given to the Military Affairs Committee.) The Appropriations Committee regained full jurisdiction over all appropriations bills in 1919. However, in the 1930s, with the passage of the Social Security Act, large parts of federal spending began to migrate to committees other than Appropriations. Social Security itself, for instance, is overseen by the Ways and Means Committee. Other entitlement spending is often in the jurisdiction of legislative committees, not appropriations. In 2009, for instance, the federal government spent about $3.5 trillion. The total of all money contained in the thirteen regular annual appropriations bills was "only" $1.7 billion.

In 1974, Congress passed the **Congressional Budget and Impoundment Control Act** (CBICA), which complicated the life of the Appropriations Committee significantly. The CBICA, first of all, established a Budget

Committee in each chamber, with the responsibility to oversee the broad parameters of taxing and spending each year. Second, the CBICA created a mechanism, called a **budget resolution**, which allowed Congress to establish spending and taxing targets each year. These two mechanisms affect all committees in the House, but the Appropriations Committee is the most affected, since it oversees the largest pots of money. Tensions between members of the Budget and Appropriations Committees have caused them to regularly play a game of "chicken" over levels of federal spending. As Table 8.7 suggests, House members would still rather be appropriators than budgeteers, but clearly most members of the Appropriations Committee would be happy if the Budget Committee did not exist.

Committee on Ways and Means The House Committee on Ways and Means is the oldest standing committee still in existence, having been created in 1795, the first major standing legislative committee to be created in either chamber. When first created, the Ways and Means Committee controlled all financial legislation in the House, but its jurisdiction over auditing the executive branch was taken away during the War of 1812 and its jurisdiction over spending and banking was removed at the end of the Civil War. What is left of its jurisdiction is still substantial: all tax legislation, plus important social programs with their own tax mechanisms, like Social Security and Medicare. The constitutional provision requiring the House to move first on tax legislation gives the Ways and Means Committee an important position in the most important of legislative activities.

From its creation until the 1970s, the Committee on Ways and Means was as much an exclusive club as a legislative committee. It was often among the smallest of House committees. It had no subcommittees, making its chair particularly influential. Indeed, for much of its history until the 1920s, the chairman of the Ways and Means Committee often was considered the floor leader of the majority party in the House, second only to the speaker. And from the 1920s until the 1970s, it also served as the "Committee on Committees" for the Democrats.

In the 1970s, many of the special prerogatives given the Ways and Means Committee were removed. The right to make Democratic committee assignments was given to a separate party committee, the Ways and Means Committee was required to create subcommittees, and the size of the committee was expanded significantly. In addition, prior to the 1970s, only "responsible" (i.e., low-taxing, moderately partisan members capable of compromise) and electorally safe members were appointed to the committee. In the late 1970s, as the committee's size was expanded, the two parties also began appointing more ideologically vocal and electorally vulnerable members to the committee.

The changes to the Ways and Means Committee in the 1970s did not alter the overall attractiveness and power of the committee, but it did change the tenor of committee deliberations and, ultimately, the nature of tax politics. Particularly in the early 1980s, the tax cuts that were part of the Reagan economic plan were made much easier because committee members were less wedded to a philosophy of protecting the Treasury at all costs and because many Democratic members of the committee were electorally vulnerable. Since the early 1980s, both parties have appointed new members who are more like the old members of the 1960s and before—electorally safe and "responsible." Still, the Committee on Ways and Means is now much less like an exclusive club and more like the other (important) legislative committees in Congress.

Budget Committee The third in the triad of important financial committees in the House is the Budget Committee. As mentioned previously, it was created (along with its Senate counterpart) by the 1974 Congressional Budget and Impoundment Control Act. Its primary function is to oversee the budgetary process in the House, particularly the budget resolutions and the **reconciliation process**. Unlike other House committees, membership on the Budget Committee is temporary, with members generally being allowed to serve only six-year terms. It also is unusual in having a membership dominated by members appointed from other committees, Ways and Means and Appropriations, plus the leadership. Its responsibility for the entire federal budget makes membership on the committee attractive. That one can not make a career on the committee limits its attractiveness, however.

The Budget Committee, like the entire budgetary process, got off to a rocky start in the mid-1970s. The perils of the committee, and the budgetary process generally, would fill several books and many articles (for a start, see Schick 1981; Wildavsky 1991). However, the Budget Committee has withstood fairly well all the assaults on its jurisdiction. The details of the budgetary process it oversees shift from year to year and so are not particularly important for our purposes. The existence of any process to guide budgeting overall each year *is* important. To the degree that the Budget Committee always is in the middle of the annual budgetary process, it is an important player in setting fiscal policy.

Senate committees

In general, Senate committees demand less time and attention from their members than House committees, and so Senate committees tend to dominate legislating in that chamber to a smaller degree than in the House. Budgets for Senate committees tend to be smaller, as are staffs. Still, the Senate committees play nontrivial roles in the legislative processes. For their chairs particularly, the Senate committees give visibility to senators who are active in policy debates. Being smaller and more visible than the House, this is a feature of the Senate committee system that should not be overlooked.

Committee on Rules and Administration The Senate Committee on Rules and Administration is the closest Senate analogue to the House Rules

Committee, since it has primary jurisdiction over the standing rules of the chamber. Beyond that, however, the analogy is weak in two ways. First, the Senate committee is weakened by the nature of the Senate's floor rules, which make it more difficult to cut off debate and restrict amendments. The House Rules Committee gains its power largely by overseeing the writing of "rules," which determine these things for important legislation. As we see in the next chapter, in the Senate the parameters of bill consideration for important legislation are determined by *unanimous consent agreements*, which usually are hammered out by party leaders, not by committees. Second, the Senate committee has jurisdiction over campaign finance legislation, which is of considerable interest to all senators. This aspect of the committee's business, not the Senate rules themselves, draws senators toward the committee.

Senate Finance Committee The Senate Finance Committee is the direct analogue to the House Ways and Means Committee. Historically, it has been more "liberal" than the Ways and Means Committee—or at least "liberal" in the classic sense. That is, while the Ways and Means Committee historically has been cast in the role of "guardian of the Treasury," the Senate Finance Committee historically has been cast in the role of loosening the purse strings a bit. This no doubt is because the Senate must move second in writing tax legislation. Groups that win tax breaks in the House, of course, do not complain about it in front of the Senate committee. Furthermore, the revenue lost from tax breaks granted by the House is spread so diffusely among the rest of the taxpaying public that no one usually appears in front of the Senate committee to complain about others' special treatment.[17] All that is left, therefore, is for the losers in the House to appeal to the Senate. Some of the House losers will become Senate winners, giving the appearance that the Finance Committee is more liberal.

Appropriations Committee The differences between Finance and Ways and Means are just like the differences between the House and Senate Appropriations Committees. By tradition, the Senate goes second in the appropriations process, leaving winners in the House *relatively* inactive when bills go to the upper chamber and concentrating Senate activity on attempts to overturn House cuts.

Budget Committee The Senate Budget Committee was created by the 1974 Budget Act, like its House counterpart. By and large, the Senate committee performs the same roles, in much the same way, as the House, but the standard pattern of House-Senate differences often breaks down when we get to the Budget Committees. First, although most budget resolutions and reconciliation agreements formally originate in the House, the Senate Budget Committee usually plays as prominent a role in budgetary politics as its House counterpart. Second, unlike the House rules, the Senate rules do not restrict the number of years a member may serve on its Budget Committee. Therefore, senators on the Budget Committee are in a better position to develop substantive and political expertise on budgetary matters than members of the House.

Judiciary and Foreign Relations Committees In discussing notable House committees, I omitted discussing the Judiciary and Foreign Affairs Committees. That is because, in the House, these legislative committees are not especially distinct from the other midrange policy committees. In the Senate, however, the Judiciary and Foreign Relations Committees have jurisdiction over major constitutional duties unique to that body. This responsibility has ramifications for the politics of these committees and makes them somewhat distinct among the Senate legislative committees.

The constitutional duties these committees oversee, of course, are to confirm judges and ambassadors and to ratify treaties. The Senate in general has the power to confirm all federal appointments, and almost every Senate committee shares in this special constitutional function. However, an especially large number of federal judges are to be confirmed each year.[18] Therefore, the Judiciary Committee has assumed a more prominent position within the politics of the Senate than its counterpart in the House.

The Senate Foreign Relations Committee, likewise, has gained in stature by virtue of overseeing a unique power of the Senate. The attractiveness of the Senate Foreign Relations Committee is a bit paradoxical, considering the well-known political heat its chairs have received over the years. Within a short period of time, three Senate Foreign Relations chairs were defeated for reelection—J. William Fulbright (D-Ark.) in 1974, Frank Church (D-Ida.) in 1980, and Charles Percy (R-Ill.) in 1984. In each case, their opponents succeeded by charging that the senators were more attentive to the matters of foreign countries than to the folks back home. In 1984, the prospect that Jesse Helms (R-N.C.) might claim the chair of the Foreign Relations Committee became a campaign issue in his home state, and he was compelled to promise to remain as chair of the Agriculture Committee.

Theoretical Perspectives on Committees

Considerable space has been consumed discussing the empirical basics of the committee system in Congress. Although this is the longest chapter in this book, I have just touched on the important details of the committee system. Because the congressional committee system is so important, the amount of empirical knowledge we have about it has been matched by theoretical work that has attempted to understand it more fundamentally and provide interpretations to explain its significance.

Traditional perspectives on committees

The first significant scholarly analysis of congressional committees was made by Woodrow Wilson in the 1880s. In *Congressional Government*, Wilson (1963 [1885]) set about to analyze the *actual* distribution of power in Congress, rather than a *hypothetical* distribution, which might be adduced from reading the Constitution. The Constitution, in Wilson's mind, specified that all member of Congress were equal. Therefore, a reading of the first article of the Constitution, without a simultaneous glance at the actual Congress, would lead one to believe that all members of Congress, from rookies to crusty veterans, had an equal say in legislating.

Furthermore, Wilson had a normative vision of Congress in his mind to supplement the constitutional ideal, against which he judged Congress. This normative vision held Congress as the nation's premier deliberative body and *responsible* for its actions.[19] By *responsible*, Wilson meant that Congress should be a body in which it was easy to assign blame or credit for legislative actions. In practice, this means that the majority party should clearly articulate its program, use its majority to pass the program, then face the consequences on election day, depending on whether the program failed or succeeded.

What Wilson actually described was a legislature that fell far short of his ideal. Congress had a clear gradient of power. Senior members dominated the junior members and committee members dominated policy in their domains to the exclusion of nonmembers. From the perspective of responsibility, Congress was lacking, too. The majority party did not use the committees as instruments to achieve well-articulated policy goals. Committees contained members from both the majority *and* minority parties and deliberated mostly in secret, obscuring their effects on policy output.

Wilson believed that the British Parliament was a legislature that deliberated and legislated in a responsible manner and found the American Congress wanting by comparison. Wilson noted that the real work of policy making in Britain was done in the government ministries, which were controlled (nay, entirely dominated) at the top by members of the ruling party. The leaders of these ministries, cabinet members drawn from the ranks of the majority party in Parliament, formed a cohesive cabinet whose actions were clear and who, collectively, offered a single vision of policy making to the electorate. The closest analogue to the ministries and the cabinet in the American case was the congressional committees, in Wilson's view. And, in the mind of Wilson, these committees were "disintegrate ministries," meaning that instead of integrating policy on behalf of the majority party, the American "ministries" created policy disintegration and, ultimately, irresponsibility.

The last sentence of the quote by Wilson that led off this chapter probably is the most frequently cited sentence in all of political science. As political science quotes go, it is a fine rendition of an important empirical truth about the American Congress that has gone unchanged for a century and a half—Congress in its committee rooms is Congress at work. When political scientists simply repeat the last sentence of that entire passage, without noting what precedes it, they miss the larger theoretical context in which Wilson cast his thinking. The first part of the passage bears rereading.

It is a great irony in the study of the American Congress that although Wilson identified congressional committees as the centerpiece of power in Congress and therefore, perhaps, of power in the American government, very few political scientists followed in Wilson's footsteps, analyzing congressional committees any further. This no doubt is because Wilson was a reformer and was appalled at what he saw. The next three or four generations of political scientists were mostly reformers, too, and therefore were also repelled by the centrality of committees in Congress. Consequently, the theoretically oriented study of congressional committees languished until the 1960s, when political scientists trained in the methods and theories of sociology began to analyze them.

To sociologically oriented students of American politics in the early 1960s, congressional committees were not so much power centers as politically important laboratories in which to test a large collection of theories to explain group behavior. The basic unit of analysis to the political sociologists who studied Congress was a group—which in this case was the congressional committee. The biggest questions these scholars sought to address were these: How do congressional committees integrate new members into the norms of the committee? How do committees protect their power and prestige against attack from outside? How do committees establish leaders so that the group can function optimally?

Note that in all these questions, it was taken as given that members of Congress just naturally would function within the group (which happened to be a congressional committee, but it could have been anything, like a bowling league), would hold the survival and success of the *group* to be an important goal, and would think about their life within Congress *first* through the perspective of group membership rather than as individuals. Although much of the sociological approach to Congress at this time was interested in the behavior of individuals within groups, as far as scholarship is concerned, the individual behavior of group (committee) members was a problem to be solved by the group, not the source of the group's collective behavior.

The best scholarship in this tradition analyzed the politics of the financial committees in Congress: Richard Fenno (1966) analyzed the two Appropriations Committees and John Manley (1970) analyzed the House Ways and Means Committee. I discuss Fenno's research briefly here to give you an idea of how the best of this work was conducted.

Fenno began by analyzing the *role* of the House Appropriations Committee in the appropriations process. The role, Fenno discovered, was that of *guardian of the purse*. In that role, the committee subjected agency appropriations to great scrutiny, whacking them back mercilessly. New members were appointed to the committee every two years, and part of Fenno's analysis was a description of how members of the committee *integrated* new members into their committee role. Another aspect Fenno analyzed was how the committee achieved its goal of guarding the public purse in a difficult environment—after all, cuts the committee made were subject to being overturned by amendment on the floor, Keep in mind that the programs cut by the Appropriations Committee already had been approved by majorities in both chambers. In this parliamentary environment, how did the committee protect its power? It did so, Fenno discovered, by couching appropriations deliberations in nonpartisan business terms and avoiding discussing policy. By doing so, its members allowed the committee to achieve its goal of maintaining its power in the chamber.

Fenno did not lose sight of the fact that the House Appropriations Committee was a policy Goliath. However, in this work, what was important was not so much the substance of the Appropriations Committee's deliberations but how the committee maintained itself internally and maintained relations with the full chamber, in an environment in which its role was to cut appropriations requests.

Modern theoretical perspectives on congressional committees

The sociological approach to studying congressional committees provided students of Congress, in and outside colleges and universities, a tremendous number of empirical insights into the functioning of these committees, all organized into intuitively understood packages. Sociological theories of committees began to fall out of favor in the early 1970s, however, due to two critical shortcomings. First, they glossed over the tension between individual and collective goals of legislators and tended to assume that group goals would be achieved because they "had to" be achieved. Second, they tended to highly personalize accounts of committee politics. No doubt, politics—even (especially!) in congressional committees—is highly personal. But the focus on the subtle nuances of group behavior includes a tendency to overlook the impersonal strategic grasping for power and advantage that seems fundamental to politics in a legislature.

In the early 1970s, scholars took a turn toward economics in the study of Congress, and that turn had its greatest effects in the study of committees. Ironically, the turn was facilitated by an important book written by the greatest exponent of the sociological approach, Richard Fenno, as he analyzed a series of committees through the perspective of the individual goals of committee members, not the goals of the group. This book, *Congressmen in Committees* (1974), allowed students of Congress to turn a corner in understanding how committees operated. Read alongside a contemporaneous essay on congressional politics more broadly considered by David Mayhew (1974), it was difficult to go back in our theoretical understanding of how committees operate.

Fenno posited that members of Congress pursued three goals—power, policy, and reelection—and the behavior of the committees was best understood in light of those goals. First, committees differed in how they could help members pursue those goals, and members were sorted into committees based on this. For instance, the Interior Committee spent a lot of time worrying about the allocation of public works projects, which made it perfect for House members who needed to shore up support with their constituents. The House Education and Labor Committee, on the other hand, was a hotbed of ideological contention and was therefore the right place for someone interested in hashing out the details of social policy, but not such a great place for someone interested in providing public works projects to the folks back home.

Within this analysis, the motivating force behind committee politics was the goals their members brought to the committees, but goals were only the starting point. Constraining the pursuit of these goals was an environment that might include the full chamber, the administration, or interest groups. The interaction of member goals with these environmental constraints produced a distinctive brand of decision rules for each of the committees and thus a distinctive brand of policy outcomes.

David Mayhew's approach to Congress was broader than Fenno's, since he was interested in explaining behavior throughout the institution, not just in the committees. Still, Mayhew's analysis of Congress has its greatest organizational implications for the operation of the committee system. Mayhew is known for studying Congress through the lens of election—he started by assuming that members of Congress were "single-minded seekers of reelection" and went from there. Mayhew further argued that in pursuit of reelection, MCs engaged in three activities: position taking, credit claiming, and advertising. **Position taking** involves public statements intended to locate the representative on the proper side of an issue. **Credit claiming** occurs when representatives bring some particular benefit back to the constituency (like a public works project) and associate their name with the particular project. **Advertising** is the dissemination of one's name around a district with the intention of leaving a favorable impression while avoiding issue content.

On the whole, a committee is structured and does its work to enhance the ability of its members to engage in these activities, especially position taking and credit claiming. Some committees are valuable a platforms from which to expound on the issues of the day; select committees are especially good in this regard. Other committees are oriented toward processing constituency requests, and these help fulfill credit-claiming goals.

The troubling part of Mayhew's analysis is that it paints a portrait of an institution whose members care only about their own political fortunes and nothing about the collective well-being of the country—not to mention the well-being of Congress as an institution. All members of Congress want to achieve certain collective goals that might be overlooked if committees are organized simply around the narrow goals of members. Therefore, both chambers of Congress (especially the House) create "control committees,"

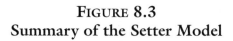

FIGURE 8.3
Summary of the Setter Model

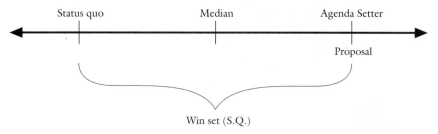

such as Ways and Means, Appropriations, Budget, and Rules, to deal with the negative consequences of uncoordinated congressional behavior. To get members of these committees to provide the public goods required of them, the chambers pay those members in terms of power and prestige.

The glimpses at committee behavior provided by Fenno and Mayhew are very general and imprecise. They were written at a time when virtually all political science was indistinguishable from history. In the intervening two decades, the theoretical and analytical tools of political scientists have become more sharply honed, and more precise theoretical statements about committee politics have been possible. The remainder of this chapter reviews the most important of those theoretical approaches.

The setter model and the study of committees The modern theoretical understanding of congressional committees is grounded in the **agenda setter model**, discussed in Chapter 1. In this simple spatial voting model, a committee votes on whether to accept a policy recommendation of an agenda setter on a take-it-or-leave-it basis. Being rational, the agenda setter will offer the median voter of the committee a policy that makes the median only marginally better off compared to the status quo but makes the agenda setter significantly better off.

An example is illustrated in Figure 8.3 with the status quo, the median, the agenda setter's spatial positions, and the win set against the status quo all as indicated. The agenda setter's chosen ideal point is the policy proposal which is accepted by the median voter despite preferring *even more* a proposal closer to his or her ideal point.

The application of the setter model to congressional committees is intuitive. A stylized fact of congressional life is that committees tend to be composed of preference outliers on the policies overseen by those committees. The rules and practices of the two chambers privilege the proposals made by the committees, and thus members are situated to make proposals of their own liking to the two chambers, with the assumption that those proposals will be passed more often than not. In other words, committees tend to act as the agenda setter in the setter model.

This thinking about congressional committees corresponds with certain commonsense impressions about congressional politics. Indeed, it is entirely consistent with Wilson's century-old complaint that the committees were "disintegrate ministries," making policy in the interest of committee members, not in the interest of political parties or more "responsible" political actors.

The setter model has formed the core of the **structure-induced equilibrium** concept, put forward by Kenneth Shepsle and Barry Weingast (1981). Moving beyond the simple unidimensional policy world embodied in the basic setter model, Shepsle and Weingast suggested that policy-making equilibria exist in Congress because of congressional institutions, and the most important of those institutions (though not the only ones) are committees.

In the realm of committees, the structure-induced equilibrium model works this way: suppose the world is multidimensional. For simplicity, we concentrate on a world that has two separate policy areas, Guns and Butter. Members of Congress have ideal points in this Guns-Butter space. Given the chaos theorem discussed in Chapter 1, we know that Congress will have no *equilibrium of tastes* with respect to Guns and Butter. Without institutions that go beyond pure majority rule, Congress will vote forever on which mix of guns and butter to enact into law and never make a final decision.

However, the hypothetical Congress has created two committees, the Committee on Guns and the Committee on Butter, both of which are charged with overseeing policy in its own domains. All changes in policy must originate with them. If a committee reports a bill to change policy in its jurisdictional domain, amendments to the bill may change policy only along the single dimension of that policy.

Figure 8.4 shows how the structure-induced equilibrium with committees might work in such a world. The ideal points of nine members of a hypothetical legislature are shown. Three members (*A, B,* and *C*) are grouped on the Butter Committee and three (*F, H,* and *I*) on the Guns Committee. The status quo is indicated by *q*. To simplify things somewhat, *q* is indicated on each axis, along with the chamber and committee medians for that dimension.[20]

The predictions we make in analyzing the figure depend on the chamber rules. Let us take one set of rules for this example. (You can try out other rules in the problems at the end of the chapter.) Suppose the committees have only **gatekeeping power**—that is, the committee can decide whether to bring a bill to the floor, changing policy in its domain. However, once on the floor, there is a *germaneness rule*, allowing the bill to be amended along that dimension. What would happen?

In general, we know that if a committee opens the gates in its policy domain, a majority on the floor will amend the bill to correspond with the chamber median on that dimension, assuming the committee bill does not propose the median to begin with. Therefore, the committee median, in deciding whether to agree to report a bill to the floor, must decide whether

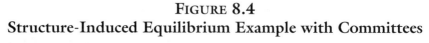

FIGURE 8.4
Structure-Induced Equilibrium Example with Committees

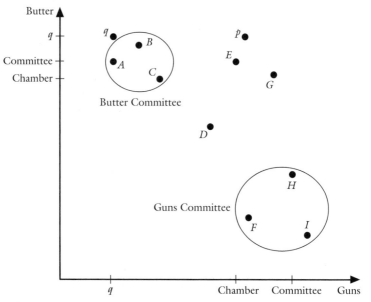

he or she prefers the status quo over the floor median in that area. If so, the member votes to report a bill to the floor, anticipating that the chamber's median will be enacted. Otherwise, the member chooses to keep the legislative gates closed, *even if he or she dislikes the status quo.*

In Figure 8.4, we see that if the Butter Committee reports a bill to the floor, the chamber will amend the bill to a position further away from the committee median's ideal point than the status quo. Therefore, the committee will keep the gates closed. However, the Guns Committee clearly would prefer the chamber median on that dimension compared to the status quo. Therefore, it will open the gates. The resulting policy in two dimensions is labeled point *p* on the graph.

This example has not been generated randomly. First, note that members with extreme preferences on the two dimensions are grouped on the committees: the Guns Committee contains members whose preferences are extreme on that dimension, compared to preferences of the chamber; likewise for the Butter Committee. We call these *outlier committees.* With special institutional prerogatives given to the committees, the effect of having outlier committees is to push policy away from the center of the chamber. You can see this by examining closely the location of *p*, the resulting policy after voting. Note that *p* lies (barely) outside the Pareto set. (The **Pareto set** is the set of all points in the policy space in which at least one of those points would receive a unanimous vote against a given alternative located outside the Pareto set. In other words, if the status quo were located outside the Pareto set, there is a policy change that the legislature would support unanimously, and it would be located inside the Pareto set.) In this example, if the chamber were allowed to vote on a policy just a bit to the southwest of p, it would support it unanimously. However, the rules of the chamber preclude this vote. Moving to the southwest from p would violate the rule that we respect germaneness and move in only "one dimension at a time." It would also violate committee prerogatives, which allow committees to take the lead in proposing policy change.

The structure-induced equilibrium perspective on committees has gained currency within political science, economics, and legal studies. The perspective is grounded in both theory and evidence. The theory has just been discussed, that of the setter model. The empirical evidence is more indirect (and subject to dispute, which we explore shortly) but based on a certain folk wisdom about Congress. That is, the committee appointment process is driven largely by self-selection. Members of Congress seek committee assignments in areas of interest to their constituents, making the committees particularly interested in constituency service, and thus preference outliers with respect to the entire chamber. The committees also have rules that protect them, many of which we discuss in the next chapter.

Research in the structure-induced equilibrium tradition has emphasized the **gains from trade** that can be extracted through the committee system. Much like nations and individuals can benefit in a market—trading what they are good at producing in exchange for what they are bad at producing—members of Congress can benefit electorally by dividing policy making into discrete arenas, allowing "interested" members to populate those arenas and dominate policy making, then allowing some sort of policy trading among the committees.

This is not always an attractive normative view of committees, since it suggests that committees do nothing more than facilitate one huge policy log roll. In defense of the log roll view, note that if MCs are electorally sensitive, this massive, committee-facilitated log roll in fact may be what a majority of Americans would want if they were in the legislature. Therefore, a criticism of this view of committees that simply notes its log-rolling potential is not all that compelling.

A more compelling criticism is this: if the "committee outlier" axiom is correct, resulting in a large number of policies far removed from what majorities of Americans want, then MCs should feel pressure to overcome the jurisdictional niceties that protect extreme policies. Consider again the world described in Figure 8.4. Here, in a Congress dominated by outlier committees with gatekeeping power, policy ends up outside the Pareto set.[21]

Why would this stylized legislature in Figure 8.4 endure this state of affairs? Clearly, if a committee system routinely produced policy outcomes that wildly diverged from the preferences of all members, the committee system would be changed.

The informational model of committees This sort of insight has motivated another robust strand of research into committees in recent years. The research, associated with Keith Krehbiel (1991), emphasizes the *informational* advantages that committees bring to policy making. Because committees potentially can improve the informational environment for *all* members of Congress, they are given special advantages in the policy-making process, including perhaps the latitude to shade policy in extreme ways.

To understand the **informational model of committees**, we backtrack to the simple one-dimensional spatial model and add a new wrinkle: uncertainty. Consider for a moment the utility function of a typical member of Congress, illustrated in Figure 8.5. Most of this figure should be familiar. An ideal point (labeled x) and a quadratic utility function are drawn for this member.

First, consider how this representative evaluates a policy, a. The dotted lines in the figure indicate the level of utility the representative associates with policy a, $U_x(a)$. In this example, the consequences of policy a are known with certainty, so the representative can simply evaluate how he or she feels about that policy, given a personal ideal point and utility curve.

Figure 8.5
Policy Voting under Uncertainty

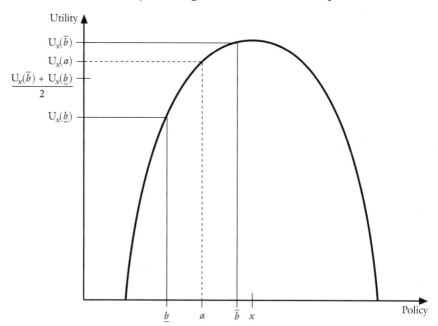

Now, consider how the MC would evaluate a policy about which he or she was *uncertain*. This new policy, b, has two possible outcomes, $\underline{b}$ and $\overline{b}$.[22]

Figure 8.5 also illustrates how this member evaluates this uncertain policy, b. On the y-axis is indicated how this representative would evaluate both policy outcomes if they were known for certain, labeling them $U_x(\underline{b})$ and $U_x(\overline{b})$. Now, because either outcome could occur with equal likelihood, the average of these utility levels also is indicated, labeled $\frac{[U_x(\overline{b})+U_x(\underline{b})]}{2}$. Note that $\frac{[U_x(\overline{b})+U_x(\underline{b})]}{2}< U_x(a)$. This is important, because the *average* policy outcomes of policy a and the lottery between policies $\underline{b}$ and $\overline{b}$ are the same. This figure illustrates, therefore, that the representative would prefer a policy that set policy at a for sure rather than a lottery that *on average* would set policy at a, but could not be predicted precisely.

This feature of voting on uncertain policies is a general finding when decision makers are risk averse. A **risk-averse** person who is given the choice between a policy that produces a for certain and one that produces a on average (sometimes better, sometimes worse) will choose the certain outcome.

What difference does this make for an understanding of committees? Actually, quite a bit. The oldest justification for committees is that they help Congress develop expertise and apply it to a problem. Stated in terms of Figure 8.5 the classic division-of-labor justification for committees looks like this: policy proposals, when they first enter the public agenda, are like the lottery between $\underline{b}$ and $\overline{b}$. The task of a committee is to study the policy to see if it can learn more precisely what will happen if the policy were adopted. When the committee reports back to the legislature, reducing the range of possible outcomes of that policy, *all* members of the legislature rate the policy more highly, even those who still believe the status quo should not be changed.

Therefore, if cost is not the issue, then a legislature should create committees to help it reduce uncertainty about proposed policies. However, creating committees is costly. Also, committees may not always do the work they promise nor do they always tell the truth. Therefore, the trick in designing a committee system is to reduce the costs of committee activity, induce committees to do the work assigned, and induce them to report the truth they discover about policies.

The costliness of creating committees was suggested earlier in this chapter. The House and Senate together spend about $600 million on their committees each Congress. If we include in this information-gathering apparatus the congressional support agencies (like the Library of Congress and the Congressional Budget Office) plus personal congressional staffs, the monetary cost of acquiring policy information is well over $2 billion each year. This amount is sufficiently large to become a campaign issue at times, as the Republicans discovered to their advantage (and the Democrats to their dismay) in 1994.

The costs are in policy terms, as well. If committee members are rational and policy motivated, nothing is automatic about the transmission of information from the committee to the floor. Suppose, for instance, that the committee investigates a policy and discovers that its most likely effects are to (1) please a majority of the committee but (2) displease a majority of the legislature. What is to force the committee to reveal what it actually knows about the likely outcomes of the proposed policy?

As this brief discussion suggests, nothing is automatic about creating informed committees, even if financial cost is not an issue. Agency costs are associated, as well. An **agency cost** is the cost incurred by a principal (in this case, the full chamber) when an agent (in this case, a committee) fails to do what the principal would have done in identical circumstances, with equivalent knowledge.

The informational approach to committees interprets many of the features of the committee system as mechanisms intended to foster and support an informative committee system. Some of these mechanisms include committee composition practices and the use of restrictive rules.

The information approach makes it clear that the entire legislature stands to gain from the appointment of committee members who share a mix of preferences. This approach first gives an informational justification for the common practice of appointing "interested" or "high-demand" members to committees, such as farmers to Agriculture or lawyers to Judiciary. Ask this question: If you were to appoint a committee that was responsible for seeing that the food supply to a quarter of a billion people was uninterrupted, would you appoint a committee dominated by representatives from farm districts, from manufacturing districts, or randomly from all districts? In all likelihood, you would appoint the lion's share of members from farm districts, for one important reason: they are the most likely already to understand food production and be best situated for learning more about it. Furthermore, they have electoral incentives to learn about the issue and stay informed. Therefore, what looks like a huge log roll to proponents of the gains-from-trade school of committee politics looks like an informational story to the informational school.

Still, if you answered "manufacturing districts" or "randomly" to the question just posed, likely it would be because you are uneasy about entrusting all farm policy to a group of people who might corrupt policy making for their own ends, not the ends of food consumers. Even though you might appoint an agriculture committee *dominated* by farmers, it would be unwise to appoint *only* farmers. While it would be impossible to appoint anyone entirely disinterested in the nation's food production and distribution, you certainly could find representatives who had no intrinsic interest in the plight of farmers and others who had experience with other parts of the food production and distribution system, such as producers, bankers, or consumers.

This diversification of committee memberships is a long-standing practice in Congress. For instance, for years it was traditional to appoint someone from New York City to the agriculture subcommittee of the House Appropriations Committee. The job of this subcommittee member was to keep the farm state interests honest and raise red flags if provisions of the bill egregiously harmed the interests of food consumers to the benefit of food producers.

Another array of resources Congress might employ to get the most information out of its committee system is restrictive rules meant to protect the legislative product of committees. The idea here may not be obvious, but it is still simple. If you want to induce committees to gather and report all the information relevant to any piece of legislation, you need to set up procedures to ensure that the time spent by committee members on information discovery is not wasted. You want to guard against what happened in the Congress of the Articles of Confederation (see Chapter 2), in which committees would work diligently on a bill, report it to the floor, and then see the bill ripped to shreds. Members of the Confederation Congress quickly realized that committee work was a massive waste of time, and so they just stopped putting a lot of effort into committees. Incompetent committees produced even worse legislative proposals, which also were shredded on the floor. Legislative proceedings were chaotic and so unproductive that members of Congress stopped showing up altogether.

The Constitution gives Congress broad latitude to set its rules in such a way that committee effort is protected. The next chapter discusses the rules of Congress and their effects on policy making. For now, just note that the rules of both chambers, but particularly of the House, give subtle strategic advantage to all bills that come from committee onto the floor. In addition, a few important bills, from a few especially powerful committees, gain even more protection under the operation of the House rules. The effect of these rules, from the information perspective, is to foster greater attentiveness by committees to policy.

The everyday parliamentary advantages to committees on the floor are many. They start with agenda setting, deciding what gets to the floor and what gets into any particular bill. Although the House, in theory, has the right to amend any bill to the fullest, time limitations restrict what practically might be targeted when a bill is considered. Moving on to amendments, committees have two advantages. In the House, an amendment passed in the Committee of the Whole is voted on again in full House session. However, an amendment that fails in the Committee of the Whole cannot be voted on again by the full House. Thus, committees get two shots at defeating amendments to its bills whereas committee opponents have no second chance if they lose in trying to amend a bill the first time. Further, committees usually are allowed to counter amendments with an *amendment to the amendment*, giving them some maneuvering room even when a majority is against them.

Finally, when bills are passed, two things advantage committees. First, most bills are passed under expedited procedures, such as suspension of the rules, in which no amendments (and practically no debate) are allowed. Therefore, for most bills, the chambers get to consider only what the committee wrote— take it or leave it. Second, committee members dominate conference proceedings, which allows them to set the contours of the final bill, subject again only to the constraint that a majority of each chamber favor, it over the status quo.

The best known (but least used) of the special committee protections is the closed rule in the House. This is a topic of Chapter 9, so it is not discussed much here. The **closed rule** is a legislative device that allows an entire bill to be brought to the floor for a single up-or-down vote. Short of such a draconian measure, modified closed rules allow some parts of the bill to be subject to amendment but close off others from the amending process. The committee that has benefited most often from the closed rule is Ways and Means. One justification for giving the Ways and Means Committee the closed rule so often is that it allows the committee to craft careful tax compromises among competing interests while protecting the overall integrity of the tax code. In return for this hard economic and political work, the House (led by the leadership, which must work hard to get a closed rule passed) grants the Ways and Means Committee added protection over its tax legislation.

It is easy to see how all these inducements for hard work are two-edged swords—they might get the information all members of Congress want, but they also can be manipulated by committee members contrary to the interests of the entire chamber.

Over the past two decades, a vigorous academic debate has emerged over proponents of the "gains from trade" and "information" approaches to committees. This debate has raged over the degree to which any of the empirical claims made by the two theories hold up to scrutiny. The gains from trade approach has been challenged to show that committees are composed of large numbers of self-selected outliers and that conference proceedings have been used to exert an inordinate influence on legislative outcomes. The informational approach has been challenged to demonstrate that the two chambers of Congress have been willing to use procedural resources to protect the legislative product of committees.

Some proponents of both approaches consider the two views to be mutually exclusive, which certainly is not true, even in theory. The gains from trade approach makes more precise how we understand the mechanisms through which individuals and small groups use the government for their private gain. The information approach makes more precise the mechanisms through which a collective body like Congress might pool its collective resources to produce a public good of informed policy. Rather than being competing approaches, together they allow us to understand more clearly the fundamental tension in all legislatures—that of balancing the needs of individuals with the needs of all citizens.

Further Reading

Cox, Gary W., and Mathew McCubbins. 1993. *Legislative Leviathan: Party Government in the House.* Berkeley: University of California Press.

Deering, Christopher J., and Steven S. Smith. 1997. *Committees i* 3rd ed. Washington, D.C.: Congressional Quarterly Press.

Fenno, Richard F. 1966. *Power of the Purse.* Boston: Little, Brov

———. 1974. *Congressmen in Committees.* Boston: Little, Brow

Hall, Richard L., and Bernard Grofman. 1990. "The Comm ment Process and the Conditional Nature of Committee Bias." *American Political Science Review* 84: 1149–66.

Kiewiet, D. Roderick, and Mathew D. McCubbins. 1991. *The Logic of Delegation: Congressional Parties and the Appropriations Process.* Chicago: University of Chicago Press.

King, David C. 1997. *Turf Wars: How Congressional Committees Claim Jurisdiction.* Chicago: University of Chicago Press.

Krehbiel, Keith. 1990. "Are Congressional Committees Composed of Preference Outliers?" *American Political Science Review* 84: 149–63.

———. 1991. *Information and Legislative Organization.* Ann Arbor: University of Michigan Press.

Mayhew, David R. 1974. *Congress: The Electoral Connection.* New Haven, Conn.: Yale University Press.

Shepsle, Kenneth A. 1978. *The Giant Jigsaw Puzzle.* Chicago: University of Chicago Press.

Shepsle, Kenneth A., and Barry R. Weingast. 1979. "Institutional Arrangements and Equilibrium in Multidimensional Voting Models." *American Journal of Political Science* 23: 27–59.

———. 1981. "Structure-Induced Equilibrium and Legislative Choice." *Public Choice* 36: 503–19.

———. 1987. "The Institutional Foundations of Committee Power." *American Political Science Review* 81: 85–104.

Wilson, Woodrow W. 1963 [1885]. *Congressional Government.* Boston: Houghton-Mifflin.

SUMMARY OF KEY CONCEPTS

1. A **select committee**, sometimes referred to as a **special committee**, is appointed on an ad hoc basis to consider a particular issue or bill.
2. A **conference committee**, consisting of members from both chambers, is appointed to reconcile differences in the text of legislation when it is passed by the two chambers in different forms.
3. A **standing committee** has a stable jurisdiction and permanent status by virtue of being written into the chamber's rules.
4. A **joint committee** has members appointed from both chambers, either to oversee internal matters (such as printing) or to consolidate investigative resources (such as tax policy). Joint committees rarely have authority to report legislation to the two chambers.

5. An important mechanism used in the House to equitably allocate committee assignments among members is the distinction between **exclusive** and **nonexclusive committees**. If a member is assigned to an exclusive committee, such as Rules, he or she may serve on no other committee. There are limits on the number of nonexclusive committees on which a member may serve, but they are not as constraining.

6. The **Johnson rule** is a practice that helps to allocate committee assignments equitably among senators. Named after Lyndon Johnson, Senate Democratic leader from 1953 to 1961, the rule requires that all freshman senators receive at least one attractive committee assignment before a senior senator is given a second.

7. The **seniority rule** is the practice of allocating committee chairs to the committee member with the longest continuous service on that committee.

8. The **subcommittee bill of rights** is a series of reforms in the House in the mid-1970s, instigated within the Democratic caucus, that transferred authority over the organization of subcommittees from the committee chairs to rank-and-file committee members. Those reforms included requirements that subcommittees have fixed jurisdictions and subcommittee chairs be chosen by the committee's majority caucus, not the chair of the full committee.

9. **Subcommittee government** is a characterization of congressional politics in the 1970s, when subcommittees experienced their greatest autonomy from full committees, with the result being a rapid decentralization of power in the institution, especially the House.

10. The **Congressional Budget and Impoundment Control Act of 1974** (CBICA) was a law that created the modern congressional budgetary process. It created budget committees in each chamber, the Congressional Budget Office, and a process for annually setting budgetary priorities within Congress.

11. A **budget resolution** is the concurrent resolution that Congress uses to set the broad parameters of fiscal policy each year. Spending targets set broad categories supposedly to guide the actions of the appropriations committees as they consider the annual appropriations bills.

12. The **reconciliation process** was created in the 1974 Congressional Budget and Impoundment Control Act to bring the budget resolutions and the annual appropriations bills into agreement. Originally designed to occur after all the spending bills had been passed, for most of the past twenty years, reconciliation measures have been passed at the beginning of the annual appropriations process to impose hard limits on the appropriations committees.

13. In *Congress: The Electoral Connection*, David Mayhew identifies three core activities in which members of Congress engage to help their reelection chances. **Position taking** is making statements on issues of the day. **Credit claiming** is associating oneself personally with material benefits

that flow from the federal government to one's congressional district. **Advertising** is getting one's name known throughout the district in a manner devoid of issue content.

14. The **setter model** is a simple application of the spatial model to cases in which an individual or group (the agenda setter) proposes a policy and an electorate (or committee) votes on the proposal, up or down, with no opportunity to amend it. An important insight of the setter model is that if the reversion point (that is, the policy that results from defeating the proposal) is sufficiently unattractive, the agenda setter is advantaged against the median voter.

15. A **structure-induced equilibrium** is a stable policy outcome produced even though a Condorcet winner does not exist, through the operation of legislative structures that preclude voting on all possible policy outcomes.

16. **Gatekeeping power** is the right of a committee to decide whether a bill will be considered on the floor of the legislature.

17. The **Pareto set** is the set of all points in the policy space in which at least one of those points would receive a unanimous vote against a given alternative located outside the Pareto set. In other words, if the status quo were located outside the Pareto set, there is a policy change that the legislature would support unanimously, and it would be located inside the Pareto set. Conversely, if the status quo is in the Pareto set, policy change cannot receive unanimous support in a vote.

18. The **gains from trade** perspective of committees emphasizes the benefits that individual legislators can derive from serving on committees that oversee electorally relevant policy areas. Within this perspective, the deference that members show toward the recommendations of committees is interpreted as supporting an implicit deal among members not to tamper with each other's electorally sensitive policy interests.

19. The **informational model of committees** posits that committees are created by Congress to improve the amount of information that rank-and-file representatives have about legislation and that the chambers craft incentives and rules to encourage committees to report truthfully what they learn about legislation.

20. I am **risk averse** if I would prefer to receive $2 for sure rather than enter a lottery in which I have a 50–50 chance of getting either $1 or $5. In general, risk-averse people are willing to pay extra to achieve a more certain outcome of lower expected value.

21. An **agency cost** generally is the price paid by a principal when he or she hires an agent to act on the principal's behalf. Agency costs include the costs of maintaining mechanisms to oversee the agent's performance and those endured when the agent's actions deviate from what the principal would have done under identical circumstances.

22. A **closed rule** is a parliamentary device in the House of Representatives that requires the chamber to vote on a bill as reported from a committee, without the option of amending it.

PROBLEMS

1. For this question, use the following definitions.

Gatekeeping power: The power of a committee to determine whether a piece of legislation changing the status quo will be let onto the floor.
Open rule: When the legislature votes on a proposal, any members of the legislature may make an amendment under pure majority rule.

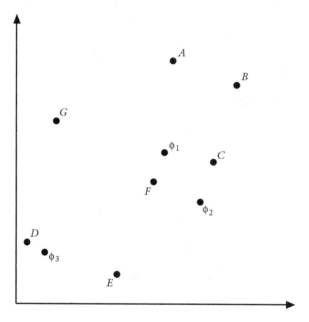

FIGURE P8.1

Closed rule: When the legislature votes on a proposal, no amendments are allowed—only a vote for or against the proposal.

Figure P8.1 maps the preferences of seven members of a fictional legislature, members A, . . . , G. Three members, A, B, and C, are members of Committee X; three members, E, F, and G, are on Committee Y. (Member D is the speaker and therefore on no committee.) Committee X has the right to propose changes in policy along the x-axis, while Committee Y has the right to propose changes in policy along the y-axis, Three status quo points, ϕ_1, ϕ_2 and ϕ_3, will be used in the problems. For all these problems, assume policy can move in only one dimension at a time.

a. Assume committees lack gatekeeping power and voting in the legislature is via an open rule. What policy proposals do the committees report to the floor, if any?

b. Assume committees have gatekeeping power and voting is by open rule. What policy proposals do the committees report to the floor, if any?

c. Assume committees have gatekeeping power and voting is by closed rule. What policy proposals do the committees report to the floor, if any?

2. Using Web or library resources, locate interest group ratings for members of the House of Representatives for the current Congress.

a. If the median member of the majority party delegation on the Rules Committee were removed and replaced by a member of the minority party located at the current median of that party delegation, how would the overall median of the committee change?

b. If the most ideologically extreme member of the majority party delegation on the Rules Committee were removed and replaced by a member of the minority party located at the opposite end of the ideological spectrum (i.e., equally extreme but in the opposite direction), how would the overall median of the committee change?

c. If the most ideologically moderate member of the majority party delegation (i.e., the majority party member most like the minority party) on the Rules Committee were removed and replaced by a member of the minority party located at the same position as the current most-moderate minority party member, how would the overall median of the committee change?

3. Using a resource that reports on political information concerning incumbent members of Congress, such as the *Almanac of American Politics* or CQPress.com answer the following questions:

a. Who is the second-ranked majority party member of the Ways and Means Committee? How might committee dynamics change if that person were to succeed into the chair of the committee, after the current incumbent steps down?

b. Repeat the preceding question, with the following committees:
   (1) Senate Finance
   (2) House Rules
   (3) Senate Budget
   (4) House Budget

4. Discuss how the chairs of Senate committees would change, using the spatial model to aid in your discussion, if

a. Party control switched hands
b. The chairs of the following committees would step down:
   (1) Finance
   (2) Foreign Relations
   (3) Government Operations

5. Find the committee assignments of your member of Congress using www.house.gov. (If you are not a citizen of the United States, pick any member of the House you wish.) Write a brief (2–3 page) paper in which you address the following questions:

a. What is the seniority status of your member on each committee and subcommittee on which he or she sits? How does this committee service relate to his or her constituency interests or characteristics? How does this committee service relate to the PAC contributions he or she received in the most recent election?

b. How have your member's committee assignments changed compared to three Congresses ago (or the first Congress of his or her service, if your member has served a shorter period of time)? If your member has changed assignments, why do you think he or she made the switch? If your member has changed assignments, has this had a discernible impact on his or her PAC contributions?

NOTES

1. There is also a line of scholarship that shows how Wilson's empirical view of congressional committees was confused, as well. See Rohde and Shepsle (1987) for one perspective on the empirical rigor of Wilson's scholarship.
2. Under long-standing parliamentary practice, the House of Representatives is considered to be a brand-new body every two years when it first convenes, because all its members are subject to biennial election. Therefore, the rules of one House do not formally carry over to the next. However, it has long been a practice of the House to adopt the previous House's rules as its own, on reconvening at the start of a Congress. Thus, while nothing in the House rules is formally permanent, except what is specified in the Constitution, it is not a big stretch to treat the House committees as permanent from one Congress to the next.

   Because only one-third of the Senate is up for election every two years, the Senate has adopted the convention of considering itself a permanent body. Therefore, in a formal sense it is even less of a stretch to consider the Senate committees permanent. Even so, well into the end of the 1800s, the Senate still adhered to the practice of appointing committees anew each *session*.
3. These two terms seem to be used interchangeably in congressional practice, with any distinction between the two being lost in the mists of time. The preferred term these days is *select committee*, which is the term I mostly use in this chapter.
4. Adding further to the confusion about the status of the Senate Indian Affairs committee is that the select committee's name was changed to the Committee on Indian Affairs in 1993 but the rules were never changed to make it a standing committee.
5. The only exception to the majority-domination practice was both chambers' ethics committees, which contained an equal number of Democrats and Republicans.
6. The *simplest* pieces of legslation might not have a conference committee at all. Conferences can be avoided (1) if both chambers simply pass the identical bill the first time around or (2) if, through a procedure that sends the bill back and

forth between the two chambers, one chamber's amendments to the bill are accepted by the other chamber. Most legislation passes Congress with no conference committee, although most "important" legislation goes through the conference procedure.

7. In 1888, when the Reed Rules were instituted, the House had 325 members, making a constitutional majority of 163.

8. The House already had created two standing housekeeping committees before this: the Committee on Elections (1789), to help judge disputed election cases, and the Committee on Claims (1794), to help judge the petitions of citizens who claimed that the federal government owed them money.

9. Keep in mind that in addition to sharing a legislative function with the House, the Senate shared executive functions with the president. The balance between the two functions can be gleaned from the relative heft of the Senate *Journal*, where legislative business was recorded, compared to the Senate *Executive Journal*, where executive business was recorded. About one-quarter of the Senate's business in its earliest Congresses can be found in the *Executive Journal*.

10. Of these practices, closed meetings were a bit of a red herring, since the House had operated under "sunshine" provisions for committee meetings for twenty years.

11. On violations of seniority over the past century, see Polsby, Gallaher, and Rundquist (1969); Abram and Cooper (1968); and Cox and McCubbins (1993).

12. Chairs of Appropriations Committee subcommittees also are subject to election by the caucus.

13. David M. Herszenhorn, "Byrd to Quit Powerful Senate Appropriations Post," *New York Times*, November 7, 2008, A19.

14. The simple ratio method is this: count the number of members who transfer onto a committee between Congresses and the number of members who transfer off it. The ratio of transfers on to transfers off is a good simple measure of that committee's attractiveness relative to other committees. See Groseclose and Stewart (1998) and Stewart and Groseclose (1999) for a discussion of several different measures, including the econometric method that produced Table 8.6.

15. Senate Rules and Administration has jurisdiction over campaign finance reform, which is of special interest to both parties, and over budgetary allocations to the other Senate committees.

16. A common mistake is to attribute the House's first move on appropriations to the Constitution. However, the House must consider first only tax bills—only by tradition does the House consider appropriations bills first. In some years, the Senate, in fact, has passed appropriations bills before the House.

17. This long-standing phenomenon is classically examined in the context of tariff legislation by E. E. Schattschneider (1935).

18. Also a tremendous number of military appointments must be confirmed each year—all officers of the armed forces must be confirmed by the Senate. In 1995, this amounted to nearly 40,000 nominations. The bulk of the Armed Services Committee's time on nominations is not spent with these relatively routine matters but rather with political appointments, such as NATO commanders and high positions in the Defense Department.

19. I use the term *responsible* advisedly, because it has taken on a popular meaning over the past century that is slightly different from what Wilson had in mind. However, this is the term Wilson used, and I use it, too.

20. On the Guns dimension, Member E is the chamber median and H is the committee median. On the Butter dimension, Member C is the chamber median and A is the committee median.

21. Some commentators have suggested that support for the 1974 Budget Act arose precisely because of problems with the appropriations process that are much like that shown in Figure 8.4. Before the Budget Act, all appropriations bills, plus bills authorizing permanent appropriations like Social Security, were acted on one bill at a time. No mechanism allowed Congress to adjust *all* the spending items simultaneously and comprehensively. One interpretation of the Budget Act, therefore, is that it created a new mechanism that allowed congressional majorities to protect themselves against the potential abuses of one-dimension-at-a-time voting rules.

22. Policies $\underline{b}$ and $\overline{b}$ are located equidistant from a, so *on average*, they produce outcome a. (Policies $\underline{b}$ and $\overline{b}$ might be two possible outcomes under a proposed welfare reform. Say, we *know* the welfare reform will cut the welfare roles but not by how much. The two possible amounts are cuts of 400,000 people ($\underline{b}$) and 600,000 people ($\overline{b}$). You might want to think of policy a, therefore, as cutting 500,000 people from the roles, for sure.

9

Doing It on the Floor: The Organization of Deliberation and What We Can Learn from It

The traditional way of discussing lawmaking in Congress is through how a bill becomes a law, in which the labyrinthine character of the legislative process is described in loving detail. One defining characteristic of legislative decision making is that it is formally sequenced. To a politician trying to attain political advantage in a legislative setting, this sequencing can become an important tool to advance or retard the development of policy. For example, because Senate committees first must conduct hearings to investigate the qualifications of presidential appointees before they are voted on by the Senate, the chairs of Senate committees can gain a strategic advantage by threatening to delay a nominee's hearing.

Therefore, we cannot avoid examining the sequencing of legislation, both in a broad scope, as in the tradition of how a bill becomes a law, and in a narrow scope, such as in examining how bills might be amended. Moreover, we cannot avoid discussing how legislation is handled once (if) it gets out of committee and onto the floor. Consequently, this chapter has two purposes. First, it takes a sequential look at legislating in Congress, starting with bill introduction and ending with bill passage. Second, particular attention is paid to what happens on the floor, explicating the strategic importance of debate, amendment, and roll call voting.

The remainder of this chapter is organized as follows. The first section takes a macro view of the overall sequencing of the legislative process. How *does* a bill become a law? How are bills bottled up? Where are the important strategic bottlenecks in the process? The second section discusses in more detail the floor consideration of legislation, paying particular attention to scheduling, debating, and amending. Finally, the last section takes a slight excursion, exploring how the record left by roll call votes can be used to inform us of the preferences of MCs, both individually and collectively.

Why a Bill Does Not Become a Law

Regardless of where we turn—to academics, courts, or journalists—the principal function ascribed to Congress in the American political system is lawmaking. The most important artifact that Congress leaves for the American political system to digest is laws. Therefore, there is no mystery about why the most hoary approach to the study of Congress is the exploration of how a bill becomes a law. If you are interested in understanding why a law has particular provisions or why a particular bill even passed in the first

FIGURE 9.1
Bills Introduced in and Passed by Congress, 1947–2010

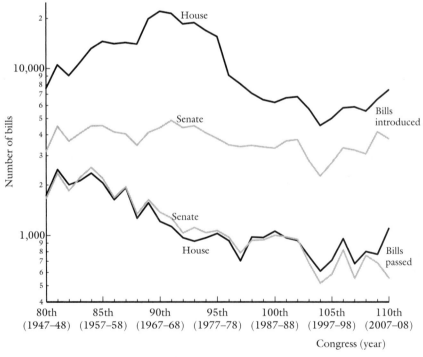

Source: Ornstein, Mann, and Malbin (2008, Tables 6-1 and 6-2); Congressional Record, *Resume of Congressional Activity,* first and second sessions, 110th and 111th Congresses.

place, it is necessary to understand the tortured path the bill took through the legislative process.

Yet this approach to studying Congress overlooks one important fact: almost no bills become law. This is illustrated in Figure 9.1, which reports the number of bills introduced into and passed by both chambers since 1947. Immediately after World War II, the Senate passed about half the bills introduced in that chamber, and the House passed about a quarter. Over time, those fractions fluctuated, but the general trend has been downward. Most recently, a little more than a tenth of the bills introduced in the House and a quarter of the bills introduced in the Senate have even gotten out of their respective chamber.

Why most bills die quiet deaths is a major subtext of this chapter. Some of the answers to this question are relatively trivial and can be dealt with simply. For instance, the rules in both chambers have varied over time in whether they allow multiple members to cosponsor legislation. Before 1979, the House limited the number of cosponsors on any bill to twenty-five. If more than twenty-five members wanted to cosponsor a bill, a duplicate would have to be filed with the additional cosponsors (and likewise if more than fifty, seventy-five, or a hundred members wanted to join in the fun). Since 1979, an unlimited number of House members may cosponsor any given bill. Obviously, allowing an unlimited number of cosponsors on a bill reduces the need to introduce duplicate versions of a bill whenever more than twenty-five representatives want to cosponsor legislation.

Another reason most bills die is a little trickier and requires us to understand the motives of members of Congress. Many members introduce bills they know will never see the light of day. This can be because members wish either to be seen as policy innovators or to use the bill introduction process as a low-cost method of demonstrating that they are on top of popular issues.

Some insight into the high death rate of congressional bills can be gleaned by examining the legislation submitted by a random House member in the 111th Congress (2009–2010), Patrick Kennedy (D-R.I.). Kennedy submitted thirty-seven pieces of legislation in the 111th Congress—eight resolutions, two concurrent resolutions, and twenty-seven bills. Kennedy represented a working-class constituency in a working-class state, and much of his legislation reflected his constituents' interests. In addition, due to his own personal background and the legacy of his family's interests, many of these bills concerned health care. An example of a bill that would have constituency bearing was H.R. 5080, which would have provided unemployment benefits during summer vacation for nonprofessional school employees. The many bills that pertained to health care—and which were all cosponsored by many other members—included bills about eliminating eating disorders (H.R. 1193), addressing autoimmune diseases (H.R. 2084), and amending the Quality of Mental and Substance Use Health Care Act of 2009 (H.R. 2369). Finally, virtually all of his resolutions singled out groups and individuals for praise by the House or proposed commemorative weeks, such as H.Res. 160, honoring Mental Health America on the 100th anniversary of its founding; H. Res.

182, expressing support for "School Social Work Week"; H. Res. 197, to commend the American Sail Training Association for "its advancement of character building under sail and for its advancement of international goodwill"; and H.Res. 716, recognizing Gail Abarbanel and the Rape Treatment Center.

Except for the last two resolutions mentioned, none of these legislative items passed. All were referred to committee. None even received a hearing.

What do we make of this activity? It certainly didn't lead to lawmaking. To some degree, the introduction of these bills allowed Kennedy to engage in what David Mayhew (1974) has referred to as "position-taking," that is, making public statements intended for back-home consumption. In other ways, bill introduction allowed the rest of Congress to gauge how broadly legislators supported certain legislative initiatives. For instance, Kennedy was one of eighty-four cosponsors of H.R. 5040, the Health Information Technology Extension for Behavioral Health Services Act of 2010. Expanding the use of information technology in health care has become an important issue, in both potential health care cost savings and in ensuring patient confidentiality as electronic records become more common. Although most sponsors of the bill were Democrats, eleven were Republicans, thus signaling this area to be one that would be fruitful for bipartisan lawmaking.

Lawmakers typically are most successful legislatively in areas that coincide with their legislative committee assignments. In this case, Kennedy, as a member of the House Appropriations Committee, was at a legislative disadvantage. Because so many of his bills were about health care, twenty-three of them were referred to the committee primarily responsible for that issue, Energy and Commerce. As the name implies, the House Energy and Commerce Committee has jurisdiction over a vast area; as the committee primarily responsible for health care, it was particularly busy in the 111th Congress. Not surprisingly, Energy and Commerce received nearly 1,500 bills by referral in that Congress. Although a representative like Patrick Kennedy may develop a reputation for caring about health care, especially mental health care, unless that representative is a member of the right committee, there is virtually no chance a bill could break through the workload clutter and even be considered, much less reported out and passed. While being on the House Appropriations Committee may ultimately help one's constituents receive a slightly larger share of federal spending, it comes at a cost of pushing more substantive legislative through the House committee system.

Let us now return to the original question: Why do so many bills die in Congress? As the example of Patrick Kennedy's bills suggests, most often bills die because they are introduced by members who are not in a position to see them through to passage.[1] When this happens, it is usually because MCs are taking positions, sometimes cynically, sometimes strategically. In other cases, bills die because the ideas embodied in them are picked up by other bills that *do* pass. In still other cases, bills actually lumber through the legislative process but die due to indifference or the press of more important business.

In spelling out the legislative process, therefore, it is more useful to think of the steps along the way as a series of hurdles rather than as steps intended to

TABLE 9.1
Legislative Hurdles

Major Hurdle / Minor Hurdle	House Detail	Senate Detail
Introduction	House originates tax bills	Senate exclusively considers executive matters
Reference to committee	Done by speaker, with no right of appeal	Done by presiding officer, with right of appeal
Committee consideration (subcommittee consideration may be nested within committee consideration)		
Hearing Mark-up Report		
Scheduling	Combination of Rules Committee and leadership negotiations	Leadership-centered negotiations
Getting on the calendar	Multitude of calendars (union, House, correction, private, D.C., discharge)	Two calendars (general orders, executive)
Getting off the calendar	Simple matters, suspension; complex matters, rules	Simple matters, suspension; complex matters, unanimous consent
Setting the parameters of debate, amendment, and voting	Rules Committee	Unanimous consent under threat of filibuster
Floor consideration	Committee of the Whole	
Debate	Constrained	Cloture
Amendment	Germaneness rules strong	Germaneness rules weak
Reconciling differences		

facilitate lawmaking. Thirty-four of Kennedy's bills failed the first hurdle (committee) with three passing the House. Because House resolutions don't need to pass the Senate, none of Kennedy's legislation faced this added set of hurdles.

Table 9.1 summarizes the hurdles that all legislation must jump in the two chambers. Each chamber possesses the same generic set of hurdles: introduction and referral, the committee process, scheduling, and floor consideration. These hurdles are listed in the first column, with important House and Senate details reported in the other two columns. Needless to say, bicameralism means that each of the generic hurdles must be jumped twice, and there is no guarantee that passage of a bill in one chamber (therefore clearing all of one chamber's hurdles) will lead to successful navigation of the other chamber's legislative obstacles. Finally, as if the parallel legislative processes in the two chamber were not enough, even if a bill passes both chambers, it must pass both chambers in *identical* form, meaning that numerous bills must be subjected to the hurdle of the conference process as well.

The remainder of this chapter addresses many of the details attending these legislative process hurdles. For the moment, simply note that although the House and Senate have identical generic legislative structures, the chambers differ in significant ways at virtually every stage of the process. (The only stage in which consideration is not materially different is in the committees.) The House's process generally is more formal than the Senate's. Senatorial informality is important substantively, because that makes it is easier for stray ideas to wander into legislation in the upper chamber than in the lower.

How a Few Bills Become Law

Introduction and referral of bills to committee

A bill starts its treacherous journey through the legislative process by being introduced then referred to committee. Bill introduction is really no hurdle—with 535 legislators in the House and Senate, a bill can count on someone, somewhere being willing to introduce virtually any idea into Congress. Unlike some state legislatures, only members of Congress may introduce bills into the U.S. Congress, which means that presidents and executive branch officials, who quite frequently are the "real" sources of major bills, must find a sympathetic MC to throw these bills into the hopper. This is no major hurdle, however, for many of the reasons already mentioned. In addition, by tradition (or shrewd political maneuvering), important administration legislation typically is introduced by senior members of the committees of jurisdiction. The annual appropriations bills typically are introduced by the chair of the House Appropriations Committee subcommittee that oversees the bill. In the first Congress of the Obama administration (111th Congress, 2009–2010), the American Recovery and Reinvestment Act (ARRA or "Recovery Act") was introduced by Representative David Obey (D-Wisc.), chair of the

Appropriations Committee, and the Lilly Ledbetter Fair Pay Act of 2009 was introduced by Representative George Miller (D-Calif.), chair of the Education and Labor Committee.

Once introduced, the bill is assigned a number and referred to committee. The number assignment process is a clerical task, but it is useful to understand the legislative nomenclature associated with bill numbers. **Bills** are assigned a number beginning with *H.R.* or *S.* in the House and Senate, respectively. As with the different types of legislation, numbers are assigned sequentially, with leaders allowed to assign "special" numbers to important legislation like vanity license plates for cars.[2] A bill, if passed, would be signed by the president and would bear the force of law. In most Congresses 80–90 percent of the measures introduced in both chambers are bills.[3]

A **resolution** involves only one chamber and lacks the force of law. Resolutions range across the map in terms of their importance. For instance, all the significant housekeeping measures are handled through resolutions, such as appointing committees, providing for the consideration of legislation in the House, and providing for appropriations for specific committees. On the other hand, purely position-taking measures also reside among resolutions, such as Representative Kennedy's resolution to honor the American Sail Training Association.

Two other types of resolutions require the concurrence of both chambers, but they differ in importance, much as bills and simple resolutions differ. **Joint resolutions** are reserved for the very few actions Congress can take without presidential concurrence, namely, proposing constitutional amendments and declaring war. **Concurrent resolutions** are reserved for matters internal to Congress itself but that pertain to both bodies. These matters range from relatively minor housekeeping matters, such as providing for the adjournment of Congress, to the significant, such as the budget resolutions that guide congressional fiscal deliberations each year.

Referral of legislation to committees is usually routine. While the formal power to refer legislation rests with the presiding officers of both chambers— the speaker of the House and the president of the Senate—in practice referral is almost always done by the parliamentarians, the employees of the chambers who specialize in seeing that the rules are applied consistently. The parliamentarians are further guided by the rules of the two chambers, which define the committees' jurisdictions, plus the precedents the chambers have followed whenever the rules are unclear or allow latitude.

While bill referral usually is routine, it need not be, and in extraordinary circumstance it is not. The classic example of an extraordinary circumstance was the 1964 Civil Rights Act, which faced tough sledding in both chambers of Congress. It is natural to think of a bill guaranteeing civil rights for African Americans to be considered by the judiciary committees of both chambers. However, in 1963 the chairman of the Senate Judiciary Committee was James Eastland (D-Miss.), a conservative opponent of civil rights legislation. To overcome Eastland's opposition to the measure, the Civil Rights Bill was drafted so that it invoked the "commerce clause" of the U.S. Constitution. Therefore, the bill also fell under the jurisdiction of the Senate Commerce Committee whose chairman, Warren Magnuson (D-Wash.), was a strong, supporter of civil rights. The House provided exactly the opposite situation: the chairman of the House Commerce Committee, Representative Oren Harris (D-Ark.), was an opponent while the chairman of the House Judiciary Committee, Representative Emanuel Cellar (D-N.Y.), was a supporter. Therefore, the Civil Rights Act was referred to the Commerce Committee in the Senate but to the Judiciary Committee in the House.

A more common special wrinkle on the bill referral process has to do with **multiple referrals** of bills to committees. Prior to 1974, speakers could refer bills to only one House committee. (Senate bills always could be referred to multiple committees. However, because the Senate rules allow more pathways for issues to be brought to a vote and added to bills, referral of legislation to multiple Senate committees rarely has been an issue.) There were many strains on this rule, but the practice came to the bursting point in the early 1970s as the House began working on complex legislation—energy regulation was the top example—that defied sorting into the House's jurisdictional rules. Therefore, in 1974, the House rules were changed, allowing the speaker to refer individual bills to multiple committees, either whole or by splitting them up into parts. Furthermore, speakers were allowed to set time limits on bills that were multiply referred, creating a process sometimes called **speaker discharge**.[4] Thus, speakers presumably not only could allow complex legislation to be considered by committees in complex ways but were also given a tool to ensure that this added complexity did not degenerate into yet another set of hurdles obstructing legislation.

The rules related to multiple referrals have changed over the past quarter century. The most important change came at the beginning of the 104th Congress (1995), when the new Republican majority took charge. The speaker no longer can refer an *entire bill* to multiple committees. However, the bill can still be split up and the *parts* referred to different committees; also, bills can be referred to various committees *sequentially* (i.e., first to Committee A then to Committee B). As in the past, when referring bills (or parts of bills) to various committees, the speaker is still allowed to set deadlines for their consideration.

Whether multiple referrals lead to "better" legislation is subject to debate, but it does seem to be true that the practice of multiple referrals has helped to better structure the mutual accommodation among competing interests in complex legislation. For instance, if the House is considering legislation to enhance the security of ports, the committee of primary jurisdiction will be the Homeland Security Committee. Without multiple referrals, the committee would likely consider the bill itself, drawing in the Transportation Committee, which otherwise has responsibility for shipping, only peripherally, or only toward the end of the process. With multiple referrals, a framework is set for both committees to work on the bill simultaneously. The prerogatives of the speaker, including her or his control of the Rules Committee, makes the multiple referral process less likely to produce fruitless delay than was commonplace a generation ago.

Allowing the multiple referral of bills to committees undermines the "structure-induced equilibrium" effects of the committee system, discussed in Chapter 8. The traditional textbook view of the committee system is that it allows complex, multidimensional issues to be reduced in complexity, thus reducing the likelihood that cycling and chaos will infect the legislative process. In reality, allowing committees with different jurisdictions to consider the same legislation must increase the dimensionality of the issue at hand and, therefore, increase the likelihood of chaos and delay.

While it is not clear whether multiple referral of bills has speeded up or improved legislation, speaker discharge has moved legislation along. The best example of how speaker discharge has expedited legislation was the consideration of the various pieces of the "Contract with America" in the early days of the 105th Congress. Elements of the contract, which consisted of a wide variety of issues spread across the legislative landscape, were referred to various committees for consideration in early 1995. Speaker Gingrich also announced that he would adhere to his promise that all contract items would be voted on within the first hundred days of Congress. This announcement clearly induced a few committees, where support for particular contract items was lukewarm, to report on contract-related legislation rather than allow the leadership to move ahead without its input.

Scheduling

Chapter 8 discussed committee consideration of legislation. Nothing will be added to that discussion here, other than a note that committee consideration (including consideration in subcommittee) is the most common source of legislative death in Congress. This regularity goes back to the earliest days of the Republic. The most pungent expression of this fact was given by Woodrow Wilson, in *Congressional Government*:

> The fate of bills committed [i.e., referred to committee] is generally not uncertain. As a rule, a bill committed is a bill doomed. When it goes from the clerk's desk to a committee-room it crosses a parliamentary bridge of sighs to dim dungeons of silence whence it will never return. The means and time of its death are unknown, but its friends never see it again. (1885, p. 63)

For that small percentage of bills reported out of committee, the next hurdle is getting scheduled for floor consideration. Here is where the major differences between the House and Senate really start to kick in.

Before we attend to details, note that the House and Senate differ in some unsurprising ways. The House is much more rule bound and structured than the Senate. The House has developed a fine set of procedures to move different types of legislation through that body, including a specialized calendar system, special days for the consideration of particular types of legislation, and a specialized committee—the Rules Committee—to facilitate legislative consideration. The Senate has developed a much simpler formal structure overall, relying instead on consensus among its members to get bills onto the floor for consideration.

The most basic queuing device for legislation is a **calendar**, which is nothing more than a list, in chronological order, of bills that have emerged from committee and are ready for floor action. The House has five such calendars. The two that see the most major legislation are the Union Calendar and the House Calendar. The **Union Calendar** is simply the list of all money legislation—appropriations and tax bills. The **House Calendar** generally includes all other public and private bills. The other calendars—Corrections, Private, and Discharges—queue up special items under the House rules. The Corrections Calendar was established in the 104th Congress (1995) when the Consent Calendar was abolished.[5] The Corrections Calendar is for legislation that addresses "laws and regulations that are ambiguous, arbitrary, or ludicrous" and "should be noncontroversial and have broad bipartisan support." The Private Calendar is for legislation that affects individuals, such as monetary claims against the government and special citizenship requests. Finally, the Discharge Calendar is for the few items that come before the House under a discharge petition (see later).

Each of these special calendars, in addition to business on the House calendar pertaining to the District of Columbia, can be called up by the speaker on **special days**. For instance, the House Rules of the 112th Congress (2011–2012) allowed for items stated to be passed via suspension of the rules to be called from the Suspension Calendar every Monday, Tuesday, and Wednesday plus the last six days of the session. To pass, a bill brought up on suspension must be approved by two-thirds of the House voting.

The **Calendar Wednesday** proceeding allows for the alphabetical "Call of Committees" each Wednesday, in which each committee is allowed to bring before the House a bill on the House calendar but not yet called up. Calendar Wednesday almost always is dispensed with via unanimous consent.

Of all these special procedures, the suspension of the rules is by far the most common. Indeed, it is the most common procedure used to get *all* legislation passed through the House. This is not surprising, since suspension of the rules is reserved for noncontroversial items, and most items that pass Congress are noncontroversial (and often trivial). At the other end of the spectrum, however, comes major legislation. Here, knowing about calendars and special days is only the starting point for a discussion of scheduling.

To begin, certain classes of legislation may be pulled off the House calendars and brought to the floor at any time. The rules of the House give the following committees "leave to report" to the House floor at any time:

- Appropriations Committee: General appropriation bills and continuing resolutions

- Budget Committee: Budget resolutions
- House Administration Committee: Enrolled bills, contested elections, printing for the use of Congress, expenditure of the House's budget, and preservation of House records
- Rules Committee: Rules, joint rules, and the order of business
- Standards of Official Conduct Committee: Conduct of House members and employees

In the nineteenth century, the privilege to report at any time was not only used frequently but was often used to the strategic advantage of the committee members with the privilege. For instance, Samuel Randall (D-Penn.), who chaired the House Appropriations Committee in the early 1880s, often would wander the House floor with appropriations bills in his pocket. If a bill Randall found objectionable was about to be called up, he would pull an appropriations bill out of his pocket, assert the privileged right for the bill to be considered, and drive the unwanted piece of legislation into hiding (Stewart 1989).

While the right to bring up its legislation at any time would seem like an unalloyed advantage to these committees, especially Appropriations and Ways and Means, there are significant drawbacks to the committees' use of this privilege. The most important drawback is that, if a bill is brought to the floor under a committee's privileged "leave to report," that bill is subject to points of order. (A **point of order** is an assertion that the rules of the House are being violated. If a bill's contents violate the rules of the House, it may not be considered.) As it turns out, most major legislation (including privileged bills) violates at least one House rule somehow. Some of these violations include the rule (actually, a law) that prohibits the House or Senate from considering tax or spending legislation until a budget resolution has passed, the rule that prohibits writing substantive legislation into appropriations bills, and the rule that prohibits a bill from being brought to the floor until three days after its report has been filed.

Therefore, important legislation that might be brought to the House floor under a special privilege rarely is brought up that way. In addition, there are many problems with bringing up other nonprivileged, yet important, legislation under the regular rules of the House. Therefore, the scheduling of the most important legislation in the House is channeled through the Rules Committee.

The House Rules Committee

Beginning in 1789, the House appointed a select committee on the rules at the start of each Congress, to write or revise the chamber's rules of procedure. This practice continued until 1880, when the Rules Committee became a permanent fixture among the House's standing committees. In very short order, the Rules Committee was transformed from a panel that simply reviewed the regular chamber rules to one that facilitated legislative action, by proposing *special rules* to govern the consideration of individual pieces of legislation.

In 1883 the role of the Rules Committee in the House was changed forever when it reported the first **special order** or **rule** concerning an individual piece of legislation. Recall from the discussion in Chapter 3 that the 1880s was a time of intense partisan division in Congress, which led the leaders of both parties to come up with innovations in the rules to get legislation passed. The same set of factors led to this enhanced role for the Rules Committee that began in 1883.

Republicans held a majority in the 47th Congress (1881–1883), but the Democrats were adept at using the tricks of the parliamentary trade, including the "disappearing quorum," to delay the consideration of legislation supported by the Republican majority. To make matters worse for the Republicans, the elections of 1882 had been disastrous, meaning that when the new 48th Congress (1883–1885) convened on March 3, 1883, the Democrats would have a nearly 2–1 advantage over the Republicans in the House. Therefore, the legislative efforts of the Republican leadership became more and more frantic during the lame duck session of the 47th Congress.[6] One important piece of legislation for the Republican leadership in this session was a tariff bill that had passed the Senate and was awaiting passage in the House.[7] Knowing that the Democrats would use every parliamentary instrument at their disposal to kill the bill, the Republican leaders decided to use a new device to get this legislation on the floor for consideration and passage.

Under the parliamentary situation that had delivered the tariff bill to the House floor, normally a two-thirds vote would have been needed to suspend the rules so that a conference committee could be appointed to hammer out a final bill. The Republicans had far fewer than two-thirds of the House, so this route was closed to them. Instead, Thomas B. Reed (R-Maine) reported a privileged resolution from the Rules Committee that, if passed, would allow the House to suspend the rules with a *majority* vote and simultaneously request a conference with the Senate to resolve differences over the tariff bill. After two days of fighting over this tactic, the House passed the resolution, and in quick order, a majority voted to suspend the rules and request a conference with the Senate. Congress passed a tariff bill at the end of the 47th Congress, which was possible only because of this parliamentary innovation.

Over the past century, this sort of tactic has ceased to be controversial and in fact has become the accepted practice in the House. The type of resolution that governs the consideration of a bill is variously called a *rule* and a *special order*. The most common term applied to this resolution is *rule*, but it is easy to confuse a rule in this special sense with a general rule of the House—that is, its regular rules of order. To minimize the possibility of such confusion, for the remainder of this chapter, when I refer to a rule, in the sense of a special order, I will refer to it as a *special rule*.

Nowadays, special rules govern when a bill will be brought up, the nature of debate on the bill, and the nature of amendments that may be offered. The major distinction among special rules is between open rules and closed rules. As the names imply, **open rules** are a class of special rules that grant very wide latitude to the amendment of bills. **Closed rules** restrict, in varying ways and to varying degrees, which amendments may be offered—if amendments may be offered at all. Over the past three decades the ingenuity of party leaders and Rules Committee members in writing special rules has been allowed to run free, leading to a variety of subspecies of open and closed rules, which are summarized in Table 9.2.

TABLE 9.2
Special Rules in the House

Type	Description
Open rule	Bill is considered for amendment under the five-minute rule, but no other special restrictions apply to its consideration beyond the Standing Rules of the House.
Open plus	Like an open rule, except this rule protects certain named amendments from points of order.
Modified open	A time limit is placed on considering amendment, but no restriction is placed on the contents of the amendments.
Modified open requiring preprinting in the *Congressional Record*	This rule does not restrict the content of amendments but encourages members with amendments to notify the chamber ahead of time about the content of those amendments.
Closed rule	No amendments are allowed to the bill, except those offered by the committee reporting the bill. Under the Standing Rules of the House, such a rule still must allow a member of the minority party to offer a motion to recommit the bill, with instructions, back to the committee.
Modified closed rule	This rule allows for the consideration of one or two amendments to a bill, which may be designated ahead of time. It may prohibit amendments to particular sections altogether or prohibit particular types of amendments.
Structured rule	This rule allows three or more amendments to a bill, which may be designated ahead of time. It may prohibit amendments to particular sections altogether or prohibit particular types of amendments.

Source: Saturno (1998).

Because formal structures are so important in determining the details of legislation, special rules are an important part of the legislative process. This is seen whenever a major bill is brought out of committee, when the hearing by the Rules Committee on the nature of the special rule to be proposed takes on great importance and often elicits press attention. This also is seen in committee transfer patterns, reviewed in Chapter 8. There, membership on the Rules Committee was shown to be just as durable and valuable as membership on Ways and Means or Appropriations Committees.

The theoretical importance of specifying whether a bill is considered under a closed or open rule is one of the easiest—and fundamental—ideas to communicate through basic formal models of legislation. An example is shown in Figure 9.2. Suppose the House Judiciary Committee was considering a comprehensive modification of the nation's immigration laws. In this example, the status quo (Q) indicates that the established law places relatively few restrictions on those immigrating into the United States to seek employment and few restrictions on those immigrating to be with their family already here. The irregular figure sketches out the win set against this status quo (W(Q)).[8] Crosshairs indicate where the median House member is located along the "work restrictions" and "family unification restrictions" dimensions.

FIGURE 9.2
Example of the Effects of Closed and Open Rules on Legislation

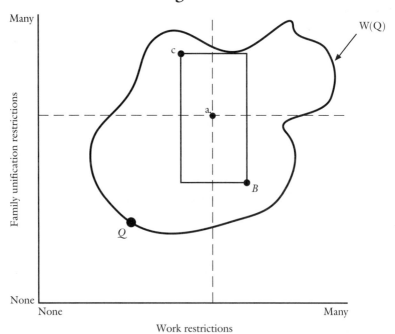

The committee reports a bill (B) that changes work restrictions much more dramatically than family unification restrictions. In fact, it provides for more work restrictions than the median wants and fewer family unification restrictions than the median on that dimension wants. B clearly is located within $W(Q)$, therefore it would pass on an up-or-down vote. However, we know that, generally speaking, B could be successfully amended via majority vote. Knowing *whether* and *how* it might be amended depends on the special rule.

For the rest of this example, assume that any amendments offered—if they are allowed to be offered—must be germane to the section of the bill being considered and that the family unification and work restriction provisions are in separate sections of the bill. Therefore, an amendment may move the bill only "one dimension at a time."

Under the theoretical open rule considered in Chapter 1, the bill eventually would gravitate to the northwest, until some of the work restrictions were loosened, some of the family restrictions were tightened, and the bill lodged at the ideal point of the medians on the two dimensions. This is illustrated as point a. Under the theoretical closed rule considered in Chapter 1, the bill simply would pass at the point where it was proposed, point B.

As the previous discussion in this section suggests, even the simplest versions of actual open and closed rules deviate somewhat from these stylized open and closed rules. For instance, open rules still provide for amendments to be considered under the "five-minute rule" and other time restrictions. Therefore, practically speaking, bill opponents have only one or two opportunities to amend a particular provision of a bill before the House has to go on to other business. Time rarely is allowed for the magic of the median voter theorem to work its will.

Suppose, therefore, that an open rule operates like this, in practice: someone (anyone) is recognized to offer an amendment to the bill on one dimension, and then someone else (anyone else) is recognized to offer an amendment to the bill on the other dimension. If these amendments are restricted (for theoretical reasons) to be in the part of the issue space where a majority of the House would support the amendment, then the final bill could end up anywhere in the box drawn in the figure. These resulting amended bills could be quite different from the bill originally reported by the committee. For instance, a bill located at point c could pass, reversing the balance struck by the committee on the emphasis placed on family reunification and work restrictions.

Further, the House rules require that all closed rules still allow the minority party to offer a motion to recommit a bill with instructions. The motion to **recommit a bill with instructions** effectively is a comprehensive amendment to the bill, offered by the minority party, that states how the minority party would have drafted the bill. It is a motion to send the bill back to the originating committee, ordering it to report back a different bill that accomplishes what the instructions in the motion to recommit dictate. In this example, a motion to recommit the bill to the Judiciary Committee, with the instructions that it report back a bill with fewer work restrictions and more family restrictions, as at point *a*, would pass the House. In fact, the motion to recommit with instructions rarely passes but that is most likely because the majority party, not the minority party, tends to have the most members close to the medians on the two dimensions and the rules generally preclude majority members from making this motion.

Finally, a modified closed rule might provide for the consideration of an amendment along one dimension and not the other. For instance, the modified closed rule might say that an amendment along the work restriction dimension is allowed but not on the family unification section. In that case, the resulting bill *could* end up to the left of *B*.

The nature of special rules passed by the House, therefore, is tremendously important for guiding the details of legislation. Is there any wonder that in times when the political parties in Congress have flexed their muscles, they have relied on the Rules Committee to be the instrument of that muscle flexing?

Although the speaker has the right to call up legislation at his or her discretion under the provisions of most special rules, it would be foolish to bring legislation to the floor willy-nilly. For a bill to pass to the liking of the majority party leaders, they not only need to craft the special rule to their liking but also to get their supporters onto the floor to support the rule and pass the bill itself. Although the speaker uses the element of surprise to advantage in rare cases, mostly he or she relies on followers to be on the floor in a legislative battle. This is done through the majority party whip organization.

Chapter 7 discussed the basic functions of the whip organizations of both parties. In this chapter it is sufficient to note that the majority whip, especially, is given the practical task of communicating the likely schedule of business to party followers, in addition to information about how the leadership feels about the bills and any amendments that might come along.

Circumventing committees

Up to this point, we have assumed that the legislation in question has been reported out of committee and placed on the appropriate House or Senate calendar. And, indeed, almost all legislation comes to the floor that way. However, sometimes popular legislation gets bottled up in committee and majorities in both chambers want to retrieve it from a hostile committee. Such moments are rare, but they do occur.

The House has developed the **discharge petition** as the primary vehicle for extracting legislation from hostile committees and bringing it to the floor. *Discharge* is the parliamentary term for ending the responsibility of a committee for a bill. Before 1910, the House had no workable procedure for discharging bills from committees. In that year, the House adopted a rule allowing a House majority to demand the discharge of a committee, via petition, and for the subsequent consideration of the legislation. The current form of the rule was adopted in 1931 (see Beth 1998).

The discharge petition currently works as follows: if a bill has been in committee for more than thirty days, it is possible for a majority to remove that bill from committee by starting a discharge petition, which must be signed by 218 House members—a majority. Once the petition has received 218 signatures, a signer may offer a motion to discharge the bill from the committee of jurisdiction. However, the motion may not be made until seven days have elapsed after the 218 signatures have been acquired *and only then* on the second and fourth Monday of the month. If the discharge motion passes, then the House may vote on whether to consider the bill immediately or put it on the House Calendar.[9]

The use of the discharge procedure is rare. From 1931 to 2010, 628 discharge petitions were filed: 372 on bills and 266 on special rules. Of these, only forty-six were put on the Discharge Calendar, having received the required number of signatures, and thirty-one were actually called up for a vote. Discharge was successfully voted twenty-six times, with the bill passing the House nineteen times. Only twice since 1931 has a discharged bill become law.[10]

The very low success rate of the discharge petition procedure suggests that discharge is a paper tiger, fairly useless for getting committees to report out legislation that the floor wants but the committee opposes. It would be unwise to jump to this conclusion, however. Just the threat of discharge may prompt a committee to action; even if the committee opposes a bill, it would rather be in control of the parliamentary situation when the bill is considered than lose control of the process altogether.

A dramatic case when the *threat* of discharge led to the eventual passage of a bill came in 1986 during the consideration of the Volkmer Gun Control Law. The National Rifle Association (NRA) and its supporters had pushed for years to weaken a series of gun control laws that had been passed in the 1960s. Support for some form of weakening carried a narrow majority in the House, but the House Democratic leaders had worked hard for nearly a decade to keep bills that relaxed gun control restrictions bottled up in the Judiciary Committee. Finally, in 1986, supporters of a bill introduced by Harold L. Volkmer (D-Mo.) to loosen gun restrictions got 209 signatures on a discharge petition; it was a matter of time before the petition would have 218.

As the number of signatures approached 218, the Judiciary Committee sprang into action. It passed a gun control measure that was a compromise between police groups (which had supported keeping the 1968 Gun Control Law unchanged) and the NRA. The bill made it to the floor and eventually was signed into law by President Reagan.

While it is impossible to know how representative the case of the Volkmer Gun Control Law is, no doubt this episode encapsulates the most common way in which the discharge procedure is significant in the House—by prompting committees to preempt the discharge procedure in the first place. The discharge petition therefore is a "club behind the door," available to be used by a majority of the House members whenever committees are seen as abusing their prerogatives.

Discharge is less of a paper tiger if we view it in another light, as well. Making public policy is only one instrumental goal among several that members of Congress pursue along the way to seeking reelection. Other goals include taking positions on issues and taking credit for federal program benefits that flow back to the district (see Mayhew 1974). Discharge rarely results in policy being changed, but it provides a useful vehicle for taking a position, both at the point of attempting to get signatures on the petition and, if the petition is successful, getting a roll call vote on the underlying bill. Bills that must be extracted from committee via the discharge petition route already face tough sledding in Congress—committees rarely just ignore the strongly held opinions of large majorities of their chambers. House members who sign discharge petitions are well aware of this and under no illusions that the real point of discharge is actually changing policy in the short term.

It is considerably easier to circumvent committee bottlenecks in the Senate because it has lax germaneness rules. Therefore, a senator whose wishes have been thwarted by committee inaction can simply move that the text of a bill be attached to virtually any other bill that makes it to the Senate floor. Furthermore, a senator whose bill is bottled up simply can reintroduce the bill and then object to the second reading of the bill, which places the bill directly on the Senate calendar for consideration.

Scheduling in the Senate

Considerable time has been spent on the scheduling and general consideration of legislation in the House for two reasons. First, and most important, scheduling legislation in the House is very rule bound. Second, some of the elements of legislative scheduling in the House are generic and therefore apply to the Senate as well. For instance, although both chambers manage the flow of amendments in different ways, restrictions on amendments— or the lack thereof—have the same effects in the Senate as in the House. Because the rules affecting the scheduling of legislation in the Senate are fewer and because some generic features of scheduling were covered while discussing the House, this section on the Senate will be appreciably shorter.

Legislation is brought up before the Senate in three major ways. Noncontroversial bills tend to be brought up and passed under **unanimous consent**. This is in contrast with the House, which tends to handle noncontroversial legislation through suspension of the rules. For controversial legislation, legislation is brought up and considered in the Senate in two ways. The most direct way is for a senator to make a motion to proceed with a bill, and then for the Senate to consider it.

Practically speaking, reliance on the motion to proceed almost always signals a breakdown in the legislative process or a defeat for the minority party. For instance, in 1999, President Clinton discovered that his judicial nominees were languishing—sometimes in the Senate Judiciary Committee, but even when the nominees were cleared by the committee, the Republican leadership in the Senate refused to bring the nominations up for a vote. This became an issue among the minority Democrats, especially when it came to delays in the consideration of minority (referring now to race, not political party) judicial nominees. Unable to get the leadership to call up nominations voluntarily, the Democrats decided to force the issue and move to proceed with the nominations. On September 21, 1999, Senator Thomas Daschle (D-S.D.) moved that the Senate go into executive session to consider, in turn, Marsha Berzon and Richard Paez to be circuit judges. Both motions failed by party-line votes, 45–54. Therefore, they were not considered.

One reason that the motion to consider is not frequently used in the Senate is that the motion itself is subject to the filibuster. Later, I discuss in detail the use of the filibuster in Senate proceedings. For now it is sufficient to know that the **filibuster** is a legislative tactic by which proceedings can be brought to a halt by a senator talking nonstop. Because a motion to proceed is subject to the filibuster, opponents of bills have two opportunities to kill legislation through the filibuster: when the motion is made to consider the bill *and* when the bill itself is considered.

Because it is so easy for a small number of senators to halt the consideration of legislation, the Senate has developed the practice of settling on the consideration of major legislation through complex unanimous consent agreements,[11] sometimes called **time agreements. Complex unanimous consent agreements** may be complex in name only or just complex in fact.

A good example of a "simple" complex unanimous consent agreement is associated with the Senate consideration of the National Missile Defense Act in March 1999. On the evening of March 11, the Senate majority leader, Trent Lott (R-Miss.) asked "unanimous consent [that] the Senate now turn to S. 257, the Missile Defense Act."[12] He further announced:

> Mr. President, for the information of all Senators, then, the Senate will be able to have the initial statement by Senator Cochran, the manager, tonight. We will resume the missile defense bill on Monday, and it is our hope that an agreement can be reached on a time agreement and that amendments will be offered during Monday's session.
>
> I urge that Members be present on Monday to make their statements on this legislation and to offer amendments, if they have them. This is a very important defense initiative. I am pleased that we are going to be able to go straight to the bill, and I hope that within short order next week we will be able to get to the conclusion of this very important national defense issue.

At the end of the evening, Senator Slade Gorton (R-Wash.) asked for unanimous consent that on the morning of March 15, "following morning business, the Senate resume consideration of S. 257, the missile defense bill."

On the following Monday, March 15, Senator Cochran (R-Miss.) moved that the Senate begin its full deliberation on the Missile Defense Bill, including general debate on the bill and one amendment that had been offered by Cochran himself. Toward the end of that day, after many senators had spoken, Senator Cochran took the floor and made the following statement:

> Seeing no other Senators seeking recognition on the floor at this time, in [*sic*] behalf of the majority leader, I ask unanimous consent that the Senate resume the pending missile defense bill at 11:30 A.M. on Tuesday and at that time there be one hour for debate on the pending Cochran amendment, with a vote to occur on or in relation to that amendment No. 69 at 2:15 P.M. on Tuesday and that no other amendments be in order prior to that vote.

This agreement was reiterated at the very end of the day when, right before adjourning for the night, Cochran asked "unanimous consent that at 11:30 A.M., the Senate resume consideration of S. 257, the missile defense bill, under the provisions of the unanimous consent agreement reached earlier today."

On the following day the "Cochran amendment" was dealt with under the provisions of this agreement and a second amendment, by Senator Landrieu (D-La.), was offered. After debate had proceeded on the Landrieu amendment, Cochran offered the following agreement:

> I ask unanimous consent that there now be 20 minutes for debate on the pending amendment, with the debate divided as follows: 10 minutes for Senator Levin; 5 minutes for Senator Landrieu; 5 minutes for Senator Cochran. I further ask unanimous consent that following that debate, the Senate proceed to a vote on, or in relation to, the amendment, with no other amendments in order prior to the vote.

On the following day, the Senate again took up the bill and considered both the Landrieu amendment and a few others, which later were withdrawn. As the day drew to a close, Senator Cochran noted:

> Mr. President, I understand from both sides that those who are listed under the order to permit them to offer amendments do not intend to offer the amendments, and I know of no other Senators who are seeking recognition. I would suggest that we have come to the time when we could have third reading of the bill. (p. S2820)

With this observation, Cochran set in motion a series of steps that led to the expeditious passing of S. 257.

The use of unanimous consent agreements in the Senate obviously is a different way of guiding the consideration of legislation from the use of special rules in the House. Note three things about the use of unanimous consent agreements in the consideration of the Missile Defense Bill. First, consideration of the bill really got rolling when the majority leader, Trent Lott, was recognized and asked unanimous consent to proceed with S. 257. By tradition, the majority leader has the right of first recognition by the presiding officer, precisely so that he or she can make these sorts of requests. Second, debate on the bill began before there was full agreement on how to proceed with the bill—about how amendments would be considered or when the bill would finally come up for a vote. Agreement over structuring debate evolved as the debate itself evolved. Third, the senator managing the bill (Senator Cochran) took the lead in developing the unanimous consent agreements that kept the bill on track. In general, although the majority leader takes an active interest in the development of unanimous consent agreements for all bills, it often falls on the bill's floor manager to work through the logistics of unanimous consent agreements.

Not obvious in this accounting of unanimous consent agreements is the role of the minority party, since all the major actors were in the majority. Needless to say, because unanimous consent agreements are adopted *unanimously*, the minority party needs to be involved in their development. The minority leader is responsible generally for protecting the interests of the minority when such agreements are established, but practically speaking, the minority party members most interested in a piece of legislation usually play more active roles in developing these agreements.

In the case of the National Missile Defense bill, the minority Democrats believed it important to make a statement in support of further negotiations with Russia over nuclear arms reductions, at the same time the Senate was voting in favor of developing a highly controversial missile defense system that the Russians strongly opposed. The Clinton administration had initially opposed the Missile Defense Bill and threatened a veto of the measure. With the veto threat looming over the Senate and the ability of the Democrats to further slow down consideration of a bill that the Republicans wanted to pass very badly, the minority party was able to use the unanimous consent mechanism to get the Landrieu amendment considered, voted on (unanimously, as it turns out), and incorporated into the bill.

The reliance on unanimous consent in the Senate to move along legislation has created a bit of a theoretical puzzle for political scientists who study Congress. Because most bills brought up under the unanimous consent mechanism are subject to opposition, why do senators who oppose a bill not object to its consideration? Traditional scholars and observers of Congress have attributed the lack of objection to a "norm" of consent—in the oft-repeated words of former Speaker Sam Rayburn, you "go along to get along." Under this understanding of legislative life, senators live in a world in which it generally is understood that everyone will, at some point, want a bill considered that others find objectionable. A senator who gains a reputation as an objector will face retaliation. Worst of all, if lots of senators routinely are objectors, there will be lots of retaliation; and business in the Senate will grind to a halt, even for noncontroversial matters.

Modern students of Congress tend to explain the observed lack of objections to unanimous consent agreements through the lens of individual utility maximization. Under this view, a senator who objects to the policy direction of a bill weighs the short-term loss in utility if he fails to object to a bill and it passes versus the long-term loss in utility if another senator retaliates in the future when she wants to bring a bill he supports to the Senate floor.

Keith Krehbiel's (1988) exploration of the strategy of unanimous consent agreements not only lays out the full logic of this perspective but provides a couple of examples in which strong opponents of bills were brought into a unanimous consent agreement through trading off the long- and short-term consequences of their actions. A straightforward example is that of Senator

Jesse Helms (R-N.C.), who had engaged in a filibuster to kill a bill in 1983 that would create a national holiday honoring Martin Luther King, Jr. With support for the bill running very high in the Senate and both senators and representatives wanting to wrap up business for an upcoming holiday, Majority Leader Howard Baker (R-Tenn.) took the floor to offer a unanimous consent agreement that the King Holiday Bill be voted on at a certain time, with an opportunity for Helms to offer a motion to recommit the bill to the Judiciary Committee.

In the midst of discussing the unanimous consent agreement on the floor, Senator Gordon Humphrey (R-N.H.) appeared to be on the verge of objecting, over provisions in the agreement that would have precluded his offering some amendments he favored. In the midst of the colloquy over the details of the agreement, Senator Helms himself urged Humphrey not to object to the agreement and to allow the bill to come to a vote.

Why was Helms, who had just led a filibuster against the King Holiday Bill, now so eager to see the bill come to a vote? One will never know the answer of this question for sure, but it is interesting to note that immediately after the unanimous consent agreement was adopted allowing for a final vote on the King Holiday Bill, the Senate considered a unanimous consent agreement allowing for the consideration of the Dairy and Tobacco Act, which Helms strongly supported. The overall package—King Holiday Bill *plus* the Dairy and Tobacco Act—was clearly preferable in Helms's eyes to the King Holiday Bill only. In addition, the coupling of the two bills in rapid succession created a mechanism for senators to retaliate against Helms should he object to the King Holiday Bill.

All in all, then, reliance on complex unanimous consent agreements in the Senate is not only a product of the egalitarian ethos and formal rules of that chamber but it also provides a setting for complex strategic maneuvers. It is no wonder, then, that the Senate has revered those senators who have mastered the rules and practices of the chamber, such as the late Robert Byrd (D-W.Va.), since the strategy is played out on the floor of the Senate, among the individual senators, rather than among a specialized group of senators, in a committee room, as happens in the House.

Floor consideration—general issues

Once legislation is scheduled in both the House and the Senate, what many people regard as the "real" business of Congress lumbers into view: debating, amending, and passing bills on the floor. These steps are reviewed next.

Before getting into the meat of legislating, it is important to know that both the House and Senate have established orders of business in their Standing Rules, which structure how each day proceeds. A summary of these orders of business appears in Table 9.3. As we have come to expect, the House's standard order of business is more detailed than the Senate's. Yet

TABLE 9.3
Daily Order of Business in the House and Senate, 112th Congress

House (Rule XIV)	Senate (Rules IV and VIII)
1. Prayer by the Chaplain.	1. Prayer by the Chaplain.
2. Reading and approval of the journal (may be waived under the rules).	2. The Pledge of Allegiance to the Flag.
3. The Pledge of Allegiance to the Flag.	3. Reading and approval of the Journal (may be waived).
4. Correction of reference of public bills.	4. Morning business (submission of various reports and messages, and the introduction of legislation).
5. Disposal of business on the Speaker's table (mostly communications from the president, executive agencies, and the Senate).	5. Consideration of bills that are on the Calendar of Bills and Resolutions.
6. Unfinished business from the day before.	
7. The morning hour for the consideration of bills called up by committees (usually dispensed with).	
8. Motions that the House resolve into the Committee of the Whole House on the State of the Union.	
9. Orders of the day.	

Source: House Rules; *Senate Manual.*

even this comparison of the formal House and Senate order of business does not reveal the most important difference between the two chambers, which involves the existential question of what constitutes a day.

In the House, there is no ambiguity about what constitutes a day. When the House adjourns for the evening, it then starts up the next day following the standard order of business, unless there is unanimous agreement to dispense with certain elements of it. The Senate, however, is able to finish its business for the day and return the next **calendar day** and to do work on a **legislative day**, which is unchanged from the day before. In general, if a chamber **recesses** rather than **adjourns**, the legislative day remains unchanged the next time the chamber convenes, even if it is on a *different* calendar day. Because it typically recesses rather than adjourns at the end of each calendar day, Senate legislative days often are out of sync with the real-world calendar.

The distinction between calendar and legislative days is important in the Senate because the standard order of business applies only to the beginning of a *legislative* day.[13] More important, at the beginning of a legislative day, the Senate must proceed with **morning business**, which is a hodgepodge of speeches, reports, and messages that must be dealt with. Dealing with morning business gives senators all sorts of opportunities to delay action; therefore the Senate has adopted the practice of simply recessing from day to day, rather than adjourning every evening. Doing so speeds up business considerably.

Committee of the Whole House

The heavy lifting of legislative floor action in the House of Representatives is done using a parliamentary device, the **Committee of the Whole**. This device actually precedes the history of Congress, going back to the early history of the English Parliament. In Parliament, Committee of the Whole proceedings were developed so that members of Parliament could exclude the speaker, who was a representative of the king, from its proceedings. As a Committee of the Whole, Parliament was not formally in session, but it did debate and provisionally alter laws, presided over by a regular member of Parliament.

Both chambers of the U.S. Congress adopted Committee of the Whole mechanisms in their earliest days, but only the House continues to rely on it. The advantage of the Committee of the Whole is primarily that a majority of the full House need not be present for the Committee to do its business. As we saw in Chapter 3, in the 1880s the quorum of Committee of the Whole was changed to 100, where it has stayed ever since. The purpose behind lowering the quorum of the Committee of the Whole to less than a constitutional quorum was to make it harder for the minority to obstruct the consideration of legislation it opposed.

And, as we saw in the discussion of special rules, most of the real work on legislation occurs in the Committee of the Whole. Amendments may be offered and debate may be held on both amendments and the whole bill. Once amending and debating in the Committee of the Whole are finished, the committee "rises" and reports what it did to the House, now in formal session. Of course, this is mostly a formality, but it does mark an important transition in the development of legislation.

The original committees of jurisdiction have an important advantage according to the rules under which legislation is considered in the Committee of the Whole. Any amendment defeated in the Committee of the Whole may not be brought back up for a vote once the House reconvenes. However, any amendment adopted by the Committee of the Whole must be reapproved by the House once the Committee of the Whole rises. Because a majority of the committee that reported the bill usually opposes floor amendments, this provides yet another small advantage to committees as they try to protect their legislative product on the floor.

Over the past generation, the most important development in Committee of the Whole proceedings has been how votes on amendments are conducted. Until the early 1970s, no provision was made for a recorded roll call vote in the Committee of the Whole. The formal name for voting in the Committee of the Whole is **teller voting**. At that time, it was common for a bare quorum to vote on amendments and for House members to use the lack of a voting record to obfuscate on the positions they had taken on amendments. Because the defeat of an amendment in the Committee of the Whole meant that the matter could not be revisited in the House, where roll calls on amendments *are* recorded, reformers charged that House members could take positions publicly but act contrary to those public positions with impunity when they voted in the Committee of the Whole. Because the 1950s and 1960s, when the issue of the unrecorded teller vote arose, was a time when liberal reformers charged that the House committee system was biased in a conservative direction, even though the House was nominally controlled by Democrats, ending the practice of unrecorded teller votes in the Committee of the Whole became a goal of House liberals.

Originally, teller voting in the Committee of the Whole was quaint: all those supporting an amendment formed a line and marched by members of the House, who recorded the number of members who favored the amendment. Then, opponents of the amendment would form a line and march by the tellers, who would count them up. At the end of this process, the number voting yea and nay would be known—only the identities of those voting yea and nay would be unknown.

The demise of this form of teller voting involved a small amount of political theater. In the 1960s, the liberal Democratic Study Group (DSG) took the lead in trying to bring about the recording of teller votes. Staff from the offices of DSG members would sit in the House galleries during teller votes and make a note of who voted with the yeas and who voted with the nays. Because the House rules prohibit writing while in the House galleries, the form of notetaking was mental. After the vote, these staff members would rush from the gallery and furiously write down the names of the yea and nay voters.

Needless to say, this mechanism was fraught with error, which is what brought it to an end; at the same time recorded teller voting was begun. In 1973, the House began the practice of **recorded teller voting**, in which House members (now) vote using an electronic system that records how everyone voted and instantly tallies the result. As a consequence of recorded teller voting, participation in Committee of the Whole roll calls became nearly universal, and the number of roll calls in the Committee of the Whole shot up severalfold.

Debate and its limitation

Debate serves many purposes in Congress. One purpose it usually does *not* serve is changing the minds of other legislators. By and large, senators and representatives come to Congress with a firmly established set of beliefs about government action that has been articulated to their constituents. Floor debate can do almost nothing to change minds in a fundamental way.

This is not to say that debate does not convey new information or that debate is a cynical charade. Debate on the floor of Congress is one setting, among many, in which the details of legislation and their anticipated consequences are discussed. Even MCs with unswerving political principles need to understand how particular pieces of legislation map onto those principles; therefore, all MCs rely on debate to help learn more about particular bills.[14]

Legislative debate also draws the attention of the media, prompting them to report on legislation, thus getting the legislation in question into the public domain. Woodrow Wilson thought this function of debate was most important when he wrote *Congressional Government*. Not only does debate periodically draw in the attention of the public; even more often debate draws the attention of other government actors, who rely on congressional debates to clarify for them **legislative intent**. Because debate is recorded, verbatim,[15] in the *Congressional Record*, it serves as a record of what members of Congress—and certainly the members of Congress who speak on an issue—anticipate will happen if a bill is passed.[16]

Therefore, while debate serves various functions, most of those functions are not unique to debate itself—information about bills can be conveyed in a wide variety of ways. Given the limited utility of debate at the end of the legislative process, the most important role of debate on the floor of the House and Senate is not informational but strategic. The most important thing about the debate of a bill on the floor of the House or the Senate is this: while the chamber is debating the bill, it is not passing the bill. Furthermore, while it is debating bill *A*, it is not considering bills *B, C, D*, and so on. Debate is a significant way to delay action. Both chambers have different ways to deal with debate-induced delay.

The House has the most rule-bound and regularized devices for dealing with debate-induced delay. The House Rules limit debate to one hour on measures that are brought before it, and to five minutes on amendments considered in the Committee of the Whole. The House has a rule allowing a majority vote to cut off debate on a bill, called the motion for the **previous question**, and of course, most major legislation is considered under the debate restrictions delineated in a special rule.

Under the Senate rules, senators usually enjoy the right of unlimited debate. Taking the floor in the Senate and talking endlessly for strategic reasons is termed the *filibuster*. Until 1917, the right of unlimited debate was absolute. That changed in 1917, when the Senate adopted **Rule XXII**, which provides a mechanism for **cloture**, the term used for cutting off debate in the Senate.

The moment that prompted the adoption of Rule XXII was a dramatic one in American history. President Woodrow Wilson had proposed arming American merchant ships, in response to the war that was raging in Europe, and a small minority of senators filibustered the bill, holding up all Senate business for twenty-three days to keep the body from acting on this proposal. The Senate's failure to adopt his proposals on the eve of America's entry into World War I prompted Wilson's famous tirade against the Senate:

> The Senate of the United States is the only legislative body in the world which cannot act when its majority is ready for action. *A little group of willful men*, representing no opinion but their own, have rendered the great government of the United States helpless and contemptible. (Quoted in Haynes 1938, vol. 1, pp. 402–3; emphasis added)

In response to Wilson's disgust, and to popular sentiment, the Senate adopted its cloture rule early in the following Congress. However, the rule as originally written did more to protect the tradition of unlimited debate than to limit it. Rule XXII originally required a two-thirds vote to cut off debate and then allowed each senator another full hour of debate before a vote could be taken. Over the next half century, the cloture procedure was rarely invoked, and when it was, it almost always failed.

Although the rule number has remained unchanged for nearly a century, Rule XXII has changed over that time, as has the practice of filibustering. The practice of unlimited debate reentered the national limelight in the years following World War II, when the issue of civil rights was current. Although guaranteeing equal legal protection for African Americans was a proposition most Americans supported, along with most members of Congress, southern representatives were vehemently opposed to civil rights legislation, and they used every parliamentary mechanism at their disposal to halt its march.

During the civil rights era, wrangling over debate and the cloture rule was as common—if not more so—as actual wrangling over the substance of civil rights legislation. The most dramatic moment in this era came in the consideration of the 1964 Civil Right Act, when the motion to consider the bill was filibustered by opponents for sixteen days. Once debate on the motion to proceed ended, civil rights opponents held the floor for fifty-seven days in a filibuster against the bill itself. In the end, two-thirds of the Senate agreed to invoke cloture, but getting to that point required great political theater, including calling the Senate into twenty-four-hour session, which necessitated senators sleeping on Army cots set up in the Capitol hallways.

Ever since the civil rights era, two important changes have overcome the filibuster. First, the practice of the filibuster changed dramatically. No longer reserved for portentous legislation, opponents often are willing to threaten a filibuster over the most minor of bills.[17] This, in turn, has led to a number of tactical changes regarding debate and filibustering. For instance, bill supporters now often try to preempt filibusters by filing cloture petitions *before* a filibuster has begun. In addition, in the 1970s, the Senate adopted a practice of allowing legislation to proceed on different tracks, in a sense allowing a filibuster to be turned off and on at will, so that it would not affect unrelated Senate business. This latter development lowered significantly the cost of filibustering and thus increased the frequency of its occurrence. The recent rise in the frequency of filibusters is illustrated in Figure 9.3, which graphs the number of cloture attempts and successes from 1919 to 2010.

The second important change in the filibuster in more recent decades has been a series of alterations in the mechanics of the cloture process, including

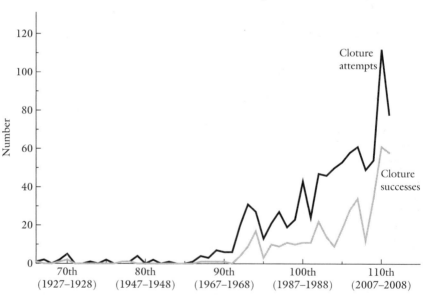

FIGURE 9.3
Cloture Votes in the Senate, 1919–2010

Source: Senate Action on Cloture Motions, http://www.senate.gov/pagelayout/reference/cloture_motions/clotureCounts.htm.

FIGURE 9.4
Example of the Effect of the Three-Fifths Cloture Rule in the Senate

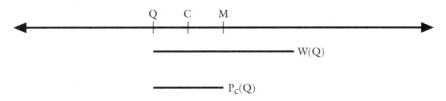

changes in the majority necessary to cut off debate. Cloture currently operates like this: sixteen senators who wish to end debate on a bill must sign a petition and present it to the presiding officer. Two days after the petition has been presented, the question is put as to whether a vote on the bill should be held. If three-fifths of the Senate *membership* votes yes, cloture is invoked.[18] When cloture is invoked, the Senate may still debate the matter for another thirty hours. At the end of that period, the Senate is then required to vote on the underlying matter.

The filibuster is such a potent parliamentary weapon that most senators try to avoid it, if possible, by accommodating the preferences of senators who might filibuster.[19] If accommodation is impossible, then the necessity to get a three-fifths vote to invoke cloture alters what type of legislation can pass the Senate. This is easily illustrated through the spatial model.

Consider the example in Figure 9.4. Here, the median senator is identified as M and the status quo is designated Q. If legislation had to pass through a simple majority, it would need to be located within the win set of the status quo, indicated on the figure as $W(Q)$. Now, suppose instead that the bill has to clear a cloture hurdle and that senators will vote to cut off debate only if they favor the bill over the status quo. In this case, the median member no longer is pivotal, but the senator who lies two-fifths of the way from the extremes of the distribution that is in the direction of the status quo, C in the figure. The preferred-to set of member C is $P_c(Q)$. Now, to pass, a bill must be located in the intersection of $W(Q)$ and $P_c(Q)$, which in this case corresponds exactly with $P_c(Q)$.

In this example, the existence of the three-fifths cloture rule constrains the amount of policy change possible compared to what a majority of the Senate would support without the three-fifths rule. While sometimes the three-fifths cloture rule does not affect the type of bill that can pass the Senate, never does the three-fifths rule give the Senate *more* latitude in writing legislation compared to a simple majority vote.

A more substantive interpretation to the example is given in Figure 9.4, as well. Assume for the moment that all Republican senators are ideologically to the right of all Democratic senators. If this is the case—and it actually was true in the 106th Congress—then the median senator will be a Republican whenever Republicans hold a majority of the chamber. What is the party identification of the pivotal senator for the *cloture vote* when Republicans hold a majority? If 60 percent or more of the senators are Republicans, then the pivotal cloture senator also will be a Republican; otherwise, it will be a Democrat. It is very unusual for the majority party in the Senate to have as many as 60 percent of the seats; and so, in most cases, the pivotal senator will be a Democrat (Republican) whenever Republicans (Democrats) control the chamber. Therefore, most of the time, whenever the status quo favors the minority party, the filibuster provides a small advantage to the minority. This suggests, finally, that senatorial decision making should be slightly more bipartisan and "moderate" than voting in the House, holding everything else constant.

Amending legislation

Although debate, in and of itself, rarely changes things, amendments do. And while many bills reported out of committee have broad support within the chamber, specific provisions may not. The amending process allows opponents of specific legislative provisions to have their say.

Because amendments often are more controversial than the bills to which they are attached, amendments themselves often are better known than the underlying bills. For instance, the "Hatfield-McGovern amendments" were well known for attempting to cut off funds for the Vietnam War. Few remember that the amendment was proposed to a military procurement bill (1970) and to the bill proposing an extension of the military draft (1971). Likewise, the "Hyde amendment" is a well-known mechanism that has been used to restrict abortions in the United States, when federal funds have been involved. The Hyde amendment is so well known that it has entered the American political lexicon as a phrase referring to any abortion restriction attached to legislation, even if not offered by Henry Hyde (R-Ill.), its original champion.

Both the House and Senate have basic rules that structure the offering of amendments. While there are important ways to skirt these rules in both chambers, the basic structure is so essential in both chambers that it is best to start there.

The rules of both chambers restrict how extensively legislation may be amended on the floor. It often is difficult to convey the structure of the amendment process verbally, and so the structure is communicated graphically through a device called an **amendment tree**. The House rules specify one general amendment tree for that body, while the Senate actually specifies four, depending on the parliamentary situation.

The House amendment tree is shown in Figure 9.5. The upper half of the figure is the traditional way of communicating the amendment tree. By its form you easily can see why it is called a *tree*. The "trunk" of the amend-

FIGURE 9.5
Two Views of the House Amendment Tree

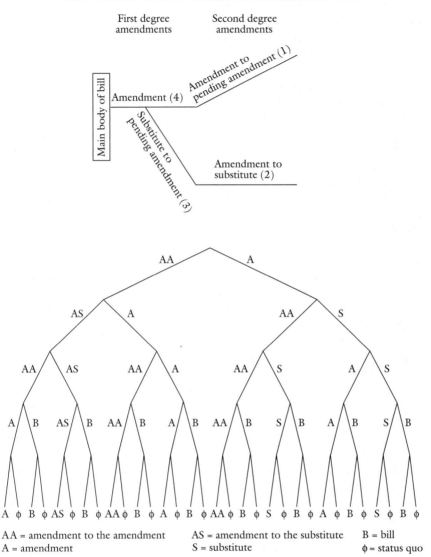

AA = amendment to the amendment   AS = amendment to the substitute   B = bill
A = amendment   S = substitute   φ = status quo

ment tree is the basic underlying bill. A House member may offer an amendment to the bill, and another House member may offer an amendment to that amendment. While the first amendment is pending, yet another House member may offer a substitute to the amendment.[20] Finally, yet another House member may offer an amendment to the substitute. The original amendment and the substitute are referred to as **amendments in the first**

degree, while the amendments to the original amendment and to the substitute are referred to as **amendments in the second degree**.

A general principle of parliamentary law is that one deals with amendment by "paring back" the amendment tree from the outermost branches to the trunk. Technically, one deals with second degree amendments first, then the first degree amendments. Another principle is that one *perfects* competing amendments before having them face off against each other. These two principles are illustrated in the House amendment tree by the order in which amendments are disposed of.

Assuming an amendment tree is fully filled out, voting on the amendments proceeds as follows: first, any pending amendment to the amendment is disposed of. If adopted, the amendment is incorporated into the original amendment, leaving one branch of the tree open. In theory, another member then could move another amendment to the amendment, and it, too, would need to be disposed of. Once all the amendments to the amendment have been disposed of in this sequential fashion, attention turns to the amendments to the substitute. Again, the pending amendment to the substitute is voted on. If passed, it is incorporated into the original substitute and another amendment to the substitute could be offered.

Once both the amendment and the substitute have been perfected, the question comes down to whether the substitute should take the place of the original amendment. Regardless of whether the substitute passes, disposing of the substitute now leaves the substitute branch empty, and *theoretically* it would be possible to fill that branch again. This is a rarity in practice.

Finally, the amendment is considered and voted up or down. Once disposed of, another amendment to the bill is possible. While it is unusual for the full amendment tree to be filled out and voted on, it is not at all unusual for several first degree amendments to be offered to a bill, one after the other.

The amending process in the Senate is simultaneously more *and* less complex than in the House. On the one hand, not one but four different amendment trees are possible in the Senate, depending on the parliamentary situation. The different trees allow for a range of two to twelve different amendments to be pending at once, compared to the four amendments possible under the House amendment tree. On the other hand, the most common amendment tree in the Senate is the most simple one under its rules—more simple, in fact, than the House tree. This tree simply allows, in order (1) an amendment and (2) an amendment to the amendment.[21]

As you can imagine, the strategic possibilities with amendments are vast. Filling out an amendment tree is just like filling out an amendment game tree of the sort explored in Chapter 1. Indeed, it is quite possible to translate the traditional congressional amendment trees into such a game tree. The lower half of Figure 9.5 does just that.

The strategic possibilities of filling out game trees periodically are used to the advantage of legislative leaders. For example, in the closing days of the 111th Congress, the Senate took up the repeal of the "Don't Ask, Don't

Tell" policy, which barred openly gay individuals from serving in the military. The repeal was brought to the Senate floor via an amendment that had been attached to an unrelated small business bill in the House, H.R. 2965. When Senator Harry Reid (D-Nev.), the majority leader, brought the repeal to the Senate floor, he simultaneously introduced a cloture petition to shut off debate on the measure. Then, he immediately offered two amendments to the House-pass repeal measure. The first inserted the sentence "The provisions of this Act shall become effective immediately" to the end. The second proposed striking the word "immediately," inserting the phrase "5 days."

Not content with protecting the repeal provision itself, Reid then dealt with the necessity to refer the repeal to committee before it could be considered on the Senate floor. He first moved that the repeal measure from the House be referred to the Senate Armed Services Committee with instructions to report back "forthwith," along with a request that the committee conduct "a study on the impact of implementing these provisions on the family of military members." Reid then amended his motion by adding the phrase "and that the study should focus attention on the dependent's children." Finally, he filled the amendment tree by offering an amendment to this amendment, adding yet another phrase, "include any data which might impact local communities."

Strategic use of amendments

Harry Reid's deft use of the Senate amendment rules is a fitting transition from a discussion about the "regular order" of amending legislation to an even broader set of issues affecting the actual use of amendments in the House and Senate. As stated many times, the House and Senate operate under different rules, which has resulted in a slightly different set of amendment issues and strategies in the two chambers. In the House, most attention has been paid to various mechanisms aimed at guiding the amendment strategy in the Committee of the Whole. In the Senate, the greatest, attention has been paid to "riders," nongermane amendments to legislation. These two issues are discussed in turn.

In the 1960s and 1970s, as the House rank and file began demanding greater influence over the legislative agenda, members began demanding greater access to the amendment process. In the Democratic caucus, for instance, this eventually led to a rule that stated that the Democratic members of the Rules Committee could not support a closed rule if the Democratic caucus objected. As the rank and file demanded greater say over the amendment process, congressional leaders, including committee leaders, began searching for amendment strategies to counteract the rank and file.

The most important consequence of this tension between the rank and file and leaders has been the growing complexity of rules. Where we once simply could talk about closed and open rules, the Rules Committee now classifies special rules into seven different categories. Most of these special rules affect which amendments are allowed to be considered in the Committee of the Whole.

One important category of special amendment rules falls under the category of *king of the hill* procedures, which has recently been replaced by *queen of the hill* procedures. The **king of the hill** procedure was developed to deal with several House members who wanted to offer a similar first order amendment to a bill. Under a king of the hill procedure, the House votes on a series of amendments, with the last amendment to receive a majority (if any) being adopted. This procedure allows members to conceivably vote to support several inconsistent amendments, knowing that the later votes count more than the earlier ones.

The newer **queen of the hill** procedure adopts a different rule for determining which amendment prevails. Under this procedure, the amendment receiving the most votes, if any receives a majority, is adopted. The queen of the hill procedure makes the sequencing of the amendments less important to the final outcome, although ties among amendments usually are resolved in favor of the last amendment voted on.[22]

A queen of the hill procedure accompanied consideration of a proposed constitutional amendment providing for congressional term limits (H.J.Res. 2) in the 105th Congress, which was considered in early 1997. The special rule that guided consideration of the constitutional amendment (H.Res. 47) allowed ten different amendments to be considered under the queen of the hill procedure. The first seven were variants of term limits that had been passed by voters in the states of Arkansas, Colorado, Idaho, Missouri, Nebraska, Nevada, and South Dakota and were proposed by representatives from those states. The amendments were offered in alphabetical order by state. None received a majority of support.

In the Senate, the most important special topic attending legislative amendments is the practice of allowing nongermane amendments to be attached to legislation; these are sometimes called **riders**.[23] Unlike the House, the Senate has very few rules requiring debate or amendments to be germane to the topic at hand.[24] This allows any senator to bypass the committee process altogether and get a bill considered directly on the floor. The use of riders is common. For instance, in fall 2009, Democrats added the Matthew Shepard Hate Crimes Prevention Act to the National Defense Authorization Act of 2010.

Reconciling differences

A bill that has survived the parallel tracks in both chambers is one step away from actually passing and being signed into law. A bill must be passed in identical form in both chambers before it can be forwarded to the president for his or her signature. The reconciliation of differences between the two chambers thus becomes the last topic, sequentially, to attend to.

How these differences are reconciled depends mostly on the complexity of the law and the controversy attending its passage. At one end of the continuum, we have simple, noncontroversial laws that often simply honor individuals in one way or the other. These bills, such as those naming federal buildings after people or proclaiming National Eat More Cheese Day, often have no differences to be reconciled and therefore the issue is moot. At the other extreme of the continuum are bills so complex and controversial that a measure may be the "same bill" in both chambers simply because it has the same bill number—and nothing more. In the middle are bills that have been changed in one or two particulars as they have moved from one chamber to the other.

In the middle range of bills, the joint rules of Congress provide two simple procedures for reconciling differences. First, a bill that has passed the House (say) and then the Senate in a slightly different form can be returned to the House, with a request that the House simply adopt the Senate bill. Second, and in a related fashion, the second chamber could return the bill to the first chamber. The first chamber then, in turn, could amend the bill and send it back to the second chambers. This legislative tennis match could continue until both chambers accepted the other's amendments.

In practice, though, complex bills regularly are taken to a conference of the two chambers immediately after passage in the second chamber. Chapter 7 briefly discussed the role and function of conference committees. Here, their behavior is discussed in a little more detail.

Formally, both chambers must agree with a conference. Once a conference has been agreed to, the presiding officers in the two chambers immediately appoint a *conference committee*, which negotiates away the differences between the two versions of the bill and reports a single version back to both chambers. For most of congressional history, the report of the *conference managers* on how the differences between the two bills were reconciled was opaque and uninformative. Nowadays, however, in addition to the **conference report**, which spells out in technical detail how provisions of the bill have been altered, compared to the two chambers' versions, a joint explanatory statement discusses the House and Senate versions of inconsistent legislative provisions and then explains how those differences were reconciled.

As mentioned in Chapter 7, the conference proceeding often sets up a tension between the original committees of jurisdiction in the two chambers and the floors. The conference committee typically is dominated by members of the original legislative committees that reported the bill to the floor. If the floor amended the bill later on, then often legislative committee members (who may have opposed the amendment) are in a position to defend the amendment. Once brought back to the floor, a conference report may not be amended. Instead, the chamber may choose to reject the conference report altogether or instruct the conferees to try again. While the floor has some control over the final content of the conference report, its ability to act if a majority of the chamber is dissatisfied with the report is limited to the blunt instruments of rejection or recommital to conference.[25]

Rules are in place that attempt to protect the floors from rogue conference committees—committees that go off and write a report that is barely acceptable to the chambers but is overwhelmingly acceptable to the original committees of jurisdiction. One such rule is the **scope of the differences** rule, under which any reconciliation of House and Senate provisions must be within the space bounded by the original House and Senate provisions. The implementation of this rule is seen most readily in appropriations bills. Suppose the House approves $50 billion for a new fighter jet and the Senate approves $100 billion for the same program. Under the rules, the conference committee must report out a bill that allows for some amount between $50 billion and $100 billion.

The difficulty in enforcing this rule should be obvious. The conferees would violate it only if the two chambers would prefer the conference report that violates the rule compared to the failure of the conference report altogether. This problem is illustrated in Figure 9.6. For this example, suppose the bill provides money to localities for education. The assistance in the bill is allocated in two ways. Some aid is based on formulas, such as population, and other aid is based on grants that localities can apply for, based on need. The status quo (Q) is shown, along with the two hypothetical win sets for the two chambers. To pass, the bill must lie within the intersection of these two win sets $W_s(Q) \cap W_H(Q)$. Finally, the location of the bill as passed in the two chambers is indicated by B_s and B_H.

Under the scope of the differences rule, the amount of money allocated based on formulas must lie somewhere in the region indicated on the x-axis,

FIGURE 9.6
Enforcing the Scope of the Differences Rule

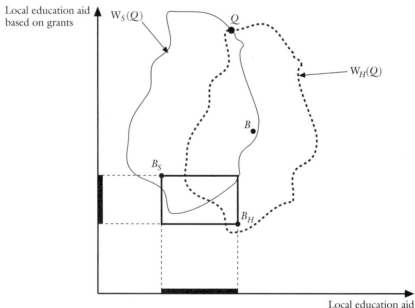

while the amount of money allocated based on grants must lie somewhere in the region indicated on the *y*-axis. All points in the policy space that satisfy this requirement are indicated by the box that is drawn in the figure. Suppose, however, the conference committee reported a bill located at *B* in the figure. What are the two chambers to do?

In theory, a point of order could be brought against the bill, since the provision for educational aid lies outside the scope of the differences on both dimensions. However, the conference report does lie within $W_s(Q) \cap W_H(Q)$. Concurrent majorities in both chambers prefer this bill to doing nothing. If the report is rejected, or recommitted, there is no guarantee that the conference committee would not do the same thing again. It would be possible for one, or both, chamber to *instruct* its conferees on how to craft these two provisions of the bill, but the only enforcement mechanism to guard this instruction would be for the floor again to threaten to reject a bill favored by majorities compared to the status quo. While it is theoretically possible for the floor to keep rejecting conference reports that fail to honor the rules about the scope of the differences, in practice, bills that violate this rule rarely are rejected.

The view of conference committees just presented suggests that they hold a very strong strategic position in legislative consideration. Because conferees typically are drawn from the legislative committees of jurisdiction, this means that the committees themselves have a great deal of strategic influence due to the conference proceeding. This is not to say that committees regularly get congressional majorities to act against their will—quite the contrary. What it does say is that, even to the end of legislating, committee influence cannot be discounted.

Roll Call Votes and What They Can Tell Us

The final stage in the consideration of legislation in both chambers is voting on it. Voting is significant for two reasons. First, votes determine outcomes. Second, votes provide evidence about how individual representatives stand on the issues. After observing a senator making enough roll call votes, we have some clue about the broad principles that the senator supports. If we compare the pattern of votes of one senator with those of others, we can quantify the degree of similarity between senators in their political principles, and therefore predict which senators will vote together in the future.

Interest groups long have been aware of this second feature of roll call voting and have used the roll call votes of MCs to rate members according to how supportive they are of the group's agenda. The granddaddy of interest group ratings is done by the Americans for Democratic Action (ADA), a liberal political organization that has been using roll call votes to rate senators and House members since the 1940s. The ADA methodology is very simple and common to all organizations that followed in its footsteps to develop their own ratings. In 2009, the ADA chose twenty "key" roll call votes in the House and in the Senate. Key votes in the Senate included voting to reauthorize the State Children Health Insurance Program (SCHIP) (the ADA supported passage), to pass the bill granting the District of Columbia voting representation in the House of Representatives (supported), and on an amendment to ban aid to international organizations that perform or promote abortions (opposed).

The ADA support score, which the ADA calls its *liberal quotient* (LQ), is calculated by adding the number of times a senator or representative supported the ADA position on one of these issues and then dividing by the number of votes it was following that year.

The ADA issues a press release every year, once it has calculated the most recent liberal quotient. In that press release, the ADA often trumpets its "Heroes" (those who have a perfect ADA score of 100 percent) and castigates the "Zeroes" (those with an ADA score of 0 percent). For anyone conversant with American politics, the identity of the Heroes and Zeroes is not surprising. In 2009, the Heroes included half the Massachusetts and New York House delegations, Senator Barbara Boxer (D-Calif.), and Senator Bernard Sanders (I-Vt.). Zeroes included Senator Jim Bunning (R-Ky.), Representative John Boehner (R-Ohio), and Representative Michele Bachmann (R-Minn.).

The ADA's conservative counterpart, the American Conservative Union (ACU), also rates members of Congress, using the same methodology, but instead of rewarding liberal votes, it rewards conservative votes. Instead of Heroes and Zeroes, its annual announcement of scores trumpets the "Defenders of Liberty" and shames the "True Liberals." The ACU's Defenders of Liberty in 2009 included Senator John Cornyn (R-Tex.), Senator Tom Coburn (R-Okla.), Representative Bachmann, Representative John Mica (R-Fla.), and Representative Randy Neugebauer (R-Tex.). The true liberals included Representative John Dingell (D-Mich.), Representative Barney Frank (D-Mass.), Representative Patrick Kennedy (D-R.I.) and Senator Al Franken (D-Minn.).

A certain amount of political theater is involved in the annual release of these scores, but a serious purpose lies behind them, as well. Members of Congress take positions on many issues, and it is difficult, if not impossible, for average voters to follow all those positions. The types of ideological ratings reported by groups like the ADA and ACU provide important information to voters about the general tendencies of their representatives.

One cautionary note must be introduced about these ratings: the issues chosen by groups like the ADA and ACU might be atypical of those considered by Congress more generally. If so, then the reports of "Heroes and Zeroes" could be fundamentally misleading and potentially dangerous. However, all the interest group ratings tend to produce support scores highly correlated with each other, even when they choose different key votes to follow. And ratings like the ADA's LQ are highly correlated with more robust techniques, like the NOMINATE technique reviewed later.

In addition to providing information about individual members of Congress, interest group ratings might be used to provide a general overview of the ideological status of the entire Congress. One such overview is shown in Figure 9.7, a histogram of ADA and ACU scores for the House in 2009. The

Figure 9.7

Interest Group Ratings of the House, 2009

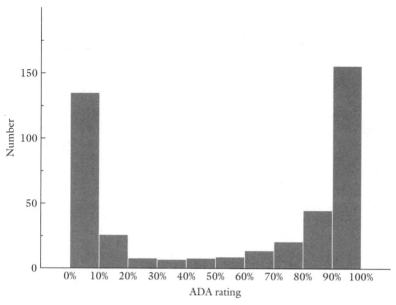

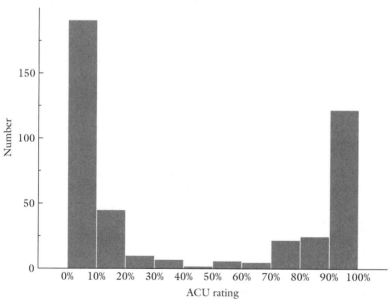

Sources: *ADA Today,* vol. 65, no. 1, Spring 2010; http://www.conservative.org/congress-ratings/.

most obvious thing about these two graphs is that both describe a legislative chamber full of extremist. Most House members had ADA or ACU scores that approached either 0 or 100, with very little in between. If we were to divide either of the graphs to show the two party contingents, we would also see that the view is one of extreme *parties*—the Democrats are virtually all extremely liberal and the Republicans are almost all extremely conservative.

Are the parties really this extreme? As I discussed in Chapter 7, many observers of Congress have remarked on the greater partisanship and polarization in Congress over the past two decades. The Congress actually might be an institution populated by nothing but ideological extremists. Before drawing such conclusions, however, we need to explore a little more deeply how interest group rankings are developed. When we do that, we will see that the interest group exercise is very good for identifying the group's friends and enemies but very bad for providing a nuanced picture of the congressional ideological landscape.

The exploration of how interest group ratings work begins by going back to the standard spatial model. Using that model, suppose that all members of Congress can be arrayed from left to right, based on how liberal or conservative they are. We can not only line up all members of Congress but we also can place interest groups on this ideological scale—certainly for groups like the ADA and ACU, which champion broad ideological stances. Where would we place the ADA and ACU on this left-right scale? While we might argue about whether they should go *all the way* to the right or left of the scale, the positions espoused by these groups certainly are pretty close to the left-right ideological anchors found in Congress. To aid in clarity in this example, therefore, I assume that we can place them *precisely* at the ends of the ideological continuum. Finally, suppose that the House is *not* composed of ideological extremists but rather members who are drawn from a uniform distribution across the ideological continuum.

With this setup, we can see how the interest group ratings are constructed. Basically, a group observes Congress voting, and whenever it finds a vote that seems to pit a clearly liberal and clearly conservative viewpoint against the other, it identifies that as a key vote. What kinds of votes are these? A vote that clearly offers liberal and conservative alternatives. Such votes typically involve a status quo that is toward one end of the ideological continuum, with the proposal being toward the other end. In such a circumstance, when a roll call vote is taken, House members will vote for the alternative closer to them. As discussed in Chapter 1, this vote will create a "cut line" that divides the House, ideologically, into those who vote yea and those who vote nay. Figure 9.8 illustrates such a clear ideological vote, with the status quo (Q), the proposal, and the cut line.

For this example, assume that the ideal points in the legislative chamber are distributed uniformly along the full ideological dimension. The feature of Figure 9.8 to focus on is the location of the cut line. Note that although the proposals are located at the extremes of the ideological dimension, the cut line is close to the center of the ideological dimension. As a consequence,

FIGURE 9.8
Cut Line for Interest Group Rating

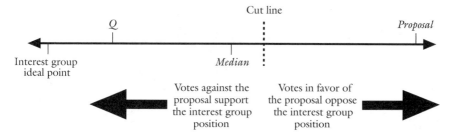

everyone to the left of the cut line, even moderates only *slightly* to the left of the median, are indistinguishably liberal while everyone to the right of the cut line, even moderates only *slightly* to the right of the median, are indistinguishably conservative.[26]

If most of the roll calls included as key votes are of the type just described— ones that create cut lines toward the middle of the ideological space—then even moderate members will seem to take "liberal" or "conservative" positions at very high rates, much higher than their underlying ideology would lead us to expect. Is this in fact what interest groups do?

Yes. The key votes that interest groups focus on are much more divisive than all roll call votes, which tends to produce artificial extremism among interest group ratings. The focus by interest groups on divisive votes, to the exclusion of frequent nondivisive votes, is demonstrated in Figure 9.9. The first panel graphs the distribution of the voting margins in all roll call votes in 2009. Note that the vote margin distribution is bimodal, indicating that most votes in 2009 were structured in two ways: either very close (mostly along party lines) or "hurrah" votes. (A hurrah vote is one that passes unanimously, or nearly so.) Yet, with so many hurrah and close (less than 60 percent) votes, still about one-quarter of all roll call votes saw the prevailing side receive between 60 and 90 percent of the vote. These were roll call votes that necessarily had cut lines away from the middle of the ideological spectrum, votes capable of distinguishing moderate liberals from extreme liberals and moderate conservatives from extreme conservatives.

The second panel of Figure 9.9 shows the distribution of voting margins for the twenty votes chosen by the ADA to construct their vote rating of House members. Two-thirds of these key votes were decided in the 50–60 percent range, which is insufficient to distinguish moderates from extremists. (In contrast, only one-third of all roll calls were decided in the 50–60 percent range in 2009.) Indeed, probably only one vote was capable of distinguishing moderates from extremists, a vote to reauthorize the SCHIP program. This vote, in which the ADA position prevailed 290–135, helped illuminate some distinction among conservatives. The ADA chose no roll call votes that similarly split *liberals*.

FIGURE 9.9
Prevailing Margins in House Roll Call Votes, 2009

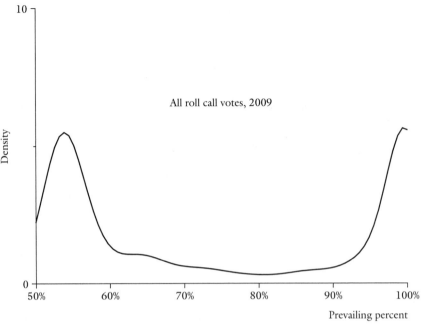

All roll call votes, 2009

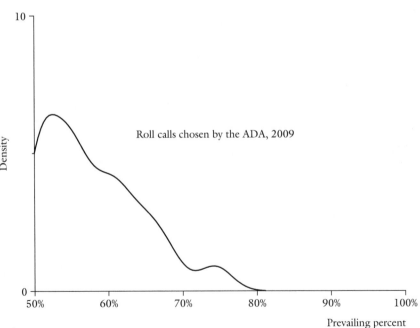

Roll calls chosen by the ADA, 2009

While interest group ratings are useful for roughly classifying Congress into liberals and conservatives, they are useless for discovering finer ideological distinctions among members of Congress (see Snyder 1992). Therefore, political scientists have sought other methods to gauge the ideology of MCs, this time using a broader sample of roll call votes. This, in turn, led to research on how to use *all* roll call votes to gauge the ideological positions of members of Congress.

The most commonly used technique to uncover the ideological positions of members of Congress was developed by Keith Poole and Howard Rosenthal (1997; 2007). They call their technique NOMINATE, which stands for NOMinal Three-stage Estimation procedure. The NOMINATE procedure starts with nothing but roll call votes, coded as 1 (yea) or 0 (nay), and an assumption that all members of Congress cast their votes based on the spatial model. If they do, then it is possible to use numerical techniques and powerful computing to uncover the issue space that MCs were voting over and the positions that MCs took on the issues.

Consider the following example. Suppose eight members of Congress were asked to vote on ten roll call votes. Suppose also that these members' ideal points could be represented in two-dimensional space. Every time a member votes yea, that is recorded as 1; every time a member votes nay, that is recorded as 0. Now, suppose we observed the following ten roll call votes:

					Vote					
Member	*1*	*2*	*3*	*4*	*5*	*6*	*7*	*8*	*9*	*10*
A	0	0	1	1	1	1	0	0	1	0
B	0	0	0	1	1	1	0	1	1	0
C	0	0	0	1	1	0	0	0	1	1
D	1	0	1	1	1	0	0	0	0	0
E	1	0	0	0	1	0	0	0	0	1
F	0	1	0	0	1	0	0	0	1	1
G	1	1	0	0	0	0	0	0	0	1
H	1	1	0	0	0	0	1	0	0	1

With no high-tech numerical techniques, we could examine this roll call record and notice certain things. For instance, some members vote together frequently, like members A and B (eight of ten times) and G and H (nine of ten times), while others almost vote against each other, like members A and H (nine of ten times) and B and G (eight of ten times). This observation might tempt us to hypothesize that A and B were extremists at one end of an ideological continuum, while G and H were extremists at the other end of the continuum. Further observing the pattern of votes, we note that the other members support either A and B or G and H at lower rates. For instance, C supports A only six out of ten times and H, four times. There-

FIGURE 9.10
Uncovering Spatial Locations Using Only Roll Call Votes

a. Preliminary ideological ordering

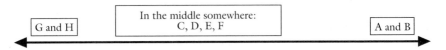

b. Ideological ordering giving rise to the observed roll call votes

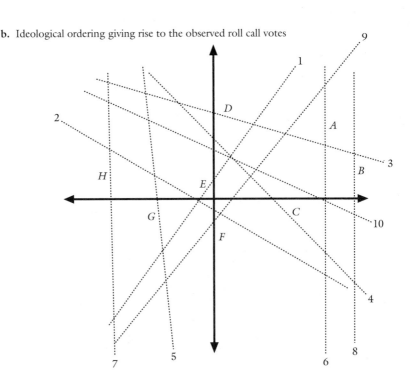

fore, it looks like members C, D, E, and F lie somewhere in the middle of this preliminary ideological continuum. We could summarize this information classification as in the top panel of Figure 9.10.

In fact, this voting pattern was generated using the ideal points specified in the lower half of Figure 9.10, along with the designated cut lines for each vote. (Cut lines are numbered according to the vote.) For instance, vote number 1 had members D, E, G, and H voting yea and A, B, C, and F voting nay. Notice that the cut line for vote number 1, oriented approximately at one o'clock on the figure, separates these two blocs of voters from each other spatially. Given the orientation of the cut line, we know that the "yea" alternative was in the northwest portion of the space, while the nay alternative was in the southeast portion of the space. However, also keep in mind that this cut line is consistent with an infinite number of locations of the yea and nay alternatives, so we cannot say for sure where the proposals them-selves were, just where the proposals divided the chamber into two blocs.

Note that the preliminary spatial locations we developed by simply looking at the patterns of 1 and 0 (A and B at one end, G and H at the other, and the rest in the middle) is highly consistent with the actual data. Along the *x*-axis, this is precisely what we find. At the same time, the ambiguity of the 1 and 0 patterns made it difficult to get a good sense of how the members were located along the second dimension, which is shown in the figure, as well. Yet without taking into account the second dimension, it would be impossible to classify all the roll call votes properly.

The Poole-Rosenthal NOMINATE procedure is a numerical method designed for uncovering the issue space, such as the lower half of Figure 9.10, from a matrix of roll call votes like those we have just seen in the text. Poole and Rosenthal assume that roll call votes are generated through the spatial model, with members voting for the closer alternative *probabilistically*. That is, they do not (cannot) assume that the spatial model operates deterministically, since no set of data ever would be consistent with such an assumption. Proceeding itera-tively, they estimate the most likely spatial location of members that would have generated the observed votes by members on the roll calls, estimate where the cut lines most likely were located on each roll call, and then start again. They finish when the procedure can do no better by continuing the exercise.[27]

Because the NOMINATE methodology uses almost all roll call votes, it is less prone to the problem of artificial extremism than interest group ratings.

FIGURE 9.11
NOMINATE Scores for the House, 2009

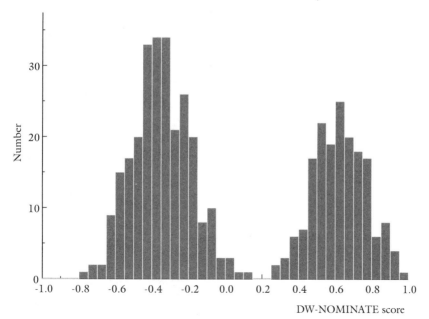

DW-NOMINATE score

With that in mind, the distribution of NOMINATE scores 2009, shown in Figure 9.11, is instructive. That figure also shows a bipolar House of Representatives, although one that is not as polarized as the ADA and ACU scores suggested.

As you research congressional decision making, you will discover several organizations that attempt to assign ideological ratings to members of Congress. These rankings fall between the interest group and NOMINATE methodologies in both sophistication and the tendency toward inflating the degree of extremism in the chamber. The most prominent of these scores are associated with *Congressional Quarterly*, a publishing concern that covers congressional news very close. Over the years, CQ has produced two other scores, the Conservative Coalition Support Score and the Party Support Score. The Conservative Coalition Support Score got its beginnings in the 1950s, when Republicans and conservative southern Democrats regularly voted together on many issues of national importance. The Conservative Coalition score measured how often this "coalition" emerged[28] and how often the individual MCs supported it. The Conservative Coalition Support Score measured the percentage of time a member of Congress voted with the Conservative Coalition whenever it "appeared" on a roll call vote. The Conservative Coalition was said to appear whenever a majority of Republicans and a majority of southern Democrats votes against a majority of northern Democrats. Although CQ ceased publishing the Conservative Coalition Support Score in 2000, the measure continues to be used in research.

As with interest group ratings, it is possible to understand the logic of the Conservative Coalition score using the spatial voting model. Figure 9.12 sketches the spatial logic underlying the Conservative Coalition Support Score. During the heyday of the conservative coalition, northern Democrats were mostly on the left, Republicans were mostly on the right, and southern Democrats were in the middle. Figure 9.12 shows a stylized version of this,

FIGURE 9.12
Spatial Analysis of *Congressional Quarterly* Conservative Coalition and Party Support Scores

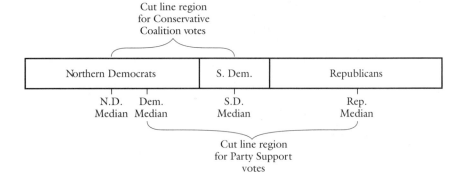

in which *all* northern Democrats are to the left of *all* southern Democrats, who are to the left of *all* Republicans. Therefore, for the Conservative Coalition to appear on a roll call vote, the cut line associated with that vote must exist in a region bounded by the median northern Democrat and the median southern Democrat.

Partisan support scores, likewise, continue to be constructed by CQ using a similar logic. Formally, a party support vote occurs when a majority of Democrats votes against a majority of Republicans. An individual's party support score is calculated by counting up the number of times a member voted along with a majority of his party whenever majorities of the two parties voted in opposite directions, dividing by the total number of **party unity votes**. Spatially, we see in Figure 9.12 that, if all Democrats are to the left of all Republicans, then party support votes will occur only when the cut line of the vote is within the region defined by the median Republican and the median Democrat.

As with interest group ratings, both scores—Conservative Coalition and party support scores—tend to produce a vision of Congress that is more polarized than reality. Yet these are superior to interest group ratings in many cases. Because of concern about artificial extremism in interest group ratings, researchers have tended to gravitate to the use of NOMINATE scores over the past decade, in addition to other similar techniques that use all roll call votes to rate members of Congress.[29] Interest group support scores and scores like the partisan support score still have their place in more popular and journalistic writing about Congress, since their intuitions are easier to convey.

Conclusion

The discussion of legislative sequencing and floor consideration in Congress is concluded. As indicated by the length of this chapter, the issues raised are considerable. More to the point, however, I hope this discussion has demonstrated the importance that the particular form of congressional organization has for making policy. As argued at the beginning of this book, preferences almost never are translated directly into policy outcomes when majority rule institutions are the instrument of decision making. Knowing that a majority approved a policy change is only the starting point for understanding how the democratic institution worked in that case. A majority may approve a single policy change, but that majority would have approved a wide variety—perhaps an infinite number—of policy alternatives. What is important to know whenever we see a bill make its way through the entire legislative labyrinth is *which* policy choices were allowed to come to a vote and *how* that was decided.

Further Reading

Bach, Stanley, and Steven S. Smith. 1988. *Managing Uncertainty in the House of Representatives: Adaption and Innovation in Special Rules*. Washington, D.C.: Brookings Institution Press.

Binder, Sarah A., and Steven S. Smith. 1997. *Politics or Principle? Filibustering in the United States Senate.* Washington, D.C.: Brookings Institution Press.

Kingdon, John W. 1989. *Congressmen's Voting Decisions.* 3rd ed. Ann Arbor: University of Michigan Press.

Krehbiel, Keith. 1998. *Pivotal Politics: A Theory of U.S. Lawmaking.* Chicago: University of Chicago Press.

Oleszek, Walter. 2011. *Congressional Procedures and the Policy Process*, 8th ed. Washington, D.C.: Congressional Quarterly.

Poole, Keith, and Howard Rosenthal. 1997. *Congress: A Political-Economic History of Roll Call Voting.* New York: Oxford University Press.

Smith, Steven S. 1989. *Call to Order: Floor Politics in the House and Senate.* Washington, D.C.: Brookings Institution Press.

Snyder, James M., Jr. 1992. "Artificial Extremism in Interest Group Ratings." *Legislative Studies Quarterly* 17: 317–45.

U.S. Congress. House Rules Committee Web site at http://www.house. gov/rules/.

SUMMARY OF KEY CONCEPTS

1. A **bill** is a measure that must be passed by both chambers of Congress and signed by the president to become law. House bill numbers are prefaced by *H.R.*; Senate bill numbers are prefaced by *S.*

2. A **resolution** is a measure that must be passed by a single chamber to deal with matters entirely within the authority of that chamber, such as its rules. House resolution numbers are prefaced by *H.Res.*; Senate resolution numbers are prefaced by *S. Res.*

3. A **joint resolution** is a measure that must be passed by both chambers of Congress to become law. Some joint resolutions are functionally identical to bills and must be signed by the president to become law, such as a continuing resolution. Joint resolutions also are used to deal with matters that do not need a presidential signature, such as proposing constitutional amendments to the states. Joint resolutions originating in the House are prefaced by *H.J.Res.*; those originating in the Senate are prefaced by *S.J. Res.*

4. A **concurrent resolution** is a measure that must be passed by both chambers of Congress to govern matters internal to Congress itself, such as the joint rules of both Houses. Concurrent resolutions originating in the House are prefaced by *H.Con.Res.*; those originating in the Senate are prefaced by *S.Con.Res.*

5. **Multiple referral** is the practice of referring a bill to more than one legislative committee in a single chamber.

6. **Discharge** is a procedure used by Congress to take a bill that has been referred to committee but not reported back and return it for consideration to the full chamber.

7. **Speaker discharge** is a procedure developed in the House of Representatives to be used whenever a bill is multiply referred, which allows the speaker to impose a deadline on a committee when it considers the bill.

8. A **calendar** is a device used by a legislature to order bills that have been reported from committee and therefore are ready to be considered on the floor. In its pure form, calendars operate like first in–first out inventory devices, insofar as legislation should be considered on the floor in the order in which it was placed on the calendar.

9. The House **Union Calendar** is the list of all bills pertaining to taxing and spending that have been reported from committee and are eligible for floor action.

10. The **House Calendar** in the House of Representatives is the list of all bills that have been reported from committee and are eligible for floor action, except bills pertaining to taxing and spending.

11. A **special day** is a legislative device used to schedule particular types of legislation in the House of Representatives, often relatively minor legislation the House otherwise might overlook. Currently, special days allow the consideration of motions to suspend the rules and pass legislation, business affecting the District of Columbia, private bills, noncontroversial corrections to existing laws, and the call of committee under the Calendar Wednesday procedure.

12. **Calendar Wednesday** is a parliamentary device created in the House in 1909 to facilitate committees bringing legislation to the floor. Each Wednesday, the clerk calls the roll of the committees alphabetically, at which time committees can bring up bills. This procedure usually is dispensed with through unanimous consent.

13. A **point of order** is made when a member of Congress challenges whether legislative activity occurring at a particular moment is according to the rules. If a bill, amendment, or the like cannot survive a challenge due to a point of order, it may not be considered any further.

14. A **special order** (or a **rule**) is a resolution passed by the House that determines the details of how a bill will be considered by the House.

15. A **lame duck** is a politician who continues in office even though he or she has been defeated for reelection or otherwise will not return to serve another term.

16. A **lame duck session** is a meeting of Congress that occurs after elections have been held but before the next Congress has convened. Before the convening date of Congress was moved back in the 1930s, from March to January, the second session of Congress typically was held in the lame duck period. Lame duck sessions now are rare.

17. An **open rule** allows free rein in making amendments to bills that come to the House floor, constrained only by the general rules of the House.

18. A **closed rule** prohibits amendments from being made to a bill that comes to the House floor but does allow debate.

19. The motion to **recommit a bill with instructions** is a parliamentary device used by the minority party to shape a bill to its liking. It is the last motion made concerning a bill before it is finally voted on for passage. The motion typically returns the bill to the committee that had reported the bill to the floor, instructing it to change the bill in particular ways, making it palatable to the minority party. Such motions rarely pass.

20. A **discharge petition** is a mechanism available to House members to remove a bill from consideration by a committee so that it can be debated and voted on by the full House.

21. **Unanimous consent** is a practice, used in most legislatures, of agreeing to an action in the absence of hearing any dissent in the chamber. In the House and Senate, minor bills, amendments, and parliamentary actions can be expedited using this practice.

22. The **filibuster** is prolonged debate solely to delay action.

23. The Senate relies on **complex unanimous consent agreements**, also known as **time agreements**, to determine how legislation will be debated, which amendments will be in order, and when final voting will occur. They serve a function similar to rules in the House. These agreements must pass without opposition and therefore often are difficult to craft.

24. **Simple unanimous consent agreements** are used dozens of times each day in the Senate to facilitate the chamber's business, such as allowing staff members to accompany a senator onto the floor during debate on a bill with which the senator is actively involved.

25. A **calendar day** is a traditional twenty-four-hour day.

26. A **legislative day** in the Senate is the period from one adjournment to the next. It is a parliamentary fiction that allows the Senate to facilitate the deliberation of legislation across several calendar days with a minimum of interruptions.

27. A **recess** is a temporary pause in legislative action that does not end proceedings for the day. The distinction between recess and adjournment is especially important in the Senate, which often recesses at the end of each calendar day.

28. An **adjournment** ends legislative activity for a day. Adjournment *sine die* ("without day") ends a year's session.

29. **Morning business** is transacted in the Senate at the beginning of each legislative day during a period called the *morning hour*, which usually lasts two hours. Morning business includes reporting the receipt of measures from the House, receiving reports from executive branch agencies, and the presentation of petitions and memorials from citizens.

30. The **Committee of the Whole** is a convenient parliamentary fiction, in which the whole House constitutes itself as a committee, allowing it to debate measures less formally and with a smaller quorum. (The quorum of the Committee of the Whole in the House is 100, compared to a

quorum of 218 for a formal meeting of the body.) The formal name is the *Committee of the Whole House on the State of the Union.*

31. **Teller voting** is a method of counting votes, in which all those in favor of a motion first march by individuals (tellers) to be counted, followed by those who oppose the motion.

32. **Recorded teller voting** is a method of counting votes in the House Committee of the Whole, instituted in 1971, in which the votes of individual members are published in the House *Journal* and *Congressional Record.* Since 1973, all recorded votes in the House, including recorded teller votes, have been taken electronically.

33. **Legislative intent** is the goal the supporters of legislation were trying to achieve when they supported a bill that passed Congress. Although this idea has intuitive appeal, many legislative and legal scholars distrust the idea of a single legislative will. Others are skeptical because the instruments often used by courts to discern legislative intent, such as committee reports and floor statements, are not subject to verification through floor vote.

34. **Revising and extending remarks** is a practice allowed in both chambers of Congress, in which a representative is allowed to edit remarks made on the floor during debate before they are inserted into the *Congressional Record.* Remarks sometimes are changed significantly between delivery and publication.

35. The **previous question** is a motion to cease debate and vote on the issue at hand.

36. **Cloture** is the procedure to limit a filibuster and bring a matter to a vote. The Senate's cloture procedure is contained in **Rule XXII**.

37. An **amendment tree** is a graphical representation of the amendments that are allowed to be offered to a bill and the order in which the amendments are considered.

38. An **amendment in the first degree** either proposes to change the original bill or substitute entirely new language for the original bill.

39. An **amendment in the second degree** proposes to amend either an amendment to the bill or the substitute.

40. A **king of the hill** amendment procedure allows a sequence of amendments to be offered to a bill. Among the amendments that receive a majority of votes, the last one receiving a majority prevails.

41. A **queen of the hill** amendment procedure allows a sequence of amendments to be offered to a bill. Among the amendments that receive a majority of votes, the one to receive the most votes prevails.

42. A **rider** is a nongermane amendment to a bill. House rules generally prohibit riders; the Senate has no such general prohibition.

43. A **proviso** is a legislative provision added to a bill, often through an amendment, that limits the conditions under which public funds may be spent. The "Hyde amendment" limiting the use of federal funds to pay for abortions is an example.

44. A **conference report** is a document issued by members of a conference committee after it has completed its work. The report delineates how differences between the two chambers were reconciled and must be signed by a majority of conferees from each chamber. Adoption of the conference report by both chambers passes the bill.

45. The **scope of the differences rule** constrains the range of choice available to conferees negotiating over differences in a bill. Features of a conference report must not exceed provisions contained in the two versions of the bill in the two chambers. If the House grants $1 billion to a project and the Senate $2 billion, the conference may not agree to less than $1 billion or more than $2 billion.

46. A **party unity vote** is a roll call vote in which a majority of the members of one party vote against a majority of the other party (sometimes, the threshold is higher, such as 90 percent). The fraction of times party unity votes appear in a Congress is a measure of overall partisan polarization. The fraction of times an individual legislator sides with his or her party on party unity votes is a measure of the party loyalty of that member.

PROBLEMS

1. Using the single-dimension spatial model, illustrate conditions under which the following statements are true:

a. The Senate filibuster influences the legislation that Congress will pass. (Ignore the effects of the presidential veto.)
b. The Senate filibuster does not influence the legislation that Congress will pass. (Ignore the effects of the presidential veto.)
c. The presidential veto influences the legislation that will be signed into law.
d. The presidential veto does not influence the legislation that will be signed into law.
e. Congress will not pass a law, because it cannot overcome a presidential veto.

2. Find a current, real-world example that illustrates each of the parts of question #1.

3. Figure P9.1 shows a status quo (ϕ), committee median (c), floor median (m), and ideal point of two members, a and b.

Suppose the House operates under the following rule: the committee can report out a bill changing policy along one dimension. A member of the

FIGURE P9.1

House—either a, b, or m—is called on to make an amendment to the bill. If that member makes an amendment, then the committee may make an amendment to the amendment. After the amendment to the amendment is made, the House votes, using its regular rules for voting on amendments.

What are the locations of the bill reported by committee, the amendment, and the amendment to the amendment (if any), if the committee *knows* which House member will be called on to offer an amendment and if the amendment maker is sincere? (In other words, answer this as if the committee knows that m will offer the amendment, if a will offer the amendment, and if b will offer the amendment.)

4. Do question 3 again, assuming the amendment makers are sophisticated.

5. A famous justification for having a relatively aristocratic Senate was that it would be like a "saucer that cools the tea" of legislative politics, implying that the Senate would tend to favor less radical legislation than the House. Using the spatial model, show the conditions under which the most important rules differences between the two chambers confirm or disconfirm this hypothesis. (*Note:* For the sake of simplicity, assume that the distribution of preferences is identical in the two chambers.)

6. Using thomas.loc.gov, find the bills your member of Congress has sponsored this Congress. (Alternatively, you can choose last Congress, if you are doing this exercise at the start of a Congress.) Write a brief (2–3 page) paper in which you address the following questions about these bills:

a. How many bills were cosponsored, and how many were sponsored by your member alone? Can you discern a pattern between bills that were single-sponsored and those that were cosponsored?
b. How many of these bills have seen some legislative action, beyond being introduced by your member? Is there anything that distinguishes these types of bills from those that have not seen any legislative action?
c. How do these bills relate to your member's constituency characteristics or interests, and how many relate to his or her committee service?

7. Visit http://www.mit.edu/~17.251/acdata.html and download the dataset Nominate_Scores.xls, which has NOMINATE scores for all House members since the 107th Congress. Keep the first dimension NOMINATE score for your member of Congress for as far back as the dataset allows. (If your member is a rookie, choose the previous incumbent. If you are the citizen of another country, you may choose any Representative you wish.) You will probably want to save this subset of the dataset on your computer.

Go to the votesmart.org Web site and navigate to the page that reports interest group ratings for members of Congress. Find your representative and select four interest groups that appear to be relevant to your district. Record the interest group ratings given by these groups and the years in which the ratings were given.

Write a short (2–3 page) paper in which you address the following questions:

a. Is your member *generally* liberal or conservative? Answer this in terms of both the House overall and the party of which your Representative is a member. Does your member's general ideology match that of your district?

b. Has your member's general ideology changed over time? If so, why do you think that is?

c. What are the interest groups you chose, how do they relate to the district's interests or characteristics, and how do they relate to your member's pattern of campaign contributions?

d. What are the scores your member received from these groups, and how do they relate to your member's overall ideology? If there is a disparity, why?

NOTES

1. Kennedy also labored under an obvious handicap in the 105th Congress: he was a Democrat in a chamber controlled by Republicans. However, typical rank-and-file Republicans had no better batting averages in getting their bills passed into law in the 105th Congress.

2. The first five House bills introduced in the 111th Congress (2009–2010) were the following:

    H.R.1.   American Recovery and Reinvestment Act of 2009
    H.R.2.   Children's Health Insurance Program Reauthorization Act of 2009
    H.R.3.   To amend title VII of the Civil Rights Act of 1964 and the Age Discrimination in Employment Act of 1967 . . . [Lilly Ledbetter Fair Pay Act]
    H.R.4.   Paycheck Fairness Act
    H.R.5.   TEACH for Our Future Act of 2009
             The first five Senate bills were these:
    S.1.   American Recovery and Reinvestment Act of 2009
    S.2.   Middle Class Opportunity Act of 2009
    S.3.   Homeowner Protection and Wall Street Accountability Act of 2009
    S.4.   Comprehensive Health Reform Act of 2009
    S.5.   Cleaner, Greener, and Smarter Act of 2009

3. The breakdown for the 111th Congress (2009–2010) was the following:

	House	*Senate*
Bill	6,550	4,038
Concurrent resolution	336	78
Resolution	1,781	704
Joint resolution	105	42

4. As we see later on, the rules of both chambers include a provision to **discharge** a committee from the consideration of a bill. When a committee is discharged, the bill becomes the property of the full chamber again, and the chamber may do with it what it likes—vote on it or refer it to yet another committee.

5. The Consent Calendar was previously for noncontroversial legislation slated to be passed under unanimous consent.

6. **Lame duck** is a term for a politician who has been voted out of office but whose term has yet to expire. Until 1933, Congress convened on March 3 of each odd-numbered year. Therefore, in the period between the fall elections and the following March, the House and Senate had many members who knew they would not return in the following Congress because they had either been defeated for reelection or had retired. During this time it was Congress's practice to hold its second session *after* the fall elections, beginning in early December and running until the following March. This session was known as the **lame duck session** of Congress. Needless to say, lame duck sessions often were quite contentious, especially when the recent election had ejected the incumbent majority party, leading the current majority to try to hasten policy change and the current minority to delay matters until the next Congress.

7. Recall that in the late nineteenth century, the tariff was probably the most heated issue dividing the two majority parties.

8. In the example, *W(Q)* has been drawn arbitrarily, since the particular location of any one member of the House is immaterial to the example. The irregularity of the figure is not particularly important, either.

9. The Rules Committee is subject to the discharge of special rules to consider substantive legislation that has been reported from committee but is languishing while waiting for a special rule to emerge from that committee.

10. Those laws were the 1938 Federal Labor Standard Act (the first minimum wage law) and the 1960 Federal Pay Raise Act.

11. A **simple unanimous consent agreement** typically is used to expedite routine business on the Senate floor, such as dispensing with a quorum call once it has begun.

12. The March 11, 1999, proceeding on S. 257 can be found in the *Congressional Record* daily edition on page S2573. Other citations to proceedings on S. 257 likewise can be found in the *Record*.

13. The House sometimes gets its calendar and legislative days out of whack, but this is much less common than in the Senate.

14. Debate generally is not the best way to learn about the consequences of legislation. Committee reports are a better source of information, for instance, as is the research of one's own office staff.

15. Characterizing the *Congressional Record* as providing a verbatim transcript of congressional proceedings is a bit generous, since representatives are often given leave to **revise and extend their remarks**, which basically means editing them to leave a more pleasant impression on the reader. In recent years, congressional rules have been changed to help the reader figure out which material in the *Record* actually was delivered on the floor and which was inserted or altered.

16. The issue of legislative intent is one of the most interesting, and contentious, subjects related to congressional lawmaking. Congress enacts only laws, not debates or committee reports. Nothing can stop a legislator from misrepresenting in debate what the majority "intended."

17. While it usually is considered bad form to threaten a filibuster outright in public, it is common for senators who oppose a bill to remark, "we will have plenty of time to explore the merits of the bill"—everyone knows what this means.

18. Note that the majority required to invoke cloture is three-fifths of the entire *membership*, not three-fifths of the Senate present and voting.

19. As already seen, the primary consequence of having to accommodate in the face of a threatened filibuster is the complex unanimous consent agreement for scheduling legislation.

20. A substitute for an amendment differs from an amendment to an amendment in the following way: the amendment to the amendment modifies some narrowly focused part of the original amendment, while the substitute is a more comprehensive alternative to the original amendment, which may differ from the original amendment on many different particulars.

21. The range in amendments allowed under the Senate rules is due to different rules, depending on whether the amendment proposes a straightforward change to the bill or striking out some provision of the bill and inserting something else. The greatest number of amendments is allowed whenever the amendment proposes to strike out the entire bill and insert a whole other bill in its place.

22. In general, the queen of the hill procedure favors the median in the chamber, since the proposal most favored by the median (assuming symmetrical utility curves) will get the most votes.

23. Do not confuse a rider with a **proviso**, which is legislation attached, usually to an appropriations bill, restricting how the funds may be spent. The Hyde amendment is a type of proviso.

24. This is not to say that nongermane amendments cannot become a strategic weapon in the House. For instance, the special rule that allowed for the consideration of campaign finance reform legislation in the House in 1998 allowed the consideration of 258 nongermane amendments to the bill, in an effort to kill the popular Shays-Meehan amendment through delay.

25. A further parliamentary detail strengthens the hand of the conference committee. When the *first* chamber considers the conference report, its options are to accept, reject, or recommit the report back to the conference committee. If the report is accepted, then the conference committee is dissolved. However, the report still needs to be considered by the second chamber. In the second chamber, there is no longer a conference committee to which the report could be recommitted. Therefore, the chamber's only choices are rejection or acceptance. If a conference report is rejected, that places the bill back where it started, and the whole conference process must begin again.

26. Note also that in this example, even a few moderate conservatives get classified as liberals. Presumably, with a lot of votes with cut lines on both sides of the ideological spectrum, this problem would even itself out, but not necessarily.

27. For the precise details about how the class of NOMINATE procedures work, see Poole and Rosenthal (1997).

28. The Conservative Coalition is not, nor has it ever been, a formal coalition; therefore, the term is a bit of a misnomer (see Manley 1977).

29. Another technique, developed by Heckman and Snyder (1997), is based on principal components factor analysis.

∽ Appendix A ∽

Researching Congress

Congressional research provides a portal into three related aspects of political science: national politics, legislative politics per se, and policy making. By *national politics*, I mean the struggle for political power waged between political elites, mostly in the electoral arena. By *legislative politics* per se, I refer to the actions of Members of Congress and those close to them (such as staff) within the institution itself. And by *policy making*, I refer to the substance of the issues that MCs contend over in the political and legislative arenas.

The purpose of this book has been to provide an introduction into congressional politics from the perspective of most contemporary students of Congress. The bulk of the material in the chapters has provided a basic grounding in the field, to enable subsequent research into congressional politics—so you might analyze Congress yourself. The purpose of this appendix is to provide a series of guideposts for your direct analysis of Congress.

Because Congress is the most public of national political institutions, a plethora of information and sources concerning legislative behavior is available. My purpose here is not to review all that information but rather to point to the most important and reliable sources of congressional information and allow your creativity and resourcefulness to pull you along. If you are looking for a comprehensive source for studying Congress, one of the best places to look is the Web site of legislative branch sources maintained by

the Documents Center at the University of Michigan. The URL is www.lib
.umich.edu/libhome/Documents.center/fedlegis.html. Of particular value
is their Legislative History Chart, which lists steps in the legislative process,
with links to information relevant to each step. The URL for that resource is
http://guides.lib.umich.edu/legchart.

If you are looking for an Internet portal that is slightly less daunting, the
Library of Congress provides a list of congressional "mega sites," which
are good places to start in doing congressional research if you do not know
where to begin. The URL is thomas.loc.gov/links. Finally, if you are looking for an edited, highly selective version of such a starting place, plus links
to data about congressional politics, my own Web site is www.mit.edu/~17
.251/. I also maintain a page with links to original datasets that are relevant
to studying Congress, at web.mit.edu/17.251/www/data_page.html.

Studying Congress Generally

The first distinction that must be made in discussing congressional research
is between primary and secondary source material. *Primary source material*
is the basic, raw stuff of politics and policy making. It is raw data, barely
digested for further consumption. In the congressional context,[1] primary
source material ranges from direct, firsthand observation of the institution
to the raw output of the legislative process, such as bills, legislative debates,
and committee reports. *Secondary sources* include most journalistic accounts
of congressional behavior and most scholarly analyses of such behavior.

Distinctions between primary and secondary sources are not all that clear,
especially at the margins. In particular, a range of sources cover congressional politics so closely and impartially that they sometimes are considered
as good as primary sources. These sources include two weekly publications
that cover Congress and Washington politics generally: *CQ Weekly* (cq.
com/displayweekly.do) and *National Journal* (nationaljournal.com). (Note
that online access to these publications is restricted, and usually only available through subscribing libraries.)

CQ Weekly deserves particular attention because of how central it is to students of the legislative process and of public policy making generally. The core
publication, *CQ Weekly,* which originally was called *Congressional Quarterly
Weekly Report,* covers legislative activity on Capitol Hill in fine detail. The topics covered range from those that affect only the members and staff themselves
(like a proposal to end the printing of bills on paper) to reports on legislative
hearings, floor deliberation of legislation (major and minor), to comprehensive
reviews of legislative activity that summarize how a policy has evolved, or is
likely to evolve. Much of this material is eventually combined into an annual
publication, entitled *CQ Almanac.* Every four years, coinciding with a presidential term, the material is combined again into a publication entitled *Congress and the Nation.* If you are studying legislative activity that is current, the
CQ Weekly is indispensable. If you are studying the history of legislation or a

policy area, the *Almanac* or *Congress and the Nation* may be the right place to start.

Recently, CQ Press (which is now separate from CQ itself) has released a valuable online resource that combines information from a wide variety of books and databases CQ has developed over the years, reaching back in some cases to the mid-1940s. The name of this resource is the CQ Press Congress Collection. (The URL is library.cqpress.com/congress, but your library will need a subscription for you to log in.) Although almost all of the material is also available in paper format, the ability this site affords to search across databases and sources to gain a comprehensive view of congressional action is unparalleled.

The second distinction to draw is between government and nongovernment publications and sources. This distinction is important because it draws attention to the ease of access to material. Government publications and sources, as the term implies, are produced by the government agencies themselves. In paper form, they usually are published by the Government Printing Office and made available through the Federal Depository Library program. Approximately 1,250 Federal Depository Libraries in the United States, usually at least one in each congressional district, provide free access to the public to U.S. government publications and expert advice on the use of these materials. Of these libraries, about fifty are designated Regional Libraries, which means that they receive all the materials distributed through the depository library program.[2] (The other libraries pick and choose materials, based on their interests, capacities, and so forth.) Many college and university libraries participate in the federal depository library program, as do many large-city public libraries. The Government Printing Office provides a search service through its Web site to locate the nearest Federal Depository Library. Information about the library programs of the Government Printing Office can be found at catalog.gpo.gov/fdlpdir/FDLPdir.jsp.

Government documents probably are the most accessible materials related to studying Congress, although they are not always the easiest to use, once they have been accessed. (Some guidance about using these materials is provided later.) Underlying this ease of access is the fact that government publications are in the public domain and, in general, cannot be copyrighted by the government. The Internet particularly has made these materials much more accessible.

Six major government Internet sites are useful for searching for government publications, both traditional (paper-based) publications and more ephemeral electronic sources. For contemporary materials, these are Web sites associated with the House of Representatives, the Senate, the Library of Congress, and the Government Printing Office. For historical material, the Library of Congress's American Memory Collection has created a site specifically for older congressional materials, A Century of Lawmaking for a New Nation: U.S. Congressional Documents and Debates, 1774–1873.[3] In addition, the National Archives Center for Legislative Archives houses original congressional documents, all the way back to the first Congress, and makes those records available to researchers. Web addresses for these sites are provided in Table A.1.

TABLE A.1
Major U.S. Government Web Sites for Searching Congressional Documents

Site Name	URL
House of Representatives	www.house.gov
Senate	www.senate.gov
Library of Congress	thomas.loc.gov
A Century of Lawmaking for a New Nation: U.S. Congressional Documents and Debates, 1774–1873	lcweb2.loc.gov/ammem/amlaw/
National Archives Center for Legislative Archives	www.archives.gov/nara/legislative/
U.S. Government Printing Office	www.gpoaccess.gov/index.html

Nongovernment publications range far and wide and include journalistic sources that cover Congress directly (*National Journal* and *Congressional Quarterly*), journalistic sources that provide excellent coverage of Congress in addition to their general political coverage (*Washington Post* and *New York Times*), and books about congressional politics and the policies that Congress considers. Accessing these materials is done through traditional library work, using a series of paper and electronic indexes, most of which already are familiar.

Because these sources are produced by commercial concerns, they are not as accessible as government publications, especially electronically. Therefore, to gain access to them, you likely will have to go to a library, either on a college or university campus or a large public library. If you are lucky, your library will have paid the large sums necessary to have a listing of important nongovernmental sources concerning congressional activity (see Table A.2).

A Further Word about Congressional Documents

If you do serious research into congressional politics and policy making, you will need to become expert in navigating through the various publications that the different subdivisions of Congress churn out in the legislative process. Following congressional activity directly has become easier in recent

TABLE A.2
Major Nongovernment Sources for Studying Congress

Source	URL
Major national newspapers	
New York Times	www.nytimes.com
Washington Post	www.washingtonpost.com
Capitol Hill newspapers	
The Hill	www.thehill.com
Roll Call	www.rollcall.com
Politico	www.politico.com
Congress-focused weeklies	
CQ Weekly Report	www.cq.com
National Journal	www.nationaljournal.com
Index of congressional documents	
Lexis-Nexis Congressional	web.lexis-nexis.com/congcomp

years, with the advent of the Internet (see the sites listed in Table A.2) and real-time television coverage via C-SPAN. (You also can watch live coverage of both chambers of Congress through the C-SPAN Web site, at www.c-span .org.) At the same time, the explosion of material emanating from Congress has obscured the fact that a limited number of congressional publications contain the official record of Congress. Therefore, whether you are doing research using paper-based or electronic sources, the following publications should form the basis of your original research of Congress.

1. *Congressional Record.* The *Congressional Record* is the (roughly) verbatim record of the floor proceedings in Congress. I say *roughly verbatim* because members of Congress usually are allowed to "revise and extend" their remarks—edit them, in other words—before they appear in print. In recent years, the *Record* has adopted some editorial conventions to help the reader distinguish between material actually delivered on the floor and material inserted into the record, including the use of different type fonts to distinguish materials and the insertion of the real time of day at regular intervals. As you move back in time in using the *Record*, you need to be more careful in figuring out what was live and what was inserted.

2. House and Senate *Journals.* The official record of both chambers is contained in their *Journals.* The *Journals* are not verbatim accounts; they simply record the official actions of the chambers. Therefore, they are especially useful in getting a quick sense about what happened on

the floor of each chamber, being a fraction of the size of the *Congressional Record*. The Senate has two journals: the *Senate Journal*, which records legislative business, and the *Executive Journal*, which records "executive business," such as treaty ratifications and consideration of executive branch nominations.

3. Committee reports. Whenever a committee sends a bill to the floor, it almost always is accompanied with a report. Reports often are voluminous documents, containing a discursive report detailing the majority opinion of the bill (usually written by staff members but endorsed by a majority of the committee), sometimes a minority opinion, and a host of supporting documents. Committee reports frequently are used by courts and executive agencies to discern "congressional intent," although this use is very controversial.

4. Committee hearings. Committee proceedings are contained in committee hearings, which usually are published whether or not a bill actually is reported to the floor for action. As the title suggests, the hearings provide the verbatim proceedings of the committees (and sometimes subcommittees), including witness testimony and an account of committee actions, such as amendments.

5. Committee prints. Committees produce many documents for their own use, which are termed *committee prints*. These are less widely circulated than hearings and reports, but they often contain the most useful and interesting information about the issue at hand.

All these documents, with the exception of committee prints and the *Congressional Record*, are combined each year into the *Congressional Serial Set*. The *Serial Set*, reaching back into the early nineteenth century, is the physical location of major congressional documents. In recent years, the emphasis has been on disseminating the *Serial Set* electronically. You can search and retrieve congressional hearings and reports, the major constituents of the *Serial Set*, starting with the 104th Congress (1995–1996) at the GPO Web site: www .gpoaccess.gov/serialset/creports/index.html. For libraries that have subscribed to it, congressional materials are available electronically through Lexis-Nexis, at web.lexis-nexis.com/congcomp. This online service continues the older paper-based index, the *Congressional Information Service*, which is still available in many libraries as an index and abstract of congressional reports, hearings, and documents.

Scholarly Research on Congress

Congressional research is among the most voluminous in political science, and so from the start, you need guidance in picking and choosing among sources. The best advice I can give you in searching through scholarly research is to be well armed by knowing how to use a small number of search tools.

Books about Congress can be searched through all library catalogues. Within the Library of Congress classification system, books about Congress lie between JK1001 and JK1443. (If your library uses the Dewey Decimal System, consult a librarian about the analogous range for that system.) Although many books have been written about Congress by scholars and others, the number is not so large that you could not browse through your library's holdings in a reasonable period of time. For a serious student of Congress, browsing through the congressional section of a library is something that needs to be done regularly.

Journals and magazine articles can be searched in many ways. Nowadays, it is common to use generic search engines such as Google and follow up where the results lead. While this is often a good way to get going, more specialized search engines and databases will deliver you quicker to deeper material. Within the Google family, for instance, Google Scholar (scholar.google.com) not only provides a valuable way to find information about scholarship in particular topics but also allows you to easily follow up on where research leads. When you search on Google Scholar, the search results are sorted more or less according to how often others have cited the work. This is a rough way to see which research is the most influential. The search results also link to other scholarship that cites the work, allowing you to quickly follow up on the most important scholarship in various topics, and to see how arguments by different scholars interact.

In addition, the *Social Sciences Citation Index* (*SSCI*), which may be accessed through Thomson Reuters' *Web of Science,* provides information that is similar to Google Scholar searches, only more focused on journals and the scholarly literature. For institutions that subscribe to the service, the URL for the *Social Sciences Citation Service* is www.isiknowledge.com. The *SSCI* captures almost every scholarly article in all the social sciences, allowing researchers to search through the literature in a number of ways. The most straightforward searches are author and keyword or title searches. An important feature of the *SSCI*, though, is that it also indexes the citations that appear in the articles (hence, the name *Social Sciences* Citation *Index*). The citation indexing feature is useful for two reasons. First, you can look at the entry for any article about a subject and see what other citations the author(s) used in doing research. This should give you a good, quick summary of the relevant scholarly literature in that field.

In addition, the *SSCI* reverses this indexing, allowing you to find all the articles ever written that cite a certain source. This is a very useful feature if you are trying to develop a quick bibliography on a topic. For instance, if you are interested in studying the historical development of the House, you could quickly look up every article that has ever cited Nelson Polsby's (1968) article "Institutionalization of the U.S. House of Representatives"—all 283 times, as of early 2011. With only a little editing and weeding, these articles would constitute a good first cut of the existing literature on the history of the House's institutional development.

A more labor-intensive way to review the journal literature about Congress is to browse through journals. Dozens of political science journals are devoted, at least somewhat, to American politics. Yet only a small handful are top-level journals in the field that a serious student of Congress should regularly consult.

The top general-interest political science journals to follow, with an eye toward congressional research, are the *American Political Science Review*, *American Journal of Political Science*, and the *Journal of Politics*. In addition, the *Journal of Political Economy* and *Public Choice* both publish research at the boundaries of political science and economics, which is where much of the theoretical work about legislative politics is reported.

Finally, serious students of legislatures follow closely the *Legislative Studies Quarterly* (*LSQ*). *LSQ* is the specialty journal within political science that focuses on legislative politics generally, ranging from subnational legislatures to national and international legislatures of all sorts.[4]

Other Electronic Sources for Studying Policy and Politics

This appendix has focused on sources that pertain narrowly to Congress and sources that exist mostly on paper and electronically. The explosion of information available through the Internet in recent years has made it much easier for students of legislatures to gather information about closely related features of politics and policy. A comprehensive review of these sources is not appropriate here, but a few points deserve mentioning for students of Congress.

First, federal government agencies and state governments have Web sites that grant easy access to a host of information relevant to congressional politics. For instance, the Federal Elections Commission has available a large list of raw data files concerning campaign contributions and expenditures that is served off its Web site (www.fec.gov). State Web sites should not be overlooked as sources of interesting information about legislative politics. If any of the material in this book is of general interest, beyond just the U.S. Congress, it should be applicable to the politics of different state legislatures. In a few cases, the Internet provides a tremendous amount of information about legislative behavior at the state level, including online versions of bills and debates, electronic versions of roll call votes, and precinct-level election returns. In other cases, state-level legislative Web sites are pretty barren.

Second, many, many Web sites approach questions of public policy from a variety of perspectives. The Lexis-Nexis Academic Web site provides access to countless news, business, and legal sources reaching back many years. Hundreds of libraries have a subscription. The URL is web.lexis-nexis.com/ universe. Good places to start in researching policy issues (especially if you lack access to the *Congressional Quarterly, National Journal,* or Lexis-Nexis sites) are the Vanderbilt University library's Web site of public policy links, located at http://www.library.vanderbilt.edu/romans/pubpol.html, and Political Information (www.politicalinformation.com).

Two congressional agencies, the Government Accountability Office (GAO) and the Congressional Research Service (CRS), engage in policy analysis and evaluation on behalf of Congress. The GAO's efforts are generally available to the public through its Web site, www.gao.gov. CRS has historically not made its reports available publicly, but CRS reports do circulate and eventually get posted on private Web sites. The opencrs.org Web site focuses solely on collecting CRS reports and posting them. A large number of CRS reports are also posted on Wikileaks.

Finally, students of Congress generally are interested in electoral politics, in both off- and on-years. Notable Web sites devoted to a wide array of political news are on the sites of CNN (www.cnn.com/POLITICS/) and the *Washington Post* (washingtonpost.com/politics). To get a brief glimpse of an Internet site that many people pay thousands of dollars a year to access, check out the *National Journal* home page (www.nationaljournal.com), which provides a few free links within a larger service that goes over policy and electoral politics with a fine-toothed comb.

NOTES

1. I emphasize the phrase *in the congressional context* because different professions and different fields of research have different standards for how they divide the world into "primary" and "secondary" source material. Many historians, for instance, would regard direct interviews, observation, and artifacts like letters and diaries as primary source material but would relegate committee reports and (perhaps) debates to secondary sources, because they are published and therefore subject to the intervention of editors.

   Discipline-specific distinctions between primary and secondary source material is much less important than the overall point behind such distinctions: Evidence about social behavior comes to us with varying degrees of filtering that intervenes between the source and the researcher. As we move from the "primary" to the "secondary" end of the source continuum, the range of issues involved in judging the sources changes. Even with primary source material, the range of issues involved in judging the sources changes. Even with primary source material, the researcher has to worry about the motivations of the individuals taking the actions being recorded, in addition to worrying about why *these* facts, and not others, have been saved for posterity. As we move more firmly into the realm of secondary source material, we have to start adding other worries about the material, particularly worries about the motivations of editors and publishers.

   In doing basic research into congressional politics—as in all social sciences— primary source material generally is to be favored over secondary sources. However, life provides us limited time, and therefore all researchers, from undergraduate term paper writers to full professors of political science, must rely somewhat on secondary sources to complete their research. Armed with the right analytical tools, the use of primary source material in studying Congress is exceptionally rewarding. As one acquires greater experience with those tools and the primary sources, one eventually comes to understand the most effective uses of the secondary sources as well.

2. The stresses facing the libraries that host the regional government depository led the body that oversees the depository library program to issue a report to the Joint Committee on Printing on the status of the regional libraries in 2008. For serious scholars, this is a very sobering report to read. The title of the report is "Regional Depository Libraries in the 21st Century: A Preliminary Assessment." It may be found at http://www.fdlp.gov/component/docman/doc_download/564-regional-depository-libraries-in-the-21st-century-a-preliminary-assessment?ItemId=45. One point made by the report is that government documents libraries are tending to be consolidated into the larger reference operations of large libraries. The number of government document specialists is declining, as all reference libraries are now being expected to know at least a little about government documents. One consequence for students of Congress at all levels is that we cannot assume the level of expertise among librarians about the unique features of legislative documents that existed even a decade ago.

3. The American Memory Web site offers fabulous access to the verbatim proceedings and journals of the House and Senate from 1789 to 1873. The Web site is misleading in one important sense, however. The site also links to original congressional bills and the Congressional Serial Set, which is the retrospective collection of all congressional documents—quite a collection. However, the digitized material under the congressional bill and Congressional Serial Set sections is quite limited and provides only a taste of what is available among the original, paper documents. Researchers hoping to use historical materials from these collections will have to rely on hard copy collections.

4. Also, one of the largest sections of the American Political Science Association is the section on Legislative Studies. An important service of the section is that it publishes a periodic newsletter, which informs its members of recent developments in legislative studies and serves as a lifeline among the dispersed community of legislative scholars around the nation. An online version of the newsletter can be found at this URL: www.h-net.msu.edu/~lss/Newsletter/.

∼ Appendix B ∼

The United States Constitution[1]

W e the People of the United States, in Order to form a more perfect Union, establish Justice, insure domestic Tranquility, provide for the common defence, promote the general Welfare, and secure the Blessings of Liberty to ourselves and our Posterity, do ordain and establish this Constitution for the United States of America.

Article 1

Section 1

All legislative Powers herein granted shall be vested in a Congress of the United States, which shall consist of a Senate and House of Representatives.

Section 2

Clause 1 The House of Representatives shall be composed of Members chosen every second Year by the People of the several States, and the Electors in each State shall have the Qualifications requisite for Electors of the most numerous Branch of the State Legislature.

Clause 2 No Person shall be a Representative who shall not have attained to the Age of twenty five Years, and been seven Years a Citizen of the United

States, and who shall not, when elected, be an Inhabitant of that State in which he shall be chosen.

Clause 3 Representatives and direct Taxes shall be apportioned among the several States which may be included within this Union, according to their respective Numbers, which shall be determined by adding to the whole Number of free Persons, including those bound to Service for a Term of Years, and excluding Indians not taxed, three fifths of all other Persons. The actual Enumeration shall be made within three Years after the first Meeting of the Congress of the United States, and within every subsequent Term of ten Years, in such Manner as they shall by Law direct. The Number of Representatives shall not exceed one for every thirty Thousand, but each State shall have at Least one Representative; and until such enumeration shall be made, the State of New Hampshire shall be entitled to chuse three, Massachusetts eight, Rhode-Island and Providence Plantations one, Connecticut five, New-York six, New Jersey four, Pennsylvania eight, Delaware one, Maryland six, Virginia ten, North Carolina five, South Carolina five, and Georgia three.

Clause 4 When vacancies happen in the Representation from any State, the Executive Authority thereof shall issue Writs of Election to fill such Vacancies.

Clause 5 The House of Representatives shall chuse their Speaker and other Officers; and shall have the sole Power of Impeachment.

Section 3

Clause 1 The Senate of the United States shall be composed of two Senators from each State, chosen by the Legislature thereof, for six Years; and each Senator shall have one Vote.

Clause 2 Immediately after they shall be assembled in Consequence of the first Election, they shall be divided as equally as may be into three Classes. The Seats of the Senators of the first Class shall be vacated at the Expiration of the second Year, of the second Class at the Expiration of the fourth Year, and of the third Class at the Expiration of the sixth Year, so that one third may be chosen every second Year; and if Vacancies happen by Resignation, or otherwise, during the Recess of the Legislature of any State, the Executive thereof may make temporary Appointments until the next Meeting of the Legislature, which shall then fill such Vacancies.

Clause 3 No Person shall be a Senator who shall not have attained to the Age of thirty Years, and been nine Years a Citizen of the United States, and who shall not, when elected, be an Inhabitant of that State for which he shall be chosen.

Clause 4 The Vice President of the United States shall be President of the Senate, but shall have no Vote, unless they be equally divided.

Clause 5 The Senate shall chuse their other Officers, and also a President pro tempore, in the Absence of the Vice President, or when he shall exercise the Office of President of the United States.

Clause 6 The Senate shall have the sole Power to try all Impeachments. When sitting for that Purpose, they shall be on Oath or Affirmation. When the President of the United States is tried, the Chief Justice shall preside: And no Person shall be convicted without the Concurrence of two thirds of the Members present.

Clause 7 Judgment in Cases of Impeachment shall not extend further than to removal from Office, and disqualification to hold and enjoy any Office of honor, Trust or Profit under the United States: but the Party convicted shall nevertheless be liable and subject to Indictment, Trial, Judgment and Punishment, according to Law.

Section 4

Clause 1 The Times, Places and Manner of holding Elections for Senators and Representatives, shall be prescribed in each State by the Legislature thereof; but the Congress may at any time by Law make or alter such Regulations, except as to the Places of chusing Senators.

Clause 2 The Congress shall assemble at least once in every Year, and such Meeting shall be on the first Monday in December, unless they shall by Law appoint a different Day.

Section 5

Clause 1 Each House shall be the Judge of the Elections, Returns and Qualifications of its own Members, and a Majority of each shall constitute a Quorum to do Business; but a smaller Number may adjourn from day to day, and may be authorized to compel the Attendance of absent Members, in such Manner, and under such Penalties as each House may provide.

Clause 2 Each House may determine the Rules of its Proceedings, punish its Members for disorderly Behaviour, and, with the Concurrence of two thirds, expel a Member.

Clause 3 Each House shall keep a Journal of its Proceedings, and from time to time publish the same, excepting such Parts as may in their Judgment require Secrecy; and the Yeas and Nays of the Members of either House on any question shall, at the Desire of one fifth of those Present, be entered on the Journal.

Clause 4 Neither House, during the Session of Congress, shall, without the Consent of the other, adjourn for more than three days, nor to any other Place than that in which the two Houses shall be sitting.

Section 6

Clause 1 The Senators and Representatives shall receive a Compensation for their Services, to be ascertained by Law, and paid out of the Treasury of the United States. They shall in all Cases, except Treason, Felony and Breach of the Peace, be privileged from Arrest during their Attendance at the Session of their respective Houses, and in going to and returning from the same; and for any Speech or Debate in either House, they shall not be questioned in any other Place.

Clause 2 No Senator or Representative shall, during the Time for which he was elected, be appointed to any civil Office under the Authority of the United States, which shall have been created, or the Emoluments whereof shall have been encreased during such time; and no Person holding any Office under the United States, shall be a Member of either House during his Continuance in Office.

Section 7

Clause 1 All Bills for raising Revenue shall originate in the House of Representatives; but the Senate may propose or concur with Amendments as on other Bills.

Clause 2 Every Bill which shall have passed the House of Representatives and the Senate, shall, before it become a Law, be presented to the President of the United States; If he approve he shall sign it, but if not he shall return it, with his Objections to that House in which it shall have originated, who shall enter the Objections at large on their Journal, and proceed to reconsider it. If after such Reconsideration two thirds of that House shall agree to pass the Bill, it shall be sent, together with the Objections, to the other House, by which it shall likewise be reconsidered, and if approved by two thirds of that House, it shall become a Law. But in all such Cases the Votes of both Houses shall be determined by Yeas and Nays, and the Names of the Persons voting for and against the Bill shall be entered on the Journal of each House respectively. If any Bill shall not be returned by the President within ten Days (Sundays excepted) after it shall have been presented to him, the Same shall be a Law, in like Manner as if he had signed it, unless the Congress by their Adjournment prevent its Return, in which Case it shall not be a Law.

Clause 3 Every Order, Resolution, or Vote to which the Concurrence of the Senate and House of Representatives may be necessary (except on a question of Adjournment) shall be presented to the President of the United States; and before the Same shall take Effect, shall be approved by him, or being disapproved by him, shall be repassed by two thirds of the Senate and House of Representatives, according to the Rules and Limitations prescribed in the Case of a Bill.

Section 8

Clause 1 The Congress shall have Power To lay and collect Taxes, Duties, Imposts and Excises, to pay the Debts and provide for the common Defence and general Welfare of the United States; but all Duties, Imposts and Excises shall be uniform throughout the United States;

Clause 2 To borrow Money on the credit of the United States;

Clause 3 To regulate Commerce with foreign Nations, and among the several States, and with the Indian Tribes;

Clause 4 To establish an uniform Rule of Naturalization, and uniform Laws on the subject of Bankruptcies throughout the United States;

Clause 5 To coin Money, regulate the Value thereof, and of foreign Coin, and fix the Standard of Weights and Measures;

Clause 6 To provide for the Punishment of counterfeiting the Securities and current Coin of the United States;

Clause 7 To establish Post Offices and post Roads;

Clause 8 To promote the Progress of Science and useful Arts, by securing for limited Times to Authors and Inventors the exclusive Right to their respective Writings and Discoveries;

Clause 9 To constitute Tribunals inferior to the supreme Court;

Clause 10 To define and punish Piracies and Felonies committed on the high Seas, and Offences against the Law of Nations;

Clause 11 To declare War, grant Letters of Marque and Reprisal, and make Rules concerning Captures on Land and Water;

Clause 12 To raise and support Armies, but no Appropriation of Money to that Use shall be for a longer Term than two Years;

Clause 13 To provide and maintain a Navy;

Clause 14 To make Rules for the Government and Regulation of the land and naval Forces;

Clause 15 To provide for calling forth the Militia to execute the Laws of the Union, suppress Insurrections and repel invasions;

Clause 16 To provide for organizing, arming, and disciplining, the Militia, and for governing such Part of them as may be employed in the Service of the United States, reserving to the States respectively, the Appointment of the Officers, and the Authority of training the Militia according to the discipline prescribed by Congress;

Clause 17 To exercise exclusive Legislation in all Cases whatsoever, over such District (not exceeding ten Miles square) as may, by Cession of particular States, and the Acceptance of Congress, become the Seat of the Government of the United States, and to exercise like Authority over all Places purchased by the Consent of the Legislature of the State in which the Same shall be, for the Erection of Forts, Magazines, Arsenals, dock-Yards, and other needful Buildings;—And

Clause 18 To make all Laws which shall be necessary and proper for carrying into Execution the foregoing Powers, and all other Powers vested by this Constitution in the Government of the United States, or in any Department or Officer thereof.

Section 9

Clause 1 The Migration or Importation of such Persons as any of the States now existing shall think proper to admit, shall not be prohibited by the Congress prior to the Year one thousand eight hundred and eight, but a Tax or duty may be imposed on such Importation, not exceeding ten dollars for each Person.

Clause 2 The Privilege of the Writ of Habeas Corpus shall not be suspended, unless when in Cases of Rebellion or Invasion the public Safety may require it.

Clause 3 No Bill of Attainder or ex post facto Law shall be passed.

Clause 4 No Capitation, or other direct, Tax shall be laid, unless in Proportion to the Census or Enumeration herein before directed to be taken.

Clause 5 No Tax or Duty shall be laid on Articles exported from any State.

Clause 6 No Preference shall be given by any Regulation of Commerce or Revenue to the Ports of one State over those of another: nor shall Vessels bound to, or from, one State, be obliged to enter, clear, or pay Duties in another.

Clause 7 No Money shall be drawn from the Treasury, but in Consequence of Appropriations made by Law; and a regular Statement and Account of the Receipts and Expenditures of all public Money shall be published from time to time.

Clause 8 No Title of Nobility shall be granted by the United States: And no Person holding any Office of Profit or Trust under them, shall, without the Consent of the Congress, accept of any present, Emolument, Office, or Title, of any kind whatever, from any King, Prince, or foreign State.

Section 10

Clause 1 No State shall enter into any Treaty, Alliance, or Confederation; grant Letters of Marque and Reprisal; coin Money; emit Bills of Credit; make any Thing but gold and silver Coin a Tender in Payment of Debts; pass any Bill of Attainder, ex post facto Law, or Law impairing the Obligation of Contracts, or grant any Title of Nobility.

Clause 2 No State shall, without the Consent of the Congress, lay any Imposts or Duties on Imports or Exports, except what may be absolutely necessary for executing its inspection Laws: and the net Produce of all Duties and Imposts, laid by any State on Imports or Exports, shall be for the Use of the Treasury of the United States; and all such Laws shall be subject to the Revision and Controul of the Congress.

Clause 3 No State shall, without the Consent of Congress, lay any Duty of Tonnage, keep Troops, or Ships of War in time of Peace, enter into any Agreement or Compact with another State, or with a foreign Power, or engage in War, unless actually invaded, or in such imminent Danger as will not admit of delay.

Article 2

Section 1

Clause 1 The executive Power shall be vested in a President of the United States of America. He shall hold his Office during the Term of four Years, and, together with the Vice President, chosen for the same Term, be elected, as follows

Clause 2 Each State shall appoint, in such Manner as the Legislature thereof may direct, a Number of Electors, equal to the whole Number of Senators and Representatives to which the State may be entitled in the Congress: but no Senator or Representative, or Person holding an Office of Trust or Profit under the United States, shall be appointed an Elector.

Clause 3 The Electors shall meet in their respective States, and vote by Ballot for two Persons, of whom one at least shall not be an Inhabitant of the same State with themselves. And they shall make a List of all the Persons voted for, and of the Number of Votes for each; which List they shall sign and certify, and transmit sealed to the Seat of the Government of the United States, directed to the President of the Senate. The President of the Senate shall, in the Presence of the Senate and House of Representatives, open all the Certificates, and the Votes shall then be counted. The Person having the greatest Number of Votes shall be the President, if such Number be a Majority of the whole Number of Electors appointed; and if there be more than one who have such Majority, and have an equal Number of Votes, then the House of Representatives shall immediately chuse by Ballot one of them for President; and if no Person have a Majority, then from the five highest on the List the said House shall in like Manner chuse the President. But in chusing the President, the Votes shall be taken by States, the Representation from each State having one Vote; A quorum for this Purpose shall consist of a Member or Members from two thirds of the States, and a Majority of all the States shall be necessary to a Choice. In every Case, after the Choice of the President, the Person having the greatest Number of Votes of the Electors shall be the Vice President. But if there should remain two or more who have equal Votes, the Senate shall chuse from them by Ballot the Vice President.

Clause 4 The Congress may determine the Time of chusing the Electors, and the Day on which they shall give their Votes; which Day shall be the same throughout the United States.

Clause 5 No Person except a natural born Citizen, or a Citizen of the United States, at the time of the Adoption of this Constitution, shall be eligible to the Office of President; neither shall any Person be eligible to that Office who shall not have attained to the Age of thirty five Years, and been fourteen Years a Resident within the United States.

Clause 6 In Case of the Removal of the President from Office, or of his Death, Resignation, or Inability to discharge the Powers and Duties of the said Office, the Same shall devolve on the Vice President, and the Congress may by Law provide for the Case of Removal, Death, Resignation or Inability, both of the President and Vice President, declaring what Officer shall then act as President, and such Officer shall act accordingly, until the Disability be removed, or a President shall be elected.

Clause 7 The President shall, at stated Times, receive for his Services, a Compensation, which shall neither be encreased nor diminished during the Period for which he shall have been elected, and he shall not receive within that Period any other Emolument from the United States, or any of them.

Clause 8 Before he enter on the Execution of his Office, he shall take the following Oath or Affirmation:—"I do solemnly swear (or affirm) that I will faithfully execute the Office of President of the United States, and will to the best of my Ability, preserve, protect and defend the Constitution of the United States."

Section 2

Clause 1 The President shall be Commander in Chief of the Army and Navy of the United States, and of the Militia of the several States, when called into the actual Service of the United States; he may require the Opinion, in writing, of the principal Officer in each of the executive Departments, upon any Subject relating to the Duties of their respective Offices, and he shall have Power to grant Reprieves and Pardons for Offences against the United States, except in Cases of Impeachment.

Clause 2 He shall have Power, by and with the Advice and Consent of the Senate, to make Treaties, provided two thirds of the Senators present concur; and he shall nominate, and by and with the Advice and Consent of the Senate, shall appoint Ambassadors, other public Ministers and Consuls, Judges of the supreme Court, and all other Officers of the United States, whose Appointments are not herein otherwise provided for, and which shall be established by Law: but the Congress may by Law vest the Appointment of such inferior Officers, as they think proper, in the President alone, in the Courts of Law, or in the Heads of Departments.

Clause 3 The President shall have Power to fill up all Vacancies that may happen during the Recess of the Senate, by granting Commissions which shall expire at the End of their next Session.

Section 3

He shall from time to time give to the Congress Information of the State of the Union, and recommend to their Consideration such Measures as he shall judge necessary and expedient; he may, on extraordinary Occasions, convene both Houses, or either of them, and in Case of Disagreement between them, with Respect to the Time of Adjournment, he may adjourn them to such Time as he shall think proper; he shall receive Ambassadors and other public Ministers; he shall take Care that the Laws be faithfully executed, and shall Commission all the Officers of the United States.

Section 4

The President, Vice President and all civil Officers of the United States, shall be removed from Office on Impeachment for, and Conviction of, Treason, Bribery, or other high Crimes and Misdemeanors.

Article 3

Section 1

The judicial Power of the United States, shall be vested in one supreme Court, and in such inferior Courts as the Congress may from time to time ordain and establish. The Judges, both of the supreme and inferior Courts, shall hold their Offices during good Behaviour, and shall, at stated Times, receive for their Services, a Compensation, which shall not be diminished during their Continuance in Office.

Section 2

Clause 1 The judicial Power shall extend to all Cases, in Law and Equity, arising under this Constitution, the Laws of the United States, and Treaties made, or which shall be made, under their Authority;—to all Cases affecting Ambassadors, other public Ministers and Consuls;—to all Cases of admiralty and maritime Jurisdiction;—to Controversies to which the United States shall be a Party;—to Controversies between two or more States;—between a State and Citizens of another State;—between Citizens of different States,—between Citizens of the same State claiming Lands under Grants of different States, and between a State, or the Citizens thereof, and foreign States, Citizens or Subjects.

Clause 2 In all Cases affecting Ambassadors, other public Ministers and Consuls, and those in which a State shall be Party, the supreme Court shall have original Jurisdiction. In all the other Cases before mentioned, the supreme Court shall have appellate Jurisdiction, both as to Law and Fact, with such Exceptions, and under such Regulations as the Congress shall make.

Clause 3 The Trial of all Crimes, except in Cases of Impeachment, shall be by Jury; and such Trial shall be held in the State where the said Crimes shall have been committed; but when not committed within any State, the Trial shall be at such Place or Places as the Congress may by Law have directed.

Section 3

Clause 1 Treason against the United States, shall consist only in levying War against them, or in adhering to their Enemies, giving them Aid and

Comfort. No Person shall be convicted of Treason unless on the Testimony of two Witnesses to the same overt Act, or on Confession in open Court.

Clause 2 The Congress shall have Power to declare the Punishment of Treason, but no Attainder of Treason shall work Corruption of Blood, or Forfeiture except during the Life of the Person attainted.

Article 4

Section 1

Full Faith and Credit shall be given in each State to the public Acts, Records, and judicial Proceedings of every other State. And the Congress may be general Laws prescribe the Manner in which such Acts, Records, and Proceedings shall be proved, and the Effect thereof.

Section 2

Clause 1 The Citizens of each State shall be entitled to all Privileges and Immunities of Citizens in the several States.

Clause 2 A Person charged in any State with Treason, Felony, or other Crime, who shall flee from Justice, and be found in another State, shall on Demand of the executive Authority of the State from which he fled, be delivered up, to be removed to the State having Jurisdiction of the Crime.

Clause 3 No Person held to Service or Labour in one State, under the Laws thereof, escaping into another, shall, in Consequence of any Law or Regulation therein, be discharged from such Service or Labour, but shall be delivered up on Claim of the Party to whom such Service or Labour may be due.

Section 3

Clause 1 New States may be admitted by the Congress into this Union; but no new State shall be formed or erected within the Jurisdiction of any other State; nor any State be formed by the Junction of two or more States, or Parts of States, without the Consent of the Legislatures of the States concerned as well as of the Congress.

Clause 2 The Congress shall have Power to dispose of and make all needful Rules and Regulations respecting the Territory or other Property belonging to the United States; and nothing in this Constitution shall be so construed as to Prejudice any Claims of the United States, or of any particular State.

Section 4

The United States shall guarantee to every State in this Union a Republican Form of Government, and shall protect each of them against Invasion; and on Application of the Legislature, or of the Executive (when the Legislature cannot be convened) against domestic Violence.

Article 5

The Congress, whenever two thirds of both Houses shall deem it necessary, shall propose Amendments to this Constitution, or, on the Application of the Legislatures of two thirds of the several States, shall call a Convention for proposing Amendments, which, in either Case, shall be valid to all Intents and Purposes, as Part of this Constitution, when ratified by the Legislatures of three fourths of the several States, or by Conventions in three fourths thereof, as the one or the other Mode of Ratification may be proposed by the Congress; Provided that no Amendment which may be made prior to the Year One thousand eight hundred and eight shall in any Manner affect the first and fourth Clauses in the Ninth Section of the first Article; and that no State, without its Consent, shall be deprived of its equal Suffrage in the Senate.

Article 6

Clause 1 All Debts contracted and Engagements entered into, before the Adoption of this Constitution, shall be as valid against the United States under this Constitution, as under the Confederation.

Clause 2 This Constitution, and the Laws of the United States which shall be made in Pursuance thereof; and all Treaties made, or which shall be made, under the Authority of the United States, shall be the supreme Law of the Land; and the Judges in every State shall be bound thereby, any Thing in the Constitution or Laws of any State to the Contrary notwithstanding.

Clause 3 The Senators and Representatives before mentioned, and the Members of the several State Legislatures, and all executive and judicial Officers, both of the United States and of the several States, shall be bound by Oath or Affirmation, to support this Constitution; but no religious Test shall ever be required as a Qualification to any Office or public Trust under the United States.

Article 7

The Ratification of the Conventions of nine States, shall be sufficient for the Establishment of this Constitution between the States so ratifying the Same.

Done in Convention by the Unanimous Consent of the States present the Seventeenth Day of September in the Year of our Lord one thousand seven hundred and Eighty seven and of the Independence of the United States of America the Twelfth In witness whereof We have hereunto subscribed our Names.

Amendments to the Constitution

Amendment One

Congress shall make no law respecting an establishment of religion, or prohibiting the free exercise thereof; or abridging the freedom of speech, or of the press; or the right of the people peaceably to assemble, and to petition the Government for a redress of grievances.

Amendment Two

A well regulated Militia, being necessary to the security of a free State, the right of the people to keep and bear Arms, shall not be infringed.

Amendment Three

No Soldier shall, in time of peace be quartered in any house, without the consent of the Owner, nor in time of war, but in a manner to be prescribed by law.

Amendment Four

The right of the people to be secure in their persons, houses, papers, and effects, against unreasonable searches and seizures, shall not be violated, and no Warrants shall issue, but upon probable cause, supported by Oath or affirmation, and particularly describing the place to be searched, and the persons or things to be seized.

Amendment Five

No person shall be held to answer for a capital, or otherwise infamous crime, unless on a presentment or indictment of a Grand Jury, except in cases arising in the land or naval forces, or in the Militia, when in actual service in time of War or public danger; nor shall any person be subject for the same offence to be twice put in jeopardy of life or limb; nor shall be compelled in any criminal case to be a witness against himself, nor be deprived of life, liberty, or property, without due process of law; nor shall private property be taken for public use, without just compensation.

Amendment Six

In all criminal prosecutions, the accused shall enjoy the right to a speedy and public trial, by an impartial jury of the State and district wherein the crime shall have been committed, which district shall have been previously ascertained by law, and to be informed of the nature and cause of the accusation; to be confronted with the witnesses against him; to have compulsory process for obtaining witnesses in his favor, and to have the Assistance of Counsel for his defence.

Amendment Seven

In Suits at common law, where the value in controversy shall exceed twenty dollars, the right of trial by jury shall be preserved, and no fact tried by a jury, shall be otherwise re-examined in any Court of the United States, than according to the rules of the common law.

Amendment Eight

Excessive bail shall not be required, nor excessive fines imposed, nor cruel and unusual punishments inflicted.

Amendment Nine

The enumeration in the Constitution, of certain rights, shall not be construed to deny or disparage others retained by the people.

Amendment Ten

The powers not delegated to the United States by the Constitution, nor prohibited by it to the States, are reserved to the States respectively, or to the people.

Amendment Eleven

The Judicial power of the United States shall not be construed to extend to any suit in law or equity, commenced or prosecuted against one of the United States by Citizens of another State, or by Citizens or Subjects of any Foreign State.

Amendment Twelve

The Electors shall meet in their respective states, and vote by ballot for President and Vice-President, one of whom, at least, shall not be an inhabitant of the same state with themselves; they shall name in their ballots the person voted for as President, and in distinct ballots the person voted for as Vice-President, and they shall make distinct lists of all persons voted for as President, and of all persons voted for as Vice-President, and of the number of votes for each, which lists they shall sign and certify, and transmit sealed to the seat of the government of the United States, directed to the President of the Senate;—The President of the Senate shall, in the presence of the Senate and House of Representatives, open all the certificates and the votes shall then be counted;—The person having the greatest number of votes for President, shall be the President, if such number be a majority of the whole number of Electors appointed; and if no person have such majority, then from the persons having the highest numbers not exceeding three on the list of those voted for as President, the House of Representatives shall choose immediately, by ballot, the President. But in choosing the President, the votes shall be taken by states, the representation from each state having one vote; a quorum for this purpose shall consist of a member or members from two-thirds of the states, and a majority of all the states shall be necessary to a choice. And if the House of Representatives shall not choose a President whenever the right of choice shall devolve upon them, before the fourth day of March next following, then the Vice-President shall act as President, as in the case of the death or other constitutional disability of the President. The person having the greatest number of votes as Vice-President, shall be the Vice-President, if such number be a majority of the whole number of Electors appointed, and if no person have a majority, then from the two highest numbers on the list, the Senate shall choose the Vice-President; a quorum for the purpose shall consist of two-thirds of the whole number of Senators, and a majority of the whole number shall be necessary to a choice. But no person constitutionally ineligible to the office of President shall be eligible to that of Vice-President of the United States.

Amendment Thirteen

Section 1 Neither slavery nor involuntary servitude, except as a punishment for crime whereof the party shall have been duly convicted, shall exist within the United States, or any place subject to their jurisdiction.

Section 2 Congress shall have power to enforce this article by appropriate legislation.

Amendment Fourteen

Section 1 All persons born or naturalized in the United States, and subject to the jurisdiction thereof, are citizens of the United States and of the State wherein they reside. No State shall make or enforce any law which shall abridge the privileges or immunities of citizens of the United States; nor shall any State deprive any person of life, liberty, or property, without due process of law; nor deny to any person within its jurisdiction the equal protection of the laws.

Section 2 Representatives shall be apportioned among the several States according to their respective numbers, counting the whole number of persons in each State, excluding Indians not taxed. But when the right to vote at any election for the choice of electors for President and Vice President of the United States, Representatives in Congress, the Executive and Judicial officers of a State, or the members of the Legislature thereof, is denied to any of the male inhabitants of such State, being twenty-one years of age, and citizens of the United States, or in any way abridged, except for participation in rebellion, or other crime, the basis of representation therein shall be reduced in the proportion which the number of such male citizens shall bear to the whole number of male citizens twenty-one years of age in such State.

Section 3 No person shall be a Senator or Representative in Congress, or elector of President and Vice President, or hold any office, civil or military, under the United States, or under any State, who, having previously taken an oath, as a member of Congress, or as an officer of the United States, or as a member of any State legislature, or as an executive or judicial officer of any State, to support the Constitution of the United States, shall have engaged in insurrection or rebellion against the same, or given aid or comfort to the enemies thereof. But Congress may by a vote of two-thirds of each House, remove such disability.

Section 4 The validity of the public debt of the United States, authorized by law, including debts incurred for payment of pensions and bounties for services in suppressing insurrection or rebellion, shall not be questioned. But neither the United States nor any State shall assume or pay any debt or obligation incurred in aid of insurrection or rebellion against the United States, or any claim for the loss or emancipation of any slave; but all such debts, obligations and claims shall be held illegal and void.

Section 5 The Congress shall have power to enforce, by appropriate legislation, the provisions of this article.

Amendment Fifteen

Section 1 The right of citizens of the United States to vote shall not be denied or abridged by the United States or by any State on account of race, color, or previous condition of servitude.

Section 2 The Congress shall have power to enforce this article by appropriate legislation.

Amendment Sixteen

The Congress shall have power to lay and collect taxes on incomes, from whatever source derived, without apportionment among the several States, and without regard to any census or enumeration.

Amendment Seventeen

The Senate of the United States shall be composed of two Senators from each State, elected by the people thereof, for six years; and each Senator shall have one vote. The electors in each State shall have the qualifications requisite for electors of the most numerous branch of the State legislatures.

When vacancies happen in the representation of any State in the Senate, the executive authority of such State shall issue writs of election to fill such vacancies: Provided, That the legislature of any State may empower the executive thereof to make temporary appointments until the people fill the vacancies by election as the legislature may direct.

This amendment shall not be so construed as to affect the election or term of any Senator chosen before it becomes valid as part of the Constitution.

Amendment Eighteen

Section 1 After one year from the ratification of this article the manufacture, sale, or transportation of intoxicating liquors within, the importation thereof into, or the exportation thereof from the United States and all territory subject to the jurisdiction thereof for beverage purposes is hereby prohibited.

Section 2 The Congress and the several States shall have concurrent power to enforce this article by appropriate legislation.

Section 3 This article shall be inoperative unless it shall have been ratified as an amendment to the Constitution by the legislatures of the several States, as provided in the Constitution, within seven years from the date of the submission hereof to the States by the Congress.

Amendment Nineteen

The right of citizens of the United States to vote shall not be denied or abridged by the United States or by any State on account of sex.

Congress shall have power to enforce this article by appropriate legislation.

Amendment Twenty

Section 1 The terms of the President and Vice President shall end at noon on the 20th day of January, and the terms of Senators and Representatives at noon on the 3d day of January, of the years in which such terms would have ended if this article had not been ratified; and the terms of their successors shall then begin.

Section 2 The Congress shall assemble at least once in every year, and such meeting shall begin at noon on the 3d day of January, unless they shall by law appoint a different day.

Section 3 If, at the time fixed for the beginning of the term of the President, the President elect shall have died, the Vice President elect shall become President. If a President shall not have been chosen before the time fixed for the beginning of his term, or if the President elect shall have failed to qualify, then the Vice President elect shall act as President until a President shall have qualified; and the Congress may by law provide for the case wherein neither a President elect nor a Vice President elect shall have qualified, declaring who shall then act as President, or the manner in which one who is to act shall be selected, and such person shall act accordingly until a President or Vice President shall have qualified.

Section 4 The Congress may by law provide for the case of the death of any of the persons from whom the House of Representatives may choose a President whenever the right of choice shall have devolved upon them, and for the case of the death of any of the persons from whom the Senate may choose a Vice President whenever the right of choice shall have devolved upon them.

Section 5 Sections 1 and 2 shall take effect on the 15th day of October following the ratification of this article.

Section 6 This article shall be inoperative unless it shall have been ratified as an amendment to the Constitution by the legislatures of three-fourths of the several States within seven years from the date of its submission.

Amendment Twenty-One

Section 1 The eighteenth article of amendment to the Constitution of the United States is hereby repealed.

Section 2 The transportation or importation into any State, Territory, or possession of the United States for delivery or use therein of intoxicating liquors, in violation of the laws thereof, is hereby prohibited.

Section 3 This article shall be inoperative unless it shall have been ratified as an amendment to the Constitution by conventions in the several States, as provided in the Constitution, within seven years from the date of the submission hereof to the States by the Congress.

Amendment Twenty-Two

Section 1 No person shall be elected to the office of the President more than twice, and no person who has held the office of President, or acted as President, for more than two years of a term to which some other person was elected President shall be elected to the office of the President more than once. But this article shall not apply to any person holding the office of President when this article was proposed by the Congress, and shall not prevent any person who may be holding the office of President, or acting as President, during the term within which this article becomes operative from holding the office of President or acting as President during the remainder of such term.

Section 2 This article shall be inoperative unless it shall have been ratified as an amendment to the Constitution by the legislatures of three-fourths of the several states within seven years from the date of its submission to the states by the Congress.

Amendment Twenty-Three

Section 1 The District constituting the seat of government of the United States shall appoint in such manner as the Congress may direct:

A number of electors of President and Vice President equal to the whole number of Senators and Representatives in Congress to which the District would be entitled if it were a state, but in no event more than the least populous state; they shall be in addition to those appointed by the states, but they shall be considered, for the purposes of the election of President and Vice President, to be electors appointed by a state; and they shall meet in the District and perform such duties as provided by the twelfth article of amendment.

Section 2 The Congress shall have power to enforce this article by appropriate legislation.

Amendment Twenty-Four

Section 1 The right of citizens of the United States to vote in any primary or other election for President or Vice President, for electors for President or Vice President, or for Senator or Representative in Congress, shall not be denied or abridged by the United States or any state by reason of failure to pay any poll tax or other tax.

Section 2 The Congress shall have power to enforce this article by appropriate legislation.

Amendment Twenty-Five

Section 1 In case of the removal of the President from office or of his death or resignation, the Vice President shall become President.

Section 2 Whenever there is a vacancy in the office of the Vice President, the President shall nominate a Vice President who shall take office upon confirmation by a majority vote of both Houses of Congress.

Section 3 Whenever the President transmits to the President pro tempore of the Senate and the Speaker of the House of Representatives his written declaration that he is unable to discharge the powers and duties of his office, and until he transmits to them a written declaration to the contrary, such powers and duties shall be discharged by the Vice President as Acting President.

Section 4 Whenever the Vice President and a majority of either the principal officers of the executive departments or of such other body as Congress may by law provide, transmit to the President pro tempore of the Senate and the Speaker of the House of Representatives their written declaration that the President is unable to discharge the powers and duties of his office, the Vice President shall immediately assume the powers and duties of the office as Acting President.

Thereafter, when the President transmits to the President pro tempore of the Senate and the Speaker of the House of Representatives his written declaration that no inability exists, he shall resume the powers and duties of his office unless the Vice President and a majority of either the principal officers of the executive department or of such other body as Congress may by law provide, transmit within four days to the President pro tempore of the Senate and the Speaker of the House of Representatives their written declaration that the President is unable to discharge the powers and duties of his office. Thereupon Congress shall decide the issue, assembling within forty-eight hours for that purpose if not in session. If the Congress, within twenty-one days after receipt of the latter written declaration, or, if Congress is not in session, within twenty-one days after Congress is required to assemble, determines by two-thirds vote of both Houses that the President is unable to discharge the powers and duties of his office, the Vice President shall continue to discharge the same as Acting President; otherwise, the President shall resume the powers and duties of his office.

Amendment Twenty-Six

Section 1 The right of citizens of the United States, who are 18 years of age or older, to vote, shall not be denied or abridged by the United States or any state on account of age.

Section 2 The Congress shall have the power to enforce this article by appropriate legislation.

Amendment Twenty-Seven

No law varying the compensation for the services of the Senators and Representatives shall take effect until an election of Representatives shall have intervened.

NOTE

1. This text of the Constitution follows the engrossed copy signed by General Washington and the deputies from twelve states. It was retrieved from the House of Representatives Web site.

References

Abram, Michael, and Joseph Cooper. 1968. "The Rise of Seniority in the House of Representatives." *Polity* 1: 52–85.

Abramowitz, Alan I. 1988. "Explaining Senate Election Outcomes." *American Political Science Review* 82: 385–403.

Achen, Christopher. 1978. "Measuring Representation: Perils of the Correlation Coefficient." *American Journal of Political Science* 21: 805–15.

Aldrich, John H. 1995. *Why Parties?* Chicago: University of Chicago Press.

———. 1999. "Political Parties in a Critical Era." *American Politics Quarterly* 27: 9–32.

Aldrich, John H., and Richard G. Niemi. 1996. "The Sixth American Party System: Electoral Change, 1952–1992." In *Broken Contract? Changing Relationships between Americans and their Government*, edited by Stephen C. Craig. Boulder, Colo., Westview Press.

Aldrich, John H., and David W. Rohde. 1997. "The Transition to Republican Rule in the House: Implications for Theories of Congressional Politics." *Political Science Quarterly* 112: 541–67.

———. 2009. "Congressional Committees in a Continuing Partisan Era." In *Congress Reconsidered*, 9th ed., edited by Lawrence C. Dodd and Bruce I. Oppenheimer. Washington: CQ Press.

Ansolabehere, Stephen, and Alan Gerber. 1994. "The Mismeasure of Campaign Spending: Evidence from the 1990 United States House Elections." *Journal of Politics* 56: 1106–18.

———. 1996. "The Effects of Filing Fees and Petition Requirements on U.S. House Elections." *Legislative Studies Quarterly* 21: 249–64.

Ansolabehere, Stephen, John de Figueiredo, and James M. Snyder, Jr. 2003. "Why Is There So Little Money in U.S. Politics?" *Journal of Economic Perspectives* 17: 105–30.

Ansolabehere, Stephen, Alan S. Gerber, and James M. Snyder, Jr. 1999. "Television Costs and Greater Congressional Campaign Spending: Cause-and-Effect or Coincidence?" Manuscript, Massachusetts Institute of Technology.

Ansolabehere, Stephen, and Shanto Iyengar. 1995. *Going Negative.* New York: Macmillan.

Ansolabehere, Stephen, and James M. Snyder, Jr. 2008. *The End of Equality: One Person, One Vote and the Transformation of American Politics.* New York: Norton.

Ansolabehere, Stephen, James M. Snyder, Jr., and Charles Stewart III. 2000a. "Old Voters, New Voters, and the Personal Vote: Using Redistricting to Measure the Incumbency Advantage." *American Journal of Political Science* 44: 17–34.

———. 2000b. "Candidate Positioning in U.S. House Elections." Manuscript, Massachusetts Institute of Technology.

Bach, Stanley, and Steven S. Smith. 1988. *Managing Uncertainty in the House of Representatives: Adaptation and Innovation in Special Rules.* Washington, D.C.: Brookings Institution Press.

Bader, John B. 1997. "The Contract with America: Origins and Assessments." In *Congress Reconsidered*, 6th ed., edited by Lawrence C. Dodd and Bruce I. Oppenheimer. Washington, D.C.: Congressional Quarterly Press.

Bailey, Stephen Kemp. 1950. *Congress Makes a Law: The Story Behind the Employment Act of 1946.* New York: Columbia University Press.

Banks, Jeffrey S., and D. Roderick Kiewiet. 1989. "Explaining Patterns of Candidate Competition in Congressional Elections." *American Journal of Political Science* 33: 997–1015.

Bartels, Larry M. 2000. "Partisanship and Voting Behavior, 1952–1996." *American Journal of Political Science* 44: 35–50.

Beth, Richard S. 1998. "Discharge Procedure in the House." *CRS Report for Congress*, April 20, 1998. Retrieved at http://www.house.gov/rules/98–394.htm on March 25, 2000.

Beveridge, Albert J. 1928. *Abraham Lincoln, 1809–1858.* Boston: Houghton Mifflin.

Binder, Sarah A. 1996. "The Partisan Basis of Procedural Choice: Allocating Parliamentary Rights in the House, 1789–1990." *American Political Science Review* 90: 8–20.

———. 1997. *Minority Rights, Majority Rule: Partisanship and the Development of Congress.* New York: Cambridge University Press.

———. 1998. "Partisanship and Procedural Choice: Institutional Change in the Early Congress, 1789–1823." *Journal of Politics* 57: 1093–1118.

Binder, Sarah A., and Steven S. Smith. 1997. *Politics or Principle? Filibustering in the United States Senate.* Washington, D.C.: Brookings Institution Press.

Birkhead, Nathaniel, Gabriel Uriarte, and William Bianco. 2010. "The Impact of State Legislative Term Limits on the Competitiveness of Congressional Elections." *American Politics Research* 38: 842–61.

Black, Duncan. 1958. *The Theory of Committees and Elections.* New York: Cambridge University Press.

Black, Gordon S. 1972. "A Theory of Political Ambition: Career Choices and the Role of Structural Incentives." *American Political Science Review* 66: 144–59.

Brady, David W. 1988. *Critical Elections and Congressional Policy Making.* Stanford, Calif.: Stanford University Press.

Brady, David W., and Charles Bullock. 1980. "Is There a Conservative Coalition in the House?" *Journal of Politics* 42: 549–59.

Brady, Henry E., and Paul M. Sniderman. 1985. "Attitude Attribution: A Group Basis for Political Reasoning." *American Political Science Review* 79: 1061–78.

Brewer, Paul R., and Christopher J. Deering. 2005. "Musical Chairs: Interest Groups, Campaign Fundraising, and Selection of House Committee Chairs." In *The Interest Group Connection: Electioneering, Lobbying, and Policymaking in Washington,* edited by Paul Herrnson, Clyde Wilcox, and Ronald G. Shaiko. Washington: CQ Press.

Brown, Robert D., and Justin Wedeking. 2006. "People Who Have Their Tickets but Do Not Use Them." *American Politics Research* 34: 479–504.

Burnham, Walter Dean. 1970. *Critical Elections and the Mainsprings of American Politics.* New York: Oxford University Press.

Butler, David, and Bruce Cain. 1992. *Congressional Redistricting: Comparative and Theoretical Perspectives.* New York: Macmillan.

Campbell, Andrea Louise. 2003. *How Policies Make Citizens: Senior Political Activism and the American Welfare State.* Princeton: Princeton University Press.

Campbell, Angus. 1966. "Surge and Decline: A Study of Electoral Change." In *Elections and the Political Order,* edited by Angus Campbell, Phillip E. Converse, Warren E. Miller, and Donald E. Stokes. New York: Wiley.

Campbell, James E., John R. Alford, and Keith Henry. 1984. "Television Markets and Congressional Elections." *Legislative Studies Quarterly* 9: 667–78.

Canon, David T., Garrison Nelson, and Charles Stewart III. 2002. *Committees in the U.S. Congress, 1789–1946.* 3 vols. Washington: CQ Press.

Carey, John M., Richard G. Niemi, Lynda W. Powell, and Gary F. Moncrief. 2006. "The Effects of Term Limits on State Legislatures: A New Survey of the 50 States." *Legislative Studies Quarterly* 31: 105–34.

Carmines, Edward G., and James A. Stimson. 1989. *Issue Evolution: Race and the Transformation of American Politics.* Princeton, N.J.: Princeton University Press.

Chambers, William Nisbet, and Walter Dean Burnham. 1967. *The American Party Systems.* New York: Oxford University Press.

Converse, Philip E. 1964. "The Nature of Belief Systems in Mass Publics." In *Ideology and Discontent*, edited by David E. Apter. New York: Free Press.

Cook, Sara Brandes, and John R. Hibbing. 1997. "A Not-So-Distant Mirror: The 17th Amendment and Congressional Change." *American Political Science Review* 91: 845–53.

Cooper, Joseph. 1970. *The Origin of the Standing Committees and the Development of the Modern House.* Houston: Rice University.

Cox, Gary W., and Samuel Kernell, eds. 1991. *Divided Government.* Boulder, Colo.: Westview Press.

Cox, Gary W., and Mathew McCubbins. 1993. *Legislative Leviathan: Party Government in the House.* Berkeley: University of California Press.

———. 1999. "Agenda Power in the U.S. House of Representatives." Paper presented at a Conference on the History of Congress, Stanford University, January 15–16, 1999.

———. 2005. *Setting the Agenda: Responsible Party Government in the U.S. House of Representatives.* New York: Cambridge University Press.

Cox, Gary W., and Michael C. Munger. 1989. "Closeness, Expenditures, and Turnout in the 1982 U.S. House Elections." *American Political Science Review* 83: 217–31.

Cutler, Lloyd. 1980. "To Form a Government." *Foreign Affairs* 59: 127–39.

———. 1988. "Some Reflections on Divided Government." *Presidential Studies Quarterly* 18: 489–90.

Davenport, Coral. 2008. "Waxman Claims a Premier Gavel." *CQ Weekly*, November 24: 3148.

DeNardo, James. 1980. "Turnout and the Vote: The Joke's on the Democrats." *American Political Science Review* 74: 406–20.

Denzau, Arthur, William Riker, and Kenneth Shepsle. 1985. "Farquharson and Fenno: Sophisticated Voting and Home Style." *American Political Science Review* 79: 1117–35.

Dodd, Lawrence C., and Bruce I. Oppenheimer. 2009. *Congress Reconsidered*, 9th ed. Washington: CQ Press.

Donald, David Herbert. 1995. *Lincoln.* New York: Simon and Schuster.

Downs, Anthony. 1957. *An Economic Theory of Democracy.* New York: Harper and Row.

Dubin, Michael J. 1998. *United States Congressional Elections, 1788–1997: The Official Results of the Elections of the 1st Through 105th Congresses.* Jefferson, N.C.: McFarland.

Duverger, Marice. 1954. *Political Parties: Their Organization and Activity in the Modern State.* New York: Wiley.

Enelow, James. 1981. "Saving Amendments, Killer Amendments, and an Expected Utility Theory of Sophisticated Voting." *Journal of Politics* 43: 1062–89.

Erikson, Robert S., and Gerald C. Wright, Jr. 1997. "Voters, Candidates, and Issues in Congressional Elections." In *Congress Reconsidered*, 6th ed., edited by Lawrence C. Dodd and Bruce I. Oppenheimer. Washington, D.C.: Congressional Quarterly Press.

Fenno, Richard. 1966. *Power of the Purse*. Boston: Little, Brown.

———. 1974. *Congressmen in Committees*. Boston: Little, Brown.

———. 1978. *Home Style: House Members in Their Districts*. Boston: Little, Brown.

Ferejohn, John A., and Morris P. Fiorina. 1974. "The Paradox of Not Voting: A Decision Theoretic Analysis." *American Political Science Review* 68: 525–36.

Finley, Paul. 1979. *A. Lincoln: The Crucible of Congress*. New York: Crown.

Fiorina, Morris P. 1977. *Congress: Keystone of the Washington Establishment*. New Haven, Conn.: Yale University Press.

Fiorina, Morris P., David W. Rohde, and Peter Wissel. 1975. "Historical Change in House Turnover." In *Congress in Change: Evolution and Reform*, edited by Norman J. Ornstein. New York: Praeger.

Fisher, Louis. 1978. *The Constitution between Friends*. New York: St. Martin's Press.

Fox, Harrison, and Susan Webb Hammond. 1977. *Congressional Staffs: The Invisible Force in American Lawmaking*. New York: Free Press.

Gamm, Gerald, and Kenneth Shepsle. 1989. "Emergence of Legislative Institutions: Standing Committees in the House and Senate, 1810–1825." *Legislative Studies Quarterly* 14: 39–66.

Gelman, Andrew, and Gary King. 1990. "Estimating Incumbency Advantage without Bias." *American Journal of Political Science* 34: 1142–64.

Gerber, Alan S., and Donald P. Green. 2000. "The Effects of Canvassing, Telephone Calls, and Direct Mail on Voter Turnout: A Field Experiment." *American Political Science Review* 94: 653–63.

Green, Donald P., and Alan S. Gerber. 2008. *Get Out the Vote: How to Increase Voter Turnout*, 2nd ed. Washington: Brookings Institution Press.

Groseclose, Tim, and Nolan McCarty. 2001. "The Politics of Blame: Bargaining before an Audience." *American Journal of Political Science* 45: 100–19.

Groseclose, Timothy, and Charles Stewart III. 1998. "The Value of Committee Seats in the House, 1946–1991," *American Journal of Political Science* 42: 453–74.

Guinier, Lani, 1989. "Keeping the Faith: Black Voters in the Post-Reagan Era." *Harvard Civil Rights–Civil Liberties Law Review* 24: 393–435.

———. 1991a. "The Triumph of Tokenism: The Voting Rights Act and the Theory of Black Electoral Success." *Michigan Law Review* 89: 1077–154.

———. 1991b. "No Two Seats: The Elusive Quest for Political Equality." *Virginia Law Review* 77: 1413–1514.

———. 1995. *The Tyranny of the Majority: Fundamental Fairness in Representative Democracy*. New York: Free Press.

Hammond, Thomas H, and Gary J. Miller. 1985. "The Core of the Constitution." *American Journal of Political Science* 81: 1155–75.

Harlow, Ralph V. 1917. *The History of Legislative Methods in the Period before
1825.* New Haven, Conn.: Yale University Press.

Haynes, George H. 1938. *The Senate of the United States: Its History and
Practice.* Boston: Houghton Mifflin.

Heberling, Eric S., and Bruce A. Larson. 2007. "Party Fundraising, Descrip-
tive Representation, and the Battle for Majority Control: Shifting Leadership Appointment Strategies in the U.S. House of Representatives,
1990–2002." *Social Science Quarterly* 88: 404–21.

Hechler, Kenneth W. 1940. *Insurgency: Personality and Politics of the Taft
Era.* New York: Columbia University Press.

Heckman, James J., and James M. Snyder, Jr. 1997. "Linear Probability Models
of the Demand for Attributes with an Empirical Application to Estimating
the Preferences of Legislators." *Rand Journal of Economics* 28: S142–S189.

Hibbing, John R. 1991. "Contours of the Modern Congressional Career."
American Political Science Review 85: 405–28.

Highton, B., and Raymond E. Wolfinger. 1998. "Estimating the Effects
of the National Voter Registration Act of 1993." *Political Behavior* 20:
79–104.

Holt, James. 1967. *Congressional Insurgents and the Party System, 1909–
1916.* Cambridge, Mass.: Harvard University Press.

Hood, M.V.III, and Seth C. McKee. 2009. "Trying to Thread the Needle:
The Effects of Redistricting in a Georgia Congressional District." *Political
Science and Politics* 42:679–87.

Hotelling, Harold. 1929. "Stability in Competition." *Economic Journal* 39:
41–57.

Howe, Daniel Walker. 1979. *The Political Culture of the American Whigs.*
Chicago: University of Chicago Press.

Jacobson, Gary. 1987. "The Marginals Never Vanished: Incumbency and
Competition in Elections to the U.S. House of Representatives, 1952–
82." *American Journal of Political Science* 31: 126–41.

———. 1997. *Politics of Congressional Elections,* 4th ed. New York: Longmans.

———. 2009. *Politics of Congressional Elections,* 7th ed. New York: Longmans.

Jacobson, Gary, and Michael A. Dimock. 1994. "Checking Out: The Effects
of Bank Overdrafts on the 1992 House Elections." *American Journal of
Political Science* 38: 601–24.

Jacobson, Gary, and Samuel Kernell. 1981. *Strategy and Choice in Congressional Elections.* New Haven, Conn.: Yale University Press.

Jameson, J. Franklin. 1894. "Origins of the Standing Committee System in
American Legislative Bodies." *Political Science Quarterly* 9: 246–67.

Jenkins, Jeffery A., and Timothy P. Nokken. 2000. "The Institutional Origins
of the Republican Party: A Spatial Voting Analysis of the House Speakership Election of 1855–56." *Legislative Studies Quarterly* 25: 101–30.

Jenkins, Jeffery A., and Charles Stewart III. 1997. "Order from Chaos: The Transformation of the Committee System in the House, 1810–1822." Paper presented at the annual meeting of the American Political Science Association.

Jillson, Calvin. 1981. "Constitution Making: Alignment and Realignment in the Federal Convention of 1787." *American Political Science Review* 75: 598–612.

Jillson, Calvin, and Cecil Eubanks. 1984. "The Political Structure of Constitution Making: The Federal Convention of 1787." *American Journal of Political Science* 28: 435–58.

Jillson, Calvin, and Rick K. Wilson. 1994. *Congressional Dynamics: Structure, Coordination, and Choice in the First American Congress, 1774–1789.* Stanford, Calif.: Stanford University Press.

Katz, Jonathan N., and Brian R. Sala. 1996. "Careerism, Committee Assignments, and the Electoral Connection." *American Political Science Review* 90: 21–33.

Kernell, Samuel. 1977. "Toward Understanding 19th Century Congressional Careers: Ambition, Competition, and Rotation." *American Journal of Political Science* 21: 669–93.

Key, V. O. 1955. "A Theory of Critical Elections." *Journal of Politics* 17: 3–18.

Kiewiet, D. Roderick, and Mathew D. McCubbins. 1991. *The Logic of Delegation: Congressional Parties and the Appropriations Process.* Chicago: University of Chicago Press.

King, David C. 1994. "The Nature of Congressional Committee Jurisdictions." *American Political Science Review* 88: 48–62.

———. 1997. *Turf Wars: How Congressional Committees Claim Jurisdiction.* Chicago: University of Chicago Press.

Knack, S. 1995. "Does Motor Voter Work? Evidence from State-Level Data." *Journal of Politics* 57: 796–811.

Koszczuk, Jackie, and David S. Cloud. 1995. "GOP Leaders Tell the Troops, It's Time to Locke Hands." *Congressional Quarterly Weekly Report*, September 16, 1995: 2769–70.

Krehbiel, Keith. 1986. "Unanimous Consent Agreements: Going Along in the Senate." *Journal of Politics* 48: 541–64.

———. 1991. *Information and Legislative Organization.* Ann Arbor: University of Michigan Press.

———. 1993. "Where's the Party?" *British Journal of Political Science* 23: 235–66.

———. 1998. *Pivotal Politics: A Theory of U.S. Lawmaking.* Chicago: University of Chicago Press.

Kurtz, Karl T., Bruce Cain, and Richard G. Niemi, eds. 2007. *Institutional Change in American Politics.* Chicago: University of Chicago Press.

Leintz, Gerald R. 1978. "House Speaker Elections and Congressional Parties, 1789–1860." *Capitol Studies* 6: 63–89.

Lincoln, Abraham. 1953. *Collected Works of Abraham Lincoln.* New Brunswick, N.J.: Rutgers University Press.

Longley, Lawrence D., and Walter J. Oleszek. 1989. *Bicameral Politics: Conference Committees in Congress.* New Haven, Conn.: Yale University Press.

Lowenstein, Daniel Hays, Richard L. Hasen, and Daniel P. Tokaji. 2008. *Election Law: Cases and Materials,* 4th ed. Durham: Carolina Academic Press.

Malbin, Michael. 1980. *Unelected Representatives: Congressional Staff and the Future of Representative Government.* New York: Basic Books.

Manley, John. 1970, *Politics of Finance.* Boston: Little, Brown.

———. 1977. "The Conservative Coalition in Congress." In *Congress Reconsidered,* edited by Lawrence C. Dodd and Bruce I. Oppenheimer. New York: Praeger.

Mann, Thomas. 1978. *Unsafe at Any Margin: Interpreting Congressional Elections.* Washington, D.C.: American Enterprise Institute.

Martinez, Michael D., and David Hill. 1999. "Did Motor Voter Work?" *American Politics Quarterly* 27: 296–315.

Martis, Kenneth. 1989. *Historical Atlas of Political Parties in the United States Congress, 1789–1989.* New York: Macmillan.

Mayhew, David R. 1974. *Congress: The Electoral Connection.* New Haven, Conn.: Yale University Press.

———. 1991. *Divided We Govern.* New Haven, Conn.: Yale University Press.

———. 2002 *Electoral Realignments: A Critique of an American Genre.* New Haven: Yale University Press.

McCubbins, Mathew D. 1991. "Party Governance and U.S. Budget Deficits: Divided Government and Fiscal Stalemate." In *Politics and Economics in the Eighties,* edited by Alberto Alesina and Geoffrey Carliner. Chicago: University of Chicago Press.

McKelvey, Richard. 1976, "Intransitivities in Multidimensional Voting Models." *Journal of Economic Theory* 12: 472–82.

McKibbin, Carroll. 1991. *Roster of United States Congressional Office Holders and Biographical Characteristics of Members of the United States Congress, 1789–1991,* Computer File, 8th ICPSR ed. Ann Arbor, Mich: ICPSR.

Miller, Warren E., and Donald E. Stokes. 1963. "Constituency Influence in Congress." *American Political Science Review* 57: 45–56.

Moncrief, Gary F., Richard G. Niemi, and Lynda W. Powell. 2004. "Time, Term Limits, and Turnover: Trends in Membership Stability in U.S. State Legislatures." *Legislative Studies Quarterly* 29: 357–81.

Mulvihill, Mary E. 1999. "House and Senate Rules of Procedure: A Comparison." *CRS Report for Congress,* 97-270 GOV, Congressional Research Service, updated April 7, 1999.

Nelson, Garrison, and Charles Stewart III. 2010. *Committees in the U.S. Congress, 1993–2010.* Washington: CQ Press.

Oleszek, Walter J. 1995. *Congressional Procedures and the Policy Process.* Washington. D.C.: Congressional Quarterly.

———. 2010. "Whither the Role of Conference Committees, or Is It Wither?" *Legislative Studies Section Newsletter* January 2010, http://www.apsanet. org/~lss/Newsletter/jan2010/Oleszek.pdf.

Ornstein, Norman J., Thomas E. Mann, and Michael J. Malbin. 2000. *Vital Statistics on Congress, 1999–2000.* Washington, D.C.: American Enterprise Institute.

———. 2008. *Vital Statistics on Congress, 2008.* Washington, D.C.: Brookings Institution Press.

Peters, John G., and Susan Welch. 1980. "The Effects of Charges of Corruption on Voting Behavior in Congressional Elections." *American Political Science Review* 74: 697–708.

Polsby, Nelson W. 1968. "The Institutionalization of the U.S. House of Representatives." *American Political Science Review* 63: 144–68.

Polsby, Nelson W., Miriam Gallaher, and Barry Spencer Rundquist. 1969. "The Growth of the Seniority System in the U.S. House of Representatives." *American Political Science Review* 63: 787–807.

Poole, Keith T., and Howard Rosenthal. 1997. *Congress: A Political-Economic History of Roll Call Voting.* New York: Oxford University Press.

———. 2007. *Ideology and Congress.* Piscataway, N.J.: Transaction.

Price, H. Douglas. 1975a. "Congress and the Evolution of Legislative Professionalism." In *Congress in Change*, edited by Norman J. Ornstein. New York: Praeger.

———. 1975b. "The Congressional Career: Then and Now." In *Congressional Behavior*, edited by Nelson W. Polsby. New York; Random House.

———. 1977. "Careers and Committees in the American Congress: The Problem of Structural Change." In *The History of Parliamentary Behavior*, edited by William O. Aydelotte. Princeton, N.J.: Princeton University Press.

———. 1985. "*Congressional Government* and the Politics of the Late 19th Century: A Retrospective View." Paper presented at the annual meeting of the American Political Science Association.

Rae, Douglas W. 1967. *The Political Consequences of Electoral Laws.* New Haven, Conn.: Yale University Press.

Rae, Nicol C., and Colton C. Campbell, eds. 1999. *New Majority or Old Minority? The Impact of Republicans on Congress.* Lanham, Md.: Rowman and Littlefield.

Rakove, Jack N. 1996. *Original Meanings.* New York: Alfred A. Knopf.

Reich, Robert B. 1997. *Locked in the Cabinet.* New York: Alfred A. Knopf.

Riddle, Donald W. 1979. *Congressman Abraham Lincoln.* Westport, Conn.: Greenwood Press.

Riker, William H. 1955. "The Senate and American Federalism." *American Political Science Review* 49: 452–69.

———. 1982. *Liberalism against Populism: A Confrontation between the Theory of Democracy and the Theory of Social Choice.* San Francisco: W. H. Freeman.

————. 1986. *The Art of Political Manipulation*. New Haven, Conn.: Yale University Press.

————. 1996. *The Strategy of Rhetoric: Campaigning for the American Constitution*. New Haven, Conn.: Yale University Press.

Riker, William H., and Peter Ordeshook. 1968. "A Theory of the Calculus of Voting." *American Political Science Review* 62: 25–42.

Rohde, David W. 1979. "Risk-Bearing and Progressive Ambition: The Case of Members of the United States House of Representatives." *American Journal of Political Science* 23: 1–26.

————. 1991. *Parties and Leaders in the Postreform House*. Chicago: University of Chicago Press.

Rohde, David W., and Kenneth A. Shepsle. 1987. "Leaders and Followers in the House of Representatives: Reflections on Woodrow Wilson's *Congressional Government*." *Congress and the Presidency—A Journal of Capital Studies* 14: 111–33.

Rosenstone, Steven, and John Mark Hansen. 1993. *Mobilization, Participation, and Democracy in America*. New York: Macmillan.

Rosenstone, Steven J., and Raymond E. Wolfinger. 1978. "The Effect of Registration Laws on Voter Turnout." *American Political Science Review* 72: 22–45.

Saturno, James V. 1998. "Special Rules and Options for Regulating the Amending Process." Congressional Research Service *Report to Congress*, July 15, 1998, viewed at http://www.house.gov/rules/98-612.htm on December 26, 1999.

Schantz, Harvey L. 1980. "Contested and Uncontested Primaries for the U.S. House." *Legislative Studies Quarterly*, 5: 547–62.

Schattschneider, E. E. 1935. *Politics, Pressures, and the Tariff*. New York: Prentice-Hall.

Schick, Allen. 1981. *Congress and Money: Budgeting, Spending, and Taxing*. Washington, D.C.: Urban Institute.

Schlesinger, Arthur M., Jr. 1971. *History of U.S. Political Parties*, 4 vols. New York: Chelsea House.

Schlesinger, Joseph. 1966. *Ambition and Politics: Political Careers in the United States*. Chicago: Rand-McNally.

Shepsle, Kenneth A. 1989. "The Changing Textbook Congress." In *Can the Government Govern?* edited by John E. Chubb and Paul E. Peterson, Washington, D.C.: Brookings Institution.

Shepsle, Kenneth A., and Barry R. Weingast. 1979. "Institutional Arrangements and Equilibrium in Multidimensional Voting Models." *American Journal of Political Science* 23: 27–59.

————. 1981. "Structure-Induced Equilibrium and Legislative Choice." *Public Choice* 37: 503–19.

————. 1987. "The Institutional Foundations of Committee Power." *American Political Science Review* 81: 85–104.

Silbey, Joel H. 1986. "'Always a Whig in Politics:' The Partisan Life of Abraham Lincoln." *Papers of the Abraham Lincoln Association* 8: 21–42.

Silver, Brian D., Barbara A. Anderson, and Paul R. Abramson. 1986. "Who Overreports Voting?" *American Political Science Review* 80: 613–24.

Snyder, James M., Jr. 1992. "Artificial Extremism in Interest Group Ratings." *Legislative Studies Quarterly* 17: 317–45.

Snyder, James M., Jr., and Timothy Groseclose. 2000. "Estimating Party Influence in Congressional Roll Call Voting." *American Journal of Political Science* 44: 193–211.

Stanley, Harold W., and Richard G. Niemi. 2010. *Vital Statistics on American Politics*. Washington: CQ Press.

Stewart, Charles III. 1989. *Budget Reform Politics: The Design of the Appropriations Process in the House of Representatives, 1865–1921*. New York: Cambridge University Press.

———. 1991. "Lessons from the Post–Civil War Era." In *The Politics of Divided Government*, edited by Gary W. Cox and Samuel Kernell. Boulder, Colo.: Westview Press.

———. 1994. "Let's Go Fly a Kite: Correlates of Involvement in the House Bank Scandal." *Legislative Studies Quarterly* 19: 521–35.

Stewart, Charles III., and Timothy Groseclose. 1999. "The Value of Committee Seats in the United States Senate, 1946–91." *American Journal of Political Science* 43: 963–73.

Stewart, Charles III., and Mark Reynolds. 1990. "Television Markets and U.S. Senate Elections." *Legislative Studies Quarterly* 15: 495–523.

Stewart, Charles III., and Barry R. Weingast. 1992. "Stacking the Senate, Changing the Nation: Republican Rotten Boroughs, Statehood Politics, and American Political Development." *Studies in American Political Development* 6: 223–71.

Sundquist, James L. 1973. *The Dynamics of the Party System*. Washington, D.C.: Brookings Institution Press.

———. 1981. *Decline and Resurgence of Congress*. Washington, D.C.: Brookings Institution Press.

———. 1992. *Constitutional Reform and Effective Government*. Washington, D.C.: Brookings Institution Press.

———. 1993. *Beyond Gridlock? Prospects for Governance in the Clinton Years—and After*. Washington, D.C.: Brookings Institution Press.

Swift, Elaine E. 1997. *The Making of an American Senate*. Ann Arbor: University of Michigan Press.

Thompson, Dennis. 1994. *Ethics in Congress*. Washington, D.C.: Brookings Institution Press.

Tullock, Gordon. 1981. "Why So Much Stability?" *Public Choice* 37: 189–205.

U.S. Congress. 1997. *Biographical Directory of the United States Congress*. Washington, D.C.: Government Printing Office.

Weingast, Barry R. 1998. "Political Stability and Civil War: Institutions, Commitment, and American Democracy." In *Analytic Narratives*, edited by Robert H. Bates et al. Princeton, N.J.: Princeton University Press.

Wildavsky, Aaron. 1991. *The New Politics of the Budgetary Process.* New York: HarperCollins.

Wilson, Woodrow W. 1963 [1885]. *Congressional Government.* Boston: Houghton Mifflin.

Wolfinger, Raymond, and Steven Rosenstone. 1980. *Who Votes?* New Haven, Conn.: Yale University Press.

Young, H. P. 1988. "Measuring the Compactness of Legislative Districts." *Legislative Studies Quarterly* 13: 105–15.

Young, James Sterling. 1966. *The Washington Community.* New York: Columbia University Press.

Index

NOTE: **Bold page numbers** refer to key concept definitions; Page numbers with an *f* or *t* indicate figures or tables, respectively.